Indigenous Philosophies and Critical Education

Studies in the
Postmodern Theory of Education

Shirley R. Steinberg
General Editor

Vol. 379

PETER LANG
New York • Washington, D.C./Baltimore • Bern
Frankfurt • Berlin • Brussels • Vienna • Oxford

Indigenous Philosophies and Critical Education

A Reader

EDITED BY George J. Sefa Dei

FOREWORD BY Akwasi Asabere-Ameyaw

PETER LANG
New York • Washington, D.C./Baltimore • Bern
Frankfurt • Berlin • Brussels • Vienna • Oxford

Library of Congress Cataloging-in-Publication Data

Indigenous philosophies and critical education: a reader /
edited by George J. Sefa Dei.
p. cm. — (Counterpoints: studies in the postmodern
theory of education; vol. 379)
Includes bibliographical references and index.
1. Indigenous peoples—Education. 2. Ethnophilosophy.
3. Education—Philosophy. I. Dei, George J. Sefa (George Jerry Sefa).
LC3715.I46   370.1—dc22   2010053219
ISBN 978-1-4331-0815-0 (hardcover)
ISBN 978-1-4331-0814-3 (paperback)
ISSN 1058-1634

Bibliographic information published by **Die Deutsche Nationalbibliothek**.
Die Deutsche Nationalbibliothek lists this publication in the "Deutsche
Nationalbibliografie"; detailed bibliographic data is available
on the Internet at http://dnb.d-nb.de/.

The paper in this book meets the guidelines for permanence and durability
of the Committee on Production Guidelines for Book Longevity
of the Council of Library Resources.

© 2011 Peter Lang Publishing, Inc., New York
29 Broadway, 18th floor, New York, NY 10006
www.peterlang.com

All rights reserved.
Reprint or reproduction, even partially, in all forms such as microfilm,
xerography, microfiche, microcard, and offset strictly prohibited.

Printed in the United States of America

This compilation of essays is dedicated to our departed ancestors who continue to guide and watch over us and strengthen us mentally, spiritually, emotionally, and materially as we navigate the treacherous waters of the academy.

Contents

Foreword by Akwasi Asabere-Ameyaw … xi

Acknowledgments … xv

Introduction … 1
George J. Sefa Dei

SECTION I: INDIGENOUS KNOWLEDGES AS PHILOSOPHY AND THE IMPLICATIONS OF DECOLONIZATION

Introduction to Section I … 15

1. Revisiting the Question of the 'Indigenous' … 21
George J. Sefa Dei

2. (Re) Conceptualizing 'Indigenous' from Anti-Colonial and Black Feminist Theoretical Perspectives: Living and Imagining Indigeneity Differently … 34
Temitope Adefarakan

3. We Are All One: Holistic Thought-Forms within Indigenous Societies Indigeneity and Holism … 53
Farah Shroff

4. Indigenous Education and Indigenous Studies in the Australian Academy: Assimilationism, Critical Pedagogy, Dominant Culture Learners and Indigenous Knowledges … 68
Marcelle Cross-Townsend

5. African Philosophies of Education: Deconstructing the Colonial and Reconstructing the Indigenous … 80
Ali Abdi

6. Space, Time and Unified Knowledge: Following the Path of Vine Deloria, Jr. … 92
Jefferey D. Anderson

SECTION II: THE QUESTION OF DIFFERENCE, IDENTITY AND REPRESENTATION AND INDIGENOUS KNOWLEDGE PRODUCTION

Introduction to Section II … 109

7. "I Live Somewhere Else but I've Never Left Here": Indigenous Knowledge, History, and Place 113
Michael Davis

8. Ruminations on Red Revitalization: Exploring Complexities of Identity, Difference and Nationhood in Indigenous Education 127
Martin Cannon

9. Identity, Representation, and Knowledge Production 142
Patience Elabor-Idemudia

10. Indigeneity in Education: A By-product of Assimilation? 157
Dennis Mcpherson

SECTION III: INDIGENOUS KNOWLEDGES AND THE QUESTION OF DEVELOPMENT: TENSIONS OF CHANGE, TRADITION AND MODERNITY

Introduction to Section III 167

11. Education for Endogenous Development: Contrasting Perspectives from Amazonia and Arabia 171
Serena Heckler & Paul Sillitoe

12. Neo-Colonial Melancholia: Alaska Native People, Education and Oil 189
Maria Shaa Tláa Williams

13. Sacred Mountains and Ivory Towers: Indigenous Pedagogies of Place and Invasions from Modernity 197
Michael Marker

14. Indigenous Knowledge in Transition: The Fundamental Laws of the Diné in an Era of Change and Modernity 212
Lloyd L. Lee

SECTION IV: INDIGENOUS KNOWLEDGE, EDUCATION AND SCIENCE: BEYOND THE FORMAL CURRICULUM

Introduction to Section IV 225

15. Bringing the Experience of Indigenous People into Alaska Rural Systematic Initiative/Alaska Native Knowledge Network 229
Gregory Smith

16. Learning Life Lessons from Indigenous Storytelling with Tom Mccallum 245
Judy Iseke & Brennus BMJK

17. Ua Lele Ka Manu; The Bird Has Flown: A Search for Hawaiian Indigenous/Local Inquiry Methods 262
Pauline Chinn, Isabella Aiona Abbott, Michelle Kapana-Baird, Mahina Hou Ross, Lila Lelepali, Ka'umealani Walker, Sabra Kauka, Napua Barrows, Moana Lee, and Huihui Kanahele-Mossman

18. The Kenyan Herbalist Ruptures the Status Quo in Health and Healing 280
    Njoki Wane

19. 'Glocalising' Indigenous Knowledges for the Classroom 299
    Ocean Ripeka Mercier

20. The Challenges of Science Education and Indigenous Knowledge 312
    Lyn Carter

Section V: Future Challenges: Centering Spirituality and Spiritual Ways of Knowing and the Discourse of Indigeneity in the Academy

Introduction to Section V 331

21. Endarkened Feminism and Sacred Praxis: Troubling (Auto) Ethnography through Critical Engagements with African Indigenous Knowledges 337
    Cynthia B. Dillard & Charlotte Bell

22. Re/Membering In—Between "Japan" and "The West": A Decolonizing Journey through the Indigenous Knowledge Framework 350
    Kimine Mayuzumi

23. Revealing the Secular Fence of Knowledge: Towards Reimagining Spiritual Ways of Knowing and Being in the Academy 367
    Riyad Shahjahan & Kimberly Haverkos

24. Knowledge, Power and Decolonization: Implication for Non-Indigenous Scholars, Researchers and Educators 386
    Soenke Biermann

25. Coyote and Raven Chat about Protecting Indigenous Intellectual Property 399
    Pat O'Riley & Peter Cole

26. Indigenous Spirituality and Decolonization: Methodology for the Classroom 411
    Eric Ritskes

27. Beyond Deconstruction: Evolving the Ties between Indigenous Knowledges and Post-Foundational Anti-Racism 422
    Zahra Murad

28. Indigenous Knowledge: Multiple Approaches 434
    Priscilla Settee

Contributors 451

Index 457

Foreword

This book is a bold attempt to challenge and make very uncomfortable the imperial procedures of knowledge making. Though there is much work concerning the transformation of schooling and education, this book gives us a genuine sense of hope. Writing through a communal spirit and engendered by the will to liberate educational philosophies, Dei and the authors address the different forms of epistemological colonization, which reifies itself through the pedagogue and resides within conventional classroom spaces. Wherever we look, Indigenous communities are making valid and legitimate claims for the recognition, authentication, and preservation of their cultures, histories, heritage, and languages. Local cultural knowledge systems are similarly being contested for validation and legitimation. All is part of the continuing struggle for identity, representation, and authentication in a search for human and collective dignity. Therefore, every knowledge system is worthy of examination in the provision of education to learners. My own foray in Indigenous knowledge goes back to my early training as a science educator when I examined the academic and practical fascination with Indigenous science and its contributions to science education in general.

Our institutions of higher learning have placed tremendous responsibility on educators to contextualize knowledge such that learners develop a deep and critical understanding of everyday social practice and the experiential reality as legitimate sources of knowledge. We work with knowledge from the known to the unknown. By working from the familiar and known, learners are able to develop a shared sense of identification and ownership in the knowledge production process. For some time now, there have also been raging contentions as to what really constitutes the "Indigenous" and the connections or disconnections with the traditional, folk, and local knowledges. The essays in this collection help sharpen our understanding of the linkages as well as the challenges of claiming Indigenousness. What is significant overall is the recognition that there are many different forms of knowledge and there is a need for education to examine these different knowledge forms rather than simply assign some forms of traditional cultural knowledges to the dustbin of history as irrelevant to contemporary experience. Local peoples use these knowledges every day. These knowledges constitute their established ways of knowing, an understanding of their communities as embedded in culture, history, science, local languages, ancestral practices, folklore and traditions, songs, riddles, and proverbs. Within communities we have custodians of important knowledge that have continued to serve communities from time immemorial. These knowledges are not static or frozen by change with the times. But they are rooted in communities' histories, heritage, and cultural repertoire, and the challenge for educators of today is to work with such knowledge as we address the tensions of tradition, change, and modernity in human societies. I commend Dei and the contributors to the collection for presenting their knowledge in ways that help move the cause of knowledge production and education. Dei being a traditional Chief in Ghana understands the importance of local cultural resource knowledge and why such knowledge should be upheld in our schools, colleges, universities, and communities.

In many contexts, claiming Indigenous knowledge in the educational system is also to promote Indigenous education. To be truly effective, such Indigenous education must reflect the political, cultural, social, spiritual, as well as pedagogic, instructional, and communicative needs and aspirations of Indigenous peoples and their communities. When these communities abandon their local epistemologies, all they are doing is committing "epistemic suicides." The responsibility of Indigenous education lies beyond a mere challenge of colonial and colonizing curricula and school texts. Indigenous education is about affirming the relevance of Indigenous knowledge. We cannot hope to educate learners of today outside their socio-cultural and political contexts and milieu. Our schools, colleges, and universities cannot deliver education that pays little or no attention to the cultures, traditions, histories, identities, and ancestral knowledges of the learners in our classrooms. Our students must be able to identify with the classroom knowledge in ways that empower, embolden, strengthen, and sustain them to become fully engaged in their education. When they are able to assert their own cultural knowings they easily develop a sense of ownership of the learning process. Thus, for many Indigenous peoples and their communities, claiming their cultural and traditional ways of knowing is part of the continuing struggle to resist and shed the vestiges of colonization and to recover who they are and remake their own destinies.

No doubt *Indigenous Philosophies and Critical Education* is an excellent addition to the existing literature on Indigenous studies. The breadth of coverage of the issues—starting with the question of knowledge as philosophy and the implications of critical education for decolonization; the question of social difference, identity, and knowledge production; the tensions of change, tradition, and modernity as conveyed in development discourses; Indigenous science education and the place of spirituality in Indigenous knowledge production—are all significant themes to be addressed in this far-ranging subject area.

The book has been exhaustive in its treatment of Indigenous philosophies, and the conscious decision to cover a wide geographical area, engage an inclusive subject matter, and to draw on the perspective of a diverse crop of academic scholars, researchers, and community educators is very impressive and commendable. The way I see it, the pressing challenge of critical education in schools, colleges, and universities is to examine different philosophies of knowing, their relative strengths and contributions to knowledge production, as well as their applicability to the resolution of human problems. Science education is no longer a question of simply training people in the technicalities of science. It is about education of learners with a much broader understanding of knowledge that embraces the sciences, arts and humanities, and literatures.

This book calls for a counter-knowledging to challenge conventional systems of education. There are huge possibilities and limitations to the study of Indigenous ways of knowing. Contributions in this volume have strived to disentangle Indigenous knowledges from the entrapments of Western/dominant configurations of knowledge. What is truly remarkable is the fact that Indigenous philosophies have not been presented as the all knowing, the panacea for the colonial episteme. Indigenous knowledges are engaged dialectically and inclusively in ways which allow for multiple centres of knowing. Ultimately, this collection is about experiential knowledge; it is about the challenges for Indigenous bodies of knowledge to assert their validity in their own right and as well make claims for moving into conventional classrooms. Presently, discussions concerning schooling and education have been regulated through the dominant edict of "Western-Enlightenment thought" steeped in colonial and colonizing ways of knowing. There is a dearth of local cultural knowledge in our classroom curricula. The authors do well to address this lacuna by highlighting the pedagogic relevance of the "Indigenous" in the context of schooling and colonial forms of education. We are continuously reminded of the need for decolonization for all bodies. The culture of globalisation engendered through the culture of capitalism *promotes* a particular culture of development that simply commodifies the human condition. Local peoples, local ways of coming to understanding and coming to make sense of the experiences of the self and community is about local cultural knowledge. Indigenous philosophy has well been historicized by local peoples through oral spaces through time and *place,* and has reflected on histories and cultures as counterpoints to dominant bodies of knowledge. Claiming a place for Indigenous philosophies in our schools, colleges, and universities is about resistance and the affirmation of the self, group, and community. Indigenousness concerns have brought to the fore of contemporary politics and social thought the experiences of colonialism. Consequently, theorizing Indigenousness necessitates knowing and understanding the experiential. It also requires writing through the vagaries of the human experience. There is the challenge of coming to know through uncertainty, coming to know through that which is incommensurable, and to think through those vexing moments to understand the relationship with the tangible, material, and non-material. As chapters in this volume show, such cogitation speaks to the spiritual self, that is, to know through that which is innate and to be intuitive in a particular way that dialogues with the infused spirit.

We must also recognize how we come to know differently through our social spaces, keeping in mind, Indigenousness is about praxis. Indigenousness is also about critical consciousness, that spirituality, for example, is not fixed, nor definite, nor operating through a set of finite locus points. Spirituality is about the governing ethic and care onto self as a form of praxis. I am encouraged that the authors are not prescribing doing away nor dismissing the present-day canon embedded within schooling and education. Refreshingly, they offer different ways of knowing in which all bodies can come to know and understand their social milieu. Central to the authors' work is seeking the interest of local and Indigenous communities. With this invested interest, the collection leaves us thinking about the relevance of activist scholarship, that we simply cannot theorize for theorizing's sake; we simply cannot theorize for academic prowess. If the collective goal concerns decolonizing and transforming schooling and education from the context of difference, then we must dialogue with knowledge from local peoples. We must speak about the colonial as it becomes revealed through all the complex forms of imposition.

Given that claiming Indigenousness is not without its politics, there are consequences, implications, and challenges for the Indigenous scholar. Notably, pedagogues claiming Indigenous frameworks have collectively struggled to have their scholarship recognized. What is needed and, as the authors here have rightly done, is to engage critical social science research without negotiating the lived experiences of the Indigenous body. They have made us aware of the danger of co-opting one's research and the need for Indigenous thought to co-exist with conventional ways of knowing. The power of this collection speaks to the deliberate accounts to miseducate learners about Indigenous, local, and cultural bodies of knowledge. The authors share their experiences and local conversations to give us a critical dialogue concerning the politics of Indigenous knowledges and the "struggles of the Indigenous peoples to be recognized as a contributing body of knowledge." We are given a writing of courage to continue the work of resistance, transformation, and decolonization.

I conclude noting that the area of Indigenous philosophy has a multidisciplinary edge that is inclusive of knowledge from the diverse sciences, arts and the humanities. As has been noted the subject area for discussion has a lot to offer Political Studies, Post-Colonial Studies, African and Caribbean Studies, Literature, Anthropology, History, Sociology, Gender Studies, Development Studies, Administrative Studies, Community Health and Medicine, Law, and Semiotics, International Development workers, and government policy officials. The special focus of the collection on the specific implications for schooling and education is welcome. Given their research interests and breadth of coverage, Dei and his excellent list of contributors have ensured that this book will have a wide appeal.

AKWASI ASABERE-AMEYAW, PHD
VICE-CHANCELLOR
UNIVERSITY OF EDUCATION, WINNEBA
GHANA

Acknowledgments

I acknowledge many have helped along the way in making this work come to fruition. First of all, I sincerely thank Shirley Steinberg for proposing my name when the idea of doing this volume was initially discussed and supporting me throughout the process. I trust this collection of essays will not disappoint the original dreams and hopes expressed. I could not have succeeded in my task without the help of Isaac Darko, whose call to duty went beyond the usual expectation of a "graduate assistant." His overall assistance has been amazing from the initial correspondence with prospective contributors to ensuring the final technical details before the draft manuscript went to the publishers. Similarly, my thanks go to Rainos Mutumba of the Faculty of Social Work, University of Toronto, Marlon Simmons, Yumiko Kawano, Eric Riskes, and Dr. Arlo Kempf, all of the Department of Sociology and Equity Studies of the Ontario Institute for Studies in Education, University of Toronto (OISE/UT), for their varied assistance including reading and making insightful comments on drafts of the manuscript before and after all the chapters from contributors were put together. I also cannot forget the anonymous reviewers! This book came about by "invitation only," and I want to thank all the contributors for being willing to share their knowledge. Even a few who could not honor the invitation sent messages wishing me well in such an intellectual undertaking.

I acknowledge that there is a growing interest in the pragmatics/praxis of Indigenous knowledges. This is attested to by the complex and diverse ways Indigenous knowledges continue to be claimed and engaged with in the academy, not to mention the evocation in everyday social practice in local communities. Personally, I have been fortunate to have Elders who have steadfastly insisted on the urgency of sustaining such knowledges for our collective survival, histories, and social development. Indigenous knowledge is about community building. It is about affirmation, resistance, and decolonization. It is also about developing respect for land, acknowledging the spirits of our ancestors and Elders, and ensuring that knowledge thrives and is used responsibly. In reading through the chapters in this collection, I could not help but feel the power and sense of pride in Indigenous knowledge. It is without saying that I came out of this entire process much better than when I entered. I end with a special thanks to my graduate students who over the years have and continue to teach me about why we as teachers, educators, students, and learners need to develop an Indigenous consciousness based on Indigenous unity. These students have always insisted on "never settling for less" as we continue to disrupt the boundaries and complacency of dominant scholarship.

GEORGE J. SEFA DEI
TORONTO, JUNE 2010

Introduction

GEORGE J. SEFA DEI

I start the "Introduction" to this important collection of essays by acknowledging First Nations and Aboriginal peoples of Canada for the space and location from which I am writing my thoughts and ideas into text. This is important especially since from time immemorial certain spaces and territories have come to be and are continually represented by colonizing practices. I will also do something unconventional for an "Introduction" to an edited collection. In this piece, I will not undertake specific discussions on the individual pieces in the book. I leave that to the various sub-themes/section in which each chapter appears. My goal here is to simply reflect in a broad sense on some general ideas that guide the direction of this book. It has been such an honor and privilege to edit this reader on *Indigenous Philosophies and Critical Education*. As an educator who has always striven to broach critical and oppositional knowledge, such moments allow for the sharing of ideas and for the opportunity to learn about multiple perspectives. Most of us are driven by an intellectual desire to diversify our academies in terms of actual physical bodies, knowledge representation, and the politics of pursuing social and educational change. Our intellectual and political projects acknowledge, validate, and legitimate Indigenous knowledges and philosophies as ways of knowing in their own right. Unfortunately, there are times when one wonders whether the present academy may ever be able to shed the chains of its past. Hence, is the goal to "transform the academy" or to "replace the academy"? (see also Kempf, 2010). I am speaking of a past which has presented particular hegemonic ways of knowledge production, validation, and dissemination and also given currency and legitimacy to certain bodies and practices. While reminded of the Fanonian exhortation of the limits of particular oppressed and colonized bodies seeking validation and acceptance in colonial spaces, I am also moved by a "pedagogy of hope" to have a newly transformed academy (see Dei, 2010).

Perhaps it is important for me to clarify from the onset why I chose as the title of this collection *Indigenous Philosophies*. I see Indigenous knowledge as philosophy, specifically as a body of Indigenous social thought embedded with critical, oppositional, and resisting knowledge and counter narratives for decolonization. In other words, Indigenous knowledge as a body of Indigenous thought has located itself contrapuntal to dominant knowledges, in that, the Indigene reveals itself through resistance, as counter-hegemonic and as tangential to conventional knowledge systems. I position philosophy as a body of knowledge central to the epistemological framework, one that accords discursive authority, power, and privilege onto the pedagogue. My claim is that (Western) philosophy as an epistemology has been historically granted a certain academic identity that endows precedence onto philosophy as a particular classification of knowledge and simultaneously locates the Indigene to the periphery of knowing. My concern with philosophy (especially Western philosophy) is not about removing philosophy as a canon, but to question the positioning/authenticity of the episteme, which reveals itself through a particular historic primacy that at the same time forms colonial relations with the "Othered" discursive episteme.

In effect, if we are to take up this trope of philosophy, philosophy must not only be about being European. Philosophy must be revisioned and rearticulated through the embodiment of different peoples, through different geographies. Philosophy in a sense then constitutes the human condition, that is, the mode of thinking, an orientation of thought imbued through all peoples alike. Philosophy, as a discursive category neither is apolitical nor does it occupy an ahistorical space. Knowledge production is not an innocent or neutral project. Every process of knowledge creation, validation, and dissemination is about the embodiment of politics. This is where Indigenous knowledge as philosophy becomes important. It challenges the normative of particular forms of knowledge while also articulating a particular politics of decolonizing dominant knowledge. I am also contending that conventional knowledge production is a hegemonic instrument which works to form colonial knowledge that reveals itself as the all-knowing universal body of knowledge.

An important academic goal is to understand on-going contestations in knowledge in the search to engage everyday social practice and experiences as well as the social barriers and approaches to peaceful human co-existence. There is a need for new, counter/alternative and multiple knowledge forms in diverse social sites to provide critical understandings to individual and collective political action. The role and importance of Indigenous knowledges and philosophies in the promotion of multi-centric paradigms are increasingly being claimed and contested. Some questions are in order: What accounts for the resurgence in Indigenous knowledges and philosophies in the academies? How does the complexity of Indigenous philosophies contribute to promoting a subversive pedagogy for educational and social change? How can we, as educators and earners, draw on the myriad intellectual traditions and philosophies of knowing to understand the nature and dynamics of imperial power relations as a necessary exercise in social, political, and intellectual liberation? This reader is an attempt to pull together ideas concerning Indigenous epistemologies (e.g., worldviews, paradigms, standpoints, and philosophies) as they manifest themselves in the mental lives of persons both from and outside the orbit of the usual Euro-American culture. The book engages Indigenous knowledges as far more than a "contest of the marginals," thereby challenging the way oppositional knowledges are positioned, particularly in the Western academy. Subsequently, this book is a call to recognize and acknowledge Indigenous knowledges as legitimate knowings in their own right, and not necessarily in competition with other sources or forms of knowledge. The project offers an opportunity for the critical thinker to continue on a de-colonial/anti-colonial intellectual journey in ways informed by Indigenous theorizing.

We place Indigenous knowledge and philosophies within the terrain of contemporary critical intellectual traditions that articulate emancipatory discourses for particularly colonized and oppressed subjects. The recognition of Indigenous knowledge as legitimate in its own right requires that we rethink the spaces that are currently in place for nurturing and sustaining a healthy multiplicity of knowledge in the academy. We would argue, then, that we not only have to decolonize existing spaces but create new non-hierarchical spaces of knowing. We cannot ask hegemonic/dominant spaces to simply make room for other knowledges to co-exist. The politics of de-centering spaces and dominant knowledge requires that we rethink new ways of creating spaces that allow for a centricity of multiple knowledge systems to contend with the asymmetrical power relations that currently exist in educational settings. If we fail to contest power, then the liberal and neo-liberal relativist stance, and to some extent, post-modernist tendency of heralding/insisting on spaces for all voices, ideas, and standpoints to be heard can only be seductive and end up actually affirming the dominance of particular forms of knowledge. Currently, not all knowledges have the same power and influence in our academies. To say that all knowledge comes to a level playing field is limiting.

What is Indigeneity and what are the possibilities of Indigenous knowledges in creating a different understanding of education that holds the promise and possibility of excellence for all? As noted, the binary tensions between so-called Western science/scientific knowledge and the Indigenous knowledge system are unproductive for learning, especially if it is acknowledged that we are dealing with multiple systems of knowledge and that no one body of knowledge can claim superiority over another. If a distinction must be made in knowledge systems, the focus should be on the processes of differentiation that set knowledge systems apart in their epistemic and philosophical emphasis, as well as on how power dynamics shape the production, interrogation, validation, and dissemination of knowledge systems, both internally and globally. The romanticization and de-contextualization of knowledges are concerns for both Indigenous and Western science knowledge. Historically, the privileging of Western ways of knowledge is accompanied by the tendency to impose such knowledge on others, while simultaneously denying or subjugating traditional/Indigenous knowledge systems. In a sense one can argue there has been a corresponding glorification of Western knowledge systems.

Currently, Indigenous and oppressed peoples are reclaiming their cultural knowledges and asserting their legitimacy in many spaces. It is clear the academy is no exception (see Abdi & Cleghorn, 2005; Kincheloe & Steinberg, 2008; Semali & Kincheloe, 1999; Wane, 2009; Waterfall, 2008; among many others). However, despite the fact that Indigeneity and Indigenous knowledge constitute a growing field of study in the academy, the relationship between Indigeneity and Indigenous knowledge is often merely assumed rather than theorized. Indigeneity is a claim to identity, history, politics, culture, and a rootedness in a place. It is about a socio-political consciousness of being as a knowing subject. It is also about an existence outside the purview of colonial encounter and the colonizing relations as over-determining of one's existence. Indigeneity is about how a body/subject is defined by self and group—a definition of an existence outside and resistant of that identity, which is more often constructed and imposed by the dominant. The politics of claiming Indigeneity in a so-called transnational context allows one to construct an identity that is beyond what is constructed within Euro-American hegemony. Consequently, to claim and reclaim an Indigenousness or an Indigenous identity is a political and decolonizing undertaking. The values, worldviews, and epistemes that govern such Indigenous existence and how we come to know and understand our communities, are appropriately termed "Indigenous knowing/knowledge."

RE-CONCEPTUALIZING INDIGENOUS KNOWLEDGE/PHILOSOPHIES

Indigenous knowledge is primarily about epistemology. Like every body of knowledge, Indigenous knowledge has its own ontological, conceptual/philosophical, methodological, and axiological groundings. Indigenous knowledge is science, philosophy, and practice of knowing about one's existence as not conscripted and scripted by simply a colonial and colonizing experience. It is also about understanding the nature of social reality as real (i.e., materially consequential for the body) as well as meaningfully in physical and metaphysical realms. Indigenous knowledge speaks of the inseparability and inter-dependence of selves and the collective. It heralds the mind, body, and spirit connections and connectedness of society, culture, and nature in the ways we come to know about ourselves and our worlds. It is based on a cosmological understanding that the elements of the universe are interrelated and intertwined (e.g., the mental, physical, spiritual, material, political, and economic). We cannot simplistically atomize and particularize the everyday living experience. The everyday experience and the social world are not always subject to the certainty of knowing. Indigenous peoples' use of their cultural knowledge system is derived from living in close relations and appreciation of nature and society. Hence the Indigenous knowledge system usually would comprise the understanding of the successful ways by which people deal with their environments and surroundings.

Culture is seen as critical to knowledge production. In fact, cultural paradigms shape knowledge; the role of local culture(s) in producing multiple ways of knowing is salient. The advancement of any one cultural perspective cannot be universally applied and/or seen as superior to other perspectives. This is the basis of the critique lodged by Indigenous knowledge regarding the ways in which hegemonic knowledges (e.g., Eurocentric ways of knowing) often masquerade as superior and "all knowing." Indigenous knowledges also affirm that there are cultural continuities as well as cultural discontinuities in a people's experiences. Knowledge does not necessarily leave the body with a relocation. Knowledge can reside in cultural memory and can be called upon/recollected to deal with contemporary pressing problems in different contexts. The belief is that all knowledges are shared and accumulated across time and space.

A culturally grounded perspective helps center Indigenous peoples' worldviews. It also helps local (oppressed) peoples to resist the dominance of Eurocentric perspectives/knowings. When reclaimed and affirmed, Indigeneity and Indigenous knowings provide intellectual agency to marginalized, colonized peoples who then become subjects of their own histories, stories, and experiences. The Indigenous philosophical tradition provides a space for colonized and oppressed peoples to interpret their own experiences on their own terms and understandings, rather than being forced through Eurocentric paradigms. The politics of Indigenous knowledge production is to (re)construct an Indigenous identity rooted in place, culture, history, and politics.

Indigenous knowledges cannot be romanticized as they are also embedded in power relations. To claim "Indigeneity" is to validate and work with Indigenous knowledges. The claiming of Indigenous knowledge is not about denying others their cultural knowledge. Given that Indigeneity and Indigenous knowledge are connected to time and place, there is no denial of their embedded intellectual politics. Historically, all groups can claim an Indigenous past and history in so far as it is outside the realm of a colonial domination and the colonizing experience. The time and space dimensions to Indigenous knowledge merely speak to the contextual basis of knowing and the fact that all knowledge is first and foremost local and needs to be situated in appropriate cultural and political contexts.

As already alluded to, knowledge exists in cultural memory and experience. Indigenous knowledge is embodied in the ability of the self and collective to call on history, cultural memory, politics, myths, stories, heritage, and traditions as important sources of knowledge. This is why discussions of Indigenous knowledge must always reference history, culture, place, social justice, colonialism, decolonization.

The Indigenous landscape articulates an Indigeneity which must be understood in terms of the society, culture, and nature nexus. Such Indigeneity is about a spiritual and spiritualized view of human existence. Indigeneity cautions that the material and non-material aspects of life cannot be dichotomized, and neither can we evade the power issues of knowledge making, validation, and dissemination. Given that knowledge "borrows" and learns from other ways of knowing, Indigeneity is about resistance to domination and colonization and a welcoming of "strangers" into existing communities. Indigeneity is not simply about rights (e.g., who has rights to a place) but more so about our individual and collective responsibilities to ensure the existence of a sustaining community. The issue of responsibility means owning up to the knowledge we produce and allowing such knowledge to compel action to bring about social transformation and change.

Questions of race, class, gender, sexuality, (dis)ability, language, religion, and spirituality are also central to discussions of both Indigeneity and Indigenous philosophies. Every knowledge form is demarcated by questions of social difference. Knowledge is power and the asymmetrical power relations are structured along lines of difference. Therefore, such differences construct multiple ways of knowing. But this understanding also implies that there are political and social contexts for knowledge, and that these subjects produce knowledge to make sense of social existence from particular standpoints. The body is also implicated in how we come to know and interpret the world. Our histories, politics, identities, social experiences, cultures, and subjectivities position us to know differently. We speak from particular contexts, out of particular experiences, and within specific, yet interconnected histories and social locations (see also Hall, 1991).

Local cultural knowledges are gendered as in cultural festivals and expectations of gender, around social norms and morals, traditional folkloric practices and the meanings embedded in oral stories, proverbs, fables, and tales. Certain traditional knowledge speaks directly to youth (e.g., rituals about age sets in African contexts). In most Indigenous communities we also learn the respective roles of women and men in safeguarding local cultural resource knowledge. In a pertinent article, exploring the relationship between conservation of biodiversity, Indigenous knowledge systems, gender and intellectual property rights, Quiroz (1994) highlighted gender aspects of Indigenous knowledge. She argued that Indigenous people have sustainably managed their environments for centuries, with women playing a key role in preserving biodiversity. Women possess an intricate knowledge about their environment that is distinctive from men's knowledge. Unfortunately, such gendered aspects of knowledge (and women's knowledge in particular) are often ignored by male-biased social science research. The author also notes that Indigenous peoples in general, and women in particular, are not adequately compensated when their own knowledge is collected and utilized by Western researchers and companies. Due to their low social status in many cultures, women are increasingly disadvantaged when dealing with issues of intellectual property rights.

LOCAL CULTURAL AND ECOLOGICAL RESOURCE KNOWLEDGES, DEVELOPMENT AND TENSIONS OF CHANGE AND MODERNITY

For Indigenous peoples, concern over the continued loss of their identities, cultures, traditions, and histories has prompted a renewed interest in their philosophies of thought. As already alluded to, such knowledge has never been frozen in time and space. They are continually relied upon in everyday challenges of human survival. Despite foreign influences and ever-changing trends of modernity and post-modernity, Indigenous knowledges have remained dynamic and evolved with contemporary challenges. In Indigenous communities, such knowledges can be found in their story forms, songs, myths and mythologies, fables, tales, folklore, riffles, and parables. They can be found in other forms of material culture, such as symbolic ornaments and body ware, and the meanings encoded in cultural artifacts. They can also be found in local cultural resource knowledges and practices associated with traditional pharmacology/plant medicine, farming technologies and agricultural methods, environmental management, soils and vegetation classification, arts and crafts, cultural norms, belief systems, social organization of families and kin groups, cultural festivals, and cultural products (e.g., weaving, pottery, poetry, folklore, music, as well as ornaments creatively fashioned from Indigenous materials). Through the power of oral traditions, we witness the flowering of a truly Indigenous literary tradition with succeeding generations of Indigenous communities. Music, drumming, dancing have been exceptional communication modes.

To reiterate, these knowledge systems do not stand apart or as distinct from Western science knowledge. Grassroots development approaches working with local knowledge have integrated different systems of thought. Knowledge is "Indigenous" to the extent that it works within the prism of local cosmologies that are localized in specific understandings of the society, culture, and nature nexus or interface. Difference is central to understanding Indigenous communities and knowledge forms. However, unlike hegemonic ways of knowing that sow the seeds of myriad forms of xenophobia (i.e., fear of the unknown or tendency to treat the unknown as undeserving), Indigenous communities (and particularly their ancestral knowledges) were rarely afraid of the strange and new. These communities and their knowledges actually welcomed strangers. But the local community was also careful not to allow influxes of different traditions and cultural practices to simply overwhelm them. (This is why most Indigenous peoples are often cautious of so-called modern influences that go a long way to devalue their cultures, heritage and histories.) Over time, local/Indigenous communities incorporated the new into the old, made over the old practices and ideas to serve the needs of the community. This speaks to the dynamism of Indigenous knowledge, and it attests to the fact that such knowledge is powerfully ingrained in local community thought and practice. Indigenous knowledge of medicinal plants (which includes information of the different kinds and functions of plants) has developed on the basis of careful observations and experimentation in local habitats. These knowledges go way back into ancestral times, and they are continually subjected to daily improvements and adaptations. Such a body of knowledge about traditional pharmacology is often contextualized on the community's historical experience with local health and illness situations and has been confirmed by their common usage and societal norms. In effect, it constitutes a collective traditional knowledge that cannot be conveniently dismissed.

Indigenous knowledge also recognizes the important role of local peoples in preserving ecological balance and biodiversity. There are customary laws (e.g., cultural taboos, rites, and rituals) governing individual and community use and relationships to social and natural environments. These customary practices and belief systems are a form of built-in protection mechanism for over-exploitation of natural resources. Local ecological sustainability works when Indigenous peoples maintain ownership status of their resources, where they can freely adopt local strategies of conservation, regeneration, and distribution and control of resources. To think otherwise is an insult to the integrity and intellectual resource knowledge of Indigenous communities. Although such practices of local food trends and 100-mile diets may be popular and seemingly new and innovative, these principles and practices pre-date the modern North American state and indeed emerged out of experience and consideration of the local environment and the food system.

Castro-Palaganas, et al. (2004) have rightly argued that "new development paradigms brought about by globalization and information technology have threatened Indigenous knowledge systems" (p. 1). The dominance of so-called modern science knowledge has largely led to an untenable situation in which Indigenous knowledge is ignored and neglected. With this trend, the authors continue "many Indigenous peoples find themselves in a transitional stage, facing the demands of an evolving and intrusive modern world but their knowledge and practices are still rooted in the traditional lifestyles of the past" (Castro-Palaganas, et al., 2004), especially in such as project planning and implementation. From time immemorial many Indigenous communities have used their own locally generated knowledge to change and to improve their circumstances (e.g., local governance and natural resource management). If local people have long plotted their own destiny, it is important to question why their knowledges are being dismissed in contemporary challenges of charting new paths for development?

Many challenges confront a critical study of Indigenous knowledge. These need to be carefully examined and engaged as our strategies for preserving and promoting such knowledge systems may actually end up leading to the (mis)appropriation of local cultural resource knowledge and heritage. For example, the capturing, documentation, and storing of such knowledge in a systematic way is not without problems. To whose benefit is such an undertaking? How and when do local peoples get to decide on the key issues affecting their lives? What happens to Indigenous knowledge when it is transformed into such codified ways from its orality (see also Dei, 2000; Domingo-Morales, 2002)? How do we include Indigenous knowledge in the modern development planning process as central building blocks of local development practice? As Castro-Palaganas, et al. (2001) note, there is little information readily available to guide project planners in using traditional knowledge. Besides, most development interventions have failed to induce Indigenous people to participate because of the absence of instruments and mechanisms that enable them to use their own knowledge.

INDIGENOUS KNOWLEDGES, EDUCATION, AND THE SCHOOL CURRICULUM

The focus on Indigenous knowledge has a politics that envisions a system of education in Indigenous traditions and philosophies. Indigenous philosophies are founded upon and express thoughts about the ways of life, traditions, and cultures of Indigenous peoples, from which all learners can, and do, benefit. For example, in an earlier work, Chinn (2007) evaluates Indigenous practices positively and critiques the absence of locally relevant science and Indigenous knowledge in the school curricula. Indigenous knowledge is about a way of life. With this reading, the author identifies local issues of traffic, air, and water quality which should be addressed, and the development of lesson plans, utilizing Indigenous prior knowledge, place, and to a lesser extent, culture, to pinpoint challenges of curricular development. The author's findings suggest that critical professional development, employing decolonizing methodologies articulated by Indigenous researchers, is critical. A methodological implication is the development of a framework for professional development which is able to shift science instruction toward meaningful, culture, place, and problem-based learning, relevant to environmental literacy and sustainability. Let me briefly focus on the pedagogic, instructional, and communicative significance of folklore and proverbs as Indigenous philosophies for educating youth. In Indigenous philosophies, spirituality and folklore are infused into everyday activities such as planting, fishing, burials, and religious and ceremonial events. But folkloric production (as in proverbs, story forms, folk music, dance, art, etc.) is about the totality of a people's experience, a way of life that speaks to the cultural, political, economic, social, and spiritual interconnections of human life and/or psycho-existential existence. Pedagogically, folkloric production can be taken up in the education of the learners. The study of Indigenous knowledge can help illustrate the ways folk culture can be positioned as a creative response to centuries of colonial oppression and exploitation. In documenting folklore as a creative response to colonialism, we can better understand the history of colonial oppression and how local folk culture emanated out of the creative imaginations of oppressed peoples.

Indigenous knowings, embedded in local religions, folklore, celebrations, healing practices, food preparation, oral tradition, pageantry, and work activities, all reveal local understandings of the connections of society, culture, and nature. Indigenous African and Diasporic cultural media, such as folk music and dance, Ananse stories, etc., can serve as useful tools for teachers. Folklore and proverbs contain a profound richness of the thought processes and language of Indigenous peoples. They constitute important communicative tools by reinforcing the epistemic saliency of peoples whose epistemologies are often devalued or negated in the formal educational arena. A careful examination of the richness of ideas carried in such cultural productions gives readers a critical insight into the moral fabric of the community. As Onuora (2009) also notes, the fact that rich proverbial sayings are usually uttered in particular contexts, along with specific explanations, makes it all the more useful as a communicative tool which teachers could use to impart invaluable lessons about the world as seen through the eyes of folk peoples. Proverbs invoke a psycho-spiritual consciousness which combines old and new strategies of addressing ongoing colonial and anti-colonial struggles. Local cultural knowings can be identity devices that shape the Indigenous consciousness of self and environment (John, 2003).

The narrative tradition of folktales can help create awareness about the political concerns of the people within a given locale. Folktales in a post-colonial and ante-colonial context also convey relevant political meanings. This provides a key resource for academics and researchers conducting research on identity formation within the context of the nation-state. Importantly, it makes explicit the connection between nation and state politics as they manifest in folkloric cultural expressions. The vitality of the art of story-telling as a legacy of Indigenous African ancestors is often conveyed in proverbs, fables, and tales. These offer an important pedagogical and communicative tool in the study of language and literature, and they relay important lessons of local history, experience, and ontological perspective on life. The retention of African cultures in the Diaspora shows the cultural continuity in knowledge systems. Indeed, Ananse stories narrated in Diasporic contexts are of importance in a social studies curriculum, as they impart lessons about work attitudes, humans, and their surroundings (see Klein, 1995; Pollard, 1985; Walter, 1966). The continuity of culture and cultural memory itself functions as a signifier of the vitality of African culture in the Diaspora today.

As educators at the classroom, administrative, board, ministry/department, regional, and federal levels debate questions of community integration, whole child education, multiple intelligence–based instruction, differentiated instruction, environmental education, and holistic pedagogy, Indigenous knowledges bring much to offer in all these areas. Understanding the learner and the teacher as embedded producers of community, who are as well produced by that community, the notion of schooling as part and product of the community is possible. Indigenous conceptions of the learner who never walks alone, and who indeed is accountable to the world around her (including the environment) address a number of the issues raised earlier. Further, as teachers and administrators struggle to understand their students and create relevant individualized approaches to instruction, the community has for too long been overlooked as a source of understanding and knowledge about its children. Educating the whole child is impossible if s/he is understood as divorced from a particular socio-cultural (and we might add environmental) context. Looking toward critical approaches in education, Indigenous approaches and knowledges are key to solving the "impossible" challenges facing educators today.

THE QUESTION OF CRITICAL INDIGENOUS METHODOLOGIES

As we seek to engage Indigenous knowledges as part of multiple ways of knowing, the question of how we secure/access such knowledge is crucial. A recent collection dealing with Indigenous and critical methodologies is helping to advance the course of Indigenous philosophy. To make a difference such methodological approaches must be anti-colonial in posture and challenge conventional assumptions that undergird Western social science research methodologies (see Smith, 1999). This book adds to the debate by highlighting the basic principles and ideas regarding Indigenous philosophies as anti-colonial, anti-racist, and anti-imperialistic. We must engage issues of responsibility and appropriation of knowledge as essential dimensions of critical social research. As much as bringing a critical gaze, locating the self, identity, and politics and affirming complicities and social responsibility are important, Indigenous research approach is about strengthening the capacity of local Indigenous peoples to undertake their own research. Indigenous research method poses some key epistemological questions and methodological concerns on critical/Indigenous research. The epistemological considerations of domination studies, conceptual and methodological issues of anti-colonial and anti-racist research; critical social research and the questions of power, difference, identity, and representation in knowledge production are all relevant to fleshing out the boundaries of Indigenous research and dominant social research.

The worth of a social theory should be judged both on its philosophical groundings/merits, as well as the ability of the theory to offer a social and political corrective. Researching Indigenous philosophies and undertaking an Indigenous research agenda must have both an academic and political component. In an Indigenous research approach, our concern is not a more conventional research agenda, using research simply to "generate knowledge about a group of (people)," or seeing our participants as "objects of knowledge." By its nature, an Indigenous research methodological approach is an activist research agenda that focuses simultaneously on ways that research allows local peoples to claim discursive agency and authority over their own lives and experiences, and which can point to discourses of resistance so as to transform the current social existence. Such a research methodological approach works with local peoples to offer their own perspectives on events, experiences, and developments in ways that can challenge dominant conceptions of everyday world and social existence. The ethical and political tensions in forging a productive Indigenist activist research agenda are part of the process of claiming multiple ways of knowing, if we are to challenge the dominance of particular ways of knowing (see Bhavnani & Davis 2000 in another context). An Indigenist research approach is itself "evolving" while in the field, rather than "moving from one predetermined step to another" (Fine & Vanderslice, 1991, p. 208).

INDIGENOUS AND SPIRITUALITY AS RESISTANCE: ASKING QUESTIONS

Resistance as part of the creation of new futures/visions of education and society is a long physical, material, metaphysical, and emotional struggle. For many of us it begins by claiming and reasserting our Indigenous identities. As mentioned earlier, for educators in general we need to develop new pedagogies anchored in our myriad identities, particularly spiritual identities. Reasserting our Indigeneity must embody the essence of ancestral knowing and geographies of cultural memory. Pedagogies of resistance (including claiming spirituality by asserting the importance of the learner's spirit) must be directed at helping young learners overcome the de-spiriting aspects of schooling (e.g., depersonalization of the learner, spirit wounding, and the everyday "humiliation rituals" including Othering of bodies) (see also Sium, 2010). We cannot disconnect ourselves from our surroundings, cultures, histories, and heritage. We must act on the basis of our history and spirituality (see also Asante, 2003).

Meaningful and genuine educational change starts with the exploration of the self of the learner. This means exploring the body, mind, and soul nexus. Conventionally, education has tended to fragment the self/learner, separating the body, mind, and the soul. To initiate change we must re-center the soul and the spirit. Spirituality as has been noted (see Smith, 1999) remains one of the clearest points of difference between Indigenous knowledge systems and Western systems of thought. Spirituality is relational and holistic and it is about a relationship with "nature, cosmos and the universe" (Mazama, 2002, p. 225). For the Indigenous scholar in the academy claiming spirituality is a form of healing, redeeming oneself and embarking upon a revolutionary journey to make the self whole again (see also Reid, 2010).

For many Indigenous and colonized peoples the politics of reclaiming and affirming our Indigenous and local cultural knowledges is a recognition of the importance and relevance of such knowledges in their own right. Yet, we also maintain that such knowledges have a right place in our academies to be shared with all learners. Therefore, in this final section of my Introduction I want to sound off a few cautionary notes as we seek to study Indigenous knowledges in the academy. There are significant challenges as to how we teach and instruct on Indigenous knowledges. Effective teaching calls for a full understanding and conceptual grounding in the systems of thought and bodies of philosophies that constitute "Indigenous knowings." So questions about who the teachers will be, who the students are and why, are very important. Furthermore, we must ask whether Indigenous teachings allow for an intellectual space for colonized and marginalized bodies in our classrooms to reclaim identity, history, culture, and space.

As we all welcome and encourage moments and pedagogic spaces to claim Indigenousness so as to subvert hegemonic knowings, we must also affirm the particularities and the shared connections of the colonial experiences among oppressed, colonized, and Indigenous peoples everywhere. There is an important caution here: In broaching Indigenous knowledges how do we avoid hyper-localization? As we make clear the local specificities of all knowledges we must also highlight the shared commonalities of Indigenous knowledges everywhere. As educators we must avoid the reproduction of colonial and re-colonial pathologies rolling out in Indigenous and anti-colonial instructional and pedagogical methods, strategies, and practices. We must meaningfully introduce Indigenous knowledges without trivializing these knowledges in the (Western) academy. We must also note the class, gender, racial/ethnic, and social difference dimensions in Indigenous knowledges. No knowledge is class, gender, race, neutral. There is always the danger for cultural custodians of knowledge to perpetuate particular patriarchal gender, class, ethnic, race, and sexual ideologies. Tradition can be invented in the service of power and oppression. Claims of Euro-modernity continue to impact the dynamics of Indigenous knowledge. As knowledges interact with each other, we see the appropriation of Western forms of modernity that may be problematic. Personally, I have always struggled with some current claims to African Indigeneity that I see as rooted in Western modernity. For example, to understand African spirituality is to distinguish such knowledge forms from syncretic religious practices. Claiming the "Indigenous" is not an end in itself. It is simply a means to an end, that is, decolonization. In effect, we must seek to repair the damage caused by colonialisms and colonial relations to all local cultural knowledge systems. Indigenousness is a search for wholeness and the repair of spiritual, emotional, physical material damage to oppressed communities through colonial practices.

I conclude by revisiting questions raised at the beginning. Can the academy "change its ways"? What are the possibilities of Indigenous knowledges co-existing in the Western academy? What capabilities (e.g., resources and spaces) exist in the academy for this to happen? Admittedly, we cannot simply make Indigenous knowledges fit into the "Eurocentric metaphorical box" by simply transforming the box into what it is not through deconstruction or reconstruction (Giambrone 2010, p. 13). What we can and should do is create a new box from the beginning and/or push for the co-existence of multiple centers of knowledges. Contributions in this book offer lessons on many issues in this Introduction. Indigenous philosophies shape the theory and practice of education (broadly defined), and help stem the tide of spiritual "dis-embodiment," particularly of learners. Indigenous knowledge forms in global and transnational contexts point to the pedagogic, instructional, and communicative implications for decolonized education. Some individual contributions begin with a brief overview of processes of knowledge production, interrogation, validation, and dissemination in diverse educational settings. There is an interrogation and critiques of theoretical conceptions of what constitutes "valid" knowledge and how such knowledge is produced and disseminated locally and externally. A particular emphasis is on the validation of non-Western epistemologies and their contributions in terms of offering multiple and collective readings of the world. Among the specific topics covered are the principles of Indigenous knowledge forms; questions of power, social difference, identity, and representation in Indigenous knowledge production; cultural appropriation and the political economy of knowledge production; Indigenous knowledges and science education; Indigenous knowledges and development in times of change and modernity; and the question of Indigenous spirituality as bedrock for transforming the academy. The book utilizes case material from diverse social settings to understand different epistemologies and their pedagogical implications. Indigenous knowledge is thus defined broadly as local cultural resource knowledge and the Indigenous philosophies of colonized/oppressed peoples.

ACKNOWLEDGMENTS

Special thanks to Marlon Simmons, Ph.D candidate, and Dr. Arlo Kempf in the Department of Sociology and Equity Studies of the Ontario Institute for Studies in Education of the University of Toronto for reading and commenting on drafts of this chapter.

REFERENCES

Abdi, A., & Cleghorn, A. (Eds.). (2005). *Issues in African Education: Sociological Perspectives.* New York: Palgrave Macmillan.

Asante, M. (2003). *Afrocentricity: A Theory of Social Change.* [Revised and Expanded] Chicago: African American Images.

Bhavnani, K., & Davis, A. Y. (2000). Women in Prison: Researching Race in Three National Contexts. In L. D. Kenny, F. W. Twine, & J. Warren (Eds.), *Racing Research, Researching Race: Methodological Dilemmas in Critical Race Studies* (pp. 227–246). New York: New York University Press.

Castro-Palaganas, E., Bagamaspad, A., et al. (2004). Mainstreaming Indigenous Knowledge Systems in Governance in the Asia-Pacific. Regional workshop on Mainstreaming IKSG, Manila, Philippines. Local Government Academy (14–16 October).

Chinn, P. W. U. (2007). Decolonizing Methodologies and Indigenous Knowledge: The Role of Culture, Place and Personal Experience in Professional Development. *Journal of Research in Science Teaching, 44*(9), 1247–1268.

Dei, G. J. S. (2000). The Role of Indigenous Knowledges in the Academy. *International Journal of Inclusive Education, 4*(2), 39–56.

Dei, G. J. S. (2010). *Teaching Africa: Towards a Transgressive Pedagogy.* New York: Springer.

Domingo-Morales, M. C. (2002). The Role of Intellectual Property Rights in Protecting Traditional Knowledge: The Philippine Experience. A Seminar on Traditional Knowledge. http://www.unctad.org/trade_env/test1/meetings/delhi/Countriestext/Philipinestext.doc

Fine, M., & Vanderslice, V. (1991). Qualitative Activist Research: Reflections on Politics and Methods. In F. B. Bryant, J. Edwards, R. S. Tindale, E. J. Posavac, L. Henderson-King, & Y. Suarez-Blacazar (Eds.), *Methodological Issues in Applied Social Psychology* (pp. 199–218). New York: Plenum.

Giambrone, A. (2010). *Indigenous Education in Intended Curriculum: Possibilities for Educators.* Unpublished course paper, Department of Sociology and Equity Studies, Ontario Institute for Studies in Education of the University of Toronto, Toronto.

Hall, S. (1991). Old and New Identities: Old and New Ethnicities. In A. King (Ed.), *Culture, Globalization and the World System* (pp. 41–68). New York: State University of New York Press.

John, C. (2003). *Clear Word and Third Sight: Folk Groundings and Diasporic Consciousness in African Caribbean Writing.* Jamaica, Barbados, Trinidad and Tobago: The University of the West Indies Press.

Kempf, A. (2010). *The Production of Racial Logic in Cuban Education: An Anti-Colonial Approach.* Unpublished Ph.D dissertation, Department of Sociology and Equity Studies, Ontario Institute for Studies in Education of the University of Toronto, Toronto.

Kincheloe, J., & Steinberg, S. (2008). Indigenous Knowledges in Education: Complexities, Dangers and Profound Benefits. In N. Denzin, Y. Lincoln, & L. T. Smith (Eds.), *Handbook of Critical and Indigenous Methodologies* (pp. 135–156). Los Angeles: Sage.

Klein, S. E. M. (1995). *The Ananse: Re-writing Oral Culture in Contemporary Caribbean Literature.* Unpublished M.A. thesis, English Language and Literature Department, University of Guelph, Guelph, Canada.

Mazama, A. (2002). Afrocentricity and African Spirituality. *Journal of Black Studies, 33*(2), 218–234.

Onuora, A. (2009). Caribbean Folktales as Indigenous Philosophy. Unpublished Paper, Department of Sociology and Equity Studies, Ontario Institute for Studies in Education of the University of Toronto, Toronto.

Pollard, V. (1985). *Anansesem: A Collection of Caribbean Folk Tales, Legends, and Poems for Juniors.* Jamaica: Longman Jamaica.

Quiroz, C. (1994). Biodiversity, Indigenous Knowledge, Gender and Intellectual Property Rights. *Indigenous Knowledge and Development Monitor, 2*(3).

Reid, R. (2010). *Leading in Meaningful Ways: Reviving the Possibilities of Spirituality in Elementary Public Schools.* Unpublished course paper, Department of Sociology and Equity Studies, Ontario Institute for Studies in Education of the University of Toronto, Toronto.

Semali, L., & Kincheloe, J. (Eds.). (1999). *What Is Indigenous Knowledge? Voices from the Academy.* New York: Falmer.

Sium, A. (2010). Assimilation, Renaming and Spirit Injury: Implications for Indigenous Bodies in Canadian Classrooms. Unpublished course paper, Department of Sociology and Equity Studies, Ontario Institute for Studies in Education of the University of Toronto, Toronto.

Smith, L. (1999). *Decolonizing Methodologies.* London: Zed.

Walter, J. (1966). *Jamaican Song and Story: Anancy Stories, Digging oings, Ring Tunes, and Dancing Tunes Collected and Edited by Walter Jekyll.* New York: Dover.

Wane, N. N. (2009). Indigenous Education and Cultural Resistance: A Decolonizing Project. *Curriculum Inquiry, 39*(1), 159–178.

Waterfall, B. (2008). *Decolonising Anishnabec Social Work Education: An Anishnabe Spiritually-Infused Reflexive Study.* Unpublished Ph.D. dissertation, University of Toronto, Toronto.

SECTION I

Indigenous Knowledges as Philosophy and the Implications of Decolonization

INTRODUCTION TO SECTIONS

Chapters in this book are written by scholars working in the areas of Indigenous knowledges and anti-colonial studies. While our focus is on education (broadly defined), we have planned for the book to have an inter- and multi-disciplinary edge. The book is divided into five (5) sections, with contributions dealing with overarching themes. A good number of the contributors speak from a position of what elsewhere (Dei, 1996, 1999) I have termed "epistemic saliency," that is, speaking with/from the authenticity of their own experiences and voices, a space that allows local subjects and scholars to speak about their informed knowledge base as opposed to being spoken for. Politically, such epistemic saliency allows us to accord salience to the voice of the oppressed, marginalized, and colonized bodies as they recount and reflect upon the experiences of colonization, oppression, marginalization, and resistance both at the local level but also in connection to larger social and theoretical frameworks.

SECTION ONE: INDIGENOUS KNOWLEDGES AS PHILOSOPHY AND THE IMPLICATIONS OF DECOLONIZATION

Section One broaches the conceptual and practical questions of Indigenous knowledges as philosophies of knowing and the implications for decolonization. It is significant to have clarity when engaging "Indigenous knowledge" as a way of knowing, especially given the voraciousness of its critics.

Such issues as the history of colonial and imperial knowledges, the perils of anti-colonial politics and discourses of Indigeneity must be approached from a critical perspective rooted firmly in discussions about knowledge, power, and decolonization. As noted in my introductory chapter, it is important for us to must move away from an essentialized, narrow, and circumscribed or bounded definition of "Indigenous" to recognize difference as well as to account for multiple and diverse experiences of Indigenous peoples under colonialism and imperialism. Particularly in Euro-American contexts we must bring a broad interpretation to Indigenous as beyond Aboriginality (e.g., inclusive of African, Hawaiian, Alaskan, Aboriginal, First Nations, Inuit, Metis, Indigenous European, and Asian). While some of these claims may be contested it serves to produce a healthy discussion of how European colonialism has positioned Indigenous knowledges as non-knowledge, backward, primitive, and inferior, as something not worthy of intellectual engagement (e.g., the denigration of Indigenous spirituality as evil, witchcraft, over-mythical, and superstitious, and hence not worthy of attention). This denigration and dismissal of Indigenous knowledges continue today, thinly veiled beneath critiques of undue romanticization, over-mythicization, overglorification, uncritical essentialism, and fetishization that are sure to accompany any claims of Indigeneity.

There have been other consequences. For example, we ask: Why is it that within the Western academy some minority/colonized and oppressed learners do not claim an Indigeneity or/and go to the extent of denying their own Indigenousness? It takes courage to openly engage Indigenous knowledge as oppositional and counter discursive in the Western academy. For many of us, we continually lead fragmented existences as learners. We are asked to put our local cultural knowledges in secluded compounds, not in the open arena of intellectual and public discourse. This is a stark reminder that a vital aspect of the decolonizing project involves the insertion of the whole self into knowledge production and the learning process; the individual experience and narrative are powerful tools in dislodging universal, colonial tropes that posit a universal subject. The Indigenous knowledge that resides in bodies and individuals is vital in securing the enduring survival of Indigenous knowledge and, in these knowledges, holds the possibility of speeding the "painful demise of Eurocentricism" (Asante, 2009).

As pointed out earlier (Dei, in this collection) (re)claiming Indigenous knowledge as a necessary exercise in decolonization is a messy, violent, contradictory, and painful undertaking. For particular oppressed, minoritized, and colonized subjects, resisting internalized racist, Euro-patriarchal notions about ourselves, cultures, traditions, and histories is a tortured undertaking. There is spirit injury on both counts (e.g., both in what the Eurocentric knowledge does to us and in the cost to us/our bodies for engaging in perpetual resistance). In resisting Eurocentric ways of knowing through Indigenous knowledges, there is the need for scholarship which not only challenges the validity of Western conceptions of "truth," "philosophy," and "objectivity," but also, the need to revisit and interrogate how Indigenous ways of knowing are taken up in the academy. This is the task of this section.

George Dei's chapter, "Revisiting the Question of the 'Indigenous'" begins with the self and the personal subject(ive) location as critical in terms of what brings him to the topic of Indigenous knowledge. He situates the self as a methodological and discursive feature of the chapter so as for the reader to examine and understand the perspective from which he is conducting the discussion of Indigeneity. The chapter then moves to pose some key questions that guide both the theorization and re-conceptualization of "Indigenous knowledge" and "Indigeneity." It is argued that "Indigenous," notwithstanding its contestations, must be applied broadly to include cultural knowledges of local and Indigenous communities globally. This includes Aboriginal, African, Hawaiian, Native American, and Australian knowledges. Such knowledge resides on the land, and in bodies, places, cultural memories, history, culture, and language. Dei briefly raises the question of who is/is not Indigenous, and/or who has Indigenous knowledge. It is pointed out that, however legitimate some of these questions are, we need to move beyond such preoccupations to ask about the politics of reclaiming Indigenous knowledge and how such politics helps subvert and/or destabilize the complacency of dominant knowings. The chapter concludes by putting forward twelve (12) principles that should form the basis of articulating an Indigenous discursive framework.

Temitope Adefarakan's chapter, "(Re)Conceptualizing 'Indigenous' from Anti-colonial and Black Feminist Theoretical Perspectives: Living and Imagining Indigeneity Differently" also takes up the notions of "Indigeneity" and "Indigenous" from anti-colonial and African feminist theoretical perspectives. She points out that these standpoints provide a critical approach by re-conceptualizing the "Indigenous" and allowing for more flexible discussions where concepts such as "migrant" or "Diasporic" Indigeneity can be imagined and framed. It is contended that this way, the unique positionings of Diasporic Africans is accorded a space to theorize the particularities of myriad experiences. Using a study of Diasporic Yoruba Indigeneity her chapter shows that an intellectual and ontological shift in current notions of Indigeneity is necessary if we are to include the diasporic African experience.

Today we are witnessing the resurgence of Indigenous forms of knowing (specifically Indigenous holistic thought) in many local communities after years of European colonial denigration of such knowledge forms. Farah Shroff's chapter, "We Are All One: Holistic Thought-Forms within Indigenous Societies—Indigeneity and Holism" briefly offers important insights about holism and holistic thought from various parts of the world, focusing on Asian schools of thought—primarily Hinduism and Buddhism. Her discussion illustrates the virtually universal, historical as well as contemporary nature of ideas such as "interconnectedness," "unity," and "oneness." In outlining Indigenous holistic philosophical foundations and working with the concepts of unity and oneness, interconnectedness, prana, panchamahabhuta theory, karma, etc., the author pinpoints the efficacy of these systems of science knowledge for education in general. Within holistic cosmologies, two notions are central: "all beings are connected" and "life is circular." By understanding and acting upon the profound nature of these ideas through visualizing all beings on Earth as one big family, Indigenous holistic thought would have a positive impact on the state of the world today.

The socio-political ideology of "assimilationism" has featured prominently in colonial discourses and colonizing projects of "civilizing" and "educating" Indigenous Australian peoples. Marcelle Cross-Townsend in his chapter, "Indigenous Education and Indigenous Studies in the Australian Academy: Assimilationism, Critical Pedagogy, Dominant Culture Learners, and Indigenous Knowledges" notes assimilationist assumptions posit Indigenous peoples, their knowledges, and practices as inferior to Western peoples' knowledges and practices. Indigenous people's survival is perceived to be dependent on wholesale assimilation into the dominant, "superior" culture and language, where the economic and social dominant culture objectives of education override any Indigenous cultural, linguistic, social, or human rights imperatives. Drawing on his own research, workplace practices, experiences, and observations over the past ten years teaching Indigenous studies in a regional Australian university, the author explores some of the divergent contextual complexities, contradictions, practical challenges, and limitations of engaging critical pedagogical approaches to challenge assimilationism and dominant ideology in Indigenous studies in the Australian higher education sector. The chapter highlights particular challenges of working with predominantly dominant culture learners, the institutional and systemic imperatives of the Academy, and the limited capacity of Indigenous studies to protect embodied Indigenous knowledges from appropriation by the disciplines of the Academy.

Ali Abdi's chapter on "African Philosophies of Education: Deconstructing the Colonial and Reconstructing the Indigenous" opines that as we speak about the general notations and assumed practices of philosophy, we must not discursively and/or analytically escape the overall conceptual and theoretical fluidities that inform the general structure, as well as the overall parameters of "philosophy." That fluidity should also assure us that, however we define and functionalize philosophy, its subjective locations will be attached to the social contexts and relationships of the human-inhabited terrains where it is physico-consciously lived. It is with this understanding that philosophical traditions would be selectively Indigenous to all spaces which people collectively inhabit. Such co-habitation refines the original meaning of philosophy from the occasionally romanticized "love of wisdom" into the more epistemically coherent perspective of critically inquiring about and relating to our world. In the colonially driven European epistemic and analytical traditions, Africa and its peoples have been located as aphilosophical, and therefore, devoid of the sophisticated knowledge categories that can create and sustain any reliable educational categories that could implicate effective social development and life management schemes that should be deployed for individual and communal well-being. Abdi challenges the false assumptions about African education and philosophies of education, African ways of knowing and attached systems of Indigenous know-how that have helped sustain peoples and development. He offers some preliminary perspectives on deconstructing the shaky colonial side of the story and reconstructing the life-affirmed context of African Indigenous philosophies of education and attached ways of knowing.

In "Space, Time, and Unified Knowledge: Following the Path of Vine Deloria, Jr." Jeffrey Anderson notes that much less attention has been paid to the philosophical line of inquiry that is integral to the writings of Vine Deloria, Jr., than to political-legal controversies and contradictions, the chasm between Euro-American and Native American metaphysics, and the multiple attacks on various Western scientific paradigms. It is contended that underlying all of these particular aims was the quest to move toward a unified knowledge that transcended the pernicious binary boundaries posed by colonization and modernity, between science and religion, Indigenous and Western metaphysics, marginal and core academic paradigms, and past and present Indigenous cultures. The grand appeal was for dialogue and reciprocity across the imagined borders of specialized and fortified epistemologies toward a unified system of knowledge that genuinely includes Indigenous, metaphysical unities and ultimate concerns, rather than simply estranging them as objects of inquiry and observation. A running thread throughout Deloria's works is to set a path for North American Indigenous communities to return ultimate concerns and turn away from the trends toward commercialization, fragmentation, and chaotically concocted forms of religion. At the core of all of these concerns is the quandary of space and time. With a particular focus on dimensions of space and time that permeate Deloria's project and others to supplement the pursuit, the chapter examines some of the fundamental ways that American Indian models of space and time move toward unified knowledge and identifies the main barriers to spatio-temporally unified knowledge.

REFERENCES

Asante, M. (2009). *Erasing Racism*. New York: Prometheus.
Dei, G. J. S. (1996). *Anti-Racism Education in Theory and Practice*. Halifax: Fernwood.
Dei, G. J. S. (1999) The Denial of Difference: Reframing Anti-Racist Praxis. *Race, Ethnicity and Education, 2*(1), 17–37.

CHAPTER ONE

Revisiting the Question of the 'Indigenous'

GEORGE J. SEFA DEI

A few opening remarks about my background and how I have come to engage this topic; I see the personal subject[ive] location as critical in terms of what brings me to the topic. The contextualization of writer/self as a methodological and discursive feature of any textual discussion is significant. It helps the reader to understand the perspective from which one is conducting the analysis. And by perspective, I do not mean just ideology or analytical framework, but a personal accounting of why I write about what I do. I am a social anthropologist by academic training who has bridged the disciplinary background with a focus on the sociology of education. I have been writing on the subject of Indigenous knowledges since the early 1980s. I also teach an advanced graduate course on "Indigenous Knowledges and Decolonization" at the University of Toronto. My long-term research interests lie in the areas of anti-colonial theory, Indigenous and anti-racism studies, minority education in Canadian contexts, and issues of African education. I have been a committed proponent of an Afrocentric school for children and youths of African descent in Canadian contexts. I find current schooling processes that depersonalize, disembody, and de-root young learners from their cultures, histories, and identities quite troubling to say the least. Of course, I am wary of race essentialism. But increasingly, I have also become skeptical of attempts to deny race as part of our identities and as consequential for knowledge production and education. I see a detailed connection between identity, schooling, and knowledge production. I have repeatedly argued that the effective education of African Canadian and minoritized youth rests on the extent to which schools can engage questions of identity, culture, spirituality, place, and history in order to give some sense of a rootedness, connectedness, and belonging to students.

In writing this chapter I seek to claim my Indigenous roots even while today living in a Diasporic context. My Indigeneity is rooted in my African experience, having been born, raised, and schooled in the surroundings and rootedness in my Ghanaian and African culture, history, and ancestry. Through the passage of time and living in different and multiple places, my local cultural resource knowledges have never left me. As a traditional elder/Chief in Ghana I respect and honor my ancestral knowledge which requires that I bring myself continually in tune with traditional customs, practices, and knowledge that have sustained many local communities over the years. It does not mean these knowledges are static. Neither does it mean that such knowledges should not be interrogated for their sites of empowerment and disempowerment for self and groups. Such knowledge resides in my cultural memory, and I know and use it to guide everyday social action. My everyday understanding and interpretations of the world around me have been shaped by Indigenous histories, cultures, heritage, myriad identities (including spiritual identity), and social experiences. My identity is steeped in my Indigeneity. With formal European schooling systems devaluing my ancestral and cultural knowledges, claiming Indigenous knowledge for me is both a political and intellectual exercise in decolonization. I, therefore, write about Indigenous knowledge as an intellectual and political exercise to subvert and resist colonial hegemonic ideologies and Eurocentric discourses masquerading in the (Western) academy as universal knowledge. I also want to understand the self and take personal responsibility to know me (the self) in order to relate holistically with others, communities and the outer world (see also Fitznor, 2005, p. 8).

As I reflected on my background training as an anthropologist over the years and my on-going engagement with Indigenous knowledges I have grappled with the following question: How might we mobilize the Indigene within the academy? I raise this question because the process of Othering and studying peoples and societies for the purpose of controlling their representation, which my institutional disciplinary background taught me, is not consistent with Indigenous knowledges. There are also tensions arising from the fact that the roots of much social science, arts, and the humanities can arguably be found in the West's historically racist tradition of exploiting, disrupting, and renaming the world of the Other. If we want to drastically change the colonial foundations of our academies, then we should rename and reimagine the academy altogether. And, we must do so in a way that connects them through a multidisciplinary approach and resonates with Indigenous ways of knowing. Pertinent to this reimagining are also discussions that explore how Western science epistemologies and academic disciplines engage questions of politics and embodiment as well as how we come to understand the intellectual practices of spiritual dismemberment and disembodiment. Similarly, issues of place are very integral. Place is more than a location of knowledge. It speaks of a past, history, culture, language, as well as to the necessity to engage with questions of materiality, spirituality, and metaphysical realms. The examination of the structure and logical coherency of Indigenous knowledge as philosophy of knowing should also respond to questions of the moral, ethical, spiritual, cosmological dimensions of knowledge (see also Kincheloe & Steinberg, 2008; Nakata, 2007a).

Postmodern, post-structural, and post-colonial theories as modes of thought have dominated the (Western) academy. The largely Eurocentric schools of thought have become the tacit norm used by everyone who purports to be "critical" to view the world. These discursive prisms/frames (if I may be allowed to name them as such) have been constructed as the sole legitimate yardstick to gauge the intellectual validity of scholarly knowledge. Consequently, they have taken on a hegemonic monopoly over what ought to constitute a legitimate logic of critique. Indigenous ways of critique and reimagination have been tangentialized by this claim of authority. However, Indigenous bodies know too well that, structures and institutions script individual lives differently and resistances are shaped by such encounters. We therefore bring different readings and experience to narrating the colonial and a supposedly "post" colonial encounter. Thus, we need to be mindful of the moments when critical and oppositional discourses are erased, denied, or discredited. Furthermore, we need to be aware of the dangers of fitting different frameworks (sometimes incompatible frameworks) (e.g., Indigenous and anti-colonial) into Western prisms or lenses that only serve to reify the dominance of Eurocentricity. We cannot use Eurocentric standards to ensure the worth of the Indigenous prism as social theory. It is intellectually foolhardy to claim that dominant standards of what constitutes theory are what theory is all about. Much of what accounted for "theory" in social science disciplines until recently (and this phenomenon persists) barely accounted for the experiences of the oppressed/minority and colonized bodies. One cannot be oblivious to this contradiction in our work. Many of us are still grappling with some of the ironies and paradoxes of our academy. [Intellectual] agency is often tied to a "mastery" of the very things one is resisting. Hence the "mastery" of dominant discourses is required in order to initiate counter-oppositional discourses. A decolonizing practice rooted in Indigenous epistemologies understands the need for this "mastery" as an intellectual impediment to the project of decolonization. An intentional and practical engagement with Indigenous knowledges from a place that views these epistemologies as critical in their own right might offer a poignant point of references for reimagining. This grounding process speaks to the centrality of claiming and reclaiming of Indigenous ways of knowing and living in the decolonization process.

By claiming Indigenous knowledges, no one is calling for a return to a mythic past or for a mythic return to a pre-colonial past. Nor is the claim a substitution of new forms of imperialist knowledge. It is a recognition of the need to renegotiate knowledge and develop multiple ways of knowing to allow us to be able to read, know, understand, and interpret our complex world.

NECESSARY QUESTIONS

Indigenous knowledges are contested. In fact, many have pointed to the futility of striving for a universal definition so I will not attempt to offer one here. All definitions are limited and it is crucial that we focus on issues and questions rather than search for neat definitions. As Battiste and Henderson (2000) rightly observed, Indigenous knowledge "is not a uniform concept across all Indigenous peoples" and we must resist the Eurocentric temptation to define, label, and categorize all human experiences (p. 35). I will instead focus on seeking some clarifications on some very familiar questions. In discussing "Indigenous knowledges" I would point out that the key issues must center around concepts of positionality and politics, identity, language, culture, and history. We also have to respond to questions around origin, authenticity, and essentialism. Language, cultural memory, and colonization always need to be evoked in a critical investigation of what is Indigenous. Fundamentally, the Indigenous should be perceived as mostly about place-based knowing, an understanding of a traditional sacred relationships between peoples and their cultures and cosmologies. These relationships offer a holistic knowledge base to operate.

There is a critique that the term "Indigenous" homogenizes and obliterates distinctiveness and that we need to offer multilayered meanings. Much of this debate seems to gloss over what the term Indigenous might reveal as opposed to what it obscures. For example, the term is a self-application by Indigenous peoples in contrast to the imposed notion of "primitive," "tribal," and "folk" knowledge (see also Purcell, 1998). Hence, the use of the term Indigenous is about a political reclamation and self-definition to challenge Eurocentric dominance. It is also significant to see Indigenous knowledge as knowledge originating from the land (Fals-Borda, 1980). Such knowledges are also dynamic, experientially based, holistic, relational, and connecting physical, metaphysical, and the cosmos (see Battiste & Henderson, 2000; Cajete, 1994; Dei, 2000; Ermine 1995; Semali & Kincheloe, 1999).

A lot of intellectual energies have been devoted to addressing such questions as What is an Indigenous perspective as opposed to a Western-centric perspective/prism or lens? What is the connection between Indigenous peoples (identified with land/territory) and Indigenous knowledges (as localized, culturally specific knowledge but not boxed in time or space, and as knowledge residing in the body)? While the questions are worthy of pursuit, the process ought to be underlined by a recognition of the limitations of binary modes of thought. At the same time it is even more important to recognize the historical and current politics of Indigenous knowledge as "discredited," "subjugated," devalued or denied. Indigenous bodies also know that Indigenous knowledges have limitations just like other ways of knowing (e.g., disempowering of certain groups, women, and ethnic minorities; and queer relationships). These limitations, however, rarely serve to undermine the Western rationalism, for example, but are persistently mobilized to discredit non-dominant knowledges.

Creating a space in the academy to discuss Indigenous knowledges in the first place constitutes a political act, a cognitive and affective imperialism (see also Battiste, 1986), it changes the meaning of what you are conveying. That is, it is a political affirmation of the relevance of the past, culture, tradition, as well as challenging and simultaneously insisting on the self of local voices and subverting the colonial and imperial ordering of knowledge. Indigenous knowledges and peoples have been colonized, and today the need for a politics of reclamation of the past, present, and for the future has never been more pressing. This begins by recognizing the degree to which this is underway in myriad places and spaces as resistance has always existed to dominant knowledges and practices.

It has at times been asked: Who is/What is not Indigenous? Who has Indigenous knowledge? These are again very significant questions that deserve critical interrogation. After all, every subject can lay an Indigenous claim to some place and location, somewhere and at some time (see also Churchill, 2003). This is especially a concern when constructions of Indigeneity that are located within historical and contemporary legacies of White conquest, colonial control, domination and occupation have become the dominant socio-political discursive order. We are compelled therefore to heed Churchill (1993, 2003) when he pushes us to think of the limitations (and I might even add possibilities) of claiming an Indigenous identity to land and territory that one is not Indigenous to. On the other hand, claims for Indigeneity that are grounded in marginalized and colonized peoples' struggles, resistance, and liberation need to be taken seriously within this context as they open up possibilities and creative designs for Indigenous bodies to re-narrate their own experiences and histories (see also Adefarakan, 2010). Furthermore, however legitimate some of the questions asked earlier might be (see St. Denis, 2004), we also need to ask who is raising these questions and why? For Indigenous bodies engaging with debates engineered by dominant bodies might end up serving as a distraction to the project of decolonization and reclamation. We must see some of this questioning as a denial of Indigeneity which serves the latest Euro-colonial project. The "Indigenous" predates colonialism and Euro-colonial impositions of dominant knowledges. Such knowledges have not remained static. In fact, colonialism and the processes of colonial imposition of knowledge transformed (or affected) Indigenous knowledges and vice versa. But such processes do not negate the existence of Indigenous knowledge, Indigeneity, and the Indigene.

Speaking directly of the Canadian context where I find myself located, we also need to discuss the relationship with the land, Indigenousness, the colonial, and what has been touted as the "Black or immigrant settler." The nomenclature of "settler" has a historic specificity to the Euro-colonial, the dominant body, that of Whiteness. Historically the settler has been installed in a particular way, which worked to erase the atrocities done onto Indigenous peoples. We cannot forget that "settler" is about hegemonic relations with Indigenous peoples, settler is about power and privilege as endowed through the Euro-American body. This is because historically settler has been and continues to be about White civility, settler is about citizenry as citizenry constitutes in a totalizing way what it means to be human. Yet concerning citizenry and the experience of the colonial in relation to settler and Indigeneity, it does not mean the racialized (Black, immigrant) body is exempt from being implicated, given the complexity of this thing we have come to know as citizenry, given that citizenry constitutes the legitimating act of belonging to the imperial nation-state. I work with the conceptualization of the "colonial" as beyond being "alien" or "foreign" to anything imposed and dominating (see Dei, 2000; Dei & Asgharzadeh, 2001). Indigeneity forms a certain relationship in and through the land, be it through the geography of time and space, or the tangible good of its materiality. Indigeneity then must be theorized through, as James (1993) notes, *dialectical histories of materialism*. In this way we can come to understand holistically the limitations, possibilities, consequences, and the implications of these historically contested sites, such as the expropriation of Aboriginal land, of what constitutes settler, of the question of immigration, of how we come to experience/understand *belonging*. As well we come to know about the experience of the Indigenous body, and about how we make sense of the colonial, not to mention how we make sense of questions of identity, the Diaspora, and the history of African enslavement as contextualized through the contemporary edict of Western globalization.

It is critical and significant for a distinction to be made between the conventional/dominant take about the need for a term/concept/notion of what constitutes "Indigenous" and what Indigenous peoples allude to when they assert their Indigenousness. This distinction is not only helpful in finding the moments when claims of Indigenousness are being denied, invalidated, or negated. But such distinction is also helpful with engaging the points of convergence and divergence, for example, between Aboriginality and Indigeneity. Indigenous is a much broader concept than Aboriginal. The latter is specific to a place. But a broader conception of Indigenous and Indigeneity (which includes understanding of Aboriginality) may also allow for discussion of Diasporic and myriad Indigeneities as well. I would argue that the distinction between "Aboriginality" and "Indigenous" allows us to bring a complex reading to the term Indigenous. One may not be "Indigenous" in the sense of an uninterrupted long-term occupancy of a place, but she or he can still work with the knowledge and politics of Indigeneity.

This clarification is important, given the sometimes-unfounded criticisms that Indigenous has come to mean a singular approach. It is pertinent to ask, for example, who imagines the Indigenous as singular? Most Indigenous peoples and their knowledge systems do not imagine their worlds as singular/undifferentiated. Therefore caution must be exercised not to theorize and "interrogate" Indigenous through the established discourses and specificities of Aboriginality and through the Eurocentric essentialization of both Indigenousness and Aboriginality. Making this assertion does not imply the connection between Aboriginality and Indigeneity is lost. Land, for example, has been integral in making any claims of Indigenousness or Aboriginality whether in occupational, territorial, relational, and affinal sense. But the Indigenous allows us to travel to varied, broader, and complex terrains and territories.

Theorizing Indigenous and Indigeneity broadly to implicate multiple bodies, spaces, and locations would bring to the fore some additional questions: for example, why is such a project of an expansive definition of Indigenous so necessary and to what intent and purposes? How do we theorize Indigeneity to recognize the ontological and epistemological lineage among some peoples dispersed in the Diasporic contexts? What are the implications for the politics of claiming and reclaiming? (see also Adefarakan, this volume). I agree with Adefarakan (2010) that theorizing Indigenous identity raises tensions with uncritical postmodern politics of identity, which presents a singularly valid or acceptable approach to how we vigorously theorize the question of identity. For example, the idea that Africans are "not Indigenous enough" or "not Indigenous at all" (see also Adefarakan, 2010) needs to be troubled. Bringing a broader reading to Indigenousness allows for displaced peoples, transitory, and migratory subjects and many others in Diasporic and transformed contexts to search and lay claim to a sense of belonging. In other words, there is a politics of re-assertion of the Diasporian Indigenous identities as a necessary exercise in our decolonization.

It is when we are able to make the connections between Aboriginality and Indigenousness, and also, draw the points of divergence that we can boldly articulate a confluence of Indigenous knowledge and the question of Indigeneity. The struggle for Indigeneity and Indigenization is about disentangling control of knowledge production from the colonizer and addressing the complicity of local Indigenous elite. It is also a struggle to retain one's identity in the call for a global sameness. As noted elsewhere (Dei, this collection) there are pitfalls and ills of the so-called modernist project and modernization. The tensions and contradictions in the narration and reclamation of Indigeneity and Indigenous knowledge exist when it is argued that one loses their Indigenous knowledge simply by being transplanted into a different space from the source of that knowledge.

The politics of resistance to such a loss means one can claim their Indigeneity as a form of identity for political and intellectual purposes. Indigenous knowledge can reside in bodies and cultural memories notwithstanding global migrations, globalization, and the emergence of Diasporic communities. Purcell (1998) points out that "as colonialism uprooted Indigenous peoples it also uprooted their knowledge systems" (p. 266). However, these knowledge systems have continued over centuries to adjust to and persist in new environments. The recognition of the specific situatedness of knowledge forms does not amount to a "fetishization of the local" or the Indigene (Ginsburg, 1994, p. 366).

For Diasporic Indigenous bodies, tensions in the use of Indigenous knowledge are the result of an incommensurability of knowledges. In other words, they are the result of unbridgeable and profound differences that cannot be easily reconciled in particular contexts, for example, some aspects of Eurocentricity and the variegated forms of Indigenous ways of living. The argument raised above has implications for knowledge integration or "cultural interface" (Nakata, 2007a, b). Cultural mixing, however, has always been a human reality/condition.

Given the discourse of "identity," such hybridity can be an articulation or fusion of two or more disparate elements to engender or create a new distinct identity. But when evoked in knowledge production, it calls for separating the politics of disrupting/interrupting binaries or dichotomous cultural differences, from an affirmation of important differences that separate knowledge forms given their unique characters and differences. In other words, while identities are not mutually exclusive, the politics of reclaiming Indigenous knowledges requires a resistance to the idea that we have somehow lost part of ourselves and our knowledge in the supposedly new and transformed spaces.

As educators within the Western (Eurocentric) academy, the key questions for us to focus on are, in bringing Indigenous knowledges to the academy, what are the specific challenges—staffing, administration, curriculum, resources, pedagogical differences, etc. and how are these problems and challenges to be resolved? Quite evidently place and context are very important to discussions of Indigenous knowledge. Colonization served to destabilize Indigenous knowledge for most communities but it does not mean their local cultural resource knowledge is lost. For example, if Africa or the African body today has no Indigenous knowledge, then what does it mean to say "Indigenous plants" of Africa? What are we to make of the ancient African civilizations, knowledges about local plant pharmacologies, local peoples' soils, climate, and vegetation classification methods and methodologies, artworks, and folkloric productions and other cultural artifacts, Indigenous proverbs, fables, talks, songs, proverbs, and local understandings of society-culture-nature nexus? Saying these are "traditional" does not convince me, as the term has historic Eurocentric baggage when made synonymous with "primitive." The discussion about what constitutes Indigenous knowledges and practices should also transcend the borders of the notion that everything Indigenous bodies practice is Indigenous.

It is imperative to recognize that there has been incessant pressure for Indigenous bodies to Indigenize Western ideologies and practices, sometimes for survival in local contexts and other times to fit into the Western-centered globalization project order. The whole issue of the absence of colonial imposition is not only significant but also necessary in claiming Indigenous knowledge. When knowledge is imposed it loses its Indigeneity. With regards to the pragmatics of Indigeneity, a recycling of colonially imposed practices is counterproductive to decolonization and serves to perpetuate Western hegemony around the discourse of knowledge production. The separation of colonially imposed ideas from knowledges originating in specific localities need not be confused with a rejection of a healthy hybridization of knowledge systems. On a different but related note, the politics of [re]claiming Indigeneity is different for human subjects (e.g., for some developing a sense of what such knowledge offers humanity in general; for others claiming knowledge to strengthen Indigenous and marginalized groups of the value of the cultural knowings in their own right). This is what the whole project of decolonization is about.

The foregoing discussion also highlights the prominence of the question of origin. How far do we go to claim an Indigenous identity? As noted earlier, a question can be a political distraction. It forces a linear thinking rather than acknowledging that what is important is the rootedness in place, culture, and politics of knowledge production. We must also be bold to question: why is it that claims to be Indigenous to certain places and locations with histories and politics of knowledge creation are contested while others are not? (see Adefarakan in this collection) We believe that origin is relevant if one is defining Indigenous solely to a place. But, as noted, Indigenous also refers to knowledge located within a body even when that body travels out of the space/place/location. Reclamation also requires a consciousness of what one has lost. This consciousness is as vital in claims of Indigeneity as reclaiming is about a past and history. There is the popular adage that it is important to know where one is coming from in order to know where one is going. In this saying I invoke the West African symbol of the "Sankofa" bird who is looking around behind while it watches ahead. The search for new answers can only succeed if we carefully dissect and understand what has failed us in the years before. It could be argued a river never returns to its source. But I like a "return to the source." Why? After all, every river contains the water from its original source. In other words, as P. Adjei (personal communication, March 5, 2010) contends, a river carries the source of its water with it! The present is constitutive of the past and we must learn from that history if we are to understand the present and contest the future (Lattas, 1993). For many of us what we seek to "reclaim" is not actually something that has been lost, rather it has been intentionally marginalized. What we are reclaiming has always been around and all we are seeking to do is to bring it to the foreground or surface.

The claim of Indigenous knowledges must be contextualized in a particular Indigenous rootedness. But Indigenous knowledges can be engaged by all learners. Hence, it is important to make a distinction between Indigenous peoples (identified with land/territory) and Indigenous knowledges (localized but not boxed in time and space, as knowledge residing in body, and also, that such knowledge can be engaged by any subject irrespective of body). There is also what I would call "the pedagogic and instructional effect for promoting educational change" through the medium of Indigenous studies. We need Indigenous bodies in the academy as a question of knowledge and representation. In the meantime as we pursue educational transformation, we can engage an inclusive politics of "and/with," and not binaries of "either/or." We can work with ideas of Indigenous knowledge to benefit from the multicentric ways of knowing without being bogged down with the important question of the "bodies and their knowledge."

I agree with Gregory Smith (personal communication, fall, 2009) that beyond creating "educational processes that make a place for the knowledge and cultural practices of Indigenous peoples within formal educational settings we must be bold and courageous and re-invent schools that help all students become [to some extent] Indigenous—of a place—acquainting them with the characteristics of their home places and cultivating in them the willingness to be responsible members of the human and natural communities that support and nurture them." While this may suggest to some that we need to move beyond the history of colonization and work with a knowledge that people, where they are, need to regain a sense of what it means to be tied to the land and specific human communities in the hopes of creating genuinely sustainable and just societies, it ought not to be so. It is neither a liberal nor a pluralist rhetoric. We can still center history of colonialism, colonization, and decolonization in discussions of Indigeneity and Indigenous knowledge. Again I share Smith's (2009) sentiments that it is important to create a truly transformative educational process aimed at developing the experience of being Indigenous—of a place—for more students. Thus, how our educational efforts can be aimed at connecting young learners to their places in ways that lead to civic participation, engagement and environmental stewardship. I argue for the need to cultivate "Indigeneity" as a means for counteracting "placelessness" and the forms of alienation and environmental carelessness so often encountered in contemporary societies (Smith, 2009, personal communication).

POSITING AN INDIGENOUS DISCURSIVE FRAMEWORK

Here I put forward some tentative ideas in the search for an Indigenous discursive framework (see also Dei, 2008). I am working with the idea that there are culturally distinctive ways of knowing. Humility of knowing is about a respect for the sacred and transcendent (i.e., spiritual sense of existence) and the axiological imperative for us to evaluate the cultural, spiritual, and ideational beliefs, values, practices in the history and contexts of communities as they search for their own moral tone. Each society has rewarded core values (e.g., rights/responsibilities; individual/community) and knowledge that reflects local capabilities, priorities, and value systems of peoples/communities.

The following twelve interrelated principles (by no means exhaustive) provide some conceptual and analytical clarity on what constitutes a critical Indigenous discursive framework:

1. Indigenous ways of knowing as a body of epistemology connect place, spirit, and body (see also Meyer, 2008). The spiritual is embodied.
2. Spiritual identity is a way of knowing. Land and spiritual identity are in fact salient/fundamental analytical concepts offering an entry point in understanding the lived experiences of those who are Indigenized.

3. Indigenous knowledge is spiritually driven or anchored. Such knowledges are embedded or imbued with the spirit. The spiritual becomes the axis on which Indigenous knowledge rests, that is, the substructure or foundation for understanding the social, cultural, economic, material, and political. Therefore, understanding the spirit constitutes an important basis of Indigenous epistemological knowing.
4. Although "land and spiritual identity" (i.e., land-based spirituality) have a special salience that salience should not lead us to a discourse of reductionism or the idea of irreducible/essentialized difference. This is because history, culture, and spiritual identities are sites and sources of asymmetrical power relations structured along the lines of difference (race, class, gender, sexuality, [dis]ability, etc.).
5. Indigenous as place-based knowledge reflected through land, history, culture, and identity has powerful explanatory powers in contemporary communities and socio-political encounters. In the politics of claiming Indigenous knowledge production we must center self, identity, representation, and history. How the self and community are represented and practiced through time, history and culture is an important source of epistemological knowing. The understanding here is that experience and practice constitute the contextual and analytical base of knowledge.
6. Indigenous knowledge is about searching for wholeness and completeness. This wholeness is a nexus of body, mind, and soul, as well as the interrelations of society-culture and nature. To understand is to have a complete, holistic way of knowing that connects the physical, metaphysical, social, material, cultural, and spiritual realms of existence.
7. Within Western cultures knowledges exist in hierarchies of power. Such hierarchies of power are themselves only meaningful in a competitive culture. The competitive nature of these communities itself helps produce "Othered subjects." Claiming local cultural resource knowledge as specific knowledge has broader implications for subverting dominance of Euro-colonial knowledges and Euro-modernity. Indigenous epistemology sees difference as embodiment of knowledge, power, and subjective agency. Creating an "Otherness" is about power and control.
8. A critical Indigenous discursive framework brings three conceptual understandings to Indigeneity: (i) colonialism, in its deep-reaching denial of history and identity, has created unequal outcomes for groups in terms of their histories, engagement of culture and traditions, and spiritual identities; (ii) there are situational variations in intensities of different identities given the effects of colonization and re-colonization; (iii) central to decolonization for Indigenized and colonized communities is the urgency of regaining our spiritual power and strength.
9. It is through a nurturing of opposing stances informed by our relative subject positions and experiences that the dominance of Westernity and Eurocentricity can be subverted. In fact, the Indigenous discursive framework claims the intellectual agency of the Indigene to define oneself. It affirms the epistemological relevance of the Indigene to set the terms of our engagement in dominant culture.
10. A critical Indigenous discursive framework is necessarily anti-colonial. It is about resistance, subject[ive] agency, and collective politics. It centers the agency, the authenticity of voice and political and intellectual interests of Indigenous and Aboriginal subjects in accounting for and resisting oppression and domination. The politics of knowledge production for

Indigenous scholars is to claim our agency through self-actualization and collective empowerment.
11. The Indigenous discursive framework highlights an ontological lineage to communities and a "spiritual ontology" that shapes the politics and forces of social change. This approach to Indigenous praxis cannot be viewed simply as a project of decolonization and the unraveling of the power relations of knowledge production, interrogation, validation, and dissemination. It is about social transformation.
12. Finally, the Indigenous discursive framework critiques the independence of "scholarship," "politics," and "activism." It does not subscribe to the luxury of the independence of scholarship from politics and activism. But the framework is also mindful of not prescribing a particular politics. The learning objective is to create a space to legitimize politics in the intellectual/academic realm.

In effect, an Indigenous discursive framework ought to promote actively living Indigenous ways and spiritualities and the validation of the concomitant embodied knowledges that come from those experiences. It is a framework for both intellectual engagement and day to day living.

THE FUTURE CHALLENGE AND RESPONSIBILITY OF INDIGENOUS KNOWLEDGE STUDIES

The examination of the structure and logical coherency of Indigenous knowledge must be matched by an engagement with the moral, ethical, spiritual, cosmological dimensions of such knowledge. Addressing the question of complicity, implication, and responsibility to Indigenous knowledge, means bringing to the foreground struggles for self-determination, cultural survival, land rights, and decolonization. The idea of a discourse of Indigeneity is among other things about the resulting material and spiritual consequences of the "processes of dispossession in a colonial world" (Johnson 2009, p. 2). Indigenous knowledge speaks to the responsibility of knowledge to promote social change. We know that decolonization is an on-going painful process. It calls for engaging discomfort and de-stabilizing knowing. It is about going where we have not been before and asking new questions. Decolonization is also about contesting futures and there are no guarantees with a decolonization project.

For Indigenous scholars we have a particular responsibility to produce, validate, protect, and defend the legitimacy of Indigenous philosophies as legitimate ways of knowing. The power of such Indigenous philosophies lies in the basis of their political and academic discussions and negotiations of identities, representations, rights, sovereignty, citizenship, and nationhood. The challenge still remains in terms of a simple question: Turner (2006) asked whether such Indigenous philosophies are articulable in the dominant's language, English (p. 116). Two domains of dissemination of knowledge in the form of translation and teaching Indigenous languages deserve special attention in responding to this question. The revitalization of Indigenous languages is key to the success of Indigenous knowledge. Colonial languages have failed miserably to articulate and frame Indigenous knowledges. However, for inter-knowledge transfers/sharing some sort of translation needs to take place. The responsibility for translating Indigenous knowledges lies in Indigenous bodies or bodies that utilize an Indigenous discursive framework. There also ought to be a protocol and ethics rooted in Indigenous ways of knowing to guide the translation of Indigenous knowledges. We only have Indigenous knowledges if we continue to teach our Indigenous languages to the younger generation. How have our school systems and our communities fared in this exercise?

What can we say about the pursuit of science when such knowledge excludes and imposes knowledge and interpretations (Wilcox, 2009)? Where and how does the whole idea of a search for a complete/holistic understanding of the history of ideas and events that have shaped and continue to shape human growth and development implicated in what we take as scientific knowledge? What is the place of identity (race, class, gender, sexuality, [dis]ability, etc.) in the construction of knowledge about a people and their past? As noted in the beginning of this chapter, I am always wary about any attempts to downplay the importance of the link between identities (racial, class, gender, sexual, disability, religious, etc.) and knowledge production. As Indigenous peoples we must seek to construct our identities outside of that which has often been constructed within Euro-American epistemic hegemony. We must claim all of our identities, inclusive of racial and spiritual identities.

The making of knowledge relating to the past for all cultures is filled with ancestral knowledges, myths and superstitions, spiritual claims, and bits of romanticism (e.g., like what is unfairly attributed solely to Indigenous peoples' past sacred histories embedded in origin place and origin myth rooted in traditions [see also Johnson, 2009]). Understanding the past is to construct knowledge about a people and their past that is holistic. But more importantly, it is to acknowledge that "a discourse of Indigeneity is among other things, the outcome of processes of dispossession in a colonial world" (Johnson, 2009, p. 2). Universal claims to a shared past or collective knowledge are often Eurocentric. The universal is also presented as natural, neutral, and reasonable to deny local variability. As Michael Wilcox (2009) also notes in another context, this "search for *universal* narratives of human cultural evolution has at times obscured historical narratives of the more recent past, that the study of this past is of limited value and that this lack of scholarly interest has led many to believe that contemporary Native Peoples have nothing to contribute to archaeological method or theory" (p. 4). Indigenous knowledge is about past, present, and future and suggests a continuum, and our understanding of the past must be rooted in local cultural knowledges of such past which offers a connection of material, physical, metaphysical, and cultural and moral concerns. The best challenge to Eurocentricity continually masquerading as universal knowledge is to posit multicentric ways of knowing.

Today, the challenge for Indigenous scholarship is more than a challenge to the "representational authority" of dominant scholars and social science disciplines and the humanities. The question of who has "discursive authority" is very much on the table. Indigenous communities are often dispossessed of their land, culture, and knowledge and tend to or are presented to have no voice. It behooves us to acknowledge the discursive authority of Indigenous peoples in speaking about/interpreting their cultures and knowledges in their perspectives "through dialogues with living subjects" (see Wilcox, 2009, p. 5 in another context).

How can an anti-colonial reading help address the intellectual quagmire of post-colonial musings over identity? The Indigenous idea of shared/collective histories, experiences, and identities was never meant to imply these histories, experiences, and identities were or are singular. I agree in part that resistance to colonialism helped foster the sense of shared/collective identities. I also concede that Indigenous identities, "like all ethnic identities are generated through a dialectical process of comparison and differentiation" (Wilcox 2009, p. 6; citing Barthes, 1969). But I would argue for an intellectual agency of the Indigenous. Africans knew who they were before the coming of Europeans. For

Indigenous communities part of knowing the "authentic self" (i.e., who one is) is through a reclaiming of the spiritual self. Why do I say this? Because Indigenous peoples resisted the colonization of their spirits despite all attempts otherwise. Our spirits have never been broken.

CONCLUSION

As we pursue a decolonizing project through claims of Indigeneity we must expect critique. But critiques should not stop us from doing this work. Resistance read simply as a reaction to colonialism/oppression removes the agency of the oppressed/minoritized/colonized. This, in our ongoing challenge to colonialism, we must work on our own terms, identifying , respecting, and working to sustain a longer historical trajectory, one not rooted in a colonial moment but in our cultural foundation. Essentialism as a practice among the oppressed is a product of European colonialism and oppression. There are historic essences we can point to advanced by the colonizer (e.g., the ranking of racial groups, community knowledges, and making claims using markers of authenticity and the inauthentic). So let us understand history and what challenges we are dealing with. Among the colonized the search for qualifying characteristics of a community does not necessarily mean a search for essences. Indigenous peoples do not only live in the past but also live in the present. There is a code of silence around the epistemic injury/violence that is being caused by colonized bodies being forced to validate their knowledges in standards set by dominant Eurocentric knowings or Western science. Such violence also plays out in both the mis-recognition and non-recognition of Indigenous knowledges.

We must open up the epistemological tool-box and situate ethics within intellectual and scientific work. This will be a recognition of how ethics and epistemology are tied. There is a danger of epistemic insularity, and it must be replaced with epistemic openness based on shared and mutual respect and recognition of multiple knowledges. We must expand the explanatory power of science and subvert the ethnocentrism of Western science. Indigenous people's mistrust of Western science is grounded in the dominant constructions of truth, validity, and rationality. These constructions are only partial stories. These have also largely been through Eurocentric and sometimes racist tropes. We must challenge the one trick pony of Western science. It must be asked: what standards are being used to validate Indigenous knowledges as science? Objectivity is culturally defined, informed, and based. Practice and experience as contextual basis of knowledge means Indigenous knowledge is lived and practiced. It is not simply based on feeling.

ACKNOWLEDGMENTS

I would like to thank Rainos Mutamba who is completing his studies at the Faculty of Social Work, University of Toronto and Marlon Simmons, Ph.D. candidate, and Dr. Arlo Kempf in the Department of Sociology and Equity Studies of the Ontario Institute for Studies in Education of the University of Toronto for reading and commenting on drafts of this chapter. I also thank the students in my advanced graduate seminar, "Indigenous Knowledges and Decolonization" (Fall, 2009) for sharing critical insights with me during class discussions.

REFERENCES

Adefarakan, T. (2010). Yoruba Indigenous Knowledges in the African Diaspora: Knowledge: Power and the Politics of Indigenous Spirituality. (Unpublished draft, Ph.D. dissertation), Department of Sociology and Equity Studies, Ontario Institute for Studies in Education of the University of Toronto, Toronto.

Battiste, M. (1986). Micmac Literacy and Cognitive Imperialism. In J. Barman, Y. Hebert & D. McCaskill (Eds.), *Indian Education in Canada: The Legacy* Vol. 1 (pp. 23–44). Vancouver: University of British Columbia Press.

Battiste, M. A., & Henderson, Y. (Eds.). (2000). *Protecting Indigenous Knowledge and Heritage: A Global Challenge.* Saskatoon: Purich.

Cajete, G. (1994). *Look to the Mountain: An Ecology of Indigenous Education.* Durango, CO: Kivaki.

Castro-Palaganas, E., Bagamaspad, A., et al. (2004). Mainstreaming Indigenous Knowledge Systems in Governance in the Asia-Pacific. Regional workshop on Mainstreaming IKSG, Manila, Philippines. Local Government Acadmy (14–16 October).

Churchill, W. (1993). *Struggle for the Land.* Monroe, ME: Common Courage Press.

Churchill, W. (2003). *Acts of Rebellion: The Ward Churchill Reader.* New York: Routledge.

Dei, G. J. S. (2000). The Role of Indigenous Knowledges in the Academy. *International Journal of Inclusive Education, 4*(2), 39–56.

Dei, G. J. S. (2008). Indigenous Knowledge Studies and the Next Generation: Pedagogical Possibilities for Anti-colonial Education. *Australian Journal of Indigenous Education, 37*, 5–13.

Dei, G. J. S. & Asgharzadeh, A. (2001). The Power of Social Theory: Towards an Anti-colonial Discursive framework. *Journal of Educational Thought, 353*, 297–323.

Ermine, W. (1995). Aboriginal Epistemology. In M. Battiste and J. Barman (Eds.), *First Nations Education in Canada: The Circle Unfolds* (pp.101–112). Vancouver: UBC Press.

Fals-Borda, O. (1980). *Science and the Common People.* Yugoslavia: International Forum on Participatory Research.

Fitznor, L. (2005). *Aboriginal Educational Teaching Experiences: Foregrounding Aboriginal/Indigenous Knowledges and Processes.* Manitoba: University of Manitoba Press.

Ginsburg, F. (1994). Embedded Aesthetics: Creating Discursive Space for Indigenous Media. *Cultural Anthropology, 9*(3), 365–382.

James, C. L. R. (1993). *American Civilization.* Cambridge, MA: Blackwell.

Johnson, M. (2009). An Indigenous Archaeology of the English? Paper presented at the Annual Meeting of the American Anthropology Association meeting, Philadelphia, December 4–6.

Kincheloe, J. & Steinberg, S (2008). Indigenous Knowledges in Education: Complexities, Dangers and Profound Benefits. In N. Denzin, Y. Lincoln & L.T. Smith (Eds.), *Handbook of Critical and Indigenous Methodologies* (pp. 135–156). Los Angeles: Sage.

Lattas, A. (1993). Essentialism, Memory and Resistance: Aboriginality and the Politics of Authenticity. *Oceania, 63*, 2–67.

Meyer, Manulani, A. (2008). Indigenous and Authentic: Hawaiian Epistemology and the Triangulation of Meaning. In N. Denzin, Y. Lincoln & L.T. Smith (Eds.), *Handbook of Critical and Indigenous Methodologies* (pp. 217–232). Los Angeles: Sage.

Nakata, M. (2007a). *Disciplining the Savages: Savaging the Disciplines.* Canberra, ACT: Aboriginal Studies Press.

Nakata, M. (2007b). The Cultural Interface. *The Australian Journal of Indigenous Education, 36*, Supplement, 7–14.

Purcell, T. W. (1998). Indigenous Knowledge and Applied Anthropology: Question of Definition and Direction. *Human Organization, 57*(3), 258–272.

Semali, L. & Kincheloe, J. (Eds.). (1999). *What Is Indigenous Knowledge? Voices from the Academy.* New York: Falmer Press.

St. Denis, V. 2004. Real Indians: Cultural Revitalization and Fundamentalism in Aboriginal Education. In C. Schick, J. Jaffe & A. M. Watkinson (Eds.), *Contesting Fundamentalisms* (pp. 35–47). Halifax: Fernwood Publishing.

Turner, D. (2006). *This Is Not a Peace Pipe: Towards a Critical Indigenous Philosophy.* Toronto: University of Toronto Press.

Wilcox, M. (2009). *Saving Indigenous Peoples from Ourselves: Separate but Equal Archaeology Is Not Scientific Archaeology.* Paper presented at the Annual meeting of the American Anthropology Association, Philadelphia, December.

CHAPTER TWO

(Re) Conceptualizing 'Indigenous' from Anti-Colonial and Black Feminist Theoretical Perspectives

Living and Imagining Indigeneity Differently

TEMITOPE ADEFARAKAN

This chapter is anchored in two theoretical frameworks: anti-colonial theory and Black/African feminisms. I draw from and build on these theoretical models of analysis to critically contextualize the experiences of Yoruba peoples in diasporic and Euro-dominant contexts. Both anti-colonial and African/Black feminist frameworks allow for a more critical and nuanced reading of how issues of race, class, spirituality, gender, language, religion, and especially notions of Indigeneity *interlock* in the lives and experiences of Yoruba peoples in the diaspora.

Within the anti-colonial discursive framework, there is a particular focus on the term "Indigenous" as a vitally significant concept in anti-colonial thought. I argue that this concept needs to be revisited and extended beyond existing ideas, where it is critically interrogated where diasporic Africans are concerned. I maintain that Indigeneity (or Indigenous identities) need to be imagined differently so that the unique positionings, especially, of diasporic Africans can be accorded a space to theorize the particularities of their experiences. In other words, there is a need for a shift in how notions of Indigeneity are taken up so that they are not imagined as singular, in the way that those who often work from exclusively Eurocentric or postmodern perspectives do. Hence, more flexible approaches with Indigeneity need to be engaged because this concept is often taken up to exclude diasporic African identities. Instead, I argue that this intellectual shift in notions of Indigeneity needs to include a variety of Indigenous peoples' experiences so that Indigeneity or "Indigenous" is engaged in ways that allow a discussion of diasporic Indigeneity.

Moving on to African/Black feminist theory, the key argument I want to get across is that gender in Indigenous, and especially the Yoruba context, differs. There is therefore the need to eschew Eurocentric and universal notions of gender in thinking about Indigenous peoples and identities.

"Indigenous" is a relatively recent term that emerged in the 1970s out of the American Indian Movement (AIM) and the Canadian Indian Brotherhood (CIB) (Smith, 1999). It came into being to give a common name to both those who exist outside the colonial domain, as well as those who were colonized (Narogin, 1995). Trevor Purcell (1998) provides further background regarding usage of the term as one that is largely self-applied because it carries less condescension than words such as "primitive" or "tribal" (p. 259). However, this concept is not unproblematic and has been seriously challenged primarily by those who work from postmodern theoretical frameworks because it may appear to homogenize unique and distinct peoples that have different experiences under imperialism (Smith, 1999). Such opposition has not come from Indigenous peoples themselves (Dei, 2000b) but rather, has originated with scholars whose work relies on Eurocentric frames of mind and analysis as the sole loci of legitimate knowledges. For Indigenous peoples, usage of the term Indigenous is a *collectivizing* political and social strategy that emerged out of anti-colonial social movements such as AIM, CIB, and Red Power, all of which were strongly influenced by the American Black Power and Civil Rights movements of the 1960s. Furthermore, "Indigenous" is employed as an umbrella term, or way of including common experiences of colonialism across various communities, language groups, and nations. Using the term "Indigenous" need not *deny* that each group's distinctiveness and unique experiences with imperialism will also be given serious attention and acknowledgment (Smith, 1999). Ultimately, "Indigenous" is a multilayered term that is informed by a multiplicity of experiences where both similarity and difference exist simultaneously; it is not a singular category, experience, or identity. Hence, my particular understanding of Indigeneity may not speak to, or include the experiences of all of those who speak from an Indigenous positionality and identity. For some, they are better suited, or more comfortable focusing on the variety of issues that surround Indigeneity rather than placing emphasis on what often can be limiting definitions. I elaborate on this further in the following section and find it important to note that while I do recognize that a multitude of claims and oppositions to "Indigenous" as an identity concept exist, it is neither my intention nor goal to resolve the conflicts and debates around this term. Instead, I offer my own multilayered working definition of how this term is used and conceptualized by me and how it specifically applies to Yoruba (African) peoples.

The first layer of my thinking comes from Mudrooroo Narogin's (1995) conception of "Indigenous" to "simply mean originating in or from a country [or land]" (p. 7). For Yoruba peoples, this land is in the south-western region of what is now known as Nigeria, as well as the neighboring borders of Togo and Benin. While according to archeologically documented knowledge, Yoruba presence in this region dates as far back as A.D. 800, Indigenous Yoruba oral literature designates this region as the site of the birth of humankind. However, the culture, language, spirituality, and worldview of the Yoruba are not bound to this one geographic space, but have traveled with Yoruba peoples in the myriad directions they have moved and migrated outside this region. For example, forced removals such as the European slave trade, which resulted in a large number of Yoruba peoples being dispersed to areas that include (but are not limited to) other parts of Africa, as well as other geographic regions such as the Americas, the Caribbean, and the continent of Europe, have inflected Yoruba identities with other lived experiences as other geographic spaces.

The second layer of my use of the term "Indigenous" concerns conceiving of cosmology or "worldview" as foundational, and borrows from George Dei's (2000a) conception of Indigenous knowledges as dynamic, experientially based, holistic, and relational in the sense that the interwoven nature of the physical and metaphysical realms of Yoruba life are common knowledge and cosmologically anchored. In Dei's words, "Indigenous epistemologies are grounded in an awareness and deep appreciation of the cosmos and how the self/selves, spiritual, known and unknown worlds are interconnected" (Dei, 2000a, p. 5). This is in keeping with the Yoruba Indigenous philosophy of maintaining links to ensure that connection between these worlds remain active and unbroken. For Yoruba people, communication occurs through a myriad of rituals and practices that utilize and evoke all bodily senses. Yoruba feminist Oyeronke Oyewumi (1997) explains the inadequacy of the term "worldview" as a synonym for cosmology in Yoruba contexts:

> The term "worldview," which is used in the West to sum up the cultural logic of a society, captures the West's privileging of the visual. It is Eurocentric to use it to describe cultures that may privilege other senses. The term, "worldsense" is a more inclusive way of describing the conception of the world by different cultural groups. . .[and] will be used when describing the Yoruba or other cultures that may privilege senses other than the visual or even a combination of senses (p. 3).

Overemphasis on the visual is also problematic for Yoruba Indigenous discourses because the Yoruba conceive of spirituality and/or spiritual forces as largely inaccessible to the human eye. Hence, the term "worldview" does not fully reflect the complexity of Indigenous Yoruba culture and how life is understood from this multi-sensed position. Cosmology or worldsense is a foundational locus of Indigenous peoples and their knowledge systems. This is so because a people's worldsense maps out how they experience and understand their world. In the Yoruba context, cosmology is complementary (Olajubu, 2003; Oyewumi, 1997; Soyinka, 1976), and interconnectedness is central, where *Orun* (the otherworld), *Aiye* (the physical world of living humans and other beings), and *Ile* (the earthworld) are all interdependent and cannot exist on their own. *Orun* is inhabited by the Supreme Being, Olodumare, who is also known as *Eleda* (the Creator) and *Olorun* (literally meaning owner of the skyworld); the 401plus *Orisa*—many of which once walked the earth as human beings with mystical powers, who were then deified through death. The lives of the *Orisa* are continued through the supernatural powers and prowess of various forces of nature such as water, wind, land/earth, fire, thunder/lightning, and the forest/trees. The Otherworld is also inhabited by a number of spirits such as *Egungun* (Ancestors), *egbe* (mirror or spiritual half/halves on the otherside), *Ebora/Iwin* (a small supernatural being with magical powers),[1] and *Ara Orun* (beings of the otherworld, including the unborn). The forces of *Orun* are always influencing and in communion with those who inhabit *Aiye*. The people of the physical world (*Aiye*) will one day die and simultaneously become one with *Ile* (the female earth/soil) because it is our last resting place, as one moves onto the spirit world. The earth and its connection to the dead are so sacred to Yoruba peoples that relatives of recently buried loved ones take small portions of soil from their grave and use it to swear oaths (Abimbola, 1997, p. 68), again, illustrating the interconnection between the living and the dead through the power of nature and earth. As is common in many Indigenous cultures, the Yoruba also hold nature and one's environment to be sacred. This is reflected in our belief in deified ancestors, the *Orisa*, and spirits that are associated with natural phenomena such as mountains, hills, earth, rivers, lakes, the ocean, trees, and wind (Awolalu, 1979, p. 45). An example of *Ile* as sacred in Yoruba life and cosmology is explained by historian J. Omosade Awolalu (1979):

> The earth is venerated in Yorubaland because it is believed to be inhabited by a spirit. The Yoruba attach great importance to the earth. In creation, the myth says, earth was spread on the face of the deep, and land appeared. Furthermore, Obatala used clay to mould man before Olodumare gave him breath. When a new born comes into the world, the first landing place is the earth; when a man grows old and dies, he is buried in the earth. The earth supplies food for human consumption, and so it keeps life going. From the Yoruba point of view, an element which has such manifold and useful functions must have a spirit dwelling there....Since most of the Yoruba depend on agriculture for their sustenance, and crops are grown in the soil,

Ile (the earth) receives special sacrifice at the time of planting and harvesting, almost in the same way as Orisa-oko does. And since the corpses of the ancestors are buried in the earth and there are powerful spirits dwelling therein, the Yoruba have the habit of pouring the first drop of any drink on the ground and of throwing some portion of food to the earth before they drink or eat in order that the spirits may drink and eat first (p. 45).

The third layer of how I conceptualize Indigeneity concerns the matter of land and how it is understood as the definitive marker of who can officially be identified or "counted" as Indigenous. Dr. Erica-Irene Daes, the chair of the United Nations Working Group on Indigenous Populations, places particular emphasis on land, or ecology as "the central and indispensable classroom" for the teaching and generational transmission of Indigenous knowledge systems (Daes as cited in Battiste & & Henderson 2000, p. 41). Many Indigenous scholars and intellectuals such as Ward Churchill, Linda Smith, Andrea Smith, Ngugi Wa Thiong'o, Ama Ata Aidoo, Ifi Amadiume, Toni Morrison, Wole Soyinka, Wande Abimbola and others have stressed the significance of land for the self-determined development and sustenance of Indigenous peoples and their systems of knowledge. On this matter, Aboriginal scholar Marie Battiste (2002) writes

Indigenous knowledge is also inherently tied to land, not to land in general but to particular landscapes, landforms, and biomes where ceremonies are properly held, stories properly recited, medicines properly gathered, and transfers of knowledge properly authenticated. Ensuring the complete and accurate transmission of knowledge and authority from generation to generation depends not only on maintaining ceremonies, which Canadian law treats as art rather than science, but also on maintaining the integrity of the land itself (p. 13).

I do not dispute that land, or rather particular lands are central to many, if not all, Indigenous peoples and the knowledge systems they maintain. Rather, it is the manner in which land is spoken of that is problematic for me here, especially where many diasporic African peoples are concerned. It is often implied, or assumed that Indigenous peoples are current residents of their countries of origin, however, just as often, they may have been displaced and pushed off their distinct territory through colonization. While imperial or colonialist settlers often forcibly remove Indigenous peoples from their *territories,* very often they remain residents of that same larger physical/geographic space or land mass—as is the case with Aboriginal peoples in the Americas, Australia, the Pacific region, as well as many South African Indigenous peoples. As scholar Trevor Purcell (1998) reminds us, to be considered Indigenous, one must be residing on, and/or in relatively close proximity to one's ancestral territory. However, what has not been given due attention—particularly in academic, as well as Indigenous grassroots activist circles in the Americas—are the Indigenous populations that have been completely displaced *off that particular land mass*; as is the case with the hundreds of millions of Africans who were enslaved by Europeans; or the current movements of continental Africans who follow global capital as a result of "globalization" (which in itself is simply a new form of imperialism). In this sense, it is one's *relationship* to his/her land that is critical, and this does not necessarily manifest as a physical marker. Yes, one's Indigeneity is undoubtedly tied to a distinct ancestral land or territory, yet, popular conceptions of Indigeneity (in the academy and otherwise) have constructed slavery and African peoples' conquest-based removal from their Indigenous lands as disqualifiers for being counted as Indigenous peoples, despite the fact that this occurred through imperialist and colonizing forces. And this disqualification occurs primarily because African Indigenous experiences under colonialism are generally not understood to be the definitive experience of Indigeneity.

By contrast, I argue that while undoubtedly tied to a distinct ancestral land or territory, Indigeneity also indicates displaced communities' *relationship* with their homeland and must include an analysis of how imperial histories and social relations of power figure(d) in the displacement of Indigenous peoples from their ancestral territories. This analysis must consider both their geographic proximity, as well as their relationship with these lands. By no means should my argument be taken as an attempt to deny the saliency and necessity of land with respect to providing self-determined sustenance for Indigenous peoples and their ways of knowing. Indeed, land theft and occupation are central to the implementation, execution, and perpetuation of colonialism and imperialist projects. Rather, what I propose here is a rearticulation of Indigeneity that permits the diverse histories and realities of distinct Indigenous groups to be seriously considered, so that the particular realities of diasporic Africans are included in this concept instead of being denied or subsumed under grand narratives or more popular notions of Indigeneity. In this regard, we move away from exclusive or hegemonizing essentialist notions of "Indigenous peoples" that are narrowly predicated on obligatory residence on one's ancestral land, to a more complicated and inclusive approach that is reflective of the varied experiences of Indigenous peoples under colonialism and imperialism.

Being attuned to how imperialism and colonialism affect various Indigenous peoples *differently,* also allows for a multifaceted conception of Indigenous identities that *anchors,* but *does not lock* them into their ancestral land or territories. I do not conceive of being "locked" and "anchored" as synonymous. In my opinion, being anchored means *being grounded* with the promise of flexible movement, and this is not limited to solely a physical state of being; interwoven in this concept throughout are psychic, emotional, and spiritual qualities of existence as well. Inversely, I conceive of the notion, or sensation of being "locked in" as a position that precludes movement, much in the same way certain definitions of Indigeneity have precluded the experiences of those who *are* Indigenous but have different, non-residential, or more transnational relationships and experiences with their ancestral lands *precisely because* their experiences with/in colonialism and imperialism have been different.

For the many diasporic Africans who have been physically and forcibly scattered, moved, and displaced out of their ancestral lands, numerous emotional, spiritual, and psychic connections to various peoples and cultures of the African continent have nonetheless been retained through reassemblages of key elements of African culture such as language, clothing, food, music, dance, spirituality, etc. Given the reality of globalization as a hegemonic process imbued with political, economic, social, and religious inequalities that induce the continued movement of peoples across multiple spaces and national borders, it becomes futile to evoke hegemonically fixed or static notions of *any form of identity* or people. My research challenges us to think about the relationship between Indigeneity and land differently. Understanding that such relationships are highly complicated and differ for African peoples across time and space opens up the possibilities for developing more nuanced analyses of the multiple, yet distinct ways that Indigenous peoples are positioned in relationship to their ancestral lands, and how colonialism and imperialism figure(d) in changing these relationships. As a project that prioritizes African Indigenous and anti-colonial perspectives in the face of dominant postmodern theorizing as the singular valid approach to "rigorously" theorizing identities imagining Indigeneity becomes quite difficult when applied to African peoples who are often seen as "not Indigenous enough" or "not Indigenous at all." These tensions become heightened when the focus is diasporic because many would argue that being in a diasporic context renders (especially) African Indigeneity impossible or, simply non-existent. In this respect, I am keenly aware that I write against the academic grain, and in the face of incredible opposition. However my aim here is not so much to engage the debate on "the politics of identity" (Indigenous or otherwise), so much as it is to engage an exploration of African, and more specifically, Yoruba Indigenous knowledges and identities *on their own terms*.

That said, folded into this third layer of my conceptualization of Indigeneity is the necessity for a conceptualization of diaspora that is also inclusive and cognizant of difference. Rather than conceiving diaspora as the exclusive preserve of specific geo-spatial regions—a position that Stuart Hall (1997) takes—I prefer Earl Lewis'(1995) suggestion that we live in "a world of overlapping diasporas" which are "interconnected and demarcated by race, class, color, and other factors" (p. 779).

Michel Laguerre (1998) and Aihwa Ong (1999) present a similar line of argument in their suggestion for "more flexible or diasporic notions of citizenship [in order] to probe the multiple belongings created in diaspora" (as cited in Braziel & Mannur, 2003, p. 6). Lewis' call helps me to think of the Yoruba communities here in Canada as a layer of diaspora that overlaps with others. What other layers precede and/or interact with that of the Yoruba in Canada?[2] The first of these are the African diasporic layers; shared and related, but different in that I am distinctly thinking about Africans who are the *direct* descendants of enslaved Africans. So there are those layers, and how that particular form of movement was traumatically enforced with no element of choice or autonomy for those who had been kidnapped away. My mind then veered toward the Indigenous peoples of "Canada" as another set of layers. As the First peoples of this land, I then wondered if they could be confined to layers? I was not sure, and frankly somewhat bemused as to how to conceptualize or approach this. I recognize that my social location as a Yoruba woman who was raised in "Canada" since the age of three, on a land that was not Indigenous to me could not to be overlooked. I wondered, what are the implications of simultaneously being Indigenous and Western, on a land that you are not Indigenous to? What does it mean to be a resident and citizen of a land where the Indigenous peoples of that land are still being oppressed and marginalized? On the whole, my reconceptualization of land and diaspora as they relate to Indigenous peoples was to underscore the central themes of difference and multiplicity. George Dei and Alireza Asgharzadeh (2001) also insist on difference as a key principle and concept in anti-colonial theorizing:

> Oppression should be looked at as a site encompassing varieties of differences, categories, and identities that differentiate individuals and communities from one another and at the same time connects them together through the experience of being oppressed, marginalized, and colonized (p. 316).

Hence, approaches to defining "Indigenous" must involve a recognition of difference, where serious attention is given to the multiple and diverse experiences that Indigenous peoples have under imperialism and colonialism. In the same way that it is necessary to acknowledge that Indigenous identity is not singular, it is necessary to recognize that Indigenous people's relationship(s) to their ancestral land or territory is also not singular. This is a call for a conceptual shift, where, instead of Indigeneity being presumptively predicated on compulsory physical residence on one's ancestral territory, this is replaced by the appreciation that notions of belonging and connection to one's Indigenous land(s) take multiple forms and should therefore not be limited to simply one experience of how belonging is manifested. This conceptualization of Indigeneity allows for the varied histories and realities of distinct Indigenous groups to be seriously considered, so that a more multifaceted and inclusive approach is utilized to reflect the nuances and varied experiences of different Indigenous peoples under colonialism and imperialism.

The fourth definitional layer of how I conceptualize "Indigenous" directly builds on the third to underscore the crucial theme of resistance and empowerment that Indigeneity holds. For this layer, I work with the idea that *colonized* Indigenous peoples can claim or evoke an Indigenous identity even when they are not on their ancestral land because such ways of knowing are *flexibly* embedded and embodied. However, before proceeding with further discussion of this layer, it is important that it not be confused with the appropriation of Indigenous identities in the way that individuals who come from dominant communities do. Linda Smith (1999) elaborates

> [Indigenous] has been co-opted politically by the descendants of settlers who lay claim to an "indigenous" identity through their occupation and settlement of land over several generations or simply through being born in that place—though they tend not to show up at indigenous peoples' meetings nor form alliances that support the self-determination of the people whose forebears once occupied the land that they have "tamed" and upon which they have settled. Nor do they actively struggle as a society for the survival of indigenous languages, knowledges and cultures. Their linguistic and cultural homeland is somewhere else, their cultural loyalty is to some other place. Their power, their privilege, their history are all vested in their legacy as colonizers (p. 7).

While everyone is Indigenous to some place, sometime, somewhere (Churchill, 2003: public lecture titled "Indigenous Strategies of Resistance" at York University), a distinction must be made between constructions of Indigeneity that are interlaced with historical and contemporary legacies of conquest, colonial occupation, and White supremacy, and those that are grounded in struggle, resistance, and decolonization. The "Indigeneity" of the former is conveniently evoked by the dominant in certain contexts, and very much shaped by power imbalances in the sense that such evocations do not disrupt their "innocence" as settlers (Razack & Fellows, 1998). Settler identities such as this are heavily anchored in romantic amnesic constructions of themselves as benevolent "founders." The Indigeneity of which I speak of is one that is anchored in being colonized on ancestral territory, or, a land mass different from the one currently residing on. Especially for African diasporic peoples, this particular (re)configuration of Indigeneity works with the salient principle that Indigenous ways of knowing and understanding the universe are dynamic, and therefore flexibly embodied and embedded.

However, an Indigenous identity where one can claim citizenship on land that one is not Indigenous to raises important questions about power. As a Canadian citizen, my Indigeneity is precariously built on the amnesic denial of "Canada" as stolen land. This is to acknowledge the paradox and complexity of being both Indigenous (Yoruba) and "Canadian" (Western) as a rather unsteady social location that does not conveniently fit popular notions of what it means to be Indigenous. Yet, I maintain that these realities do not make African peoples any *less* Indigenous, rather, it is a *different form* of Indigeneity that inevitably highlights the third definitional layer which emphasizes difference. I conceptualize this particular type of difference through something I term as a type of "migrant Indigeneity," where one retains their Indigeneity through cultural embeddedness and embodiment. I'm remembering that constructions of Indigeneity vary and are not singular but diverse and dynamic. Therefore including the Indigenous identities and knowledges of people who *carry* this information with them in their physical bodies is legitimate and considering how this operates *in concert with* their cultural histories and memories is worthy of study. And this transpires despite the fact that they may not be residing on their Indigenous lands.

Thomas Heyd (1995) has argued that Indigenous knowledges are "embedded in distinctive social practices and cultural frameworks" (p. 70) such as one's cultural memory (Dei, 2000a). Some of the most profound examples of the retentions and reconfigurations of African Indigenous knowledges are found in the older African diasporic communities that were forcibly removed from the African continent during the Maafa, more popularly known as the European transatlantic slave trade.³ Nevertheless, despite the flexible dynamism of Indigenous knowledges as "living knowledge systems that are continually responding [and adapting] to new phenomena and fresh insights" (Battiste, 2002, p. 12), the evocation of an Indigenous identity remains highly contested with continual charges of essentialism equating the term with colonialism and imperialism—particularly in academic spaces. I echo the contrasting standpoint of scholars Isidore Okpewho, Ali Mazrui, and Carol Boyce-Davies who insist that memory of Africa and a sense of roots are, in fact "political statements" and "psychological necessities" that serve(d) exiled Africans well, particularly when the conditions of oppression and colonization seemed intolerable (Okpewho, Davies, & Mazrui, 1999, p. xv). Similarly, Dei and Asgharzadeh (2001) maintain that many aspects of Indigeneity act as "profound sites of empowerment, struggle and resistance against imposed hegemonies" (p. 318). However, in "Essentialism, Memory and Resistance: Aboriginality and the Politics of Authenticity" Andrew Lattas (1993) presents one of the most thought-provoking positions on this issue. In agreement with Okpewho et al. and Dei and Asdharzadeh, Lattas also posits that "cultural and political significance is always constituted through a past" where "a sense of continuity with the past might be a way of resisting assimilation" (p. 246). Of principal significance is Lattas' response to charges of essentialism, which he establishes through a rearticulation of Indigenous identity *from an Indigenous worldsense standpoint*:

> An enormous amount of intellectual energy is currently directed at establishing Aboriginality as something that is invented through European involvement. What is often ignored is the sense of autonomy from the control of the "Other" conferred by images of the past and indeed the necessity to have an image of the past if one is to have a sense of ownership of oneself. Yet when Aborigines seek to give a mythological content to, or to reclaim, a primordial past for themselves then they are accused of essentialism and of participating in their own domination. Aboriginal culture here is set up to be de-mythologised and rationalized by the white intellectuals working in Aboriginal studies. It is to be stripped of its essentialising mythology and folklore and introduced to modern theoretical ideas which emphasize the contextual and relative nature of any identity. This is identity without content and without a primordial past; it is identity stripped to the bare logic of being simply a relation. The demand that Aborigines produce their popular consciousness along the lines of a social theory of identity is a request that they become conscious of themselves as purely relational identities; they are to be resisters without producing an essence for themselves. They are to situate themselves in opposition to Whites without fetishising themselves. They are to become a pure system of difference, an oppositional form that does not stabilize itself except through being a subversion of the other. There is no positivity and content in this form of Aboriginality, it is a relationship of opposition responding to the terms and agenda set yet again by white society. In effect, a white moral gaze refuses Aborigines an identity politics that is grounded in them taking up their bodies as an imaginary space (pp. 247–248).

Lattas' brilliant discussion highlights the empowering possibilities of Indigenous knowledges as central decolonizing tools of resistance against domination and colonization. In placing Indigenous ways of knowing at the center, Lattas refuses the conventional Eurocentric yardsticks of academic identity construction and, instead, carves out a space to reconstruct an Indigenous identity *on its own terms*; that is, from an Indigenous perspective that affirms the past through descent, the body and generational transmission of one's memories and ancestors. Lattas helps me to think about engaging Indigeneity as a decolonizing terrain of intellectual engagement. He also demonstrates that essentialisms that are grounded in Indigenous constructions of the self cannot be *solely* and simply measured *in relationship* to Whites, but rather, Indigeneity also exists autonomously to serve important "cultural and political functions" (p. 246) that are empowering—for example, being conscious of one's connection to one's past, one's land, and one's body as strategic ways of resisting colonialism and assimilation (p. 245). This is not to say that relational readings and constructions of identity should be jettisoned or dismissed, rather, what is being advocated here is the necessity to take seriously Indigenous constructions of identity on their own terms and to be aware of the dangerous re-colonizing implications if these ways of knowing continue to be denied and delegitimized. In this sense then, essentialisms are "strategic" (Spivak, 1990) and cannot be sloppily grouped with and subsumed under the oppressive and dangerously subjugating essentialisms of the dominant/colonizers. In effect, certain essentialisms are evoked differently because these formulations serve the function of strategic resistance, particularly in the necessary and eventual decolonizing shift toward healing from oppression. Such essentialisms are also therapeutic in that they provide physical, psychic, spiritual, and emotional ways of knowing and understanding oneself through a sense of community, groundedness, connection, and stability. In other words, certain essentialisms are empowering Indigenous constructions of identity that must be taken *on those terms,* and according to *those ways* of knowing the world, ways which are deeply anchored in their own unique Indigenous worldsense. Finally, Lattas'(1993) discussion reminded me that taking a staunch and absolutely anti-essentialist position where people are continually reduced to "pure systems of difference" (p. 248) is a form of essentialism in and of itself because one remains *fixed* in that system. Indigeneity here is conceptualized both as an empowering resistant identity, and *as part of a diverse range of identities.* The fact remains that there are a myriad of ways to understand our existence and identities in this world, and to exclude Indigenous identities or slap them with charges which ring of some type of subtextual "primitive" essentialism while engaging in a particular type of one's own essentialism is to participate in exclusionary hierarchical politics which (intentionally or not) continue to deny Indigenous peoples' right to self-identify. In the end, such accusations are misguided and, in addition to reifying dominant Western knowledges, they fail to recognize the empowering and decolonizing possibilities of Indigenous knowledges and identities.

The fifth conceptual layer of my understanding of Indigeneity involves the premise that binaristic thinking around Indigenous and Western knowledges as clearly demarcated needs to be avoided (Dei, 2000b; Purcell, 1998).[4] However, it is also important to recognize the current position of Indigenous knowledges and identities as "discredited" (Morrison, 1984) and subjugated, particularly in relation to dominant Western discourses about "truth" (Foucault as cited in Purcell, 1998, p. 260). To bring it back to the African context, the two monotheistic religions of Christianity and Islam have historically constructed African Indigenous religion—this includes that of the Yoruba—as "inferior," "uncivilized" and "backward." Where Islam relegated African Indigenous religions to *al-Jahilliyya,* the time of Barbarism, Christianity viewed it "as pure paganism" (Olupona, 1991, p. 1). Needless to say, these hegemonic constructions persist to date, as evidenced in the often ostracizing and antagonistically hostile attitude toward proponents of African Indigenous spirituality. The fact that most Africans have internalized, converted to, and consequently live out Christian or Muslim identities in allegiance to these colonizing religious traditions poses some interesting questions around how African Indigenous religions figure in liberation and decolonizing projects. Accordingly, an anti-colonial theoretical framework becomes imperative to my study because it engages a critique of the denigration and disparagement of Indigeneity, particularly since such pathologizing is carried out in the name of "modernity" (Dei & Asgharzadeh, 2001, p. 301). In short, the anti-colonial discursive framework appreciates, and therefore takes the position that Indigenous knowledges and identities carry crucial elements of empowerment, resistance, and the basic human right to simply be who one is. In this sense, justice and social change are attendant imperatives when working with/in this framework. Scholars Ladislaus M. Semali and Joe L. Kincheloe (1999) elaborate:

> A central tenet [is] our belief in the transformative power of indigenous knowledge, the ways that such knowledge can be used to foster empowerment and justice in a variety of cultural contexts. A key aspect of this transformative power involves the exploration of human consciousness, the nature of its production, and the process of its engagement with cultural difference (p. 15).

The sixth layer of my conceptualization of Indigeneity involves a synthesis of the salient Black feminist principle where the various forms of oppression in our world, such as patriarchy, White supremacy/racism, classism, ablism, and heterosexism are conceptualized as interlocking and mutually sustaining forces of dominance (Collins, 1990; hooks, 1981; Lorde, 1984). Against the traditionally masculinist grain of anti-colonial theory, George Dei and Alireza Asgharzadeh echo Black feminist sentiments in their rearticulation of anti-colonial discourse to assert the necessity that *all* forms of oppression be approached as interlocking and therefore of equal importance in anti-colonial theorizing. However, given such rearticulations, it should not be assumed that research which may focus more extensively on one or more sites of oppression is immediately doing so at the expense of others and therefore reproducing these same forms of oppression. Instead, attention must be paid to *the manner* in which this is done and ways in which certain forms of oppression and domination are salient in certain contexts, or, the need for focus and emphasis on certain sites because they remain under-researched and scantily theorized. Dei and Asgharzadeh (2001) provide a lucid articulation of how this can be done in a strategic and anti-hegemonic manner:

> The anti-colonial thought forwards a notion of critical gaze which could be maintained on any single category such as race, class, or gender, at the same time can refrain from subduing or subordinating other categories and sites of oppression. Such a gaze is not concrete and fixed. It is fluid and transparent. It constantly sees and observes colonial relations of power and domination, shifts from one site onto the other, resists all of them, but maintains a relatively heavier presence on any chosen category in a strategic gesture to be more effective (pp. 312–313).

As mentioned earlier, scholarship that premises *contemporary* Indigeneity from an African diasporic perspective remains quite scant and under-researched. My present research gives the concept of contemporary African diasporic Indigeneity the same consideration that other social identities and forms of domination are given when thinking through the interlocking nature of oppressions. Said another way, what I am suggesting here is that, as a social location and identity that one both celebrates, yet is systematically oppressed under, through colonialism, African diasporic Indigeneity needs to be included as a category of analysis. Doing so could only enrich and nuance one's scholarship, but more importantly, doing so indicates a counter-hegemonic political act in academic spaces. That is, one is aware of, and contesting the (destructive) dominance of Western knowledges as normative. Finally, to do so (whether one identifies as Indigenous or not) would be taking a powerful alliance-based standpoint that signals to others the importance of speaking out against the continued oppression of Indigenous peoples, their knowledges, and lands.

The seventh and final conceptual layer of my understanding of Indigeneity is two-fold and builds on the sixth. The first portion entails an awareness that any critical analysis which seeks to understand the interlocking social relations of power in diasporic Yoruba identities requires us to put aside the seductive lull of romanticizing our Indigeneity. We must recognize that some Indigenous knowledge systems carry sites of disempowerment, which are often evoked against women and other cultural or ethnic minorities (Dei, 2000a, p. 8).[5] These evocations also tend to be erected in the name of "tradition" or under that banner of "culture," as justifications for inequitable social relations. With a conscientious awareness of how colonialism figures, these sites of oppression also need to be critically engaged and examined, not disregarded.

The second portion of this final layer emphasizes the importance of working with a philosophy of humility, acknowledging the incompleteness of knowledge. This means embracing the power of not knowing (Dei, 2000b). In my opinion, this is one of the most important lessons that scholars in the academy and Western world can learn from African and other Indigenous knowledge systems. In a space where one's worth and status are judged on an overevaluation of the primacy of the mind and "knowing it all," opening oneself up to the humbling position of viewing oneself as a perpetual learner rather than an eternal expert can be a transformative tool for many in the academy and beyond. As a core element for Indigenous knowledge systems, humility challenges us to think *and feel* outside our individual selves by engaging circle-centered epistemologies that focus on our interconnectedness with each other. The hope is that this will assist us in developing a critical reflexivity and sustaining deeper critical understandings of how these connections among one another reinscribe our position(s) in this world.

Ultimately, anti-colonial theory is central to African diasporic identities because it privileges Indigeneity as an empowering and crucially significant standpoint from which to understand the world. Further, this theoretical framework produces scholarship that addresses colonialism, imperialism, and other inequitable social relations of power to allow for a more historicized, contextualized, and nuanced understanding of how specifically Yoruba Indigenous knowledges and identities are constructed, and how they might be reinscribed as empowering decolonizing tools.

AFRICAN/BLACK FEMINIST THEORY

My argument is also anchored in African and Black feminist theoretical frameworks, both of which complement and contribute to anti-colonial theory. These frameworks explicate and further nuance the complexity of African life and experience on the African continent and its diaspora through their commitment to dismantling forms of oppression such as patriarchy, White supremacy, classism, and heterosexism. These discourses emerged largely from the unique positions Black women hold, where, on the one hand we face the racism and White supremacy of White feminists, while, on the other we face the (often internalized) sexism and patriarchy of African/Black men, all within the larger contexts of capitalism and Eurocentric societies (Amadiume, 1997; Collins, 1990; Combahee River Collective, 1983; Davis, 1983; hooks, 1981; Mama, 1997).

While African and Black feminisms do have distinct histories in terms of their academic development,[6] it is important to point out that they also heavily overlap and dialectically inform each other.[7] As Black feminist contributions to transnational feminist theory continue to gain a foothold in academic circles, the emphasis on critically examining, as well as crossing national, economic, political, and cultural borders has grown and consequently induced a shift toward focusing on how the local affects the global and vice versa. This shift has, in turn, increasingly lent itself to shining a spotlight on the impact of inequitable social relations in African women's lives everywhere. Black/African feminisms are indispensable to my argument because they provide frames of analysis that allow me to critically interrogate and expose the entanglements of masculinist, patriarchal, and White supremacist knowledge systems that deny and oppress the voices, contributions, and experiences of African women. These feminisms are powerful because they place Black women at the center of analysis (Amadiume, 1987; Collins, 1990; hooks, 1981) while simultaneously employing the concept of intersectionality; where categories of identity, oppression, and analysis such as race, gender, class, sexuality, and ability are conceptualized as inextricably interdependant, mutually sustaining, and of equal importance (Collins, 1990; Combahee River Collective, 1983; hooks, 1981; Lorde, 1984). The term "Intersectionality" enables me to think through the complex experiences of Yoruba migrants without hierarchically prioritizing either gender- or race-specific oppressions (Amadiume, 1997; Boyce-Davies, 1994; Collins, 1990), while eclipsing others. In contradistinction to White feminist or Black male-centered articulations of oppression which inevitably wind up positioning African women's experiences and knowledges at the lower ends of such hierarchies, thereby obscuring Black female presence and voice, African/Black feminisms, and their concept of intersectionality become crucially imperative because they offer frameworks through which to situate the diverse realities, experiences, and knowledges of Black/African women as central, both historically and contemporarily.

A melding of African feminist theory and anti-colonial scholarship is also of necessity for my work given that this chapter considers Indigenous knowledges as crucial entry points and sites of resistance and empowerment against Eurocolonial oppression. African/Black feminist theory complements, overlaps, and builds on anti-colonial frameworks because it allows for more nuanced attention to be paid to the entanglements of gender and power, and how they figure(d) in colonizing and imperialist systems of oppression. However, while there is a proliferation of African and Black feminist literature that explores the question, meaning, and significance of gender as a primary social category, for this chapter my entry point is African/Black feminist scholarship that draws on and engages the category of gender from Indigenous perspectives. African/Black feminisms are a powerful and necessary conceptual tool here because they critically interrogate spaces of inequity within Indigenous knowledge systems, while simultaneously recognizing that these spaces of disempowerment are challenged and critically interrogated *in the promise of transformation and hope for more equitable change.* African feminist frameworks that embrace Indigenous knowledges and ways of knowing appreciate that these spaces of disempowerment do not then become "backward" or "primitive" all-encompassing representations of the whole network of Indigenous knowledge systems—as they are often framed in colonialist discourses. Ultimately, Black feminisms which utilize, and are anchored in Indigenous-centered philosophies understand that Indigenous ways of knowing are not singular, monolithic epistemologies, and that the impact of colonialism and imperialism on these knowledges must be given critical attention, especially given the reality that these hegemonic systems continue to oppressively impact our choices, voices, and overall lives. This is not to deny our own agency and forms of resistance, but rather, to highlight the insidious nature of the legacy of colonialism, how it often obscures our access to knowledges—particularly Indigenous ones—and the assorted fields of empowerment that such knowledges offer.

CONCEPTUALIZING GENDER IN INDIGENOUS YORUBA CONTEXTS

In this research, I draw on African/Black feminist literature that prioritizes and engages gender from Indigenous perspectives. Since imperialism and conquest (and their legacies) are the realities that many Indigenous peoples live with, much Indigenous feminist scholarship has focused on the devastating impact of colonialism; namely how it has displaced and warped Indigenous constructions of gender. Such arguments then conveniently explain patriarchal dominance and violence against women in Indigenous communities. Oyeronke Oyewumi (1997), Bibi Bakare-Yusuf (2003), and Oyeronke Olajubu (2003) are all African/Black feminist scholars whose work addresses the meaning and significance of gender in Indigenous Yoruba contexts. Oyewumi's work addresses the naturalization of Western knowledge production processes in African studies. Specifically, she focuses on the epistemological underpinnings of Western notions of sex and gender, where gender-specific English is written into gender-free Yoruba, as foundational evidence that gender, and particularly the category, "women" does not operate in Yorubaland in the same way it does in Western discourses (1997, pp. x–xi). In Oyewumi's estimation, seniority, not gender, is the primary power relation in Yorubaland. Oyewumi's groundbreaking exposition of concealed Western social categories—particularly the category of "woman"—as universal, is a staunch reminder of the need to remain cognizant of how the naturalization of culturally specific (Western) categories prevail even in analyzing Indigenous cultures. In this sense, Oyewumi's work acts as a decolonizing model for my research around gender, as well as other social categories. Oyewumi's deconstructive resistance against Western universalisms reinstalls the need to use Yoruba Indigenous knowledges as central sites from which to theorize and produce knowledge about Yoruba people.

However, Yoruba feminist Bibi Bakare-Yusuf contests Oyewumi's position that gender is not one of the primary organizing principles in Indigenous Yoruba societies. Bakare-Yusuf argues that Oyewumi reduces Yoruba cultural life and experience to discourse, semiotics, and representation, without taking into account the lived effect of language on embodied subjects as sexuated bodies. For Bakare-Yusuf, Oyewumi fails to address "how agents live through and are positioned within the field of power, language, discourse and social practice" (p. 120). Bakare-Yusuf's attention to power, embodiment, and social experience is key for my work, in that, not only are they of prime relevance when discussions around sex, gender, and anatomy are raised, they are also important analytical tools necessary for gaining a deeper understanding of what Yoruba Indigenous identities and lived experiences in diasporic contexts entail. Because these features are missing from Oyewumi's study, she is not able to address how the gendered and age-identified body *interlocks with power*.

Bakare-Yusuf argues that Oyewumi's failure to seriously consider the social relations of power also means that she will not be able to address the complex nuances of how power figures with respect to seniority and gender. Oyewumi and Bakare-Yusuf's positions are not mutually exclusive however, and their approaches remind us of the principal importance of intersectionality as a fundamental tool of critical inquiry, to tease out and better understand how power and privilege shape our experiences and identities. The concept of intersectionality is critical for this research because age and seniority are not categories that exist devoid of their entanglements with other social categories such as gender and class, for example. Of particular significance to my work is Bakare-Yusuf's position that these social relations are continually shaped by differences in power, and the often violent consequences of such inequities:

> ... [Oyewumi] cannot discuss the fact that the ideology of seniority is very often used as a way of masking other forms of power relationship. It is in this sense that her theorisation of seniority may be seen as politically dangerous. The vocabulary of seniority often becomes the very form in which sexual abuse and familial (especially for the aya/wife in a lineage) and symbolic violence are couched...where victims are reluctant to challenge the abuser in the name of "disrespecting their senior" (p. 132).

Bakare-Yusuf notes that the Indigenous Yoruba category of seniority can become a *conciliatory* site of patriarchal oppression and disempowerment for the "sexuated" (Bakare-Yusuf, 2003) or "ana-female" (Oyewumi, 1997) body otherwise known as "woman." According to Oyewumi, there is no Yoruba category of woman that is equivalent to the Western sense of the word/social identity. However, as Bakare-Yusuf points out, what does exist are notions of seniority that, in practice, can leave women vulnerable and prone to abuse and violence under the guise of seniority. In other words, while abuse and oppression are not epistemically visible in Yoruba Indigenous philosophy, the marginalization of women is practiced. Here, Oyewumi's argument is both right and wrong: right in that gender does not operate in Yorubaland in the same way it does in Western society and discourse; wrong in her denial of gender as a primary social relation in Yoruba society. In the end, Bakare-Yusuf's discussion echoes Dei's (2000a) sentiment that "sites of disempowerment" in Indigenous knowledge systems cannot be left unexamined and must be critiqued, albeit with keen cognizance of the larger colonial context.

Perhaps the most useful and flexible discussion of gender in Yoruba contexts is that of Yoruba feminist scholar Oyeronke Olajubu (2003), who understands gender as a dynamic *process* that is mutably constructed and therefore interdependent on other social systems (p. 7). She states

> ... gender as construed by the Yoruba is essentially culture bound and should be differentiated from notions of gender in some other cultures. It is a gender classification that is not equivalent to or a consequence of anatomy at all times. Yoruba gender construction is fluid and is modulated by other factors such as seniority (age) and personal achievements (wealth and knowledge acquisition). Its boundaries are constantly shifting, and reconfigurations attend its expressions constantly (p. 8).

Olajubu's emphasis on the flexibility of Yoruba gender construction is the most relevant for my research here because such flexibility allows for discussions about gender to be taken out of narrow binarized conceptions that either deny, or decontextually overemphasize gender as a primary social category in Yoruba culture and society. In this sense, Olajubu's articulation of gender as mutable, and process-oriented provides an effective conceptual model for how to utilize and approach gender in my research. However, note that Olajubu's argument of Yoruba gender construction as culture-bound is somewhat contradictory to her position that it is flexible since culture itself is not static, but flexible. What Olajubu neglects to mention is how, through the violence of colonialism and imperialism, *Eurocentric* notions of gender have also influenced how the Yoruba construe gender. So the question becomes, *to which culture(s)* are Yoruba gender constructions bound, when the fact of dominating processes such as colonialism and imperialism are taken into account? Further, while Olajubu recognizes that Yoruba gender construction is modulated by other social factors such as age, wealth, etc., nowhere in her statement does she address colonialism or imperialism. In neglecting to do so, she fails to account for the fact that the fundamental impetus behind colonialism and imperialism was to conquer, destroy, and annihilate. In this context Indigenous Yoruba gender constructions must have been *somehow* impacted and modulated; that is, in some way, they were shifted and displaced according to patriarchal Eurocentric constructions of gender. Regrettably, Olajubu does not engage what I think is a crucially fundamental aspect of the varied *flexible* manifestations (be they Eurocentric, hegemonic, Indigenous, or the complicated entanglements of these) of Yoruba gender construction processes. Unlike Olajubu, I conceptualize the various social relations that modulate Yoruba gender construction to be one that *includes* and is therefore cognizant of oppressive systems such as colonialism and imperialism, systems which, in all likelihood, have almost certainly warped Indigenous Yoruba constructions of gender.

Ultimately, this complicated debate about gender in Yoruba contexts is of significance because it underscores the fact that such a discussion is not solely about gender but rather, is also bound up with spirituality and issues of imperialism, colonialism, embodiment, power, culture, and the uncritical acceptance of Western discourse as normative. While Oyewumi convincingly cautions against the dangers of Western universalisms, Bakare-Yusuf reminds us that continued focus on differences of privilege and power imbalance is imperative in understanding the embodied and material realities of Yoruba women, and society on a whole. Meanwhile, Olajubu's argument that Yoruba gender constructions are flexible, fluid, and process-oriented, serves as a significant reminder that Indigenous knowledges are complex and dynamic and cannot be reduced to narrow binaries. The debate on gender and how it figures in Yoruba society has not been resolved, and it is not my intention to settle these tensions. Rather, it is more useful to reflect and build the works of these scholars by expanding on the convergent and divergent discussions around gender as a significant social category in Yoruba society. Thereby giving serious attention to the spiritual, material, and embodied realities of how gender intersects with other social categories, such as race, class, seniority, and age, all within the larger contexts of colonialism and imperialism.

In conclusion, the concept "Indigenous" needs to be imagined differently and more flexibly where diasporic Africans are concerned, so that these distinctive social positionings can be theorized in a manner where the particularities of these experiences are also investigated. In other words, there is a need for a shift in how notions of Indigeneity are taken up so that they are not imagined as conventionally singular, thereby excluding the unique realities of Africans in the diaspora.

NOTES

1. Fama's Ede Awo: *Orisa Yoruba Dictionary*, p. 97.
2. I am aware that this particular layer I speak of is not the first Yoruba diaspora in "Canada." I acknowledge that many other Yoruba peoples who were enslaved preceded this, however, for the purposes of this research project I focus on the most recent Yoruba speaking communities who "voluntarily" migrated from the African continent in the late 60s to the early 70s and on.
3. See Patricia Jones-Jackson, *When Roots Die*; Melville J. Herskovits, *The Myth of the Negro Past*; Marion Kraft, *The African Continuum and Contemporary African American Writers: Their Literary Presence and Ancestral Past*; Maureen Warner-Lewis, *Guinea's Other Suns, Trinidad Yoruba and Central Africa in the Caribbean*; Robert Farris Thompson, *Flash of the Spirit*; Edward Kamau Brathwaite, *History of the Voice*; John W. Pulis (ed.) *Religion, Diaspora and Cultural Identity: A Reader in the Anglophone Caribbean*; Albert J. Raboteau, *Slave Religion: The "Invisible Institution" in the Antebellum South*; Sterling Stuckey, *Slave Culture*; Catherine A. John, *Clear Word and Third Sight: Folk Groundings and Diasporic Consciousness in African Caribbean Writing*; Jason R. Young, *Rituals of Resistance: African Atlantic Religion in Kongo and the Lowcountry South in the Era of Slavery* for excellent studies of how Indigenous African culture is reassembled, yet retained and continued in the African diaspora.
4. This is important primarily because Indigenous knowledges are often co-opted, appropriated, and subsumed under "Western" knowledges, without being acknowledged in their own right.
5. For example, whilst not the focus of my study, I ask, how does homophobia, or the silence and denial of same gender relationships in African Indigenous knowledge systems limit itself as a source of empowerment and decolonization? As I make this assumption around the denial of homosexuality in African traditional societies, I feel the urge to unsay it because, yes, although Africans do share many cultural and spiritual values, epistemologies and histories, it is also vastly important to not homogenize African peoples, or see the continent as an undifferentiated monolith. The differences and specificities of distinct African societies need to be seriously considered. For example, Malidoma Somé has discussed the key role spiritual gatekeepers—who are often gay men—play among the Dagara people of Burkina Faso. He is also currently writing a book on gays and lesbians as spiritual gatekeepers in traditional Dagara society. See his Web site, www.malidoma.com for more

information. Also see, Boris de Rachewiltz, *Black Eros: Sexual Customs of Africa from Prehistory to the 1964 Present Day*. Despite the heavily anthropological construction of African societies, the pictures and images in this text give some insight into the diverse ways different African societies value, manage, respond to, and deal with sexuality and, the dangers in assuming that the markers of sexuality in the West can easily be transferred to African societies. According to this text, homosexuality is accepted in some societies and severely punished or seen as unnatural in others. Additionally, the often metaphorical, indirect, and proverbial salience of African languages and oral traditions must be seriously engaged where analysis and discussion of sexuality in African contexts are raised.

6. On the ancestral shoulders of the long history of Black enfranchisement and Black abolitionism, the academic concept of Black feminism emerged largely from the historically activist-based and grassroots experiences of Black women in the United States. See Zora Neale Hurston, *Their Eyes Were Watching God; Folklore, Memoirs and Other writings*; Gloria T. Hull et al, *All the Women are White, All the Blacks Are Men, But Some of Us are Brave: Black Women's Studies*; bell hooks, *Ain't I a Woman?: Black Women and Feminism*; Audre Lorde, *Sister Outsider*; Angela Davis, *Women, Race and Class*; Patricia Hill-Collins, *Black Feminist Thought* for in-depth discussion and theorizing of Black feminism, as an important site for critical analysis of Black female experience within oppressive social relations of power. This is not to deny the long-standing grassroots activism and resistance of Black women on the continent, the Caribbean, Europe, and North and South America—which occurred simultaneously and alongside their African American sisters—rather, it is simply to say that the emergence of academic and text-based Black feminist discourses were initially conceived in primarily U.S. contexts.

Similarly, see Ifi Amadiume, *Male Daughters, Female Husbands; Reinventing African: Matriarchy, Religion and Culture; Daughters of the Goddess, Daughters of Imperialism*; Amina Mama, *Beyond the Masks; Race, Gender and Subjectivity*; Patricia McFadden, *Gender in Southern Africa: A Gendered Perspective* for academic texts which explicate and theorize African feminism. To contribute to the dearth of written literature placing Black women as subjects at the centre, these texts emerged largely from the historical and contemporary experiences of continental African women. Also, in light of the significance of narrative as central to African Indigenous culture and ways of knowing, many other African feminist intellectuals have theorized and voiced African women's experiences through narrative or storytelling. See works by Ama Ata Aidoo, Buchi Emecheta, Tsitsi Dangarembga, Mariama Ba, Flora Nwapa, Yvonne Vera, and Bessie Head (to name a few).

7. Despite contentious debates over the distinct specificities of the terms "Black" and "African," they do overlap, are highly interconnected, and therefore cannot be clearly demarcated as separate. Hence, I use these terms interchangeably as a political signifier in specific reference to the various and multiple Indigenous peoples of the African continent—to indicate both, those who were stolen away through the horrific European transatlantic slave trade, and those who remained on the African continent, and were forced to undergo the atrocious traumas of colonialism and imperialism. In the spirit of unity and community, I also use these terms interchangeably as a counter-hegemonic and political identity to critically underscore the unique positionings and social locations of Indigenous Africans in Africa, Europe, the Caribbean, North and South America, and Asia. This is not to mobilize a conflated conception of "Africans" and "Blacks," where we are homogenized as one large monolith that exists absent of difference, rather, my aim is to discuss and theorize the complex nuances of Indigenous African life—wherever that may be—through usage of these terms as the larger politically unifying milieux under which Black/African people can be named and identified.

REFERENCES

Abimbola, Wande. (1997). *Ifa Will Mend Our Broken World: Thoughts on Yoruba Religion and Culture in Africa and the Diaspora.* Roxbury, Massachusetts: Aim Books.

Alexander, M. J. (2005). *Pedagogies of Crossing: Meditations on Feminism, Sexual Politics, Memory and the Sacred.* London: Duke University Press.

Amadiume, I. (1987). *Male Daughters, Female Husbands: Gender and Sex in an African Society.* London: Zed.

Amadiume, I. (1997). *Reinventing Africa: Matriarchy, Religion and Culture*. London: Zed.
Anzaldúa, G. (1987). *Borderlands /La Frontera: The New Mestiza*. San Francisco: Aunt Lute.
Anzaldúa, G. E., & Cherrie L. M. (Eds.). (1983). *This Bridge Called My Back: Writings by Radical Women of Colour*. New York: Kitchen Table, Women of Color.
Appiah, K. A. (1992). *In My Father's House: Africa in the Philosophy of Culture*. New York: Oxford University Press.
Awolalu, J. O. (1979). *Yoruba Beliefs and Sacrificial Rites*. Essex, UK: Longman.
Bakare-Yusuf, B. (2003). Yorubas Don't Do Gender': A Critical Review of Oyeronke Oyewumi's *The Invention of Women: Making an African Sense of Western Gender Discourses*. *African Identities, 1*(1), 119–140.
Battiste, Marie & James (Sa'ke'j) Youngblood Henderson. (2000) *Protecting Indigenous Knowledge and Heritage: A Global Challenge*. Saskatchewan: Purich Publishing Ltd.
Battiste, Marie. (2002). *Indigenous Knowledge and Pedagogy in First Nations Education: A Literature Review with Recommendations*. Ottawa: Apamuwek Institute.
Boyce-Davies, C. (1994). *Black Women, Writing and Identity: Migrations of the Subject*. London: Routledge.
Brand, D. (2001). *Map to the Door of No Return: Notes to Belonging*. Toronto: Vintage Canada.
Brown, L. (1981). *Women Writers in Black Africa*. Westport, CT: Greenwood.
Braziel, Jana E. & Anite Mannur. (2003) *Theorizing Diaspora: a reader*. Massachusetts: Blackwell.
Carby, H. (1987). *Reconstructing Womanhood: The Emergence of the Afro-American Woman Novelist*. New York: Oxford University Press.
Castellano, M. B. (2000). Updating Aboriginal Traditions of Knowledge. In G. J. S. Dei, B. L. Hall, & Rosenberg, D. G. (Eds.), *Indigenous Knowledges in Global Contexts: Multiple Readings of Our World* (pp. 21–36). Toronto: University of Toronto Press.
Centre for Contemporary Cultural Studies. (1982). *The Empire Strikes Back: Race and Racism in 70s Britain*. London; Hutchinson: University of Birmingham.
Christian, B. (2000). The Race for Theory. In J. James, & T. D. Sharpley-Whiting (Eds.), *The Black Feminist Reader* (pp. 11–23). Boston, MA: Blackwell.
Churchill, W. (1996). *From a Native Son: Selected Essays on Indigenism*. Boston: South End.
Churchill, W. (1997). *A Little Matter of Genocide: Holocaust and Denial in the Americas, 1492 to the Present*. San Francisco: City Lights.
Churchill, W. (1999). *Struggle for the Land: Native North American Resistance to Genocide, Ecocide and Colonization*. Winnipeg: Arbeiter Ring.
Churchill, W. (2003). *Indigenous Strategies of Resistance*. Toronto: York University.
Collins, P. H. (1990). *Black Feminist Thought: Knowledge, Consciousness and the Politics of Empowerment*. New York: Routledge.
Combahee River Collective. (1983). The Combahee River Collective Statement. In B. Smith (Ed.), *Homegirls: A Black Feminist Anthology* (pp. 272–282). New York: Women of Color Press.
Davies, C. B., & Graves, A. A. (1986). *Ngambika: Studies of Women in African Literature*. Trenton, New Jersey: Africa World .
Davies, C. B. (1994). *Black Women, Writing and Identity: Migrations of the Subject*. London: Routledge.
Davis, A. (1983). *Women, Race and Class*. New York: Vintage.
Dei, G. J. S. (1996). *Anti-racism and Education: Theory and Practice*. Halifax: Fernwood.
Dei, G. J. S. (2000a). African Development: The Relevance and Implications of "Indigenousness." In G. J. S. Dei, B. L. Hall, & D. G. Rosenberg (Eds.), *Indigenous Knowledges in Global Contexts: Multiple Readings of Our World* (pp. 70–86). Toronto: University of Toronto Press.
Dei, G. J. S. (2000b). Rethinking the Role of Indigenous Knowledges in the Academy. *International Journal of Inclusive Education, 4*(2), 111–132.
Dei, G. J. S., & Asgharzadeh, A. (2001). The Power of Social Theory: Towards an Anti-colonial Discursive Framework. *Journal of Educational Thought, 35*(3), 297–323.
Dei, G. J. S., Hall, B. L., & Rosenberg, D. G. (Eds.). (2000). *Indigenous Knowledges in Global Contexts: Multiple Readings of Our World*. Toronto: University of Toronto Press.
Eboh, M. P. (2000). The Woman Question: African and Western Perspectives. In E. C. Eze (Ed.). *African Philosophy:*

An Anthology (pp. 333–337). London: Blackwell.
Enloe, C. (1990). *Bananas, Beaches and Bases: Making Feminist Sense of International Politics*. Berkeley, CA: University of California Press.
Eze, E. C. (1997). Toward a Critical Theory of Postcolonial African Identities. In E. C. Eze (Ed.). *Postcolonial African Philosophy: A Critical Reader* (pp. 339–344). London: Blackwell.
Eze, E. C. (Ed.). (1998). *African Philosophy: An Anthology*. Oxford: Blackwell.
Fafunwa, B. A. (1974). *History of Education in Nigeria*. Ibadan, Nigeria: NPS Educational.
Falola, T. (1999). *Yoruba Gurus: Indigenous Production of Knowledge in Africa*. Trenton, NJ: Africa World.
Fanon, F. (1967). *Black Skin, White Masks*. Translation by C. L. Markmann. New York: Grove.
Fanon, F. (1963). *The Wretched of the Earth*. New York: Grove.
Hall, Stuart. (1997). Subjects in History: Making Diasporic Identities. In *The House That Race Built*. New York: Vintage. 289–299.
Heyd, T. (1995). Indigenous Knowledge, Emancipation and Alienation. *Knowledge and Policy: The International Journal of Knowledge Transfer and Utilization, 8*(1), 63–73.
hooks, b. (1981). *Ain't I a Woman: Black Women and Feminism*. Boston: South End.
Higgins, T. E. (2001). *Religiosity, Cosmology, and Folklore: The African Influence in the Novels of Toni Morrison*. New York: Routledge.
Hull, G., Scott, P. B., Smith, B. (1982). *All the Women Are White, All the Blacks Are Men, but Some of Us Are Brave: Black Women's Studies* (pp. xvii–xxxi & pp. 13–22). New York: Feminist.
Hurston, Z. N. (1978). *Mules and Men*. Bloomington, IN: Indiana University Press.
Hurston, Z. N. (1990). *Their Eyes Were Watching God*. New York: Harper & Row.
Idowu, B. (1996). *Olodumare: God in Yoruba Belief*. Lagos, Nigeria: Longman.
Imbo, S. O. (1998). *An Introduction to African Philosophy*. Lanham, MD: Rowman & Littlefield.
Laguerre, M. S. (1998). *Diasporic Citizenship: Haitian Americans in Transnational America*. New York: St. Martin's.
Lattas, A. (1993). Essentialism, Memory and Resistance: Aboriginality and the Politics of Authenticity. *Oceania, 62*, 249–263.
Lewis, Earl. (1995). To Turn as on a Pivot: Writing African Americans into a History of Overlapping Diasporas. In *The American Historical Review, 100*(3) 765–787.
Lorde, A. (1984). *Sister Outsider*. New York: Crossing.
Mama, A. (1997). Sheroes and Villains: Conceptualizing Colonial and Contemporary Violence Against Women in Africa. In A. Jacqui, & C. T. Mohanty (Eds.), *Feminist Genealogies, Colonial Legacies, Democratic Futures* (pp. 46–62). New York: Routledge.
Mikell, G. (1997). Conclusions: African Women and State Crisis. In G. Mikell (Ed.), *African Feminism: The Politics of Survival in Sub-Saharan Africa* (pp. 333–346). Philadelphia: University of Pennsylvania Press.
Miller, I. (1995). We the Colonized Ones: Kukuli Speaks. *Third Text: Contemporary Perspectives on Art and Culture, 32*(Autumn), 94–102.
Minh-ha, T. (1989). *Woman, Native, Other: Writing Postcoloniality and Feminism*. Bloomington, IN: Indiana University Press.
Morrison, T. (1984). Rootedness: The Ancestor as Foundation. In M. Evans (Ed.), *Black Women Writers: 1950–1980, A Critical Evaluation* (pp. 339–345). New York: Doubleday.
Morrison, T. (1987). *Beloved*. New York: Plume.
Narogin, M. (1995). *U.S. Mob History, Culture, Struggle: An Introduction to Indigenous Australia*. Australia: Angus and Robertson.
Nwikale, K. (1996). Homesick or Eurocentric? Alice Walker's Africa. In F. Ojo-Ade. (Ed.), *Of Dreams Deferred, Dead or Alive: African Perspectives on African-American Writers* (pp. 157–169). Westport, CT: Greenwood.
Ogundipe-Leslie, O. (1985). Women in Nigeria. In Women in Nigeria (Organization). (Ed.), *Women in Nigeria Today* (pp. 119–131). London: Zed.
Okpewho, I., Davies, C. B., & Mazrui, A. A. (1999). *The African Diaspora: African Origins and New World Identities*. Bloomington, IN: Indiana University Press.
Olajubu, O. (2003). *Women in the Yoruba Religious Sphere*. New York: State University of New York Press.

Olupona, J. K. (Ed.). (1991). *African Traditional Religions in Contemporary Society.* New York: Paragon House.

Ong, A. (1999). *Flexible Citizenship: The Cultural Logics of Transnationality.* Durham, NC: Duke University Press.

Oyewumi, O. (1997). *The Invention of Women: Making an African Sense of Western Gender Discourses.* Minneapolis: University of Minnesota Press.

Philip, M. N. (1989). *She Tries Her Tongue: Her Silence Softly Breaks.* Charlottetown: Ragweed.

Philip, M. N. (1991). *Looking for Livingstone: An Odyssey of Silence.* Toronto: Mercury.

Purcell, T. W. (1998). Indigenous Knowledge and Applied Anthropology: Question of Definition and Direction. *Human Organization, 57*(3), 258–272.

Razack, Sherene & Mary Louise Fellows. (1998). The Race to Innocence: Confronting Hierarchical Relations Among Women. In *The Journal of Gender, Race & Justice.* Spring 1998.

Richards, D. (1990). The Implications of African-American Spirituality. In M. Asante, & A. S. Bandi. (Eds.), *African Culture: The Rhythms of Unity* (pp. 59–79). New Jersey: Africa World.

Richards, D., & Ani, M. (1994). *Let the Circle Be Unbroken: The Implications of African Spirituality in the Diaspora.* Trenton, NJ: Red Sea.

Smith, L. T. (1999). *Decolonizing Methodologies: Research and Indigenous Peoples.* London: Zed.

Soyinka, Wole. (1976). *Myth, Literature and the African World.* Cambridge: Cambridge University Press.

Spivak, G. C. (1990). Practical politics of the open end. In S. Harasym. (Ed.), *The Post-colonial Critic: Interviews, Strategies, Dialogues.* London: Routledge.

Steady, F. C. (1989). African Feminism: A Worldwide Perspective. In R. Terborg-Penn (Ed.), *Women in Africa and the African Diaspora* (pp. 3–31). Washington DC: Howard University Press.

Taussig, M. T. (1987). *Shamanism, Colonialism and the Wild Man: A Study in Terror and Healing.* Chicago: University of Chicago Press.

Taylor-Guthrie, D. (1970). *Conversations with Toni Morrison.* Jackson, MS: University Press of Mississippi.

Terborg-Penn, R., & Rushing, A. B. (Eds.). (1996). *Women in Africa and the African Diaspora.* Washington, DC: Howard University Press.

Warner-Lewis, M. (1997). *Trinidad Yoruba: From Mother Tongue to Memory.* Trinidad and Tobago: The University of the West Indies Press.

CHAPTER THREE

We Are All One

Holistic Thought-Forms within Indigenous Societies
Indigeneity and Holism

FARAH SHROFF

> Once one is one no more, no less: error begins with duality; unity knows no error
> —SANAI, 11TH CENTURY PERSIAN POET

The holistic concept of social, psychological, and spiritual interconnectivity is a central aspect of Indigeneity. In this chapter, we explore holistic thought-forms as one way of deepening our understanding of Indigenous societies. Various scholars who theorize Indigeneity mention the importance of valuing relationships between people (communal belonging) and the earth, holistic and circular understandings of the world, and ultimately, about spirituality (Agrawal, 2010; Ball, 2004; Cajete, 2005; Dei, 2008). This chapter concretizes some of these ideas.

While this chapter does not focus on this, concepts of interconnectivity within Indigenous ways of knowing translate into various values: relationships with others and self and ultimately to helping others and being of service—kindness and compassion. The implications of teaching these ideas within educational settings are profound; if the intellect and the heart were engaged in educational settings, the leaders of the world would come to their positions with values that would challenge greed and the lust of power.

Greetings within various languages of Africa, Asia (including the Middle East), the Americas and elsewhere, include such concepts as "*gorbanet*" which in Arabic and Farsi means "I sacrifice myself for you." Most contemporary Farsi speakers utter this word virtually every time they are saying goodbye so for most people the connotations of "gorbanet" are about the importance of their relationship with that person. However, embedded within the language is the importance of relationships and giving of oneself (albeit somewhat extreme) for the wellbeing of others. Within traditional Iranian culture, the highest praise bestowed upon a person was to say that s/he was kind. Kindness was a highly valued cultural tradition and those who were kind—compassionate, generous, hospitable, friendly, and giving—were upheld as model citizens.

HOLISM FROM THE INSIDE OUT

The emphasis of this chapter is on Hindu and Buddhist concepts of holism while referring to the relationships that exist with these philosophical traditions and African, First Nations, and systems science theories. Although divergences exist within Asian (including Middle Eastern), African, First Nations, and other scientific theories, our purpose here is to illustrate the similarities. Hindu and Buddhist doctrines are parallel in several ways, to the point that some Hindus believe that Buddha was an incarnation of Krishna, one of the Hindu Gods.

The reason that Hinduism and Buddhism are featured is because of my knowledge base in this area. I am a Kenyan-born Parsi who was raised in Canada. I have been practicing yoga (which was born of Hindu cosmo-visions) since I was a very young child as my parents were, and continue to be, daily students of yoga. I am now a yoga teacher and am passionately engaged in the pursuit of more knowledge, from the inside and the outside, about spirituality from Hinduism and Buddhism and other traditions; this involves traveling regularly to India to learn more. In Canada and many other parts of the world—Turkey, Cyprus, Jordan, Syria, Dubai, Egypt, India, Sweden, Bulgaria, Greece, Thailand, Malaysia, Korea, and elsewhere—I have been teaching *asana* (postures), *pranayama* (breathing exercises that enhance life energy), meditation, *yoga nidra* (deep relaxation), Indian massage, dance, martial arts, and more—to people of all ages.

Living on the unceded land of the Musqueam people, I am continually grateful for their stewardship. Having genuine relationships with the people from this nation is an important part of my life. I have worked with the natives of Turtle Island as a professional since 1986 and believe that one of the reasons that I live on this continent is to be in relationship with them.

On a recent five-week trip to Guatemala I was thrilled to connect with Mayan peoples and see how actively they seek to learn these Indian forms of knowledge from me; I taught three classes a day in some places. I was amazed at how Guatemalans took to me so quickly because of my Indian heritage. They were not as interested in spending time with me if they heard I was from Canada. When they met me they asked *where else* I was from and when I told them that my heritage was from India, their eyes lit up. Many people asked almost immediately if I knew anything about yoga and within seconds we had set up a class for them. I taught campesinos, medical professionals, university professors—people from various parts of the country, all ages, and a great diversity of Guatemalans. I am very clear that my path in this lifetime is to spread knowledge that brings people to a place where they feel healthy or healthier through this form of holistic praxis. It brings me endless joy to see the results of this type of knowledge—greater inner peace, improved personal relationships, better focus at studies/work, a smiling heart, the ability to express inner thoughts and emotions, a desire to serve others, greater flexibility of body and mind, and more.

My Ph.D. thesis, completed in 1996, was on ayurvedic medicine, a branch of Indian knowledge related to yoga. Since then, my scholarly work has continued along this path. Immersing myself in this world of spiritual ideas has shown me how much more I have to learn. While I was a graduate student it took lots of effort to grasp the concepts with my mind; now I am absorbing these concepts with both head and heart.

As a Parsi, I am not a Hindu or a Buddhist by religion. Our community has been in India for about 600–1000 years. Parsi means "from Pars" or Persia. Our religion is Zarathustrianism (or Zoroastrianism as is more commonly stated in English as the ancient Greeks renamed our prophet Zoroaster); our name for him is Zarathustra. My identity as a Parsi is a central part of who I am; the religious part of this is less important than the cultural aspect. I *do* embrace the foundational tenet of Zarathustrianism: *humata, hukta, hvarstha*—good thoughts, good words, good deeds. This mantra illustrates the connections between thoughts, words, and actions and reminds us to continually reflect on our praxis. Intrinsic to Parsi identity is Zarathushti identity so, like all the known generations before them, our children have performed the *navjot,* the ceremony that welcomes them into the religion and thus they are full-fledged members of our tiny community that has ancient roots in the Middle East.

My spiritual journey is one that integrates yoga (including meditation), Buddhist practices, being amidst nature, and learning from various traditions. Being married to an Iranian I have been fortunate to delve into our old cultural traditions which most Parsis have lost; one of these traditions is Shabe-Yalda, the longest night of the year—winter solstice—in which we read old Persian poetry, drawing from the complete works of Hafiz. Recently I have discovered other Persian poets whose verse is consonant with yogic philosophy and I am falling in love with it. That is the reason this chapter begins with Sanai; Rumi, the well-known Persian mystic poet, cites Sanai and Attar (another Persian poet whose words have spiritual resonance) as his inspiration. Thus it is my own heritages that continue to enrapture me in a search for more knowledge.

As an anti-racist, feminist, eco-activist, educator, and researcher, I seek to shore up the "underdogs" of the world today and make us all feel stronger, deeply rooted in who we are; one of the ways of doing this is to rediscover the beauty of traditional knowledges. I am sure that one lifetime is not enough to learn the wisdom from these truly brilliant cosmologies. Thankfully, I will have more lives!

INDIGENOUS CONCEPTS OF HOLISM FROM ASIA, AFRICA, AND THE AMERICAS

The word "holistic" is often spelt as "wholism," denoting its intimate relationship with the concept of wholeness.[1] Holistic schools of thought vary from region to region, and throughout time but are more similar than different. A number of principles unite them. Entities and systems in the universe, including humans, are considered part of a unified whole, which cannot be understood by the isolated examination of its separate parts (Mayes, 2003). These parts are actively interrelated. Similarly, matter is interlinked, interconnected, and dynamic; it is constantly changing and it is this transformation that denotes time (Mayes, 2003).

Holistic worldviews thus do not focus exclusively upon atoms or organisms but on the larger world—the universe—and are often associated with spiritual or religious thought-forms. At the heart of holism, there is the awareness of the unity and mutual interrelation of all beings and events. All beings are seen as interdependent and inseparable. Indigenous traditions refer to this ultimate, indivisible reality. It is called *Brahman* in Hinduism, *Dharmakaya* in Buddhism, *Tao* in Taoism. Because it transcends all concepts and categories, Buddhists also call it *Tathata*—Suchness (Deshmukh, 2006): That Which Is, or Is-ness, the sum of all forms.

In Hinduism, applying the concept of interconnectivity of all life is a critical part of living the philosophy. "[T]o the Indian sage the only heresy there can be is the heresy of separateness, from which stems all the evil of the world. It is characteristic of the Vedas, for example, that the oneness which is the hallmark of spiritual life is subtly, but constantly, brought out, especially by means of such a grand figure as Agni, the all-pervading fire, which burns in all things, animate and inanimate"

(Feuerstein & Miller 1971, p. 43.). One of the Hindu texts, the *Isa-Upanisad* states: "[b]ut he (sic) who beholds all beings in his (sic) own Self, and his (sic) own Self in all beings, does no longer hate (*vijugupsate*)" (stanza 6).

These views are echoed in other traditions. According to African holistic views, for example, the cosmos is one, a spiritual totality and spirit is not separate from matter, as everything is connected (Janzen & Green, 2003; Nkudu-N'Sengha, 2009). In African holistic thought, all things are considered to be related and connected through one divine force (Janzen & Green, 2003). They are alive, giving and receiving energy, with all life and matter are created for a specific purpose.

First Nations' philosophies are also similar. First Nations' peoples see themselves as part of a Sacred Hoop or Circle of Life, not having control over it; they are careful to maintain a balance with life (Hunter, Logan, Goulet, & Barton, 2006; Mehl-Madrona, 2003). Human beings are considered to be a part of nature. The Creator produced all life forms as interdependent: people are dependent on nature for survival and nature is dependent on people for survival (Cyr, 2010). All life forms have a spirit that is connected to, but separate from the physical body (Thunderbird, 2010). This spirit is one of the ways in which we are all connected.

Elder Shannon Thunderbird (2010) maintains that traditional philosophies are integral to the survival of modern peoples:

> Traditional teachings are as relevant today as they were in the time of my Ancestors. They are blueprints for human behaviour—they connect us to the teachers of the natural and supernatural worlds, celestial beings, plants, animals, earth, air, fire, water—respected equals, in other words, whose unique traits provide models for living in a "good way." There are lessons to be learned from both the supernatural and secular worlds—to be passed down from generation to generation through songs, stories, sharing, caring, medicine wheel teachings and ceremony. *Wilwilaaysk, All My Relations.*

Just as we impact the broad cultural climate in which we live, our physical emotional, and psychological health is influenced by that very climate. Social harmony thus influences individual wellbeing in many First Nations' cosmo-visions. First Nations' healers advise people to see everyone as a family member or friend, thus encouraging social integration (Musqueam Elder Shane Pointe, personal communication, November 5, 2006).

The "medicine wheel" as mentioned above, representing harmony and connectivity, is a good example. It represents all of creation: all planets, stars, peoples, animals, and plants. It is the basis of community health, with the circle symbolizing cycles of the seasons and of life, and wholeness and perfection. Black Elk, an Oglala Sioux born in 1863, spoke of the importance of the circle:

> You have noticed that everything an Indian does is in a circle, and that is because the Power of the World always works in circles, and everything tries to be round. In the old days when we were a strong and happy people, all our power came to us from the sacred hoop of the nation, and so long as the hoop was unbroken, the people flourished....The sky is round, and I have heard that the earth is round like a ball, and so are all the stars. The wind, in its greatest power, whirls....The sun comes forth and goes down again in a circle. The moon does the same, and both are round. Even the seasons form a great circle in their changing, and always come back to where they were. The life of man (sic) is a circle from childhood to childhood, and so it is in everything where power moves. (Neihardt, 2008, p. 155)

First Nations peoples' healing circles, sweat lodge ceremonies, and other healing rituals are all done in a circle. The circle emphasizes togetherness and community unity, without which the individual cannot be well.

Life, death, and rebirth are also part of a larger circle. Most First Nations traditionally believed in reincarnation and the continuous dance of life force within an individual (Thunderbird, 2010).

In a vision for creating a sustainable and harmonious world, the Four Worlds International Institute put forward the following guiding principles (Lane, 2010):

Interconnectedness. Everything is connected to everything else; therefore, any aspect of our healing and development is related to all the others (personal, social, cultural, political, economic, etc.). When we work on any one part, the whole circle is affected.

No Unity, No Development. Unity means oneness. Without unity, the common oneness that makes (seemingly) separate human beings into "community" is impossible. Disunity is the primary disease of community.

Spirit. Human beings are both material and spiritual in nature. It is therefore inconceivable that human community could become whole and sustainable without bringing our lives into balance with the requirements of our spiritual nature.

Morals and Ethics. Sustainable human and community development requires a moral foundation centered in the wisdom of the heart. When this foundation is lost, morals and ethical principles decline and development stops.

The Hurt of One Is the Hurt of All: The Honor of One Is the Honor of All. The basic fact of our oneness as a human family means that development for some at the expense of well being for others is not acceptable or sustainable.

Development Comes from Within. The process of human and community development unfolds from within each person, relationship, family organization, community or nation.

No Vision, No Development. A vision of who we can become and what a sustainable world would be like, works as a powerful magnet, drawing us to our potential.

These principles, created by Indigenous Elders around the world in concert with others, illustrate the application of theories of holism. For example, in noting that injuries to one person are injuries to all people, these sages are showing in practice that interconnectedness is at the root of human existence: we are an interdependent species who need other humans and the support of the entire ecosystem to survive.

Many prophecies from the Hopi, Mayans, Cherokee, and other nations state that we are at the threshold of a massive planetary transformation; this change will be destructive in some ways and will bring forth a new world. Mayan elders liken this transformation to childbirth—a painful event which ends in a joyous result (personal communication, Mayan guide Juan Diaz, February 27, 2010). As the prophecies predict, the earth will suffer in untold ways: war, famine, drought, and more. We are living through those times. Now more than ever, the people of this planet need the wisdom of these elders to ensure that the upcoming transformation will bring peace to all.

PRANA

As noted above, in many parts of the world, holistic theory is posited on the notion that an energetic force connects all life in the universe, and that this energy is responsible for the life of all beings. The concept of *prana* has equivalents in approximately forty-seven languages (Grossman, 1985), including Chinese (*chi*), Japanese (*ki*), Hawaiian (*mana*), Ancient Egyptian (*ka*), and Ancient Greek (*pneuma*). In Chinese, the concept of *chi* is linguistically embedded in various terms: the character for friendly translates to "peaceful *chi*"; the character for healthy translates to "original *chi*" and the character for vitality is "high-quality *chi*" (Reninger, n.d.). There is no equivalent concept in the English language. The English language and the dominant North American culture and religion which embrace this language are different from those of many countries around the world.

The concept of *prana* has been translated into English as life force, vital energy, or breath; these translations do partial justice to this concept. *Prana* is that which gives us life; it is the vehicle of life, the cosmic breath, the rhythmic oscillation effective on all levels of conditioned existence. Restoring and keeping this life force flowing is one way of keeping people healthy.

Prana is manifested in air, breath, wind, and elsewhere and is responsible for giving life to all sentient beings. It connects all beings that are "alive." Yogananda (1968) called it creative lifetronic force. In the Hindu Vedas, life is defined as having four essential aspects: *shariram* (the physical body, or that which decays); *indriyam* (the senses); *manas* (mind); and *atman* (soul or self). The dialog between these aspects of life is *prana* (personal communications, Dr. Acharya, April 2, 2010).

Vasant Lad (1984), a leading ayurvedic physician and philosopher, defines *prana*:

> It is vital energy (life-energy) which activates the body and mind. *Prana* is responsible for the higher cerebral functions, and the motor and sensory activities. The *prana* located in the head is the vital *prana*, while *prana* which is present in the cosmic air is nutrient *prana*. There is a constant exchange of energy between vital *prana* and nutrient *prana* through respiration. During inspiration, the nutrient *prana* enters the system and nourishes the vital *prana*. During expiration, subtle waste products are expelled (p. 169).

When *prana* flows throughout the body easefully, a person is said to be in harmony and in good health. When the flow of *prana* is blocked, that person is in a state of disease. So it is with the flow of *prana* in the universe. When it moves easily the universe is in a state of balance.

KARMA

Another concept that shows the interconnectivity of time and lifetimes is that of *karma*. It is a widely held belief within the Asian continent and other parts of the South. While it is a highly complex idea, *karma* functionally means "action" and is derived from the Sanskrit *kri*, to do. Technically, *karma* also denotes the effects of actions (Vivekananda, 1991). Hindu cosmological theory states that all actions are "recorded," and each one produces a concomitant reaction. Positive or good action will generally produce positive actions in the future. The reverse is generally true for negative actions. The *karmic* effects of all deeds shape the past, present, and future.

In essence, the concept of *karma* empowers human beings to make behavioral choices that they can live with, literally—as each action creates a reaction. Contemporary physics mirrors *karmic* theory, which is at least 3000 years old, with the principle of action/reaction.

Karma offers an explanation to many questions that begin with *why?*: why is that person living on the street with all their belongings in a small bag and why am I living in this well-furnished house?; why did that car accident happen to that person?; why does this person excel in music, love, career, and everything seems easy for her/him? Answers to these questions are not easily answered by scientific inquiry, which is good at describing answers that begin with *how?*

Typically, within Hindu, Buddhist, and related philosophies, the answers to these types of questions are related to the *karmic* path that each being walks upon. Deeds of the past have come to fruition in the present and that is why some people suffer and others do not.

> Everything which goes up must come down
>
> —OLD INDIAN SAYING

So the king who has treated his subjects poorly, overtaxed them, and provided little by way of services, will eventually suffer the consequences of these deeds, in his current life or in another life. Having a belief in *karma* aids people in being hopeful as eventually, all wrongs will be righted and all good deeds will be rewarded.

Furthermore, *karma* connects one life to the next. It means that an act has a meaning beyond its apparent consequences. There are past, present, and future dimensions of *karma*. At death, *atman* (soul) survives while the material body decays.

Unfortunately this concept has been manipulated and abused to serve those in positions of power. In India, "lower-caste" peoples are kept within disenfranchised positions, partly due to the notion that they had accumulated negative *karma* in previous lives and this is the reason that they are suffering now. According to this way of thinking, it is their "destiny" to carry human waste or perform other such undesirable acts; their "destiny" will only change if they accept this position in society and comply with the expectations placed upon them. This notion—that the only way to improve negative *karma* from the previous life in the current life is to behave subserviently to the powerful—serves to prohibit rebellion by the working classes, bottom rungs of the caste system, and women of all social strata (when everyone buys into this way of thinking). This is a corrupt interpretation and negative implementation of the concept of *karma*.

Questions about the "afterlife" are not easily researched. The concept of *karma* is directly in opposition to global hegemonic religious discourses which state that negative actions may be forgiven by a priest (by admission of guilt and repentance) or by generous donations to a particular church or other similar gestures. (Within Hindu religious practice, too, priests and the priestly caste hold a great deal of power.) Other hegemonic discourses note that only God has the power to decide someone's destiny.

It is a profound thought to consider that each action has a response which manifests itself on the physical, mental, or spiritual plane and that this response can last over lifetimes. Cause and effect are the products of *karma* and the entire cycle of deeds; the ever-turning wheel of existence, is called *samsara*—reincarnation.

REINCARNATION

The concept of rebirth is well formulated within many spiritual traditions, including Hinduism and Buddhism. Buddhists of the Tibetan tradition believe that there are five stages of life (Sogyal Rinpoche, Gaffney, & Harvey, 1992): birth, living, death, the *bardo* (the intermediate state between death and rebirth), rebirth.

Individuals can be reborn as plants, reptiles and insects, birds, animals, including aquatic creatures, and humans. The notion that life is cyclical and not linear has profound implications. The belief that we will return to live on the earth after dying means that it is not in our best interests to destroy this planet or do harm to other life forms. It forces us, at least, to rethink the way in which we treat others and the way in which we "use" the resources of the earth.

It is conceivable that people who believe that they will never return to earth will also treat the ecosystem and its inhabitants kindly, and certainly, such people exist. However, the thought that this is not the only time that we are here may be an incentive for kindness or gentle walking on the earth.

Reincarnation echoes the notion that life is a circle and beings continue around this wheel of existence until reaching a point where the *atman* (soul) becomes part of the universal soul (*Brahman*). This is a final dissolution of the individual *atman* and is considered as the pinnacle of spiritual existence. This is where *samsara* ends; the *atman* is not going to be reborn. It is often likened to a drop of water becoming part of a vast ocean. This state of being has many names: *moksha, nirvana,* and others. *Moksha* is a Sanskrit word which means to release or let go, inferring a release of the individual being from *samsara*—the cycle of life and rebirth and a release of the concept of individuality, separation, duality; now all is one: one universal consciousness. Arriving at this state is to be continually in bliss and living as pure consciousness (*satcitananda*).

Nirvana is essentially the same idea: enlightenment. Being free of suffering, a being in a state of nirvana has a calm mind and does not react to negative or positive stimuli. *Nir* means not or out and *vana* refers to wind so *nirvana* literally means windless, as in a windless lake: no waves, no movement, complete stillness of the water and all around it. This tranquil state of mind is the ultimate objective of life and can be reached through meditation and related spiritual practices such as yoga.

PUNCHAMAHABHUTAS

The basis of holism within various holistic arts and sciences such as yoga, ayurveda, and traditional Chinese medicine is embodied within the concept of *punchamahabhutas*. *Pancha* in Sanskrit means five. *Maha* means great. *Bhutas* means elements or states, in the ancient sense; they are sometimes known as proto-elements. (*Bhutas* are thus not to be confused with the elements as they appear on the periodic table; within modern chemistry these would be considered as compounds.) *Punchamahabhutas* are thus the five great "elements." This "Five-Element Theory" states that **ether, air, fire, water,** and **earth**, the *punchamahabhutas*, are the foundations of all existence. They are contained in all animate and inanimate entities. Energy and matter are considered interchangeable.

The concept of *punchamahabhutas* embodies the philosophical foundations of these holistic practices: all parts of the universe are created by five elements (earth, fire, air, ether, and water). The microcosm—the human being—is thus a reflection of the macrocosm—the universe—as the essential building blocks are the same.

Although the elements themselves and how they combine are different, Chinese Five-Element Theory parallels this: "[e]verything on earth is dominated by one of these elements, and their constant interplay, combined with those of *yin* and *yang*, explain all change and activity in nature" (Vogel, 1991, p. 180). Briefly, the qualities of each *bhuta*:

- Ether (*akash*): non-resistance, sound/essence
- Air (*vayu*): expansion, sound + touch
- Fire (*agni*): heat, luminosity, sound + touch + color
- Water (*ap*): liquidity, sound + touch + color + taste
- Earth (*prthvi*): roughness, sound + touch + color + taste + smell

Prthvi helps the other four by being their support. *Ap* helps the other four by moistening. *Agni* assists the others by ripening. *Vayu* is the drying agent. *Akash* helps by providing space (Ray, 1937). In the human body, the hard parts are earth (bones, etc.); the liquid parts are water (kidneys, etc.); the hot parts are fire (stomach, small intestine, etc.); the air/wind parts (respiratory tract, etc.); and the vacuous parts are all pervasive.

The human body, food, all plants, animals, and minerals contain the *bhutas*. From the *bhutas*, the *dhatus* (constructing elements) are formed.

According to holistic principles, the smallest particle of the universe is the universe in miniature. The interaction between the universe and the individual takes place through input and output of matter. The universe is thus the macrocosm and other entities, including human beings, are the microcosm. To illustrate this simple yet profound concept, the words of one of the world's spiritual teachers follow:

> . . . it has been said in the Vedas, "[k]nowing one lump of clay we know the nature of all the clay that is in the universe." Take up a little plant and study its life, and we know the universe as it is. If we know one grain of sand, we understand the secret of the whole universe. Applying this course of reasoning to phenomena, we find, in the first place, that everything is almost similar at the beginning and the end. The mountain comes from the sand, and goes back to the sand, the river comes out of vapor, and goes back to vapor; plant life comes from the seed, and goes back to the seed; human life comes out of human germs, and goes back to human germs. The universe with its stars and planets has come out of a nebulous state and must go back to it (Vivekananda, 1896/1989b, p. 218).

UNITY AND ONENESS

The essence of *punchamahabhuta* principles lies in their spiritual import. Holistic principles state that there is a unity and oneness in the universe and all is connected. Following are words of some of the experts in this internationally celebrated theory:

> My face is the land.
> . . . my face was well known.
> It was known to the squirrel that heard a twig break under my foot while I walked into the woods. It was known to the porcupine that sat in the tree top and watched me pass underneath.
> . . .
> It was known to the wind that brought me messages from other creatures and plants.
> . . .
> It was known to the rain that feeds the spring where I quenched
> my thirst day after day.
> It was known to the lakes whose waters blended with the sky who
> speaks to all of freedom.
> The trees also knew my face. I was told by my father that some day
> when the skin of my face takes on the furrows of pine bark, my
> spirit will leave my body and seek a new home in a tree.
> But like the wolf that soon will be gone from here, my face is the
> face of a vanishing kind.
> You see, what is the wilderness is in my face, and what is in my
> face is in the wilderness.
> My face is the land!
> If you misunderstand one you will neglect the other!
> If you harm one you scar the other!

If you despise one you will disgrace the other!
If you shame one you will cause the other to weep!
If you look at one and cannot call its name you will never know
the other!
But how can you not know my face?
How can you not know the land?
Is it not all around you?
Is it not part of all you do and live for?
Is it not within your heart, where the yearning for brotherhood (sic)
takes its beginning?
Are we not all living in times of enlightenment when no one
should have a nameless face any longer, not even an Indian? (George & Hirnschall, 1989, pp. 19–20).

[T]his Oneness of life, this Oneness of everything. We shall see how it demonstrates that all our misery comes through ignorance, and this ignorance is the idea of manifoldness, this separation between *wo/*man and *wo/*man, between nation and nation, between earth and moon, between moon and sun. Out of this idea of separation between atom and atom comes all misery. But the Vedanta says this separation does not exist, it is not real. It is merely apparent, on the surface. In the heart of things there is Unity still. If you go below the surface, you find that Unity between *wo/*man and *wo/*man, between races and races, high and low, rich and poor, gods and *wo/*men, and *wo/*men and animals. If you go deep enough, all will be seen as only variations of the One, and *s/*he who has attained to this conception of Oneness has no more delusion....All is Perfect Union and Perfect Bliss (Vivekananda, 1896/1989a, p. 129).

All the spiritual teachers of humanity have told us the same thing, that the purpose of life on earth is to achieve union with our fundamental, enlightened nature...to realize and embody our true being (Sogyal Rinpoche, Gaffney, & Harvey, 1992, p. 127).

When one is in direct contact, do you know what happens? Space disappears, the space between two people disappears and therefore there is immense peace—and this is only possible when there is freedom, freedom from the making of images, from the myths, the ideologies, so that you are in direct contact. Then, when you are directly in contact with the actual, there is transformation (Krishnamurthi, 1991, p.108–109).

The words of these sages speak for themselves. From varying angles, they describe the spiritual concept of the confederacy of all matter and life. This concept has extremely profound implications. If human beings behaved as if all members of the universe were connected and the interests of all were the interests of one, then conflicts, wars, colonialism, patriarchy, and other forms of oppression would be greatly reduced if not eliminated; the South African slogan, "an injury to one is an injury to all" would have genuine meaning in such an ideal world.

Table 3.1 is an attempt to explain the properties and essence of *punchamahabhuta* concepts. The "elements" are connected by *prana* (life-force) and *atman* (soul). They are created out of a union of *prakriti*, the female principle, and *purusha*, the male principle, according to *samkhya* philosophy.

Life is considered to be a reflection or reaction from within due to stimulus from the outside. The *Charaka Samhita,* an ayurvedic text, states "The wise considers the entire universe as his (sic) preceptor. It is only the unwise who finds enemies in it" (Dash & Junius, 1983, p. 22).

Table 3.1 Qualities of the *Punchamahabhutas*

	Ether (*akash*)	Air (*vayu*)	Fire (*tejas*)	Water (*ap*)	Earth (*prthvi*)
Definition	The space in which events occur; no physical existence; the field from which everything is manifested & into which everything returns	Existence without form	Transformation	Force of cohesion	Solidity
Essence	Sound/essence	Sound + touch	Sound + touch + color	Sound + touch + color + taste	Sound + touch + color + taste + smell
Properties	Motivity, inertness, distance, non-resistance, vacuousness	Movement, vibration, oscillation, gaseousness, expansion, dynamism	Color, heat, radiation, appearance, form without substance, can convert substances	Liquid, fluid, moist, force of cohesion, flux, without stability	Firm, rough, heavy, offers resistance, solid, stable, odorsome, coarse, rigid
Corresponding ▢form and ▢function	Vacuous parts ▢hollows/cavities: organs of speech (tongue, vocal cords, mouth), reverberant areas in body and ears	Dry/airy parts ▢touch, respiration, winking of lids, contraction & relaxation of movements, lightness of body, hands, fear	Hot parts ▢digestion, pigmentation, sharpness, bravery, sight, heat & temperature of body, anger, luster, feet, appearance, sex	Liquid parts ▢reproductive fluid, genitals, urine, blood, marrow, brain	Solid parts ▢nails, nose, enamel, bones, flesh, hair, nerves, arteries, anus, lymph
Main sense	Hearing	Touch	Vision	Taste	Smell
Helps other *bhutas* by	Giving space	Drying	Ripening	Moistening	Being their support
Corresponding *tridosha*		Vata		Pitta	Kapha

The sameness (*samanya*) of self (*purusha*) and nature (*prakriti*) is thus the underlying principle of these holistic practices (Heyn, 1987). This ecological principle, which embodies the understanding that the human body/mind/spirit is connected to all other life forms in the universe, is articulated in different forms through health promotion, disease prevention, and curative care.

SYSTEMS SCIENCE

Interestingly, we find the very same ancient principles exist in contemporary science. Francesco Varela, for example, observes that Buddhist ideas are prevalent within scientific principles—in physics and biology, for example, the basic ideas are Buddhism in disguise (Wallace, 2003). During the past few decades, scientists from various disciplines, such as Ilya Prigogine, Erich Jantsch, Gregory Bateson, Humberto Maturana, and Manfred Eigen (Francois, 1999) developed emerging systems views of the world and made the study of living systems, organisms, social systems and ecosystems their focus.

The systems view focuses on integration and relationships and sees systems as integrated wholes whose properties cannot be reduced to its smaller units. Every organism, from the smallest bacterium to plants, animals, and humans, are integrated and considered as living systems. Families and communities are also considered as systems. Gregory Bateson (1972), for example, was interested in studying patterns, which connect crabs to lobsters, orchids to humans, and in seeing the interrelatedness of life forms. For 2000 years, much of Western science concentrated on isolating the world's basic building blocks. Now that this has been achieved to some extent, the systems approach emphasizes principles of organization (Bateson, 1972), creating a more ample understanding of matter, from macro and micro perspectives. Systemic properties are lost when a system is dissected, either physically or theoretically, into isolated elements. Although it is possible to discern individual parts in any system, the nature of the whole is always different from the mere sum of its parts (Bateson, 1972). This understanding ties in very well with principles of holism.

Connected to systems science, some physicists also make connections between their work and holistic thought-forms. Notable physicists such as David Bohm (Bohm & Hiley, 1993) and Fritjof Capra (2002) emphasized the similarities between their newest theories of the indistinguishability of field and force, mind and matter, with the spiritual traditions of Buddhism, Confucianism, Hinduism, and Taoism. Over the past 2000 years or more, Buddhists have developed philosophical, phenomenological, and epistemological sophistication, and they have found a very practical way to apply it (Brockman, 2002). Aforementioned Varela's (1997) view of the mind has been profoundly influenced by his interest in Buddhist thought, and he has worked to establish empirical correlations between Buddhist practice and scientific work (Varela, 1996). Western tradition has avoided the idea of a selfless self, of a virtual self. This egolessness, or selflessness, is at the very core of Buddhism.

Capra (2002) also extends the framework of systems and complexity theory to the social domain, akin to the foundational principles of holism. He uses this extended framework to discuss some of the critical issues of our time—the management of human organizations, the challenges and dangers of economic globalization, the scientific and ethical problems of biotechnology, and the establishment of ecologically sustainable communities and technologies (Capra, 2002).

Bohm (1980) conceptualizes an implicate order to the universe composed of frequencies beyond time and space that has been hidden from people. Bohm's paradigm is a form of ontological holism. In this conception of order, primacy is given to the undivided whole and the implicate order inherent within the whole rather than to parts of the whole (Healey, 2010).

These scientists emphasize in their work the same notions as holism: the whole is greater than the sum of its parts. The natural world is seen to interact synergistically. It is thus not possible to understand whole systems by knowing the properties of their individual components (although it is intrinsically useful to study individual components). Powerful descriptions of isolated fragments of the world have been made but reductionist science has not yielded a metatheory of how the universe operates (Meadows, 2008).

Quantum mechanics researchers have found that "the basic oneness of the universe is not only the central characteristic of the mystical experience, but it is also one of the most important revelations of modern physics. It becomes apparent at the atomic level and manifests itself more and more as one penetrates deeper into matter, down into the realm of subatomic particles" (Capra, 2000, p. 131).

The observer of a scientific experiment, according to quantum theory, can change the outcome of an experiment, simply by observing, for the observer puts energy into the system. Just as Buddhist and Hindu philosophy have stressed, the observer and observed are in the new physics seen as connected, as are mind and matter, field and force. Gary Zukav (1979) explains the new physics:

> Observer and observed are interrelated in a real and fundamental sense. The exact nature of this interrelation is not clear, but there is a growing body of evidence that the distinction between the "in here" and the "out there" is illusion. The conceptual framework of quantum mechanics, supported by massive volumes of experimental data, forces contemporary physicists to express themselves in a manner that sounds, even to the uninitiated, like the language of mystics (p. 92).

The new physics thus emphasizes the interrelational, indeterminate, and probabilistic qualities to matter and energy. As Zukav's quotation above shows, it challenges components of the scientific method related to Newtonian mechanics, such as determinism and linear causality as well as reductionism and dualism. Using laboratory techniques these modern day scientists have concluded that "we are all one"—the same conclusion arrived at some thousands of years ago by Buddhists and Hindus whose Indigenous knowledge systems were derived from meditation practices, knowing the world within. We have come full circle. Knowledge from inside is consistent with knowledge from outside.

HOLISM: THE HEART AND SOUL OF INDIGENEITY

The concept of holism is international and ancient. Virtually all societies on the planet have upheld some of the holistic principles addressed here. Crossing countries and historical periods, holistic thought, and practices based on these thought-forms flourished for centuries and declined over the past 400 years, in part due to the growth of reductionist thinking and its off-shoot, allopathic medicine.

Currently there is a global re-emergence of holistic thinking and holistic practices. This chapter analyzed the historical as well as contemporary basis of holism as interconnectedness, unity, and oneness.

With respect to education, those who apply holistic principles to formal classrooms have found various benefits, including: respecting and listening to self and others; to grow positive thoughts and good humor; maintaining the health of the body and mind; to straighten the spine and develop correct posture; to learn that physical activity can lead to relaxation of body and mind; to develop correct breathing; to manage stress and regulate energy levels; learning to relax and rest the body and mind; to install periods of silence and structured rest; to improve receptivity to teaching and to enhance learning; learning to concentrate, develop visual memory, and creativity; to raise the pleasure of learning (Flak, 2010).

Given that the basis of holistic philosophy is unity and oneness, it provides a platform for world peace. Returning to holism would positively transform the planet. In the words of an Indigenous scholar and sage:

> Look at those trees standing over there; the alder does not tell the pine tree to move over; the pine does not tell the fir tree to move over; each tree stands there in unity, with their mouth pressed toward the same Mother Earth, refreshed by the same breeze, warmed by the same sun, with their arms upraised in prayer and thanksgiving, protecting one another. If we are to have peace in the world, we too must learn to live like those trees (Lane, 2010, p. 2).

NOTE

1. Here we use the conventional spelling without the "w" as it is simpler.

REFERENCES

Agrawal, A. (2010). Indigenous and Scientific Knowledge: Some Critical Comments. Retrieved from http://www.nuffic.nl/ciran/ikdm/3-3/articles/agrawal.html

Ball, J. (2004). As if Indigenous Knowledge and Communities Mattered: Transformative Education in First Nations Communities in Canada. *American Indian Quarterly, 28*(3/4), Autumn, 454–479.

Bateson, G. (1972). *Steps to an Ecology of Mind: Collected Essays in Anthropology, Psychiatry, Evolution, and Epistemology.* San Francisco: Chandler.

Bohm, D. (1980). *Wholeness and the Implicate Order.* London: Routledge and Kegan Paul.

Bohm, D., & Hiley, B. J. (1993). *The Undivided Universe*: *An Ontological Interpretation of Quantum Theory.* New York: Routledge.

Brockman, J. (2002). *The Next Fifty Years: Science in the first Half of the 21st Century.* New York: Vintage Books.

Cajete, G. (2005). American Indian Epistemologies. *New Directions for Student Services, 109,* 69–78.

Capra, F. (2000). *The Tao of Physics: An Exploration of the Parallels between Modern Physics and Eastern.* Boston: Shambhala.

Capra, F. (2002). *The Hidden Connections: A Science for Sustainable Living.* New York: Doubleday.

Cyr, A. (2009). Understanding First Nations' Spirituality: Teachings from the Elders. Retrieved from http://canadian-first-nations.suite101.com/article.cfm/understanding_first_nations_spirituality

Dash, B., & Junius, M. (1983). *A Handbook of Ayurveda.* New Delhi: Concept.

Dei, G. J. S. (2008). Indigenous Knowledge Studies and the Next Generation: Pedagogical Possibilities for Anti-colonial Education. *Australian Journal of Indigenous Education, 37,* 5–13.

Deshmukh, V. D. (2006). Neuroscience of Meditation. *The Scientific World Journal, 6,* 275–289.

Feuerstein, G., & Miller, J. (1971). *A Reappraisal of Yoga—Essays in Indian Philosophy.* London: Rider.

Flak, M. (2010). Research on Yoga in Education. Retrieved from http://www.ryeuk.org/

François, C. (1999). Systemics and Cybernetics in a Historical Perspective. *Systems Research and Behavioral Science, 16,* 203–219.

George, D., & Hirnschall, H. (1989). *My Spirit Soars.* Blaine, WA: Hancock House.

Grossman, R. (1985). *The Other Medicines.* Doubleday and Co, USA.

Healey, R. Analysis (2010) *Science without representation.* 70 (3): 536-547. doi: 10 .1093/analys/anq039;

Heyn, B. (1987). *Ayurvedic Medicine—The Gentle Strength of Indian Healing.* New Delhi: Indus.

Hunter, L. M., Logan, J., Goulet, J. G., & Barton, S. (2006). Aboriginal Healing: Regaining Balance and Culture. *Journal of Transcultural Nursing, 17*(1), 13–22.

Janzen, J. M., & Green, E. C. (2003). Continuity, Change and Challenge in African Medicine. In H. Selin and H. Shapiro (Eds.), *Medicine Across Cultures: History and Practice of Medicine in Non-Western Cultures* (pp. 1–26) (Vol. 3). London: Kluwer.

Krishnamurthi, J. (1991). *On Freedom.* San Francisco: Harper.

Lad, V. (1984). *Ayurveda: The Science of Self-Healing.* Boston: Lotus.

Lane, P. (2010). Sixteen Guiding Principles for Co-creating a Sustainable and Harmonious World. *Four Worlds International Institute.* Retrieved from http://www.fwii.net/profiles/blog/show?id=2429082%3ABlogPost%3A27426&xgs=1&xg_source=msg_share_post

Mayes, C. (2003). *Seven Curricular Landscapes: An Approach to the Holistic Curriculum.* Lanham, MD: University Press of America.

Meadows, D. H. (2008). *Thinking in Systems: A Primer.* White River Junction, VT: Chelsea Green.

Mehl-Madrona, L. (2003). Native American Medicine: Herbal Pharmacology, Therapies, and Elder Care. In H. Selin and H. Shapiro (Eds.), *Medicine Across Cultures: History and Practice of Medicine in Non-Western cultures* (pp. 209–224) (Vol. 3). London: Kluwer.

Neihardt, J. G. (2008). *Black Elk Speaks: Being the Life Story of a Holy Man of the Oglala Sioux.* Albany: State University of New York Press.

Ray, D. N. R. (1937). *The Principle of Tridosha in Ayurveda.* Calcutta, India: SC Banerjee.

Reninger, E. (n.d.). *What Is Qi (Chi)? The Vibratory Nature of Reality.* Retrieved from http://taoism.about.com/od/qi/a/Qi.htm

Sanai, H. (2000). The Walled Garden of Truth. In P. Washington (Ed.), *Persian Poets* (pp. 41–47). Toronto: Knopf.

Sogyal Rinpoche, S., Gaffney, P., & Harvey, A. (1992). *The Tibetan Book of Living and Dying.* San Francisco: HarperSanFrancisco.

Thunderbird, S. (2010). *Tribal Knowledge, Supernatural & Ceremonies.* Retrieved from http://www.shannonthunderbird.com/tribal_beliefs.htm

Varela, F. (1996). The Early Days of Autopoiesis: Heinz and Chile. *Systems Research, 13*, 407–417.

Varela, F. (1997). A Science of Consciousness as if Experience Mattered. In S. Hameroff, A. Kazniak, & A. Scott (Eds.).*Towards the Science of Consciousness: The Second Tucson Discussions and Debates* (pp. 31–44). Cambridge: MIT Press.

Vivekananda, S. (1896/1989a). God in Everything. *Jnana Yoga*. Calcutta, India: Advaita Ashrama.

Vivekananda, S. (1896/1989b). The Cosmos—The Macrocosm. *Jnana Yoga*. Calcuta, India: Advaita Ashrama.

Vivekananda, S. (1991). *Karma Yoga—The Yoga of Action*. Calcutta, India: Advaita Ashrama.

Vogel, H. G. (1991). Similarities between Various Systems of Traditional Medicine. Considerations for the Future of Ethnopharmacology. *Journal of Ethnopharmacology, 35*(2), 179–190.

Wallace, A. B. (2003). Introduction: Buddhism and Science—Breaking Down the Barriers. In A. B. Wallace (Ed.), *Buddhism & Science: Breaking New Ground* (pp. 1–31). New York: Columbia University Press.

Yogananda, P. (1968). *Spiritual Diary: An Inspirational Thought for Each Day.* Los Angeles: Self Realization Fellowship.

Zukav, G. (1979). *The Dancing Wu Li Masters: An Overview of the New Physics*. New York: Morrow.

CHAPTER FOUR

Indigenous Education and Indigenous Studies in the Australian Academy

Assimilationism, Critical Pedagogy, Dominant Culture Learners, and Indigenous Knowledges

MARCELLE CROSS-TOWNSEND

Currently, gaps between Indigenous and non-Indigenous Australians in key areas of education, such as access, retention, completion rates, and employment outcomes continue to be highlighted as enduring, long-term critical concerns in national and state education policies as well as many policy reviews and research analyses (see, for example, Bradley, Noonan, Nugent, & Scales, 2008; DEEWR, 2005, 2006; IHEAC, 2006; Storry, 2007). These issues are historical and current at once, having persisted for as long as Indigenous Australian ("Indigenous") people have engaged, either willingly or by coercion, in Western style, or "dominant culture" education since the early nineteenth century (Beresford & Partington, 2003, p. 41). Equally persistent, historical and current are the attitudes, approaches, theories, education policies, and initiatives employed by government, educators, and researchers to address Indigenous educational disparity.

In particular the socio-political ideology of "assimilationism" has been prominent in social and political discourse throughout the continuing colonial project of "civilizing" and "educating" Indigenous Australian peoples, referred to here as "Indigenous Education" (McConaghy, 2000, p. 151). Assimilationist assumptions posit Indigenous peoples, their knowledges, and practices as inferior to Western peoples, knowledges, and practices. Indigenous people's survival is perceived to be dependent on wholesale assimilation into the dominant or "superior" culture and language, where the economic and social dominant culture objectives of education override any Indigenous cultural, linguistic, social, or human rights imperatives (McConaghy, 2000, pp. 186–187). Assimilationism has been similarly influential in Australia and elsewhere through research and public education about Indigenous Australian peoples, referred to here as "Indigenous Studies." Until more recently, Indigenous Studies has largely promoted dominant epistemological superiority and actively undermined Indigenous identities, societies and knowledges (Mooney & Craven, 2005, p. 3). In short, it is assimilationist ideology that has entrenched and continues to sustain racism in Australian society.

By tracing the history of assimilationist ideology in both Indigenous Education and Indigenous Studies the following discussion will put forward that, despite rapid and ongoing social, economic, political, and technological changes over the course of this history, assimilationist ideology remains the most powerful influential trend in relation to Indigenous peoples' inequitable socio-political positioning within modern Australian society. In the higher education sector, Indigenous Studies has been identified as having the potential to become an important emancipatory tool for combating racism and challenging dominant ideology. Engaging in the discussion of critical theorists who work to define and articulate emancipatory education, I attempt to understand the direction that Indigenous Studies must take to challenge assimilationism and positively influence Indigenous peoples' opportunities and outcomes in education specifically, and in society generally.

Drawing on my own research, workplace practices, experiences, and observations over the past ten years teaching Indigenous Studies in a regional Australian university, I explore some of the divergent contextual complexities, contradictions, practical challenges, and limitations of engaging critical pedagogical approaches to challenge assimilationism and dominant ideology in Indigenous Studies in the Australian higher education sector. I conclude by positing critical approaches to Indigenous Studies as not only highly relevant but crucial for the emancipation of Indigenous people and knowledges from assimilationist ideology and practice, albeit limited in the capacity to protect Indigenous knowledges from continued appropriation, disembodiment, and dislocation by the filtering systems of the disciplines of the Academy.

INDIGENOUS EDUCATION AND ASSIMILATIONISM

At the time of the earliest colony in Australia in the late eighteenth century, Europeans failed to recognize or appreciate that Indigenous Australians maintained complex formal education systems that successfully supported thousands of generations of people to live in social and environmental sustainability. Indigenous people were regarded as primitive savages destined to die out in the face of "civilization," and many did die defending their land in the frontier violence of the first century or so of colonization (see Newbury, 1999). Missionaries flocked to Australia to "civilize and Christianize" Indigenous peoples, and early colonial "Protection" policies legislated the forced removal of many Indigenous peoples from their homelands to these missions. Others fled their homelands to missions to survive frontier violence. Despite the implied intent to protect and care for Indigenous people, missions were institutions where the assimilationist goal of "civilizing and Christianizing the natives" was overtly pursued. While some Indigenous children did attend public schooling, "Exclusion on Demand" practices established by the Minister for Education in 1902, and continuing until at least the early 1970s, prevented thousands of Indigenous people from accessing a public education. "Exclusion on Demand" meant that any objection by a non-Indigenous parent to an Indigenous pupil at their child's school enabled the school principal to "exclude" the Indigenous pupil from attending. This resulted in the establishment of Indigenous-only schools on missions and reserves (Board of Studies, NSW, 2010) where assimilationism was fervently established and where students had little opportunity for education beyond basic tuition required for manual or domestic service (Parbury, 1999, p. 70).

Anthropological and scientific discourses posited Indigenous peoples as a "child-like race," regarding them as unable to be mature, independent citizens. The intellectual abilities of Indigenous people were measured by their physical appearance—"full-bloods" were considered least intelligent whilst "half-castes" were considered potentially fit for education (Parbury, 1999, p. 72). The accepted notion of Indigenous peoples' intellectual inferiority easily led to the widespread acceptance and application of "cultural deficit theory" to explain Indigenous peoples' difficulty with, or perhaps more accurately their rejection of, the Eurocentric and assimilationist ideology, curriculum, and education practices of the Australian education system. Assimilationism was formalized through the adoption of "Assimilation" policies in some Australian states in the late 1930s and in all states by 1951 (McConaghy, 2000, p. 151). Policies of assimilation were motivated by Australia's increasing spotlight on the world stage during World Wars I and II where, after having fought against the racism of oppressive regimes elsewhere in the world, it became too shameful to continue to exclude Indigenous people from public life and public education (Gray & Beresford, 2008, p. 207). The move from protection to assimilation policies was further motivated by Indigenous population growth that called into question the flawed "dying race" theory (Parbury, 1999, p. 68). Even more concerning was the growing population of people of mixed Indigenous and European descent who were seen as a real threat to "White" Australia (p. 69). Assimilation policies legislated that Indigenous people were to adopt European cultural and social beliefs and practices, while forsaking or extinguishing their own. Education is an important vehicle for social control and was certainly perceived as crucial for the purposes of enacting assimilation policies (p. 186). State authorities were urged to invest "all efforts" toward the education of Indigenous children *"under the same conditions as whites with a view to their taking their place in the white community"* (Native Welfare Conference, 1937, cited in Parbury, 1999, p. 69).

Legislated assimilationism entrenched the popularity of cultural deficit theory to explain ongoing disparity in Indigenous education outcomes. Subsequent "compensatory education" for Indigenous Australians became widespread by the 1970s (Gray & Beresford, 2008, p. 208) and continues to be entrenched in Indigenous education policy and practice today. The "truth" of cultural deficit theory is "evidenced" by ethnocentric competency-based standards that result in Indigenous students' segregation into "special classes" for "underachievers" (p. 209). These classes generally offer a simplified and reduced curriculum (Parbury, 1999, p. 72) combined with pastoral support and experiences perceived to be lacking in the familial and socio-cultural environment of the student (p. 76). The endurance of cultural deficit theory is revealed in a recent Australian education policy review document that suggests Indigenous peoples are disadvantaged, not because of an unfair society, but because of the *"circumstances of their birth"* (Bradley, Noonan, Nugent, & Scales, 2008, p. xi). The language of cultural deficit theory has merely been shifted or "softened" from describing Indigenous peoples and epistemologies as "deficient" to instead describe being an Indigenous person a "disadvantage." Cultural deficit theory is basically a "blame the victim" campaign (Cummins, 2003, p. 42).

"Learning styles theory" is an assimilationist theory that developed from the field of cognitive psychology, largely in the United States, from around the middle of the twentieth century (Halse & Robinson, 1999, p. 202). Learning styles theory involves the development of learning style taxonomies based on essentialized and stereotyped racial and cultural differences and was applied in earnest to the problem of poor education outcomes for colonized Indigenous people (Stewart, 2002, p. 16). The development of learning styles theory in relation to Indigenous education in Australia gained momentum from the mid-twentieth century (see Harris, 1984, 1990; Hughes, 1987) and is still influential in current Indigenous education research and program design (see, for example, Beresford & Partington, 2003, p. 256; Hughes, More, & Williams, 2004; Mellor & Corrigan, 2004, p. 35; Nichol,

2005; Pearce, 2008, p. 133; TAFE NSW, 2008, para. 19; Tranby Aboriginal College, 2008). McConaghy (2000, pp. 125–126) argues that learning style theory maintains Indigenous peoples constructed position as "other" and "lesser," while Coffield, Moseley, and Ecclestone (2004, p. 137) describe education based on learning styles theory as largely *"labeling, vested interests and overblown claims."* Certainly, the learning styles identified as Indigenous Australian could just as easily be found to be consistent with many cultures (Stewart, 2002, p. 17). It seems to me that many educational theorists and policy makers have misinterpreted and misconstructed holistic and embodied Indigenous philosophies, values, and epistemologies as "Indigenous learning styles."

Decades of sustained political activism and social justice campaigns by Indigenous activists and organizations led to the establishment of new advisory and consulting groups to inform Indigenous Education policy-making. Groups such as the National Aboriginal Education Committee (NAEC) and Aboriginal Education Consultative Groups (AECG) bore out the eventual development of state and federal Aboriginal Education Policies (AEP), effective in all State and Territory governments since 1990. Despite extensive consultation with Indigenous educators, the twenty-one long-term goals fail to acknowledge that "equity" is more than the ability to access and participate in dominant culture education and pursue dominant culture objectives. Equity for Indigenous Australians must be understood as something beyond the potential for Indigenous Australians to be "more like" dominant culture Australians in terms of their ability to access acknowledged dominant cultural rights, freedoms, and privileges (McConaghy, 2000, pp. 187–188). A true shift away from assimilationism means the right to define and engage education that is founded on Indigenous objectives, philosophies, epistemologies, values, and language literacy with an acknowledgment that Indigenous objectives in education might include goals that both include and extend beyond dominant culture objectives of English language literacy and employment outcomes. The structural change of introducing the AEPs did not therefore affect an ideological shift away from assimilationism.

In the current neo-liberalist climate, assimilationist ideology in Indigenous education is articulated in terms of "what works" and "best practice" as informed by dominant cultural notions of educational success. This is well illustrated in a recent policy analysis report that focuses on "successful education initiatives" in "good schools" in remote Indigenous Australian communities (Storry, 2007). Students from the schools are described in the report as generally having very low English language, literacy, and numeracy standards as well as being "socially and materially" ill prepared for school education (Storry, 2007, p. 12). The report does not mention language skills (other than English) or culturally specific skills or strengths that students may bring to the school environment. Successful initiatives are described as *"Attendance Sticks and Carrots"* approaches. The "stick" approach involved threatening to withhold parent's welfare allowances if their children did not attend school or if they were not adequately prepared for school (Storry, 2007, p. 14). The "carrot" approach involved sport or cultural activities as enticements for students to attend school. Cultural activities were seen, however, to "dilute mainstream education outcomes" (Storry, 2007, p. 15).

That assimilationism maintains epistemic authority in Indigenous education ideology today is because assimilationism enjoys a healthy relationship with neo-liberalism and notions of citizenship and nationhood that presents assimilation for Indigenous Australians as a seemingly reasonable and socially just goal (McConaghy, 2000, p. 152). National policy goals for Indigenous education in Australia continue to proffer assimilation as the only educational option, the only valid educational goal (see, for example, MCEECDYA, 2010).

INDIGENOUS STUDIES AND ASSIMILATIONISM

History attests to the significant impact that assimilationist ideology continues to have on Indigenous Studies. Assimilationism has been particularly influential in the education of non-Indigenous Australians in public education by promoting dominant cultural superiority and actively undermining Indigenous identities, societies, and cultures (Mooney & Craven, 2005, p. 3). Indigenous Studies was clearly defined and articulated in the Australian Institute of Aboriginal Studies Act 1964, as *"anthropological research and study in relation to the Aboriginal people of Australia"* (Nakata, 2004, p. 3). Neither the policy nor the anthropologically based practices of the Institute involved Indigenous people as knowledgeable agents but rather as ethnographic subjects. Later policy reform agendas applied theories and approaches that continued to exclude Indigenous voices by privileging dominant assimilationist educational and psychological theories (p. 4). However, an important shift came about in 1982 when a Commonwealth Aboriginal Studies Working Group articulated that Indigenous Studies should now focus on "contemporary Aboriginal concerns" by referencing Indigenous as well as non-Indigenous sources (p. 5).

With this shift there came a growing awareness that the ignorance and ideological assumptions that fuel racism in the majority society were major contributing factors to socio-economic disparities experienced by Indigenous Australians. This was recognized in a further target of the Aboriginal Education Policies that all students should be taught about Indigenous Australia—that Indigenous Studies should become part of mainstream curricula as a way to combat racism and effect social change (Beresford & Partington, 2003, p. 20). In response, Indigenous Studies as an academic discipline has increasingly developed in the higher education sector over the past three decades, either as specialized Indigenous Studies subjects, award courses, or through the "Indigenization" of curriculum across academic disciplines. Many universities today include mandatory Indigenous Studies subjects in mainstream undergraduate coursework programs such as education, health, humanities, and social science programs. "Indigenization" is the most recent catch-cry for Indigenous Studies where the strategy is to inject "authentic Indigenous content" across the disciplines of the academy (see, for example, Carey, 2008; Williamson & Dalal, 2007). Consequently, Indigenous Studies is now the concern of a myriad of Western academic disciplines where anthropology, education, and psychology are joined by history, cultural studies, Australian Studies, legal studies, health studies, environmental sciences, literature, fine arts, the social sciences, and more. This is the fundamental basis upon which Indigenous Studies courses and Indigenized curricula are constructed today, and in many instances dominant culture learners (non-Indigenous learners) make up the greater percentage of students undertaking Indigenous Studies in the Australian higher education sector (Nakata, 2004, p. 5).

However, wholesale inclusion of mandatory Indigenous Studies and Indigenization of discipline-specific curriculum will not automatically create authentic, equal, or secure Indigenous knowledge spaces nor miraculously work to combat racism. Indigenous Studies continues to been framed and delineated by dominant epistemology, theories, and academic disciplines (Nakata, 2004, pp. 11–12) and reinforced by dominant ideological assumptions. Indigenous Studies, in many instances, continues to be informed by a preponderance of research where Indigenous peoples are the sole focus of predominately ethnographic analysis that fails to critically examine or problematize the impact of dominant culture ideologies, theories or practices on Indigenous peoples' knowledges and socio-economic realities (Flowers, 1996, p.19). Indigenous knowledges in the academy have been disembodied, dismembered, and synthesized through dominant culture conceptual, ideological, and theoretical assumptions and appropriated by the disciplines of the academy. Indigenous people continue to be pathologized as the "problem," the focus for remedy and therapy to improve "their" socio-economic disadvantage.

Without a critical approach, Indigenous Studies can and does work to sustain the socio-political power imbalances and hegemonic ideologies that oppress Indigenous opportunity. Conversely, by engaging critical theoretical and pedagogical approaches, Indigenous Studies has the capacity to be an important site of resistance to assimilationism in the academy.

INDIGENOUS STUDIES—CRITICAL DIRECTIONS

Critical theoretical assumptions are highly relevant to Indigenous epistemologies and diverse Indigenous standpoints. Brookfield (2005) describes critical theory as having three "core" assumptions: firstly, that modern democracies are inequitable societies; secondly, that dominant ideologies maintain inequity; and thirdly, that this situation must be revealed, challenged, and changed (p. 370). These assumptions fit neatly with Indigenous standpoints, in that it is dominant ideology and hegemony that have continued to repress Indigenous Australians in all areas of civic life, and particularly in education. The critical tradition posits the "ideal" society against the revealed reality of oppression, inequity, immorality, and injustice of modern societies. Due to this normative grounding, critical theory attracts criticism that it is *"not a genuine theory at all but a set of preferences, prescriptions, and platitudes"* that arrogantly presume to know and understand "true democracy," to know what constitutes an "ideal" society (Brookfield, 2005, p. 27). Horkheimer (in Brookfield, 2005) opines the impossibility of "verifying" critical theory,

> . . . until the social vision it inspires is realized. . .there can be no corresponding concrete perception of it until it actually comes about. If the proof of the pudding is in the eating, the eating here is still in the future (p. 29).

It is just this point of "knowing" true democracy in an ideal society, however, that makes critical theory highly relevant to Indigenous epistemological perspectives. The distinction is that until a little over two centuries ago, we'd been "eating pudding" for eons. Indigenous epistemologies do not just "posit" or "prescribe" a socially just or ideal society, but *remember knowing* social justice, freedom, morality, and equality. Indigenous epistemologies have a "concrete perception" of the fundamental goal of critical theory that has been realized in the recent past. In this way, Indigenous epistemologies validate critical theoretical assumptions.

INDIGENOUS STUDIES AND CRITICAL PEDAGOGY

The relevance of critical pedagogical approaches is pronounced here as crucial if Indigenous Studies is to contribute to the emancipation of Indigenous knowledges in the academy. Indigenous Studies must engage a sharply focused critical expose, deconstruction, and analysis of dominant culture hegemonic ideologies, power relations, and constructions of "aboriginality" in relation to Indigenous Australian peoples (Williamson & Dalal, 2007, p. 52). The focus must shift to recognizing Indigenous knowledges as diverse, current, and relevant, informed by generations of experiences of eco-cultural sustainability (Stewart, 2002, p. 15). Diverse Indigenous individual, communal, and societal knowledges and experiences across time and place must be contextualized.

Through analysis of the tensions and contested nature of the relationships within and between Indigenous and dominant epistemologies, ideologies, and experiences, diverse Indigenous knowledges can be illuminated as contextual, contingent, and indivisibly embodied in people and places. Nakata (2007) usefully defines this contested space of converging multiple and overlapping epistemologies and standpoints as "the cultural interface"(p. 195–210). Whilst critical pedagogical approaches for Indigenous Studies using the multi-faceted analytical lens of the cultural interface have the potential to facilitate students' problematization of their own relationship to dominant ideologies and hegemony (McGloin, 2008, p. 83) and for the possibility of challenging assimilationism, this approach is not without limitations.

CRITICAL INDIGENOUS STUDIES PEDAGOGY: CHALLENGES AND LIMITATIONS

There are three main challenges to engaging critical Indigenous Studies pedagogy in the context of higher education in Australia: dominant culture learners, the institutional and systemic imperatives of the academy and the limited capacity to protect embodied Indigenous knowledge from being appropriated and segmented by the disciplines of the academy. Whilst there is a proliferation of literature highlighting examples of successfully engaging critical social pedagogy in the context of mass societal poverty, oppression, and injustice, there remains a paucity of literature addressing the specific theoretical concerns and practical applications of engaging critical pedagogy for dominant culture learners in the Western academy. Uncritical application of Freirean approaches when working with dominant culture learners can be problematic because the social reality of Indigenous oppression and inequity can be difficult to intellectually and emotionally relate to for dominant culture learners. The individualizing culture of neo-liberalism has "deinstitutionalized failure, poverty, and racism," where now individuals are seen as accountable for their own personal misfortunes, without recognition of the institutional, political, and hegemonic forces that sustain inequality (McGloin, 2008, p. 83). Deeply critical deconstruction and analysis of dominant culture from Indigenous standpoints can work to threaten and alienate dominant culture learners (Choules, 2007, p. 166).

Further, by encouraging the equal privileging of all learners' individual voices as is traditional in Freirean pedagogy, dominant discourse can be asserted to the exclusion of minority perspectives and standpoints. Individualizing discourse in relation to inequality and prejudice can work to deny the impact of dominant ideological and institutional discrimination where dominant culture learners can "mis-position" themselves as "victims." Wholesale application of Freirean pedagogy risks facilitating a learning environment where dominant culture learners merely engage in repressive tolerance and reproduce the "oppressive relations" that contribute to Indigenous societal and educational disparity. In this context it is important to engage a high level of critical analysis, abstraction, and theorizing to balance the narratives of individual standpoints (Choules, pp. 168–172).

From my teaching practice it has become apparent that Indigenous values in education are not only obviously relevant for Indigenous Studies pedagogy but are also highly relevant to critical pedagogical approaches. Whilst Indigenous epistemologies and axiologies are diverse across Indigenous Australian nations, the importance of relatedness and relationships in learning is common across the continent (see, for example, Hogan & Randall, 2007; Waltja Tjutangku Palyapayi, 2001, pp. 23–24). The development of safe, trusting, and respectful learning relationships is equally crucial to critical pedagogical approaches (GHFP, 2006, para. 16), particularly when working with dominant culture learners. It can be extremely difficult and taxing work undertaking the learning tasks of critical pedagogy in the context of the cultural interface. This type of pedagogy requires learners to commit to the "personal work" of continual "critical self-reflection" (Brookfield, 2005, p. 2; Williamson & Dalal, 2007, pp. 52–55). Ongoing critical deconstruction of dominant culture processes of meaning-making can be intensely confronting and exceptionally distressing for dominant culture learners (Williamson & Dalal, 2007, p. 57). Therefore prioritizing the time needed to develop trusting learning relationships and safe learning environments is vital to the facilitation of this difficult work and the amelioration of the potential negative impacts on learners.

Critical pedagogy is grounded in the goals of graduating critical thinkers able to identify, resist, and advocate against injustice, community members who value, respect, contribute to, and engage productively with diversity and learners who will continue to value learning as a life-long endeavor. In many ways the moral economies of both Indigenous values in education and critical pedagogy are at odds with the competitive, prescriptive, and conformist rules and regulations of the current neo-liberalist economy of user-pays model of higher education in Australia today. Institutional and systemic imperatives of Australian higher education institutions are major impediments to achieving the goals of critical Indigenous Studies pedagogy. Institutional restrictions on time, place, space, and technological demands inhibit opportunities for the development of safe, trusting, and respectful learning relationships so vital to Indigenous and critical approaches to education. The potential for learning facilitators to develop meaningful learning relationships is significantly restricted by timetabling practices of institutions where the lecture and follow-up tutorial model is entrenched. Immersion or block studies can afford the substantial time necessary for any learning group to create an "environment of reciprocity and sociability" or "cultural safety" (Bin-Sallik, 2003) but can be difficult to negotiate within the limits of institutional timetabling imperatives.

At many if not most universities in Australia today, the physical teaching and learning spaces are generally configured to facilitate what Freire (1996) described as the "banking method" of education where many students face the lone teacher, listening as s/he instructs (p. 7). This environment tends to evoke the perception that the teacher's authority overrules learner agency and does not abet the development of equitable learning relationships. Where student cohorts are large, as is the case with many of my own classes, there is no option but to gather in large lecture theatres where the teacher must stay in the front of the class so that s/he can be heard over the microphone. Further, many classes must now be video-streamed live to students who are at different locations. This further prescribes the spatial arrangements in that the teacher must remain in front of the camera, while the students sit quietly watching and listening to the "talking head" on the video screen. Small student cohorts and face-to-face immersive block-style classes are essential for the development of meaningful group learning relationships and for engaging the difficult work of critical learning. Small cohorts allow for easy rearrangement of teaching spaces and for alternate teaching and learning locations to be accessed.

Formal education is an important ingredient in successful social change education; however, it is but one component of a much more holistic, embodied, and emotive educative process. Learners can only develop mutually rewarding critical learning relationships through the immersive practices of "continuous contact" and "democratic discussion" where they mentor and learn from each other (Maddison & Scalmer, 2006, pp. 55–62). Effective critical pedagogy must motivate learners "by head, heart and spirit" (Kovan & Dirkx in Ollis, 2008, p. 9).

Arguably the most profound limitation of critical Indigenous Studies pedagogy is the inability to effectively protect Indigenous knowledges from the appropriating capacities of the academy. Indigenous knowledges transcend the disciplines of the academy through the holistic conceptual embodiment of knowledge in people and in places. Embodied knowledge is contingent on *where* it is known and the relationship of the knower to specific knowledge places. When embodied Indigenous knowing is transplanted from specific knowledge place,s the relevance, currency, and agency of the knowledge are immediately in danger of being appropriated and further disembodied. On the one hand, critical Indigenous Studies is vital and necessary for challenging assimilationism and contributing to the development of an environment of "epistemological equality" (Dei, 2008, p. 8) in the academy. On the other hand, continuing to expose holistic, embodied knowledges to the disciplines of the academy through Indigenous Studies risks the continued colonization and appropriation of Indigenous knowledges.

CONCLUSION

Assimilationist ideology remains powerfully influential in education policy and practice for both Indigenous and non-Indigenous learners in Australia today. Assimilationist objectives based on theories of the "deficit other" can be clearly identified throughout the history of Indigenous education policy and practice. Government policy objectives continue to focus on assimilationism, and money continues to be thrown at Indigenous education programs that rehash and revive failed theories and practices of the past. Indigenous education policy and practice continue to disregard Indigenous people's rights to be Indigenous, to engage their own epistemologies and languages and to control and manage their own education systems in their own knowledge environments (Harrison, 2000, p. 1; Partington, 1998, p. 4). Assimilationist ideology works to mask both the hegemonic nature of dominant culture education and the spectacular long-term failure of public education in Australia to facilitate Indigenous emancipation.

In recent decades Indigenous Studies has been promoted as an antidote for societal racism, and critical pedagogical approaches certainly have the potential to effectively challenge the epistemological bias toward dominant knowledge constructions (Dei, 2008, p. 10) and the institutional imperatives of the academy that "circumscribe" Indigenous knowledges and sustain assimilationist ideology (Nakata, 2004, pp. 11–12). Critical theoretical approaches are relevant to Indigenous Education in terms of reflexivity. Through the concrete perception of an ideal society, Indigenous epistemology is well positioned to expose the hegemonic socio-historical justifications that underpin assimilationism and oppress Indigenous opportunity. Critical Indigenous Studies pedagogy should be viewed as a crucial and necessary site of resistance to assimilationist ideologies and the epistemic authority of dominant culture in the academy.

Nonetheless, critical approaches must be problematized in relation to the particular context of Indigenous Studies, Indigenous knowledges, dominant culture learners, and the broader neo-liberalist culture of modern Australia. The indiscriminate implementation of critical pedagogy in Indigenous Studies has the potential to inadvertently empower and sustain dominant ideologies whilst further marginalizing and silencing Indigenous standpoints and voices (Dei, 2008, p. 6). Critical approaches to Indigenous Studies do have the potential to make a significant and valuable contribution to challenging assimilationism and effecting social change but are always inhibited by the dominant ideological, institutional, systemic, and disciplinary imperatives of the academy. While critical Indigenous Studies pedagogy can contribute to breaking free of the ideological shackles of assimilationism, Indigenous Studies remains limited in its capacity to protect contextual and embodied Indigenous knowledges from being appropriated by the academic disciplines. Indigenous Studies in the academy then, is a crucially important site of resistance to assimilationist ideology and the oppression of Indigenous peoples and knowledges, whilst remaining a dangerous and hostile environment for diverse holistic and embodied Indigenous knowledges.

REFERENCES

Beresford, Q., & Partington, G. (Eds.). (2003). *Reform and Resistance in Aboriginal Education—The Australian Experience.* Western Australia: University of Western Australia Press Crawley.

Bin-Sallik, M. (2003). Cultural Safety, Let's Name It! *Australian Journal of Indigenous Education, 32*, 21–28.

Board of Studies NSW. (2010). *Aboriginal Education Timeline 1900–1966, Aboriginal Education.* Sydney: New South Wales Government.

Bradley, D., Noonan, P., Nugent, H., & Scales, B., (2008). *Review of Australian Higher Education.* Canberra: Commonwealth of Australia.

Brookfield, S. (2005). *The Power of Critical Theory for Adult Learning and Teaching.* Berkshire, UK: Open University Press, McGraw-Hill.

Carey, M., (2008). Indigenisation, Interdisciplinary and Cultural Competency: Working the Dialogic Space between Indigenous Studies and Other Disciplines at Curtin University. *Psychology and Indigenous Australians: Teaching Practice and Theory Conference.* Curtin University, Western Australia.

Choules, K. (2007). Social Change Education: Context Matters. *Adult Education Quarterly, 57*(2), 159–176.

Christie, M. (1985). *Aboriginal Perspectives on Experience and Learning: The Role of Language in Aboriginal Education.* Melbourne: Deakin University Press.

Coffield, F., Moseley, D., & Ecclestone, K. (2004). *Learning Styles and Pedagogy in Post-16 Learning—A Systematic and Critical Review.* London: Learning and Skills Research Centre.

Cummins, J. (2003). Challenging the Construction of Difference as Deficit: Where Are Identity, Intellect, Imagination and Power in the New Regime of Truth? In P. Trifonas, (Ed.), *Pedagogies of Difference: Rethinking Education for Social Change* (pp. 41–59). New York: Routledge.

Dei, G. (2008). Indigenous Knowledge Studies and the Next Generation: Pedagogical Possibilities for Anti-colonial Education. *Australian Journal of Indigenous Education, 37*(Supplement), 5–13.

Department of Education, Employment and Workplace Relations (DEEWR). (2005). *National Report to Parliament on Indigenous Education and Training.* Canberra Commonwealth of Australia.

Department of Education, Employment and Workplace Relations (DEEWR). (2006). *National Aboriginal and Torres Strait Islander Education Policy.* Canberra: Commonwealth of Australia.

Flowers, R. (1996). Can Competency Assessment Support Struggles for Community Development and Self-Determination? *Partnerships in Assessment Conference.* Auckland Institute of Technology, New Zealand.

Freire, P. (1996). *Pedagogy of the Oppressed.* London: Penguin.

Gray, J., & Beresford, Q. (2008). A Formidable Challenge: Australia's Quest for Equity in Indigenous Education. *Australian Journal of Education, 52*(2), 197–223.

Guerrand-Hermes Foundation for Peace (GHFP). (2006, July). *A Vision for Transformative Education.* Paper presented at the meeting of Rethinking Educational Change, Third Vittachi International Conference, Al Akhawayn University in Ifrane (AUI), Morocco.

Haebich, A. (1988). *For Their Own Good: Aborigines and Government in Southwest of Western Australia 1900–1940.* Nedlands: University of Western Australia Press.

Halse, C., & Robinson, M. (1999). Towards an Appropriate Pedagogy for Aboriginal Children. In R. Craven (Ed.), *Teaching Aboriginal Studies* (pp. 199–213). St Leonards, NSW: Allen & Unwin.

Harris, S. (1984). *Culture and Learning—Tradition and Education in North-East Arnhem Land.* Canberra: Australian Institute of Aboriginal Studies.

Harris, S. (1990). *Two-Way Aboriginal Schooling: Education and Cultural Survival.* Canberra: Aboriginal Studies Press.

Harrison, N. (2000). Where Do We Look Now? The Future of Rresearch in Indigenous Australian Education. *Australian Journal of Indigenous Education, 36,* 1–5.

Hogan, M. (Producer, Director), & Randall, B. (Writer). (2007). *Kanyini* [Motion picture]. Australia: Reverb Films.

Hughes, P. (1987). Aboriginal Culture and Learning Styles—A Challenge for Academics in Higher Education Institutions. *The Second Frank Archibald Memorial Lecture,* University of New England, Armidale, NSW.

Hughes, P., More, A., & Williams, M. (2004). *Aboriginal Ways of Learning,* Adelaide: Flinders.

Indigenous Higher Education Advisory Council (IHEAC) (2006). *Report to the Minister for Education, Science and Training—Improving Indigenous Outcomes and Enhancing Indigenous Culture and Knowledge in Australian Higher Education.* Canberra: Commonwealth of Australia.

Janke, T. (1998). *Our Culture: Our Future, Report on Australian Indigenous Cultural and Intellectual Property Rights.* Sydney: Australian Institute of Aboriginal and Torres Strait Islander Studies (AIATSIS) & Aboriginal and Torres Strait Islander Commission (ATSIC).

Maddison, S., & Scalmer, S. (2006). *Activist Wisdom: Practical Knowledge and Creative Tension in Social Movements.* Sydney: UNSW.

McConaghy, C. (2000). *Rethinking Indigenous Education—Culturalism, Colonialism and the Politics of Knowing.* Flaxton, QLD: Post Pressed.

McGloin, C. (2008). Recontextualising the Award: Developing a Critical Pedagogy in Indigenous Studies. *The International Journal of Humanities, 6*(4), 81–88.

Mellor, S., & Corrigan, M. (2004). *Australian Education Review—The Case for Change—A Review of Contemporary Research on Indigenous Education Outcomes.* Sydney: Australian Council for Educational Research (ACER).

Ministerial Council for Education, Early Childhood Development and Youth Affairs, (MCEECDYA) and Curriculum Corporation. (2010). *Indigenous Education Action Plan Draft, 2010–2014, for Public Comment.* Carlton South, Victoria: MCEECDYA.

Mooney, S., & Craven, R. (2005). *Teaching Aboriginal Studies: Producing Inclusive Australian Citizens,* Sydney: Australian Association for Research in Education.

Nakata, M. (2004). Indigenous Australian Studies and Higher Education. *The Wentworth Lectures.* Canberra: Australian Institute of Aboriginal and Torres Strait Islander Studies.

Nakata, M. (2007). *Disciplining the Savages, Savaging the Disciplines.* Canberra: Aboriginal Studies Press.

Newbury, P. (Ed). (1999). *Aboriginal Heroes of the Resistance: From Pemulwuy to Mabo,* Surry Hills, NSW: Action for World Development.

Nichol, R. (2005). *Socialization, Land, and Citizenship among Aboriginal Australians—Reconciling Indigenous and Western Forms of Education.* New York: Edwin Mellen.

Ollis, T. (2008). The "Accidental" Activist: Activism, Community and Social Change. *Paper Presented to Community Development and Ecology: Engaging Ecological Sustainability through Community Development.* Melbourne, Australia.

Parbury, N. (1999). Aboriginal Education: A History. In R. Craven (Ed.), *Teaching Aboriginal Studies* (pp. 63–86). St Leonards, NSW: Allen & Unwin.

Partington, N. (1998). *Perspectives on Aboriginal and Torres Strait Islander Education.* Melbourne: Thomson.

Pearce, S. (2008). Critical Reflections on the Central Role of Indigenous Program Facilitators in Education for Social Change. *Australian Journal of Indigenous Education, 37,* 131–136.

Stewart J. (2002). The Relevance of the "Learning Styles Debate" for Australian Indigenous Students in Mainstream Education. *Australian Journal of Indigenous Education, 30*(2), 13–19.

Storry, K. (2007). What Is Working in Good Schools in Remote Indigenous Communities? *Issue Analysis, 86.*

TAFE NSW, Training and Education Support. (2008). *Promoting Emerging Practice.* Sydney: New South Wales Department of Education and Training.

Tranby Aboriginal College. (2008). *Diploma of Community Development.* Sydney: Tranby College.

United Nations (UN). (2007). *United Nations Declaration on the Rights of Indigenous Peoples.* Geneva: UN.

Waltja Tjutangku Palyapayi. (2001). *Pipirri Wiimaku—"For the Little Kids"—Innovative Child Care Report 2000–2001,* Alice Springs: Waltja Tjutangku Palyapayi Aboriginal Corporation.

Williamson, J., & Dalal, P. (2007). Indigenising the Curriculum or Negotiating the Tensions at the Cultural Interface? Embedding Indigenous Perspectives and Pedagogies in a University Curriculum. *Australian Journal of Indigenous Education, 36*(Supplement), 51–58.

CHAPTER FIVE

African Philosophies of Education

Deconstructing the Colonial and Reconstructing the Indigenous

ALI ABDI

Philosophy, which was at one point appreciated as the quasi-straight line of the love of wisdom, has been defined in many ways, and with as many analytical, pedagogical, and socio-cultural intentions and emphasis. At least within and around the parameters of academic projects, philosophy might be seen as the fluid but ongoing study and analysis that pertain to all aspects of the way we live in a given time and space, how we critically inquire about social contexts and relationships that would, either in alignment, or in contrario, describe and institutionally locate the intersections of those life systems. With that understanding, and with education being an important component of social life, one would assume that no group, nation, or continent would be denied upon laying some claim on the philosophical viability of its life systems, and how learning to live and succeed (in relative terms) would be defined by formalized or informal clusters of the philosophy of education, which would comment upon, and potentially shape the qualities as well as the structures of all indigenous systems of education. In factual terms, that should not be a difficult theme to understand, but in the history of extensively colonized Africa, the imposition of European philosophies and theories of knowledge, complemented by the denial that the ancient continent had any philosophy, philosophy of education, or other coherent thought systems (Abdi, 2008; Achebe, 2000; Mudimbe, 1988), has perhaps done as much damage as any other project of the imperial enterprise. Indeed, as Nyerere (1968) and Rodney (1982) cogently discussed, the ontological as well as the epistemological colonization of Africa led to the ongoing de-development of the continent, and in Ngugi wa Thiongo's terms, the educational terrain, especially the de-Africanization of that terrain, has affirmed the processes of mental colonization that are still afflicting the lives of Africans (wa Thiongo, 1986, 2005).

It is also central to note here that one of the main plunders (there are many) of the postcolonial African elite was the continuation of colonial philosophies and epistemologies as the main definers of education and development in the continent. In this chapter, I intend to challenge the false assumptions about African education and philosophies of education, ways of knowing and attached systems of life. I will start by talking about educational types, with some focus on how pre-colonial informal systems of learning in Africa were effective platforms of educational and social development, and as Nyerere (1968) among others have pointed out, Africa's stunted progress in the past two centuries could actually be traced back to those moments when people's learning and social development platforms were deliberately destroyed by the colonial forces. From those observational platforms, I will introduce select descriptive and analytical points that pertain to the pedagogical revitalization of African philosophies of education, and how, from both historical and contemporaneous terms, African education was steeped in indigenous philosophies that were not necessarily structured as Europe's but were put into place to serve the situation-specific needs of the African people. In all the analysis I deploy in this chapter, the subjectivity of the case should be clear.

As an African man myself, I have lived through and continue to live in the thick of the early formations of the major philosophical and pedagogical discourses that have affirmed the theoretical supremacy of the ideas of the West as they related to the world of the colonized (Bessis, 2003) and as they were later perforce practicalized to effect the global ontological and physical life divisions that exist today. As I interact with these realities, I can clearly locate the beginnings of the conceptual and philosophical lines that have suppressed the place of Indigenous philosophies of education, which because these were the carriers of and conductors of indigenous knowledge, the capacity for indigenous advancement in educational, political, and economic terms was to be stunted for many centuries and into the writing of this chapter. This does not necessarily mean that African knowledge systems would have always developed better by themselves; indeed, knowledge, as I will note later, is a human project that was only achievable in the spirit as well as the actions of human togetherness, and it is via this reality, that it can serve well the lives of people. But by disallowing the expansive and essential contributions of whole populations, not only in Africa but as well in many other places including the highly developed systems that existed in pre-Columbian Americas (Mann, 2006), the issue will be so much more than just marginalizing the evolving epistemic space of those societies, and it certainly speaks about the minimalization of the direct contributions these knowledges could make to the well-being of the humano-ecological systems that attach us to the overall cosmologies we inhabit. With the extensive subjective locations that heavily inform this chapter, the work will also extensively benefit, for its general observations, perspectives, and conclusions, from the voluminous literature that has been mostly produced by postcolonial writers who have, like me, lived through the discursive and practical experiences presented here.

GENERAL EDUCATIONAL TYPES AND CHARACTERISTICS

In speaking about the types of education used in different learning situations, one may discuss formal systems of education, informal systems of learning, and non-formal systems of education. As global learning systems are structured today, the most institutionalized of these is formal education which has been, especially in its current form and structure, introduced to the African continent by European colonialism. This does not mean, though, that some formal instructional and learning arrangements were never in place in pre-colonial Africa. As students of African civilizations including the man who may be the doyen of the area, the late Senegalese scholar, Cheikh Anta Diop, have shown the world, for many years before Europeans decided to carve up Africa for their economic benefits, the continent was highly endowed in its intellectual development and had some of the first comprehensive learning institutions including those achieved by the Mali kingdoms in the early centuries of the second millennium. While these systems of higher education and some of the earliest library systems located there have been known to many of us for a number of years, the newest discoveries actually accentuate how the level of epistemic and epistemological sophistications achieved there was more impressive than was ever thought. That being as it is, one can still safely say that current programs of formal education, as they are practiced in the world, fairly follow a European way of philosophizing, teaching, and knowing. With my focus below more on the historical validity and current importance of indigenous informal education, let me briefly note that non-formal education is probably the least ubiquitous of the three types of learning, as it usually focuses on limited, seminar-style training programs that organizations and institutions design and implement for the knowledge advancement of their employees. Occasionally, though, one might come across this type of learning being used interchangeably with informal education. My own understanding is that the two should be different, and that should become clearer as I say more about the latter in the following lines.

The focus (albeit briefly here) on informal education is important in any historical, philosophical, and cultural studies of the African continent. As the most extensive, temporally longest, and therefore, socially most effective learning systems in pre-colonial African traditional societies, this type of education has shaped the developmental and general life management schemes of the African people (Abdi, 2002; Semali, 1999). One important characteristic of this type of learning is its openness where it is not restricted by any organizational or governance conditionalities, and as such accords all the chance as well as the selective capacity to learn. Beyond the individual or the group level, informal education would always have a regional or even continental quality that makes it conform more to the geographical and related environmental needs of the populace. In terms of the assumed randomness of informal education, one needs to qualify the point. While informal education was not as structurally restricted as, say, current forms of schooling, it is clear that in some community-sanctioned contexts, it actually has had select and ongoing time- and age-bound expectations, even restrictions and evaluative measures that assured its relevance, timeliness, and effectiveness in relation to the needs for which it was undertaken (see, inter alia, Achebe, 2000; wa Thiongo, 1993, 2005). As Semali (1999) pointed out, traditional African education also had an effective knowledge and scientific repertoire that allowed it to effectively respond, not only to social and governance needs of the community, but as well, to the ecological literacy, and to the agricultural and medical needs of people. Indeed, it is via this form of learning that Africans have thrived and constructively managed their lives over millennia. Yet, with the arrival of colonialism, all African systems of learning and modes of development were derided as useless and not fit to be used. From there, these highly reliable and time-tested projects of learning were perforce rescinded from all learning contexts, and European systems of education, languages, educational philosophies, and epistemologies were imposed on colonized populations. The history of this tragic story is well known to many, it has been magisterially discussed and multi-perspectively studied and critiqued by such brilliant thinkers as Julius Nyerere who in his book, *Freedom and Socialism* (1968) analyzed the lasting effects of these extensive colonial projects on the being of the persona Africana. These issues have also been studied by the late Guyanese scholar Walter Rodney, who in his classic, *How Europe Underdeveloped Africa* (1982), emphasized the centrality of indigenously induced, designed, and implemented systems of learning for both the immediate needs as well as the long-term well-being of the community. As I have done few times before, I will still quote Rodney's (1982) cogent and timeless points in this regard:

The following features of indigenous African education can be considered outstanding *for the specific indigenous contexts it was designed for*. Its close links with the social life, both in material and spiritual sense; its collective nature *where it focuses on the whole of the person and the community*; its many-sidedness, and its progressive development in conformity with the successive stages of the physical, emotional and mental development of the child. There was no separation of education and the productive activities *of people*. Altogether, through many informal means, pre-colonial African education matched the realities of pre-colonial African society and produced well-rounded personalities to fit into that society (p. 239, emphases added).

Rodney's points are not just a descriptive exercise of what this education did for the people, he also engages a number of philosophical points. Indeed, the main questions of the philosophy of education would engage, in diverse global contexts, what we could call the big questions of its concern, that is, the WHATs, WHYs, and HOWs of education. Initially, it should be expected that the establishment of any new educational enterprise will begin with the question: what type of education do we, or the community, need? Without that taking place, Rodney's points will not be realized. Indeed, with the consensual point that education leads to some form of social well-being, one cannot negate the fundamental philosophistic nature of all learning projects. From there, the other major philosophy of education question, why do we need this type of education (with the assumption that the first question has already been answered), would form the basis for the establishment of educational contexts; without that happening, then one will be taking away the inherent learning agency of the human. And if any reader is experiencing any analytical dissonance in terms of whether these were built into the informal systems of education that were in place in Africa, the answer should be a categorical yes. Even in spaces where the normative semi-structure of traditional education (with all its socially binding but formally non-codified sanction-and-prohibition mechanisms), there would be so many tacitly agreed-upon notations and practices that govern the way people learn, value knowledge, and use that knowledge for specific intentions and locations that are embedded within the political, social, and cultural platforms of the places they inhabit.

With respect to the third question, the HOW, this could be selectively described as the most important educational philosophical conjecture, for it affirms how both the general and particular messages of education would be conveyed to learners, who will use such information for their livelihoods and for the psychological and existential constructions of the realities that define their communities and the time- and space-dependent achievements they intend to accrue as a result of their education. Indeed, all these important philosophical questions concerned African traditional societies, and to fit their learning programs into the living spaces of their societies, they were able to answer those questions by themselves, for themselves, and for future generations. The main difference in terms of what has happened since colonialism, is that instead of the community answering those questions by themselves and as such, achieving through education what Walter Rodney described above, colonizing Europe decided to answer the questions on behalf of Africans. And to clarify now, the latter actually did not seek any help with any learning concerns and surely did not invite any foreigner to tell them how to manage their resources and developmental schemes.

Actually, the last sentence above could be seen as rhetorical but it is an important rhetoric. Of course we should know why African systems of education were destroyed by colonialism, why new and alien philosophies of education were imposed, and we of course, need to talk about why the de-philosophizing process was important for the colonizers. But to perhaps repeat some of the stuff we have to know by now, mainly for the sake of reminding ourselves of the complexity of colonialism and how its architects thoughtfully designed and implemented it, this psychosomatically destructive project was perhaps anything else (at least initially) but psychological in that it extensively demeaned and value-wise diminished anything that was African; by doing so, and by elevating the place of everything European, it aimed to convince Africans of their need for the colonizing project. As one should effectively imagine, people will not submit to colonialism unless they had some belief in its superiority. And when the psychological persuasion was not yielding the needed results, the deployment of the undoubtedly superior instrument was always an immediately ready option. The second item on the menu of colonialism that the colonized had to avail themselves, was cultural: the psychological persuasion and other more concrete forms of convincing were to advance some form of an assumed cultural precedence (sometimes called, with clear contradiction in terms, a more advanced moral profile) for the colonizers.

The cultural insertion in the early stages of colonialism was very important, for culture actually mediates the structure as well as the functionalities of everyday life and had, therefore, the added effect of slowly normalizing the uneven colonial relationships. Concomitant with the cultural, was the educational where formalizing quickly the already established psychological and related persuasions was important. Indeed, the following two stages of colonialism, the political and the economic, would not have been as successful without the affirmation of everything they stood for, via the educational systems that were established to teach natives their self-negation and the heavy belief systems that de-ontologized their world and attritionally pushed them to become psycho-culturally and pedagogically conscripted participants in the overall project. As Fanon (1967, 1968) and Memmi (1991) noted, extensive processes of corporeal objectification would eventually lead to the formations of new creatures who would behave in ways that would have been alien to their former selves. Undoubtedly, such outcomes from so much de-culturalization would affirm the creation of emergent psycho-pedagogically subjectivities that behave in new ways, expect less of themselves, and are continually located in shifting but firmly oppressing borderlines that assure their exploitation as if they only exist for such realities.

Interestingly and especially for the European de-philosophizations of African life and education, the onslaught actually started much earlier than the first colonial settlers. In a written form at least, it was actually the Roman historian, Pliny the Elder, who, in his book, *Historia Naturalis* (1982/1856), philosophized about Africa as a place inhabited by an uncultured monstrous race. How did he know that? He, of course, did not know anything about Africa, but such sayings became the basic knowledge about Africa and they were accepted as true and real scholarship. The second wave of European writers about Africa was composed of some of the most important European philosophers and thinkers, who especially, because of the times in which they lived, had a great influence on how their governments and the public in their countries saw this huge landmass which to them was terra incognita. Apparently, though, their null knowledge somehow became more than that via their unsubstantiated and false assumptions about Africa. Indeed, when one comes across the writing of, inter alia, G. W. F. Hegel, Immanuel Kant, Thomas Hobbes, and yes, even the so-called philosophers of liberty, the Frenchmen Voltaire and Montesquieu, it is nigh impossible to view them as decent thinkers whose scholarship deserves any measure of attention. As I have written before (Abdi, 2006), the writings of these "luminaries" of social thought were greatly responsible for the constructions of the colonial project where the outright demeaning of whole populations and their lands as barbaric and worthy of subjugation would have removed any moral screen that might have restrained the fateful invasion of the merchants, the soldiers, and the clergy, which led, not only to the physical and environmental destructions we see now, but more so, and more enduringly, to the deep diminishing of the onto-existential, philosophical, epistemological, and other life plateaus that would have sustained the educational and social development platforms of *dadka Afrikaanka ah*. Hegel (1965), for example, was sure of the following about Africa:

> Africa is not interesting from the point of view of its own history, but because [in Africa] is in a state of barbarism and savagery which is preventing him from being an integral part of civilization. Africa, as far back as history goes, has remained closed and without links with the rest of the world. It is the country of gold which closed in on itself, the country of infancy, beyond the daylight of conscious history, wrapped in the blackness of night (p. 247).

In these few sentences, the number of errors (actually descriptive crimes) the "great" German philosopher commits against Africa are impressive. Without setting a foot in the continent and apparently without reading a single concrete point about it, he concludes that it has no history, no civilization, no understanding of the rest of the world, no links with anything outside itself, no agency, no knowledge, and by extension, no education, and no philosophy. Technically and for all pragmatic undertakings, this is nothing short of an organized attempt in the total dehumanization of everything African, and via the power of the text produced by Hegel and his racist cohorts, the belief systems this has established in the European public space would be enormous and it was enormous, with much of the belief system still intact. And all of it was of course absolutely false. As I have indicated earlier in the chapter, how could populations thrive over millennia, productively manage their lives, and actually achieve some of the most important civilizations in the world (for more on Africa's breakthrough achievements including the invention of human civilization itself, see Bernal, 1987/2002; Diop, 1974, 1987, 1990; Jackson, 1970). As Bernal notes in Volume II of his multi-volume *Black Athena* (1982/2002), which exclusively focuses on solid archaeological and documentary evidence, the origins of European civilizations actually came from Africa. Moreover Cheikh Anta Diop (1974, 1987, 1990), who has perhaps studied both the strength as well as the validity of African civilizations more than anyone else, also used archaeological, linguistic, and related evidence, to affirm once and for all, how Africa's achievements on the human civilizational ladder were, for many centuries, either at par or even superior to other things undertaken elsewhere in the world.

If, for example, as Chamberlain (cited in Jackson, 1970) noted, iron smelting and therefore, the mass use of iron was first developed in Africa, and if that invention became the spark that catapulted modern civilizations into what they are today, then how do we locate African civilizations vis-a-vis everything that came after that? Diop (1987) indeed noted how in many parts of Africa, "active blast furnaces [first] produced the iron that was required for economic and technological activity (p. 204). It is almost certain that wood was the fuel used, and the use of metallurgy in black Africa dates back to time immemorial."

In the pre-colonial processes of paving the way for colonialism, though, the prominent European thinkers mentioned earlier were not interested in elevating the lot of Africa in either the philosophical or other select epistemic platforms of life. That, as we should clearly understand, would have problematized the still-continuing project of global imperialism and could have occasionally stunted the forward march of the diabolic and grossly misnamed *"mission civilsatrice"* (see Said, 1993). But despite the abundance of facts that would point otherwise, the organized processes of denying Africa any historical and philosophical platforms continued from many angles, and I will suggest that itself is still affecting how ideas and any resulting knowledge systems produced there are valued in the world today.

RE-PHILOSOPHIZING AFRICAN EDUCATION: THE MISSED LINK

With most African countries gaining their political independence (albeit nominal as they found out quickly) from late 1950s to early 1960s, the point of re-philosophizing and re-indigenizing African systems of learning should have been at hand, and with education seen as an important vehicle for social development, the basic philosophical questions of what education different countries needed, why they needed those types of education and how these would be done, should have been extensively asked, analyzed, and inclusively dealt with. That, of course, did not happen. By and large, African educational policy makers somehow missed the crucial point that colonial education was not going to develop Africa; it was actually designed and implemented to underdevelop it. Indeed, without any of the essential questions about indigenous African education and possibilities of local development being raised, the postcolonial situation continued to be dominated by the colonial curriculum, colonial languages, and colonial structuring and distribution of educational resources. Here, one can sense how the psychological and cultural designs mentioned above, and that were affirmed through colonial educational programs, were at play.

The leadership of the supposedly liberated natives, who were almost entirely schooled in colonial colleges, many with advanced degrees from the few first-rate universities in the North, technically understood and seemingly appreciated the dominant systems of learning, were clearly de-linked from traditional systems of education and local languages and fully knew that their political privilege and economic well-being were both functions of their European education. As should be ascertained, therefore, they were not willing to popularize learning systems, for that would have endangered their cultural and political capital. Undoubtedly, that colonial way of thinking was majorly instrumental in blocking effective ways of African development. This also instilled in the minds of the new African elite select negative ontological relationships with the masses, where just like European colonialists, they saw all those not schooled and "cultured" like them as inferior and not worthy of the rights that free citizens should enjoy. This could be a mini-controversial point, but I once again submit, that some deep psycho-cultural formations were instilled in the minds of these Black rulers, and they decided, not only not to modify oppressive colonial systems of education but to massively oppress the populace, take away people's basic political and economic rights, and punish any opponents at will. And the overall story might not be far from the extensive inculcations in their minds that anything non-European or deficient in European manners was not worthy of respect, rights, freedom, even basic socio-economic well-being. Was this specific to the African context? Not necessarily, but at least in many other places, the package was mixed. In some Asian countries, for example, including Malaysia, Indonesia, and Singapore, postcolonial rulers might have accumulated too much political power, but they were at least sensitive to the educational and social development needs of their peoples. As Kwapong (1994) pointed out, many countries in Asia that have done well, did not only focus on some portions of indigenous economic development but also selectively re-cultured their educational systems so these fit both the historical and actual needs of the public. In Africa's case, the exceptions were not many, and even where there was a singular political and policy effort, the global intervention in the form of international capitalism vigorously opposing it was, unlike in the Asian cases, extensive and immediate.

One important singular attempt to change the situation was undertaken by Julius Nyerere, Tanzania's first postcolonial President, and a thoughtful philosopher-statesman who although, he went through colonial education including doing a graduate degree in the United Kingdom, was critically aware of the need to indigenize African education. In his widely referenced essay "Education for Self-Reliance," Nyerere prospectively analyzed the problems of continuing the colonial education system in post-independence Tanzania. He fully understood that such was not appropriate for the future of free Tanzania, and that the future of Africa was to be designed on the basis of the needs of the people and not on the preferences of those who have subjugated them for so long. Indeed, Nyerere (1968) understood as much as anyone that learning programs should be contextualized and should respond to the specific tempo-spatial needs of their recipients. He wrote

> The educational systems in different kinds of societies in the world have been, and are, very different in organization and content. They are different because the societies providing the education are different, and because education, whether it is formal or informal, has a purpose. The [main] purpose is to transmit from one generation to the next, the accumulated wisdom and knowledge of society, and to prepare the young for their future membership of that society and their active participation in its maintenance and development (p. 268).

Undoubtedly, Nyerere knew what Tanzania and the rest of Africa needed in the arenas of education and social well-being. Needless to add, he was not without his detractors, who accused him of engaging in grand social designs that were not practical in the real world. As we wrote not long ago, though, (Mhina & Abdi, 2009), the counter-Nyererean perspective is basically the highly neo-liberalized economic and political programs that are in full force in most of Africa today. These do at least one thing well: they promote an already determined rhetorical "survival of the fittest" notations that reward those who are already advantaged. In that sense, today's Tanzania may be described as post-Nyererean, but it is also highly hierarchical in economic terms at least, and the number of people who benefit from its abundant natural resources are few in relation to those who are marginalized. And it is possible that some would see such situations as the normal order of things, which is precisely what Nyerere was not willing to accept.

RECONSTRUCTING THE TERRAIN THROUGH THE RE-AFRICANIZATION/RE-INDIGENIZATION OF LEARNING PROGRAMS

Before I go into specific analyses of the possibilities of Africanization (always in relative terms), let me briefly relay some pointers on epistemology. Before I even do that, though, let me say one more thing about the emerging philosophical debates. I believe that African philosophical responses, with the respect to the writing of colonialist thinkers, have been effective (see, among others, Abiola, 2009; Eze, 1998; Serequeberhan, 1997; Wiredu, 1997), with many of these works critically located to challenge the baseless scribbling concocted by ill-informed foreigners about Africa and its people. In addition, while African philosophies and African philosophies of education could have select similarities with other philosophies from other parts of the world, one must also note some specificities that may be particular to the former. One stream of philosophy that might represent this particularity is Sage Philosophy, which was actually the title of the book by the late Kenyan scholar, Henry Odera Oruka (1991) who systematically showed the world how African men and women without any formal schooling were capable, not only in engaging philosophical inquiry, but in producing, in their places of residence and for their communities, extensive philosophical treatises that defined, critiqued, and located their existentialities as effectively and as comprehensively as anything produced in the European metropolises.

From a generalist theoretical and analytical perspectives, any organized discussion on education and educational philosophies, should contain at least few pointers on epistemology, which should be crucial in that it speaks about the descriptions and related analysis that explain the way we locate and attach comprehensible meaning to things, immediately complemented by how we transfer and exchange those meanings. It is because of this that one needs to appreciate how issues of epistemology usually deal with concerns that try to untangle, analytico-praxically speaking, theories of knowledge, and how these establish or situationally mediate ways of knowing. It is with regard to this reality that we should adhere to the practices of different and at times, detached epistemic possibilities and diverse ways of knowing. As such, Almeder (1992), for example, reminds us how propositional knowledge directly corresponds with epistemology, where in some contexts, such knowledge points to someone knowing something. From a different perspective, epistemic concepts, evidence, rationale for acceptance, and related justifiable possibilities, are things that we can discern and believe and other constructs that might be known through some of those (Fumerton, 2006).

With this in mind, it should be impossible to accord one system of education or one way of knowing the sole legitimacy of epistemic paradigms and epistemological platforms. Here, even unique ways of creating text-based knowledge, oral knowledge, linguistic characteristics, and all the social, political, and economic contexts that influence all of these, should affect, not only the way knowledge is expressed and used but as well the relational assumptions that derive from these. Knowledge, as Allen (2004) correctly noted, "cannot be limited to what is linguistically articulated, because everything we talk about tacitly should also refer to the wider world of artifactual culture" (p. 260). This is indeed what should increase, has actually already increased, the usefulness of such epistemological realities as contextualism or situationalism. As such, the rich diversity and developmentally viable possibilities of different epistemologies should be given a viable space in the contemporary world's knowledge and learning platforms. Especially in Africa, this is more urgent than ever. With the continent dealing with a host of social development liabilities, most of which have not been so far addressed by national or even private education systems, we should not only focus on re-doing the philosophical foundations of education but as well the epistemological re-aligning of learning spaces and programs so as to aim for more Africanized possibilities (in inclusive terms) of education and development.

Select Africanizations of knowledge

In speaking about the possible Africanizations or indigenizations of knowledge, let me categorically state that I do not adhere to any theoretical or practical constitutions or conventions that want to present knowledge as either African, Asian, European, or Pacific Islander, for that matter. I think it will be pragmatic to agree with, inter alia, Sandra Harding (1998, 2008) that knowledge is a collective human heritage and is produced by all societies, and selectively with Longino (2002) and Koch (2002) that the way we create and use knowledge is, by and large, socially constructed and managed. As I have discussed in other forums, therefore, the type of knowledge I am discussing here, or the educational outcomes and philosophies that might be achieved thereof, shouldn't have been a priori African and need not become a posteriori African. In these *post-facto* spaces of life, especially (that is, in relation to the irrecoverable wealth of knowledge that colonialism has distilled from the world of the Africans), my intention is to deliberately appreciate what is good and constructively functional in current systems of education but also intermesh with these the ideas and practices that are extracted from African languages, literature, historical and cultural studies, and scientific and mathematical achievements. It is via this inclusive and epistemically polycentric approach that the space of indigenous knowledges in postcolonial learning contexts could be elevated. That would undoubtedly engender the emergence of indigenous epistemes and epistemological platforms that enhance, not only the overall quality of the pedagogical and instructional endeavors, but as well, the psycho-cultural and existential relationships African learners would have with their schooling contexts.

In addition, the issue of the selective indigenization of education is also related to the well-argued social capital and cultural capital theories popularized by the French sociologist Pierre Bourdieu. As he effectively expounded in a number of highly referenced sociological writings (Bourdieu, 1984; Bourdieu & Passerson, 1990), the social characteristics of the family and community spaces we occupy, and the cultural capitals we harness thereof, could be strong determinants of the extent to which we succeed in our educational settings, and by extension, to what length we can exploit the societal networks that are formed and reformed in the quotidian intersections of life. And to expand on this point, it will not be that Africans, who through lacking the right cultural capital in current spaces of schooling, might just be disadvantaged in their local contexts, they could also be marginalized in the open-border realities of today's rapidly globalizing world, where the so-called knowledge societies will outdo others in the competition for development and well-being. As Africa's doyen of contemporary letters (of course, conveyed in English as today's dominant medium of expression), Chinua Achebe (2000) noted, the plight of current African locales is the directly deforming "de"-writing (read de-Africanizing) of our cultures, ontologies, and overall being by those who did not understand that much of what they were talking about.

It is in response to this need to inclusively (not exclusively) indigenize knowledge systems and philosophies of knowledge in African learning settings and in the wider society at large that we could look at some new possibilities in the situation. One example we can cite in the context of indigenizing the contents of schooling, which will also affirm new ways of philosophizing about African education, are media of instruction. While the world system induced advantages accrued from learning English or French in today's global system are situationally useful for iterant intellectuals like myself, the facts still remain that one's language is not only socially and culturally liberating, it is also, as Ngugi wa Thiongo has repeated many times, a powerful constitution that affirms people's histories, identities, even expectations, and aspirations. As such, no matter how one masters and uses English, it still does not belong to Africans, and in Frantz Fanon's seminal pointers, if the world would belong to those in whose languages it is expressed, Africans might find it difficult to achieve viable re-philosophizing of their educational systems or to harness social development possibilities that could be triggered by the learning programs they are exposed to. Indeed, Fanon's point has now been factualized: the world already belongs to those whose languages have become the dominant media of culture, economics, politics, and technology. So while I am not intending to go into too much detail in this area as I am conluding my writing here, the need for a linguistic turn in Africa's educational and social development terrains cannot be overstated. And to remind us all, Africa still remains the most linguistically colonized global space in the world, and while it may be wise to avoid quickly drawing any direct inferences from the case, I will take the risk, anyway: it is also the most developmentally depressed continent.

CONCLUSION

In this chapter, I have started with some discussions on colonialism and African educational histories, possibilities, and problematics. Clearly, the denial of Africa to lay any claim on viable philosophies or philosophies of learning, has been a part of the overall European project which dominated the continent via its psycho-cultural, educational, and politico-economic grand re-engineering. Technically, one must also ascertain the fact that all societies that have successfully managed their lives, as Africans have done for thousands of years, would not have done so without indigenous and contextually effective ways of thinking about the world, critically ascertaining their cosmological and environmental relationships with it, interactively managing their spaces and resources, and devising educational projects that effectively responded to both their immediate and long-term needs. Thus all societies, including Africans, have had effective philosophical treatises and philosophies of education, complemented by select epistemologies of learning that would have minimally assured their historiographical survival. With the profit-driven programs of colonialism, though, Africans had to deal with imposed systems of learning that have diminished their being and living personhoods and that have imposed on them alien forms of life that assured the needs of the colonizer. For philosophical, epistemological, and by extension, ontological redemptions, therefore, Africans need to re-indigenize not only the contents of their education but their philosophies of education. As I have pointed out, the postcolonial African elite terribly missed this important correction in the life of the African child, and the task is now long overdue. It is by achieving this educational turn, I submit, that Africa could achieve viable and inclusive projects of social well-being in today's selectively interconnected but still socio-developmentally disjunctured world.

REFERENCES

Abdi, A. A. (2002). *Culture, Eeducation and Development in South Africa: Historical and Contemporary Perspectives.* Westport, CT: Bergin & Garvey.

Abdi, A. A. (2006). Culture of education, social development and globalization: Historical and current analyses of Africa. In A. Abdi, K. Puplampu, & G. Dei (Eds.), *African Education and Globalization: Critical Perspectives* (pp. 13–30). Lanham, MD: Rowman & Littlefield.

Abdi, A. A. (2008). Europe and African thought systems and philosophies of education: "Re-culturing" the trans-temporal discourses. *Cultural Studies, 22*(2), 309–327.

Abiola, F. I. (2009). *Francophone African Philosophy: An Introduction.* New York: Routledge.

Achebe, C. (2000). *Home and Exile.* Oxford: Oxford University Press.

Allen, B. (2004). *Knowledge and Civilization.* Boulder, CO: Westview.

Almeder, R. (1992). *Blind Realism: An Essay on Human Knowledge and Natural Science.* Lanham, MD: Rowman & Littlefield.

Bernal, M. (1987/2002). *Black Athena: The Afroasiatic Roots of Civilization* (*Vol. II: The Archaeological and Documentary Evidence*). Toronto: Scholarly Book Services.

Bessis, S. (2003). *Western Supremacy: Triumph of an Idea?* London: Zed.

Bourdieu, P. (1984). *Distinction: A Social Critique of the Judgement of Taste.* Cambridge, MA: Harvard University Press.

Bourdieu, P. & Passerson, J-C. (1990). *Reproduction in Education, Society and Culture.* (R. Nice, Trans.) Thousand Oaks, CA: Sage.

Diop, C. A. (1974). *African Origins of Civilization: Myth or Reality?* Brooklyn, NY: Lawrence Hill.

Diop, C. A. (1987). *Pre-colonial Black Africa: A Comparative Study of the Social and Political Systems of Europe and Black Africa from Antiquity to the Formation of Modern Nation States.* Brooklyn, NY: Lawrence Hill.

Diop, C. A. (1990). *Civilization or Barbarism: An Authentic Anthropology.* Brooklyn, NY: Lawrence Hill.

Eze, E. (Ed.). (1998). *African Philosophy: An Anthology.* Cambridge, MA: Blackwell.

Fanon, F. (1967). *Black Skin, White Masks.* New York: Grove.

Fanon, F. (1968). *The Wretched of the Earth.* New York: Grove.

Fumerton, R. (2006). *Epistemology*. Malden, MA: Blackwell.
Harding, S. (1998). *Is Science Multicultural? Postcolonialisms, Feminisms and Epistemologies*. Bloomington, IN: Indiana University Press.
Harding, S. (2008). *Science from Below: Feminism, Postcolonialities and Modernities*. Durham, NC: Duke University Press.
Hegel, G. W. F. (1965). *La raison dans l'histoire.* Paris: UGE
Jackson, J. (1970). *Introduction to African Civilizations*. Secaucus, NJ: Citadel.
Koch, A. (2002). *Knowledge and Social Construction*. Lanham, MD: Lexington.
Kwapong, A. (1994). Culture, development and democracy: Role of intellectuals in Africa. In S. Soermardjan & K. Thompson (Eds.), *Culture, Development and Democracy* (pp. 145–154). New York: United Nations University.
Longino, H. (2002). *The Fate of Knowledge*. Princeton, NJ: Princeton University Press.
Mann, C. (2006). *1491: New Revelations of the Americas Before Columbus*. New York: Vintage.
Memmi, A. (1991). *The Colonizer and the Colonized*. Boston: Beacon.
Mhina, C. & Abdi, A. A. (2008). Mwalimu's mission: Julius Nyerere as (adult) educator and philosopher of community development. In A. Abdi & D. Kapoor (Eds.), *Global Perspectives on Adult Education* (pp. 55–69). New York: Palgrave Macmillan.
Mhina, C. & Abdi, A.A. (2009). Mwalimu's mission: Julius Nyerere (adult) aducator and philosopher of community development. In A. Abdi & D. Kapoor (Eds.), Global perspectives on adult education. New York: Palgrave.
Mudimbe, V. Y. (1988). *The Invention of Africa: Gnosis, Philosophy and the Order of Knowledge*. Bloomington, IN: Indiana University Press.
Nyerere, J. (1968). *Freedom and Socialism: Selection from Writing and Speeches, 1965–67*. London: Oxford University Press.
Oruka, H. O. (1991). *Sage Philosophy: Indigenous Philosophies and Modern Debate on African Philosophy*. Nairobi: ACTS.
Pliny, The Elder (1982/1856*). Historia Naturalis*. London: Sidgwick & Jackson.
Rodney, W. (1982). *How Europe Underdeveloped Africa*. Washington, DC: Howard University Press.
Said, E. (1993). *Culture and Imperialism*. New York: Vintage.
Semali, L. (1999). Community as classroom: Dilemmas of valuing African indigenous literacy in education. *International Review of Education, 45*(3/4), 305–319.
Serequeberhan, T. (1997). *African Philosophy: The Essential Readings*. Salt Lake City, UT: Paragon.
wa Thiongo, N. (1986). *Decolonising the Mind: The Politics of Language in African Literature*. London: Heinemann.
wa Thiongo, N. (1993). *Moving the Centre: The Struggle for Cultural Freedoms*. London: James Curry.
wa Thiongo, N. (2005). Europhone or African memory: the challenge of the pan Africanist intellectual in the era of globalization. In T. Mkandawire (Ed.), *African Intellectuals: Rethinking Politics, Language, Gender and Development* (pp. 115–164). London: Zed.
Wiredu, K. (1997). *Cultural Universals and Particulars: An African Perspective*. Bloomington, IN: Indiana University Press.

CHAPTER SIX

Space, Time and Unified Knowledge

Following the Path of Vine Deloria, Jr.

JEFFEREY D. ANDERSON

Vine Deloria, Jr. was perhaps the foremost Native American thinker of the twentieth century. In many of his later writings, he looked back on a career in which he had gained some reaction after publication of *Custer Died for Your Sins* (1969), but soon after, as he reflected later in life, he "hit the glass ceiling that minority writers eventually hit when American white intellectuals no longer pay attention to them" (Bender et al., 1998, p. 24). At most, relevant academic disciplines responded to his works on an ad hoc basis, usually only for nominal citation, in defense of their model or discipline, or to take one of his particular calls to action seriously. As Treat points out, Deloria's works on religion drew little attention from theologians (Deloria & Treat, 1999, p. 3), despite his solid background in comparative theology and his primary aim to engage dialogue about religion in *God Is Red* (1994) and *The Metaphysics of Modern Existence* (1979).

Following an ancient academic tradition, his opponents labeled, caricatured, and discarded his work by exaggerating a partial reading and contrasting it to the current, if always transient, state of the art in their disciplines. The book *Red Earth, White Lies* (1995), for example, only attracted the defensive posturing of archeologists united to defend their science as a whole, while disregarding his ultimate concerns. It should be noted that some of the cherished theories about Native American prehistory at the time have since proved to be challengeable and falsifiable in the ways Deloria suggested. Major social theorists have also ignored his work, even though that his critique of the universality and progressiveness of Western epistemologies predates subsequent attempts in various fields at reflexivity, deconstruction, decolonization, and anti-essentialism.

In cultural anthropology, Deloria's call for dialogue has often been cited in contexts of research ethics, but the remainder of his work has been ignored or at most stereotyped. Similarly, a quick review of anthropology's reflexive period finds that none of the major figures in that movement recognized Deloria's or other Native American scholars' views in what was really an exclusively in-house clean-up job. During Deloria's career, mainstream anthropology also moved further away from the older traditions of Sapir, Whorf, Hallowell, Lee, and others who at least aimed at the unifying phenomenological knowledge of Native American metaphysics that he advocated.

Philosophy has also similarly disregarded Deloria and indigenous philosophies in general. Some quick searches of published works in philosophy reveal only several references to Deloria's work over the past forty years. Those few works connecting to Deloria's philosophical thought are about ethics, environmentalism, and human rights, with only rare engagements in metaphysics. Along with other Native American philosophers, he participated in the recent edited volume *American Indian Thought* (Deloria, 2004, p. 3) that seeks to break through the "bastion of white male supremacy" still reigning in philosophy.

Most decolonizing scholars in Native American studies embrace his work in name but only primarily to deploy the political or academic oppositional levels of his work to reify indigenous versus Western differences. Few have embraced the full range and ultimate concerns of his intellectual background and mission. Much more important than political discourse at a national level or academic word-games is the concern for revitalizing indigenous philosophies in local communities that are losing them. Toward that end, Deloria's ultimate concern was not just to identify the deeper divergent metaphysical premises underlying all political, academic, legal, scientific, religious, and moral gaps of understanding and conflicts between Native American and Euro-American peoples but also to find a bridge across the chasm by identifying common as well as contested ground. Defenders of the borders on both sides have tended to prevail, though, over those, like Deloria, seeking a unique dialogue and epistemological pluralism.

My own connection to Deloria's quest for unified knowledge resulted from direct, concrete experience. During 1988–1994 I worked in several jobs and conducted dissertation fieldwork in the Northern Arapaho community on the Wind River Reservation in Wyoming. Every new situation and project posed contradictions surrounding knowledge in a whirlwind of competing claims to authority and validity both within the community and between the reservation and the non-Indian world on the outside. The Arapaho strategy of maintaining consensus in political and ceremonial leadership, well documented by Loretta Fowler (1982) for the period before the 1970s, had given way to factionalism in the cultural and linguistic revitalization programs in which I actively participated. Revitalization efforts in the community tended to simplify and reduce language and culture for educational programs to single or superficial levels in ways dictated by older approaches in academic linguistics and anthropology, such as in the reduction of language through standardization to code and lexicon without concern for pragmatics and semantics. At the same time, none of the anthropological models I had studied were of any use in understanding the contradictions. By the 1990s, anthropology had also joined the wave of postmodern reflexivity by deconstructing and defining as colonial projects all sociocultural totalities and claims to unified knowledge. This one-sided effort, as many realize now, did not make the contradictions go away for Native American communities, but paradoxically may have proliferated them by preserving false binaries of researcher versus native people. That binary and its presumed associated contradictions were such a small part of my experience and concerns while working in the Arapaho community. The contradictions I confronted were not those of the short-term field experience that most anthropologists take home or the academic gaze they then engage in the bounded-off and estranged playground of ideas back at the department. For example, most of the buzz-words, fads, and major issues I encountered when I returned to academia in 1994 I found had nothing to do with praxis in the lived world of Native American communities.

One reliable source for understanding all of this, though, was the work of Vine Deloria, Jr., to which I kept returning. In and of the everyday situational flow of intercultural contact, I saw not just a constructed difference of ways of speaking or values, but the chasm between two different metaphysics that Deloria described, including deeply inculcated orders of time, space, and epistemology. I repeatedly observed and pondered that Deloria's ideas were not just "gratuitous games" with language, as Bourdieu (1990) defines the practice of *Homo academicus*, but that "this stuff really happens" (p. 381). I observed many non-Indian agencies, professionals, and educators distance themselves from local contexts by holding fast to orders of linear time through blind faith in schedules, agendas, and, progress, as well-specialized bureaucratic spaces for particular functions and types of knowledge to be stored and taught. As Deloria realized and as I developed for the Northern Arapaho more fully in *The Four Hills of Life* (2001), such frames of space-time and knowledge exclude more knowledge than they include and combine to move understanding in the opposite direction from unified knowledge.

In the Arapaho community, I also observed that the challenges of cultural revitalization are huge and require unified knowledge. For one thing, many folks live in collective denial about the rate and extent of culture loss. While more—but still too little—attention has been paid to language loss, much less has been expended on the issue of loss of metaphysics, ethics, and epistemologies. In my experience, many efforts at local cultural education were either framed in terms of generic pan-Indian precepts or were empty scattered, disconnected, and even often random in orientation. Many projects had little connection to specifically Arapaho ultimate concerns, though elders and others often discussed the need to make those connections. As Deloria notes (2004), "The task today is that of intensive research and study to enable people to project what the various tribal peoples probably meant when they described the world around them" (pp. 4–5). Revitalization efforts are fraught with the politics of knowledge in the fray of competing and often conflictual claims to expertise, credentials, and identity to engage in such research. Both Indian and non-Indian researchers readily meet with controversy with each new project or publication, whether from native communities, academic institutions, or both at the same time.

To some extent, native communities have embraced reified models of language and culture from imposed anthropological or other social scientific paradigms that are no longer even accepted in the academic world but persist as "survivals" of a former stage of intellectual history. In short, renewal efforts typically reduce culture or language to a standardized object in which multiple views are often eschewed for a single, abstracted one. Out of this a neotraditional purism develops, which, as Deloria (2004) recognized, "Here the idea of philosophy certainly derives from the popular American notion that if a person has certainly staunchly held opinions he or she has a 'philosophy'" (p. 5). One's efforts, as a result, are preoccupied with defending small factual points, debunking counter-philosophies, or even struggling to be heard. In both indigenous communities and academic contexts, discourse must appropriate Western dialectical strategies and thus move away from unified knowledge toward factional enclaves in which dialogue across boundaries of culture, disciplines, indigenous nations, and communities is precluded. The research Deloria (2004) proposed requires a commitment to the view "that there is something of value in any tribal tradition that transcends mere belief and pride" (p. 5).

Most ignored of all has been Deloria's ultimate concern for unified knowledge, which pervades his myriad works spanning four decades, from the earlier *God Is Red* and *Metaphysics of Modern Existence* to the posthumously published *C. G. Jung and the Sioux Tradition*. This concern is critical, he believed, to healing native communities, the earth, and the human species. Unified knowledge will, he firmly believed, overcome the exile for native peoples from tradition, as well as the alienation of the modern non-Indian world from nature, spirituality, and the majority of non-Western peoples.

Needed, then, with cultural revitalization in indigenous communities is a move toward collective healing. Culture and language loss are intricately overdetermined by connections to human loss, both for individuals and peoples as wholes. In my own extensive research in the Northern Arapaho community, all oral historical, ethnographic, and even linguistic interviews evoked from elders memorializing pauses for ancestors now passed, tragic experiences in hard times, and the loss of cultural knowledge they had seen in their lifetimes. Ironically, the depth of those moments does not end up in the published or recorded works.

Unified knowledge is consistent with, but often ignored by, new culturally relevant psychotherapeutic approaches that aim toward healing "historical trauma" experienced by many oppressed groups or the "soul wound," as it is called, in Native American contexts. The movement toward what Duran (2006) calls "liberation psychology" realizes the necessity or enormity of recovering unified knowledge in native communities (pp. 13–15). Hybridized ethno-therapeutic approaches could follow paths set by Deloria's work, such as his final major work (Deloria, Deloria, & Bernstein, 2009) on convergences and divergences between Jung's psychoanalytic theories and Lakota metaphysics with the ultimate concern of moving toward deeper collective healing and reconciliation. To achieve holistic remediation, Deloria advocated a (re)unification of knowledge and expansion of modes of experiences beyond those differentiated in established Western epistemologies. Revision of the canon meant for him more than just adding Native American content to the prevailing disciplines, appending a new cultural studies program to the curriculum, or waging a full-scale decolonizing ruthless attack on all mainstream ideas, often ironically using the conceptual weapons inherited from Western critical theories. Rather, Deloria imagined a genuine intertribal, intercultural, and interdisciplinary inquiry that draws on Western and indigenous pathways toward understanding the unifying reality underlying all existence.

While unified knowledge requires metaphysical inquiry in all the mainstreams of contemporary disciplines, metaphysics today is commonly a mystified or even taboo subject. For one thing, the shift over the long duration toward reductionism in natural and social sciences precludes unification. More recently, too, metaphysical discourse has been preempted by a ruthless postmodern critique of any proposed cultural or social totality or unity, based on the presumption that any total system must be constructed by a Western colonial gaze. Totalities, including those that indigenous peoples have maintained for centuries, are thus framed as imagined, ahistorical, constructed, or essentialist. There is a great publishing industry now devoted to debunking indigenous cultures as fabricated for political, economic, or other base human ends. To semantically redirect Benedict Anderson's concept (1991), if only academic disciplines themselves would realize that they, too, are "imagined communities," not actual territories anchored to some empirical ground of the things themselves.

All of the relations Deloria drew upon from a vast landscape of intellectual fields were so broadly interdisciplinary as to resist the accepted discursive borderlines between disciplines, denominations, sciences, and philosophies. He followed paths toward unified knowledge set by Western thinkers as far afield as Cassirer, Tillich, Barbour, Lévi-Strauss, Jung, Heisenberg, Feyerabend, and many others, including a good number of obscure or marginal thinkers with no seats in the halls of any discipline. Following indigenous rather than Western dialectical paths of critical inquiry, which in the mainstream stay in the boundaries of the leisurely life of the *shkolè* and confine thought to the Socratic-Hegelian continuum of dialectical reasoning (Bourdieu, 1990), Deloria's works aimed to unify knowledge that has been sliced up by pernicious, dead-end dichotomies and dialectics of modern thought, including Western versus Native American world views, religion versus science, time versus space, abstract versus primary experience, *kairos* versus *chronos*, history versus nature, objective versus subjective, and metaphysics versus experience.

Throughout Deloria's work, foremost among barriers to unification is that Euro-American epistemologies have relegated indigenous ways of thinking to an external, diminutive, or "Other" category. Native American culture is a resource to be tapped as needed for data in turn as a means to assumed larger aims of theory or hypothesis testing. Historically, indigenous knowledge systems have been confined to "conceptual reservations" as primitive, mythological, prelogical, and closed systems of thinking, that is, as nonscientific views regarded at most as confused systems of classification, a logical mode of reasoning but with a closed set of unscientific premises, or an intuitive, even "mystical" awareness as an alternative to Western rationality. In anthropology, other social sciences, and the humanities, Native American knowledge is often only an object of research, analysis, and even critical inquiry but rarely recognized as epistemologies to be placed on the shelf of prevailing paradigms or theoretical orientations. The truth-value of indigenous epistemologies is always already bracketed as a non-question by partitioning them as constructed for social, cognitive, psycho-emotional, symbolic, or practical functionality.

To even suggest that one could adopt Hopi metaphysics to understand the world economic system or a Lakota model to understand the human psyche appears absurd and unthinkable to a "serious" academic mind. The typical, reasonable Western mind will respond that such epistemologies are not to be included because they are nonempirical, that is, based on nonfalsifiable premises. Yet, many nonempirical remnants of Western intellectual history are still embraced even though they have long proved to be quite outlandish in empirical terms. Deloria challenged some of these, but many more remain to be exposed. Metaphysical realities are simply embraced without question, such as constructs of history, nature, being, and causality. Most disciplines claim to be sciences because their epistemologies rest on Popper's (1959) principle of falsifiability, but rights to engage in falsification and critique can be claimed by only those initiated to their respective cloisters. Throughout his works, Deloria called upon modern defenders of science to consider that Popper's distinction between falsifiable and nonfalsifiable knowledge does not simply correlate with science and religion as a fixed and universal binary. There are scientists who hold fast to their models, individually or collectively, even when the evidence should have falsified them long ago. Conversely, religious experience, at least in Native American contexts, draws on immediate experience and can actually be open to new knowledge and views.

Another barrier to metaphysical inquiry is the tendency in Western minds to elevate all varieties of metaphysics on a vertical axis. To a Western orientation that reifies ultimate realities in complex, abstract, or transcendental terms, metaphysics takes on spatially vertical otherness, usually in the metaphorical sense of being "above" or "beyond" experienced reality. As such, metaphysics is either in one extreme eschewed by empirically minded thinkers as nonsense or, on the other, mystified by Western alienated consciousnesses in search of unified knowledge through "alternative" experiences that actually, without groundedness, dissipate into a mystical cloud. From deep in Western history extending back to classical roots, metaphysics is also commonly framed as the most extreme form of privilege or *skholé*, a term Bourdieu (1990, p. 381) follows to its etymological connection with "school," as "an institutionalized situation of studious leisure," as in Plato's tradition of *spoudaios paizein*, "to play seriously." Unified knowledge is thus, in Western frames, accessible only to elite minds freed from the immediate, practical concerns of everyday life. In short, one must be freed in the Platonic sense from the majority of actual experiences, such as emotions, appetites, dreams, and so forth to engage only rational thought and draw from an intellectual heritage rooted in Greece, biblical tradition, and European thought. If we remove this vertical placement, uproot the classical biases, and cast aside "frightening" notions, Deloria (1979, p. 12) suggests we can consider metaphysics, as Ian Barbour concretely defined it, as quite simply "the search for a coherent set of categories for the interpretation of experience" (p. 12).

Toward this aim, the first and perhaps deepest chasm Deloria (1994) identifies between indigenous and Western metaphysics is that between space and time, or nature and history, respectively:

> When one group is concerned with the philosophical problem of space and the other with the philosophical problem of time then the statements of either group do not make much sense when transferred from one context to the other without proper consideration of what is taking place (p. 63).

The locus of all Native American unified knowledge was and is the land. Space as concrete landscape, as opposed to an abstract projection or extension of space, Deloria and Treat (1999) observe, "has the ability to short-circuit logical processes; it enables us to apprehend underlying unities we did not suspect" (p. 251). Such a connection to the land of North America is rare for non-Indians because they have not resided on it long enough and in that short time modified colonized space to serve an image of progress in time. As such, too, Euro-Americans have imposed invasive time-oriented epistemologies on the land: "Thousands of years of occupancy on their lands taught tribal peoples the sacred landscapes for which they were responsible and gradually the structure of the ceremonial reality became clear. It was not what people believed to be true that was important but what they experienced as true" (Deloria, 1994, p. 67).

Almost all Native American varieties of metaphysics are grounded in sacred places of various types. Many cultures retain one or multiple sacred centers of the cosmos that orient all space and time. In many Native American ceremonies, orientation to the four directions, zenith, nadir, and center is the first and repeated action. As such, the locus for unified knowledge is placed outside the individual ego but yet accessible to the focused, collective consciousness. In ceremonies and everyday experience there is a strong emphasis on all thoughts focusing on one ritually or mythically centered point or thing, which is also usually the axis mundi along which humans can communicate with other levels of reality. A sacred center can be below in some cases or above in others, often serving as central gathering for all types of being and nexus of many types of knowledge. The axis is variously the pathway for shamanic journeys, point of emergence of humans from below to this earth, the nodule of earth's creation, and a center from which life is generated in myriad forms. While Western religions often have sacred places, Deloria (1994) recognizes, they "are appreciated primarily for their historical significance and do not provide the sense of permanency and rootedness that the Indian sacred places represent" (p. 67).

Deloria argues that most non-Indian deep engagements of the land, as well as a good number of contemporary Indian ones, are limited to reflective experience, but that to native peoples such sites may offer the most profound sort of revelatory experiences for select individuals in tribal communities. Reflective experiences are actively sought and offer a sense of self-world integration and associated ecstatic state. Revelation, Deloria distinguishes, is an experience of a powerful force in a place, which is not univocally positive. Such power can actually keep medicine men and women away most of the time, because of the sheer *mysterium tremendum* of dread and foreboding engendered. Approached correctly, a sacred space can offer life and clarity, but if approached incorrectly, the results can be negative. To generate life itself as motion, growth, and health, sacred places are essential to Native American religions. Through sacred practitioners' sacrifices, offerings, gifts, and petitions at sacred places, relations to all other existences and the life-force they share can be achieved. Deloria (2006) describes the underlying force:

> We can begin with the recognition that the fundamental reality in our physical world is a strange kind of energy that is found within everything—from stars to humans to stones to quantum energy fields. This energy is personal—or can be experienced personally. It is mysterious, and so potent and varied that it is useless to explore all the possible ways to define it. If we say anything about this power or energy, we say that the world we live in, sustained by this power, is ultimately spiritual and not physical. Here we have the opportunity to unite psychology and religion with the energy fields of quantum physics (p. 184).

In Lakota, this force is *wakan,* in Algonquian languages *manitu,* and to the Iroquois *orenda.* Deloria posits the reality of life-force beyond the Newtonian world of matter and space-time absolutes, which circumscribes narrowly empirical Western views and even folk ideologies.

The knowledge acquired in sacred places, Deloria (2006) refers to as the "mind-stuff" of existence, meaning "an energetic mind undergirding the physical world, its motions, and that provided energy and life in everything that existed" (p. 197). Contact with such mind-stuff was carefully reserved for those who had been prepared for ceremonies, sacrifices, or vision experiences, which were in turn needed to generate life, return the cosmos to balance, or avert crisis. To demonstrate the reality of this phenomenon, Deloria (2006) finds convergence toward this Native American knowledge in "a reasonable number of Western scientists and thinkers who subscribe to the idea that the ultimate constituent of the universe is mind, or mind-stuff." Exploring this bridge between Native American and Western knowledge, he discovers connections in Plato's forms, Jung's concept of psychic energy, the wave-particle of quantum physics, warping of space and time in Einstein's theory of relativity, the life-energy-knowledge carried in DNA, and many others (Deloria, 2006, pp. 195–197).

In most Western views, though, such convergence is ignored. Native American concepts of power and mind-stuff are most often reduced to functionality in the individual or collective mind. Following William James' (1936) call for suspending existential judgment about religious metaphysics and turning to its value in pragmatic terms informs almost all social scientific levels of inquiry. The individual or collective human psyche is posited as the generative source and beneficiary of its own creations or imaginings. As such, scientific approaches reserve epistemological sovereignty over access to subjective or objective things-in-themselves with ontological status out there in the world, while religious knowledge is reduced to "useful fictions."

The foremost barrier to unified knowledge in Deloria's view is the turn in Western metaphysics toward time as the ultimate concern and away from space. Combining influences of Christian and Greek linearity, Western thought invests intellectual capital in history as various forms of *telos* that require belief or faith in the actual occurrence of past events as moments of *kairos,* a time of miracles, revelation, and prophecy foretold or realized, breaking out of the linear normal time of *chronos* and changing the course of future events:

> Christian theology has made a fetish of distinguishing between two modes of time, traditional characterized as *kairos,* the fullness of time when qualitative experiences are present and *chronos,* the mathematical time of clocks, seasons, and sequences....Apart from revelation, Christian theologians would argue, our species is trapped within a chronology that makes little sense and is ultimately demonic (Deloria, 1979, p. 25).

Western knowledge systems, both religious and scientific, in turn universalize the temporal significance of revelatory events:

> In the western tradition, revelation has generally been interpreted as the communication to human beings of a divine plan, the release of new information and insights when the deity has perceived that mankind has reached the fullness of time [*kairos*] and can now understand additional information about the nature of our world. Thus, what has been the manifestation of deity in a particular local situation is mistaken for the truth applicable to all times and places (Deloria, 1994, p. 66).

In Native American religions, ceremonies, myth, and other sacred forms engender fullness of time through relations among all diverse beings and persons who are called to participate in the event and contribute their knowledge. Lakotas refer to this connectivity as *mitakuye oyasin*, "all my relations." In the Western logic of *kairos*, a newfound truth from a turning point event carries with it the ultimate concern to universalize that truth as the set course of history, compelling believers to convert all humans to the truth revealed and transform all local space for that higher purpose. Past *kairos* thus becomes a future-oriented *telos*, a move toward universal actualization of the discovered truth in all space and time beyond and detached from the context of its realization.

Simultaneously, modern Western time appropriates control of *chronos* as a powerful organizer of work, thought, and human relations through the standardized, abstract time objectified in the clock and calendar (see Thompson, 1967). Only in hierarchical societies is time used as mode of domination, which thus becomes a "demonic" or dreadful reality to escape. There is thus a great binary tension between time as meaningful and as meaningless in Western metaphysics, which was only intensified by the secularizing shift in authority over time from church to economic institutions beginning in the Middle Ages (see LeGoff, 1982). Time with the Industrial Revolution became a mechanism of unprecedented power for unifying and dividing people, knowledge, and space. In experience, time became abstract and scarce, a form of labor to be sold, a flux beyond individual control, and a wedge for estrangement from the local concrete realities of life, nature, and actual human relationships. The effects on Native peoples were often profound, as Deloria and Treat explain (1999):

> Not only did their geographic confinement work to destroy the sacred calendars of tribes, but the effort to perpetuate traditional life within the confines of the reservation was vulnerable to overtures by the federal government, seeking to make the people abandon old ways and adopt new practices which were carefully orchestrated by a new sense of time—a measured time which had little to do with cosmic realities. It is debatable which factor was most important in the destruction of tribal ceremonial life: the prohibition of performances of traditional rituals by the government, or the introduction of white man's system of keeping time (p. 246).

Modern measured time is a wholly artificial construction removed from what in anthropology has been defined as "ecological time" (Evans-Pritchard, 1940), a type of time in which human activities are correlated to actual changes in space. In Native American contexts, it involved not just astronomical observation and changes in weather, but also close observations of many plants and animals, changes in the land itself, and the rhythms of life within the camp itself. Camp movements, plantings, ceremonies, war parties, gathering, fishing, and many more social and subsistence activities were scheduled with these changes. Time in this way unified human knowledge with animals, plants, and celestial beings. In this sort of existence, chronology was not considered demonic and time was not scarce and harsh. As Deloria and Treat (1999) relate:

> The old traditional Indians were in tune with the rhythms of life. They were accustomed to bringing in and relating the whole picture of the land, the plants, and the animals around them. They responded to things as a part of a larger whole which was a subjective reality to them. We could say the traditional Indian stood in the center of a circle and brought everything together in that circle. Today we stand at the end of a line and work our way along that line, discarding or avoiding everything on either side (p. 275).

Modern Western orders of time alienate individuals and groups from the actual experienced flow of time. Just as space becomes a Euclidean abstract extension, time becomes a reified machine with power over everything, and thus ideologies proliferated to try to connect isolated individuals trapped in *chronos* to larger missions and quests in the unfolding of history. However, the wedge is ever obdurate, and thus the fullness of time can never be achieved in the present. Deloria and Treat (1999) observe the profound truth of this moving contradiction for native peoples:

> Unless time is understood as sacred, experienced in all its fullness, and so dominant a consideration in the life of a people that all other functions are subservient to it, it is impossible to have a complete and meaningful ceremonial life. Rituals lose their efficacy because they are performed within a secular time which does not always make room for them or give them the status they deserve. They soon take on the aspect of mechanical adjustments made to solve problems which occur within that kind of time. Forced adaptation to secular mathematically measured time has produced a fundamental sense of alienation (p. 247).

Through modernization, time also becomes a trajectory against which to measure indigenous and other subaltern individuals and groups in terms of the degree to which they are out of sync, behind in development, anachronistic, and resistant to progress. Superiority of knowledge in science, fashion, economic development, politics, and perhaps all other modes of knowledge is measured by individuals' or groups' position relative to the edge of present currency. As Fabian (1983) recognized, tribal peoples were and are denied coevalness with the dominant group and thus placed in an "Other" time. Conversely, the highest form of Western conscious is synchronized with current knowledge, whether in science, fashion, or news. To be coeval in the movement of one's thought, research, reading, or discourse with current knowledge is to be modern, well-informed, cosmopolitan, and intellectually grounded. Currency is the measure of intellect, merit, utility, and moral value. Much of that knowledge in the bubble of current interest is ironically transient and unrelated to ultimate concerns or a fullness of time, though it often poses as such in the passing moment of attention to it.

Rather than unifying reality, the movement of linear time has been used to alienate individuals and divide groups into intelligent and slow, saved and unsaved, believer and heathen, developed and undeveloped, and civilized and primitive, thus excluding most of the world's people and their knowledge from history and thus metaphysical interest. This division, often buttressed by the so-called great thinkers of Europe and America, was the foundation for the Doctrine of Discovery, Providence, Manifest Destiny, and Progress, all which were used to justify conquest, environmental transformation, forced assimilation, war, and almost all major cataclysmic events in Western history over the past six centuries or more. Deloria (1994) contrasts this dependency on a utopian future as the ultimate concern to that of indigenous ethics, in which "there is little dependence on the concept of progress either on an individual or community basis as a means of evaluating the impact of religious practices" (p. 68).

Anything or anyone not coeval with history in motion must thus be converted, saved, assimilated, developed, or improved. This principle has been the most powerful and destructive force in Western history of colonization, and, as Deloria notes, has transmuted into many other universalizing doctrines that are not obviously religious or explicitly tied to the original Doctrine of Discovery. These include progressive and conservative ideologies alike that aim to universalize a brotherhood of humankind, global democracy, capitalism, scientific thinking, and sundry other world improvement projects. At the same time, Western knowledge systems generate a multiplicity of doctrines or models that futilely and at times violently compete with one other to become universal in space and time. They also require that individuals and groups sever their religious connections to local space and time. For the individual or group to develop along the path of history, he or she must be isolated from inferior parochial sources of knowledge residing in family, village, and even nation.

To accomplish the separation of experience, a complementary order to history evolved to compartmentalize and thus divide knowledge through the temporalization of space. Access to knowledge was distributed among what Giddens (1984) calls "time-space zones" such that knowledge and its acquisition are divided up into compartments within bureaucracies, factories, and schools. Western epistemologies came to parallel this same order and believe in the reified boundaries between fields or subfields. Widely dispersed zones become increasingly integrated by the authority of time rather than space. Schedules, clocks, calendars, and so forth dictate when one engages in particular knowledge forms. When one leaves one zone to enter another at the appointed time, then connection to that knowledge must be replaced with another. Students, workers, researchers, and scholars thus acquire, process, and critically assess knowledge in their specialized domains without the need for any unified knowledge of the entire system, which looms large and powerful in distanciated massive forms and authorities (e.g., libraries, databases, and archives). These forms and access to them increasingly become commodities that knowers must purchase with money, whether as books, tuition, or online databases. While Western society boasts of its massive accumulation of knowledge, few if any knowers can grasp it all as a unified system.

While Western metaphysics have moved away from them, microcosmic models once prevailed in Native American metaphysics and knowledge systems. Namely, among many if not most Native American religions, unifying knowledge was based on a similar form, shape, or structure for ordering space, time, or both dimensions interdependently on all levels from the very smallest particle to the cosmos at large and from the micro-level to the epochal level of time. Microcosmic thought may even be a universal rubric for unifying knowledge, since hundreds of examples are found throughout the world, but in each culture and era it takes on a unique emphasis and function. As discussed above, a majority of Native American cosmologies recognize the same order to space and time through the four or seven directional and phased model. Domestic space, artistic design, ritual action, territory, and cosmos on the spatial side are often oriented to the four cardinal directions, with zenith, nadir, and center often added for a total of seven. Time is homologously oriented on multiple levels, including stages of ritual action, the seasonal cycle, the life trajectory, and epochs of cosmic history are also often phased according to the same four- or seven-part model. Temporal phasing was thus grounded in the same order as for space, such as the four- or seven-directional model that was also applied to quotidian, seasonal, life cyclical, and epochal levels of time. These are also often overlain with other levels of significance, such as colors, animals, sacred beings, and forces. Such homologous orders allow for ritually activated interconnectivity of all levels of reality, forms of being, and underlying forces.

In an obscure but remarkably rich work, George P. Conger (1967) traces the intellectual history of microcosmic theory in Western theology, philosophy, and science from the pre-Socratics to early nineteenth-century thinkers. He concludes that

> The philosophies apparently most favorable to microcosmic theories have been, in chronological order, hylozoism, Pythagoreanism, probably Stoicism, the work of Philo, Neo-Platonism, the medieval Jewish philosophy and the *Encyclopedia* of the Arabian Brethren of Sincerity, the work of Paracelsus, Boehme, Leibnitz, Schelling, Schleiermacher, Schopenhauer, Fechner, and the absolute idealists (Conger, 1967, p. 134).

While implicit or mentioned occasionally, Greek and Christian roots of microcosmic thinking are not clearly discernible. I agree with his assessment that later scholarship tends to exaggerate microcosmic thinking in early Greek and Christian modes of thought, which, among all cultures in the world perhaps, Conger adds, set the course for the movement away from it. Early examples of systemic microcosmic thinking tend to be more closely associated with Babylonian, Judaic, and Islamic influences, such as the effort of Philo of Alexandria to synthesize Greek philosophy and Judaism. Western microcosmic theories that do appear tend to privilege the human body, mind, or soul as the primary nexus interconnecting God, nature, the cosmos, and celestial bodies. Most examples situate humans on a Chain of Being between animals and God or a universal form. In general, they tend to be organismic, anthropocentric, and hierarchical, as well as limited in inclusiveness to only one or several dimensions of space and time.

Throughout much of Western colonial history, the central microcosmic order for ontological distinctions has been a scaled order epitomized by the Great Chain with God at the top followed by angels, humans, animals, plants, and minerals in descending order. Borrowing from Plato, Plotinus, and Aquinas in turn, the Great Chain of Being ranked types of being vertically from the most perfect, rational, and immutable at the top to the least perfect, least sentient, and most changeable at the bottom. Vestiges of ranked orders of this sort still persist in secularized forms today, mostly in subtle and less obvious variations.

Conger also identifies the sources of the modern trend away from microcosmic theory and unified knowledge, which was one of his ultimate concerns. On both points his work anticipates the ideas of theologians like Barbour and Tillich, from which Deloria himself borrows much direction. Unified space-time theories in Western thought have themselves become particularized as metaphorical (Lakoff & Johnson, 1980), mythological (Cassirer, 1953), or mathematically based, as in unified field theory in physics or fractal theory in mathematics. Conger suggests that the turn to the dominance of empiricism and humanism eliminated microcosmic theorizing from mainstream Western thought. In general, modern Western theories have estranged non-Western and all non-scientific variations of microcosm for unifying knowledge, including indigenous ones, as outside of empirical sensory experience and thus invalid. In various theories of mythical and magical thought since the nineteenth century, indigenous microcosm-macrocosm connections have been interpreted in sundry ways as confused primitive thinking, whether as prelogical thinking for Lévy-Bruhl, an expression of the disease of language for Max Müller, or a sense of the childish "omnipotence of thoughts" to Freud. Theorists who have come to respect such microcosmic systems in the history of religions, anthropology, and other social scientific orientations commonly propose that the underlying truth resides not in empirical or rational experience, but in an "Other" kind of objectivity. The epitome of this approach is Cassirer's (1953) work on mythical thought, which embraces the Kantian notion of "objectivization," according to which homology and other features of space and time are regarded as given a priori in an intuitive type of experience.

Retaining the same binary of us versus them, most modern philosophical and social scientific approaches to time and space recognize "Other" systems as extensions or constructions, borrowing in all instances the concept of pure reason from Kant, Guyer, & Wood (1998):

We can accordingly speak of space, extended beings, and so on, only from a human standpoint. If we depart from the subjective condition under which alone we can acquire outer intuition, namely that through which we may be affected by objects, then the representation of space signifies nothing at all (pp. 159–160).

More precisely, Kant, Guyer, & Wood posited the transcendental ego as the unifying locus of knowledge and reality, including space and time. Time and space, they note, are expressions of our uniquely human intuition. Any ground for space and time in concrete realities, such as land in Native American metaphysics, gives way to a generative source in human consciousness.

Kant's thought is at the center of Western knowledge about time and space and persists through many subsequent lines of academic thought that view all forms of metaphysics as human constructions and thus relative in history and culture. Time and space are human constructions and the individual or collective consciousness is at the center of it all. Different disciplines have in turn placed different boundaries on human consciousness. Philosophy and psychology generally turned to the individual, while anthropology and sociology turned to collective consciousness.

As Deloria and Treat (1999) note accompanying modern philosophy's turn to reason and empirical knowledge, the "generic" rather than actual individual became the locus of all knowledge in its legal, political, moral, religious, and scientific contexts (p. 186). This idea reigns despite the very basic fact, he continues, that "we never find the individual as a solitary being." Through the equivocation of consciousness as human, Western epistemologies and pedagogies presume, as George Tinker (2004) writes, that "a highly developed neocortical human brain is somehow the ultimate achievement in terms of consciousness" (p. 112). Human consciousness is held as the standard for all consciousnesses and, in the spirit of the scale of being, among humans the Western, formally educated consciousness is exalted as the ideal of perfectibility for the whole species. As such, myriad other forms of consciousness are degraded, excluded, or submitted to mechanisms of improvement.

Native American microcosmic systems by and large have different dimensions and purposes. The human body, mind, or the soul is not the locus for moral, aesthetic, and epistemological unifications of knowledge. The aim is not to unify human with universal levels of space-time to understand the former in either religious or humanistic terms. Rather, the land itself is typically the focal level for space and time in indigenous metaphysics. It is the geometer of all levels of space and the chronometer for all levels of time.

Conversely, with the center of consciousness situated in human consciousness, Western thought can elevate time and space to abstractions that preclude unity. The tendency is to see unified systems as abstract rather than concrete in this sense, such that the task of unified theories, as for example in physics today, takes on the highest level of abstraction through mathematics. By contrast, Conger (1967) notes that in past Western philosophies favorable toward microcosmic theories, "the tendency is toward concrete, as distinguished from abstract speculation" (p. 134). Paradoxically, the more Western knowledge systems become specialized and presume to access empirical unities, the more abstract their models and language become, at least to the degree that actual space-time no longer presides and the major portion of the range of direct experience and thought are set aside.

As Deloria and Treat (1999) argued, Western abstractions of time and personhood have found their way into contemporary Native American religious improvisations as a deteriorative force that works against unified knowledge, while ostensibly moving toward it. This is especially salient in New Age and Pan-Indian religious forms that regard the function of revelation as solely for self-world integration and treat microcosmic forms as abstract, universal, and even mystical entities in themselves. (Deloria & Treat, 1999, p. 177) cites the example of Lakota "Red Road" traditions, such as the four directions and "medicine wheel" philosophy in the work of Hyemeyohsts Storm (1972, p. 263). In many contemporary indigenous religious variations, the sacredness attributed to forms in themselves, such as the "circle" or "medicine wheel," simplifies the more complex geometry of traditional microcosmic systems in which there were many more other meanings, shapes, and dimensions involved. This dilution of microcosmic forms is akin to the simple dimensionality of Euclidean geometry, but forms in traditional local contexts were and are comparable to non-Euclidean space that involves shapes of space beyond three dimensions. Deloria concurs with Cassirer on this distinction: "The primitive easily comprehends the places of his or her experience, but he or she does not abstract from them a scheme of space in a Euclidean or Newtonian sense" (quoted in Deloria, 1979, p. 158). The primitive person is thus in direct immediate relationship with his or her environment but fails to extend abstract principles continuously to conceive of "endless" dimensional existence. Locally situated microcosmic theories, rather, are involuted with a rich, dense field of local knowledge. Cassirer (1953) adds that the difference between mythical and mathematical thought is that, in the latter, the "space of perception, the space of vision and touch, does not coincide with the space of pure mathematics" and that the latter requires "*negation* of what seems immediately given in sensory perception" (p. 83). Mythical thought is analogous in form to pure mathematics but diverges greatly in content, though Western thought tends to attribute greater truth and experiential content to the latter. In mythical space, Cassirer proceeds, each element retains content accessible to perception in the form of accent, tonality, motion, and feeling. In short, mythical space is a concrete product of consciousness, not something simply accessible in and through abstracted forms.

Thus, projection of indigenous microcosmic space-time as geometric is the map but not the territory. The one-to-one association of forms with experientially circumscribed abstract meanings "misplaces concreteness," to use a phrase Deloria borrows often from Whitehead. To assert that a shape, such as a circle, or a color, such as red for a particular direction on a medicine wheel, means this or that, is only a thin level of meaning. Within the struggle to preserve or renew indigenous unified knowledge systems is the need to retain well-placed concreteness in the primary experiential ground to which they have been anchored for perhaps millennia, rather than removing them to circulate freely in any and all spaces and times.

Native American orders of space-time and knowledge must be situated in actual locations. Accordingly, another profound difference to be resolved is that while some Western epistemologies can accept relativism with respect to history and culture, very few readily move toward the type of epistemological pluralism that pervades Native American religions. Deloria and Treat (1999) explicate this unique side of indigenous knowledge:

> Tribal peoples, on the whole, have a very tolerant attitude for other religious traditions, for other peoples, and for the rest of creation. This attitude is based upon the recognition of our limitations and acceptance that many things cannot be explained under any conditions that satisfy us. There is great mystery to the world and our most hopeful sign is that we can come to understand the environment in which we live and the creatures that live with us. Here the tribal concept of revelation is very helpful. A sacred experience always has a specific content and a direct focus to it (p. 158).

The Western ontological stance juxtaposes an individual or collective self to a total entity, whether God, nature, society, the human species, or even a reflection of the self writ large. Once some new knowledge is acquired, it is thus generalized to an entire field of relevance and situated as a break from all past history. The uniqueness of the particular becomes then a universal and eternal truth to be shared with all humankind in the name of progress. But, multiple Western knowledge systems all following this same course, invariably collide with each other in their universalizing efforts, thus often further legitimating their causes. Accordingly, to situate knowledge in and of a local place and time is judged parochial and thus anachronistic. Particularity is to be expunged because it defies the principles of "objectivity, impartiality, and fairness" that Deloria and Treat (1999) argue is the Western big three in the "world of systems" (p. 177). Modern Western epistemologies claim superiority over folk knowledge by virtue of excluding types of experience considered "idols of the mind," to borrow Bacon's terms, that are always already defined as nonobjective, biased, and unfair because they are of limited scope in space and out of sync with current knowledge. To be modern, cosmopolitan, and objective one must adopt a transcendent gaze that hovers above reality but not in it and synchronize one's consciousness with the current state history in motion. In my own fieldwork I tried to sustain this "floating" gaze for the first year or so, because I thought avoiding attachment to one group, organization, area, or community would help me preserve an impartial, objective view of things. As I learned, both from Arapaho people who told me this and from direct experience, one needs a "place" from which to know anything or get anything done. The floating White man's gaze actually produces the most distorted knowledge of all in native communities. Attachment to family, place, and community engages relations for the exchange of knowledge.

Following the relational principle of Native American religions, epistemological pluralism extends to beings other than humans and the types of knowledge such beings can offer human beings. Contrary to the Great Chain scheme of existence, all species and individual members of them were created uniquely, as Shooter (Lakota) states, "because each is placed here by Wakan Tanka to be an independent individuality and to rely upon itself" (quoted in Deloria, 1994, p. 89). In prayers, seasonal ceremonies, curing, sweating, rites of passage, songs, and all other forms of medicine for generating life, all beings, both sacred and natural, must be called to the occasion, not just symbolically, but to represent, participate, and contribute their various types of knowledge. Different knowledge systems at all levels from the individual to the collectivity and even species level have identities and "places" of their own defined by geography, experience, and unique time-frames. Native American mythology is replete with stories emphasizing that the transfer of knowledge from one species, people, or place to another requires carefully circumscribed boundaries, ceremonial exchange, and ritual controls. Each type of knowledge and associated being must be respected. Distinguishing it from simple relativism in which "anything goes" or "no unity is ever possible," Deloria recognizes epistemological pluralism as a type of pragmatism that defines boundaries beyond which one should not extend one's own knowledge. Deloria (2004) notes that in Black Elk's famous vision, "he saw many peoples, each having their own circle in which they lived" (p. 9). Each person, family, band, nation, gender, age group, species, and sacred being can have its own knowledge, which may be irrelevant or even dangerous to others not in the right frame of reference. In turn, to know, learn, and act in indigenous communities, one must have a "place."

In the traditional Arapaho life cycle, (see Anderson, 2001) there was a type of knowledge, mode of personhood, and way of communicating that, as elders explained to me, that was right for each stage of life, though it was not that one stage was superior to all others. Children have knowledge that is right for them, and others for their stages. In speaking in public, the late Pius Moss once explained, one must be careful to put one's words in the right place, meaning that one must put the right boundaries on one's statements. As among other indigenous nations, one must frame reported knowledge by clarifying, "This is how Arapahos see it," or if it is personal knowledge, one gives the background about how one acquired that knowledge. Before telling a story, for instance, one must explain how one acquired it. Many Native American languages have obligatory validity forms and aspectual markers in grammar, as well discourse routines in practice, to situate knowledge one is conveying in space, time, and type of experience. The shift from native ways of speaking to English forms, though, is in many communities weakening the requirements of situating knowledge upon which epistemological pluralism rests. As Arapaho elders repeated many times, you can just say anything you want in English, but in Arapaho you have to be careful. In many contexts, the attenuation of epistemological pluralism and the requirements to locate one's knowledge in places have created much confusion and distortion that stands in the way of unified knowledge. Knowledge once confined to one indigenous people or even one family is often extended to other peoples or families as a much broader truth that it was originally. As discussed above, this often happens through standardization and cultural pluralism that accompanies cultural revitalization efforts.

Also related to pluralism, is the unique indigenous dialectic in which it is always possible to imagine "another way of looking at anything." One must always be aware of these other ways of seeing in order to avoid danger or to take advantage of blessings. Nonetheless, because of the mystery that always lies beyond the boundaries of one's knowledge, it is not always possible to do so. This dialectical parallax pervades ancient trickster stories and persists in much modern Native American literature, such as Sherman Alexie's popular works. What initially appears as good, true, or beautiful may shift in form to something bad, false, and ugly in the next phase of awareness. Thus, an animal can appear as a human, a human as an animal, and either as a spirit form.

Localized knowledge can be transmitted across boundaries, but only through well-defined paths of exchange. Animals shared knowledge with humans in the beginning of time, such as buffalo who gave culture in many forms to Arapahos and other Plains peoples. In visions, humans can acquire the knowledge of animals or spirits. In history, native peoples acquired knowledge from each other, such as in exchange of ceremonies, social dances, songs, stories, art forms, designs, and more, often through ceremonial exchanges of bundles or objects representing and containing the acquired knowledge. Knowledge can be shared as gifts among animals, humans, and other beings but only when the donor recognizes that the recipient is ready and the latter has moved into a state of being that demonstrates that readiness. The most powerful knowledge embodied in sacred objects or stories could thus only be transmitted to those who had been initiated or reached a necessary stage of preparation. Otherwise, that knowledge and its associated objects were carefully bundled, hidden, or placed safely away from others. In turn, knowledge once acquired must not be used to extremes or beyond limits. Though paradoxical from a Western perspective, unified knowledge through pluralism often required maintaining boundaries rather than universalizing truths to all.

Sharing this pragmatic pluralism, Chief Lone Bear, an early twentieth century Arapaho leader and life-long Catholic and traditionalist describes what he called the "many roads to God":

> I pray according to the way I was taught by the church and when I get through I pray the Indian way. Wherever I go and there is a church and time to go to that church and if I do not belong to that church, it does not make any difference. I go over there and go to that church. It is all one God. We are all heading for the same God. There is no contradiction involved in holding multiple faiths at the same time. Different roads can lead to the same place, and that truth defined much of Deloria's life work (cited in Fowler, 1982, pp. 136–137).

In conclusion, Deloria's ultimate concern was to explore the many roads in modern existence and ancient indigenous religions that can converge in the direction of truth and reality for unifying knowledge. Western academic knowledge is able to map those roads but never follow them. It can engage relativism toward philosophies and cultures outside their well-beaten paths and study them objectively but resist including those other paths as part of a genuine epistemological pluralism. Indigenous cultures can be studied as world views but not be deployed in or for the inquiry itself. Deloria et al. (1999) report that a major publisher rejected the title of their work *Metaphysics of Modern Existence* "because no one will buy a book on metaphysics written by an Indian" (p. 5). Given the defensive borders set up by Western academic disciplines against anomalies, critiques, or "ramblings of madmen," Deloria's proposal for unified knowledge seems ambitious and idealistic. Save for a few marginal subfields, fields, and scholars, the tendency over the past half century has been toward increasing specialization accompanied by denial or silence about what highly specialized accumulations of data and theoretical investigations contribute to ultimate concerns beyond those fields themselves, let alone to the concrete challenges of existence.

To move against this push away from unified knowledge, those involved in educational praxis at all levels should, I suggest, consider these seven lessons taken from the works of Vine Deloria, Jr. First, it is important to not only engage reflexivity about knowledge by holding up what you know or your predecessors knew against abstract political, moral, and critical concerns expressed in a half dozen buzz-words by a few elite consciousnesses in the academic mainstream but also to consider the relation of the knowledge at hand to the lived world of indigenous peoples themselves. Second, this requires broadening the range of voices involved in critical review of knowledge beyond the elite or cloister of a discipline or academia writ large toward inclusion of indigenous modes of discourse, dialectics, and argument. Third, it is good to ask how one's own frames of space and time are accepted as given, universal, and natural but actually exclude other shapes of space-time and block access to sources of knowledge. Fourth, in each field, research project, course, or lesson it is crucial to consider at every juncture how knowledge is connected to other domains of knowledge and, especially, to ultimate concerns. Fifth, all educators and educational institutions should examine how their actions and institutional systems marginalize unifying thinkers, publications, courses, and programs. Sixth, it is good to make direct and not just gestural connections to the world in which one actually lives rather than the simulated world one studies or thinks about as an academic, including the natural environment, local indigenous communities and histories, and the full range of sensory data available. Seventh and last, as Deloria (1979) notes less rather than more effort must be exerted:

> When Western thinkers start confronting knowledge directly without feeling obliged to trace origins, to applaud our present efforts to gain information while rejecting past syntheses of knowledge, and see the value in discontinuities as well as uniformities, then we can bring about unity of human knowledge (p. 211).

REFERENCES

Anderson, B. R. O. (1991). *Imagined Communities: Reflections on the Origin and Spread of Nationalism*. London: Verso.

Anderson, J. D. (2001). *The Four Hills of Life: Northern Arapaho Knowledge and Life Movement*. Studies in the anthropology of North American Indians. Lincoln: University of Nebraska Press.

Bender, T., Bernstein, C., Bromwich, D., Brown, W., Cornell, D., Deloria, V., Jr., Wiener, J. (1998). Thinking in public: A forum. *American Literary History, 10*(1), 1–83.

Bourdieu, P. (1990). The scholastic point of view. *Cultural Anthropology, 5*(4), 380–391.

Cassirer, E. (1953). *The Philosophy of Symbolic Forms*. New Haven: Yale University Press.
Conger, G. P. (1967). *Theories of Macrocosms and Microcosms in the History of Philosophy*. New York: Russell & Russell.
Deloria, V. (1969). *Custer Died for Your Sins; An Indian Manifesto*. New York: Macmillan.
Deloria, V. (1979). *The Metaphysics of Modern Existence*. San Francisco: Harper & Row.
Deloria, V. (1994). *God Is Red: A Native View of Religion*. Golden, CO: Fulcrum.
Deloria, V. (1995). *Red Earth, White Lies: Native Americans and the Myth of Scientific Fact*. New York: Scribner.
Deloria, V. (2004). Philosophy and tribal peoples. In A. Waters (Ed.), *American Indian Thought: Philosophical Essays* (pp. 3–11). Malden, MA: Blackwell.
Deloria, V. (2006). *The World We Used to Live in: Remembering the Powers of the Medicine Men*. Golden, CO: Fulcrum.
Deloria, V., Deloria, P. J., & Bernstein, J. S. (2009). *C. G. Jung and the Sioux Traditions: Dreams, Visions, Nature and the Primitive*. New Orleans: Spring Journal.
Deloria, V., Deloria, B., Foehner, K., & Scinta, S. (1999). *Spirit & Reason: The Vine Deloria, Jr., Reader*. Golden, CO: Fulcrum.
Deloria, V., & Treat, J. (1999). *For This Land: Writings on Religion in America*. New York: Routledge.
Duran, E. (2006). *Healing the Soul Wound: Counseling with American Indians and Other Native Peoples*. Multicultural foundations of psychology and counseling. New York: Teachers College Press.
Evans-Pritchard, E. E. (1940). *The Nuer, A Description of the Modes of Livelihood and Political Institutions of a Nilotic People*. Oxford: Clarendon.
Fabian, J. (1983). *Time and the Other: How Anthropology Makes Its Object*. New York: Columbia University Press.
Fowler, L. (1982). *Arapahoe Politics, 1851–1978: Symbols in Crises of Authority*. Lincoln, NE: University of Nebraska Press.
Geertz, C. (1973). *The Interpretation of Cultures: Selected Essays*. New York: Basic.
Giddens, A. (1984). *The Constitution of Society: Outline of the Theory of Structuration*. Cambridge: Polity.
Hallowell, A. I. (1955). *Culture and Experience*. Philadelphia: University of Pennsylvania Press.
James, W. (1936). *The Varieties of Religious Experience: A Study in Human Nature*. New York: Modern Library.
Kant, I., Guyer, P., & Wood, A. W. (1998). *Critique of Pure Reason*. Cambridge: Cambridge University Press.
Lakoff, G., & Johnson, M. (1980). *Metaphors We Live by*. Chicago: University of Chicago Press.
LeGoff, L. (1982). *Time Work and Culture in the Middle Ages*. Chicago: University of Chicago Press.
Popper, K. R. (1959). *The Logic of Scientific Discovery*. New York: Basic Books.
Storm, H. (1972). *Seven Arrows*. New York: Harper & Row.
Thompson, E. P. (1967). Time, work discipline, and industrial capitalism. *Past and Present, 38*, 56–97.
Tinker, G. (2004). The stones shall cry out: Consciousness, rocks, and Indians. *Wicazo Sa Review, 19*(2), 105–125.
Waters, A. (2004). *American Indian Thought: Philosophical Essays*. Malden, MA: Blackwell.

SECTION II

The Question of Difference, Identity and Representation and Indigenous Knowledge Production

Section Two situates questions of identity and representation in Indigenous knowledge production. Indigenous knowledges are themselves also demarcated by questions and trajectories of social difference (race, gender, class, sexuality, [dis]ability, language, religion, and culture). Indigenous knowledge is about claims of local authenticities, power, and the construction of social meanings. Given the increasing importance and awareness of Indigenous knowledge among, particularly, colonized peoples, we cannot downplay the relevance of putting such questions as the (mis)appropriation and ownership of local knowledges on the table for discussion. We must examine the socially constructed ways of making meaning in today's highly racialized, gendered, sexualized, classed, (re)-colonial, and imperial settings. All Indigenous knowledges speak about race, class, gender, sexual, (dis)ability, and sexuality questions (e.g., the social meanings conveyed in proverbs, songs, fables, tales, medicinal practices, and ethno-music). How the world is read is itself a political act, and it implicates us all (as readers and learners) in how we come to appreciate, interrogate, and challenge established hegemonic ways of knowing.

The academic project of affirming difference and identity is primarily to examine how we can promote multi-centric knowings. As already noted, Indigenous knowledges are increasingly being claimed and resisted. But why? There is the idea of an Indigenous discursive framework as another way of knowing that challenges the historic dominance of particular ways of knowing. Indigenous knowledge is about representation—who, what, and how. All forms of representation are political and contested. The ideological colonization of Western knowledge base is on-going and today is being fiercely contested by many (Indigenous) scholars. Even the methods for studying such Indigenous knowledges point to the central place of difference and representation. Methods of listening and talking to people, knowing about Indigenous stories through interviews, field observations, through documentation, and study of documents or the acquisition of such knowledge through apprenticeship all bring to the fore questions of power, representation, and identity (see Antweiler, 2004).

Hall (1992) long ago reminded us that a theory is not truth, but must be seen as a "set of contested, localized, conjectural knowledges which have to be debated in a dialogical way" (p. 286). A theory of Indigeneity must connect identity, selfhood, culture, and history to the processes and politics of knowledge production. The politics of claiming Indigeneity is a critique of the Manichaen conception of social life using a binary mode of thought, as in the identification between material/ideological; body/spirit; power/resistance; or as Mitchell (1990) puts it, the false idea that ". . .the metaphysical realm of structure or meaning. . .stands apart from what we call material reality" (pp. 560–562). Also, to paraphrase Moore (1997, p. 5) we must acknowledge that Indigenous knowledge presented as a "text" does not reside in a fixed, static, metaphoric site or space removed from practice, performance, power, and process. If Indigenous knowledge is also about power, identity, and representation then we must ask: What are the "power-saturated aspects of identity" and knowledge production (Moore, 1997, p. 1)? In the Western academy Indigenous knowledge is contested because of the politics of the subject and the identities of those who lay claim to such knowledge. Thus, identity can be articulated in a place, and with the particular politics of place. So we must deal with the "situated [political] practices through which identities and places are contested, produced and reworked in particular localities" (Moore, 1997, p.1). The concreteness of a place/space lies in its historical specificities. Definitions of a place/locality and belongingness are not fixed, but imagined and fiercely contested. Spaces are contested because there are places about producing knowledge, ideas, images, and imagining (see also Said, 1993, p. 7). The examination of the historical specificities attest to the grounded struggles and resistance of gender, sexual, racial, ethnic, and class groups as they construct and contest places, spaces, and social identities to produce legitimate and valid knowings.

Michael Davis's chapter, "'I Live Somewhere Else but I've Never Left Here'—Indigenous Knowledge, History and Place" acknowledges that Indigenous knowledge is represented in Western discourses in multiple ways. Yet this knowledge also continues to be subjugated and regarded as subordinate in many Western discourses and in the contexts of hegemonic dominant knowledges that are enacted through the regulatory and governmental regimes of the State. Indigenous peoples produce, and articulate their knowledge in other ways, especially through expressions of difference, and connections to, and being on (and in) country, identity, memory, and history. Davis explores some of these different discourses and considers the possibilities for finding some common ground, equal validity, and legitimacy for the different knowledges. In discussing these competing narratives and discourses, he turns to some of the literature on theories of place and how they contribute to understandings of Indigenous knowledge and identity formation. The chapter also draws attention to the powerful role that Indigenous knowledges can have in the formal academy and in contributing to more equal ways of knowing and understanding the world. The discussion is situated in his on-going work with Aboriginal Traditional Owners and Elders of the Tubba-Gah people in Dubbo, a large regional centre in New South Wales, Australia.

Martin Cannon's "Ruminations on Red Revitalization: Exploring Complexities of Identity, Difference, and Nationhood in Indigenous Knowledge Education" highlights the myriad challenges facing educators involved with decolonizing education and bringing Indigenous knowledge into the academy. He dwells on his own personal experiences as an Indigenous person faced with reconciling federally imposed categories of identity and belonging with intergenerational displacement and language loss, histories of colonial injustice and dislocation, and the de-valorization of Indigenous identities. Cannon positions Indigenous knowledge not as a static or unchanging entity, but rather a dynamic and fundamentally place-based or location-based set of knowledges, tied inherently to histories of the land and Indigenous nationhood. Central to his argument is the need to break with fictitious and/or homogeneous "Indian" identities and to focus instead on the vast array of heterogeneity and Indigenous knowledge bases, which are as numerous as they are nation specific in what is now called Canada. He argues that to achieve the ultimate goal of a respectful, decolonized education, Indigenous curricula must be developed from the bottom-up, emerging from local or community-based partnerships, rather than the top-down importing of academics who—while knowledgeable about some aspects of Indigeneity—cannot possibly embody the place-based knowledge specific to local nations to which they do not belong.

Patience Elabor-Idemudia in "Identity, Representation, and Knowledge Production" shows how the questions of identity and representation have implications for power in knowledge production in terms of their effects as frames of reference. She examines how relations of power shape knowledge production and how people's multiple identities and their ever-changing tendency to fit into occasions in a postmodern society influence the positionality taken in knowledge production. Using intersectionality framework, standpoint theory, insider's perspective, and anti-racist discourse, the author examines the implications for knowledge production (by "otherized" persons) of transnationality, multiple/hybridized identities, and other mediating factors of representation. In doing so, the marginalization and delegitimation of the knowledge produced by "otherized" persons from curriculum in the mainstream education system are interrogated in compliance with a principle of anti-racist education.

Dennis McPherson in "Indigeneity in Education: A By-product of Assimilation?" argues that Indian control of Indian education is in fact just as harmful to Native students and just as destructive of Native culture as anything attempted by the Indian Residential Schools. He substantiates this claim through a careful examination of legislation concerning child welfare and so forth showing how Native communities have fallen into applying the legislation of the dominant society on themselves and their children, motivated primarily by the funding rather than the well-being of their children. The chapter offers some suggestions as to the direction to take in order to rectify this unacceptable situation. Indigenous education is about educating youth to know the world in which they live in and ensuring that Indigenous values promote the continued survival of Indigenous peoples and their cultures.

REFERENCES

Antweiler, C. (2004). Local Knowledge Theory and Methods: An Urban Model from Indonesia. In A. Bicker, P. Sillitoe, & J. Pottier (Eds.), *Investigating Local Knowledges* (pp. 1–34). Aldershot: Ashgate.

Hall, S. (1992). Cultural Studies and Its Theoretical Legacies. In L. Grossberg, C. Nelson, & P. Treichler (Eds.), *Cultural Studies* (pp. 277–294). London: Routledge.

Mitchell, T. (1990). Everyday Metaphors of Power. *Theory and Society, 19*, 545–577.

Moore, D. S. (1997). Remapping Resistance: Ground for Struggle and the Politics of Place. In S. Pile & M. Keith (Eds.), *Geographies of Resistance* (pp. 87–106) London: Routledge.

Said, E. (1993). *Culture and Imperialism.* New York: Vintage.

CHAPTER SEVEN

"I Live Somewhere Else but I've Never Left Here"

Indigenous Knowledge, History, and Place

MICHAEL DAVIS

Indigenous knowledge is represented and constructed in multiple ways in Western discourses. Anderson, for example, has examined the intersections between Indigenous knowledge and Western legal discourses on intellectual property (Anderson, 2009). The dominance of Western discourses of archaeology and cultural heritage management vis-a-vis Australian Aboriginal knowledge and narratives is a focus in work by Smith (2007), who writes about what she describes as an 'authorized heritage discourse.' This is characterised as emphasising "the material, or tangible, nature of heritage, along with monumentality, grand scale, time depth and aesthetics" (Smith, 2007, p. 163). This authorised heritage discourse is, says Smith (2007) "informed by archaeological concerns with materiality and assumptions about the representational relationships between material culture and identity, [and] obscures or marginalizes or misrecognizes those identities created using conceptualizations of heritage that sit outside of the authorized heritage discourse" (p. 164). The unequal engagement between Indigenous knowledge and development discourses is a subject of inquiry by Sillitoe (1998, 2002, 2007) among many others.

Indigenous people produce and articulate their knowledge in other ways, especially through expressions of difference, connections to, and being on (and in) country, identity, memory and history. In this chapter I explore some of these different discourses, and consider the possibilities for finding some common ground between them. In discussing these competing narratives and discourses, I turn to some of the literature on theories of place, as these can contribute to understandings of Indigenous knowledge and identity formation. In exploring these themes and connections, I will draw on some of my recent work with Aboriginal Traditional Owners and Elders of the Tubba-Gah people in Dubbo, a large regional centre in New South Wales, Australia.

The regional rural town of Dubbo, some 400 kilometres west of Sydney, is located in the region referred to as the Western Plains of New South Wales, which is a flat, relatively dry landscape. Here, in what is the centre of their traditional territory or 'country,' Aboriginal Traditional Owners, the Tubba-Gah people of the large Wiradjuri Nation, are actively reclaiming their sense of identity and belonging. Tubba-Gah people speak today with authority about their connections to their country, deploying a vocabulary that includes specific references to types of material culture, land and environment-related practices, and knowledge of local ecology and topography. This discourse contributes to ways in which Tubba-Gah articulate their self-representation and recognition and reaffirm both to themselves and to the outside world their cultural continuity. What is also of interest is the way in which Tubba-Gah people's discourse embodies a sense of place both as a particular geographical locality, and also as a metaphor for their ideas of belonging, and formation of identity. Their Indigenous knowledge thus encompasses place, person and cultural heritage.

The idea that knowledge resides not only in institutions, academies and texts, but in *place,* is captured in the following autobiographical fragment by the English poet John Clare (maintaining his original spelling and absence of punctuation):

> Knowledge gives us a great number of lessons for nothing like Socrates she is not confined to Halls or colledges or forum(s) but like him accompanys us in our walks in the fields and attends on us at our homes…in fact she is every where with us ready to instruct and assist our enquireys...we have only to feel a desire to come at the means of her acquaintance and she is instantly ready to instruct us how to meet with the matter (Robinson & Powell, 2004, p. 242).

Although this extract suggests that knowledge may reside everywhere, for Clare, as will be seen next, knowledge was as much about being in a specific place. This localising aspect of knowledge is important for Tubba-Gah people in Dubbo, who refer to themselves as belonging to a place that they identify with red or yellow ochre. This is a reference to a significant element of material culture, and it is also a signifier of group and language, as essential components of their identity. This relationship between knowledge (e.g., also encompassing a remembered knowledge of uses of ochre), identity and place also presents some notion that, as suggested by John Clare, knowledge resides in all places, including in memory. Yet this sense of constructing an identity is also troubling, since it suggests a discursive construct based on an essential, or absolute, set of intrinsic attributes or qualities. An 'essentialist discourse' comprising features including inherent rights, and sense of separateness or distinctiveness is a common way in which Indigenous peoples might define and identify themselves. While this kind of essentialist discourse renders difficult any exchange or dialogue, it can be, and often is important as a strategic way of positioning themselves as a distinct group, resisting oppression and subjugation, and mobilising against development (see, e.g., Ashcroft, Griffiths, & Tiffin, 1998; Spivak, 1985, for discussion on essentialism and strategic essentialism in post-colonial critique).

There is also a sense in which Indigenous people, such as Wiradjuri and Tubba-Gah, are discursively constructed in the Western imagination by means of their absence, or silence, in a European landscape. Their 'presence' (or 'non-presence') is, in this sense, constructed on the basis of disappearances, or traces, remnants or fragments; gaps in the record. This trope of disappearance figures powerfully throughout Europeans' discourses on Aboriginal people in the landscape and persists in the construction of Tubba-Gah and Wiradjuri country and identity (e.g., Macdonald, 1998, p. 183).

Set in opposition to the various totalising and homogenising authoritative discourses, as enacted through, and formed by the State, Indigenous peoples' own discourses and self-representations of their identity are equally varied and complex. While they are expressed in very different articulations, as I suggest later in this chapter they are also formed out of the intertwined discourses of Indigenous/European encounters, texts, readings and interpretations.

A sense of being in place is at the heart of their construct of identity. Tubba-Gah peoples' discourses are constructed from a diverse set of oral historical traditions, implicit cultural values and understandings. Coursing alongside, and intertwined in complex ways with what I shall call this Aboriginal discourse, are other discourses that also construct or (re)-construct a Tubba-Gah cultural-historical past and present. These alternative discourses are fashioned from non-Aboriginal texts, statements and cultural and socio-political formations, located within the (largely) formal Western disciplinary and institutional domains of archaeology, history, government, museum-heritage bureaucracy. I am using 'texts' here in the wider sense of referring to both written and verbal statements and utterances. It is in the intersections between these parallel discourses—Indigenous, and what I shall refer to as 'Western'—that there reside possibilities for finding common ground. A movement between and to and from Indigenous, and non-Indigenous (what I have referred to occasionally here as 'European,' or 'Western,' terms that themselves require some interrogation) discourses produces a new and emerging 'other knowledge,' one that allows for what cultural critic Mignolo has called a 'border thinking' and 'double critique.' 'Border thinking' entails what Mignolo has termed (borrowed from Moroccan philosopher Abdelhebir Khatibi) an 'other way of thinking,' in which a space is opened up for critique from positions outside of particular ways of knowing. As a mode of postcolonial critique, 'border thinking' recovers subjugated and subaltern knowledges by forming a 'double critique' that is beyond, or outside, the established discourses. In Mignolo's (2000) scheme, referring to critiques of Western and Islamic ways of thought, or traditions, a 'double critique' implies to "think from both traditions and, at the same time, from neither of them" (p. 67). These notions of 'border thinking' and 'an other thinking' (Mignolo, 2000, pp. 66-68)...offer useful frames for understanding the ways in which a particular body of knowledge can be fashioned that enables a critique of specific discourses, while itself residing outside those.

Before I move on, to consider some aspects of Tubba-Gah peoples' discourses, I want to say a little about my own position in writing this chapter—my speaking position. If we are to consider the juxtaposition of texts, narratives and discourses, then my own position needs to be articulated here too. I write as an English-born male of secular European-Jewish descent. In my writing and thinking on Indigenous peoples, and in my work with Aboriginal communities and individuals in Australia, I am informed subconsciously by my feelings of 'outsiderness' or of being 'other.' In this context, my work is influenced by what Grosz (1993) refers to as an 'ethics of Otherness,' in an exploration of, as she puts it, "the ways in which the lived experience of Jewishness contributes to understanding that position of social marginality or exile which the Jew shares in common with other oppressed groups" (p. 57). In my case, this Jewishness does not derive from a religious or devout basis in practice, as my family have been separated from the religious tradition for at least a generation, and 'assimilated' into English and Australian society. My outsiderness stems instead from what I might describe as a cultural Jewish identity based in ideas and feelings about difference and a sense of being apart. My writing standpoint in thinking about difference, outsiderness and otherness is a critical factor in my interpretation of the play of discourses that I am exploring in this chapter.

Tubba-Gah peoples' constructions of their ways of knowing, their sense of identity and belonging are shaped, in addition to cultural and oral traditional factors, by their own readings and interpretations of 'Western' historical, ethnographic, anthropological and archaeological texts, artefacts and other discourses. This movement between discourses—Indigenous and Western—fashions from Tubba-Gah peoples' readings and innovative interpretations of the extant historical, ethnographic and archaeological discourse, a creative formulation of self-knowledge and identity.

The complex articulation of place and being by Tubba-Gah is articulated powerfully by one Traditional Owner in conversation, who expressed her identity to me by stating 'I live somewhere else, but I've never left here.'[1] This statement captures a sense that identity resides both in place and out of place. It is also referenced to Tubba-Gah history, which has been one of dispossession, dislocation, exile and loss of knowledge. The Traditional Owner who expressed this sentiment currently lives away from Dubbo in another part of Australia but retains her strong connections to her country and its people.

It is perhaps a complex intertwining of knowledge with place that enables an individual to maintain identity as attachment to a particular locality while being geographically distant from that place. Thus John Clare's notion of knowledge being 'every where with us ready to instruct' enables us to think about a connection to country for Indigenous people being articulated without necessarily residing in that place. This also suggests a greater need to consider Indigenous knowledge as something more than, or different from, an entity that is 'defined' or constructed in terms of its need for protection.

THE EDUCATIVE POWER OF INDIGENOUS KNOWLEDGE

The idea that knowledge can, as John Clare wrote, be 'ready to instruct' is an important one. This is certainly the case with Indigenous knowledge, which has great pedagogical value. Globally, historically, and in continuing ways, Indigenous peoples' knowledge is at worst subordinated and subjugated, or at best assimilated within the hegemonic and dominant discourses.

The State legitimates the devaluing of Indigenous knowledge as Battiste (1998), for example, has pointed to the 'cognitive imperialism' wherein the dominant discourses tend to be validated 'through public education,' while at the same time devaluing alternative knowledges such as those of Indigenous and local peoples (p. 20). Yet, as Semali and Kincheloe (1999a) argue, Indigenous knowledge has 'transformative power' and "can be used to foster empowerment and justice in a variety of cultural contexts" (p. 15).

Indigenous knowledge has for decades been a subject of increasing attention and interest across a wide range of domains and disciplines including governmental, administrative, scientific, ethnographic, legislative and activist. Areas for discussion include the role of Indigenous knowledge in development (e.g., Briggs, 2005; Briggs & Sharp, 2004; Sillitoe, 1998, 2002), questions about the intersections between, and 'cultural politics' of, Indigenous knowledge and law (e.g., Anderson, 2009; Brown, 2003; Davis, 1997, 1998; Gibson, 2005; Whitt, 2009), and the relationship between Indigenous, and other forms of knowledge (e.g., Agrawal, 1995a, 1995b; Davis, 2006), as well as a burgeoning literature (mostly in the anthropological and ethnographic fields) on using, collecting and documenting Indigenous knowledge. As well as discussions on Indigenous knowledge that fall within the disciplines of anthropology, ethnography, political science and development studies, a major area of scrutiny is conducted within a legal framework, in regard to the regulation, recognition and protection of Indigenous knowledge. Related to those inquiries, yet another prominent focus is on the classification of Indigenous knowledge and questions of definition. It is discussed in the literature using a range of terms including 'Indigenous ecological knowledge,' 'traditional ecological knowledge,' 'traditional environmental knowledge,' 'traditional knowledge' and 'Indigenous knowledge.' This 'problem of nomenclature' is in itself sometimes a topic for discussion (e.g., Heckler, 2009; Zent, 2009). The variety of terms used suggests, or reflects, the variety of disciplines within which

Indigenous knowledge is located as a subject for discussion. More significantly, it indicates a sense of unease that many writers about this subject perhaps experience—albeit unconsciously—in the subject matter's unwillingness to be readily categorised or labelled within a single or specific discipline or approach. While discussions about Indigenous knowledge tend to be scattered across many disciplines and areas of methodological and theoretical interest, in general, those discussions construct it as though it is a unitary, homogenous entity or subject for analysis.

The focus in much of the literature on Indigenous knowledge is on the relationship between Indigenous knowledge and legislative regimes for protection, predominantly intellectual property rights. I have written elsewhere about some of the problems I perceive in too great a reliance on notions of 'protection' in regard to Indigenous knowledge (Davis, 2008). This discourse on Indigenous knowledge articulated in legal concepts around property and protection is a significant component of the official, State-authorised discourse that serves the technologies of government in its construction of Indigenous identity. This discourse consists of official statements, laws and legislative amendments, legal commentaries and discussions, government and parliamentary documents and reports and submissions produced within the context of the legal, bureaucratic and administrative domains. These have been formulated and maintained mostly by the authoritative, official structures of government and its machinery of legislation and regulation. This State-authorised discourse is entrenched primarily in legislative frameworks, especially intellectual property rights, and operates as a 'technology of government' legitimated by structures and processes of power/knowledge (Gordon, 1991).

At the same time as that official discursive production, there has emerged at least one parallel discourse, which, while having been developed as a distinct alternative to the official one, also intersects with that in important ways. I refer here to what has been termed Indigenous cultural and intellectual property rights—a term used to denote Indigenous peoples' cultural heritage in both its physical and intangible aspects (Janke, 1998). This discourse of Indigenous cultural and intellectual property rights, discussed and advocated most recently by Janke, an Australian Indigenous legal expert, is also increasingly being taken up in a wider domain of research, writing and policy development. It allows a possibility for at least providing a critique, if not a challenge to the prevailing authoritative discourses.

The State-sanctioned official discourse deploys dominant knowledges and legislative regimes based in archaeology, cultural heritage management and planning, that often have the effect of limiting the capacity of the State to effectively allow for the expression and articulation of alternative knowledges including those of Indigenous peoples. The governance and regulation of Indigenous heritage in Australia illustrates the tensions between imposed, authoritative State-based regulatory regimes, and the assertion of rights in control, management and decision making over their own knowledge and other forms of heritage by Indigenous peoples.

The authorised discourse of Indigenous heritage was beginning to be articulated many decades ago in Australia (Davis, 2007). Some early ethnologists and collectors of Aboriginal cultural material had identified a need for legislative protection of what was sometimes referred to as Indigenous 'antiquities'; but more rigorous attempts to develop preservation legislation did not occur until around the 1950s. Despite this early interest in legislative 'protection' of Indigenous heritage, those moves were still conducted in a milieu in which the predominant notion in Europeans' minds of Indigenous heritage was as a physical or object-based entity. The shift during the 1950s towards a growing awareness of the sacred as an important dimension of Indigenous heritage was a significant development. In Europeans' discourses, the 'sacred' in Aboriginal heritage was focussed on specific places, or sites—the sacred site. This resulted in what is today an emphasis on 'sites' as an indicator or identity marker for Indigenous people, constructed through discourses of archaeology and heritage assessment. It was not until the 1970s that awareness developed among Europeans of the close interdependence between physical, object-based Indigenous heritage and other elements, including the intangible. This latter component or dimension came to their consciousness not so much through their awareness of the sacred but by their growing perception of the need to 'protect' Indigenous peoples' artistic expressions. Also around this time, there began to take shape an idea that Indigenous peoples had certain kinds of property rights; the growth of the land rights movement during the 1960s attested to this realisation. In a move that seemed to be 'ahead of its time,' in 1969 a proposal was developed by prominent bureaucrat Herbert ('Nugget') Coombs that sought to recognise Indigenous property rights in art, sites, ceremony and elements of material culture (Davis, 2007, pp. 281–284). The proposal for 'Traditional Aboriginal Property' legislation did not progress, but it did signal future developments that would seek recognition of Indigenous property rights. Laws and regulations for the protection of Indigenous heritage, in various forms, had already been introduced by some state and territory governments through the 1950s and 1960s (such as the Northern Territory's *Native and Historical Objects and Areas Preservation Ordinance* 1955–1960). Subsequently, legislation was developed at the Commonwealth level, with two pieces of legislation being particularly relevant: the *Aboriginal and Torres Strait Islander Heritage Protection Act 1984*, and the *Protection of Movable Cultural Heritage Act 1986*. However, none of this legislation provides recognition or protection for Indigenous knowledge, whether considered as a component of cultural heritage, or as a form of 'intellectual property.' Instead, these legislative regimes contribute to the formation of an official discourse on Aboriginal culture and heritage. These legislative developments, as well as more recent Commonwealth and State-based regimes (such as the NSW *Aboriginal Land Rights Act 1983*, and the Commonwealth Government's *Native Title Act 1993*) have continued to play an important role in the formation of official constructs of Indigenous identity.

Within the domain of official intellectual property rights-based discourses, concerns by artists, policy makers and some people in government and bureaucracy about the misuse of what came to be referred to in official discourses as 'Indigenous intellectual property rights' became more prominent during the 1970s, with attention being drawn to the unlawful appropriation of Aboriginal peoples' designs on artworks, and (during the 1990s) Aboriginal peoples' claims for wrongdoing made under the *Copyright Act*. Those developments prompted the growth of a discourse that was subsequently referred to in terms of Aboriginal peoples' traditional designs as their 'intellectual property.' Developments seeking to reform laws relating to what is now commonly referred to as Indigenous peoples' 'intellectual property' began to advance, with the establishment in the 1970s of a Working Party to "examine the nature of legislation required to protect Aboriginal artists in regard to Australian and international copyright" (Davis, 2007, p. 252). At that time, the debate was couched in terms of Aboriginal 'folklore,' that term having been explained as pertaining to a recognition "that traditions, customs and beliefs underlie forms of artistic expression, since Aboriginal arts are tightly integrated within the totality of Aboriginal culture" (Davis, 2007, p. 295, quoting the Report of the Working Party on Aboriginal Folklore). That development was critical in its recognition of the intangible Indigenous heritage, and of the close interconnections between various elements of that heritage, unfortunately, once again it did not result in any legislative framework. All this legislative activity established an authoritative discourse for the regulation of Indigenous heritage, primarily if not exclusively in regard to its physical or intangible aspects. There was now, by the 1990s a relatively comprehensive suite of laws and policies governing Indigenous heritage, and providing possibilities for its 'protection.'

Constructions of identity for Indigenous people can emphasise both diversity and unity. Read (1988) has suggested that for Wiradjuri, although they were diverse within the group, they also displayed unity "Within the Wiradjuri borders too there were different cultural traditions....Yet for all the diversity there were strong unifying forces. The great religious ceremonies brought hundreds of people together, sometimes from distances of hundreds of kilometres" (pp. 2–3).

As a defined group, Wiradjuri have been constructed in a variety of historical and geographic discourses. For example, 'the Wiradjuri' has been constructed through discourses of bounded regions and topographical and geographical features as Read (1988) suggests

> Who were the Wiradjuri people....Geographical features formed their boundaries—the Blue Mountains in the east, the foot of the western slopes in the south, and away to the north and north-west, Wiradjuri was no longer spoken as a first language where the open eucalyptus forest gave way to the grassy plains and mallee scrub (p. 2).

In this framework, Wiradjuri identity is closely associated with geographical and topographical features, especially rivers. "Three great rivers, the Macquarie, the Lachlan and the Murrumbidgee, intersected Wiradjuri country and gave to the families associated with them some common bonds as river people" (Read, 1988, pp. 2–3).

Read (1988) suggests that for Wiradjuri, identity is formed by connection between people, name and place:

> These associations between people and local area are for the most part ancient....The essence of modern Wiradjuri unity, therefore, is not boundaries on a map, not even a common Aboriginal culture, (which is shared by near neighbours) but the old Wiradjuri kin-groupings, now bearing European names, which identify with certain regions (pp. 2–3).

A similar point is made by anthropologist Macdonald (1998) who wrote

> Wiradjuri consciousness of space, and of the ways in which it is constructed, is a system of knowledge that Wiradjuri people share but, like all systems of knowledge, it is not equally accessed or distributed. Various discourses are available by which Wiradjuri speak of the divisions within the landscape that make that landscape meaningful. These are frequently and not unexpectedly contradictory. They may emphasise the autonomy of the local area but also the commonalities of the region. They may prioritise economic or political or spiritual relations at different times, depending on context....(p. 163).

Geography and environmental features also figure significantly in State-based planning and management regimes. For Wiradjuri, and Tubba-Gah, their identity has been constructed through various European discourses, and regulated and governed through the machinery of New South Wales legislation for cultural heritage and parks management, mostly the *National Parks and Wildlife Act 1974* which 'protects Aboriginal objects and places in NSW.' Similarly, Wiradjuri are also constructed in terms of officially recognised and corporate entities for the purpose of administration of land rights regimes:

> The idea of Wiradjuri country, which now includes approximately 20 different communities associated with rural towns and cities, has taken on new institutional expression since the passing of the New South Wales

Aboriginal Land Rights Act 1983. This Act required that Local Aboriginal Land Councils be clustered into regions (Macdonald, 1998, p. 163).

Despite these official legislative and administrative constructions of Wiradjuri (and Tubba-Gah) identity, as Macdonald observes, a sense of place and being in the landscape figures as the central motif in Indigenous peoples' own self-representations. She states "but what really makes Wiradjuri space their space is their presence. The idea of land is the idea of presence, a writing of oneself onto the landscape; it is a humanising and socialising of that within which one is embodied" (Macdonald, 1998, p. 164).

Macdonald (1998) writes that Wiradjuri peoples' presence in their landscape includes "heritage sites where Wiradjuri people of the past have left the marks of their presence, and sites which, even without those visible marks, they strongly believe are places their ancestors would have favoured and frequented" (p. 164). However, there is a risk of constructing what Porter (2006) has described as a 'sites discourse' as a way of defining these people.

While discursive constructions of the wider Wiradjuri presence and identity have been a significant contributing factor in fashioning 'the Wiradjuri' in the European imagining, similar narratives perform a construction of Tubba-Gah identity.

In Dubbo and the surrounding region, cultural heritage assessment and archaeological reports are produced, many of which draw upon a mixture of anecdotal, historical and ethnographic accounts, and linguistic and archaeological studies for their depictions of Tubba-Gah. One recent cultural heritage report presents the following summary of Dubbo-based Wiradjuri, as a defined cultural/linguistic group associated with specific country:

> According to Tindale's map of tribal boundaries (1974), the Dubbo area falls within the northern limits of Wiradjuri country, as defined by the limits of the Wiradjuri language group. Bordering to the west is Wongaibon country, and to the north Kawanbarai country. According to Horton (1980), the boundary of the Wiradjuri extends somewhat further to the north and west to encompass Gilgandra, Nyngan and most of the Bogan River (OzArk, 2009, p. 12).

In this report, early local historical and anecdotal texts, combined with archaeological reports (Garnsey, 1942; Koettig, 1985; Pearson, 1981) are deployed to construct a 'picture' of Tubba-Gah:

> The Dubba-ga group were part of the broader Wirruh-Jah-Mine tribe (Wiradjuri–Possum men territory). Such groups were thought to have comprised about 30–40 people, although various sized groups have been reported (Koettig 1985: 21–22). The territory said to have been traversed by this group generally lies to the east of the Macquarie River, south of the Macquarie River and north of Eulomogo creek.

According again to Garnsey,

> ... the Dubba-ga mob were named after a pigment found in their territory called Dub-bo, which refers to the red or blood pigment found within their territory. This was a valuable and prized commodity, bartered widely and found at a place called Dub-am-bil (place of pigment) located about two miles up stream of the Macquarie River, on its right bank (OzArk, 2009, pp. 13–14).

A feature of these types of discourse is their tendency to reify Indigenous culture as though it is captured forever in some imagined past (Fabian, 1983). The presentation of perceived ethnographic features defines 'a people,' which then becomes reinforced and perpetuated through successive representations, texts and discourses.

References to the material culture of Tubba-Gah contribute a significant element to discourses on their identity, both in their self-representations, and in the imposed, outsider discourses. One example of this emphasis on material culture is the stated presence and use of yellow and red ochre. Ochre was, and still is important not only as a marker of place for Tubba-Gah Wiradjuri people but also as a signifier for the name they give themselves. Ochre was a very significant resource, and the Dubbo area was noted for quarries for red and yellow ochre. This material was important in Tubba-Gah society for ornamentation for body and material culture items, for ceremonial and ritual use. It was also an important trade item, and its access and use were governed by strict cultural norms. An early local historian Garnsey had written that "the ochre was traded extensively along trade routes [and] there is evidence of it being located hundreds of kilometres distant from Dubbo" (1942). The association between the Tubba-Gah people and ochre is important in linguistic as well as symbolic and cultural senses. The clan/band name Tubba-Gah, rendered as *Dubboga* by Garnsey, was named for the red ochre deposits "quarried from the banks of the Macquarie River near Eulomogo Creek." The ochre quarry "was also the site of the *Dubboga* axe grinding industry" (Garnsey, 1942).

These powerful associations between place, identity, language and naming return us to the significance of place, in its fullest sense. In *Getting Back to Place* Edward Casey (1993) writes that "place serves as the *condition* of all existing things"(p. 15). Casey (1993) "this means that, far from being merely locator or situational, place belongs to the very concept of existence...to be is to be bounded by place, limited by it"(p. 15). This has important implications for landscape, and for the Indigenous concept of 'country.' Casey (1993) makes an argument about the relationship between place and landscape. "A landscape seems to exceed the usual parameters of place by continuing without apparent end; nothing contains it, while it contains everything, including discrete places, in its environing embrace" (p. 15). There is also a powerful connection between body and place, as Casey (1993) explains

> The body, on the other hand, seems to fall short of place, to be 'on this side,' the near edge, of a given place. Nevertheless, body and landscape collude in the generation of what can be called 'placescapes,' especially those that human beings experience whenever they venture out beyond the narrow confines of their familiar domiciles and neighbourhoods (p. 25).

In this way, it would seem that Tubba-Gah Traditional Owner's notion that they can live away but never have left a place suggests that place-based identity resides in the human person as much as in a specific locality. There is also an important point here about memory; that identifying with place as locality is a remembered quality, one that is transportable. This takes us into a different path to that in Casey's argument, to suggest that we are not necessarily always taken 'back to place'; rather, it seems more like the thesis proposed by David Morris (2004), who suggests instead, that our sense of 'space,' rather than 'place' is not anchored to a particular locality, as he puts it, "...our sense of space is something we take away from place, even in careful dwelling" (p. 181). He says "we cannot fully get back into place, because at its limit place exceeds us" (Morris, 2004, p. 181). It is in this combination of movement and place Morris (2004) suggests, that we find a concept of 'space' that expresses greater plasticity than place: "our sense of space is the living sense that we take away from our movement in place" (p. 179). These place, and space, worlds invite greater contemplation as they suggest a more nuanced and integrated notion of knowledge, knowing and being in constructions of Indigenous identity.

Understanding Indigenous peoples' identity with location, and the notion of possibility of attachment to place as a way of thinking requires that we conceptualise a (re)unitary sense of physical space—that of living in a place—with an imaginary or 'mental place' (Lefebvre, 1991, p. 3). In poet Gary Snyder's (1995) terms, this might be a kind of 'reinhabitation,' a "knowledge of place that enables the knowledge of self" (p. 189). As Snyder (1995) puts it "knowing who we are and knowing where we are are intimately linked" (p. 189). Lefebvre's notion of a sensory or mental idea of space is well developed by Bachelard, whose 'poetics of space' offers an appreciation of the 'dialectics of outside and inside' between space as exteriority, and as an experienced, intimate space (Bachelard, 1994).

A knowledge of being in place weaves together a powerful story about Indigenous peoples' knowledge tradition as they experience it, and express it to outsiders. Being in place is much more than living there, occupying and inhabiting the place. As Malpas argues, it is experience in place that gives us meaning and depth. Experience in place encompasses memory, histories and a sense of self versus others.

This sense of rootedness in place brings us back to John Clare. A sense of a bounded, familiar world that contains all ones' knowledge is captured powerfully in the following fragment of Clare's autobiography (I have retained Clare's distinctive spelling and absence of punctuation in this quote):

> I lovd this solitary disposition from a boy and felt a curiosity to wander about the spots were I had never been before. . .I remember one incident of this feeling when I was very young. . .it was in summer and I started off in the morning to get rotten sticks from the woods but I had a feeling to wander about the fields and I indulgd it. . .I had often seen the large heath calld Emmonsales stretching its yellow furze from my eye into unknown solitudes when I went with the mere openers and my curiosity urged me to steal an oppertunity to explore it that morning. . .I had imagind that the worlds end was at the edge of the orison and that a days journey was able to find it. . .so I went on with my heart full of hopes pleasures and discoverys expecting when I got to the brink of the world that I could look down like looking into a large pit and see into its secrets the same as I believd I could see heaven by looking into the water. . .so I eagerly wanderd on and rambled among the furze the whole day till I got out of my knowledge when the very wild flowers and birds seemd to forget me and I imagind they were the inhabitants of new countrys. . .(Robinson & Powell, 2002, p. 40).

Here Clare has articulated his profound expression of knowledge in place. As Malpas (2007) has suggested, ". . .the very possibility of understanding or of knowledge resides in locatedness and in a certain embeddedness in place" (p. 189).

Malpas (2007) has elaborated on this connection between identity and place, writing that

> the sense. . .in which identity is tied to place (and so to a spatio-temporal realm in which persons and things can be encountered and a world can be grasped) is not just the sense in which a sense of identity might be tied up with a certain 'emotional reminiscence,' but derives from the way in which the very character of subjectivity, in the general and the particular, and the very content of our thoughts and feelings, is necessarily dependent on the place and places within which we live and act (p. 188).

There is a dynamic interplay between Aboriginal peoples' self-representations (e.g., "I am Tubba-Gah"), representations of them by others, and their representations of other peoples and texts. Tubba-Gah people distinguish themselves apart from other clan groups in the Wiradjuri. In talking about themselves, their connection to place, Indigenous people are also both drawing on and further shaping their knowledge. This intricate connection between language, knowledge, self and place is the essence of a phenomenology of attachment to place. As Abram (1996) puts it "the sense of being immersed in a sentient world is preserved in the oral stories and songs of indigenous peoples—in the belief that sensible phenomena are all alive and aware, in the assumption that all things have the capacity of speech. Language, for oral peoples, is not a human intervention but a gift of the land itself" (pp. 262–263). In Abram's (1996) framework, "language, in indigenous oral cultures, is experienced not as the exclusive property of humankind, but as a property of the sensuous life-world" (p. 154).

This intricate and intimate connection between place, history, identity and self is enriched by a shift away from understanding place solely as territory or landscape towards more nuanced interpretations. Ingold's (1993) notion of what he calls a 'dwelling perspective,' for example, allows us to perceive of the landscape as "constituted as an enduring record of—and testimony to—the lives and works of past generations who have dwelt within it, and in so doing, have left there something of themselves" (p. 153). Memmott and Long (2002) too have called for a better understanding of the theory of place for "any scientific, political or professional analysis of the cultural heritage values of places or sites" and "issues in the maintenance of Indigenous places in contemporary Aboriginal Australia" (p. 39). Massey (2004) advocates for a thinking of space 'relationally,' stating that

> an understanding of the relational nature of space has been accompanied by arguments about the relational construction of the identity of place. If space is a product of practices, trajectories, interrelations, if we make space through interactions at all levels, from the (so-called) local to the (so-called) global, then those spatial identities such as places, regions, nations, and the local and the global, must be forged in this relational way too, as internally complex, essentially unboundable in any absolute sense, and inevitably historically changing (p. 5).

The construction of an 'Indigenous peoples' has also been purveyed through a series of shared experiences, dispossession, shared concerns for protection of culture and heritage, notions of difference, survival in the face of great traumas. This politics of identity is a complex mix. Niezen (2003), for example, points to one of the many elements that may comprise this identity formation: "Indigenous peoples, like some ethnic groups, derive much of their identity from histories of state-sponsored genocide, forced settlement, relocation, political marginalisation, and various formal attempts at cultural destruction" (p. 5).

What I have sought to explore in this chapter, however, is an idea that identity construction for Indigenous peoples, incorporating powerful representations of cultural knowledge, and a sense of place and being, is not unitary and homogeneous, and especially is not based singly on notions of destruction and loss.

My intention here has been not to focus, in this chapter at least, on the important role of political and strategic mobilisations for Indigenous identity, or on seeking understandings of the powerful and contested notions of shared oppression; rather, I have sought to (re)find a role for the sense of place, in its fullest meanings of both physical and sensory, as a significant element of Indigenous knowledge and identity formation. I have argued that Indigenous knowledge plays a vital part in constructions of Indigenous peoples' identity, especially in terms of its relationship to a sense of place, as a location and also as a way of knowing, thinking and speaking. This knowledge is utilised both as a 'marker' of difference but also as part of a strategy by Indigenous people to develop a challenge to prevailing authoritative discourses relating to land, heritage and environment, and in education.

The role of Indigenous knowledge in rethinking education and learning is a particularly crucial one (Dei, 2000; Dei, Hall, & Rosenberg, 2000; Semali & Kincheloe, 1999b). Recognition and understanding Indigenous knowledges as alternative ways of knowing and engaging the world, and acknowledging these as having equal validity with other, currently dominant epistemologies and learning, can enhance a wider knowing and understanding of the world.

These Indigenous knowledges offer a critical site of resistance, engagement and re-connection for Indigenous peoples in neo-colonial and post-colonial situations and articulate key expressions of difference and relatedness to place and identity. Striving to allow a plurality of knowledges inside the formal classrooms, academies, institutions and organisations, and in less formal contexts presents powerful possibilities for developing greater notions of ethical cosmopolitan social formations.

I have endeavoured in this chapter to move towards an argument that in the intersections between Indigenous peoples' constructions of their identity and those of State-sanctioned and authoritative discourses, some common ground might be recovered wherein a kind of 'border thinking' can be articulated that enables shared understandings about knowledge, place and belonging in situations of plurality and equality.

Note

1. Mrs Narrell Boys. I am grateful to Mrs Boys for giving me permission to quote her for this chapter. I also thank Traditional Owner Mrs Coral Peckham for allowing me to draw on conversations with her and other Traditional Owners, Elders and members of Tubba-Gah, Wiradjuri for this chapter.

REFERENCES

Abram, D. (1996). *The Spell of the Sensuous: Perception and Language in a More-than-Human World*. New York: Vintage.

Agrawal, A. (1995a). Dismantling the divide between indigenous and scientific knowledge. *Development and Change* 26(3), 413–439.

Agrawal, A. (1995b). Indigenous and scientific knowledge: Some critical comments. *Indigenous Knowledge and Development Monitor* 3(3), 3–6.

Anderson, J. E. (2009). *Law, Knowledge, Culture: The Production of Indigenous Knowledge in Intellectual Property Law*. Cheltenham, UK: Edward Elgar.

Ashcroft, B., Griffiths, G., & Tiffin, H. (1998). *Key Concepts in Post-colonial Studies*. London & New York: Routledge.

Bachelard, M. (1994). *The Poetics of Space*. (M. Jolas, Trans.). Boston: Beacon.

Battiste, M (1998) Enabling the autumn seed: Toward a decolonized approach to Aboriginal knowledge, language, and education. *Canadian Journal o fNative Education* , 22(1), 16–27.

Briggs, J. (2005). The use of indigenous knowledge in development: problems and challenges. *Progress in Development Studies* 5(2), 99–14.

Briggs, J., & Sharp, J. (2004). Indigenous knowledges and development: A postcolonial caution. *Third World Quarterly* 25(4), 661–676.

Brown, M. F. (2003). *Who Owns Native Culture?* Cambridge: Harvard University Press.

Casey, Edward (1993). *Getting back toPplace: Toward a Renewed Understanding of the Place-world*. Bloomington: Indiana University Press.

Davis, M. (1997). Indigenous Peoples and Intellectual Property Rights. Research Paper No. 20. Canberra: Department of the Parliamentary Library.

Davis, M. (1998). Biological Diversity and Indigenous Knowledge. Research Paper No. 17. Canberra: Department of the Parliamentary Library.

Davis, M. (2006). Bridging the gap or crossing a bridge? Indigenous knowledge and the language of law and policy. In W. V. Reid, F. Berkes, T. J. Wilbanks, & D. Capistrano (Eds.), *Bridging Scales and Knowledge Systems:*

Concepts and Applications in Ecosystem Assessments (pp. 145–182). Washington DC: Island.
Davis, M. (2007). *Writing Heritage: The Depiction of Indigenous Heritage in European-Australian Writings*. Melbourne and Canberra: Australian Scholarly Publishing and National Museum of Australia Press.
Davis, M. (2008). Indigenous knowledge: Beyond protection, towards dialogue. *Australian Journal of Indigenous Education* 37S, 25–45.
Dei, G. J. S. (2000). Rethinking the role of Indigenous knowledges in the academy. *International Journal of Inclusive Education* 4(2), 111–132.
Dei, G. J. S., Hall, B. L., & Rosenberg, D. G. (Eds.). (2000). *Indigenous Knowledges in Global Contexts: Multiple Readings of Our World*. Toronto: University of Toronto Press.
Fabian, J. (1983). *Time and the Other: How Anthropology Makes Its Object*. New York: Columbia University Press.
Garnsey, E. (1942). A Treatise on the Aborigines of Dubbo and District: Their Camp-Life, Habits and Customs. Dubbo Museum and Historical Society.
Gibson, J. (2005). *Community Resources: Intellectual Property, International Trade and Protection of Traditional Knowledge*. Aldershot, UK: Ashgate.
Gordon, C. (1991). Governmental rationality: an introduction. In G. Burchell, C. Gordon & P. Miller (Eds.), *The Foucault Effect: Studies in Governmentality* (pp. 1–51). London: Harvester Wheatsheaf.
Grosz, E. (1993). Judaism and exile: the ethics of Otherness. In E. Carter, J. Donald and J. Squires (Eds.), *Space and Place: Theories of Identity and Location* (pp. 57–71). London: Lawrence & Wishart.
Heckler, S. (2009). Introduction. In S. Heckler (Ed.), *Landscape, Process and Power: Re-evaluating Traditional Environmental Knowledge* (pp. 1–15). New York & Oxford: Berghahn.
Ingold, T. (1993). The temporality of landscape. *World Archaeology* 25(2), 152–174.
Janke, T. (1998). *Our Culture, Our Future: Australian Indigenous Cultural and Intellectual Property Rights*. Canberra: ATSIC.
Koettig, M. (1985 July). Assessment of Aboriginal Sites in the Dubbo City Area, Report in conjunction with a Planning Study undertaken by Cameron McNamara P/L.
Lefebvre, H. (1991). *The Production of Place*. (D. Nicholson-Smith, Transl.). Massachusetts & Oxford: Blackwell.
Macdonald, G. (1998). Master narratives and the dispossession of the Wiradjuri. *Aboriginal History* 22, 162–179.
Malpas, J. E. (2007). *Place and Experience: A Philosophical Topography*. Cambridge: Cambridge University Press.
Massey, D. (2004). Geographies of responsibility. *Geografiska Annalar* 86(B)(1), 5–18.
Memmott, P., & Long, S. (2002). Place theory and place maintenance in Indigenous Australia. *Urban Policy and Research* 20(1), 39–56.
Mignolo, W. D. (2000). *Local Histories/Global Designs: Coloniality, Subaltern Knowledges, and Border Thinking*. Princeton, NJ: Princeton University Press.
Morris, D. (2004). *The Sense of Space*. Albany: State University of New York Press.
Niezen, R. (2003). *The Origins of Indigenism: Human Rights and the Politics of Identity*. Berkeley: University of California Press.
OzArk Environmental and Heritage Management Pty Ltd. (July 2009). Aboriginal Heritage Assessment: Tracker Riley Cycleway extension, Dubbo, NSW.
Pearson, M. (1981). *Seen through Different Eyes: Changing Land Use and Settlement Patterns in the Upper Macquarie River Region of N.S.W., from Prehistoric Times to 1860* (PhD Thesis), Canberra, ANU.
Porter, L. (2006). Rights or containment? The politics of Aboriginal cultural heritage in Victoria. *Australian Geographer*, 37(3), 355–374.
Read, P. (1988). *A Hundred Years War: The Wiradjuri People and the State*. NSW: ANU.
Robinson, E., & Powell, D. (2004). *John Clare: Major Works*. Clarendon: Oxford University Press.
Semali, L. M., & Kincheloe, J. L. (1999a). Introduction: What is Indigenous knowledge and why should we study it? In L. M. Semali and J. L. Kincheloe (Eds.), *What Is Indigenous Knowledge? Voices from the Academy* (pp. 3–57), New York & London: Falmer.
Semali, L. M., & Kincheloe, J. L. (Eds). (1999b). *What Is Indigenous Knowledge? Voices from the Academy*, New York & London: Falmer.
Sillitoe, P. (1998). The development of Indigenous knowledge: A new applied anthropology. *Current Anthropology*

39(2), 223–252.

Sillitoe, P. (2002). Globalizing indigenous knowledge. In P. Sillitoe, A. Bicker, & J. Pottier (Eds.), *Participating in Development: Approaches to Indigenous Knowledge* (pp. 108–138), London & New York: Routledge.

Sillitoe, P. (2007) Local science vs. global science: An overview. In P. Sillitoe (Ed), *Local Science vs. Global Science: Approaches to Indigenous Knowledge in International Development* (pp. 1–22). New York & Oxford: Berghahn Books.

Smith, L. (2007) Empty gestures? Heritage and the politics of recognition. In H. Silverman & D. F. Ruggles (Eds), *Cultural Heritage and Human Rights* (pp. 159–171), New York: Springer.

Snyder, G. (1995). *A Place in Space: Ethics, Aesthetics and Watersheds, New and Selected Prose*. Washington, DC: Counterpoint.

Spivak, G. C. (1985). Criticism, feminism and the institution: An interview with Gayatri Chakravorty Spivak. Thesis Eleven 10 (11), 175–187.

Whitt, L. (2009). *Science, Colonialism, and Indigenous Peoples*. Cambridge: Cambridge University Press.

Zent, S. (2009). A genealogy of scientific representations of Indigenous knowledge. In S. Heckler (Ed.), Landscape, *Process and Power: Re-evaluating Traditional Environmental Knowledge* (pp. 19–67). New York & Oxford: Berghahn.

CHAPTER EIGHT

Ruminations on Red Revitalization

Exploring Complexities of Identity, Difference and Nationhood in Indigenous Education

MARTIN CANNON

This chapter considers the importance and challenges associated with bringing Indigenous knowledge into postsecondary institutions of learning. I also provide an in-depth discussion of colonialism and racism, and the way this has shaped my own identity as an Indigenous (Onyota'a:ka, Six Nations) person. I then chronicle my involvement in developing a degree specialization from 2002 to 2007 offering undergraduates at a Canadian university an opportunity to think and work within Indigenous traditions, conceptual frameworks, and knowledge. The goal of the chapter is to provide greater clarity and specificity about the individual and institutional challenges facing some of us as scholars engaged in developing programs that incorporate Indigenous knowledge and ways of knowing. I want to raise critical questions about identity, difference, and belonging, the way this shapes knowledge production as well as the definition, delivery, and development of Indigenous knowledge education in the academy. In the conclusion to the chapter, I offer my own personal and scholarly reflections on the mobilization of Indigenous knowledge, and the vision and praxis of decolonizing Aboriginal education.

FIRST WORDS: WHERE IT IS THAT WE COME FROM

In his article "Indigenous Knowledge and the Cultural Interface," Martin Nakata (2002) asks educators to take seriously an oversimplification that has pervaded much of intellectual thinking about Indigenous knowledge in the academy. In raising the question "what is Indigenous knowledge?" he does not contest the existence of these knowledges but is rather concerned with the tendency to regard them as standing in dichotomous, either/or relation with "Western" or "scientific knowledge" (Nakata, 2002, p. 283). Like others who have criticized a cultural/Western, Indigenous/scientific nexus (Agrawal, 1995), Nakata is focused on matters involving the exchange, diversity, development, and transformation of knowledge systems (Nakata, 2002, p. 284). He contests an Indigenous/

Western dualism because it assumes fixity across time and space, a falsehood given the diversity and transformation among all knowledge-based and societal systems (Nakata, 2002; see also Wolf, 1997).

In choosing to focus on questions of Indigenous knowledge as "systems of knowledge" or as epistemology, Nakata (2002) is steadfastly resistant to a view of knowledge that is static and unchanging. In order to truly appreciate Indigenous knowledge, emphasis must be placed on the life-world—the places we live in, and the conditions that shape us as Indigenous peoples. The intersection of Western and Indigenous domains is what Nakata refers to as "the cultural interface," a space that if closely considered will lead to a much more dynamic definition and understanding of Indigenous knowledges. He writes: "Viewing the Cultural Interface as the beginning point accepts that inevitably Knowledge systems as they operate in people's daily lives will interact, develop, change, and transform" (Nakata, 2002, p. 286). He explains:

> At the interface, traditional forms and ways of knowing, or the residue of those, that we bring from the pre-contact historical trajectory inform how we think and act and so do Western ways...for many of us a blend of both has become our lifeworld (Nakata, 2002, p. 285).

The culture/knowledge interface raises important issues for the academy in terms of decolonization and reform. Most importantly, it causes us to reflect on the multitude of Indigenous and other knowledge systems and the way these have evolved and continue to develop over space and time. The process as experienced by us as Indigenous people involves much "rejection, resistance, subversiveness, pragmatism, ambivalence, accommodation, participation [and] cooperation" (Nakata, 2002, p. 285). Although Nakata is not the only scholar to define Indigenous knowledge in such dynamic and transformative ways (see Dei, 2008), he shows us that it is precisely these sorts of definitions that ought to shape current theoretical underpinnings of pedagogy and practice. It needs to transform the way that Indigenous knowledge is acted upon and contemplated within the academy.

Indigenous knowledge cannot be understood as "another information set from which data can be extracted to plug into scientific frameworks" (Nakashima & de Guchteniere, quoted in Nakata, 2002, p. 283). Nor can the human sciences afford to "celebrate" Indigenous knowledges as "less inferior" while failing to recognize precisely what makes them different (St. Denis, 2004, 2009). Indeed, much can be gained from seeing Indigenous knowledge in all of its dynamism, heterogeneity, and diversity, including the refusal to have our knowledge positioned as simply cultural or Other. It is precisely at this complex juncture of time, space, and cultural hybridity that I wish to begin this chapter. I want to explore issues of identity, colonialism, and nationhood, and the way these factors shape the production of Indigenous knowledge systems, and the development and delivery of Indigenous knowledge education.

In general, it is important to look to the particularities of lived experience when it comes to thinking about Indigenous knowledge. In order to truly appreciate the kinds of Indigenous knowledge we possess as Indigenous peoples, it is important to contemplate the complexity of the self and history, our varied experiences of colonialism, including the places where we make decisions and express agency (Nakata, 2002, p. 286). For me, the knowledge I possess as an Indigenous person has developed over time, and it has been influenced by changing circumstances, especially as this relates to matters of identity and belonging. Colonialism has caused me to think in deeply reflective ways about what it means to be an Indigenous person in Canada and also, the knowledge I possess as a Haudenosaunee,[1] or Six Nations person.

When I think of what it means to be an Indigenous person, the history of colonialism cannot be underestimated. I am referring specifically to the impact of colonial policy and legislation that has effected legal categories onto the identities of Indigenous nations and peoples in Canada—a process whereby Indigenous peoples went from being sovereign nations to "Indians" for state administrative purposes (Magnet, 2003), and to dispossess us of land (Lawrence, 2004). I have written elsewhere about Canada's Indian Act, and the matter of federally imposed categories of identity (Cannon, 2006, 2007, 2008). Here I wish to point out that the experience of acquiring federal recognition as an Indian represented a life-altering moment, one that shaped and motivated the recovery of traditional knowledges concerning my own identity and belonging.

The experience of being an Indigenous person extends far beyond federal and colonial legislation. Over the years, I have realized that it rests instead within the stories we tell ourselves about who we are as nations. The ones that I prefer to have stick with me are rooted in an ancient set of understandings and stories that are shared in common in my nation. The story of creation is one such story. Although the story takes days to tell, and is normally orated, our elders tell us that before this earth was created, there was only water and water beings (Thomas & Boyle, 1994). There also existed the sky world and sky beings. Sky Woman fell one day from this world and brought with her the medicines: the corn, beans, squash, tobacco, and strawberries that sustain us. The water beings laid her and her medicines on a turtle's back—and at that time—Mother Earth was created.

How we came to occupy the world is almost as important as how we got to be situated where we are today spatially. Indigenous peoples did not create Indian reserves in what is now called Canada. Indeed, our territories extend far beyond the physical and ideological boundaries constructed by governmental policy aimed at easing our administration as Indians. The coming of my nation to the banks of the Grand River in what is now Ontario, Canada is rooted in early historical alliances that pre-date colonialism. In an exchange of gratitude for our complicated partnership with the British during the American War of Independence, Sir Frederick Haldimand granted to us a sizable six-mile portion of land on either side of the Grand River from its mouth to its source on 25 October 1784. This story is familiar to me and others in my community.

The way we understand ourselves, individually and in relation to each other, is fundamental to our identities as nations. For the Six Nations, the story that describes how best to live with one another is contained in the *Kayanerenhkowa*, or in English, the Great Law of Peace. The *Kayanerenhkowa* tells the story of events in the life of a wise man—The Great Peacemaker—who first brought words of peace to Ukwehuwe at an estimated date of 1192 (Johansen, 1995). The *Kayanerenhkowa* cannot be summarized in a few short pages. As Hill (2008) writes, the story itself takes between eight and eleven days to recite (p. 26). The *Kayanerenhkowa* is of fundamental importance to understanding traditional governance, or as Seneca legal scholar Rob Porter (1998) writes

> [I]t sets forth a variety of mechanical rules governing the process by which member nations address confederate affairs, including the management of diplomatic and military relations with the other continental powers, trade relations with governmental and private interests and colonial relationships with client tribes (p. 817).

The Great Law of Peace is a story that details our very origins as Haudenosaunee. The story itself tells how a Confederacy of Six Nations gained its authority, definition, organization, and functioning as an independent sovereign confederacy of nations (see Haudenosaunee Confederacy, 1983, 31A:13). Like many stories, the *Kayanerenhkowa* was recorded in beaded wampum (Cannon, 2007).

Wampum are of great significance to Haudenosaunee because they functioned to formalize agreements. Furthermore, and as Mohawk scholar Patricia Monture (1999) writes, wampum were neither easily forgotten nor destroyed. Wampum represent the strength of the Haudenosaunee (p. 36–37). They are rooted in the Indigenous knowledge we possess as present, past, and future generations of Haudenosaunee.

It is nothing short of remarkable that we continue as Haudenosaunee to preserve these rich cultural knowledges of our ancestors. The story of Sky Woman, who we are as people, and most importantly, who we want to become, remain on the minds of many. In responding to federally imposed categories of identity and citizenship, some of us look to traditional stories in a way that invariably transforms knowledge production. Our stories shape the way we think about identity and belonging, and they are especially relevant to decolonizing colonial understandings of citizenship. They are also relevant to challenging patriarchy and gender discrimination. In seeking to show that Indigenous knowledges are dynamic and transformative, I want to emphasize that our stories tell us as much about governance and nationhood, as they do about the roles and responsibilities of men and women.

My decision to talk about gender relations, and men's and women's roles, is not simply attached to a scholarly or academic pursuit concerned with fitting one's theoretical work into a feminist tradition or thought paradigm. When I speak of the history of sex discrimination, I am not simply adopting a feminist lens or engaging in a debate concerning "men in feminism" (Jardine & Smith, 1987). Rather, my aim is to speak about histories that have affected me personally because of the gender of my ancestors and also because of the everyday lived particularities that shape my experience and location as an Indigenous person. I am concerned with histories of sex discrimination—in particular how these interlock with histories of racialization—because they are tied to patriarchal strategies that attempted to colonize us as Haudenosaunee peoples.

I have written elsewhere that men's decision to challenge sexism and gender discrimination is not only based on an academic interest in anti-sexist education (Cannon, 2008). Rather, there is ancient context for describing women's status, and for being concerned about gender imbalance and exclusion. It is rooted in the philosophies we use to shed critical light on contemporary contexts as Indigenous peoples. I am not the first Haudenosaunee writer to suggest that it is the responsibility of men to combat patriarchy (Alfred, 1993, p. 8; Kane & Maracle, 1989; Monture, 1999). Indeed, the knowledge we possess as Haudenosaunee peoples requires us to exercise our responsibility in opposing patriarchy—a strategy employed by settler colonials to disrupt the balance of gender and complementarity in our nation (Cannon, 2007).

It is imperative that we look beyond categories of identity and belonging imposed upon us by colonialism in Canadian legislation, especially when it comes to matters of identity and belonging. Federal legislation is modeled on a patrilineal model of descent reckoning, common to Europeans in the mid-19th century. Under the patriarchal model, a person's identity was determined through the male line of descent. For Haudenosaunee, we look to relatives on the female side of the family in order to understand who we are as nations. A person's clan affiliation is matrilineal if it is determined through one's mother and grandmothers. This is something many elders have made clear to us as a nation (North American Indian Travelling College, 1984, 1993), and it was also of great interest to anthropologists who were determined to document it over time.

Under the Indian Act, I must bifurcate my identity into impossible either/or categorizations. I am not an "authentic" or "real" Indian (Lawrence, 2004) because my father is White. Traditionally, however, it is of no matter that my father is of Anglo-British descent. It matters only that my mother and grandmothers are from the Oneida nation, each of them belonging to the Turtle Clan. I believe my ancestors would have wanted me to think seriously about these systems of kinship organization when it comes to matters of intermarriage and the trouble brought on by the Indian Act, both currently, and in the past. The knowledge we possess as Haudenosaunee people is important to mobilize, especially where matters of identity, nationhood, and belonging are concerned.

Indigenous knowledge is fundamental to who we are as nations. It shapes the way we view the world and people around us. The knowledge we possess as Indigenous peoples has been passed along through many generations and is of vital importance to our sense of cultural identity, heritage, and the history of our peoples. Combined, these things tell us how we got to a specific territory or place and also where we are going. Indigenous knowledge is local or place-based. To be clear: the knowledge I possess as a Haudenosaunee person is altogether distinct and different from other Indigenous nations in Canada. I wish to emphasize this latter dimension of Indigenous knowledge because it provides a much needed corrective to practices that routinely treat Indigenous peoples as if we were all the same.

The history of Canada is one that is distinctly colonial in nature, and in that sense, it is one that has been oblivious to the subtle and often substantial differences between us as Indigenous nations. Sunera Thobani (2007) aptly describes colonialism as a condition that "produces homogeneity out of heterogeneous populations" (p. 24). As Goldberg writes "Colonialism…was about managing heterogeneity, dealing with difference through imposition and restriction, regulation and repression" (quoted in Thobani, 2007, p. 24). State practices remain focused on creating homogeneity of our populations, though this can be contested by affirming that Indigenous knowledges are specific to a collection or nation of people. Indeed, the idea of Indigenous knowledge as placed-based knowledge is one that the academy needs to take seriously if it hopes to address the needs of Indigenous peoples in the territories where their educational institutions are hosted.

In summation, the knowledge we possess as Indigenous peoples is neither static nor unchanging. As Nakata (2002) suggests, it is dynamic and has changed over time. Moreover, it has been profoundly impacted by histories of colonization and genocide, the nature of which has affected Indigenous peoples differently across what is now called Canada. Like many Indigenous peoples, my own familial history tells an altogether familiar story of the displacement brought on by colonialism, the nature of which is complicated at its best, and painful to tell at its worst. In the next section of this chapter, I detail some of this history in an effort to contextualize my own positionality as an Indigenous scholar entrusted with the responsibility of developing a program for undergraduates on Canada's prairies to think and work within Indigenous knowledge and conceptual frameworks. I then describe the program in further detail, offering some thoughts about Indigenous knowledge education.

REVISITING HISTORIC PASTS: MEMORY, CHANGE, AND COLONIZATION

Who has Indigenous knowledge? The question, while seemingly benign, is of profound importance and inevitably must be dealt with by Indigenous scholars charged with the duty of decolonizing curricula and claiming a space in the academy for Indigenous knowledge education. In her 2004 article "Real Indians," Cree/Metis scholar Verna St. Denis suggests that Indigenous scholars take this question seriously, something that inevitably requires us to grapple with our own personal identities when answering it. She reminds us that our histories have been complicated by colonialism, placing some of us into complex positions relative to language maintenance, reclamation, and the doing of Indigenous knowledge in classrooms. She observes "Aboriginal teachers charged with the responsibility of supporting the development of a positive and strong cultural identity...must struggle with their own challenges of reclamation and revitalization" (St. Denis, 2004, p. 38).

It is incumbent upon us to think seriously about the way that colonialism has shaped our identity as Indigenous peoples. The matter itself requires in part a look inward at the intricacies of seemingly mundane familial histories. Many writers, some of them Haudenosaunee, have already engaged in this process (Maracle, 2005; Schwager, 2003; Spears, 2003). It has also been the subject of considerable artistic expression and criticism. In his 1994 Brazilian soapstone sculpture "I Can't Speak My Language," Inuk artist Angus Kaanerk Cockney calls on spectators to think seriously about the colonization of Indigenous peoples. He is concerned with the loss of Indigenous languages because of educational, policy-based, and genocidal practices. When I first saw Cockney's sculpture at the Prince of Wales Museum in Yellowknife, NWT, it reminded me of a long history of colonial domination and language loss in Canada. Like many Indigenous peoples, I can relate to the impact of language loss because it is something that has affected me personally.

The displacement of Indigenous peoples has a long history. This history varies regionally in Canada, but in many cases, and in the first instance, it involved the movement of people from traditional territories to reserve lands created for them by the colonizer. For later generations, my grandfather's in particular, it involved the migration from reserves to cities for the purposes of employment and economic sustainability. These histories in particular are important when it comes to thinking about the maintenance of language, as well as the transmission of Indigenous knowledge. In order to mark spaces as urban, Indigenous bodies were—and are still today—regulated through practices of difference-making (Cannon & Sunseri, in press). These are material and symbolic practices intended to effect the removal of Indigenous peoples from their lands and territories. The history is lengthy and complex, but it shaped the choices available to our ancestors, providing in turn the basis for culture and language loss.

The history I am describing has impacted on my own family. One of the earliest recollections I have of my grandfather are times spent in the backyard of his house in Brantford, Ontario. It was there that I would busy myself with childhood pursuits, outdoors on weekends, while he socialized at the kitchen table with my great-grandfather in the Mohawk language. Whether inadvertently, or by conscious determination to ensure that my generation did not acquire the Mohawk language, my grandfather chose ultimately not to teach me—or let me—or any of his children (my mother included) listen in on his native tongue. This meant that, effectively, the ability to communicate in Mohawk ended in my family when my grandfather passed in March of 1984. While my grandmother would succeed him in this world, her own life journey was complicated by a loss of language and culture.

My grandmother attended the Mohawk Institute with her brother and sister from 1924 to 1934. The New England Company—a non-sectarian Protestant missionary organization—formally established the Mohawk Institute in 1829 (Miller, 1996, p. 73). By the late 1830s, the Mohawk Institute, or "mush hole" functioned as a fully developed "residential school" (ibid.). The curricula were strictly gendered in accordance with Eurocentric understandings: boys received training in carpentry and other trades, and girls, instruction in sewing and general housekeeping (Miller, 1996, also see Graham, 1997, pp. 18–21). My grandmother's time at this school prohibited her from using her Oneida language and most surely devalued her Haudenosaunee culture. In fact, I am struck to this day by my grandmother's refusal to talk at all about being a Haudenosaunee person. I attribute her reluctance as being tied to her experience of education. Determined as she seemed to have been to forgo the ways of her people, my grandmother never spoke to me, or any of her children, about being Haudenosaunee.

We are obliged to think seriously about the familial histories I am describing. Over time, I have come to realize they are not specific to my own experience or even to my nation. Nor do these histories reflect the experience of my grandparent's generation across the board. They do not foreclose, for that matter, histories of resistance by older generations to oppose the forces of colonialism. They do not furthermore preclude a determination by a current generation to revitalize our culture or even to embark on the lengthy and sometimes difficult task of re-learning our Indigenous languages. What these complex histories do suggest is that our ancestors made choices—deliberate or inadvertent—themselves shaped by histories of colonial dominance and genocide. For well over a century, our ancestors were subject to cognitive, pedagogical, and linguistic supremacy of a sort that continues to shape our identities as Indigenous peoples today. These histories cannot help but shape our experience and identities today.

Residential schools were aimed at making people like my grandmother productive members of an emerging capitalist economy. Like others of her generation, this was a particularly violent and disruptive process, involving in some cases, though not in my grandmother's, the forcible removal of children from their homes and communities. Our ancestors were subjected to instruction premised on colonial superiority, in turn marking their cultures and knowledge as inferior. It is perhaps therefore not surprising that my grandmother elected to concentrate her efforts on city life, the Anglican faith and calendar (though sometimes United or Pentecostal), and speaking to her children, and grandchildren, in English. I have struggled at different times in my life to understand these choices with frustration, confusion, and anger, especially in my efforts to claim my Haudenosaunee identity.

The intergenerational impacts effected by residential schooling, and the refusal by our forebears to teach or otherwise speak to us in our languages, cannot be underestimated. A public apology by Canada's Prime Minister to former students of residential schools on June 11, 2008, cannot reverse the loss of language weighing on my own and other generations of Indigenous peoples. Despite ameliorative efforts, many of us still struggle to acquire an ability to communicate in our languages and to piece together cultural practices that are relevant to us when sorting through issues such as spirituality, ceremonial matters, even clan-based belonging. It is precisely these kinds of traditional practices that were pushed out of educational institutions premised on colonial superiority. Many of us seek to revitalize these knowledges and to incorporate them as cultural understandings into our everyday life.

As nations of individuals, we are determined to recover our languages and culture. Many work tirelessly in communities to maintain our stories, and to transmit our knowledge to future generations. Collectively, we have envisioned a way forward based on traditional teachings. Our communities offer programs that are culturally specific and appropriate, many of them seeking to reclaim and revitalize the customary ways of our people. These successes demonstrate our perseverance as peoples and our resistance to colonialism. They are indicative of widespread resurgence in our nations to maintain our Indigenous ways of knowing, our stories and our ways of being. Having said that, I am mindful of the choices available to our ancestors in the face of racism and colonial injustice. In light of my own familial history, I want to think seriously about the identities produced out of colonialism, and furthermore, to identify how a politics of cultural authenticity disregards the impact of this history upon them.

The impact of colonial injustice on our identities concerns me greatly. Exactly what are the implications of colonial injustice and its impact on personal and familial histories? What impact furthermore does this have for educational practice and reform? In the next section of this chapter, I pay close critical attention to these questions based in part on my own life history, as well as my experience as an Indigenous scholar charged with the responsibility of developing an undergraduate degree program focused on Indigenous knowledge and traditions. I center my discussion on two broad assertions. First, post-secondary institutions should endeavor to focus on the local or place-based knowledge of the nations whose territories they find themselves hosted. Second, the academy must better acknowledge the impact of colonialism on the identity of Indigenous peoples, and endeavor to realize the challenges and complexities this presents for some of us in the doing of Indigenous knowledge education.

The questions I am raising must be taken seriously. What does it mean for an Indigenous scholar who is familiar with the history and protocols of one nation to live and teach in another nation or territory? What do Indigenous scholars need to take into consideration when it comes to formal education and instruction? What sets of pedagogical strategies and protocols are available to us in imparting knowledge that is respectful of an Indigenous territory or place? How might the academy better exercise a degree of understanding on matters of difference, identity, and nationhood in ways that are responsive to the multiplicity of Indigenous nations and their aspirations as divergent peoples? It is to an examination and discussion of these questions that I now turn.

INDIGENOUS KNOWLEDGE AND THE ACADEMY: EMBRACING DIFFERENCE, IDENTITY, AND NATIONHOOD

In 2002, I was appointed to a tenure stream position at the University of Saskatchewan, a mid-sized university located on the Canadian prairies. Saskatchewan is comprised of some seventy-four First Nations communities with populations that live on and off reserves. There are approximately 130,000 people who identify as Aboriginal peoples in the province, although many prefer to identify as nations. Saskatchewan is home to six principal nations including the Cree, Metis, Dene, Saulteaux, Lakota, and Nakota nations. Although collectively they share the land and are connected together historically, the nations of Indigenous peoples living in Saskatchewan are diverse. The stories they tell—and pass on to succeeding generations—are different than in my own nation. These are knowledges rooted in the land and nations making up the territories we now call Canada. These differences must be taken seriously when contemplating Indigenous knowledge education.

As Indigenous peoples, we are familiar and conscious of the differences that I am describing. When introducing ourselves to one another, we typically acknowledge the territory and/or people who host us. If we do not know this information, we find out, and we in turn share with them something about our specific history, nationhood, and identity. My arrival in Saskatchewan was very quickly marked by these kinds of exchanges, both academically and in community-based settings. At an Elder's gathering held early on in my academic appointment, I quickly realized that my colleagues knew of histories different than my own and that Saskatchewan was home to people whose histories were distinct from my own. The province itself is marked by linguistic differences: Cree itself is nothing like the Mohawk spoken by my grandfather. Numbered treaties form the basis of nation-to-nation agreements; and the stories—including that of creation, or how it was that the people came to occupy this earth—are remarkably distinct.

I feel very strongly about identifying Indigenous peoples as different by nation. Despite what colonialism has taught us about "Indians" being the same in nature and historicity, the nations that have called Saskatchewan home for generations, share in common a unique set of linguistic, political, and historical differences unique from those of, say, the Mikmaw or Onondaga nations.

Educators cannot underestimate this matter. In order to be truly decolonizing, the planning, development, and doing of Indigenous knowledge education must start first by acquiring a familiarity with a given territory or place, as well as the set of stories held by nations in the area. Second, a set of trusts—and institutional supports—enabling community involvement, local input, and a community of elders from local nations to participate in the development of education aimed at Indigenous youth and local citizens needs to take place.

If Indigenous knowledge is specific to a territory or place, then emphasis should be placed on local knowledges. Out of respect to Indigenous peoples alone, time should be taken to understand the Indigenous knowledge systems local to a given history and land-base. These kinds of partnerships need to be considered by the academy in the very first instance of conceptualizing an Indigenous knowledge program. These partnerships take time to develop within institutions of higher learning, and they have often been excluded from formal history and learning. Histories of exclusion are not the only set of challenges facing the academy in the development and definition of Indigenous knowledge education. It is also urgent that a series of critical pedagogies intent on having people think about the self and history, including local Indigenous knowledges and the varied experience of colonialism as well as people's position relative to settler colonialism take place.

As a pedagogical strategy aimed at having people think about the knowledge they possess as Indigenous peoples—and as a way of highlighting Indigenous knowledges in contemporary contexts—I used classroom activities aimed at rendering biographical details involving identity and history visible to both Indigenous and non-Indigenous students in my classroom. Much of this was accomplished through autobiographical discussions and assignments where I asked all students to think about where they stood in relation to the history of Indigenous peoples in Saskatchewan. Haig-Brown (2009) discusses her use of "decolonizing autobiographies" to historize land and engage discourses of diasporic studies and Indigeneity. I used them in a similar fashion, as a way of introducing myself as an Indigenous person with a history altogether unique from the Lakota, Nakota, Dene, Cree, and Saulteaux nations. I was intent on having non-Indigenous students speak of their unique treaty relationships.

Having students think in general about their relationship to a territory or place, as well where they stand in relation to histories of colonialism, territory, or place is a powerful pedagogical tool. In my classroom, Indigenous students were often struck by my experience of federally imposed categories of identity, and they shared stories similar to my own, but altogether different with respect to the histories of displacement and colonial policy (see Cannon, 2007). They also spoke of treaty relationships, not altogether different than the nation-to-nation agreements we share with the British as Haudenosaunee, but yet unique in their own right. These are the kinds of dynamic knowledges spoken of by Nakata (2002). They are precisely the kinds of "lived experience" and "particularities of location" noted by Dei (2008) that need to inform the theory guiding the teaching and learning process.

Asking people to position themselves as Indigenous peoples is entirely consistent with Indigenous ways of knowing. When we introduce ourselves, as mentioned, we ordinarily tell each other where we are from, and what nation we belong to. Pedagogically, it is important to position ourselves in these ways as Indigenous peoples because it allows us to sort out what makes our histories and traditions both similar and unique. These are important discussions to have between us, especially in light of colonial dominance, where the tendency has been to treat us the same and as Indians. Positioning ourselves also allows non-Indigenous students to think critically about where they stand in relation to a territory or place and how they are implicated in White settler colonialism. These are the kinds of pedagogy I chose to implement in my classroom. Even still, the doing of Indigenous knowledge and especially its reception in the academy is by no means easily determined.

CULTURE, COMPLEXITY, AND INDIGENOUS KNOWLEDGE: A CRITICAL INTERROGATION

The university in general faces considerable challenges where the implementation of Indigenous knowledge is concerned. In addition to the differences between nations, and the need to account for them, the academy is built on Western knowledge systems (Battiste & Henderson, 2000) thought always to stand in dichotomous—and more valued—relation to Indigenous knowledge. When a university decides to offer courses enabling undergraduates with an opportunity to think and work within Indigenous knowledge and traditions, it does not easily overcome a set of dualisms that have served historically to delegitimize Indigenous ways of knowing. Despite ameliorative efforts, the university does not simply transcend its own structural advantage or epistemological power, nor does it remedy histories of colonial injustice or racism by merely incorporating Indigenous knowledge into its curriculum. With respect to the latter issues of power, I view Indigenous knowledge as a bit of a double-edged sword.

When I think about the knowledge we possess as Indigenous peoples, I am conscious of the very traditions that were pushed out of educational institutions and that—in the case of my own family—have represented a significant barrier in fully realizing my own identity. At the same time, I am conscious of the institutional challenges attached to bringing Indigenous knowledge into the university. Much of this stems from what Cote-Meek (2010) and others (LaRocque, 2001; St. Denis, 2004, 2009) have observed as a tendency to view Indigenous peoples as being of culture and not mind. As St. Denis (2009) has suggested, we cannot as Indigenous scholars allow for the development of Indigenous knowledge or "culturally relevant education" when colonialism or critical race analysis is left unexplored in other parts of the curriculum (p. 164).

Comanche curator Paul Chaat Smith provides the conceptual context for issues I am raising. With respect to the relationship between Indigenous knowledge, racism, and colonialism, his concern is with romanticism. In his book *Everything You Know about Indians Is Wrong,* Chaat Smith (2009) defines romanticism as "a specialized vocabulary created by Euros for Indians" ensuring in turn "a status as strange, primitive and exotic" (p. 17). While romanticism cannot in itself explain the motivation—or fascination—by educational institutions to incorporate Indigenous knowledge and cultural perspectives into their curricula, it does give us cause for concern about the difference that Indigeneity makes, including some historic context for demanding clarification about culture-based educational initiatives. The racism we need to challenge as Indigenous scholars has as much to do today with the disavowal of Indigenous knowledge as it does with culture especially the role it has played in the naming and marking of others as different.

The binary of mind/culture depends ultimately on the definition provided of Indigenous knowledge and on whether the academy chooses to pay attention to histories of colonialism and difference-making. I believe that my experience at Saskatchewan led me to appreciate the complexity of cultural knowledges and how much of the knowledge we possess as Indigenous peoples resides in our everyday lived experience. As Nakata (2002) explains, Indigenous knowledge has been discussed as a commodity, "something that can be value-added, something that can be exchanged, traded, appropriated, preserved, something that can be excavated and mined" (p. 283). In order to challenge this way of thinking, it will be necessary to redefine Indigenous knowledge in ways I discussed earlier in this chapter and informed by the exchanges we share together as Indigenous peoples about identity, belonging, and citizenship. This is precisely the kind of cultural complexity that should be read into Indigenous knowledge.

The incorporation of Indigenous knowledge into the university cannot alone combat histories of racism, colonial injustice, and exclusion. But this does not mean that it should be dismissed altogether. Instead, we need to simultaneously incorporate anti-racist and anti-colonial pedagogy into our curricula and to raise a series of critical questions within the academy involving the construction of racial and gendered difference, and the historic representation of Indigenous peoples as cultural, exotic Others. I am not the only Indigenous scholar to raise this matter. Mohawk scholar Taiaiake Alfred (2009) describes how culture-based solutions can work to maintain—or leave unquestioned—oppressive practices within institutions of Eurocentric power (also see Deloria, 1969; LaRocque, 2001; St. Denis, 2004, 2009). He writes

> [T]he state celebrates paint and feathers and Indian dancing, because they reinforce the image of doomed nobility that justified the pretense of European sovereignty on Turtle Island. Tribal casinos, Indian tax immunity, and Aboriginal fisheries, on the other hand, are uncomfortable reminders that—despite the doctrine of state sovereignty—indigenous identities and rights continue to exist (Alfred, 2009, p. 83).

There has been an historic tendency, as Alfred suggests, to treat cultural knowledge as though it were a static and unchanging entity. He also draws attention to a politics of representation that shapes our everyday lives, and to the academy as an institution of power and privilege. If culture itself has allowed the colonizers to imagine themselves as civilized but only insofar as they establish themselves in contrast with the mythical construction of Indigeneity in the colonial imaginary, then what is to be done with culture? Culture should not become irrelevant, but instead, we should engage the interface of culture, mind, and soul as inseparable, dynamic, and continually evolving.

A singular focus on Indigenous knowledge education aimed at the incorporation of Indigenous culture makes possible a caricature of Indigeneity. At worst, it forecloses any real thinking about the naming and marking of others as different, the role of difference-making practices, and the production of rigid binaries between Indigenous and Western ways of knowing. Having said that, we should not abandon the work we do in communities, and in the academy, to incorporate Indigenous knowledge, language, and culture. Instead, we need to be mindful of when—and how—our knowledge is regarded as "cultural knowledge" (Battiste & Henderson, 2000), while Western knowledges pass as invisibly the norm. The emphasis placed on culture and cultural revitalization (St. Denis, 2004, 2009) should not foreclose critical thinking about the breadth of knowledges present in colonial pasts in modern day milieu.

In general, I think that change starts with the academy realizing that a person who identifies as an Indigenous person may not necessarily possess knowledge about a particular nation or territory. Nor should it be assumed that an Indigenous person understands the proper protocol for acquiring this knowledge. There are two reasons for this. First, and as I have shown in this chapter, we do not always have access to the language and stories of our people depending on the choices made available to our ancestors in the face of racism and white supremacy. Second, Indigenous knowledge is place-based knowledge that is tied to a particular land, language, and nation. The knowledge we possess as Indigenous peoples is different across Canada. Together, these are challenges that must serve as starting points whenever a scholarly institution or person is charged with the responsibility of defining Indigenous knowledge, decolonizing education, and of bringing Indigenous knowledge, culture, and traditions into the academy.

The integration of local or place-based knowledge requires institutional supports, and proper protocol should be followed for acquiring this knowledge. This can be accomplished by forming an advisory committee of elders to advise the university on how best to incorporate Indigenous knowledge and also the sorts of knowledges that are specific to a territory or place, including the types of traditions and knowledge deemed important by its Indigenous citizens. These are "infrastructural issues" that need to begin early on in the planning stages of curricular development and follow on from the hiring of faculty charged with the teaching of courses. On the other hand, we need to broaden the definition we have of Indigenous knowledge to incorporate, though by no means restrictively, the breadth of experiences we have as Indigenous peoples, including the types of knowledges we possess as a result. As Semali and Kincheloe (1999) point out "the Indigenous cultural experience is not the same for everybody; Indigenous knowledge is not a monolithic epistemological category" (p. 24).

Semali and Kincheloe (1999) define subjugated knowledge as one particular dimension of Indigenous knowledge. As they put it, "use of the term, subjugated knowledge, asserts the centrality of power in any study of Indigenous knowledge and any effort to include it in the academy" (Semali & Kincheloe, 1999, p. 31). The matter to which they draw attention is important and useful both historically and pedagogically. Historically, their definition allows us to account for the colonialism and the way it has shaped Indigenous identities. It allows us to see that not every person in Canada realizes what it means to have acquired Indian status, as an example, or what it means to be impacted by residential schools in terms of language and culture loss. Pedagogically, this is a useful starting point for me in trying to address issues of difference, identity, and nationhood. Furthermore, mixed Indigenous/non-Indigenous classrooms—like the ones I instructed at University of Saskatchewan—also allow important discussions about positionality.

The choice of what to include in a course is never an easy process; however, when it involves making decisions about knowledge and traditions that do not belong to you, or about which you are unfamiliar, the process itself can be daunting. These matters are not only complicated by how much (or little) we know of our own traditional protocols and culture, they are made difficult by what sets of community involvements have been made possible and the time we have had to build a rapport with other nations of people or to familiarize ourselves with the ways of a people. Even despite the knowledge we might come to possess in this regard, we can only ever hope to teach about the local and place-based knowledge of peoples located in another territory or place. To teach the local knowledge would in fact be impossible, not to mention decidedly disrespectful to the lands and/or people. These are the kinds of cultural complexities that must be acknowledged by the academy in the definition, delivery, and incorporation of Indigenous knowledge.

CONCLUSION

It is by no means easy to relocate oneself to a territory belonging to a series of different nations and, as part of that experience, develop an Indigenous knowledge program. There are several reasons for this, but in this chapter, I have shown how some of the difficulty is rooted in our own personal and familial histories and the way they have been impacted by colonialism. The tendency to conceive of Indigenous knowledge as a "monolithic epistemological category" makes matters additionally complex. As an example of the contrast between Indigenous knowledges, the story of Sky Woman, the coming of the Great Law of Peace, the relationship we share with the land through nation-to-nation agreements are vastly different from the Cree story of Wisakecahk, the significance of the buffalo, as well as the treaty-making process. At the same time, I am not suggesting that these differences—or the complexities I have outlined—ought to preclude the incorporation of Indigenous knowledge into formal education.

Based on my experience, I think that priority should be placed on the hiring of Indigenous faculty who are familiar with, or already situated in, a territory, nation, or place. The hiring of faculty is not the only initiative that needs to be put into place. We are not all the same as Indigenous nations, therefore, the hiring of faculty needs also to take place inseparably from—and not before—the development of advisory and institutional supports. As an inseparable part of the hiring process, and not just in token ways, it is incumbent on the academy to involve local Indigenous communities, in the very first instance, in ways that make possible local input about the definition, development and delivery of Indigenous knowledge. From an administrative point of view, elders, traditional peoples, and community members who can teach Indigenous knowledge, or otherwise bring its pedagogies to the university in ways that some of us are unable to—or cannot possibly accomplish—must take precedence.

For reasons I have discussed with respect to identity and nationhood, it is impossible to define, develop, or realize Indigenous knowledge programs without first building a series of relationships with the nations specific to a given territory or place. In order to be truly decolonizing, the academy must work to facilitate partnerships between Indigenous peoples and the university itself. These are not the only steps that need to be taken when incorporating Indigenous knowledge. Before the curriculum can be transformed in ways that incorporate Indigenous knowledge, it will be necessary to compile and review resource and curricular materials and to identify local people who can advise us about them. These initiatives are invaluable to us in teaching Indigenous knowledge and in learning about the history specific to a territory or place. Having said that, some of us will be limited in what we can teach due to the availability of materials, their suitability, or our own inability to instruct using Indigenous languages and pedagogies.

In conclusion, there are a number of critical initiatives, each with their own strengths and limitations, which can work in combination to incorporate Indigenous knowledge into the academy. The promotion and development of educational materials aimed at the revitalization of our knowledge and traditions must be prioritized. At the same time, the university needs be mindful of colonialism, identity, and difference. The compiling of culturally relevant resources cannot take place in isolation from assembling materials and courses aimed at understanding the history of difference, nationhood, racism, and settler-colonialism specific to a region or province. Students need also to think critically about culture and difference-making and the role it has played in maintaining colonialism. The doing of Indigenous knowledge remains therefore as much urgent as it is complicated. As Paul Chaat Smith (2009) suggests, it "requires invention, not rewriting"—it may even require "a final break with a form that was never about us in the first place" (p. 52).

Note

1. The word Haudenosaunee, meaning "People of the Longhouse" (a reference to the distinctive houses in which our ancestors once resided), may differ depending on the Six Nations person or community to whom one is

speaking. For example, Taiaiake Alfred refers to his people (the people of Kahnawake Mohawk Nation) as Rotinohshonni (1995, p. 38; 1999, p. xi). Doxtator (1996) chose the word Rotinonhsyonni. I use the word Haudenosaunee as it is one that is familiar to me, and also one that has been used by the Six Nations people in political dealings with the Canadian government (see Haudenosaunee Confederacy, 1983). Several words used henceforth in this paper, including the word Ukwehuwé (the Original ones) are in my grandmother's language, the Onyota'a:ka (Oneida) language, and I am grateful for the advice that has been provided to me in this regard by several Oneida speakers.

REFERENCES

Agrawal, A. (1995) Dismantling the Divide Between Indigenous and Scientific Knowledge. *Development and Change*. (26) 413–439.

Alfred, T. (2009) *Peace, Power, Righteousness: An Indigenous Manifesto* (2nd Edition) Toronto: Oxford University Press.

Alfred, T. (1999). *Peace, Power, Righteousness: An Indigenous Manifesto*. Toronto: Oxford University Press.

Alfred, T. (1995). *Heeding the Voices of Our Ancestors: Kahnawake Mohawk Politics and the Rise of Native Nationalism*. Toronto: Oxford University Press.

Alfred, T. (1993). The People. In North American Indian Travelling College (Eds.), *Words That Come Before All Else: Environmental Philosophies of the Haudenosaunee* (pp. 8–14). North American Travelling College.

Battiste, M., & Henderson, J. S. Y. (2000). *Protecting Indigenous Knowledge & Heritage: A Global Challenge*. Saskatoon: Purich.

Cannon, M. (2008, May). *Revisiting Histories of Gender-Based Exclusion and the New Politics of Indian Identity*. A Paper Written for the National Centre for First Nations Governance. Vancouver, B.C. .

Cannon, M. (2007). Revisiting Histories of Legal Assimilation, Racialized Injustice, and the Future of Indian Status in Canada. In J. P. White, E. Anderson, W. Cornet, & D. Beavon (Eds.), *Aboriginal Policy Research: Moving Forward, Making a Difference*, Volume V (pp. 35–48). Toronto: Thompson Educational.

Cannon, M. (2006). First Nations Citizenship: An Act to Amend the Indian Act (1985) and the Accommodation of Sex-Discriminatory Policy. *Canadian Review of Social Policy (25th Anniversary Edition) 56*, 40–71.

Cannon, M. J. & Sunseri L. (2011) *Racism, Colonialism, and Indigeneity in Canada*. Toronto: Oxford University Press.

Chaat Smith, P. (2009). *Everything You Know about Indians Is Wrong*. Minneapolis: University of Minnesota Press.

Cote-Meek, S. (2010). *Aboriginal Colonial Violence: Exploring the Implications in the Postsecondary Classroom*. (Unpublished Ph. D. Dissertation). Department of Sociology and Equity Studies, Ontario Institute for Studies in Education of the University of Toronto, Toronto.

Dei, G. J. S. (2008). Indigenous Knowledge! Any One? Pedagogical Possibilities for Anti-colonial Education. In G. J. S. Dei (Ed.), *Teaching Africa towards a Transgressive Pedagogy* (pp. 89–103). Dordrecht: Springer.

Deloria, V. Jr. (1969). *Custer Died for Your Sins: An Indian Manifesto*. Norman: University of Oklahoma Press.

Doxtator, D. (1996). *What Happened to the Iroquois Clans? A Study of Clans in Three Nineteenth Century Rotinonhsyonni Communities*. (Unpublished Ph.D. Dissertation), University of Western Ontario, Canada.

Graham, E. (1997). *The Mush Hole: Life at Two Indian Residential Schools*. Waterloo, ON: Heffle.

Haig-Brown, C. (2009). Decolonizing Diaspora: Whose Traditional Land Are We on? *Cultural and Pedagogical Inquiry 1* (1), 4–21.

Haudenosaunee Confederacy. (1983). Statement of the Haudenosaunee Concerning the Constitutional Framework and International Position of the Haudenosaunee Confederacy. In House of Commons Minutes of Proceedings and Evidence of the Special Committee on Indian Self-Government, Issue # 31, Appendix 36. Ottawa: Queen's Printer.

Hill, S. M. (2008). Travelling Down the River of Life Together in Peace and Friendship Forever: Haudenosaunee Land Ethics and Treaty Arrangements as the Basis for Restructuring the Relationship with the British Crown. In L. Simpson (Ed.), *Lighting the Eighth Fire: The Liberation, Resurgence, and Protection of Indigenous Nations* (pp. 23–45). Winnipeg: Arbeiter Ring Publishing.

Jardine, A., & Smith, P (Eds.). (1987). *Men in Feminism*. New York: Methuen.

Johansen, B.E. (1995). Dating the Iroquois Confederacy. *Akwesasne Notes 1* (3&4), 62–63.

Johnston, D. M. (1986). The Quest of the Six Nations Confederacy for Self-Determination. *University of Toronto Faculty Law Review 44*(1), 1–32.

Kane, M. (Osennontion), & Maracle, S. (Skonganleh:ra). (1989). Our World: According to Osennontion and Skonaganleh:ra. *Canadian Woman Studies 10*(2 & 3), 7–19.

King, T. (2003). *The Truth about Stories: A Native Narrative*. Toronto: Anansi.

LaRocque, E. (2001). From the Land to the Classroom: Broadening Epistemology. In J. Oakes, R. Riewe, M. Bennett & B. Chisholm (Eds.), *Pushing the Margins* (pp. 62–75). Winnipeg: Native Studies.

Lawrence, B. (2004). *"Real" Indians and Others: Mixed-Blood Urban Native Peoples and Indigenous Nationhood*. Vancouver: University of British Columbia Press.

Maracle, D. (2005). A Story Untold: A Community-Based Oral Narrative of Mohawk Women's Voices from Point Anne, Ontario. In U. Lischke, & D. T. McNab (Eds.), *Walking a Tightrope: Aboriginal Peoples and their Representations* (pp. 53–98). Waterloo, ON: Wilfrid Laurier University Press.

Magnet, J. E. (2003). Who Are the Aboriginal People of Canada? In J. E. Magnet, & D. A. Dorey (Eds.), *Aboriginal Rights Litigation* (pp. 23–91). Markham: LexisNexis Canada.

Miller, J. R. (1996). *Shingwauk's Vision: A History of Native Residential Schools*. Toronto: University of Toronto Press.

Monture, P. (1999). *Journeying Forward: Dreaming First Nations Independence*. Halifax: Fernwood.

Nakata, M. (2002). Indigenous Knowledge and the Cultural Interface: Underlying Issues at the Intersection of Knowledge and Information Systems. *IFLA Journal 28*(5–6), 281–291.

North American Indian Travelling College. (1984). *Traditional Teachings*. Cornwall Island: North American Indian Travelling College.

North American Indian Travelling College. (1993). *Clanology: Clan System of the Iroquois*. Cornwall Island: North American Indian Travelling College.

Porter, R. B. (1998). Building a New Longhouse: The Case for Government Reform within the Six Nations of the Haudenosaunee. *Buffalo Law Review 46*(3), 805–945.

Schwager, L. (2003). The Drum Keeps Beating: Recovering a Mohawk Identity. In K. Anderson & B. Lawrence (Eds.), *Strong Women Stories: Native Vision and Community Survival* (pp. 36–54). Toronto: Sumach.

Simpson, Audra (1998). The Empire Laughs Back: Tradition, Power, and Play in the Work of Shelley Niro and Ryan Rice In Doris I. Stambrau, Alexandra V. Roth and Sylvia S. Kasprycki (eds.) *Iroquois Art: Visual Expressions of Contemporary Native American Artists* (pp. 48–54) Altenstadt, DE: European Review of Native American Studies.

Semali, L. M. & Kincheloe, J. L. (Eds.). (1999). *What Is Indigenous Knowledge? Voices from the Academy*. New York: Falmer.

Spears, S. (2003). Strong Spirit, Fractured Identity: An Ojibway Adoptee's Journey to Wholeness. In K. Anderson, & B. Lawrence (Eds.), *Strong Women Stories: Native Vision and Community Survival* (pp. 81–94). Toronto: Sumach.

St. Denis, V. (2009). Rethinking Culture Theory in Aboriginal Education. In C. Levine-Rasky (Ed.), *Canadian Perspectives on the Sociology of Education* (pp. 163–182). Oxford University Press.

St. Denis, V. (2004). Real Indians: Cultural Revitalization and Fundamentalism in Aboriginal Education. In C. Schick, J. Jaffe, & A. M. Watkinson (Eds.), *Contesting Fundamentalisms* (pp. 35–47). Halifax: Fernwood,

Thobani, S. (2007). *Exalted Subjects: Studies in the Making of Race and Nation in Canada*. Toronto: University of Toronto Press.

Thomas, J., & Boyle, T. (1994). *Teachings from the Longhouse*. Toronto: Stoddard.

Wolf, E. R. (1997). *Europe and the People without History*. Berkeley: University of California Press.

CHAPTER NINE

Identity, Representation, and Knowledge Production

PATIENCE ELABOR-IDEMUDIA

Knowledge is power that begins with the self and in interaction with others. The fact remains, however, that knowledge production processes traditionally and in contemporary times, have been dominated by Western philosophical thought and worldviews that undermine or devalue indigenous philosophical thoughts that are equally relevant. The dynamics of identity and social difference (race/ethnicity, class, gender, and sexuality) that significantly mediate how knowledge creation experts and practitioners come to produce and validate the use of "knowledge" about marginalized communities and groups have been left highly unaddressed. The result of this practice is a colonial education system that denies peoples' identity and negates their knowledge of self through shifts in focus to only prestigious functions. The problems with this practice is the asymmetrical power relations between educators and the subjects of education, and in the differing frames of reference adopted in the knowledge production process. For example, the failure to recognize the epistemic saliency of the subject of subjective knowing has contributed to maintaining relations of domination in educational practices.

It should be noted that hegemonic knowledge that promotes the interest of powerful, elite groups often obscures its value premises by masquerading as totally objective. Despite occupying positions of considerable status, power, privilege, and authority in the eyes of local peoples, the roles of (Western) experts ". . .may seem of dubious value" to marginalized communities (Heron, 1996, p. 4). Dei (2004) warns that the threat of Western dominance over what constitutes valid knowledge in schools, in addition to marketing knowledge and culture, should call for greater concern among scholars and activists dedicated to the transformation of education and indigenous education in particular. It is therefore, a position taken in this chapter that both identity and representation have implications for power and legitimacy in knowledge production in terms of their effects as frames of reference for validation of such knowledge. The chapter aims to deconstruct knowledge production processes in order to decolonize and challenge its political economy according to Dei and Calliste (2000) that accords certain privileges and legitimacy to certain forms of knowledge while invalidating those whose point of departure is located in insider's perspective and indigeneity.

Using insider's perspective and anti-racist discourse, the chapter critically examines how identity and relations of power shape knowledge production that lead to validation or (de)validation of such knowledge based on identity (race, class, and gender) and location. The author is aware that countering exclusion and Eurocentrism often produces an anxiety framed by *content* rather than grappling with the *modalities* of knowledge production. The chapter therefore addresses the modalities of knowledge production and the implications for students in multicultural classrooms. This is significant because if we are to create a liberatory, transformative knowledge, educators must not only be aware of the body of knowledge that has been produced, they must also understand that the producers of that knowledge are located within particular social, economic, and political contexts of the society called positionality (Tetreault, 1997).

INTERROGATING KNOWLEDGE CONSTRUCTION PROCESS

Code (1991) claims that knowledge involves both subjective and objective dimensions and calls for knowledge created by the knower to reflect both perceived subjective and objective phenomena. She also argues that the "objective/subjective dichotomy in knowledge construction is but one of several dichotomies that have structured mainstream Euro-American epistemology . . ." (p. 158). Therefore, any attempt to sharply distinguish between the two elements of knowing and to label objective knowledge legitimate and subjective knowledge as mere interpretation is inconsistent with how human beings know. In interrogating this trend both subjective experiences and objective knowledge must be emphasized as equally relevant to holist representation of subjects and communities under study (Smith, 1999). There seems to be an underlying problem with perceptions of Western philosophical thoughts and the indigenous knowledge of non-Western cultures. According to Ghanaian philosopher Kwesi Wiredu (1980), indigenous knowledge is generally perceived in knowledge production processes as "doomed to self-damnation unless it can be subjected to the therapeutic benefits of dialectical and critical reflection and re-evaluation. This view if based on existing perceptions that people in traditional setting are lacking in inspiration for critical thinking about theoretical and practical matters of everyday life" (as cited in Karp & Masolo, 2000, p. 7).

We need to bear in mind that recognizing the subjective/objective nature of knowledge does not mean that we must abandon the quest for the construction of knowledge that is as objective as possible. What is called for is the recognition of insider scholarship of the non-Western cultures described "as the production of knowledge by a scholar about a group with which s/he identifies as a member" (Anyidoho, 2008, p. 26). The idea of insider scholarship often evokes a series of queries about who produces what knowledge, about whom and for whom, the link between location and scholarship, between belonging and knowledge production, between identity and representation? These queries, long subjects, sometimes subtexts of debate, are not ones we can afford to dismiss as we look back over the state of knowledge production, in order to chart new courses (Anyidoho, 2008).

Insider scholarship involves shared struggles and calls for research to be inclusive of indigenous ways of knowledge as knowledge should not be an imposition of one's agenda on others (Aguilar, 1981). The struggle itself has to be a process of negotiation. It involves recognizing that the presuppositions, the ideas, interests, and values with which we invariably enter into research[1] may not be those of the people with whom we do research. I am mindful of this in my own work because of my presumption to speak on behalf of "my" research participants. Research agendas should be motivated by dissatisfaction with existing paradigms that are applied, sometimes indiscriminately by governments and international development agencies. I am wary of the harm they cause when they do not take into account the context of people's lives. Alcoff (1991) cautions that "the practice of speaking for others is often born of a desire for mastery, to privilege oneself as the one who more correctly understands the truth about another's situation" (p. 29). This is an indictment we should avoid if we intend to engage in scholarship that affirms people as centers of power and knowledge. Self-reflexivity is always a key. With self-reflexivity and with intentionality, insider scholarship can be an important basis of knowledge production.

Foucault's (1980) work on power and the formation of subjects is useful in the interrogation of knowledge production process. Specifically, he alludes to the fact that there is a contradictory reality of hierarchical arrangement of power in research and that power is exercised rather than possessed, as not primarily repressive but productive and best analyzed from the bottom-up. He sees power as a set of relations dispersed throughout social formation. He argues that the "normal" mode of power is how it works at the micro-level of practice. He proposes that power relations be analyzed by looking for strategies, tactics, and procedures. He also calls for attention to be focused on its effects and not on the intentions of the "powerful." In other words, Foucault instructs us to look at what he describes as the "micro-dynamics of power," that is, the detailed mechanisms of power as they actually work at the lowest level (Foucault, 1980) in this case, in the knowledge production industry.

Collins (2002) calls for any scholar—especially one who is in a position of marginality—to map a personal epistemology for his/her work. At various points in our careers, and for specific research ventures, we should ask ourselves: "On what basis do I claim insider status?" There is the need to allow that others in the research context also define our positionality. If we fail to recognize the ways in which subjective factors—such as race, class, and gender—influence the construction of knowledge, we are unlikely to interrogate established knowledge that contributes to the oppression of marginalized and victimized groups (Elabor-Idemudia, 2002).

IDENTITY, REPRESENTATION, AND KNOWLEDGE PRODUCTION

Knowledge creation practitioners have conveniently denied that they have a stake in which narrative/voice to highlight or privilege. With the pervasive trend toward the commoditization of knowledge under intellectual property law, what is being challenged here is the very ideal of the educational-cultural sphere as the locus of mutual understanding in a pluralist society (Holmes, 2009). Questions about one's identity,[2] culture and history, and politics and the relations to the process can no longer be left unanswered as researchers have assumed the role of "others," without questioning the "right" to go into local communities to conduct social research. But why are identity and knowledge production issues for a new generation of scholars of color? It is not because these are novel concerns, but precisely because they are perpetual challenges that require every generation to offer responses peculiar to their circumstances.

Discursive approaches in knowledge production that allow us to avoid presupposing the subject, thus illuminating the ad hoc reality—that identity is a tool utilized in negotiations between individuals and between individuals and knowledge experts—need interrogating. Support for this argument emerges from claims that emancipation can be reduced to arguments for identity-based rights rather than social justice claims. Identity and discourse are central components of a minority problematic. Any group impacted on by the state on the grounds of a politicized group identity becomes forced to engage with the state in terms of that group identity regardless of group cohesion, thereby creating a minority problematic. Within available discourses, individuals need to consider their perceived position with the position they want and make demands within the constraints of the discourse—in other words, how individuals perceive their interests influences their bid for power. This involves examining what social science scholars take for granted in studies that deal with identity. Ultimately, if one considers identity to be innate, then it becomes less likely that explanation will capture how strategies evolve.

The intimate nature of today's society demands attention to events on one end of the world that may have a ripple effect on the other end. The events of the past few years have shown that we cannot afford to think of "the global village" as merely a cliché (Anyidoho, 2008, p. 27). As bilateral and multilateral agencies move away from obviously coercive modes of neo-liberalism to more subtle, but perhaps even more effective control strategies, the local becomes integrated into the global. Alongside these trends are theoretical perspectives that laud the fusion of ideas and cultures. According to Anyidoho (2008), "it is imperative that we maintain an awareness of the confluence of political, social, economic with identity and ideological forces that influences our scholarship" (p. 27).

In his work on Caribbean immigrants in Britain, Stuart Hall (1999) noted that:

> Identity is not a fixed essence, lying unchanged outside history and culture. It is not some universal and transcendental spirit inside us on which history has made no fundamental mark and it is not one-and-for all. It is not a fixed origin to which we can make some final absolute return (p. 226).

Hall's observation is perceptive, emphasizing the dynamic nature of identity and the potential difficulties of any attempt to problematize or analyze the construct. The questions of what knowledge is for and what knowledge does cannot be answered in their generality. Likewise, as Hall pointed out many years ago, there are "no pedagogies in general" (Hall, 1999). This does not suggest that we simply valorize the "local," whether as a counter to the charge of Eurocentrism or champion specificity as an antidote to hegemony of the universal. The pursuit of the particular—for example, in the demands for separate multicultural schooling in the United Kingdom or "Ethnic studies" in the United States of America and Canada—often leads to a reductive mode of identity politics bearing suspect claims of cultural authenticity on behalf of racialized groups (Puwar & Sharma, 2007).

It is therefore, pertinent to note that the globalized world we live in today is a diasporic reality where identity is "dynamic, fluid, multiple, historically situated and involving of processes that are always changing to fit moods or personality changes" (Henry & Tator 1991, p. 99). The conditions in which a particular "culture," "identity," or "knowledge" emerge, and the constant negotiations, dissonant exchanges, and operations of power which inscribe particular differences should underwrite our pedagogies. Cultural difference cannot be reduced to the consensual unity or the banality of pluralized knowledges (see Hall, 1996; Madood & Pnina, 2007). To practice pedagogy means risking antagonistic exchanges in a classroom with incommensurable points of view and knowledges not being diffused in the moment of their expression (Puwar & Sharma, 2007).

QUESTIONS OF LOCATION AND POSITIONALITY

The idea of identity is at the heart of analysis of location and positionality. Positionality refers to the identities of the researcher in relation to the "researched" (Wolf, 1996). In other words, positionality indicates contextualized and relational locations such as nationality, ethnicity, race, class, education, religion, family affiliation, ideological leanings, epistemological perspectives, and philosophical orientations. It is contextual because it takes account of the circumstances in which knowledge is produced and is relational because it concerns both the subjectivity of the researcher and the subjectivities of others. The focus on positionality is important because of its implications for the nature of knowledge produced and how that knowledge is received. This has been painfully self-evident in writings about non-Western societies whereby missionaries or administrators, non-Westerners made representations about colonies from self-declared locations of authority.

"Situated knowledge" acknowledges differentiated locations, and affirms location as starting points for the production of knowledge. The question of where you stand is important because every research project, and indeed all scholarship, has its basis in the personal. Locations are, however, mobile because each person inhabits multiple locations within and across time. To avoid an identity trap, the question of what you stand for is as important as where you stand. In this way, a discursive space should be created for "an imagined community of…intellectuals that rise above national, racial, and gendered boundaries in the articulation of politically responsible presentations" (Lal, 1996, p. 200).

The commoditization of knowledge is the driving force and central goal of the Schumpeterian competition state, to the precise extent that the leading edge of capitalist production is redefined as technological and managerial innovation (particularly in the financial sphere). All the flowerings of human aspiration and experience can then be treated not just as commodities but as investments in an entrepreneurial self as the economist Gary Becker (1962) has shown with his notion of "human capital." One of the ways Europeans now experience capital failure is when education and culture come packaged with a price tag that disfigures them, even when it doesn't leave them completely out of reach.

Mohanty (1991) appeals to the notion of imagined communities of resistance, proposing that it is not color or sex which constructs the grounds for these struggles. Rather it is the way we think about race, class, and gender—the political links we choose to make among and between struggles. Thus, potentially, "[scholars] of all colors…can align themselves with and participate in these imagined communities. However, clearly our relation and centrality in particular struggles depend on our different…locations and histories" (Mohanty, 1991, p. 4). Henry A. Giroux (2008) posits that "critical pedagogy attempts to understand how power works through the production, distribution, and consumption of knowledge within particular institutional contexts" (p. 28). As the institutional context of educational organizations expands to include virtual environments it is important to probe and to raise questions regarding the relationship between power, technology, and education. A critical pedagogy approach compels one to ask questions about these very "material realities." However, some of the implicit claims of proponents of this technology warrant a friendly interrogation in order to better position ourselves as educators who will be confronting increasingly multicultural classrooms (Vander-Valk, 2008). This is what the analysis in this chapter is attempting to do.

CURRICULUM AND THE REPRODUCTION OF EUROCENTRIC KNOWLEDGE

In academia, racial minorities' experience of education is determined by the assumed superiority of Eurocentric masculinist forms of knowledge. There is a disturbing failure to recognize that minority people do theorize in their communities as part of their community life and that they not only can articulate but also interpret their experiences (Elabor-Idemudia, 2002). The result of failure to recognize this fact is that "knowledge becomes mystified; losing sight of people's needs" (Escobar, 1992, p. 420). In our educational training, knowledge of and knowledge produced by non-Western racialized scholars remain as invisible in the text as we are in classroom discussions. White instructors have always found it possible to write about life where minorities, like women in general, are not present or have had their roles subordinated. This invisibility assumes that the experience of White men is the norm for the entire population and is the only experience that counts.

As Blacks and visible minorities, we see our humanity being reduced to claims that we are a population of ignorant, uncivilized, lazy, childlike, and illiterate peoples (Brittan & Maynard, 1984). The construction of the Negro or the color Black suggests no situatedness in time, history, or space, that is, ethno- or politico-geography. Distortion of facts and the invisibility of peoples from the so-called developing and colonized world characterize much of the learning by White students about the social world. People of color as well as peoples from the developing and colonial world are often shown to be architects of their own disadvantage. Both these views represent a culture that is manufactured by and for those who benefit from racism and sexism. Like other forms of oppression, race and sex oppression are expressed and reproduced at the ideological level as though they were natural processes. Unfortunately, uncovering and exposing the truth could take many generations.

A comprehensive analysis of school textbooks shows how Eurocentrism and racism operate through curriculum (Klein, 1987). In the curriculum, the history of people of color begins when Whites "discover" them. Human civilization is portrayed as an evolutionary process in which Euro-American culture—the Western legal system, democratic forms of government, and a capitalist economy—is considered the best in the world. This perspective is also manifested in the learning resources, which often fail to reflect alternative viewpoints. Daenzer and Dei (1994) argue that the assault on racial-minority students' identity is the direct consequence of bias and exclusion of indigenous knowledge from other cultures from curriculum content. Along with other authorities (Cummins, 1994; Lee, 1985; Moodley, 1984; Solomon, 1992), they share the view that the reproduction of knowledge in the classroom perpetuates racist thinking among both White students and their teachers. Viswanathan (1989) posits that until curriculum is studied less as a receptacle of texts than as activity, that is, as a vehicle of acquiring and exercising power, descriptions of curricular content in terms of expression of universal values on the one hand, or pluralistic, secular identifier on the other, are insufficient signifiers of their historical realities.

Since the 1960s and 1970s, efforts to revise curriculum in North American schools, colleges, and universities to reflect the ethnic, cultural, and gender realities of the population and societies have stimulated heated debates about the nature of knowledge. Banks (1994) identifies five types of knowledge (personal/cultural, popular, mainstream academic, transformative learning, and schooling), which he proposed should be taught in the academy. This proposal has met with a lot of challenges from academics who contest his conceptualization and argue that personal/cultural knowledge is not legitimate. He was accused of not making an essential distinction between the actuality of what occurs and how people interpret their experiences and observations. As an example, the production and organization of knowledge by academicians linguistically and institutionally alienates women of color especially Black women. Often, the language used references the White, upper-middle-class world. Black women's (and other women of color's) daily experiences with racism and sexism mean that their lives are less embedded in the linguistic and institutional hierarchical structures which define academia.

The knowledge developed by this group—as with many other marginalized groups—does not depend solely on the dominant society's thought validation process because it is knowledge which is used outside of and in opposition to dominant society's domain and constitutes the everyday interactions of the group's social world. It is what Foucault refers to as "subjugated knowledges," which are "located low down on the hierarchy." They are far enough away from and sufficiently non-challenging to the mainstream that their "validity is not dependent on the approval of the established regime of thought" (Foucault, 1982, p. 210). It is this same knowledge, derived from everyday experiences that Black women and other women of color bring into the academic arena only to find that such knowledge forms are unacceptable.

MAKING A DIFFERENCE: TEACHERS' ROLE IN RIGHTING THE WRONG

A vital part of preparing individuals to become teachers in multicultural classrooms is helping them to discover how they are experiencing direct contact with students who are culturally different from themselves. Increasingly, educators of color are asking how pre-service students understand diversity, broadening analysis from the quantitative measures that were used a decade ago, to include qualitative indices that add depth and texture to what we know. Researchers have framed their analysis of pre-service students' perspective in different ways which, when taken together suggest that they conceptualize children in individualistic terms, seeing little connections between their demographic "characteristics" and pedagogy. Traditional educational course work does not necessarily help pre-service teachers learn to perceive children of diverse backgrounds in substantially more helpful ways.

Specific teacher education course work designed to address multicultural education is not consistently integral as many programs add on course work about different cultural groups. Noordhoff and Kleinfeld (1991) made particular note of the inadequacy of preparing teachers using additive processes that provide knowledge about different cultural groups and expect pre-service teachers to relate content contained therein to students from diverse cultures. Not only have such efforts proved ineffective in helping pre-service teachers make the intended associations and become more resistant to stereotypes, but in some cases, this type of approach may have strengthened the tendency to overgeneralize and stereotype groups of students from diverse cultures (Cazden & Mehan, 1989; Grant, 1981; McDiarmid & Price, 1993). Avery (1993, p. 16) has concluded that pre-service students would be "unlikely to implement knowledge about particular ethnic groups into curriculum" based on their lack of knowledge about ethnic groups.

A point of departure in teacher education, then can be helping pre-service students learn to observe children carefully and to make their interpretations of them explicit and helping them learn more appropriate and meaningful interpretative frameworks for behavior that they actually see children exhibit in the classroom. Borrowing from Paine's (1990) framework, this would entail assisting pre-service students in moving from individualistic orientation toward children, toward contextual and pedagogical orientations. A first step would be to teach pre-service students, ethnographic skills and to have them begin to learn about children by collecting and interpreting data as an ethnographer would.

Field experiences in culturally diverse classrooms need to be much more extensive and more effectively conceived than many teacher education programs currently provide. These experiences should be closely associated with designated courses that are designed to assess student progress in specific ways. This is to prevent "free-floating" episodes that reinforce stereotypes based on culture, race, gender, and other aspects of diversity. Expecting that pre-service students will naturally intuit how course work is related to teaching children from diverse cultures and backgrounds, even when a plethora of professional literature, as made available and studied in university classes, is neither expedient nor effective. Identifying schools with diverse student and teacher populations that can provide immersion encounters appears requisite if pre-service teachers are to have many opportunities to examine their distortions and their truth about students who are different from them.

Teachers' education course work often covers a great deal of theoretical knowledge in survey fashion, more so than helping students learn to think like, for example, a cognitive psychologist, a sociologist, or an anthropologist. Rather than bombarding students with results of numerous research studies, courses in teacher education programs should focus on helping pre-service students learn to think objectively and systematically about children. Teachers in the field should be selected partly on the basis of their ability to explain their teaching behaviors with reference to learning theory. When there is no explanation provided to pre-service students for children's classroom behavior that they observe, they tend to fall back on their own explanations, which appear to be significantly influenced by strongly held stereotypes and fears associated with surviving the teaching experience. To prepare pre-service students to teach in culturally diverse classroom, course work should begin with the contact between the teacher and children.

PEDAGOGY AND TRANSFORMATIVE LEARNING ABOUT DIFFERENCE AND DIVERSITY

Students need to know and understand that the meaning given to difference is a social construction that reflects both the objective reality as well as the subjectivity of the knower. Students should examine ways in which the construction of race/ethnicity, class, gender, ability, sexuality, and religion reflects the social context, the historical times, and the economic structure of the society. Students should also understand that the concepts are still in the process of change and reconstruction.

A lesson that students can learn from examining the historical development of social science concepts like race, class, and gender, is the relationship between knowledge and power. It is the hegemonic groups with power who tend to construct ideas and conceptions that reinforce their power and position within society. Mannheim (1971) calls the view of knowledge constructed by groups with power *ideology*. Groups with little power within a society that are marginalized and oppressed tend to construct ideas and concepts that will enhance the liberation and empowerment of their group. Mannheim calls this kind of knowledge *utopia*. Mannheim points out how each of these perspectives can lead to the distortion of events and actualities.

Students, who have a keen understanding of how knowledge is constructed, how it reflects both subjectivity and objectivity, and how it relates to power, will have important skills needed to participate in the construction of knowledge that will help the nation to participate in the democratic ideals. Students with these skills will also be able to interrogate the assumption of the knower and consequently will be less likely to be victimized by knowledge that protects hegemony and inequality. Students must not only be able to interrogate and reconstruct knowledge but must be able to produce knowledge themselves if they are to be effective citizens in a multicultural world of the twenty-first century.

Although it has been shown that knowledge is a social construction, which is culturally influenced and invented and re-invented through time, knowledge in the school curriculum is often presented to students as a body of unchanging facts that are not to be questioned, critically analyzed, or reconstructed. E. D. Hirsch (1987) and other neo-conservative scholars critical of schools, believe that students should be taught a list of facts so they will become culturally literate and effective citizens.

In a democratic, pluralistic society, educators and scholars from a broad range of cultural and ethnic groups need to participate in determining the knowledge that will be taught in the school curriculum. Rather than teach students a predetermined list of facts, theories, and principles, teachers should help students to understand the knowledge construction process that is used to invent and re-invent knowledge (Elabor-Idemudia, 2001). The knowledge construction process consists of the methods, activities, and questions that teachers use to help students to investigate, understand, and determine how implicit cultural assumptions, frames of reference, perspectives, and biases within a discipline influence the ways in which knowledge is constructed (Banks, 1994). When teachers teach knowledge construction processes in the classroom, the cultural assumptions, frames of references, and the perspectives of the knower influence the knowledge that is produced. The school curriculum is transformed when the knowledge construction process is taught because students learn that knowledge is not certain and static but is dynamic, changing, and contextual. The centrality of racialized discourses in the constitution of geo-political relations allows Eurocentrism to dominate the discourse about what constitutes valid knowledge (see Comaroff & Comaroff, 1988). This trend needs interrogation as indicated in this chapter's discussion.

THE SIGNIFICANCE OF ANTI-RACIST EDUCATION IN KNOWLEDGE PRODUCTION AND ACQUISITION

Anti-racism education may be defined as an action-oriented strategy for institutional and systemic change needed to address racism and the interlocking systems of social oppression. It emerged as a discourse through the pioneering works of Justice Rosalie Abella (1984), Barb Thomas (1985), Enid Lee (1985), and George Dei (1996) and its objective was to transform schooling and education experiences for all. The impetus for change came from local community political struggles that challenged the Canadian state to live up to the true meanings of democratic citizenship, social justice, equity, and fairness.

Anti-racism education takes the position that every form of education needs to provide for a holistic understanding and appreciation of the human experience, comprising of social, cultural, political, ecological, and spiritual aspects. It posits that in order for this to be manifested, educators need to instill in their students the importance of collective responsibility in relation to upholding the virtues of the social and natural worlds. The connection between the inner and external (social) self is of utmost concern to the anti-racism struggle for change. This involves the development of a spiritual consciousness that arises from collective consciousness of community membership (e.g., mutuality, collective responsibility, solidarity, and individual responsibility to the community).

Anti-racism education further calls for a focus on an explication of the notion of "identity" and how it is linked to knowledge production and acquisition. "Identity" in this context refers to the individual self and personhood; it implies both uniqueness (selfhood) and sameness (relations with/to others). The identity of the self involves more than the individual, and it is important for educators to understand how issues of individual and group cultural identities intersect. Anti-racism education links identity with schooling in different ways in order to give meaning, place, context, origin, and history to discussions of who we are as teachers, administrators, students, parents, and members of a community. Race identity formation and the associated struggles at both individual and collective levels are part of critical anti-racism discourse (Dei, 2004). The process of identity is, therefore, intertwined with the processes of knowledge production.

Anti-racism education problematizes the marginalization of certain voices in society and, specifically the delegitimation of the knowledge and experiences of marginalized groups in the education system. It critiques the Euro-Canadian/American dominance of both what constitutes valid knowledge and how such knowledge should be produced and disseminated internally and internationally. The teachings and pedagogy of anti-racist strategies engage the different and multiple ways of knowing in our world in order to advance the course of social knowledge and calls for the creation of spaces for everyone, but particularly for marginal voices to be heard. The task of anti-racism educators, therefore, is to create safer spaces for studens to be able to develop some solutions to social problems.

Further, anti-racism education teaches that one cannot understand the full social effects of race without a comprehension of the intersections of all forms of social oppression including how race is mediated with other forms of social difference. It acknowledges the traditional role of the education system in producing and reproducing not only racial, but also gender-, sex-, and class-based inequalities in society. Schools are part of the institutional structure sanctioned by society and the state to serve their material, political, and ideological interests as well as those of industrial capital. The public school system serves as a site for the production and reproduction of the ideological hegemony of the state and of the economic interests of global capital. Meritocracy still has a central place in educational practice and theory. Anti-racism discourse, therefore, incorporates an intersectionality lens which views gender, class, and sexuality as fundamental and relational aspects of the human experience that intersect both in the historical and contemporary reality of people's lives.

Anti-racism education acknowledges the pedagogic need to confront the challenge of diversity and differences in Canadian society. It recognizes the urgent need for an education system that is more inclusive and is capable of responding to minority and Aboriginal concerns about public schooling. The idea of inclusive schooling sees schools as "working communities" in that the powerful notion of "community" and "social responsibility" is brought from the margin into the centre of the processes of delivering education. Inclusive schools respond to the needs and challenges of diversity in their education of youth by tapping into the cultural knowledge of parents, guardians, and community workers. Anti-racism pedagogy does not seek to nullify power and social difference; it recognizes that everyone speaks from places which have real power differences that can be used as resources. Therefore, a critical anti-racism discursive framework helps us to understand the nature of the interaction existing between the labor demands of the competitive global economy and the processes of schooling that accord differential treatment and educational outcomes for students of diverse racial and economic backgrounds.

CONCLUSION

The analysis done in this chapter has attempted to show that the process of producing knowledge is a process of making politics. If knowledge is power, then decolonizing knowledge production should be a process of challenging dominant power (Adjei 2007). Individuals engaging in the project of decolonizing the academy need to assess themselves if they are ready to face the consequences of their actions. Spivak (1990) has rightly warned that the task of changing the academy is difficult and only when one begins to take a whack at shaking the structure that one sees how the opposition is well consolidated. The failure of scholars, researchers, and teachers to examine their own subjective positions in the process of knowledge construction and dissemination constitutes a problem for promoting well-rounded and all-inclusive knowledge. Recognizing the ambiguous consequences of imbalances in power relations between creators of knowledge and their subjects is a first step toward altering the manner in which knowledge is perceived. As Gandhi (1993, p. 202) reiterates, it is "far better for a learner to remain unlettered and break stones for the sake of liberty than to go in for a literary education [colonial education] in the chains of slaves." Knowledge of self is very important in education. Therefore, teachers and other educators must look beyond material rewards of colonial education to seek knowledge that enhances the liberty and self-respect of learners.

This calls for recognition of the ambiguous consequences of imbalances in power relations between knowledge producers and their subjects as a first step toward altering the manner in which knowledge is perceived. An acceptance of a politics of difference—as opposed to a politics of "othering"—is, in my opinion, a necessary condition for restructuring of the epistemological validity of the knowledge of the "other" (Elabor-Idemudia, 2002). This means that an acceptance of a politics of difference is crucial for the radical changes necessary for the production of knowledge. To reach this stage, researchers—Western or non-Western, Whites or non-White, feminists or non-feminists alike, others involved in the knowledge production process—have to go through a process of what bell hooks terms "meaningful contestation and constructive confrontation" (hooks, 1990, p. 133). As a transformative framework, an anti-racist prism theorizes education beyond what happens in the classroom to issues emerging in the community (see Dei, 1996). Indeed, education potentially confers simultaneously two rewards on its graduates: a personal knowledge and an improvement.

This chapter concludes by highlighting the need to take into account that people's multiple identities and their ever-changing tendency to fit occasions in a globalized world influence the positionality taken in knowledge production. As such, as the institutional context of educational organizations expands to include identity and representation, it is important to probe, and to raise questions regarding, the relationship among power, identity, representation, and knowledge production. The implications for knowledge production of transnationality, multiple identities, and other mediating factors of representation need to be explored. In doing so, the absence and/or marginalization of other ways of knowing including indigenous knowledge from curriculum in the mainstream education system will be interrogated in compliance with the principles of anti-racist education.

Notes

1. Much of what we identify as our research agendas derives from questions that we have a personal interest in finding answers to, phenomena that fascinate us, and points we want to prove. There is no such thing as disinterested research.
2. It is important to note that the identity of the scholar is informed not only by her/his own self-identification but also by the identities imposed on her/him by the circumstances of, and the people involved in, the process of knowledge production. While acknowledging that one's identities are not wholly self-determined, for the purposes of this particular discussion I foreground that aspect of positionality that is somewhat within the conscious decision-making of the scholar.

REFERENCES

Abella, R. (1984). Equality in Employment: A Royal Commission Report. Government of Canada: Ontario Commission on Equality in Employment.

Adjei, P. B. (2007). Decolonizing Knowledge Production: The Pedagogic Relevance of Gandhian Satyagraha to Schooling and Education in Ghana. *Canadian Journal of Education 30*(4), 1046–1067.

Aguilar, J. (1981). Insider Research: An Ethnography of a Debate. In D. Messerschmidt (Ed.), *Anthropologists at Home in North America: Methods and Issues in the Study of One's Own Society* (pp. 15–26). Cambridge: Cambridge University Press.

Alcoff, L. (1991). The Problem of Speaking for Others, *Cultural Critique, Winter,* 5–32.

Anyidoho, K. (1983). *Death and Burial of the Dead: A Study of Ewe Funeral Folklore* (Unpublished masters' thesis), Bloomington: Indiana University Press.

Anyidoho, N. A. (2008). Identity and Knowledge Production in the Fourth Generation. *Africa Development XXX–II*(1), 25–39.

Appiah, K. (1997), Cosmopolitan Patriots, *Critical Inquiry 23*(3).

Asante, M. K. (1997). More Thoughts on the Africanists' Agenda. *Issues 23*(1), 11–12.

Avery, P. G. (1993). Prospective Teachers' Perceptions of Ethnic and Gender Differences in Academic Achievement. *Journal of Teacher Education 14*(1), 12–37.

Banks, J. A. (1994). *Multi-ethnic Education: Theory and Practice* (2nd ed.). Boston: Allyn and Bacon.

Becker, G. S. (1962). Investment in Human Capital: A Theoretical Analysis. *The Journal of Political Economy 70*(S5).

Bourdieu, P. (1977). *Outline of a Theory of Practice*. Cambridge: Cambridge University Press.

Brittan, A., & Maynard, M. (1984). *Sexism, Racism and Oppression*. New York: Blackwell.

Cazden, C., & Mehan, H. (1989). Principles of Sociology and Anthropology: Context, Code, Classroom and Culture. In M. C. Reynolds (Ed.), *Knowledge Base for the Beginning Teacher* (pp. 47–57). Oxford: Pergamon.

Code, L. (1991). *What Can She Know? Feminist Theory and the Construction of Knowledge*. Ithaca, NY: Cornell University Press.

Collins, P. H. (2002). *Black Feminist Thought: Knowledge, Consciousness and the Politics of Empowerment* (2nd ed.). New York: Routledge.

Comaroff, J., & Comaroff, J. (1988). Through the Looking Glass: Colonial Encounters of the First Kind. *Journal of Historical Sociology 1*(1), 6–32.

Cummins, J. (1994). Lies We Live by: National Identity and Social Justice. *International Journal of Sociology of Language 100*, 145–154.

Daenzer, P. & Dei, G. J. S. (1994). *Issues of School completion/Dropout: A Focus on Blacks in Ontario Schools and Relevant Studies*. Background paper submitted to the Ontario Royal Commission on Learning, Toronto, Ontario.

Dei, G. J. S. (1996). *Theory and Practice: Anti-racism Education*. Halifax, NS: Fernwood.

Dei, G. J. S. (2004). *Schooling and Education in Africa: The Case of Ghana*. Trenton, NJ: Africa World.

Dei, G. J. S. & Calliste, A. (2000). *Power, Knowledge and Anti-racism Education: A Critical Reader*. Halifax, NS: Fernwood.

Elabor-Idemudia, P. (2000). The Retention of Knowledge of Folkways as Basis for Resistance. In G. S. Dei, B. Hall, & D. G. Rosenberg (Eds.), *Indigenous Knowledge in Global Context: Multiple Readings of Our World* (pp. 102–119). Toronto: University of Toronto Press.

Elabor-Idemudia, P. (2001). Equity Issues in the Academy: An Afro-Canadian Woman's Perspective. *The Journal of Negro Education: A Howard University Quarterly Review of Issues Incident to the Education of Black People*. Black Women in the Academy: Challenges and Opportunities *70*(3), 192–203.

Elabor-Idemudia, P. (2002). Participatory Research: A Tool in the Production of Knowledge in Development Discourse. In K. Saunders (Ed.), *Feminist Post Development Thought: Rethinking Modernity, Post-colonialism and Representation* (pp. 227–242). London: Zed.

Escobar, A. 1992. Reflections on Development: Grassroots Approaches and Alternative Politics in the Third World, *Futures 24*, 411–434.

Fonow, M. M. & Cook, J. A. (Eds.). (1991). *Beyond Methodology: Feminist Scholarship as Lived Research.* Bloomington: Indiana University Press.

Foucault, M. (1980). Power/Knowledge: Selected Interviews and Other Writings, 1972–1977. In C. Gordon (Ed. and Trans.), *Power/Knowledge* (pp. 78–108). Brighton, UK: Harvester.

Foucault, M. (1982). Afterword by Michel Foucault: The Subject and Power. In H. L. Dreyfus & P. Rabinow, *Michel Foucault: Beyond Structuralism and Hermeneutics* (pp. 208–226). Chicago: University of Chicago Press.

Gandhi, M. K. (1993). *Gandhi: An Autobiography. The Story of My Experiments with Truth* (M. H. Desai, Trans.). Boston: Beacon.

Giroux, H. A. (1981). *Ideology, Culture and the Process of Schooling.* Philadelphia: Temple University Press.

Giroux, H. A. (2008). Academic Repression in the First Person: The Attack on Higher Education and the Necessity of Critical Pedagogy. *CUNY Graduate Center Advocate,* January.

Grant, M. (1981). Education That Is Multicultural and Teacher Preparation: An Examination from the Perspective of Pre-service Students. *Journal of Educational Research 4*, 197–204.

Hall, S. (1983). Education in Crisis. In J. Donald & A. M. Wolp (Eds.), *Is There Anyone Here from Education* (pp. 2–10). London: Pluto.

Hall, S. (1990). The Emergence of Cultural Studies and the Crisis in the Humanities. *The Humanities as Social Technology* 53, 11–23.

Hall, S. (1999). Thinking the Diaspora: Home-Thoughts from Abroad. *Small Axe 3*, 1–18.

Hall, S. and Paul Du Gay, eds. (1996). Questions of Cultural Identity. London: Sage.

Henry, F., & Tator, C. (1991). *Multicultural Education: Translating Policy into Practice.* Ottawa: Multiculturalism Canada.

Henry, F., Tator, C., Mattis W., & Rees, T. (2000). *The Color of Democracy: Racism in Canadian Society* (2nd ed.). Toronto: Harcourt Brace Canada.

Heron, J. (1996). *Co-operative Inquiry: Research into the Human Condition.* London: Sage.

Hirsch, E. D.(1987). *Cultural Literacy.* Boston: Houghton Mifflin.

Holmes, B. (2009). The Politics of Knowledge Production. *Europa Magazine*: European Alternatives.

hooks, b. (1990). *Yearning: Race, Gender and Cultural Politics.* Boston: South End.

hooks, b. (1993). Keeping Close to Home: Class and Education. In M. Tokaiezyk and E. Fay (Eds.), *Working Class Women in the Academy: Laborers in the Knowledge Factory* (pp. 99–111). Amherst: University of Massachusetts Press.

hooks, b.(1994). *Teaching to Transgress: Education as the practice of Freedom.* New York: Routledge.

Karp, I., & Masolo, D.A. (2000). *African Philosophy as Cultural Inquiry.* Bloomington & Indianapolis: Indiana University Press.

Klein, R. (1987). The Dynamics of Women's Studies Classrooms: A Review Essay of the Teaching Practice of Women's Studies in Higher Education. *Women's Studies International Forum 10*(2), 187–202.

Lal, J. (1996). Situating Locations: The Politics of Self, Identity, and "Other" in Living and Writing the Text. In D. L. Wolf (Ed.), *Feminist Dilemmas in Fieldwork* (pp. 185–241) Boulder, CO: Westview.

Lee, E. (1985). *Letters to Marcia: A Teacher's Guide to Anti-racist Education.* Toronto: Cross-Cultural Communication Center.

Madood, T., & Pnina, W. (2007). *Debating Cultural Hybridity: Multi-cultural Identities and the Politics of Anti-racism.* London and Atlantic Highlands, NJ: Zed.

Mannheim, K. (1971). *Ideology and Utopia: An Introduction to the Sociology of Knowledge.* New York: Harcourt Brace.

McDiarmid, G. W., & Price, J. (1993). Preparing Teachers for Diversity: A Study of Student Teachers in Multicultural Programs. In M. J. O'Hair & J. Odell (Eds.), *Diversity and Teaching: ATE Yearbook I* (pp. 31–59). Fort Worth, TX: Harcourt Brace Jovanovich.

Mkandawire, T. (1995). Three Generations of African Scholars: A Note, *CODESRIA Bulletin 28*.

Mkandawire, T. (1997). The Social Sciences in Africa: Breaking Local Barriers and Negotiating International Presence. The Bashorun M. K. O. Abiola Distinguished Lecture Presented to the 1996 African Studies Association

Annual Meeting. *African Studies Review 40*(2), 15–36.

Mohanty, C. T. (1991). Cartographies of Struggle: Third World Women and the Politics of Feminism. In C. T. Mohanty, A. Russo, & L. Torres (Eds.), *Third World Women and the Politics of Feminism* (pp. 1–47) Bloomington: Indiana University Press.

Mohanty, C. T. (2002). Under Western Eyes Revisited: Feminist Solidarity through Anti-capitalist Struggle. *Signs: Journal of Women in Culture and Society 28*(2), 499–535.

Moodley, K. (1984). The Ambiguities of Multicultural Education. *Currents: Readings in Race Relations 2*(3), 5–7.

Moodley, K. (Ed.). (1992). *Beyond Multicultural Education: International Perspectives*. Calgary: Detselig.

Narayan, K. (1993). How Native Is a "Native" Anthropologist? *American Anthropologist 95*, 671–686.

Narayan, U. (1987). The Project of Feminist Epistemology: Perspectives from a Non-Western Feminist. In A. M. Jaggar, & S. R. Bordo (Eds.), *Gender/Body/Knowledge: Feminist Reconstructions of Being and Knowing* (pp. 224–255) New Brunswick, NJ: Rutgers University Press.

Narayan, U. (1997). *Dislocating Cultures: Identities, Traditions, and Third-World Feminism*. New York: Routledge.

Noordhoff, K., & Kleinfeld, J. (1991). *Preparing Teachers for Multicultural Classrooms: A Case Study in Rural Alaska*. Paper presented at the annual meeting of the American Educational Research Association, Chicago, IL.

Obbo, C. (1990). Adventures with Field Notes. In R, Sanjek (Ed.), *Field Notes* (pp. 290–302). Ithaca: Cornell University Press.

Paine, L. (1990). Orientation towards Diversity: What Do Prospective Teachers Bring? (Research Rep. No. 89–9). East Lansing, MI: National Center for Research on Teacher Education.

Power, K. (2005). *Conflicts in the Production of Knowledge*. Debate for *Edu-factory e-journal*.

Pratt, M. L. (1992). *Imperial Eyes: Travel Writing and Transculturation*. London & New York: Routledge.

Puwar, N., & Sharma, S. (2007, May). Short-Circuiting Knowledge Production. *Darkmatter: In the Ruins of Imperial Culture*, retrieved from http://www.darkmatter101.0rg/site/2007/05/13/short-circuiting-knowledge-production/

Reed-Danahay, D. E. (1997). Introduction. In D. E. Reed-Danahay (Ed.), *Auto/Ethnography: Rewriting the Self and the Social* (pp. 1–17). Oxford: Berg.

Rosenau, P. M. (1992). *Post-modernism and the Social Sciences: Insights, Inroads, and Intrusions*. Princeton: Princeton University Press.

Said, E. (1978). *Orientalism: Western Conceptions of the Orient*. London: Penguin.

Said, E. (1993a). *Representations of the Intellectual* (The Reith Lectures). New York: Vintage.

Said, E. (1993b). *The World, the Text and the Critic*. London: Vintage.

Sangren, S. (1988). Rhetoric and the Authority of Ethnography. *Current Anthropology 29*, 505–424.

Sawicki, J. (1991). *Disciplining Foucault: Feminism, Power and the Body*. New York: Routledge.

Slater, D. (1995). Challenging in Western Visions of the Global: The Geo-Politics of Theory and North-South Relations. *European Journal of Development Research 7* (2), 366–388.

Smith, D. E. (1987). Women Perspective as a Radical Critique of Sociology. In S. Harding (Ed.) *Feminism and Methodology* (pp. 84–96). Bloomington: Indiana University Press.

Smith, L. T. (1999). *Decolonizing Methodologies: Research and Indigenous Peoples*. London: Zed.

Solomon, P. (1992). *Black Resistance in High School: Forging a Separatist Culture*. New York: SUNY Press.

Spivak, G. C. (1988). Can the Subaltern Speak? In C. Nelson, & L. Grossberg (Eds.), *Marxism and the Interpretations of Culture* (pp. 271–313). Urbana: University of Illinois Press.

Spivak, G. C. (1990). In S. Harasym (Ed.), *The Post-colonial Critic : Interviews, Strategies, Dialogues*. London: Routledge.

Tetreault, M. K. T. (1997). Classrooms for Diversity: Rethinking Curriculum and Pedagogy. In J. A. Banks, & C.A. M. Banks (Eds.), *Multiculturalism Education: Issues and Perspective* (3rd ed., pp. 150–170). Boston: Allyn and Bacon.

Thomas, B. R. (1985). States of Consciousness: A New POTPOURRI Intellectual Direction, a New Teacher Education Direction. *Journal of Teacher Education 36*, 55–59

Vander-Valk, F. (2008). Identity, Power, and Representation in Virtual Environments. *Merlot Journal of Online Learning and Teaching 4* (2), 205–211.

Viswanathan, G. (1989). *Masks of Conquest: Literary Study and British Rule in India*. New York: Columbia University

Press.

wa Thiong'o, N. (1993). *Moving the Centre: The Struggle for Cultural Freedoms*. London: Heinemann.

Westkott, M. (1983). Women's Studies as a Strategy for Change: Between Criticism and Vision. In G. B. Bowles, & R. Duelli-klein (Eds.), *Theories of Women's Studies* (pp. 210–218), London: Routledge.

Wiredu, K. (1980). *Philosophy and the African Culture*. Cambridge: Cambridge University Press.

Wolf, D. L. (1996). Situating Feminist Dilemmas in Fieldwork. In D. L. Wolf (Ed.), *Feminist Dilemmas in Fieldwork* (pp. 1–55). Colorado: Westview.

CHAPTER TEN

Indigeneity in Education

A By-product of Assimilation?

DENNIS MCPHERSON

According to Prime Minister Stephen Harper, "We...have no history of colonialism. So we have all of the things that many people admire about the great powers but none of the things that threaten or bother them..." (as cited in Ljunggren, 2009). Yet colonialism is a fact of life for Native people and it reached its peak within the Indian Residential School system. There are many testimonials to the atrocities suffered by individuals attending these schools, but perhaps the greatest harm of all is the intentional cultural disruption of Native people as described by a Cree Elder

> What happened in the residential school...was to assimilate. It didn't matter whether they called it integration or whatever. It all boiled down to one thing, and that was to assimilate the native people into the non-native culture. Either you're going to train them to be little farmers, and the girls to be maids in homes, or whatever...that was the mandate (Stonebanks, 2008, p. 230).

With the human rights movement of the 1950s and 1960s, desegregation became the policy of the day, and the Department of Indian Affairs began the lengthy process of shutting down the Indian Residential Schools across the country. As Indians began to gain a political voice in the latter part of the 1960s we began to hear more loudly of "Indian Control of Indian Education."

Desegregation also created a new problem for Indian Reserve communities. When the Indian Residential Schools were closed, children returned to the reserves where they were apprehended by the thousands by well-intentioned social workers who set out to save the children from the effects of crushing poverty, unsanitary health conditions, poor housing, and malnutrition; an era known as the "Sixties Scoop" (Johnston, 1983, p. 23).

Some 25 years ago I had the pleasure of representing the Rainy Lake Region Tribal Chiefs before the Standing Committee on Social Development for the Province of Ontario. The message I was carrying to Queen's Park was in regard to our concern for the large number of Native children who had been apprehended and adopted under the *Child Welfare Act*. It was our impression that we could provide for them much better under the principle of "Customary Care."

The Committee wanted to know how if we were given the opportunity to look after our own children could we guarantee that our children would in fact be looked after? My response was that the only thing we could guarantee was that if given the opportunity, "we could kill our children just as good as they were doing."

Since the changes in child welfare legislation in the Province of Ontario in 1985, the *Child and Family Services Act* (CFSA) provides for inclusion of Indian and Native peoples throughout, with an onus on Children's Aid Societies and the courts to inform the bands when an Indian or Native child is taken into care. Indian and Native people are referenced at least 32 times in the first 9 sections of the CFSA, and Part X of the Act pertains specifically to Indian and Native interests. Part X provides for a scheme wherein the Indian or Native community can delegate an Indian or Native child welfare authority with whom the Minister shall negotiate. If the authority chooses to provide soft services the Ministers may, at the authority's request, designate the authority as a Children's Aid Society. On the other hand, the authority has the option through the regulations, to be exempted from the Child and Family Services Act in order to provide child welfare services in accordance with customary care.

Today, more Indian children are in the care of Indian- or Native-run Children's Aid Societies than were resident in the Indian Residential Schools, and no Indian or Native child welfare authorities have negotiated exemptions to the Act in order to provide child welfare services in accordance with customary care.

It is interesting to note that in the year 2008 alone in the Province of Ontario, 90 children died while in care. Since the major proportion of children in care in the Province are Indian or Native children it is a high probability that the higher proportion of the children who died in care were Native children. I would say that we are killing our children just as good as they did.

The challenge we face as Indian or Native people is that we have to overcome our fear of oppression and stop being like the colonizers. We need to liberate ourselves and humanize our oppressors. As Paulo Freire says "Only as they discover themselves to be "hosts" of the oppressor can they contribute to the midwifery of their liberating pedagogy. As long as they live in the duality in which *to be* is *to be like,* and *to be like* is *to be like the oppressor,* this contribution is impossible" (Freire, 2003, p. 48).

It is well known that there are problems with literacy and numeracy in Indian country, and we are over 28 years behind the educational norms of the rest of Canadian society. Funding is a problem. There is a shortage of teachers and most teachers are not culturally sensitive in their approaches. For those of our children who make it through a primary school, there is difficulty in a transition to secondary and post-secondary education. All of this leads to political strife within our communities.

As Frances Widdowson and Albert Howard (2008) have stated in their recent book, *Disrobing the Aboriginal Industry,* "Political pressure to increase the number of aboriginal peoples with credentials has created a fertile ground for disguising low educational levels. While there certainly is much lip-service paid to the cause of educating native people, in practice deeply entrenched checks mean that the 'educated' native will still need lots of help. The demand of native control over curriculum assures that traditional cultural practices have precedence over modern communication requirements so that students remain unprepared for the disciplines of secondary education. The secondary schools are then adjusted to allow aboriginal peoples to graduate artificially. And why stop there? Many undergraduate programs are now specifically designed for natives, where the application of 'Aboriginal' signifies the lower standard of the degree" (Widdowson & Howard, 2008, p. 193).

According to Widdowson and Howard (2008) "The fact that aboriginal societies in North America had not surpassed the Neolithic period (and the stage of barbarism) when they encountered Europeans, who had already experienced thousands of years of civilization, is generally ignored in the literature because it is perceived as being demeaning to native people." They go on to say "it must be recognized that all aboriginal groups have been influenced by modernity, and therefore their cultural development is uneven. Native peoples in Canada have had the ministrations of the church for hundreds of years and have been schooled for generations. . . .However, much of the aboriginal participation in modern societies is as consumers, not producers. Isolation from economic processes has meant that a number of Neolithic cultural features, including undisciplined work habits, tribal forms of political identification, animistic beliefs, and difficulties in developing abstract reasoning, persist despite hundreds of years of contact"(p. 13).

It is difficult to dispute Widdowson and Howard's claims given the recent events at the First Nations University of Canada. Funding from both the Provincial and Federal governments for the institution has been withdrawn. The First Nations University of Canada in the beginning "was a dream of our elders and previous leaders to see this," proclaimed Perry Bellegarde, Chief of the Federation of Saskatchewan Indian Nations. But, "It was a 'politicized board,'" says James Turk, executive director of the Canadian Association of University Teachers, "It was too large, and too political, to permit the necessary academic independence and freedom." "It's a bit foreign to them that there are things they can't be sticking their nose into," says a former senior official at the Department of Indian and Northern Affairs who worked in the ministry when the university was christened. "They don't get the importance of academic independence. They were told over and over to get their governance straightened out. They just refused" (as cited in Libin, 2010).

Widdowson and Howard (2008) proclaim ". . .education is not only important because it enables people to make a 'good living' in modern society. Education is worthy in its own right as it enables us to develop critical thinking and independent thought to further our understanding of the universe and our place in it. Aboriginal people, like all other human beings, need to acquire this understanding in order to fully self-actualize in the contemporary world. Regression to the teaching of primitive survival skills denies aboriginal children a fundamental prerequisite to their development" (p. 197).

In reviewing educational options and asking what is to be taught, Howard Gardner (1991) states that "First, you must determine the realm of society that seems most crucial to preserve. You can decide to focus on the fulfillment of certain societal roles (How does one learn to be a parent, a priest, a poet?); on the transmission of cultural values (What does it mean to be a virtuous person? What is the good life? Which behaviors are approved of or at least permitted? Which sanctions must be invoked if laws are violated?); or on passing on different varieties or forms of knowledge that have been achieved over the millennia (the printed word, the craft of magic, the findings of science)" (p. 116).

The options laid out by Gardner were addressed 150 years before by Egerton Ryerson, Superintendent of Schools for Canada West (known as the "Founder of the School System of Ontario"), in his report of 1846 entitled "Report of a System of Public Elementary Instruction for Upper Canada." (Wilson et al., 1970, 217). Education for Ryerson was to be Christian, universal, free, and compulsory. "By religion and morality," Ryerson made clear, he did not mean "sectarianism in any form, but the general system of truth and morals taught us in the Holy Scriptures." For Ryerson the schools were proper vehicles for the dissemination of Christian principles; these Christian principles were, however, virtually synonymous with Protestant values. "Education is a public good, ignorance is a public evil" and therefore every child rich or poor should receive an education sufficient to overcome "the evils of want and poverty," and to "fit him to be an honest and useful member of the community. This conviction led Ryerson to assert that education should be compulsory—'if the parent or guardian *cannot* provide him with such an education, the *State is bound* to do so'" (Wilson, Stamp, & Audet, 1970, p. 217). Ryerson's blueprint of 1846 was to a large extent realized within his 30-year term of office.

There is the appearance that perceptions from Ryerson's blueprint for education were written into statute in *An Act to Encourage the Gradual Civilization of the Indian Tribes in This Province, and to Amend the Laws Respecting Indians.* Under this law, the visiting superintendent of each tribe of Indians, the Missionary, or such other person appointed to be Commissioners were to report in writing to the Governor of their examination of "any such Indian of the male sex, and not under twenty-one years of age, is able to speak, read and write either the English or the French language readily and well, and is sufficiently advanced in the elementary branches of education and is of good moral character and free from debt then it shall be competent to the Governor to cause notice to be given in the official Gazette of this Province, that such Indian is enfranchised under this Act" *(An Act to Encourage the Gradual Civilization of the Indian Tribes in This Province, and to Amend the Laws Respecting Indians,* s. III).

The "elementary branches of education" spoken to in the Act were attained by the Indians attending schools within the Province. In fact, the first teaching done in Ontario was conducted in French and Indian dialect by the Jesuit missionaries in Huronia (1639–1649) (Wilson, Stamp, & Audet, 1970, p. 232). And the first known Indian school using English was opened at Fairfield on the Thames River by David Zeisberger in 1793 (Wilson, Stamp, & Audet, 1970, p. 232). As of "the *Common School Act* of 1824, government grants were available for Indian education. Prior to 1824 support of Indian education had come from the king and missionary societies" (Wilson, Stamp, & Audet, 1970, p. 205).

Although *The Indian Act* of 1876 provided for "The chief or chiefs of any band in council to frame, subject to confirmation of the Governor in Council, rules and regulations for....The construction and repair of school houses . . ." (*The Indian Act*, 1876, s. 63). The Act also stated that "Any Indian who may be admitted to the degree of Doctor of Medicine, or to any other degree by any University of Learning, or who may be admitted in any Province of the Dominion to practice law either as an Advocate or as a Barrister, or Counsellor or Solicitor or Attorney or to be a Notary Public, or who may enter Holy Orders or who may be licensed by any denomination of Christians as a Minister of the Gospel, shall *ipso facto* become and be enfranchised under this Act" (*The Indian Act*, 1876, s. 86.1).

By 1880, *An Act to Amend and Consolidate the Laws Respecting Indians* stipulated that "The chief or chiefs of any band in council may frame, subject to confirmation by the Governor in Council, rules and regulations....As to what religious denomination the teacher of the school established on the reserve shall belong to; provided always, that he shall be of the same denomination as the majority of the band; and provided that the Catholic or Protestant minority may likewise have a separate school with the approval of and under regulations to be made by the Governor in Council..." (*The Indian Act*, 1880, s. 3).

Segregating Indians from the rest of society was not enough. To be sure of cultural separation, amendments to the *Indian Act* in 1884 deemed that "Every Indian or other person who engages in or assists in celebrating the Indian festival known as the 'Potlach' or in the Indian dance known as the 'Tamanawas' is guilty of a misdemeanor, and shall be liable to imprisonment for a term of not more than six months nor less than two months in any gaol or other place of confinement"; in addition, "any Indian or other person who encourages, either directly or indirectly, an Indian or Indians to get up such a festival or dance, or to celebrate the same, or who shall assist in the celebration of the same is guilty of a like offence, and shall be liable to the same punishment" (*Indian Act*, 1880, Assented to 1884).

Applying Gardner's (1991) criteria for determining what is to be taught to the time period of the late nineteenth century, first you must determine the realm of society that seems most crucial to preserve, but it is clear that the legislators of the day dictated that no elements of Indian society were crucial to preserve. Quite to the contrary, they prescribed that all Indian societal roles should be left behind; the good life could only come to Indians by becoming Christians, their ceremonies were banned by law and Indians could be jailed failing to comply with these restrictions.

As a result of a conference held in Ottawa on November 8, 1910, the manner in which the government intended to deal with Indians is clearly expressed in the following extract from a letter, dated Ottawa, November 25, 1910, sent to the representatives of the several religious bodies in Canada interested in Indian education.

> When Indian education was taken up seriously in western Canada in the eighties, the policy of the government was to establish industrial schools, erected at the cost of the government, to be conducted under the auspices of the several religious bodies interested; the government contributing to the maintenance of the schools a fixed sum per head. In pursuance of what was then believed to be sound policy, these schools were, generally speaking, located at points distant from Indian reserves, and for this reason there was frequently considerable difficulty in securing a sufficient attendance of Indian pupils to earn the grant adequate for their upkeep.
>
> To meet the educational needs of the Indian children who could not for one reason or another be provided for in the industrial schools already mentioned, from time to time boarding schools were established on a number of reserves at the charge of the various religious bodies. It was a foundation principle in the case of the industrial schools that the government erected the buildings at government cost, while in the case of the boarding schools the church erected the buildings at the cost of the church. In recognition of the efforts towards Indian education by the erection of these boarding schools, and to substantially assist the churches in their work, a grant per head was made by the government towards their support.
>
> As time went on, it became more and more apparent that the boarding schools were filling a want that the industrial schools had not filled, and for this reason instead of the number of industrial schools having been increased, the number of boarding schools has been increased. With this increase in the number of boarding schools, the burden of their support upon the various churches has correspondingly increased, and as the buildings which were erected in the first place by the churches have required repair or enlargement the government has from time to time, and in many cases, been called upon to provide these enlargements, improvements and repairs. Besides, there have been occasions when the difference between the contribution of the government and the actual cost of maintaining the school was greater than the church interested in the school felt itself able to provide, and the government was called upon to meet the deficit.
>
> This was not a desirable condition from the point of view either of the church or of the government. If there had been a prospect of these conditions being improved, there might not have been need of change, but all reports tended to show that, far from the probability that this condition would improve, it was likely to become aggravated year by year. Realizing the importance of the educational work being done by the boarding schools and the serious burden that the support of these schools is upon the various churches interested in them, the government concluded and the conference agreed that it would be wise to substantially increase the grant per head to boarding schools conducted under church auspices, but in doing this it was

necessary that the unbusinesslike lack of arrangement whereby the government repaired and added to mission buildings and met deficiencies in mission management should cease (Department of Indian Affairs, 1911).

The draft contract that was attached to the memorandum embodies the conditions upon which the increased grant would be paid. The conditions required that the school buildings would be sanitary, and that the school management would be conducive to the "physical, moral and mental well-being of the children…" and as far as education is concerned the conditions of the contract required operators

> To provide at the said school teachers and officers qualified to give the pupils religious instruction at proper times; to instruct the male pupils of the said school in gardening, farming, and care of stock, or such other industries as are suitable to their local requirements; to instruct the female pupils in cooking, laundry work, needlework, general housewifery and dairy work, where such dairy work can be carried on; to teach all the pupils in the ordinary branches of an English education; to teach calisthenics, physical drill and fire drill; to teach the effects of alcoholic drinks and narcotics on the human system, and how to live in a healthy manner; to instruct the older advanced pupils in the duties and privileges of British citizenship, explaining to them the fundamental principles of the government of Canada, and training them in such knowledge and appreciation of Canada as will inspire them with respect and affection for the country and its laws (Department of Indian Affairs, 1911).

Fast track the clock for a 100 or so years to the present and ask the question, what has changed? From a policy point of view, surely there is evidence that the policies of the past in regard to Indian education are different today than they were a 100 years ago, or are they? The assimilative policies which were entrenched in law in 1857 under *An Act to Encourage the Gradual Civilization of the Indian Tribes in This Province, and to Amend the Laws Respecting Indians* can no longer be fulfilled. From 1857 through to 1985, Indians could be enfranchised under the *Indian Act*. But in 1985, the government took a progressive step backward in Indian jurisprudence by repealing the enfranchisement section of the *Indian Act* in order to be compliant with the changes to the constitution in 1982 and remove violations of the equality sections of the *Charter of Rights and Freedoms*—discrimination based on gender. What repealing enfranchisement means under the present regime is that once you are a status Indian, you will always be a status Indian, there is no escape. Looking back, a literal translation of the Act in 1857 meant that being an Indian equated to being uncivilized for the intent of the Act was to "gradually" civilize Indians. With repealing enfranchisement in 1985, there now is no hope of status Indians ever enjoying the same legal rights and liberties of an ordinary citizen within Canadian civil society.

Under the Constitution Act, 1867, powers for education were conferred on the provinces under section 93. Responsibility for Indians, and Lands reserved for Indians fell to the Federal government under section 91(24). James C. MacPherson has written in the *MacPherson Report on Tradition and Education: Towards a Vision of Our Future,* that "the general principles of interpretation of the Canadian constitution establish a theoretical starting point of broad and substantial jurisdiction for both the federal and provincial governments in the field of Indian education." (MacPherson, 1991, p. 23) However, "In constitutional terms, in the field of Indian education the federal government has an open field; the provincial field is mined with potential constitutional bombs." (MacPherson, 1991, p. 28) The reality today is that the federal government's involvement in Indian education is defined within sections 114 to 122 of *The Indian Act*, R. S., 1985, which reads not unlike the wording of the earlier version initiated way back in the 1800s. For example, *The Indian Act* requires "every Indian child who has attained the age of seven years shall attend school," and the Act allows for "A Protestant or Roman Catholic minority of any band. . ., with the approval of and under regulations to be made by the Minister, have a separate day school or day school classroom established on the reserve unless, in the opinion of the Governor in Council, the number of children of school age does not so warrant." In accordance with the Act, Indian children today are the only children in Canada who, by law, are required to attend school, a requirement stipulated by the state. They are also the ones who most closely represent an actual manifestation of the vision for education as Ryerson said education should be; "Christian, universal, free, and compulsory." However, their education, though it is Christian and compulsory, it is anything but universal, and certainly is not free.

Colin J. Burke, an Australian Aborigine and Chairman of the Indigenous Australian Higher Education Association, a group formed in 1994 to try to give aborigines control of their own education, asks "How can you expect your culture and identity to survive if you give all the responsibility for education to another group of people? It is absolutely essential, if we are to know what it is to be aboriginal, to take charge of the education system . . ." (Burke, 1995, p. 47).

"Taking charge of the education system" in the Canadian context has evolved mainly into a fiscal debate. Arguments abound around the differences between the costs of a provincial system of education as compared to what is offered on reserves. What seems to be lost in the discussion is the fact that provincial education systems for primary and secondary schools are governed in accordance with provincial standards for education set by the governing party of the day and supported within a particular fee schedule. There are no standards for the delivery of education on reserves and there is no governing debate about what such standards should look like. Instead, Indian and Northern Affairs Canada has promoted Indian education with emphasis on local First Nations control as part of the Department's policy of devolution by which the Department endeavors to give control of educational programming over to the individual bands, an initiative started in the 1950s.

Education programming for Indians began as early as 1956 when Indian School Committees had been formed on some reserves and received some funding from the then Indian Affairs Branch. These committees were specifically responsible for matters like truancy and care of school property and slowly evolved in other areas such as school attendance and scholarships from band funds. By the mid-1970s, a number of Indian bands took initiatives to establish and manage schools on their own reserves. Typical of these schools are problems in securing qualified teachers, diverse standards in education levels, relevant curriculum content, and overcoming funding deficiencies. It is argued that the on-reserve student receives $2000 less funding than their provincial counterpart without the provision of any rationale or justification of why this is the case.

According to the *2006 Census of Canada*, 32 percent of Aboriginal peoples 25–34 years old had not completed high school compared with 10 percent of non-Aboriginal Canadians of the same age. In terms of university attainment, only 3 percent of those with Registered Indian status had a university degree, compared to 6 percent of the broader Aboriginal identity population and 18 percent of the entire population.

Alex Usher writes, on behalf of the Educational Policy Institute, in *The Post-Secondary Student Support Program: An Examination of Alternative Delivery Mechanisms* that "there are a variety of barriers to increased [Post Secondary Education] participation among First Nations and Aboriginal peoples, of which financial barriers are just one. Though clearly insufficient on their own to erase the gap in participation between Aboriginal and non-Aboriginal Canadians, programs which assist students with their finances are necessary parts of the policy tool-kit and need to be run as efficiently and effectively as possible in order to assist as many people as possible" (Usher, 2009, p. 8).

Along with Usher and others, even "the leader of Canada's First Nations people says he wants to see more money for their education…Shawn Atleo, national chief of the Assembly of First Nations, wants the government to increase funding for First Nations youth in an attempt to bring the high school graduation rate up from 49%, closer to the 87% of their contemporaries. He also wants to increase university graduation rates and estimates improving First Nations education would work out to an extra $179 billion in the Canadian economy by 2026. Bringing the graduation rate in line with that of other Canadians would mean 65,000 First Nations university grads over five years. He says even when the government is tightening its purse strings, the investment is worth it" (as cited in Payton, 2010).

In "Supporting Better Education Outcomes for First Nations" outlined in the 2010 Budget the Government says it "is committed to working with First Nations and provinces to ensure that First Nations children receive the education they require for success. Budget 2010 provides $30 million over two years to support an implementation-ready tripartite K-12 education agreement. This agreement will ensure First Nations students benefit from comparable education and achieve comparable results whether the classroom is located on or off reserve. The Government will work with First Nations groups and other willing partners to develop options, including new legislation, to improve the governance framework and clarify accountability for First Nations elementary and secondary education. In addition, the Government will engage in a new approach to providing support to First Nations and Inuit post-secondary education. The new approach will be effective and accountable, and will be coordinated with other federal student support programs" (Department of Finance, Government of Canada, 2010).

There is no question that finances are a major concern and an important part of any educational reality, but like the century-old battle for a multiplicity of Indian rights, inquires into fraudulent use of education dollars, claims of insufficient funding, etc., are no more than knee-jerk reactions in response to the financial system for Indian education that was put in place as a constitutional responsibility of the Federal government under section 91(24) and which Indians themselves have, over the years, made major contributions.

As Bourke says "It is absolutely essential, if we are to know what it is to be aboriginal, to take charge of the education system…," but taking charge of the education system must mean more than just the administration and distribution of dollars to support a foreign education system.

I suggest that the fundamental issue blocking the success of Aboriginal students is a question of identity. This problem is front and foremost a blockage to success as delineated by a former student of mine, Dr. Lorraine Mayer, who writes "No Aboriginal student can read the literature 'about' us without feeling physically, mentally, and spiritually sick" (DePasquale, Eigenbrod, & LaRocque, 2010, p. 103).

Lorraine goes on to say that "in the words of John Dewey, 'education is brutal competition.' Not much has changed since Dewey's writing in the early 1900s. In fact, education, at any level, is aimed at promoting and sustaining brutal competition, which is probably why so many Aboriginal students balk at entering institutions that have the propensity to destroy our identity. It is hard enough to walk a racist world every day, but to deliberately put ourselves in front of a mental firing squad, day in and day out, is questionable. Many times I had to question whether it was the lack of sleep, the tired body, or the exhausted mind that kept feeding me with bitterness? I would recall literature that was particularly insulting, like the debate between Sepulveda and Las Casa in the 1500s. According to

Sepulveda, 'being slaves by nature, [the Indians], uncivilized, barbarian and inhuman, refuse to accept the rule of those civilized [the Spaniards].' Or I'd think about Tom Flanagan, who, in our own time, claimed that Aboriginal peoples were not civilized like Europeans and therefore were not Nations and had no right to sovereignty. I would recall how even Richard Maundrell, a former professor of mine, made claims similar to Flanagan's. After recalling such views, I would again be overwhelmed with rage, then depression (DePasquale, Eigenbrod, & LaRocque, 2010, p. 104).

Sadly, Lorraine's experience is not an exception; it reflects the norm for Aboriginal students. Almost all aboriginal students will feel "physically, mentally, and spiritually sick" when they read the literature. Like Widdowson and Howard (2008) say; "Many undergraduate programs are now specifically designed for natives, where the application of 'Aboriginal' signifies the lower standard of the degree." By and large most undergraduate programs which are "designed for natives" are founded on the research efforts of non-Aboriginals, and anthropologists in particular. These programs which are based on such theories or myths as a lack of antiquity for Indians; an interpretation that paleo-Indians could have crossed Beringia; the myth of the noble savage; the Hollywood Indian; or even the trusted stewardship of Mother Earth made famous by the hippie generations of the 1960s do a disservice not only to the Aboriginal learner but to all students in general interested in the world around them. Yet it is these types of programs that flourish in mainstream institutions, well supported financially, perpetuating the propaganda based on the fear of the colonizers of anything Indian, a fear which has been deeply embedded in the education system over the last 150 years.

If the education system is to change, if Indians are to be academically successful we have to stop being susceptible to the false generosity of the government. We neither have a standard for education in our schools, nor do we know what the unit cost of a successful education program would be, yet, we cannot simply replicate the institutions of the mainstream and maintain the status quo as we have done in child welfare merely for the monetary benefit which may accrue to a chosen few. If Gardner (1991) is correct that "you must determine the realm of society that seems most crucial to preserve" to determine what is to be taught, then at the end of the day we are left with one very important question; if we cannot educate our own children to know the world in which they live, while maintaining our Native values, then the question that must be asked is what does all the rest of it matter?

REFERENCES

1911. *Correspondence and Agreement Relating to the Maintenance and Management of Indian Boarding Schools.* Ottawa, ON.: Government Printing Bureau. 6656–1.

2010 Budget. March 4, 2010. Ottawa, ON.: Department of Finance, Government of Canada.

An Act to encourage the gradual Civilization of the Indian Tribes in this Province, and to amend the Laws respecting Indians, S. Prov. C. 1857, c. 26.

Depasquale, Paul, Renate Eigenbrod, and Emma LaRocque, Editors. 2010. *Across Cultures, Across Boarders: Canadian Aboriginal and Native American Literatures.* Peterborough, ON.: Broadview Press.

Fraser, S. Auditor General of Canada. 2010. Opening Statement to the Standing Committee on Aboriginal Peoples, Indian and Northern Affairs Canada—Education Program and Post-Secondary Student Support. Retrieved from http://www.oag-bvg.gc.ca/internet/English/oss_20100512_e_33879.html.

Freire, Paulo. 2003. *Pedagogy of the Oppressed.* New York: Continuum.

Gardner, Howard. 1991. *The Unschooled Mind: How Children Think & How Schools Should Teach.* New York: Basic Books.

Johnston, Patrick. 1983. *Native Children and the Child Welfare System.* Ottawa, ON.: Canadian Council on Social Development, #147.

Libin, Kevin. Feb 20, 2010. "A First Nations dream soured; An aboriginal-run university is in turmoil over loss of funding, staff and students, as well as charges of corruption," *National Post*, Don Mills, ON. . p. A. 4. Retrieved from http://proquest.umi.com/pqdlink?RQT=572&TS=1283371332&clientId=29636&VType=PQD&VName= PQD&VInst=PROD&PMID=38532&PCID=50913911&SrtM=0&SrchMode=3&aid=1

Ljunggren, David. Sept 25, 2009. "Every G20 nation wants to be Canada, insists PM," *Reuters*,. Retrieved from http://www.reuters.com/article/idUSTRE58P05Z20090926.

MacPherson, James C. . Sept. 1991. MacPherson Report on Tradition and Education: Towards a Vision of our Future, Ottawa, ON.: Department of Indian Affairs and Northern Development.

Maslen, Geoff. October 6, 1995. "Progress for aborigines," *The Chronicle of Higher Education* v.42 . p. A47–8. Retrieved from http://vnweb.hwwilsonweb.com/hww/results/getResults.jhtml?_DARGS=/hww/results/results_common.jhtml.34.

Payton, Laura. March 3, 2010. "AFN chief wants money for education," *Toronto Sun*. Retrieved from http://www.torontosun.com/money/2010/03/03/13096061.html.

Stonebanks, Christopher. 2008. *James Bay Cree Students and Higher Education: Issues of Identity and Culture Shock*. Rotterdam: Sense Publishers.

The Indian Act, S.C., 1876.

The Indian Act, S.C., 1880.

Usher, Alex. 2009. The Post Secondary Student Support Program: An Examination of alternative Delivery Mechanisms. Ottawa, ON.: Department of Indian and Northern Affairs Canada.

Widdowson, Frances and Albert Howard. 2008. *Disrobing the Aboriginal Industry: The Deception Behind Indigenous Cultural Preservation*. Montreal & Kingston: McGill-Queen's University Press.

Wilson, J. Donald, Robert M. Stamp, and Louis-Philippe Audet. 1970. *Canadian Education: A History*. Scarborough, ON.: Prentice-Hall.

Section III

Indigenous Knowledges and the Question of Development: Tensions of Change, Tradition and Modernity

The noted dynamism of Indigenous knowledges convey the realization that every knowledge moves through time and space confronting and sorting out the tensions in tradition, change and so-called modernity. This is not some post-modern project of intellectual hybridity but one rooted in place, history, and politics. There needs to be explicit recognition that the project of reclaiming Indigeneity in contemporary times has both possibilities and pitfalls for the learner. Indigenous knowledges are explicitly political and, in being so, necessarily engage with other knowledges and the tensions that are revealed through this engagement. The conflict, tensions, contestations, and contentions of knowledge point to the value of close interrogation and searching for the relevance of Indigenous knowledge at any point in time. Indigenous knowledge is about everyday survival and moving forward for self, community, group, and nation. This is what social development is also about. What Indigenous knowledge helps us to do then is rethink the processes of social development and embrace the contradictions of human existence. For example, in re-thinking "development" and challenging the imperial dance existent within it, the survival of Indigenous knowledge systems through time helps bring to the fore the tensions of globalization, transnationalism, and modernity, while still managing to ground this interrogation in history.

We know that the local, cultural resource knowledge bases of Indigenous peoples have been the least analyzed for their contributions to the so-called development process. Starting development from what people already know and what they think ought to be an important entry point to discussion about future development. The use of local creativity and resourcefulness as a cornerstone for development suggests the existence of local cultural resource knowledge. Such recognition also suggests shifting development away from a top-down approach to a bottom-up undertaking and means affirming what local peoples know and do. This means seeing local peoples as producers of knowledge and active agents in claiming the power of Indigenousness and Indigeneity. Local peoples understand changes taking place in their lives. They have their own ideas about how to resolve the tensions and contradictions in everyday existence. The authenticity of local voices needs to be respected as we collectively search for ways for social development for a global humanity.

Today, Indigenous knowledge is about a struggle to retain one's identity in the call for a global sameness. It is also about developing awareness of the pitfalls and ills of the so-called modernist project and modernization. The poetics and practice of Indigenous knowledge today also brings into focus struggles of Indigeneity and Indigenization in global competitive spaces. This entails wresting control of knowledge production from the colonizer and the imperial savior while addressing the complicity of local Indigenous elites who shamefully partake in the denigration of local cultural resource knowings. Indigenous knowledge is about resistance, not in the romanticized sense, but resistance as struggle to navigate the tensions of today's modernized, globalized world while seeking to disrupt its universalizing, hegemonic norms.

Part of the Indigenous identity are local peoples' continuing struggles for access to land, political channels, markets, and education to defend themselves in "….[a competitive, hierarchical]….non-Indigenous world" (Nash, 1995, p. 11). Indigenous peoples' strive for recognition of their ethnic distinctiveness and dignity in an era of marked global capital encroachment. In some communities "...forced acculturation has conditioned Indigenous responses" (Nash, 1995, p. 9) to their integration into the global market. These challenges offer important lessons for understanding how we move ahead into the future as a community of nations. There are challenges of dealing with change and modernity and how we speak about the relevance of knowledge. For example, how can we arrest the disastrous consequences that Western-style development (e.g., tourism, mining, and other mineral-extracting activities driven by market-oriented economic development practices) are having on Indigenous cultural knowledge systems, cultural property, and heritage? What does development that uses Indigenous knowledges as its base look like? Can we even still think in terms of "development" without imposing a Eurocentric imperial world view?

Serena Heckler and Paul Sillitoe's chapter on "Education for Endogenous Development: Contrasting Perspectives from Amazonia and Arabia" takes up the question of the role of higher education in supporting "endogenous development." The discussion is anchored in the authors' own involvement in Indigenous education in two different contexts: amongst the Indigenous people of Ecuador—particularly the Intercultural University in Quito—and the Arabs of the Gulf—particularly at Qatar University in Doha. They argue that "endogenous development" differs from "participatory development" in the centrality of Indigenous worldviews setting and defining the goals of development. It is pointed out that one of the primary objectives of "endogenous development" is to create an appropriate education system that enables people to interact effectively with the structures that determine the distribution of resources and afford them some agency in drawing on their own identities as sources of empowerment and well-being.

Indigenous people have been subject to U.S. laws that govern Native American/American Indians in terms of land alienation, imposed Western education, and laws that restrict traditional religious practices, hunting/fishing, and have severely affected cultural practices such as language, and music/dance since the nineteenth century. Alaska is no exception. In her chapter on: "Neo-colonial Melancholia: Alaska Native People, Education and Oil" Maria *Shaa Tláa* Williams focuses on the Alaska Native Claims Settlement Act (ANCSA) which when signed into law radically changed the political and cultural map of Alaska's Indigenous peoples. She argues that the main purpose of ANCSA was to extinguish aboriginal claim to Alaska's lands to pave the way for oil development. Since the passage of the Act, oil companies have made extraordinary profits, yet the Alaska Native population remains in the lower economic and educational ranks. In the rural villages, nearly 70%

of Alaska Native students continue to drop out of high school and have high teen suicide rates and other social traumas that are vestiges of their colonial histories. Her chapter is a critique of the oil colony of Alaska and its undue influence on policies, even in the area of education. As Alaska Native people have adapted to the change and eventually have become players in the political scene, the issues of education still come to the forefront, even in the twenty-first century. Public education continues to propagate a system that does not serve the Indigenous population and the K-12 education curriculum needs to radically change.

Michael Marker's "Sacred Mountains and Ivory Towers: Indigenous Pedagogies of Place and Invasions from Modernity" describes how the efforts to bring pre-contact community knowledge into a culturally responsive pedagogy are challenged by the historic effects of colonization. He shows how Indigenous scholars are working in academic spaces as conduits to community projects that are decolonizing local elementary and high schools. Drawing on experiences and examples from the Coast Salish region, the chapter examines the ways that Indigenous knowledge merges ecological and spiritual principles that bond the physical and metaphysical in practical ways connected to resource management. It is noted that modernity's invasion of Coast Salish territory brought policies such as the potlatch laws that attempted to eradicate the ceremonies, remove the people from the land, and assimilate them into the margins of a "universalized" society. Lockean principles of property ownership along with the culture of empire relegated Indigenous knowledge systems to the categories of primitive and outmoded beliefs. Marker pinpoints the ways Coast Salish educational projects are working with youth to explore the ecological knowledge of ancestors and recreate something of the cognitive geographies of their borderless traditional territory.

Lloyd Lee's chapter "Indigenous Knowledge in Transition: The Fundamental Laws of the Diné in an Era of Change and Modernity" argues that notwithstanding the ways Europeans, and later Americans have traumatically impacted Indigenous peoples way of life, Indigenous peoples have been able to maintain many aspects of their cultural knowledge. In 2002, the Navajo Nation codified ethical standards their ancestors lived by since their emergence to Diné Bikéyah (Navajo land). These ethical standards are known as the Fundamental Laws of the Diné. Since its codification, Navajo people have interpreted these laws in various ways. The Navajo council, the court system, and the people have different angles in their understanding of the Fundamental Laws. Lee's chapter interprets and analyzes these laws paying attention to how the council, the court system, and various grassroots environmental organizations apply them for their particular needs. The Navajo Nation is in an era of modernity and change but these laws represent a cultural knowledge that has sustained Navajo people for many generations. More and more young Navajos are not able to speak their cultural language fluently or participate in the rituals and ceremonies to strengthen their identity. Will these laws continue or will they succumb to modernity and change? This is a key question.

REFERENCE

Nash, J. (1995). The Reassertion of Indigenous Identity: Mayan Responses to State Intervention in Chiapas. *Latin American Research Review, 30*(3), 7–41.

CHAPTER ELEVEN

Education for Endogenous Development

Contrasting Perspectives from Amazonia and Arabia

SERENA HECKLER & PAUL SILLITOE

Our concern in this chapter is the role of higher education in supporting particular types of development, notably the paradigm of endogenous development. We explore the topic of this volume, namely Indigenous knowledge (IK) and education, vis-à-vis the following questions: what is the role of Indigenous knowledge in endogenous development; what is the role of education in endogenous development; and what does an education for endogenous development look like? We address these questions with particular reference to our involvement with endogenous development in two radically different contexts: amongst the Indigenous peoples of Ecuador and the Arab population of Qatar. We argue that endogenous development differs from participatory development in the centrality of IK, or rather Indigenous worldviews, which should form the perspectives that set the goals of development. The people involved—previously considered the "recipients" of development—set out to identify the barriers to their own identified goals, what they, not outsiders, perceive as progress. These barriers often involve education. Consequently, one of the primary objectives of endogenous development is to create appropriate educational systems that enable people to interact effectively with the structures that determine the distribution of resources and afford them some agency in drawing on their own identities as sources of empowerment and well-being.

Both authors have long-standing interests in the role of Indigenous knowledge in development contexts which have recently extended to an interest in education as a means of supporting, resisting, or outright challenging existing development paradigms. Sillitoe's regional focus in this chapter came about less by intentional design than unforeseen destiny. He was invited to accept a chair at the University of Qatar to establish a program of teaching and research in sustainable development. An ironical challenge, for the chair is not only endowed by the energy giant Shell, which along with other oil companies many see as culpable for supplying the world with climate-changing fossil fuel, but the program is also located on the Arabian Gulf, where life today depends on unsustainable socio-economic arrangements that feature the exploitation of environmentally damaging non-renewable hydrocarbon resources. During his time at the university he has become fascinated by the contradictions inherent in an institution seeking to become a university to be reckoned with globally, which means playing by foreign occidental rules, while simultaneously trying to remain true to its oriental cultural legacy—not a clash but a confusion of civilizations.

Heckler's interest in Indigenous ways of knowing and being began as a small child when she spent many of her days with her grandmother on Fort Hall, a Shoshone-Bannock reservation in South East Idaho. Her grandmother taught her to respect Shoshone-Bannock ways of knowing, particularly those things that chimed with her grandmother's own left-wing political beliefs and love of the land.[1] Nevertheless, when she began working with Amazonian Indigenous people as a Ph.D. student, she had romantic notions of coming into contact with the exotic other. During the subsequent years of sharing people's daily lives and concerns, coming to consider some of them as dear friends, and experiencing first hand not only the challenges that they face, but also the creativity, resourcefulness, and determination with which they face it, she has come to see that it is not her job to speak for or champion Indigenous people. Instead, she has worked to develop collaborative relationships with a range of Indigenous organizations, one of them being the Intercultural University written about here, in which she acts as a consultant to help them find their own pathways to empowerment and well-being. The university organizers have asked her, among other things, to write about their educational project, thereby helping them to gain legitimacy in academic and political circles, the importance of which will become clear later in the chapter. She has shown a draft of this chapter to the UINPI organizers, has discussed it with them, and they have encouraged her to publish it in this book.

Endogenous Development

In relatively recent years, the development theory called post-development has critiqued sustainable and participatory development, not only arguing that these paradigms are subject to manipulation, but also that their very conception is a fallacy (Cooke & Kothari, 2002; Escobar, 1995; Rahnema & Bawtree, 1997). In the wake of this disillusionment, a few practitioners and scholars have become involved with projects that can be glossed as "alternative development" (Nederveen Pieterse, 1998), including "endogenous development," "self-determined development," or "development with identity" (Corpuz, 2008). The idea of alternative development has gained ground in international policy circles, with a wide range of organizations and donors supporting alternative development initiatives (Nederveen Pieterse, 1998).

Alternative development is in danger of achieving "buzzword" status. According to Jan Nederveen Pieterse (2001), it does not comprise a coherent paradigm but consists of a range of development practices, theories, and philosophies that share nothing more than a rejection of modernist and neoliberal development approaches. The same may be said of endogenous development, one of the many types of alternative development being championed today. Although the term has been around for some time, it appears to mean something different in different contexts. For instance, Nederveen Pieterse (2001) uses it to refer to "an endogenous process" that predates "externally induced change, under the aegis of imperialism, capitalism, globalism" (p. 43). Whereas, in the EU's famous LEADER program, it is seen to be roughly synonymous with participatory or bottom-up development (Ray, 1999, p. 521), while set in a context of decentralization and an increasing emphasis on localities, rather than the nation-state, as sites of development (Ray, 1999, p. 524). In Venezuela, on the other hand, the use of the term forms part of a discourse of ideological rejection of Western capitalism, with reference to the strong, central nation-state.

Recently, a definition of endogenous development based on an explicit recognition of the power differentials inherent in both economic marginalization and classical development paradigms has begun to gain prominence in international development institutions. This recognition has ramifications for development practice, including a shift in the goal of development projects from simply meeting the material and health needs of local people to empowering them to demand social and environmental justice, or, at the very least, to find their own paths to development. Recently this approach has been brought into mainstream development with the human rights–based approach (HBRA) currently promoted by the UN agencies amongst others (e.g., Pettit & Wheeler, 2005; UNHCR, 2006), but many endogenous development advocates insist that the HRBA and the international institutions and tools upon which it draws are more effective when they support, rather than initiate and control, development projects (Bradshaw, 2006). It thus follows that local groups, communities, and societies must be able to effectively engage with and utilize these tools and determine and enact their own development projects. There is therefore a strong emphasis on empowerment, capacity-building, and education in this type of endogenous development.

The Comparing and Supporting Endogenous Development (COMPAS) network[2] illustrates this approach. This international consortium of NGOs and universities accepts that "endogenous development" is similar to other participatory approaches, but stresses on its Web site that it differs from them in "its emphasis on including spiritual aspects in the development process, in addition to the ecological, social and economic aspects."[3] The Web site continues:

> Endogenous development is mainly based on local strategies, values, institutions and resources. Therefore priorities, needs and criteria for development may differ in each community and may not always be the same as those of the development worker.
>
> Key concepts within endogenous development are: local control of the development process; taking cultural values seriously; appreciating worldviews; and finding a balance between local and external resources. The aim of endogenous development is to empower local communities to take control of their own development process. While revitalising ancestral and local knowledge, endogenous development helps local people select those external resources that best fit the local conditions. Endogenous development leads to increased bio- and cultural diversity, reduced environmental degradation, and a self-sustaining local and regional exchange.

This is an ambitious statement and there are several points that could be questioned. For instance:

- Is there a contradiction between seeking to support local/ancestral knowledge and external resources (for instance, external pedagogical models)?
- What, if any, is the contemporary role for ancestral/Indigenous/local knowledge?
- How does revitalizing ancestral knowledge empower local communities?
- What about when local concerns are at odds with international priorities, notably environmental issues?

We will deal with these questions throughout, but here, we wish to establish this view of endogenous development as a characterization of that type of alternative development that is increasingly figuring in the practice and discourse of Indigenous social movements around the world (Tebtebba Foundation, 2004). Key to this perspective is the explicit recognition that, from a local perspective, the solutions, perception of the problems, and goals of development may be quite different from those that feature in an exogenous point of view. These are embedded within worldviews and epistemologies that mainstream development may systematically and structurally exclude to the point of rendering them invisible to those working within that system. The endogenous development approach, unlike classical development paradigms, holds that only focusing on economic prosperity will not achieve these goals. Rather, it maintains that by also focusing on social, cultural, and emotional well-being—in other words, by placing the maintenance of distinct and empowered identities at the center of the development project, well-being for all peoples may be improved.

While this view of endogenous development fits the Ecuador context, it is not, at first glance, a good fit for the Qatar context. Specifically, the emphasis on empowerment and grassroots activism is not appropriate in Qatar. Although there is a certain sense of disempowerment among some Qataris, the civil institutions are largely tribally based, and any grassroots initiatives work through this system. Moreover, the cultural context is much less conducive to the sort of large-scale protest that is regularly seen in Ecuador. Nevertheless, we do contend that certain aspects of the COMPAS definition are relevant to Qatar. For instance, the central question remains how groups and individuals in different social, political, and historical contexts may determine their own pathway to what they consider to be a better standard of well-being.

INDIGENOUS KNOWLEDGE IN DEVELOPMENT

Its shortcomings notwithstanding, mainstream development has made some efforts to incorporate Indigenous perspectives. Indeed, Indigenous knowledge (IK) has been part of development discourse for at least two decades (Ellen & Harris, 2000; Heckler, 2009; Sillitoe, 1998). What exactly is meant by IK, however, is a matter of considerable debate. For instance, in academia, different disciplines have different understandings of what IK is (Zent, 2009), while in applied contexts, it has taken on a highly politicized significance (related to identity, rights, etc.), in which its definition and application change depending upon the perspective and agenda of the involved parties (Alexiades, 2009). Of course, the same may be said for the academic approaches, which are often grounded in a particular ideology (Battiste & Henderson, 2000, pp. 35–38; Sillitoe, 2004). This instrumental plasticity and a concern over whose ends the concept serves has led some to be highly skeptical of the incorporation of IK into development (Battiste & Henderson, 2000; Briggs & Sharp, 2004).

A widely known critique of the incorporation of IK into development is that by Arun Agrawal (1995, 1999). He argues that those approaches to IK that see it as discrete bits of technical or taxonomic data that can be extracted from the context in which they were derived and applied to particular problems in a scientific manner fundamentally change and appropriate that knowledge. For example, the incorporation of certain agricultural techniques into development initiatives, or recording the names and uses of medicinal plants or crop varieties in different contexts represent a cooption of that knowledge. Similarly in education initiatives, it is sometimes assumed that IK can be transmitted by bringing scientifically extracted IK data into a formal education setting, an approach that has been critiqued widely (Bates, 2009; Dei, Hall, & Rosenberg, 2000, p. 7; Rival, 1997).

However, several IK researchers and professionals have emphasized the holistic nature of IK, repeatedly demonstrating that discrete taxonomic or technical data are nothing more than emergent indicators of rich and complex worldviews that inform every facet of lived experience (Ellen & Harris, 2000; Heckler, 2009; Sillitoe, 1998). To understand and appropriately incorporate IK, it is not enough to package "data" in a scientific or pedagogical model that is external to that data. In contrast, it must be elicited, understood, and transmitted in ways that are appropriate to the particular epistemology whence it arose (Battiste & Henderson, 2000, pp. 35–36; Cajete, 2000).

In many Amazonian and Andean societies, well-being is grounded in a moral and aesthetic imperative to work hard, share food, and not seek to dominate others (Overing & Passes, 2000). This morality is supported by and grounded in Indigenous worldviews, including mythology, ontology, epistemology, and everyday practice. The last named often bears a semi-ritualistic significance, in that the manner in which everyday tasks are enacted has important ramifications for the spiritual and affective well-being of the enactor, their family, and their community (Overing, 2003). For instance, the way in which a woman weeds a garden, a man moves through the forest while hunting, or a child learns is informed by rich mythologies, rituals, and sacred places—sometimes called "cultural codes" by Ecuadorian Indigenous intellectuals (Kowii, 2007, p. 117; Macas, 2009, p. 84)—that transmit the mundane know-how and deeper knowledge that ensures the health and well-being of the family and community (Universidad Intercultural Amawtay Wasi, 2004, pp. 166–167). Any development project that increases household income at the expense of the broader significance of these actions will not improve well-being (see also Astvaldsson, 2002).

Moreover, as Ishizawa and Rengifo (2009) note for communities in the Peruvian Andean and Amazonian regions, "there is a recognition among traditional authorities...that their present lack of well-being is due to a generalized loss of respect for each other, for their deities and nature" (p. 60). From this perspective, economic and rights-based development can only occur if the proper moral enactment of social relationships—embedded within a particular cultural context—is healthy and functional. This puts cultural elements, such as ritual, religion, language, storytelling, and other ways in which social relationships are enacted, at the center of endogenous development.

Similarly, in the Arab world, IK[4] accords with Islamic religious beliefs and practices. These are prominent in the Gulf region, with prayers and associated rituals marking daily rhythms. The holy Koran informs moral codes, social relationships, and humans' relationships with nature. But since the mid-twentieth century with the exploitation of large oil and gas reserves, life has changed dramatically and with it IK. The region is in the throes of a development construction boom and nearly all the population are now urban dwellers. While people are resistant to any changes that they perceive go against the Koran's divinely inspired teachings, they have witnessed staggering rates of technological and social change. Knowledge and experience have transformed too, particularly between the generations. The majority of men know far more about four-wheel drive vehicles than they do about camels.

Desert and marine environments are under threat with such rapid industrial and urban development, and IK and associated culture are disappearing in its wake, traditions that for centuries have enabled the people of the Gulf and Middle East to survive sustainably in a harsh climate without degrading the natural environment. Whereas previously, pastoralists had an intimate knowledge of their environment, relying on locally available pasture and water wells, today those who continue to keep animals rely on imported fodder, deep tube wells, desalination plants, and employ migrant labor to herd their stock. But in other domains of life, IK and traditional values remain strong. While apparently embracing much industrialized change and associated consumer culture, with large shopping malls a prominent feature of the urban landscape, people look apprehensively at Western capitalist society, particularly its erosion of family values. Kin remain central to Gulf social life, and any threat to the family, clan, and tribe will be strongly resisted, just as any threat to Islamic teachings.

In both Ecuador and Qatar, then, Indigenous knowledges can only be understood as holistic and dynamic worldviews. This perspective renders many assumptions about the role of IK in development problematic. For instance, viewing IK as processual, historically contingent, and largely socially constructed questions the appropriateness of plugging "Indigenous solutions" into development projects that were conceived of and designed exogenously; the use of decontextualized methodologies—such as pile sorts, tree trails, among others—to extract IK data (Heckler, 2007); or the emphasis on a particular type of institution-building while remaining ignorant of the worldviews and complex socio-political factors that shape endogenous institutions. How, then, are we to incorporate IK into the development process? We believe that in both Ecuador and Qatar an appropriate education system that transmits not only technical knowledge but also encourages and valorizes social, spiritual, and environmental aspects of IK is central to this endeavor.

EDUCATION FOR ENDOGENOUS DEVELOPMENT

By way of illustrating how this works in diverse contexts and what, if anything, unifies endogenous development, we now consider two universities which both purport, in different ways, to valorize IK. They both seek to gain international recognition as high-quality education institutions while combining external and endogenous pedagogical models, intellectual histories, and value systems. As we demonstrate, however, they do this in two very different ways. These examples also illustrate the importance of education in transmitting or at least enabling the cultural codes and practices that serve as moral and social guidelines to well-being.

Higher Education for Endogenous Development: Two Case Studies

In Ecuador, we collaborate with an Indigenous university, the Intercultural University of Indigenous Nations and Peoples of Ecuador-Amawtay Wasi (UINPI by its Spanish initials), which operates a branch in Amazonia. Since 2007, Heckler has been carrying out ethnographic research with UINPI in the various Indigenous communities where it works. And in Qatar, we work in the national university located in a north Doha suburb, where Sillitoe has held the Shell Chair in Sustainable Development in the Social Sciences Department of the College of Arts and Sciences since 2008.

The overall objectives of UINPI are three-fold: (1) to refute the undeniably prevalent perception in Indigenous society today that Ecuadorian IK and ways of being and knowing are somehow inferior to exogenous ones; (2) to teach certain elements of IK that serve as cultural codes after several generations of intentional suppression; and (3) to teach technical skills and knowledge derived from both Indigenous and external sources in a complementary manner to enable students to better their own lives and society generally. The second purpose is generally referred to by UINPI educators as the "revitalization of ancestral knowledge." The first purpose, refuting the supposed superiority of exogenous culture and knowledge, often has an element of Indigenous activism. For instance, this quote by a UINPI organizer, during an interview with Heckler in 2010:

> UINPI. . .is going to. . .sensitize [national leaders] [to see Indigenous people as equals]. Or maybe not even to sensitize our current leaders. . .but to create new conditions, new ethics for the future generations so that we can advance together, or rather with other forms of power, with more horizontal relations. Two or three generations in the future, perhaps we will see. And even better if there will be other universities that are intercultural. I believe that the universities, more than anything, can contribute immensely to this project, in this activity of sensitizing our future generations (Quito, 3/3/2010).

In recent decades, a range of scholars have turned their attention to the inequality embedded within hegemonic conceptions of knowledge (Dei, Hall, & Rosenberg, 2000). In these analyses, culturally appropriate education is seen as a crucial element of identity politics in which people learn to improve their societies using perspectives and ideas derived from IK (Garcia, 2005; Jackson & Warren, 2005; Turay, 2000, p. 248; Wangoola, 2000). From this perspective, empowerment, citizenship, dignity, and community become primary goals of education (Llanes-Ortiz, 2009). IK is seen as being central to this process in that it values the worldview(s) of the student, thereby contributing to the development of an empowered person (Howard, Barbira-Freedman, & Stobart, 2002, p. 3). It also is seen to engage more directly with the student by presenting information within a framework with which the student is already familiar, or perhaps more accurately, to not use study paradigms and worldviews developed in one cultural context to teach people from another (Thaman, 2003, p. 2). Finally, UINPI seeks to demonstrate the possibility of more ecologically sustainable and socially egalitarian ways of living to non-Indigenous people.

In this case, intercultural education is an overtly political project, in which one of the main aims is resistance to an exogenous system that has caused great damage to the well-being of local communities. It is sometimes admitted that the knowledge that is transmitted in such contexts is hybridized. However, considerable effort is made to transmit knowledge within an epistemological framework that is appropriate for the knowledge being transmitted. This, say the deans of UINPI, is central to the second purpose of revitalizing ancestral knowledge. In other words, by grounding the teaching of IK in frameworks that make explicit reference to Indigenous worldviews (for instance, using the Southern Cross as the model for organizing the curriculum, onto which Indigenous conceptions of "wisdom" and "knowledge" are mapped), the holistic nature of Indigenous epistemologies are brought to the students' attention, thereby encouraging a more profound appreciation of them.

In Qatar University, on the other hand, social action and new social movements are not on the agenda. The Gulf educational institutions, instead of directly confronting these globally dominant views with alternative Arab ones, seek to develop in ways that can match them, indeed make them serious global players in the higher education field—the Ivy Leaguers of the Middle East—while remaining true to certain core Arab values and beliefs that the West's particular tradition of enquiry might challenge, posing some intriguing conundrums. The prospectus of Qatar University (2009) makes this clear, stating on its opening page that it "seeks to be a model national university that offers high quality, learning-centred education to its students" and that while promoting "the cultural and scientific development of Qatari society" it aims at "preserving its Arabic characteristics and maintaining its Islamic cultural heritage"(p. 2).

There is an awareness in the University that it is necessary to safeguard Arab heritage in the face of the rapid Westernization of its curriculum (with all the burdensome bureaucracy that this implies); for instance, following pressure from some staff, the University has recently ruled that all communications must be in Arabic followed by English translations as necessary, which some speak of overtly as protecting Arabic ways and ensuring that they remain dominant in their homeland. People are alive to these issues beyond universities in the Gulf region regarding aspirations to protect cultural values. The 2030 National Vision of Qatar,[5] for instance, which sets out the country's aims "to be an advanced society capable of sustaining its development and providing a high standard of living for all of its people" identifies five major challenges facing the country of Qatar, the first of which is "modernization and preservation of traditions."

Pedagogical Issues in Higher Indigenous Education

The teaching method developed by UINPI differs significantly from the lecture-based style normally associated with universities. Firstly, the central campus only hosts some post-graduate courses. Most of the teaching and learning is coordinated in a series of "Learning Communities" based around the country so that they are accessible to Indigenous people, the majority of whom cannot afford to leave their work, their farms, and their families to study at a faraway campus. Moreover, the communities of learning offer more exchange of knowledge, information, and practical results between home communities and the university. In fact, the deans consider the real "experts" in culture not to be academics but rather the elders for whom leaving the communities to teach in Quito or Guayaquil would be unthinkable.

A primary aim is to avoid the alienation from communities that Indigenous students often experience and the hostility that local communities sometimes feel toward "elitist" universities. To this end, only a small amount of time is spent in classroom contexts and even that time mostly takes the form of discussion sessions on particular themes, such as Indigenous rights, traditional architecture, culinary arts, mythology, and cosmology. These topics are presented formally then integrated into ordinary narratives through informal storytelling sessions that can go on for hours. These are not mere repetitions of myths or established narratives. Instead, they incorporate bawdy anecdotes, gossip, jokes, and everyday tales interwoven with discussion of the pedagogical topics of the day, a narrative style that is important in making sense of everyday experience for many Indigenous people (Overing, 2000). But they are also settings where students can negotiate and contest attitudes toward their own identities. Combining these sessions with post-colonial studies and practical engagement with the elders in their own communities enables students to think about and express their ethnic identities in new ways.

Indeed, what Heckler found through a series of unstructured interviews with thirty UINPI students is that UINPI serves as a catalyst which offers legitimacy and value to their own IK, sometimes for the first time in the student's life. The students become enthusiastic to bring their learning into the community, interrogate his/her lifestyle and begin to talk to other community members about the role of IK in their contemporary lives. In other words, rather than teaching IK per se, UINPI teaches students to value and be interested in IK and teaches them methods (such as interviewing elders and carrying out certain key rituals) that enable them to reflect upon and integrate IK into their contemporary lives in new ways. In this way, the students begin also to identify themselves as part of a particular ethnic group, culturally, socially, and politically, that is currently engaged in a struggle for recognition and respect on its own terms.

For the Arabs, on the other hand, the nature and duration of contact with European civilization are different, enabling a different relationship between the two pedagogical traditions. Indigenous Ecuadorians have only relatively recently come into contact with Euro-American epistemologies and that in the context of subjugation and oppression, whereas for the Arabs there is a long history of interaction, notably in the Levant and North Africa, extending to the Moorish occupation of parts of Spain in the first millennium A.D. . Consequently, there is some overlap regarding knowledge traditions and beliefs, for while Christianity and Islam may be portrayed as antagonistic faiths since the Crusades, they share a common Abrahamaic heritage. And Arab scholarship, notably in the sciences, heavily informed European knowledge. The Arab world has a long history of scholarship—influenced by ancient Greek and Roman philosophy in the West and Indian science and mathematics in the East—that burned like an intellectual light during the European Dark Ages, and featured such scholars as al-Kindi, al-Farabi, and Ibn Sina to al-Ghazzali, Nasir al-Din al-Tusi, and Mulla Sadra.

The Middle East also has a long history of educational institutions, collectively *madrasah* (literally "place for lessons"), often associated with mosques, as formal learning and enquiry were integral to Islam, for all knowledge ultimately concerns some aspect of Allah's presence. Universities made their appearance in the Arab world in the eighth century A.D.; such institutions of higher education are called *jameah* today. There is a certain irony for a contribution to a volume that seeks to promote the independence and distinctiveness of Indigenous/other pedagogy, to note that these Muslim universities heavily influenced the foundation and curricula of medieval European universities, and that today they are wrestling to establish their relationship with the globally dominant Euro-American system of higher education that has resulted.

At Qatar University, therefore, they seek to adopt Euro-American approaches to pedagogy, rather than break free from these and forge their own, albeit they are doing so in ways that comply with Arab values. The state of Qatar is investing huge sums in education with a view to achieving these aims and equipping its citizens for the future. The national University of Qatar is undergoing rapid, well-resourced expansion. These developments include an entire new Doha suburb—called Education City—where educational and research facilities are being constructed that will rival anything elsewhere in the world, and several U.S. universities have branch campuses there. These franchise campuses are intended specifically to raise through example the standards of Qatari educational institutions to international levels. But currently they stand strangely isolated in another part of the city, are poorly attended and are in danger of becoming something of anomalies partly because they are perceived as foreign institutions that are not engaging like Qatar University with issues on Arab terms. There is a need for them, in seeking to include local students in their programs, to embrace their worldviews, not expect them somehow to put aside their cultural heritage.

These Arab traditions concern issues such as a respect for the teachings of the Koran and wish to have Islamic beliefs guide teaching and research, or at least for these not to be challenged sacrilegiously; an awareness of the importance of the family to Arab life and respect for their culturally specific familial arrangements, which with respect to gender relations are strikingly different from Europe and America; and an allowance for political arrangements that appear undemocratic to Westerners, which feature an unelected and fabulously wealthy emirate monarchy that works together with a tribal system featuring sheik representatives. These cultural arrangements have aspects that are readily misunderstood by foreigners, such as veiling and cousin marriages (El Guindi, 2003), and as currently evident in the tragic association of Muslim beliefs and practices with terrorism, rooted in fears that we can trace back to the Crusades of the twelfth century. They inform the organization of university campuses in ways that are strange to the Euro-American tradition. For instance, regarding gender relations, the campus of Qatar University is split in two, one half for female students and the other for male students. A large wall marks the divide and entrances in it are policed by security guards to ensure that men do not wander into the women's side. All teaching is duplicated with separate lectures and classes for male and female students. No respectable family would allow its daughters to attend an institution where they mixed freely with unrelated males, given the strong sentiments of honor and shame that inform family life.

Thus we have two distinct models of culturally appropriate education which have distinct aims. The model for Indigenous education in Ecuador is explicitly political, with a strong emphasis on empowerment of Indigenous people and valorization of IK with the aim not only to redefine development for Indigenous people but to change society as a whole. In Qatar, on the other hand, the goal is to beat the globally dominant Euro-American universities at their own game while valorizing Islamic values, kinship, and family structure. Euro-American universities seem to overlook or exclude consideration of such issues given their *modus operandi*. In both contexts, the assumed superiority of Euro-American institutes is interrogated and challenged.

Empowerment in Education: Combating Intellectual Domination as a Human Right

There is a tendency for Euro-American style education to assume that it is superior, largely because of its technological associations. Its hegemony derives from the application of certain knowledge, which has resulted in awesome industrial capacity that allows humans unprecedented ability to intervene in the world. This informs one strand of efforts to interface Indigenous with scientific knowledge in development contexts, namely to facilitate the up-take of assumed technological benefits, by representing IK more effectively to development agencies and practitioners, winning it respectability so that it can play its part in this process.

It is this perceived superiority that prompts Gulf educational institutions, such as Qatar University, to develop teaching and research programs that match those of globally prominent Euro-American universities, while remaining true to Arab worldviews. Indeed many persons in this part of the world conceive of development—*tanmia*—in narrow technological terms, epitomized in the current frenetic construction of high-rise buildings, multi-lane highways, state-of-the-art airports and docks, etc., employing many foreign builders, engineers, and architects to oversee the work, and large armies of migrant laborers, predominantly from poor Asian countries, to do the manual work. This view of development as largely a technological issue has a further intriguing gender dimension at Qatar University with male students largely interested in studying engineering subjects and business and economics, while female students predominate in the arts and sciences.

This perspective on development is slowly changing with Qatar's national vision acknowledging the importance of sustainable development and the preservation of tradition. Indeed, Qatar University has recently initiated a program of teaching and research in sustainable development, which Sillitoe is helping to establish. The response of both faculty and students suggested there was a certain discordance at the association of development with sustainability. While they could readily conceive of *tanmia* "development"—largely as technological progress, as related previously—and everyone was happy with the idea of something being *mustadama* "sustainable," there seemed to be some dissonance when the two words were put together as *tanmia mustadama* "sustainable development," in that persons' comments suggested a strange lack of awareness of the implications.

The differences became further evident when teaching a class of students and exploring the related ideas of sustainability (*mustadama*) and conservation (*weqaia*) which from their comments also seemed strangely out of sync, as if they had trouble seeing the close connection between them. It transpired that *mustadama* had the connotation for them of "forever" and *weqaia* of "save." The source of confusion slowly became clearer. While it is possible to think of saving something forever, it is difficult to conceive of this in the context of development, which implies progressive change. We can appreciate how the idea of everlasting technological progress conflicts with that of sustainable development which, in aiming to achieve a steady state with respect to the use of the world's resources, is in some senses the antithesis of development forever; it is more the view that informs capitalist economic approaches to development that worryingly overlook the finiteness of the earth's resources and logical limit to growth, as is now becoming increasingly and urgently evident with environmental damage.

Formal education is both fomenting and resolving this cognitive dissonance. In raising these issues and promoting debate about them it may help to work out confusions; for instance in encouraging people to discuss aspects of social change that worry them, such as threats to the integrity of family and tribe, and how they might resist them. But in bringing these issues into conscious focus it may foster further confusions; for instance in contrasting the idea of capitalist economic growth with its associated technological wizardry and desirable consumer goods with other approaches to being in the world, such as that of the Bedouin who traditionally exploited resources sustainably. In doing so in a university context there is a danger of casting the issues in an occidental framework. The program at Qatar University is aware of this and seeks to encourage discussion with an eye to sustainable endogenous development, to use the terms we have employed in this chapter. In this context, acutely aware of the importance of IK in the wide holistic sense used here, we encourage students to draw on their own cultural heritage in considering issues relevant to development and not to confuse technological change with progress necessarily, particularly if it appears to conflict with values they hold important but to discuss and consider the implications.

It is important to point out that the founding of this program was not the result of a grassroots movement but rather gradually changing priorities and perspectives at the top of Qatari society, partly as a result of international discourses. Nevertheless, the slow uptake of foreign universities in Doha's Education City suggests that this discourse is only effective because Qataris are able to relate to it, culturally and socially, and therefore are able to define for themselves the terms of their own development and its related pedagogical models. This gives them the autonomy and self-determination to decide to what extent and in which way they wish to engage with such international agendas.

In Ecuador, on the other hand, there is a much more overtly political element to the formal education offered at UINPI. During the social events and storytelling sessions that form a prominent part of formal learning and teaching events, students, and facilitators from all over the country talk of their unity, their plans for and contribution to a unified social struggle. One Shuar facilitator lecturing at the primarily Shuar[6] learning community, once told a group of eighty students that they were a non-violent "army" ("ejercito") that would bring, through peaceful activism, a new era of prosperity to the Shuar people.

The role of IK in this new, non-violent, Shuar army is absolutely central. Shuar concepts and symbols are used as rallying points, touchstones of common ground that can facilitate this new unity and serve as a guide for a morally and socially appropriate development. For instance, the Shuar god, Arutám,[7] has become a symbol of strength, wisdom and the ability to overcome adversity and shape one's own destiny. Meanwhile, *nijiamanch* (chicha or manioc beer) is seen as a symbol of the ties and responsibilities that contribute to a supportive, caring and strong family life.[8] Several students told Heckler that they had started making *nijiamanch* again, or had encouraged their female relatives to do so, as a result of learning during class discussions of its profound significance. As they drink *nijiamanch* or evoke Arutám, they also talk about how by doing so, they are encouraging Shuar people to be strong, to respect themselves and to demand their rights. In this sense, then, these symbols have become vehicles of meaning "around which political struggle is organized in [an] effort to negotiate the legacies of colonial occupation, incorporation into modern national projects, and the pressures of globalization" (Greene, 2004, p. 212).

While some see this objectification of IK as negative, even a distortion or pollution of IK, it must be accepted that Indigenous lifeways are changing and the question is not how to maintain IK in some pristine, ancestral state, but rather what its significance is to those Indigenous people, such as those in Ecuador, who wish to have access to the same opportunities offered to other members of Ecuadorian society. And of course, its role, as we stated above, is empowerment to demand those opportunities if they are denied through structural or informal racism.

Although this resonates with the human rights–based approach (HRBA) to development, endogenous development in the Ecuadorian context actually takes the HRBA a step further. One of the criticisms of the HRBA is that, despite the rhetoric of empowerment and equality, it originates from institutions that disempower local and Indigenous communities in the first place (Bradshaw, 2006). One of the reasons for this is that, like various development paradigms, the problems and solutions to lack of well-being in local communities are still determined externally. Endogenous development, on the other hand, is driven by local people who determine their own problems and their own solutions. IK is, of course, central to this process, in that analysis of a particular situation may be completely different from a local perspective than from an external one. Rather than educating people to see development from the external/international perspective, an education for endogenous development, at least in the UINPI setting, enables people to see development from both perspectives, to compare and contrast them, to be able to initiate, negotiate, accept, or contest development initiatives on their own terms. Local people thus become the drivers, rather than the recipients of development. The enthusiasm that local people have for such an approach is demonstrated in a recent surge of Ecuadorian Indigenous NGOs that focus on a range of development and cultural initiatives (Andolina, Laurie, & Radcliffe, 2009).

UINPI follows a pedagogical technique inspired in part by problem-based learning. The central problem is often the inadequacy of income for families and communities. This concern for increasing income could lead the casual observer to assume that IK is taking a back seat to material concerns. However, the key—and innovative element—of the UINPI pedagogical model is the manner in which IK is applied to problems that many see as contemporary and exogenous, hence outside the IK remit. For example, the degree in agro-ecology requires students to develop, on family land, IK-inspired agricultural systems that provide a wide range of products for household consumption, sale, or barter. For many students, this represents a radical departure from the high-input, low-diversity systems that have been promoted by government, missionary, and development agents. The return to diverse systems, based upon spiritual and cosmological principles that infused so-called ancestral farming systems, not only improves nutrition and household economy, but also reinforces an all too often latent sense that the student's parents or grandparents were more knowledgeable than the student had thought. This, then, gives the student a basis from which to reject any equation of IK or Indigenous lifeways with ignorance and poverty. In this way, endogenous development, Indigenous knowledge, Indigenous education, and social action all converge.

Again, these two case studies demonstrate two distinct approaches to combating intellectual domination. The differences in the approach can be attributed to any of a number of contextual and historical differences. For instance, in Ecuador, UINPI educators are attempting to engage and negotiate with their own national government and in many cases calling in international allies (such as European development funds and universities) to help them in this. In Qatar, the university is largely aligned with the national government in a project to defend and protect Islamic values from the onslaught of the international community. Of course, its ability to do this is greatly helped by the country's vast hydrocarbon resources and consequent economic wealth available to support Qatar University, as opposed to UINPI which receives no public funds, so must operate on an extremely small budget. The difference in resources explains why in Qatar debate about the aims of development takes a dominantly ideological turn. In Ecuador, on the other hand, externally and superficially, the focus is on increasing the material wealth of Indigenous communities. While this is important to UINPI organizers—one organizer has said that it is impossible to teach someone whose belly is empty—it seems all too often to occlude UINPI's ideological message. After all, the aim of UINPI's founders was no less than to offer a viable alternative development model for all society, not just for Ecuadorian Indigenous peoples.

SOME CHALLENGES FACING EDUCATION FOR ENDOGENOUS DEVELOPMENT

Any education and development initiative that seeks to counter hegemonic structures inevitably faces considerable challenges. Indigenous pedagogy of the Ecuadorian variety, for instance, has received strong mainstream criticism. In a 2009 government evaluation of Ecuadorian universities, UINPI was graded as failing and was threatened with closure. The evaluation, which used the Euro-American universities as its model of excellence, held that the lack of a fixed central campus, a permanent and research-active faculty, and a relative lack of academic publications indicated low intellectual standards and academic rigor. As we pointed out earlier, all of these features are a direct result of the attempt to make UINPI more relevant and appropriate to Indigenous lifeways and knowledge. Hence, there is a sense among UINPI organizers that their project is fundamentally at odds with the goals of mainstream education and development currently favored by government and business leaders.

This is in sharp contrast to Gulf efforts to develop internationally recognized universities, which aim to comply with Euro-American standards of excellence and academic rigor, while retaining a distinctly Arabic cultural perspective. In this regard, one sometimes hears reference to re-establishing Arab scholarly traditions, which once led the world in mathematics and astronomy, medicine and biology, and kept alive aspects of ancient Greek scholarship. The Web site of the Qatar National Research Foundation, which is investing millions of dollars annually in competitively tendered research programs (in the region of $86 million for 2010), has a rotating banner headline that refers to "contributing to the Arab scientific renaissance" and "creating a knowledge-based society."[9] However, there is no sense that this is inherently at odds with Euro-American–style pedagogy. In both cases, however, Indigenous scholarship questions some Euro-American intellectual pre-occupations, which we should surely welcome, with Indigenous scholars and sensitive ethnography opening up and adding new dimensions to Euro-American scholarship.

The problems faced in gaining the respect of dominant Euro-American institutions are evident in the difficulties that Indigenous scholars face in publishing their work in prominent international outlets (such as academic journals and university presses) because it is not considered to be of sufficient intellectual merit—as defined by a particular epistemological perspective. This is made worse by the fact that they are often struggling to express themselves in a foreign language. It is often a question of mere survival, for example, with UINPI there is a constant negotiation with national authorities about how to fit their pedagogical approach into nationally established norms. The costs may be high, recognition demanding many compromises in their representation and transmission of Indigenous philosophies that are often inimical to structuring along the formal, hierarchical lines expected in Euro-American universities.

The costs for Gulf institutions are only slowly becoming evident, as they begin to realize that adopting the Euro-American canon challenges core Arab beliefs. For example, the theory of evolution challenges both the Koranic and Biblical versions of human origins and this can make both Muslim and Christian believers uncomfortable. The related point that evolution suggests that there is no such supreme being as God or Allah, other than as a figment of the human imagination, is blasphemous. Similarly, some New World Indigenous activists contend that the scientific theory that the New World was populated by people crossing the Bering Strait land bridge conflicts with their own origin myth and is therefore offensive to them. Any debate on these issues is consequently not allowable, which conflicts with the cornerstone principle of academic freedom that is central to the Euro-American idea of a university as a place that safeguards free speech and argument, where any and all such issues may be explored and debated.

In both contexts, then, the development of a culturally appropriate higher education involves direct challenges to some of the ideological principles of the dominant higher education paradigm. We do not argue that these issues are easily resolved or that any model of higher education will do as long as it is justified by being locally relevant. Instead, we argue for opening up the dominant paradigm to more fundamental questioning and enabling meaningful negotiation that admits the possibility other, equally valid, ways of learning, teaching, and doing research.

QATAR AND EDUCATOR: DIVERSE PERSPECTIVES ON ENDOGENOUS DEVELOPMENT

After considering these two case studies in some detail, we return to the definition of endogenous development proposed by COMPAS. To summarize, COMPAS is primarily concerned to empower local communities who are seen to be victims of conventional development processes and, if given more agency, will develop a more ecologically sustainable and socially equitable system. This idealizing language seems more realistic if it is acknowledged that the empowerment of local communities and Indigenous peoples often involves negotiating and adapting IK to contemporary contexts. In this way, IK can often lead to entirely new behaviors based on Indigenous principles and ideals, which can improve the economic well-being of Indigenous people even during times of extreme exogenous transition (Dei, 1991, p. 334). This certainly holds true for the Ecuador case, where UINPI is focusing on adapting and reconciling elements of external and Indigenous resources to bring the contemporary relevance of IK to light for local, national, and global communities alike. It seeks to do this while ensuring that the university operates alongside and in support of local communities, rather than taking students from those communities to gain largely abstract knowledge in a separated and isolated space. Certainly, Heckler's interviews with a range of UINPI organizers, students, and facilitators suggest that the relevance of IK in a contemporary context is dependent upon that IK being live and fluid, able to adapt to new challenges, and situations. Hence, rather than teaching IK as something unique and delimited to the boundaries of their cultural group, they teach it as something that can use and be used by external systems. The primary challenge, then, is to imbue IK with the prestige that is given to scientific knowledge. This would lead to a negotiation of the problems, pathways, and goals of development between IK-bearers and scientists as equals in which IK-bearers are allowed to influence the type of development that their communities and societies undertake (a central tenet of IK in development research for some two decades now) (Sillitoe, 1998).

In Qatar, on the other hand, the Qatari already have the political-economic power to determine the direction of development in their country; the primary question becomes, which direction and which values should be upheld? In the recent past, Qatar certainly moved away from some tenets, such as environmental sustainability, that feature in the COMPAS proposal. Indeed, some may argue that Qatar is not a genuine model of endogenous development, as its development path was and is largely informed by foreign authorities. Nevertheless, unlike for Ecuadorian Indigenous peoples, a large part of the nation's resources are under Qatari control and the resulting wealth is distributed widely amongst its citizens. As a result, they have drastically improved their material well-being in the last half century. Only now are they beginning to consider other facets of development—for instance, environmental sustainability and the utility and wisdom of Arab knowledge. Of course, acknowledging the potential benefits is not the same as returning to a Bedouin lifestyle, a move that would be unthinkable to the majority of Qatar University students. Nevertheless, the cosmology that supported that lifestyle, at least in the shape of Islamic beliefs and practices, is still alive and strong. It is through valuing and making visible the particularities of Islamic epistemologies and social structures that an education promoting a less destructive development may unfold at Qatar University. In some senses, then, this is the perfect definition of endogenous development, with Qatar University at the center of debating and negotiating how that development should occur. This only remains endogenous development, however, as long as the education system remains a place where new ideas are introduced, debated, and negotiated within a culturally relevant framework, without attempting to insist on particular pathways or visions of development. This is obviously a fine line, where there is a tendency to defer to foreign authorities (for instance, Qatar University has arranged for various programs to undergo accreditation by outside bodies and places great store by the "branding" that results).

CONCLUSION

We now return to the questions posed at the beginning of this chapter. The first two regarding the role of IK and higher education in endogenous development are easily summarized. IK, defined as holistic worldview(s), is central to endogenous development in that, ideally, it informs the perspectives that define the problem, set the goals, and determine the means of development. In order to do this, people must be empowered to challenge the models of education and development that have marginalized them. They do this through revaluing and drawing on their cultural and spiritual heritage, in other words, their IK. In this view, IK is the start and endpoint of endogenous development. Hence, one of the primary objectives of endogenous development must be to create appropriate educational systems that empower people to interact effectively with the structures that determine the distribution of resources and afford them some agency in drawing on their own identities as sources of empowerment and well-being in the widest sense.

The third question, what an education for endogenous development looks like is less straightforward, especially given the necessity of local control of development. We explore this question vis-à-vis two case studies and find that both struggle with similar questions but formulate diverse locally appropriate answers, thereby illustrating the dangers of sweeping generalization. However, it can be said that in both contexts, the goal is a negotiation of the problems, pathways, and goals of development with IK-bearers and outsider authorities as equals.

At first glance, the aims and positionality of Qatar University differ from the model of endogenous development being adopted by Indigenous leaders and activists. Nevertheless, the university and its sustainable development program are more successful than nearby Euro-American universities in part because it is concerned to present the issues within a worldview largely informed by Islam and Arabic social values. Given that Qatar University is at the center of debating and negotiating how development should occur, it is, in some ways, an excellent example of endogenous development.

By combining exogenous pedagogical methods, such as problem-based learning, with Indigenous ways of knowing and doing, UINPI has created an innovative model that puts social action and empowerment at the center of education and economic development. Students learn to see development from both perspectives, to compare and contrast them, to be able to initiate, negotiate, accept, or contest development initiatives on their own terms, thereby becoming the drivers of development. In this example, endogenous development, Indigenous knowledge, Indigenous education, and social action all converge.

The establishment of Indigenously framed education programs epitomizes attempts to break free of distorting Euro-American intellectual views and dominance and to wrestle back control of the representation and reproduction of local ways. This is particularly so where people have been colonized and find themselves in the role of second-class citizens, such as Indigenous Ecuadorians. They contrast with autochthonous Arab populations in the Gulf that remain firmly in control of their countries politically and economically. The result is different sets of problems and priorities in establishing education programs that are true to IK and serve locally appropriate development goals, which is surely the fundamental ideal of endogenous development. However, it is obvious in both contexts that the key is to create a space in both education and development institutes where IKs—as holistic *ways of knowing and doing*—can be reaffirmed, negotiated, and reflected upon respectfully and in a fully engaged manner. This type of pedagogical project contributes to a plurality of empowered persons, which in turn is an essential aspect of endogenous development.

NOTES

1. Hilde Heckler, who passed away in April 2009, was the daughter of leading socialist politicians from Bavaria. Those of her parents' party who were not murdered were forced to flee the Nazis. She always said of her long association with the Bannock-Shoshone that "they were the only ones who understood her point of view" in South East Idaho.
2. http://www.compasnet.org/
3. http://www.compasnet.org/ed_1.html
4. There is some question as to whether the term "Indigenous" is appropriate to describe traditional knowledge in Qatar; it is not a locally used concept. Nevertheless, there is certainly a Gulf Arab culture and knowledge tradition that is widely acknowledged in present-day Qatar. Given that the term "Indigenous knowledge" is used throughout this volume, we will use it here. For more discussion on appropriate terminology, see Heckler (2009) and Sillitoe (2000, p. 145–160).
5. http://www.gsdp.gov.qa/portal/page/portal/GSDP_Vision_Root/GSDP_EN/GSDP_News/GSDP%20News%20Files/QNV2030_English_v2.pdf
6. The Shuar are an Amazonian Indigenous people who live in Southeast Ecuador and across the border in Peru. They are renowned for their history of bellicosity, clan warfare and resistance to colonialism well into the twentieth century (Harner 1984; Hendricks 1993; Perruchon 2003; Rubenstein 2002).
7. Although there is considerable debate about the equivalence of the Shuar concept of Arutám with the Christian God, every Shuar person that Heckler has spoken to (and she has interviewed more than fifty people on this topic), have equated Arutám with the Christian God. Whether this was true in the past is irrelevant for the way the symbol is used in the contemporary context.
8. The fact that women chew manioc, adding their saliva as a way to stimulate fermentation was seen by Christian missionaries and Ecuadorian mestizos as dirty. Unfortunately, many Shuar were thus influenced to give up making *nijiamanch* during the second half of the twentieth century.
9. http://www.qnrf.org/

REFERENCES

Agrawal, A. (1995). Dismantling the divide between Indigenous and scientific knowledge. *Development and Change, 26,* 413–439.

Agrawal, A. (1999). Ethnoscience, "LK" and Conservation: on power and Indigenous knowledge. In D. A. Posey (Ed.),

Cultural and Spiritual Values of Biodiversity (pp. 177–184). London: Intermediate Technology Productions.

Alexiades, M. (2009). The cultural and economic globalisation of traditional environmental knowledge systems. In S. Heckler (Ed.), *Landscape, Process and Power: Re-evaluating Traditional Environmental Knowledge* (pp. 68–98). New York: Berghahn.

Andolina, R., Laurie, N., & Radcliffe, S. (2009). *Indigenous Development in the Andes: Culture, Power and Transnationalism*. Durham, N.C.: Duke University Press.

Astvaldsson, A. (2002). Coming to power: knowledge, learning and historic pathways to authority in a Bolivian community. In H. Stobart & R. Howard (Eds.), *Knowledge and Learning in the Andes: Ethnographic Perspectives* (pp. 109–126). Liverpool: University Press.

Bates, P. (2009). Learning and Inuit knowledge in Nunavut, Canada. In P. Bates, M. Chiba, S. Kube, & D. Nakashima (Eds.), *Learning and Knowing in Indigenous Societies Today* (pp. 95–106). Paris: UNESCO.

Battiste, M., & Henderson, J. Y. (2000). *Protecting Indigenous Knowledge and Heritage: A Global Challenge*. Saskatoon: Purich.

Bradshaw, S. (2006). Is the rights focus the right focus? Nicaraguan responses to the rights agenda. *Third World Quarterly, 27(7),* 1329–1341.

Briggs, J., & Sharp, J. (2004). Indigenous knowledges and development: A postcolonial caution. *Third World Quarterly, 25(4),* 661–676.

Cajete, G. (2000). *Native Science: Natural Law of Interdependence*. Santa Fe, N.M.: Clearlight.

Cooke, B., & Kothari, U. (Eds.). (2002). *Participation: The New Tyranny?* London: Zed.

Corpuz, J. (2008). Consultation workshop and dialogue on indigenous peoples' self-determined development or development with identity. Permanent Forum on Indigenous Issues. E/C.19/2008/CRP. 11

Dei, G. (1991). The re-integration and rehabilitation of migrant workers into a local domestic economy: Lessons for "endogenous" development. *Human Organization, 50(4)*, 327–336.

Dei, G. J. S., Hall, B., & Rosenberg, D. (2000). Introduction. In G. J. S. Dei, B. Hall, & D. Rosenberg (Eds.), *Indigenous Knowledges in Global Contexts: Multiple Readings of Our World* (pp. 1–17). Toronto: University Press.

El Guindi, F. (2003). *Veil: Modesty, Privacy and Resistance*. Oxford: Berg.

Ellen, R., & Harris, H. (2000). Introduction. In R. F. Ellen, P. Parkes, & A. Bicker (Eds.) *Indigenous Knowledge and Its Transformations* (pp. 1–33). Amsterdam: Harwood Academic.

Escobar, A. (1995). *Encountering Development: The Making and Un-making of the Third World*. Princeton: Princeton University Press.

Garcia, M. E. (2005). *Making Indigenous Citizens: Identity, Development and Multicultural Activism in Peru*. Stanford: University Press.

Greene, S. (2004). Indigenous people incorporated? Culture as politics, culture as property in pharmaceutical bioprospecting. *Current Anthropology, 45(2)*, 211–237.

Harner, M. (1984). *Jívaro: People of the Sacred Waterfalls*. Berkeley: University of California Press.

Heckler, S. (2007). On knowing and not knowing: the many valuations of Piaroa local knowledge. In P. Sillitoe (Ed.) *Local Science vs. Global Science: Approaches to Indigenous Knowledge in International Development* (pp. 91–107). Oxford: Berghahn.

Heckler, S. (2009). Introduction. In S. Heckler (Ed.), *Landscape, Process and Power: Re-evaluating Traditional Environmental Knowledge* (pp. 1–18). New York: Berghahn.

Hendricks, J. (1993). *To Drink of Death*. Tucson: University of Arizona Press.

Howard, R., Barbira-Freedman, F., & H. Stobart. (2002). Introduction. In H. Stobart & R. Howard (Eds.), *Knowledge and Learning in the Andes: Ethnographic Perspectives* (pp. 1–13). Liverpool: University Press.

Ishizawa, J., & Rengifo, G. (2009). Biodiversity regeneration and intercultural knowledge transmission in the Peruvian Andes. In P. Bates, M. Chiba, S. Kube, & D. Nakashima (Eds.), *UNESCO, Learning and Knowing in Indigenous Societies Today*. Paris: UNESCO.

Jackson, J., & Warren, K. (2005). Indigenous movements in Latin America, 1992–2004: controversies, ironies, new directions. *Annual Review of Anthropology, 34*, 549–573.

Kowii, M., A. (2007). Memoria, Identidad e Interculturalidad de los Pueblos de Abya-Yala: El caso de los Quichua Otavalo. In Claudia Zapata Silva (Ed.), *Intelectuales Indígenas Piensan América Latina* (pp. 113–125). Quito: Abya-Yala.

Llanes-Ortiz, G. (2009). Encouraging the mind to sprout? Maya learning and the challenge of intercultural learning processes in an Indigenous university in Mexico. Presentation given at the symposium, "Indigenous Studies and Engaged Anthropology: Opening a Dialogue," held at Durham University, Durham, UK, 14–17 September, S. Heckler & P. Sillitoe (organizers).

Macas, L. (2009). Construyendo desde la Historia: Resistencia del movimiento indígena en el Ecuador. In A. Acosta & E. Martínez (Eds.), *Plurinacionalidad: Democracia en la Diversidad* (pp. 81–98). Quito: Ediciones Abya-Yala.

Nederveen Pieterse, J. (1998). My paradigm or yours? Alternative development, post-development, reflexive development. *Development and Change, 29,* 343–373.

Nederveen Pieterse, J. (2001). *Development Theory: Deconstructions/Reconstructions.* London: Sage.

Overing, J. (2000). The efficacy of laughter: The ludic side of magic within Amazonian sociality. In J. Overing & A. Passes (Eds.), *The Anthropology of Love and Anger: The Aesthetics of Conviviality in Native Amazonia* (pp. 64–81). New York: Routledge.

Overing, J. (2003). In praise of the everyday: Trust and the art of social living in an Amazonian community. *Ethnos, 68(3),* 293–316.

Overing, J., & Passes, A. (2000). Introduction: conviviality and the opening up of Amazonian anthropology. In J. Overing & A. Passes (Eds.), *The Anthropology of Love and Anger: The Aesthetics of Conviviality in Native Amazonia* (pp. 1–30), London: Routledge.

Qatar University. (2009). *Welcome to QU: Undergraduate Prospectus.* Doha: Qatar University.

Perruchon, M. (2003). *I Am Tsunki: Gender and Shamanism among the Shuar of Western Amazonia.* Uppsala Studies in Cultural Anthropology 33. Uppsala: Acta Universitatis Upsaliensis.

Pettit, J., & Wheeler, J. (2005). Developing rights? Relating discourse to context and practice. *IDS Bulletin, 35(1),* 1–8.

Rahnema, M., & Bawtree, V. (1997). *The Post-Development Reader.* London: Zed.

Ray, C. (1999). Towards a meta-framework of endogenous development: Repertoires, paths, democracy and rights. *Sociologi Ruralis, 39(4),* 521–537.

Rival, L. (1997). Modernity and the politics of identity in an Amazonian society. *Bulletin of Latin American Research, 16(2),* 137–151.

Rubenstein, S. (2002). *Alejandro Tsakimp: A Shuar Healer in the Margins of History.* Lincoln: University of Nebraska Press.

Sillitoe, P. (1998). The development of Indigenous knowledge: A new applied anthropology. *Current Anthropology, 39(2),* 223–252.

Sillitoe, P. (2000). *Indigenous Knowledge Development in Bangladesh: Present and Future.* London: Intermediate Technology.

Sillitoe, P. (2004). Introduction: hunting for theory, gathering ideology. In A. Bicker, P. Sillitoe, & J. Pottier (Eds.), *Development and Local Knowledge: New Approaches to Issues in Natural Resources Management, Conservation and Agriculture* (pp. 1–18). London: Routledge.

Tebtebba Foundation. (2004). *Reclaiming Balance: Indigenous Peoples, Conflict Resolution and Sustainable Development.* Baguio City, Philippines: Tebtebba Foundation.

Thaman, K. H. (2003). Decolonizing Pacific studies: Indigenous perspectives, knowledge and wisdom in higher education. *The Contemporary Pacific, 15*(1), 1–17.

Turay, T. (2000). Peace research and African development: an indigenous African perspective. In G. J. S. Dei, B. Hall, & D. Rosenberg (Eds.), *Indigenous Knowledges in Global Contexts: Multiple Readings of Our World* (pp. 248–264). Toronto: University Press.

UNHCR. (2006). *Frequently Asked Questions on a Human Rights-Based Approach to Development Cooperation.* Geneva & New York: United Nations.

Universidad Intercultural Amawtay Wasi. (2004). *Aprender en la Sabiduría y el Buen Vivir.* Quito: Imprenta Mariscal.

Wangoola, P. (2000). Mpambo, the African multiversity: a philosophy to rekindle the African spirit. In G. J. S. Dei, B. Hall, & D. Rosenberg (Eds.), *Indigenous Knowledges in Global Contexts: Multiple Readings of Our World* (pp. 265–277). Toronto: University Press.

Zent, S. (2009). A genealogy of scientific representations of Indigenous knowledge. In S. Heckler (Ed.), *Landscape, Process and Power: Re-evaluating Traditional Environmental Knowledge* (pp. 19–67). New York: Berghahn.

CHAPTER TWELVE

Neo-Colonial Melancholia

Alaska Native People, Education and Oil

MARIA SHAA TLÁA WILLIAMS

For thousands of years Alaska Native people survived and even flourished in a region of the world that is often considered extreme. I grew up hearing oral histories of great leaders, of Raven's great adventures (our trickster-hero), and how my father grew up along a trap-line along the Alaska/Canada border, of a life that was built upon the collective work of extended families and on detailed knowledge of the environment. The Indigenous knowledge base enabled survival and continuity throughout all regions of Alaska. Native people know their environment, surrounding flora/fauna, weather, and climate changes intimately—we can read the tides, use the star systems to navigate, employ math systems to make elaborate baskets and textiles. All Alaska Native people developed ways to smoke and dry fish and preserve summer foods such as berries through the long winters. We have beautiful songs, stories, and dances that set us apart as unique peoples. Our epistemologies and scientific knowledge have been perfectly attuned to our landscape. The Arctic and sub-Arctic hunters who use the winter sea ice to hunt have dozens of terms for ice and developed ingenious footwear and hunting techniques for the different types of ice. Marine mammal hunters in Alaska invented the kayak (found all over the world today) and still use open skin boats for whale hunting; these watercraft all use waterproof stitching for the hide boat covers.

There is ample evidence of Native science and engineering in every single village in Alaska. I have had the opportunity to travel to rural parts of Alaska beginning in the early 1990s. In 2007 I went by boat to numerous villages along the Tanana and Yukon rivers and spent two seasons at a summer fish camp.[1]

I saw amazing independent people and extended families—who can travel hundreds of miles on one of the world's largest rivers with no maps, know how to use and gather special materials for their smoke houses, meat caches, and have a self-sufficiency that is perfection. I saw many young people, who were smart, and had remarkably agile minds; I wondered why the majority of them did not graduate from high school. What is wrong? As I traveled from village to village, I visited the schools—which always had a White principal, and White teaching staff, using curriculum that did not provide any link to the local knowledge base. It was clear to me that the young people were seeing their own cultures either ignored or devalued. The reductivist scenario, compounded by satellite American TV, did not include anything close to their village societies. I understood why they dropped out—why not? The school curriculum appeared to be a gate-keeping strategy that did not inspire the Native students to master the subject matter, make plans for college, or encourage them to think of their futures. The school system appears to make them feel devalued and instills a crippling lethargy. Thus, high teen suicide rates abound, along with drug and alcohol abuse and the tragic legacy of colonialism continues—neo-colonialism. As an Alaska Native educator, this grieves me greatly and inspired me to do additional research on the history of Western education in Alaska in order to understand how we arrived at the 21st century and to identify what needs to be changed in order to have higher graduation rates and ultimately more Native youth attend college.

CRITIQUE OF EUROCENTIRC SCHOOLING IN ALASKA

Western education was introduced in various parts of Alaska in the 19th century. Initially Russian Orthodox priests arrived and set up churches and schools. Most of the limited schooling was bilingual in Russian and the local Indigenous language.[2] In 1867, the Treaty of Cession ended Russian control over the territory, and beginning in the 1870s and 1880s American missionaries began to arrive; their philosophy and approaches were markedly different than the Russians. The various denominations believed in strict English-only policies, with the exception of the Moravians who came to the Yukon/Kuskokwim areas. Mission schools were quickly established in all regions of Alaska between the 1880s and 1920s. Their main focus was to remake the spiritual landscape, eradicate traditional religions, languages, shamanism, and indoctrinate the Indigenous children into the Western world (Williams, 2009, p. 153). Most of these activities were supported by the U.S. government, and often subsidized by federal funds. The Bureau of Indian Affairs also began to establish schools beginning in the early 20th century. This was alongside territorial schools established for the White population.

It was not until 1928 that a group of Native people sued the territorial government over education. The Alaska Native Brotherhood (ANB) of southeastern Alaska sued the territorial government because they would not allow Native students in their classroom. By the 1920s there were nearly two dozen communities that had segregated schools. The case, filed by the ANB and their Tlingit attorney, William Paul, allowed the Native children in southeastern communities to attend the formerly White-only schools established by the territorial government and integrated the classrooms. It also established one of the first integrated school systems in the country at that time. This lawsuit did not cover issues such as the lack of schools in the 200-plus villages. Between 1920–1970 hundreds of children were sent to boarding schools in Sitka, Alaska, and the Lower 48 states to Oregon, Arizona, and Oklahoma where there were federal Indian Boarding schools. Children were sent away as early as seventh grade, often for years at a time.

By the 1960s and 1970s the State of Alaska established two new initiatives for Alaska Native students, a Boarding Home Program and the creation of regional high schools. The Boarding Home Program compensated families in urban locations to house rural students to attend high school. The state built three regional boarding high schools for village students.[3] These efforts were directly aimed at removing Native youth from their villages. The program was intent on destroying the Native villages, and to eliminate "...dispersed and isolated communities which do not offer opportunities for other than subsistence economy." A State of Alaska report claimed, ". . .residence in urban areas appears to accelerate the breakdown of old village patterns, patterns which may retard the development of rural folk into a disciplined and reliable workforce" (State of Alaska Regional Secondary School System, 1967, p. IV-9–12).

It is not a surprise that the regional high schools and the Boarding Home Program were disasters. Dropout rates were close to 50%, along with other more serious social problems such as suicide and rampant substance abuse. In 1972, the Alaska State Commission for Human Rights investigated the Nome-Beltz Regional High School dormitory after a particularly violent outbreak fueled by alcohol. The commission found the situation to be "epidemic." The school nurse's solution was to inject the students with Thorazine (Cotton, 1984).

In 1972, a group of 27 rural students filed a suit against the State of Alaska, now known as the *Molly Hootch Case*, or *Tobeluk v. Reynolds*. The students sued the State of Alaska for failing to provide schools in their villages, rejecting the Boarding School programs. The lawsuit included 126 villages and was settled in 1976; the State of Alaska consented to start a massive construction project that would build high schools throughout the villages included in the lawsuit. By 1982, 101 of the villages in the lawsuit had high school programs and 84 of them had newly constructed schools. The village schools provide a center for various village activities outside of school. Beginning in the 1970s and 1980s the schools became the centers for dance festivals and were part of the renaissance in traditional dance/music. The village schools are also a place where youth can play basketball games and a place for other village activities, such as potlatches and other traditional gatherings. They have become in many cases vital community centers.

DEMOGRAPHICS AND EDUCATION IN ALASKA

Although Alaska has the largest percentage of American Indian/Alaska Native students at 26.3% (Faircloth & Tippeconnic, 2010, pp. 8–9), graduation rates for Alaska Native students hovers around 37.9% in the rural areas (where the greatest concentration of Native people live), and 46% for the urban Indigenous population. The graduation rate for Whites is 67.6%. This fact clearly illustrates the continued struggle with education.

General demographics show that Alaska's Indigenous population is young and growing:

- The Alaska Native population is a young demographic; one-third of the population is under the age of 18 years—the K-12 age group.
- The median age of Alaska Natives is 24 years.
- More than 44% of Native people are under the age of 19 years.
- Of the entire Alaska Native population 58% lives in rural villages.
- In the rural villages 82% of the population is Alaska Native.
- In 2004, there were 100,000 Alaska Native people, which is about 16% of the overall population of the state.
- Expected population in the 2010 census is 140,000.

(Alaska Native Policy Center, 2004)

There are 500 public schools in Alaska and 55 school districts, spread throughout an area that encompasses over 440 million acres of land, with no major road systems and a challenging physical environment. There are over 200 Alaska Native villages. Yet less than 5% of the teachers are Alaska Native and 80% of Alaska K-12 teachers are recruited from outside of Alaska (C. Englom-Bradley, personal communication, March, 2010). Major job fairs are sponsored in cities such as Seattle, and Minneapolis, as well as Anchorage, Alaska, to recruit teachers.[4] So, the average Native student in Alaska will have a non-Native teacher that is not from Alaska and not familiar with the history, cultures, and Indigenous languages, or the village social protocols. Additionally the curriculum is another alienating factor, as math, science, English are introduced and taught using a Western pedagogical approach that devalues the local Indigenous knowledge systems.

Alaska Content Standards were developed by the State of Alaska's Department of Education in the 1990s. These standards are incorporated into public and charter schools. In addition, the federal policies also have set standards and these are measured through testing. The 2002 federal No Child Left Behind (NCLB) policy enacted by President Bush was built upon a model that impacted the already negative situation. Testing of students in an attempt to grade the school's success and/or failure resulted in "...Indian children...internalizing the system failures as their personal failure..." (NIEA, 2005, p. 8). The NCLB is being phased out by President Obama's administration, but a new federal educational framework has not been clearly laid out yet.

The 1971 Land Settlement and Oil

In the 1971 ANCSA settlement, Alaska Native people received 44 million acres or 10% of Alaska's land base, and $947 million in order to extinguish aboriginal claim to the land. The Act also mandated the establishment of Native for-profit corporations, built on the Wall Street capitalist model, rather than the traditional reservation model that had been the basis of land settlements between Native Americans and the U.S. government. One of the major outcomes of the 1971 land settlement, and the main purpose of ANCSA, was to lease out large tracts of the North Slope area to oil companies for drilling. By 1977, construction of the 800-mile-long Trans-Alaska Pipeline System (TAPS) was complete. Estimated profits are around $70 billion to oil companies, such as ARCO, British Petroleum, and Exxon/ConocoPhillips.[5]

Between 1977 and 2009 the profit for three oil companies in Alaska is roughly $70 billion (R. A. Fineberg, personal communication, March 2010). The oil industry averages 55% of the net profits, with the State of Alaska receiving about 32% and the federal government about 13% (Fineberg, 2005, pp. 5–6). Profits from oil go to areas well outside of Alaska and certainly not into the hands of Alaska's Indigenous people. Neither the State of Alaska nor the oil industry is forthcoming on the exact amount of profits from oil. "The difficulty in getting specific information on this is a demonstration of the inordinate power of the industry" (R. A. Fineberg, Personal communication, March 2010).

As resource revenues such as oil continue to generate enormous profits from rural Alaska, the Indigenous people who make up 87% of the rural population, remain in the lower economic spheres, and their cultures, languages, and life ways continue to be misunderstood and devalued by the Western society. Education is often a source of tensions and the Alaska State legislators have consistently taken aim at rural education and its associated costs. In 2001 the legislature attempted to pass a bill that would limit the amount of funds the Native-majority North Slope Borough could obtain that would have directly impacted school construction, maintenance (Kizzia, November 26, 2001). In 2006, the legislature enacted a tax because "...rural Alaska needs to start paying their 'fair share' for public schools." (Matt, March 3, 2006). There are many more examples of the political mechanizations that have aimed to limit and in some cases completely extinguish state funding for public education K-12 in the rural villages. The often contentious debates pit the urban population, which is majority non-Native against the minority rural Native population. Most of the legislators who support or have proposed cutting rural educational funding and other initiatives, such as school construction and maintenance, use the argument of majority-rule. Meaning the White-majority urban population should get most of the funding, leaving rural schools with the slimmest slice of the fiscal pie. The legislators and representatives who have continued to attack rural Alaska and the cost of delivery education have election campaigns funded by special interest groups, such as oil. Oil has proven to be a corrupting force for elected officials in Alaska, and recent investigations have sent legislators to trial and jail for taking bribes from the oil industry (PBS, 2008).

Education has become a commodity in the capitalistic sense, but also a political wedge that seeks to force the Indigenous population to leave their villages and become urban dwellers. The economic life in rural Alaska is a mixed economy, with minimal cash-paying jobs that include the school employees and teachers (mostly non-Native and not even from Alaska), the post-office employees, and perhaps some part-time positions with the local tribal government. Western food is exorbitantly expensive in rural areas because it has to be flown in. Most of the food on the table in rural areas is hunted or gathered by the local residents. Ironically fuel costs are the highest in rural Alaska and in 2009, gas averaged $10.00 a gallon, but in Anchorage $3.00. So with fuel costs three times higher and food costs about eight times higher, the out-migration from villages to urban centers in Alaska is creating a scenario in which the Indigenous population must give up their traditional way of life, their family and kinship connections, and the environmental and spiritual connection to their land bases. This is particularly alarming because the demographic trend indicates that the Alaska Native population is a very young population.

The shift from a subsistence-based economy to a capitalistic cash-based economy has been a rocky and painful road. This is especially obvious in the rural villages where most residents are Alaska Native and practice traditional hunting and fishing. The 1971 ANCSA was a social engineering effort to change Indigenous people into resource exploiters who would develop oil, gas, and other natural resources in the corporate-system. This has been a mixed failure, with three or four of the thirteen corporations regularly making profits and the other eight or nine in the red. The ANCSA has also created a Native corporate elite as board members of these corporations hold the positions for 20 years or longer, some living outside of the state of Alaska. Because of oil, the 1971 Act was passed and because of oil, Alaska's politics have a tendency to be skewed. As the politicians support more oil development, resulting in lawsuits to protect Alaska's lands, a David and Goliath battle has emerged. A prime example is the two-decade battle to open up the Alaska National Wildlife Refuge (ANWR), which has pitted anti-oil Native people against pro-oil Native people and created a schizophrenic economic scenario in which they have been presented with one option—oil development for economic gain at the sacrifice of their subsistence-based cultures. The end game is to erase the Native; to engage them into a capitalistic model and become resource exploiters rather than living in concert with their environment as hunters/fishers which they have done admirably since the Pleistocene age. Thus, it is amply clear that oil, the new colonial force in Alaska does not have any respect for Native worldview, culture, and language. The oil industry and other resource exploiters want access to the land to develop more oil fields, gas, coal and re-invigorate the mining industry

To counter the neo-colonial legacy, it must mentioned that there are positive programs in place, including a new PhD program created in 2009 at the University of Alaska Fairbanks that is targeting Alaska Native students. There are several charter schools that are focused on Alaska Native education and initiatives such as the Future Teachers of Alaska Program, the Alaska Native Knowledge Network, and other innovative programs. There are 24 charter schools in Alaska, and 3 have an Alaska Native focus. They are located in Anchorage, Fairbanks, and Bethel.[6]

In 1998, the Alaska Native Knowledge Network published *Alaska Standards for Culturally Responsive Schools.*[7] There are also many dedicated teachers who have worked hard at working within the confines of the limiting curriculum and the NCLB policies and they deserve recognition.

Despite positive strides in the area of Indigenous education, there still needs to be a radical step away from the current paradigm. At the heart of this is a curriculum that alienates Indigenous students, and for the most part renews the negative cycle of colonialism, resulting in high dropout rates. Perhaps we, as Alaska Native people, need to take control of the K-12 curriculum. We can look at other examples, such as the Maori of New Zealand; in the 1970s they took strong political action and successfully protected their language and culture. We, as Alaska Native people, need to start writing our own curriculum, establish long-term programs in which we can see more Native K-12 teachers, and more educators writing and creating a culturally relevant curriculum.

Without an education, Native students will not be able to become teachers, doctors, engineers, architects, inventors, veterinarians, and we will not re-gain control of the destiny of our communities. As oil companies continue to make staggering profits, other resource-exploiting global corporations are starting mining projects in Alaska. Pebble Mine, and others are using the same model established by oil companies in Alaska. Who is in the way for resource exploitation? Native people. Mine owners do not want to see empowered Native people. Big oil companies support politicians who will allow them to continue making tremendous profits, pay a minimum of tax, not be responsible to environmental damage, and have created a corrupt state government. Beginning in December 2006, over a dozen politicians in Alaska were investigated and charged by the FBI and Department of Justice for corruption—all were tied to oil companies. These included Alaska legislators who accepted bribes from oil companies to vote in favor of oil-friendly tax bills; also indicted, convicted, though later acquitted was Senator Ted Stevens.

CONCLUSION

Alaska Native people have been dealing with an imposed educational system since the 19th century. Although there are certainly improvements, it is still a gate-keeping mechanism that propagates a system that negates Indigenous identity. Through the various programs designed by the state and federal governments, as well as Christian missionaries, the Alaska Native voice has been muted. A monolingual culture—a philosophy of uniformity in which all cultures, all peoples, must be uniform is causing major disconnections in the 21st century (Shiva, 2009). This is a very apt description of the K-12 curriculum in Alaska. The cookie-cutter approach does not work for the multitude of Alaska Native cultures, especially in the rural areas. What needs to change? First and foremost the curriculum, secondarily, the pedagogical approach, thirdly, access to funding, and lastly, the powerful influences of oil needs to be limited.

We need to

1. Develop new curriculum that is reflective of Alaska Native ideas of science, math, astronomy, art, language, and music. Students can learn English, grammar, math, and other

requirements of Western education, but Indigenous knowledge must be presented in a methodology and approach that is reflective of an Indigenous-based pedagogy.
2. We need more Native teachers in the classroom, so that students can identify better with the instructor, and the classroom becomes an extension of the village rather than the current model, in which the teacher does not know anything about Alaska or Indigenous languages, arts, sciences, and village and cultural protocols.
3. Schools must fairly apportion budgets, especially in the rural school districts; urban schools now get the lion's share of funding, leaving the rural schools with small budgets that doom them to failure.
4. The skewed politics of oil have created an apartheid atmosphere in Alaska and without better public policy and laws that limit the lobbying influences of special interest, such as oil, education will continue to be a losing battleground for Indigenous peoples in Alaska.

In conclusion, we as Indigenous people need to take control of the K-12 curriculum and make it our own. By rethinking and remaking schooling and education we can critically engage Indigenous education in a neo-colonial context that empowers Native youth. The challenges for creating a new curriculum are that we will not see immediate results, and need to think in the long term. If we do not create an alternative vision for education for Alaska Native youth, our survival as a people is at stake.

NOTES

1. The Yukon River is 3185 km long and is the fifth longest river in North America; its drainage area is almost 800,000 km.
2. Russian priests were the first to develop written alphabets in several Alaska Native languages, including Unangan, Yup'ik, Sugpiaq, Athabascan, and Tlingit.
3. These were located in Nome (1966), Kodiak (1967), and Bethel (1972).
4. According to their Web site, over 3000 teachers have been placed in Alaska over the past 3 years as a result of these job fairs (http://www.alaskateacher.org/doku.php?id=alaska_job_fairs).
5. ARCO, British Petroleum and Exxon/ConocoPhillips own 91.5% of the Trans-Alaska Pipeline (TAPS) and 93% of the Alaska North Slope production (Fineberg, 1993, p. 11). ConocoPhillips controls 40% of North Slope production and 28.3% of TAPS. Exxon controls 36% of North Slope production and 20.3% of TAPS. British Petroleum controls 30% of North Slope production and 46.9% of TAPS (Fineberg, 2005, p. .9).
6. The Alaska Native Charter School was approved in 2007 in Anchorage and has an enrollment of 153 in grade levels K-6 (http://www.asdk12.0rg/schools/anccs/pages/). The Ayaprun Elitnaurvik Yup'ik Immersion school located in Bethel was approved in 1999 and has an enrollment of 145 from K-6. Yup'ik is one of the 20 different Alaska Native languages and is spoken through the southwestern mainland of Alaska in the Yukon/Kuskokwim Delta (http://www.lksd.org/ayaprun/). The Effie Kokrine Charter School based in Fairbanks, was approved in 2005 and has 102 students from grades 7–12 (http://ekc.k12northstar.org/). In addition, there is the Mount Edgecumbe high school, a boarding school in Sitka, Alaska (http://www.mehs.educ.state.ak.us/), which has over 400 students from a number of different communities throughout Alaska with 94% Native students. It is a residential high school that was originally part of the national system of Indian boarding schools. It opened in 1947, and was eventually taken over by the State of Alaska. It has grades 9–12.
7. This is a philosophy or guide and does not include curriculum or references to existing curriculum that highlight Indigenous knowledge systems.

REFERENCES

Agreement of Settlement at 8, Tobeluk v. Lind, C.A. No. 72–2450 (Alaska Super. Ct., 3rd Dist., approved October 27, 1976).

Alaska Native Policy Center. (2004). Our Choices, Our Future: Analysis of the Status of Alaska Natives Report 2004. Prepared for the Alaska Federation of Natives.

Bristol Bay Alliance. Pebble Mine Threatens World's Greatest Salmon Rivers. Retrieved from http://www.bristolbayalliance.com/

Complaint, Hootch, v. Alaska State-Operated School System, C.A. No. 72–2450 (Alaska Super. Ct., 3rd Distr., filed August 10, 1972; First Amended Complaint filed October 5, 1972).

Cotton, S. E. (1984). Alaska's "Molly Hootch Case": High Schools and the Village Voice. *Educational Research Quarterly, 8(4),* 30–43.

Faircloth, S. C., & Tippeconnic, J. W. III. (2010). *The Dropout/Graduation Crisis among American Indian and Alaska Native Students: Failure to Respond Places the Future of Native Peoples at Risk.* The Civil Rights Project/*Proyecto Derechos Civiles* at UCLA and the Pennsylvania State University, Center for the Study of Leadership in American Indian Education.

Fineberg, R. A. (2005, April). The Profitability and Economic Viability of Alaska North Slope and Associated Pipeline Operations. Paper prepared for the Prince William Sound Regional Citizens' Advisory Council.

Fineberg, R. A. (1993, October). Alaska North Slope Oil Profits and Proposed Environmental Mitigation Measures. Paper at the 15th Annual North American Conference of the International Association for Energy Economics, Seattle, WA.

Kizzia, T. (2001, November 26). Mayor Calls Bond Bill a Slap at North Slope. *Anchorage Daily News.*

Matt, V. (2006, March 2). Rural Tax Bill Aiming to Finish "Free Lunch." *Anchorage Daily News.*

National Indian Education Association (NIEA). (2005). Preliminary Report on No Child Left Behind in Indian Country. Washington, D.C. Retrieved from http://www.niea.org/issues/policy.php

PBS. (2008). Timeline: Alaska Corruption Scandal. Retrieved from http://www.pbs.org/now/shows/347/alaska-corruption.html

Shiva, V. (2009). Shakti: Feminine Power for Change. Alternative Radio, Denver, CO.

State of Alaska Regional Secondary School System. (1967). Implementation Plan, Final Report. Falls Church, VA: Training Corporation of America.

Williams, M. (2009). The Comity Agreement. In M. S. T. Williams (Ed.), *The Alaska Native Reader: History, Culture, Politics* (pp. 151–162). Durham & London: Duke University Press.

CHAPTER THIRTEEN

Sacred Mountains and Ivory Towers

Indigenous Pedagogies of Place and Invasions from Modernity

MICHAEL MARKER

Indigenous scholars, having recently arrived to the academy, have brought their communities with them. That is, they have been trying to wedge a space for the voices of their ancestors and elders to be heard in the halls of universities. Indigenous academics have been trying to introduce conversations from their elders about the meanings of history, place, and spirit. The academy, an architect of the colonial erasure of Indigenous worldviews, has been a precarious place for Indigeneity. In their struggles to make space for silenced and marginalized histories, Indigenous intellectuals have presented distinct challenges to mainstream assumptions about knowledge and social progress. They have brought their memories of community realities with them to their positions at universities. Consciously and unconsciously, the Indigenous community lives within them.

This distance between the Indigenous communities and the academy is one the deepest felt problems for Native academics. My own experience as a high school teacher and faculty member at a tribal college has propelled much of my inquiry about what education can do to change things for Indigenous communities. I have heard people talk about what was wrong with schools, and I have listened to elders and parents discuss what education should provide for their youth and for the revival of the community. The Indigenous scholar not only brings the community with her/him, but the community draws the scholar back from the ivory tower into the intellectually messy world of day-to-day, on-the-ground dilemmas. Said (1994), tells us that "no one has ever devised a method for detaching the scholar from the circumstances of life, from the fact of his involvement (conscious or unconscious) with a class, a set of beliefs, a social position, or from the mere activity of being a member of a society" (p. 136). For the Indigenous scholar, the pedagogical repositioning of traditional knowledge is not supplementary but rather the core element of political engagement both in the academy and in the community.

Following Vine Deloria's (1991) point that Indigenous people may misunderstand, but they do not misexperience, the academy is experienced as a place where the senses of time, space, and spirituality are in opposition to the values of the community. For Indigenous people, the universities are the palaces of their colonizers. They contain all of the assumptions of modernity and the rationalizations for the conquest of the Indigenous world. In using the term modernity, I am not only referencing the ideas and structures of life that emerged in European and American cities in the 19th and early 20th centuries, but I want to focus particular attention on the rationalizations for the domination of Indigenous peoples that accompanied—and still accompany—this technocratic social order. Eric Wolf (1982), in reflecting on Max Weber's prognosis of social evolution, explained that

> modern society would sever people from inherited ties and allocate the newly mobile population to specialized and differentiated roles responding to the changing needs of an overarching universal society....Those capable of generating such new arrangements would find themselves launched into modernity. Those incapable of doing so would find their society arrested at the point of transition or mired in traditionalism (p. 12).

I want to underscore the term "universal society" in this quotation since this idea of universalism is one of the persistent problems that modernity still poses for Indigenous communities. The demands of this universalism in education and technology have led to the eradication of unique local knowledges and languages.

The economic foundations for modernist and colonial assumptions about social hierarchies were famously articulated by John Locke who asserted that labor put to transforming land—into the culturally specific image of British agricultural and industrial contexts—was the *only* recipe for ownership of land. Indigenous cultures, who lived on the land within a cosmology of relationships and ecological/spiritual belief systems were defined as not utilizing the land and so, by this ethnocentric argument, they had no claim or rights to the land which could then be taken by those who followed the Lockean formula. While assumptions about private property were central to the advance of colonization, it is also important to note that, particularly in places like British Columbia, the broad culture of empire probably had a more important overall effect on the beliefs about Indigenous peoples and the suppositions of Western—especially British—superiority (Harris, 2002). Edward Said (1979) has thoroughly described this history and the conditions of self-assured imperial self-interest. Webbed to these assumptions about property, labor, and empire are the 19th-century legacies of scientific racism and beliefs about "progress." As Maori scholar Makere Stewart-Harawira (2005) puts it, "next to genocide, and enclosures, the undermining of Indigenous ontologies and cosmologies was the most persistent strategy of the first wave of colonization" (p. 79). The regimes of truth and genealogies of knowledge (Foucault, 1970) that accompanied the technologies of supremacy disqualified Indigenous local, place-based ecological knowledge, replacing it with a universalizing way of life.

In contradistinction to Western education's tendency to universalize knowledge toward transportable careers, Indigenous learnings center the collecting of pre-contact local knowledge, weaving these ancestral insights into a curriculum that inspires people back to traditional ways of life in their homelands. It is oriented toward encouraging youth to stay put instead of leaving the community for alluring opportunities in the globalized economies. "Ideas about progress are grounded within ideas and orientations towards time and space....Deeply embedded in these constructs are systems of classification and representation which lend themselves easily to binary oppositions, dualisms, and hierarchical orderings of the world" (Smith, 1999, p. 55). From an Indigenous perspective, modernist education has been predominantly a centrifugal force that has depleted their communities stressing individualism and the abandonment of place and traditional culture.

Indigenous scholars are working in academic spaces acting as conduits to community projects that are decolonizing local elementary and high schools. Communities are at work researching the pre-contact knowledge of ancestors and weaving this information into revised curriculum replacing erroneous portrayals of the Indigenous past. Some of their educational goals include guiding youth to understand how practical the skills and insights of the old people were toward living sustainably.

In the efforts to bring pre-contact community knowledge into a culturally responsive pedagogy and educational revival, the Indigenous scholar is much like a diver who often becomes tangled in the underwater nets, sunken boats, and submerged refuse of colonization. The waters of the past are murky and cluttered with centuries of oppression. There is much to be recovered and the community has a memory about what was lost. But, sorting out Indigenous knowledge from the debris of colonization is tricky business; bringing it to the surface and demanding its inclusion within the dominant ethos that pushed it under in the first place becomes a perilous task to be undertaken by vulnerable Indigenous academics. Linda Smith (1999) has described this condition well:

> Why then has revisiting history been a significant part of decolonization? The answer, I suggest, lies in the intersection of Indigenous approaches to the past, of the modernist history project itself and of the resistance strategies which have been employed. Our colonial experience traps us in the project of modernity. There can be no 'postmodern' for us until we have settled some business of the modern (p. 34).

In this chapter I survey two broad themes of tensions between Indigenous knowledge and modernity. Again, this is not to apply binaries that simplify a complex situation, but to recognize that there are distances between things, and they are experienced within the politics of Indigenous-settler state relations. The first theme is concerned with how epistemologies, founded on relationships with a *sentient* landscape, shape a pedagogy of place, giving local knowledge a pre-eminence over imported, abstract and techno-globalized knowledge. The second theme reflects on how spiritual substance is infused in all processes of knowledge acquisition and application. Elders and traditional knowledge keepers reference a unified spiritual dimension that has no divide between sacred and secular experience. In the Indigenous communities this is not considered a "mystical" position, but rather a commonsense methodology for a form of conscientization. Centering the local and spiritual in a set of educational goals is the basis for Indigenized praxis and a decolonized pedagogy. Indigenous scholars, traveling back and forth from the communities to the academies, must be attendant to how these concerns are experienced within the context of local knowledge in the communities and recognize the myriad forms of modernist institutional retrenchments that characterize the barriers to Indigenous efforts at transformation.

While knowledge production in the academy has emphasized more abstract theorizing, Indigenous scholars have tended to give attention to the concrete realities of their own communities, producing works that have immediate utility toward improving the educational circumstances there. As Sandy Grande (2000) explains, "most American Indian scholars feel compelled to address the political urgencies of their own communities, against which engagement in abstract political theory appears as to be an unaffordable luxury and privilege of the Whitestream, academic elite" (p. 354).

Because of my own fieldwork and community affiliations, I will focus on the Coast Salish region for examples of the themes of resistance to modernity and the reimagining of Native space. To make Indigenous space in the academy requires that the academy recognize its physical location on the land that is Native space (Kuokkanen, 2007). Reflecting on how Indigenous scholars travel back and forth to the communities, it is essential that the intellectual work of integrating Indigenous knowledges not remain purely in the academy but be able to travel into the surrounding territories and learn from these communities that contain the local memories and meanings of the landscape. In my work at both Northwest Indian College at the Lummi reservation and at the University of British Columbia, I have come to learn something of the historic and contemporary intricacies of the Coast Salish communities that surround these institutions located on opposite sides of a colonially imposed border.

The Coast Salish territory is divided by the Canada-U.S. border and presents a remarkable illustration of Indigenous people who are reframing their collective and individual identities based on their traditional conceptions of territory. Despite colonization and urbanization, the Coast Salish world of interconnected villages has remained, in many ways, a vital and separate reality from the mainstream dominant societies that surround them. Families experience the geography of the region based on their connections to traditional ways of life, ceremonies, and cultural relationships to other families and communities across borders and waterways. It is through the intricate regional connections of families, villages, and ceremonies that traditional knowledge has been protected and nourished.

While, in one sense, the border has been fairly invisible to the Coast Salish, it has also been a powerful signifier of differences between government policies and national cultures. Recently, environmental groups have joined with Aboriginal communities in renaming the entire ecosystem the "Salish Sea." Such alliances between environmentalists and Aboriginal leaders are part of a movement beyond the immobilizing politics of modern nation states to a consideration of Indigenous knowledge as a framework for reconceptualizing connections between human economies and the natural ecosystems. Meanwhile, as Coast Salish peoples are reclaiming their sense of a borderless shared territory, each community must deal with the political conditions of either the Canadian or American governments. The circumstances for settling land claims, treaties, and the demands for health care and education are confined within parallel but separate national cultures, not within traditional territories that cross borders. Coast Salish people, intermarried and entirely interconnected across the border, maintain the traditional sense of an undivided territory, but they must navigate the differences in policies and national cultures in British Columbia and Washington State. Coast Salish people are transnational and often reside in two or more communities on opposite sides of the border.

The Coast Salish experience with colonization has been unique in two ways that have intensified their resistance to modernity. First, the imposition of the international border dividing the territory in ways completely inconsistent and contradictory to the traditional relationships between villages meant that people had to ignore the nation states' attempts to confine them in order to travel and be present for ceremonies and events that maintained the pre-modern versions of community life. Second, the overwhelming forces of urbanized settlement caused elders and traditional knowledge keepers to create micro worlds of secluded segregated spaces in order to teach languages and traditional knowledge, resisting assimilation. In some respects, the Coast Salish, with their land reduced to miniature reserves within the avalanche of urban expansion have been more resistant to absorption into modern nation state culture than many other groups who have been more geographically isolated from "civilization." Because of intense surveillance from church and government as well as from curious crowds of outsiders, much of the culture is kept private, and there is a strong commitment to protecting information from public access (Rasmus, 2002).

These Indigenous communities, on the margins of a surging urban geography are continuing their traditional ways of seeing space, time, and social relations within an intersecting set of relationships layered by eras of subjugation. Their histories of resistance to colonization include the efforts to bring back languages suppressed and forbidden in residential schools, the revival of ceremonies and winter spirit dances, and the creation of community schools that emphasize traditional ecological knowledge. Schooling, as a weapon of imperialism, is one of the most recognized sites of symbolic violence and trauma for Coast Salish people. Schools, both residential and integrated public schools that Coast Salish people attended, were places where the state not only attempted to dislodge the Indigenous students' culture and connections to the land, but they were locations where the modernist ideologies of individualism and Western science were forcefully asserted as a superior way of life. Elsewhere I have described how differences in colonial policies created parallel, yet distinct kinds of educational experiences on both sides of the Canada-U.S. border (Marker, 2009).

DECOLONIZING MODERNIST ACCOUNTS OF INDIGENOUS SPACE AND TIME

Many of the ethnographic accounts of 19th-century Coast Salish life are focused around the questions posed by anthropologists who were interested both in salvaging earlier pre-contact knowledge and in understanding how individual Aboriginal people were adapting to culture conflict brought about by the imposition of modernity on their lives. The anthropologists had their own projections and expectations about what Aboriginal informants were telling them. The researchers often wanted to fit the stories of their Native informants into frameworks that corresponded to their own ideas of chronology, epistemology, and what constituted publishable accounts for an academic audience. Historian John Lutz (2008) has written about how the attempts by 19th-century ethnographers to direct questioning, arrange information, and translate Coast Salish languages into English have created a body of anthropological work that tells us a great deal about the goals of anthropologists but leaves us guessing about the perspectives of Aboriginal people. Furthermore, these texts are often the sources for stereotypes about the contemporary values and beliefs of Aboriginal people. Sakej Youngblood-Henderson (2000) points out that "so strong are the ethnographer's written views that often one can predict from them what modern society will demand of Aboriginal people; much too often these classic notions organize the lives of Aboriginal people for them and limit their future" (p. 255). Hence, the use of texts from early ethnographers to create curriculum that re-establishes Indigenous knowledge as a centerpiece for educational development is a challenge of cross-cultural interpretation for Indigenous scholars and community leaders. Later in this chapter I offer some examples of how curriculum from non-Indigenous sources must be critiqued and challenged. Sorting out the modernist voices of anthropologists from the often-misunderstood conversations of their Aboriginal informants remains an important job for scholars wanting to decolonize interpretations of the past and bring accurate traditional knowledge into the present educational environment.

Because anthropologists, clergy, and government agents have done most of the writing about Indigenous people, it has been difficult to understand the context and purpose for ceremonies and events that were described in the 19th and early 20th centuries. For example, from the colonial gaze, the potlatch, a central part of the Coast Salish world, was one of the most misunderstood and misinterpreted performances. Potlatches were complex ceremonials that often lasted many days and served a multitude of functions including the distribution of wealth and the validations of inherited and earned status within the multi-village social system. Dances, namings, feasts, and gift giving were the outward manifestations of these events. The potlatch was a complex cultural and economic activity that corresponded to the Coast Salish cosmology but was antithetical to the goals of Western capitalist development. Colonists, if they even considered Indigenous standpoints, rejected an elaborate economic system that upheld individual accumulations of wealth only for the purpose of gifting all away to fulfill the unseen obligations of the Indigenous social order. Anthropologist Wayne Suttles (1987), who did the most prominent studies of the Coast Salish potlatch, notes the ways that the "potlatch is part of a larger socio-economic system that enables the whole social network, consisting of a number of communities, to maintain a high level of food production and to equalize its food consumption both within and among communities. The system is thus adaptive in an environment characterized by the features indicated before—spatial and temporal variation and fluctuation in the availability of resources" (p. 25). In other words, it was an environmental management system that holistically responded directly to the ecological conditions of the multi-village cosmos to redistribute wealth and avoid both economic and ecological collapse in times of environmental fluctuations. For the Coast Salish, the potlatch was required for confirming the status of leaders and their traditional influence in community relationships. The potlatch was central to maintaining both the human and natural ecologies. Social and ecological chaos would result if these ceremonies could not be conducted.

Potlatching was prohibited by the Canadian government in 1885, as part of a policy to force Aboriginal people into modern wage occupations and promote individualism. It was prohibited precisely because it maintained an Aboriginal social economy in contradiction to a capitalist economy and was viewed as an impediment to assimilation into the imperial order. However, Native peoples were already active participants in the wage economy of the advancing colonial society, deploying the wealth earned from jobs in logging and commercial fisheries toward their *own* cultural goals associated with the potlatch and collectivist sensibilities. All the same, racism limited their participation in the colonial economy and they were only employed during periods of labor shortage (Lutz, 2002).

Government agents could not understand how vital the ceremonies were for sustaining fisheries, hunting, harvests of crops, and agreements between powerful families who preserved the necessary resources of an entire region. As the Coast Salish landscape was being invaded by overwhelming numbers of settlers, Native people adapted the potlatches to purposes that reflected the loss of land and the struggle to retain at least the spiritual vision of the peoples' relationship to the land.

> The main economic incentive for the potlatch, the need to pass on the rights to valuable resource sites, diminished as the sites were lost to urbanization and the new state regulations, which appropriated control over hunting and fishing. Hereditary names continued to be passed down, but the focus had shifted to spiritual accomplishments and the winter dance (Lutz, 2008, p.105).

Modernity's invasion of Coast Salish territory made it impossible for the colonizers to understand the sublime utility of Indigenous cultural practices that were being transformed by waves of immigrants while they were being observed. The settlers were unknowingly watching a culture being changed by the crowd of so many White invaders. Anthropologists, clergy, and government officials, if they tried to imagine a pre-contact Coast Salish world, projected their own values, particularly about land and history. The Coast Salish epistemologies were outside the scope of the colonial mind which was busy manufacturing history while re-arranging the Indigenous geographies. The settlers, not understanding how conditions were changing for the Aboriginal world, saw only a reworked version of the potlatch that highlighted spiritual powers, but not the practical aspects of ecological conduct. They miscomprehended the ways that the potlatch functioned to maintain social cohesion and sound environmental resource management at the same time.

What is important to note is that versions of the same 19th-century misunderstandings about Indigenous practices and principles continue in the present moment. Indigenous people's relationships with environmentalists show an adjusted modern discourse of misunderstanding about language, goals, and purposes:

> Many Euro-North Americans also interpret First Nation people's talk of "respect" to mean that they have feelings of love and reverence for an environment that they regard as sacred and that these beliefs in turn keep them from exploiting and/or destroying it. But terms like *sacred* and *reverence,* like *respect,* are English terms used to approximate aboriginal concepts. It is dangerous to judge First Nation people's behavior against the meanings of these English terms as generally accepted by Euro-North Americans (Nadasdy, 2005, p. 303).

In the 19th century, church and government officials saw community members who, after hosting a potlatch, became destitute. This was, to the colonizers, an unacceptable social condition, and the agents of the state could not understand how the Coast Salish cultural systems would function to provide for the well-being of these people. Paige Raibmon (2005) points out that one of the reasons missionaries pushed to eradicate the potlatch was that they too often arrived at a village to evangelize and found everyone away at another village attending a potlatch. Indian agents, trying to perform colonial inspections of villages, were likewise frustrated by the Indigenous mobility central to the potlatch.

The Potlatch Law, section 149 of the Indian Act, was eventually repealed in 1951. For participation in the banned potlatch, the minimum penalty was two months in jail; the maximum was six months. In British Columbia it was so essential for certain individuals to attend and perform traditional roles such as giving customary speeches that they ended up spending months in jail as a result. While this history is considered remote within the mainstream public consciousness and within the educational systems of the region, it is close at hand as an elemental aspect of contemporary Indigenous identities. These histories of domination and the attempts to eradicate Coast Salish social practices are present in the minds of Aboriginal people as they evaluate and describe social conditions in their communities. Daisy Sewid-Smith's (1997) response to anthropologist Harry Wolcott is an example of an Indigenous scholar explaining the historic and contemporary significance of the potlatch and the broader context of how ethnographers continue to misunderstand the intricacies of community and desire.

This history of cultural suppression is also resonant in the awareness of community leaders who are working to bring back traditional knowledge and reconnect people and places in Coast Salish territory. For example, in July 2007, Lummi Nation in Washington State hosted a tl'aneq or potlatch/feast gathering of 68 canoe families from communities up and down the West Coast. It was the first potlatch to be hosted at Lummi since 1937, and brought together communities throughout the region and from both sides of the border.

It is instructive to use local and regional examples of nation state policies tracing their trajectories of domination into the present moment. An Indigenous version of Fanon's call for an analysis of the colonial situation would have us decolonize intellectual work away from the universalizing tendencies of Eurocentric history and from modernity's privileging of time over space (Soja, 1993). The language we use to describe reality is constructed from our assumptions about the processes of history and the meanings of geographies. Dale Turner (2006) has said we need to understand how normative language—that is, the language that makes substantive claims about 'what is the case'—is put to use in a particular way of perceiving the world. Once we do understand, we can assess whether this normative language is useful for us as Indigenous intellectuals. (p. 114)

Turner's comments lead us to consider whether Indigenous scholars can actually understand the processes of modernity and colonization without understanding something of the morphological frameworks of Indigenous languages that tend to be verb-oriented, rather than noun-oriented. "Aboriginal languages express an awareness of a local ecology and are directed to understanding both external life forms and the invisible forces beneath them.... These sounds create a dynamic consciousness between ease and unease of inner life" (Youngblood-Henderson, 2000, p. 262). Moreover, not only do Aboriginal languages have precise ways of describing the epistemologies of landscape (Basso, 1996; Cruikshank, 2005; Kawagley, 2003), they also uniquely describe the processes of colonization.

Jay Miller (1999), in writing about the Lushootseed Coast Salish language points out how the linguistic structure and traditional metaphors present the local understandings of how the land was taken. An elder he interviewed used a Lushootseed word which means "to wedge" in describing colonization from a Coast Salish point of view:

> In other words, in the native view as confirmed by the language, whites took over the Northwest by acting as expanding wedges set in the most desirable areas, generally those long occupied and developed by resident native communities. As a descriptive image, it is both vivid and telling, especially when compared with academic history (Miller, 1999, p. 37).

As Indigenous communities begin to reclaim lost cultural space, there is an advancing focus on the revival of Indigenous languages as a centerpiece for curriculum development. Stories that feature the pre-contact worldview and the places within the Coast Salish territory are being used with language education that emphasizes traditional ecological knowledge. For example, Snuneymuxw Nanaimo elder Ellen Rice White (2006) has inscribed stories handed down to her from her grandparents that are from the ancient Coast Salish cosmologies. A recognized authority from a prominent family, she wrote the stories in English but interspersed them with words from her Hul'q'umin'um' Coast Salish language. Important messages of honoring the spiritual dimension of landscape as a kind of morality text are conveyed through narratives about the creator/transformer Xa:ls.[1]

The stories contain messages that challenge modernity and ask Aboriginal youth to respond to the values of tradition, elder knowledge, and animal and spiritual beings as teachers. After each story, she explains how place-based knowledge of materials, processes, and spirituality is woven into a holism of learning self, community, and land. For example, in the story of the boys who became a killer whale, a group of teenagers is resentful that they have not been given sufficient knowledge and responsibility to perform adult tasks which require speaking to inanimate objects. Angry at not being given the sacred teachings, and wanting to make a show of their presumed capacities to the village, they find a whale skin and, with incomplete powers, they transform themselves into a whale. Disaster follows as the boys are not recognized as boys but as a whale that is then killed for food. Overflowing with sadness, the entire village, through the grandfather's explication, comes to understand what happened. Ceremonies are conducted and the location becomes an honored place of teachings on the landscape.

The story includes references to substances such as *tumulh* (red ochre) which have transformative powers: "It is taught that when water hits certain kinds of dirt or minerals, it becomes different in substance, 'two in one,' or maybe more than two. *Tumulh* was used so much because it united many different forms of energy into one" (White, 2006, p. 40). In these, and other oral traditions, there is a seamless merging of both spiritual content and place-based knowledge as the region's animals, plants, and landmarks are described in ways that stress Coast Salish commitments to healing both land and the people. Names and concepts recovered from pre-contact times by listening to elders are invaluable resources for both community education and for ongoing land claims and treaty negotiations in British Columbia.[2]

Place-based and sacred traditional relationships to landscape may be in contradistinction to Western, modernist approaches to land and society, but colonization has, as was noted earlier, made this a very complex situation and one that should not be expressed in terms of Western environmental ethics or aesthetics. Julie Cruikshank (1998) has described Indigenous connections between the natural world and human societies:

> In a framework where animals and humans are understood to share common states of being that include family relationships, intelligence, and common responsibility for maintenance of a shared world, the rights and obligations obtaining to relationships among people also extend to the natural world. Interaction with the physical world, then, *is* a social relationship, and consequently it is rarely straightforward (p. 60).

A Saanich elder was recently explaining to me how his family, in the old days, used to travel the distance from his village on Vancouver Island to visit relatives at the Lummi community in Washington State over 30 nautical miles away paddling on open water in canoes. He told me that they had deep knowledge of the tides and could use them "just like you catch a bus nowadays. We had names for the tides and currents just like they were people." This is not just reminiscence from a different time, but rather a way of speaking that summons a view from the "real" world, the Coast Salish world that still exists under the deposits of modernity which has eroded the ability of the people to understand the deep meaning of the land.

When this revived knowledge is welded to an understanding of the political conditions of colonization, it focuses the educational goals of Aboriginal peoples in ways that are dissimilar from those of the dominant society. Indigenous communities also understand that reviving traditional practices is a political move toward broader paradigm transformation. Indigenous youth are becoming committed to a praxis that reclaims both lost knowledge and lost land. Julie Cruikshank (1998), in explaining the way that storytellers in the Yukon use songs and place names, along with descriptions of "land and kinship as attachment points for memory" (p. 158), reports on how these pre-contact understandings of place are inspiring youth toward the political efficacy of traditional knowledge:

> A story now heard in the Yukon describes how a visitor invited to a primary school classroom in the early 1990s asked children what they hoped to do when they finished school. One youngster waved his hand enthusiastically. His occupational choice? "A land claims negotiator!" (p. 159)

The revival of pre-contact knowledge and traditional practices are not without significant caustic debate in educational sites. Elsewhere (Marker, 2006) I have written about the backlash environment for Coast Salish students from communities involved in treaty negotiations or controversial cultural practices protected by treaties. For example, the Makah boy who proclaimed in the classroom his desire to be a whale hunter like his cousins is an example of an expression of Indigenous identity that was pounced upon by the Whitestream hegemony of the schools.

SPIRITUALITY, RELIGION, AND MODERNIST EDUCATION

The discussions of land and place-based knowledge as a core of Indigenous life is, in many ways, inseparable from considerations of spirituality. Indigenous scholars and place-based educational thinkers have noted the connections between modernist approaches to land and the institutional expulsions of place-based spirituality. David Orr (1992) has commented that:

> other than as a collection of buildings where learning is supposed to occur, place has no particular standing in contemporary education....Place is nebulous to educators because to a great extent we are a displaced people for whom our immediate places are no longer sources of food, water, livelihood, energy, materials, friend, recreation, or sacred inspiration (p. 126).

For Indigenous peoples, Western education is not simply an encounter with a placeless institution devoted to abstract knowledge, it is an environment where their sense of spirituality connected to the land is relegated to the category of exotic or primitive beliefs. Gregory Cajete (1999) employs the terms biophobia and biophilia to set down the divide between Indigenous and Western outlooks on knowledge, place, and spirit:

> The biophobic tendency is associated with a kind of "urbanity of the mind" that seem to be learned and internalized as a result of living a life largely disconnected from nature and propagated by the advent and development of cities. Because biophobia underlies aspects of the prevailing mindset of modernism, it influences the "hidden curriculum" of modern Western education. Indeed, the evolution of biophobia as expressed in the attempt to control and subdue nature has its own unique historical progression in Western religious, philosophical, artistic, and academic traditions (p. 190).

Cajete (1999) explains that biophilia, by contrast, refers to human desires to affiliate with other forms of life. This is part of a pre-contact way of life and "has long been the guiding paradigm of Indigenous forms of education found throughout the world" (p. 191). This way of life is founded on reverential relationships to land.

The Western education that was employed to assimilate Indigenous people into modernity was founded on an amalgam of religious principles and modern national interests. In Canada, the Christian churches were the tools of the state in administering residential schools, but the contradictions were abundant in preparing the students to participate in a gritty social Darwinist industrial secularism while proselytizing them to the divine moral principles of the Churches. While many Indigenous peoples successfully amalgamated Christianity with their own belief systems, the tensions between Indigenous spirituality and Christianity remained. The religious indoctrination students received at the residential schools was based on abstract and universalized beliefs about spiritual truth. This contrasted with place-specific understandings that are central to Indigenous ceremony and revelation. Vine Deloria (1994) has described contradictions between Indigenous and Christian theologies explaining that:

> what has been the manifestation of deity in a particular local situation is mistaken for a truth applicable to all times and places, a truth so powerful that it must be impressed upon peoples who have no connection to the event or to the cultural complex in which it originally made sense (p. 66).

Further, he explains how Indigenous religions are embedded in place and responsibility:

> The vast majority of Indian tribal religions, therefore, have a sacred center at a particular place, be it a river, a mountain, a plateau, valley, or other natural feature. This center enables the people to look out along the

four dimensions and locate their lands, to relate all historical events within the confines of this particular land, and to accept responsibility for it. Regardless of what subsequently happens to the people, the sacred lands remain as permanent fixtures in their cultural or religious understanding. (Deloria, 1994, p. 67)

It is an enormous undertaking to wedge spaces into educational settings for a consideration of Indigenous spirituality, place, and history. Claude Denis (1997), in his study of Coast Salish collisions with Canadian modernity, examined the ways that spirituality and social cohesion were welded together in the winter spirit dances. He observed the advantages of Indigenous holistic systems of integrated spiritual and social structuring in contrast to nation state forms of secular control. He concluded that, "we ought to listen to what is being said so loudly, and take it seriously: modernity's marginalizing of spirituality is a severely debilitating flaw" (Denis, 1997, p. 143). While the history of residential schooling shows the function of religion as a weapon of conquest, the present secularized nature of Western education has been caustic to Indigenous values as well. Indigenous knowledge systems resist the Western sacred-secular dichotomies, and elders invoke spirituality as a way to give deep meaning and substance to their teachings. This is seen as a contrast to school-based knowledge which is commonly regarded as superficially technical and distanced from the fundamental concerns of life.

However, the observations about spirituality must be accompanied with a firm cautionary message. Without the appropriate cultural interpretations of spiritual values from elders and traditional knowledge specialists, classroom teachers frequently descend into untrue interpretations of the pre-contact Indigenous world drawn from the accounts of anthropologists and the writings of textbook authors. Julie Kaomea (2005) has illustrated how modernity and colonization continue to operate as an overlay to push Indigenous histories of religious and cultural practices into the category of barbarism in a public school curriculum on Native Hawaiian studies. The pre-contact world of Indigenous peoples is portrayed in classrooms as violent, dark, and chaotic. The religious ceremonies and beliefs are represented as primitive; replaced by a more enlightened modern era with the arrival of White settlers and missionaries. She explains

> such lessons, through the reiteration of familiar colonial discourses, simultaneously discredit Hawaiian rulers of the past and present, building within the children an appreciation for the democratic government of today and a fear of ever returning to the days of fierce Hawaiian monarchs. (p. 34)

While she argues for the need to replace the colonially influenced textbooks with new works by Native Hawaiian scholars, she is skeptical about the prospects for real change because of the embedded nature of Indigenous stereotypes and the elusive modernist hegemony of the mainstream classrooms.

CONCLUSION

When I was a high school teacher on the Lummi reservation in the late 1980s and early 1990s, one of the main problems was the lack of accurate curriculum for students to read about the history of colonization in the Coast Salish region. I taught history and language arts for Lummi, Swinomish, and Nooksack youth who were finishing high school through a grant-funded program at the tribal college. I would show books and articles to elders and language teachers. They helped me to understand both the directly incorrect works as well as the writings that, by taking cultural and religious practices out of context, made Aboriginal knowledge seem outdated and supplanted by modern ideas in a historical progression that was made to seem natural. My students, many of whom had dropped out—or, more accurately, had been pushed out—of the local public schools, saw me struggling to find materials that would help them build academic skills while critiquing the mainstream textbook assumptions about Aboriginal people. I eventually abandoned the idea of using textbooks and instead assembled readings from the tribal college library. I was fortunate to have the help of community elders who talked to the students about how the ancestors solved problems in realms of technology and human relations.

With consultation, I developed courses that revived some of the relevancy of pre-contact knowledge and provided a culturally responsive space for students to gain a high school diploma. Nearly all the students did graduate and some of them are presently involved with the ongoing cultural resurgence of the community. For example, one of the graduates from this program is now the Xwelemi Chosen (Lummi language) teacher at the local public high school. I spent a morning in his classroom recently and watched him explaining to the students how essential the language was to thinking in Coast Salish space and time. His students, like the students I worked with nearly twenty years ago, struggle to validate an Indigenous identity in classrooms that are soaked in modernity and the ideologies of progress. The high school, with over a thousand students attending, is a swirl of youth and non-Indigenous teachers who know very little about the history of the land that surrounds the institutional buildings. The Lummi language class, offered in a mainstream high school, is a kind of Indigenous intellectual island. It is a safe place for the students to learn to express themselves apart from the identities that are assigned to them in the halls and other classrooms of the high school.

Indigenous scholars, acting as conduits between the divided worlds of the university and the community, are often more engaged with the local, concrete concerns of the communities they come from and work with than with the abstract, specialist knowledge of the academy. However, in bringing ideas from their communities to the academy, they are having a particular effect on the universities they work at. For example, at the University of British Columbia, because of the work of Indigenous scholars and the participation of the local Coast Salish communities, the university is explicitly acknowledging the institution's location on the "unceeded territory of the Musqueam people" through mission statements and policy documents. The First Nations House of learning (the longhouse) at UBC hosts many events, and Musqueam elders provide the welcome to the territory and the opening prayers, often in the Hunquminum Coast Salish language.

Through these events that groups of non-Indigenous faculty attend, there is a growing awareness of the Indigenous protocols which honor both place-based knowledge and local spirituality. Whether these gestures of Indigenous acknowledgement actually represent a transformation or simply a perfunctory wave is central to the question of whether Indigenous scholars and their communities' knowledges will be admitted or rejected by the increasingly globalized academies. Rauna Kuokkanen (2007) has reported on the significant moments when the Musqueam were not invited to be part of events such as the Asia Pacific Economic Cooperation Summit (APEC) in 1997. The affairs of international and multi-national economic systems are considered to be outside the domain of Indigenous knowledge.

> Beyond its somewhat random attempts to acknowledge the Musqueam, and except for the fact that the university is located on their territory, UBC tends to disregard this relationship and the responsibilities attached to it....The Musqueam are recognized when it is convenient for the university; when it is not, they are ignored, neglected, and pushed aside, especially when the university wants to represent itself—walk in the spotlight—as the sovereign master to the outside world (Kuokkanen, 2007, p. 135).

One of the most recent developments in place-based Coast Salish education is the Lummi Youth Academy. Located on the Lummi reservation, the Academy is a tribally administered boarding school for Coast Salish students who are completing high school. Some of the students have come from foster homes and are recovering from alcohol and drug abuse. While the residential school concept has been a controversial element of the project, there is an urgent need to provide a sanctuary for Coast Salish youth who have inherited the multigenerational legacies of both church-operated residential schooling and racist public schools. The Lummi Youth Academy provides a safe place from conditions of family violence and drug and alcohol addiction as well as a place where their traditional culture and homeland is woven into their education. The Academy houses students from Coast Salish communities on both sides of the border and recognizes the shared regional families and histories. Director, and former Lummi Tribal Chair, Darrell Hillaire has emphasized the need to re-establish a traditional, borderless, sense of self and place for youth; a Coast Salish citizenship.

Other projects in the Coast Salish region are also combining traditional ecological knowledge with the goal of reorienting youth to the traditional meaning of the cross-border territory. The "Tribal Journey" is an annual summer event that has canoe families traveling from one community to another as they recreate aspects of ancient relationships between villages within the region. Youth who participate in these extended canoe voyages are exposed to language and ideas from elders and traditional knowledge keepers. Places on the landscape are named and narrated as the canoes pass by. Ceremonies are conducted that connect people with the interwoven spirituality of the Coast Salish world. These are the present-day pedagogies of place; endeavors to reclaim pre-contact knowledge and decolonize Coast Salish learning. Recently, environmental scientists have come to understand the value of traditional canoe travels for gaining a vision of a bioregion and a deeper ecological insight into climate change. The canoes are participating in an emerging partnership with the United States Geologic Survey (U.S.G.S.) helping with scientific research on the water quality changes in the "Salish Sea." Canoe skippers are given water quality probes and global positioning system devices to carry on board during the summer canoe journeys. The canoes are well suited for research on water quality because they move at a slow speed that is ideal for the use of the probes. And, because the journeys cross the border frequently, they can help give a vital snapshot of the region that could replicate the way Aboriginal people see a borderless world (Grossman & Gibbons, 2008).

With advancing globalization, Indigenous communities face increasing pressure to provide academic and technical training for youth while protecting their homelands through the revival and application of traditional knowledge. The traditional Coast Salish values and the ecological sense of space are shared across the border. We must consider how Indigenous knowledge was practical toward the goals of sustainability. Indigenous perspectives on history, culture, and power challenge the universities to learn about the local knowledge of the local people and consider the imaginative possibilities for new/old ways of thinking about the inextricable spirit of social and natural ecologies. If we are to take Indigenous knowledge seriously in the academy, we must also take the Indigenous communities seriously and listen to what they have to say.

NOTES

1. Because the name of the creator is pronounced somewhat differently and because different orthographies evolved throughout the region, each Coast Salish language group uses different spellings for this name. I use the most common spelling among the northern Straights Salish here. The Transformer is a universally accept-

ed creator and teacher who transforms people and animals into stone or places them as landmarks to show locally based universal truths. The word is pronounced with a backward "x" and then dropping the strong "h" sound in the word halls, hulls, or other variations depending on the dialect.
2. The Delgamuukw decision, handed down by the Supreme Court of Canada on December 11, 1997, is a prominent example of how vital traditional knowledge is to the ability of indigenous peoples to protect and reclaim their lands. Oral tradition, in this decision, was considered to have the same weight as written evidence and the Gitxsan and Wet'suwet'en Nations demonstrated both their occupancy and ownership of their land, 58,000 square kilometers of Northern British Columbia, through the use of their adaawks, traditional creation stories.

REFERENCES

Basso, K. (1996). *Wisdom Sits in Places: Landscape and Language among the Western Apache*. Albuquerque: University of New Mexico Press.
Cajete, G. (1999). Reclaiming biophilia: lessons learned from Indigenous peoples. In G. Smith and D. Williams (Eds.). *Ecological Education in Action: On Weaving Education, Culture, and the Environment* (pp. 189–206). Albany: SUNY.
Cruikshank, J. (1998). *The Social Life of Stories: Narrative and Knowledge in the Yukon Territory*. Lincoln: University of Nebraska Press.
Cruikshank, J. (2005). *Do Glaciers Listen? Local Knowledge, Colonial Encounters, and Social Imagination*. Vancouver: UBC.
Deloria, V. (1991). Foreword to (Ed.) Peter Nabokov, *Native American Testimony: A Chronicle of Indian-White Relations from Prophecy to the Present*. New York: Penguin.
Deloria, V. (1994). *God Is Red: A Native View of Religion, the Classic Work Updated*. Golden, CO: Fulcrum.
Denis, C. (1997). *We Are Not You: First Nations and Canadian Modernity*. Peterborough: Broadview.
Grande, S. (2000). American Indian identity and intellectualism; The quest for a new red pedagogy. *International Journal of Qualitative Studies in Education, 13*(4), 343–359.
Grossman, E., & Gibbons, H. (2008). USGS will collaborate with coast Salish Indigenous peoples to measure water quality in the Salish Sea (Puget Sound, Strait of Georgia, and Strait of Juan de Fuca). Sound Waves. Available at http://soundwaves.usgs.gov/2008/05
Foucault, M. (1970) *The Order of Things: An Archaeology of the Human Sciences*. New York: Random House.
Harris, C. (2002). *Making Native Space: Colonization, Resistance, and Reserves in British Columbia*. Vancouver: UBC.
Kaomea, J. (2005). Indigenous studies in the elementary curriculum: A cautionary Hawaiian example. *Anthropology & Education Quarterly, 36* (1), 24–42.
Kawagley, A. O. (2003). Nurturing native languages. In J. Reyhner, O. Trujillo, R. Carrasco, & L. Lockard (Eds.). *Nurturing Native Languages* (pp. vii–x). Flagstaff, AZ: Northern Arizona University.
Kuokkanen, R. (2007). *Reshaping the University: Responsibility, Indigenous Epistemes, and the Logic of the Gift*. Vancouver: UBC.
Lutz, J. (2002). Work, sex, and death on the great thoroughfare: Annual migrations of "Canadian Indians" to the American Pacific Northwest. In J. Findlay & K. Coates, (Eds.). *Parallel Destinies: Canadian-American Relations West of the Rockies* (pp. 80–103). Seattle: University of Washington Press.
Lutz, J. (2008). *Makúk: A New History of Aboriginal-White Relations*. Vancouver: UBC.
Marker, M. (2009). Indigenous resistance and racist schooling on the borders of empires: Coast Salish cultural survival. *Paedagogica Historica, 45*(6), 757–772.
Marker, M. 2006). After the Makah whalehunt: Indigenous knowledge and limits to multicultural discourse. *Urban Education, 41*(5), 482–505.
Miller, J. (1999). *Lushootseed Culture and the Shamanic Odyssey: An Anchored Radiance*. Lincoln: University of Nebraska Press.

Nadasdy, P. (2005). Transcending the debate over the ecologically noble Indian: Indigenous peoples and environmentalism. *Ethnohistory, 52*(2), 291–331.

Orr, D. (1992). *Ecological Literacy: Education and the Transition to a Postmodern World.* Albany: SUNY.

Raibmon, P. (2005). *Authentic Indians: Episodes of Encounter from the Late-Nineteenth Century Northwest Coast.* Durham, NC: Duke University Press.

Rasmus, S. (2002). Repatriating words: Local knowledge in a global context. *American Indian Quarterly, 26*(2), 286–307.

Said, E. (1979). *Orientalism.* New York: Vintage.

Said, E. (1994). From orientalism. In P. Williams & L. Chrisman (Eds.). *Colonial Discourse and Post-colonial Theory: A Reader* (pp. 132–149). New York: Columbia University Press.

Sewid-Smith, D. (1997). The continuing reshaping of our ritual world by academic adjuncts. *Anthropology & Education Quarterly, 28*(4), 594–603.

Smith, L. T. (1999). *Decolonizing Methodologies: Research and Indigenous Peoples.* Dunnedin: University of Otago Press.

Soja, E. (1993). History, geography: modernity. In S. During (Ed.). *The Cultural Studies Reader* (pp. 135–150). London: Routledge.

Stewart-Harawira, M. (2005). *The New Imperial Order: Indigenous Responses to Globalization.* London: Zed.

Suttles, W. (1987). *Coast Salish Essays.* Seattle: University of Washington Press.

Turner, D. (2006). *This Is Not a Peace Pipe: Towards a Critical Indigenous Philosophy.* Toronto: University of Toronto Press.

White, E. (2006). *Legends and Teachings of Xeel's, the Creator.* Vancouver: Pacific Educational.

Wolf, E. (1982). *Europe and the People without History.* Berkeley: University of California Press.

Youngblood-Henderson, J. (2000). Ayukpachi: Empowering Aboriginal thought. In M. Battiste (Ed.), *Reclaiming Indigenous Voice and Vision* (pp. 248–278). Vancouver: UBC.

CHAPTER FOURTEEN

Indigenous Knowledge in Transition

The Fundamental Laws of Diné in an Era of Change and Modernity

Lloyd L. Lee

For over five hundred years, Indigenous peoples have been fighting to maintain their identity as distinct human beings. It has been a struggle and a challenge for Indigenous peoples in the Western hemisphere. Our languages, rituals, ceremonies, protocols, and ways of life have been disrupted and disheveled. Colonization has also impacted Indigenous knowledge yet Indigenous peoples have maintained elements of their epistemology and philosophy. Indigenous scholars and intellectuals such as Greg Cajete, Vine Deloria, Jr., Linda Tuhiwai Smith, Manulani Aluli Meyer, Daniel R. Wildcat, Taiaiake Alfred, Dale Turner, and other Indigenous writers continue to engender Indigenous knowledge. This knowledge is viable and key to native nation re-building yet questions and possibly doubts surround the dynamic of Indigenous thought amid tensions in an era of change and modernity in Indigenous communities today. Some Indigenous peoples and non-Indigenous peoples question the validity of Indigenous knowledge to overcome the many socio-economic problems facing their communities. Some Indigenous leaders advocate a practical and modern approach to resolving these problems while others choose to follow their core values to help them alleviate the issues.

Some Indigenous scholars and intellectuals, elders, and Indigenous peoples in general advocate using Indigenous knowledge to help rectify the challenges facing Indigenous communities. For instance, Cajete's *Look to the Mountain*, *Native Science*, and several of his other texts utilize Indigenous knowledge to promote ways to re-build Indigenous education for a holistic experience. Deloria, Jr.'s work also uses Indigenous knowledge to propose many ideas to sustain Indigenous communities in the areas of governance, philosophy, and religion. Alfred advises Indigenous communities to use their cultural knowledge toward re-building their governments and political systems. Smith also advocates using Indigenous knowledge when developing research protocols, methodologies, and projects to help re-build their nations and communities. Their thoughts and words represent a knowledge foundation where Indigenous peoples can seek guidance yet some Indigenous peoples do not want their cultural knowledge to be translated into a Western paradigm.

One example of this is on the Navajo Nation, which all of my intellectual work focuses on. I, too, want to help the Navajo Nation address the socio-economic challenges they are facing in the twenty-first century, and I advocate the usage of Diné cultural knowledge as the guiding path in this endeavor. Helping to re-build the Navajo Nation is an important part of my scholarship because, like Cajete, Deloria, Jr., Smith, Alfred, Meyer, and the many other Indigenous scholars who use Indigenous knowledge in their work, the business of Indigenous scholars is to work for the sustainability of an Indigenous peoples' way of life. This essay contributes to thinking about a way to help sustain the Navajo Nation and to the continuation of Indigenous knowledge in general. For the past forty years, the Navajo Nation like many other Indigenous nations is interacting with challenges impacting all aspects of their society and way of life. The Diné people including the government have devised ways to employ their cultural knowledge to alleviate their challenges. One idea was the Fundamental Laws of the Diné (FLD).

In 2003, the Fundamental Laws of the Diné were codified into Title One of the Navajo Nation Code. These laws are meant to enhance Diné leadership, sovereignty, and governance. For the first time in history, Diné ethical laws were classified for government usage. For some Diné people, this was the first time they heard of the Fundamental Laws, others knew of these laws and followed them on a daily basis, and other who thought FLD had nothing to do with their own lives. The medicine people who explained these laws to the lawmakers at first were resistant to the idea of writing these laws in the code. They knew the danger of sanctioning the Fundamental Laws, which were meant to be passed down orally. However, they changed their minds when representatives were able to persuade them on the concern this knowledge was fading, and the lack of this knowledge may be the primary reason why the people experienced many negative forms of behavior and certain natural events (i.e., the Holy People visitation in 1996) would not have occurred if the people had been observing and living by these laws.

The Navajo Nation Council, a foreign government system created in 1938, and the court system use the Fundamental Laws to help them govern and to analyze legal issues. Many other Indigenous nations in the United States also have a foreign government system. In the mid-1930s, numerous American Indian tribes adopted the Indian Reorganization Act (IRA) although the Navajo Nation rejected it; nevertheless, the government system created in 1938 was similar to the other IRA governments. Several Native nations have been able to maintain parts or all of their traditional governance (e.g., O'Brien, 1993; Wilkins, 2003) such as the Iroquois Confederacy and various Pueblo nations in New Mexico.

The Navajo Nation court system has been successful in helping families and individuals rectify many challenges ranging from domestic violence to robbery. We also see Diné citizens and grassroots organizations using the FLD for specific claims.

In May 2007, the Navajo Nation Supreme Court rendered its decision in the Laverne Wagner grievance. The case concerned Leonard Tsosie's election to the Navajo Nation Council. In November 2006, Leonard Tsosie was elected to one of two seats representing the chapter houses of Torreon, Whitehouse Lake, and Pueblo Pintado. At the time of his election, he was a New Mexico State Senator. The Navajo Nation Election Code prohibits individuals from serving simultaneously as a council delegate and a member of another government entity. Tsosie wanted to serve both governments. The Navajo Nation Supreme Court ruled that Tsosie could not serve both and ordered him to choose one position.

In the ruling, the court analyzed Tsosie's contention that in the Fundamental Laws it clearly states voters may choose leaders of their choice. The court recognized voters may choose leaders of their choice but the choice requires two other criteria. The first requirement is the selection of the person by the voters themselves, and the second is the person chosen must accept the position, and that acceptance comes from taking an oath to serve the laws of the Navajo Nation. According to the Navajo Nation Supreme Court, only when a person is properly installed as a leader, can the individual be called a leader. In Diné, it's called "Diné binant'a'í bee bi'doosziid" or "Diné binaat'áanii bee bi'doosziid."[1] Because the individual swears an oath to support, obey, and defend the Navajo Nation and all its laws, it is absolute and allows for no conflict in loyalty. Therefore, a person cannot serve both the Navajo Nation and another governmental entity. The court stated this prohibition to serve two government entities is consistent with the Fundamental Laws of the Diné, and it is not improper for the Election Code to require Tsosie to make a choice and serve only one position. He did not agree with the opinion but chose to take the Navajo Nation Council Delegate oath and he resigned his New Mexico State Senator seat.

Many questions abound on the meaning of the Fundamental Laws. Several Diné environmental grassroots groups such as Eastern Navajo Diné against Uranium Mining (ENDAUM), Diné CARE (Diné Citizens against Ruining our Environment), Dooda Desert Rock, and Black Mesa Water Coalition have evoked the natural law provision of the FLD to help with their causes. ENDAUM was successful in using the FLD to justify a prohibition on uranium mining and milling on the Navajo Nation. President Joe Shirley signed into law the Diné Natural Resources Protection Act of 2005 banning future uranium mining and milling on Diné Bikéyah (Diné land). This was a collaborative effort by activists, government officials, and state officials.

Diné CARE and Dooda Desert Rock are currently using the Fundamental Laws to stop the Desert Rock Energy Project and to lay out an economic and energy alternative to a proposed coal-fired power plant. President Joe Shirley stated Diné CARE and Dooda Desert Rock incorrectly interpreted the Fundamental Laws.[2] The Navajo Nation Council also supports the energy project because of the need for economic opportunity and job creation, however, the U.S. Environmental Protection Agency revoked the Desert Rock Power Plant's permit in October 2009. The Navajo Nation and their corporate partner, Sithe Global, proposed the Desert Rock Energy Project, a 1500-megawatt coal-fired power plant southwest of Farmington, New Mexico, on the reservation. The permit revoke means the Navajo Nation and Sithe Global must start the review process again.

In the summer 2009, Navajo Nation Council session, Council Delegate Raymond Joe, who represents the Tachee, Blue Gap, and Whippoorwill chapters, introduced legislation (number 0368–09) to repeal the Fundamental Laws of the Diné. It was tabled until the fall session. The legislation was not discussed at the fall session because Joe removed it from the agenda. It re-appeared in January 2010 at the winter session. The new legislation was amended to restrict the court's usage of the Fundamental Laws to only the peacemaking courts and the rest of the court system could only use council statutes in their legal analysis. The legislation passed 56–17. President Shirley vetoed the legislation. The council overrode Shirley's veto by a vote of 69–11. The council only needs fifty-nine out of eighty-eight delegate votes to override a Presidential veto.

Joe's rationale for the legislation was that people were misusing, misinterpreting, and abusing the Laws.[3] Apparently, Diné citizens evoke the Fundamental Laws to check the Navajo Nation Council. The council did not approve the Fundamental Laws for citizens to hold the council accountable. The Fundamental Laws of the Diné apparently differentiate between government officials and

Diné citizens. But what are these Fundamental Laws the council feels citizens are abusing, misusing, and misinterpreting? A discussion and analysis of the chapters of the Fundamental Laws follow.

CHAPTERS IN THE FUNDAMENTAL LAWS

The Fundamental Laws of the Diné are a part of the Navajo Nation Code. The Navajo Nation Code is the "de facto" constitution of the Navajo Nation government. However, neither the Navajo Nation Council nor the public has ever approved of a constitution or the Code itself. The Code was established in 1938 to function as the law-making rules of the Navajo tribal council. Since 1938, it has become the laws of the land. The council attempted in the 1950s and 1960s to approve a constitution but both attempts failed.

The Fundamental Laws are rooted in Indigenous cultural values, traditions, and ancestral knowledge. First, FLD is discussed in the Diné language. Words, phrases, and meanings are in the Diné language and not in any other language. When the medicine people spoke with political representatives on the drafting of the resolution to codify FLD, the discussion was in Diné. Second, Diné epistemology and identity acknowledge and respect all elements on the earth and in the universe; the foundation of the Fundamental Laws. Third, the Fundamental Laws represent a Diné paradigm; a pathway guiding the people on how to live on the earth. Fourth, oral tradition is the primary teaching method for the Fundamental Laws. Diné ancestral knowledge directs the Fundamental Laws to this day.

In chapter one of the Fundamental Laws, the council declared the foundation of Diné law. The declaration is in the Diné language followed by the English translation. Here is the English translation of the declaration:

> We, the Diné, the people of the Great Covenant, are the image of our ancestors and we are created in connection with all creation.
>
> The Holy People ordained, through songs and prayers, that Earth and universe embody thinking, Water and the sacred mountains embody planning, Air and variegated vegetation embody life, Fire, light, and offering sites of variegated sacred stones embody wisdom. These are the fundamental tenets established. Thinking is the foundation of planning. Life is the foundation of wisdom. Upon our creation, these were instituted within us and we embody them. Accordingly, we are identified by:
>
> Our Diné name, Our clan, Our language, Our life way, Our shadow, Our footprints. Therefore, we were called the Holy Earth-Surface-People. From here growth began and the journey proceeds. Different thinking, planning, life ways, languages, beliefs, and laws appear among us, but the fundamental laws placed by the Holy People remain unchanged. Hence, as we were created and with living soul, we remain Diné forever.[4]

This declaration is the rationale for the Fundamental Laws. It also reflects the identity of the Diné people.

The council ratified the Fundamental Laws to acknowledges the duty of the leadership to preserve, protect, and enhance the Diné way of life, and they believe by incorporating the Fundamental Laws into the code it would generate interest in learning about FLD and contribute to the continuance of Diné thought. The council at the time did not believe FLD contravene the Navajo Nation Code itself. They believed the adoption of the Fundamental Laws did not sanction government religion nor prohibit the free exercise of religion. The council also believed it was the responsibility to teach the meaning of the Fundamental Laws and to openly observe FLD in public functions. Today, questions surround the meaning of the Fundamental Laws and how they should be interpreted both by the council and the general public.

Chapter two of the Fundamental Laws lays the groundwork to understand traditional law, customary law, natural law, and common law:

> The Diné bi beenahaz'aanii embodies Diyin bitsaadee beehaz'aanii (traditional law), Diyin Dine'é bitsaadee beehaz'aanii (customary law), Nahasdzaan doo Yadilhil bitsaadee beehaz'aanii (natural law), and Diyin Nohookaa Diné bi beehaz'aanii (common law). These laws provide sanctuary for the Diné life and culture, our relationship with the world beyond the sacred mountains, and the balance we maintain with the natural world. These laws provide the foundation of Diné bi nahat'a (providing leadership through developing and administering policies and plans utilizing these laws as guiding principles) and Diné sovereignty. In turn, Diné bi nahat'a is the foundation of the Diné bi nahat'a (government). Hence, the respect for, honor, belief and trust in the Diné bi beenahaz'aanii preserves, protects and enhances the following inherent rights, beliefs, practices, and freedoms.[5]

The rights, beliefs, practices, and freedoms are both for the individual and the collective group. Some people might interpret the Fundamental Laws to mean it is a political and legal document similar to the Bill of Rights in the United States. The council codified FLD in response to the concerns that many concepts in Diné thought and ethics were no longer part of the Diné public. The council thought by writing these important and sacred laws it would help ensure a distinct Diné way of life. Instead, many disagree with this act, because the Fundamental Laws are now laden with Western concepts of rights, freedoms, and self that do not reflect historical Diné thought and experiences. In other words, the Fundamental Laws cannot be explained or understood within a contemporary structure foreign to a Diné matrix though these rights, beliefs, practices, and freedoms are interwoven. The following is a list of rights and freedoms for each Navajo person listed in the FLD:

A. The individual rights and freedoms of each Diné (from the beautiful child who will be born tonight to the dear elder who will pass on tonight from old age) as they are declared in these laws; and

B. The collective rights and freedoms of the Diyin Nihookáá Diné as a distinct people as they are declared in these laws; and

C. The fundamental values and principles of Diné Life Way as declared in these laws; and

D. Self-governance; and

E. A government structure consisting of Hózhoojí Nahat'á (Executive Branch), Naat'ájí Nahat'a (Legislative Branch), Hashkééjí Nahat'a (Judicial Branch), and the Naayee'jí Nahat'á (National Security Branch); and

F. That the practice of Diné bi nahat'á through the values and life way embodied in the Diné bi beenahaz'áanii provides the foundation of all laws proclaimed by the Navajo Nation government and the faithful adherence to Diné Bi Nahat'á will ensure the survival of the Navajo Nation; and

G. That Diné bi beenahaz'áanii provides for the future development and growth of a thriving Navajo Nation regardless of the many different thinking, planning, life ways, languages, beliefs, and laws that may appear within the Nation; and

H. The right and freedom of the Diné to be educated as to Diné Bi Beenahaz'áanii; and

I. That Diné Bi Beenahaz'áanii provides for the establishment of governmental relationships and agreements with other nations; that the Diné shall respect and honor such relationships and agreements and that the Diné can expect reciprocal respect and honor from such other nations.[6]

While some may argue the Fundamental Laws were never to be codified and then interpreted through a foreign government structure, the reality is they are being utilized in this fashion. What does this mean for future definitions and translations? It means more discussion and debate will transpire both inside and outside the government system.

Chapter three is on Diyin Bits'áadee Beehaz'áanii (Traditional Law). In this chapter, it states it is the right and freedom of the Diné to choose leaders of their choice and for the leaders to carry out their duties and responsibilities in a moral and legal manner. It lists the duties of the leaders of the executive, legislative, judicial, and security branches. It calls for the people to respect and honor the elders and medicine people. The elders and medicine people can be called upon to cleanse, protect, pray, and bless the leaders and the operation of the government. It also calls for the government and the people to respect the spiritual beliefs and practices of any person and to allow input and contribution of any religion. Finally, it allows the people and government to incorporate practices, principles, and values of other societies foreign to the principles and values of Diné Bi Beenahaz'áanii in the best interest and those necessary to provide the physical and mental well-being for each person.

In this chapter, the leaders of the executive, legislative, judicial, and security branches shall work to ensure public trust and confidence and adhere to the values and principles of Diné Bi beenahaz'áanii. Yet recently, the Diné people have been losing their trust and confidence in the executive and legislative branches of their government. In October 2009, the President was put on administrative leave by the Navajo Nation Council for alleged violations of Navajo Nation ethics laws. The Navajo Nation attorney general called for a special prosecutor to investigate the charges against the President. Prior to the President being put on administrative leave, several stories printed in *The Navajo Times* focused on the abuse by several individuals in acquiring thousands of dollars from several Navajo Nation Council delegates. The Council, along with the President, has a discretionary fund account. According to the chapter, each delegate's share of the discretionary fund amounts to $92, 821. The President's share is $360,000.[7] Because of these stories, the Navajo Nation's White Collar crime unit and the Ethics & Rules Office launched a joint investigation of the council's discretionary fund. Initially, the Ethics & Rules committee subpoenaed all discretionary fund records of all of the eighty-eight council delegates. Four days later, the Ethics & Rules committee rescinded the subpoena at the request of the Chief Legislative counsel. No reason was given to the Ethics & Rules director as to why the subpoena was taken back.[8] The total amount in the discretionary fund for a four-year period was over $35 million.[9] The ethics and responsibilities of being a leader are clearly defined in the traditional law chapter yet questionable behavior is evident.

Furthermore, in the third chapter, it states Diné people and the government itself can blend foreign practices, principles, and values into Diné thought to help the people with their physical and mental well-being. While it may be perceived as a virtuous thing to live by, this honorable way of living can be viewed as counterproductive, unhealthy, and continuing a traumatic and painful history. The people suffered a traumatic experience at Fort Sumner from 1864 to 1868. Thousands of people died either walking to or returning from the concentration camp or at the camp itself. Another horrifying experience occurred in the 1930s when thousands of goats, sheep, cattle, and horses were destroyed or taken from many families by the U.S. federal government. This experience resulted in many families being no longer self-sufficient. It forced many Diné men to find work off the reservation and many women lost wealth and happiness. The livestock reduction traumatically altered the Diné way of life. These two negative experiences have impacted how Navajo society lives today; although, it is respectful to forgive the oppressor it is rather difficult to do so when you know thousands of ancestors died to ensure the people live today. In contrast, the Fundamental Laws does not appear to recognize the terrifying history in the 1860s and 1930s.

The laws allow the people today who have been acculturated into American thought and way of life, a way to be part of Diné Bi Beenahaz'áanii. While diversity was part of society in the past and still is today, these laws are codified to ensure Diné continuance. Can a foreign perspective assist with Diné continuance? Diné people from the 1940s until 1970s might argue yes; that is, an American education can aid Diné continuance.

In 2010, thousands of Diné children do not speak their Indigenous language and do not practice their ceremonies; nonetheless, the language still lives and the ceremonies are still being conducted—but for how long? The incorporation of foreign thought into the Diné perspective is neither new nor different for the people. Diné people have always allowed foreign ways to be incorporated into Diné thought and way of life. The people have always shaped and molded these foreign perspectives into a distinct Diné perspective. Is that what is happening today in Diné society? It does not appear to be so because many children are learning to speak English first, and many of those individuals do not know the history or cultural traditions of their ancestors. Some are learning the language, history, and culture but will it be enough to ensure Diné continuance for hundreds of years. It may not be.

In the fourth chapter, the Fundamental Laws declare the principles and teachings of Diyin Diné Bits'aadee Beehaz'áanii (Customary law). It states the following:

Diné customary law declares and teaches that:

A. It is the right and freedom of the people that there always be holistic education of the values and principles underlying the purpose of living in balance with all creation, walking in beauty and making a living; and
B. It is the right and freedom of the people that the sacred system of k'é, based on the four clans of Kiiyaa'áanii, Todich'iinii, Honaghaahnii and Hashtl'isihnii and all the descendent clans be taught and preserved; and
C. It is the right and freedom of the people that the sacred Diné language (nihiineí) be taught and preserved; and
D. It is the right and freedom of the people that the sacred bonding in marriage and the unity of each family be protected; and
E. It is the right and freedom of the people that every child and every elder be respected, honored and protected with a healthy physical and mental environment, free from all abuse.
F. It is the right and freedom of the people that our children are provided with education to absorb wisdom, self-knowledge, and knowledge to empower them to make a living and participate in the growth of the Navajo Nation.[10]

This chapter works to ensure the language, culture, traditions, and history are taught to the children. While this is an important and worthy goal, it is difficult to implement when most of the schools on the reservation are controlled by non-Diné governmental entities and many families are not teaching the language, culture, and history to their children. In the past, the Navajo Nation Council encouraged schools on the reservation to teach the language, culture, and history without enforcement. All the schools on the reservation are state controlled (public) either by the states of Arizona,

New Mexico, or Utah, federally controlled (Bureau of Indian Education), parochial controlled (churches), or are contract grant schools where the funding comes from the federal government and the schools adhere to state and federal standards. A few schools have been able to implement Diné language, culture, and history courses, but when they do offer these courses, they are electives and not part of the core curriculum.

Navajo Preparatory School in Farmington, New Mexico does offer Diné language and history courses as part of their curriculum along with the mandatory courses of English, math, social studies, and science; however, it is a small private school, where about twenty to thirty students graduate each year. By far, the majority of Diné students attend public schools on the reservation and many of those schools only offer Diné language and history as an elective.

The other difficulty of achieving what is stated in the customary law is many families do not want their children to learn their distinct language, culture, and history. Many of these families believe by learning the language, culture, and history they will be holding back their children from being successful in the larger society. While this attitude is not new, it is still very prevalent in many Diné people's thinking. While a growing number of Diné people are advocating for the language to be taught to the younger generation today, it has not resulted in a growing number of fluent speakers for the past twenty years. In the next twenty years, we will see if the language revitalization movements taking place in many communities in Indian Country, including Diné, will build a critical mass of fluent tribal speakers.

In section E of the fourth chapter, it states children and elders should be respected, honored, and protected. They are to be free from all abuse. In many Native communities including the Navajo reservation, children, women, and elders are being physically, verbally, and mentally abused.[11] It is a continuing and debilitating problem. Diné communities are trying to resolve this but it is a challenge. The abuses to children, women, and the elderly are a consequence of American colonization on Indigenous peoples. The historical trauma of what occurred at Fort Sumner and the devastation of livestock reduction in the 1930s continue to impact the Navajo Nation. While the Navajo government recognizes this and wants the people to have the right and freedom to be respected and protected, the problem has yet to be resolved.

Chapter five focuses on Diné natural law, Nahasdzaan doo Yadilhil Bits'aadee Beehaz'áanii. In this chapter, air, light/fire, water, earth/pollen, the six sacred mountains, and the attendant mountains all must be respected, honored, and protected. All of creation on earth and in the universe has a right and freedom to exist and the Diné people have a sacred obligation and duty to respect, preserve, and protect all.

Diné CARE, Black Mesa Water Coalition, and ENDAUM use the natural law chapter in their work to protect the land from pollutants including the Navajo Nation Council itself. As stated earlier, the council and the court system criticize these groups mainly in terms of how they are interpreting the natural law chapter.

In section E of the chapter, it states, "Mother Earth and Father Sky is part of us as the Diné and the Diné is part of Mother Earth and Father Sky; the Diné must treat this sacred bond with love and respect without exerting dominance for we do not own our mother or father." In analyzing this section, Diné people are not to dominate over any part of the earth or sky in any matter whatsoever, including extracting natural resources from the earth. In contrast, section F states, "The rights and freedoms of the people to the use of the sacred elements of life as mentioned above and to the use of the land, natural resources, sacred sites and other living beings must be accomplished through the proper protocol of respect and offering, and these practices must be protected and preserved for they are the foundation of our spiritual ceremonies and the Diné life way."

Section F allows the government and the people to benefit from the natural resource extraction through a proper protocol of respect and offering. While many if not all Indigenous peoples have the same ethical approach when it comes to the usage of natural resources, in many cases concerning the Navajo Nation, non-Indigenous peoples and entities are the ones who are extracting the natural resources without proper protocol of respect and offering. The Navajo Nation along with other Indigenous nations in the United States have decided to work with corporations, state governments, local municipalities, and the federal government to receive royalties from companies who are extracting natural gas, oil, coal, timber, and uranium from their lands. While history shows Indigenous nations had no choice when these operations started in the twentieth century, the Navajo Nation and other Native nations do have a choice now, and it appears the Navajo Nation Council has decided to continue with the natural resource approach to ensure economic stability.

In section G of the fifth chapter, it states the Diné people have a duty and responsibility to protect and preserve the beauty of the natural world for future generations. The people and families who are working against uranium and coal mining and the opening of a new coal-fired power plant are trying hard to convince the President and the council to take this last section of the Diné natural law to heart. They want the Navajo Nation to live by these standards rather than concerning themselves with economic development projects that contravene Fundamental Laws. It is a challenge but there are positive signs it is working.

In 2005, the Navajo Nation banned all uranium mining activities within the reservation boundaries and for the past four years the tribal government has been fighting to protect Dook'o'oosłííd, San Francisco Peaks in Flagstaff, Arizona, from the usage of treated waste water to make snow for the Snow Bowl ski facility. The tribal government is also interested in developing a wind turbine project outside of Flagstaff to generate power for communities and homes on the reservation.[12] However, the President and the council fully support the Desert Rock Energy Project.

Chapter six is on Diyin Nohookáá Diné Bi Beehaz'áanii (Common law). This chapter is the shortest of the chapters. It is also a reflection of how life is today in the twenty-first century and of the constant interactions with other peoples. It states:

Diné Common Law declares and teaches that:

A. The knowledge, wisdom, and practices of the people must be developed and exercised in harmony with the values and principles of the Diné Bi Beenahaz'áanii; and in turn, the written laws of the Navajo Nation must be developed and interpreted in harmony with Diné Common Law; and

B. The values and principles of Diné Common Law must be recognized, respected, honored, and trusted as the motivational guidance for the people and their leaders in order to cope with the complexities of the changing world, the need to compete in business to make a living and the establishment and maintenance of decent standards of living; and

C. The values and principles of Diné Common Law must be used to harness and utilize the unlimited interwoven Diné knowledge, with our absorbed knowledge from other peoples. This knowledge is our tool in exercising and exhibiting self-assurance and self-reliance and in enjoying the beauty of happiness and harmony.[13]

All written laws in the Navajo Nation Code are presumed to follow Diné Common Law. In 2005, the Navajo Nation Council overrode the President's veto of the Diné Marriage Act. The Diné

Marriage Act of 2005 voided and prohibited plural marriages, marriages between relatives, and marriages between persons of the same sex. The legislation intent is to promote strong families and preserve and strengthen family values. The definition of strong families and family values was never explained in the legislation. If this marriage act is supposed to reflect Diné Common Law, the question of how beauty and harmony, which is the essence of the Fundamental Laws, is maintained with a law based on a foreign culture needs to be explained.

In the act under plural marriages, it states, "All plural marriages contracted, whether or not in accordance with Diné custom, shall be void and prohibited." This statement reveals the impact of other beliefs, values, and worldviews distinct from the Fundamental Laws. While Diné Common Law allows for the absorption of other people's knowledge to help exercise and exhibit self-assurance and self-reliance, it does not reflect enjoying the beauty of happiness and harmony in relation to Diné thought. If the government denies a part of the culture and history of the people, does it mean all parts of Diné culture and history are renounced? The Fundamental Laws of the Diné do not reflect this nullification but the actions of the government appear not to be in compliance with the FLD in relation to the Diné Marriage Act of 2005. It appears to be a reflection of the influences of Christianity, Western thought, twenty-first-century life ways, and a distinct perspective not reflective of past Diné custom and tradition.

In 2004, the people voted to expand gaming. Prior to 2004, the electorate voted twice against the production of casinos and gaming within the boundaries of the Navajo Nation. When Joe Shirley was elected President of the Navajo Nation in 2002, he along with the council pushed for the building of casinos. In 2003, they announced gaming operations would commence soon and by 2004, a referendum on whether or not to expand gaming passed. President Shirley and the council were not going to retreat from the gaming operation. The people could not voice their opinion against the gaming operation in the referendum. It was going to happen. It did. Fire Rock Casino, east of Gallup, New Mexico, opened in November 2008.

According to the Navajo Nation, it had a very successful first year.[14] The majority of the customers are Diné and the majority of the employees are Diné as well. Plans for additional gaming enterprises are in preparation now. An announcement was sent out in February 2010 for architectural design plans for a casino and hotel in Fruitland, New Mexico between Shiprock and Farmington. The Navajo Nation expects to operate six gaming facilities, two in New Mexico and four in Arizona, by the end of 2012.

In Diné Common Law, the need to compete in business for sustenance is acknowledged and encouraged. The casino operations as well as other business enterprises are supposed to create self-reliant individuals and communities and in turn a self-sufficient Navajo Nation. This self-sufficient approach is also expected to produce self-assured peoples resulting in the creation of a happy and harmonious Diné society. While some enterprises appear to be working out very well such as the Fire Rock casino operation and the Navajo Agricultural Products Industry, the jury is still out as to whether it has created a self-sufficient Navajo Nation and if all the people are happy and in harmony with life.

The last part of the Fundamental Laws is a diagram of a Diné original law structure. The structure has a distinct Diné perspective many people might misinterpret. If you view the diagram from a Western perspective, it appears to be a hierarchy in which the people are on top, leaders beneath the people, next the laws, and then under the specifics of the laws: traditional, customary, natural, and common. This is not an incorrect interpretation from a Western perspective, but if you examine the diagram from a Diné angle, you will observe a distinct historical outlook on Diné governance.

The law structure should be viewed as a circular motion. Traditional law, customary law, natural law, and common law are the essential elements of life and these elements help the people live in this world. The people are not above the laws but rather live by them. The laws set a path for which the people follow to ensure happiness, prosperity, and harmony. By diverging from these laws, challenges and difficulties will ensue for the people. The diagram is a creative metaphor to which Diné people can refer to for clarity and meaning.

These are the chapters of the Fundamental Laws. These ethical laws designed for the people to live by in this world. In the twenty-first century, several different worldviews impact how Diné people think and act in this world. These worldviews create a distinct Diné society, which produced changes in how the people live. What does this mean for the Fundamental Laws fifty years, one hundred years, two hundred years, and five hundred years from now? If you examine the last five hundred years of Diné history, you can form a preliminary prospect on what the future holds.

CHANGE AND MODERNITY

Council delegate Raymond Joe wanted the Fundamental Laws repealed. He was successful in limiting their recognition and usage. The Navajo Nation Supreme Court stated environmental organizations such as Diné CARE and Dooda Desert Rock do not interpret the Fundamental Laws correctly. Some Diné people are not exactly sure of the meaning of the Fundamental Laws. Most likely, medicine people are probably saying to themselves this is why we do not codify FLD. Still, some people do not even know about the Fundamental Laws. Instead, what we have is a society in a state of disorientation and in need of clarity when it comes to the Fundamental Laws.

The Navajo Nation has socio-economic challenges such as poverty, unemployment, domestic violence, gang violence, and health problems to name a few. The Fundamental Laws are designed to prevent these socio-economic challenges. While the laws have only been codified recently, these standards have been around since the beginning of time. In 2010, Diné society is radically different. Does this excuse why all people do not follow these laws? No. Is it the responsibility of all people to know the FLD and to live by them today? If the Navajo Nation believes these laws will help the people overcome many of the socio-economic challenges today, it might be advantageous to do so.

Meanwhile, many Diné people are impacted by their experiences living in an American world distinct from a Diné matrix in which these laws originated. The current situation is that these laws are not taught to the children and Western education has taken over as the dominant form of teaching in Diné society. Some families think the schools can teach the language, culture, and history. Other families do not teach their children any Diné knowledge. They may believe Western knowledge is the only teaching the children need to know. Diné, and in general Indigenous, knowledge is in tension with change and modernity today. What does the future hold for Diné and all Indigenous knowledge? The tension between Indigenous knowledge and modernity exemplifies the need for intergenerational communication in Indigenous communities.

Diné elders can teach the younger generation the cultural knowledge that has sustained Diné identity. The younger generation can learn this knowledge to help them overcome the challenges facing them in the twenty-first century. This type of intergenerational communication is key to maintaining and revitalizing Diné knowledge. While language revitalization programs today are in various Diné communities, people will not know their success until another generation or two. Furthermore, Diné cultural knowledge might not be taught at the same time.

Presently, families predominantly teach cultural knowledge and many schools might not have the resources to do this presently. Furthermore, schools on the reservation have to follow the same educational standards as other public schools in the country. The Fundamental Laws are not part of the core curriculum. Navajo government implemented these laws to ensure continuation; yet, it is the individual's responsibility to learn FLD. Hopefully, more and more people will learn the meaning of the FLD and teach it. Indigenous knowledge and more specifically Diné knowledge is a factor in maintaining Indigenous and Diné identity.

Because of the actions by the Navajo Nation Council to codify the Fundamental Laws, more Diné and non-Diné people know about them. The laws have become an important tool for the people; they are using these laws to hold the government accountable for their actions. Joe might interpret this as abusing the intention of these laws, but the people, who utilize the laws to help them fight for these causes, might view it as actually abiding by these laws. These laws will continue to be interpreted in different ways for the coming years, and the council might fully repeal them but these laws will not disappear. The laws' heart has not succumbed to changes, modernity, and colonization. While some people are not clear on how to use these laws in an era of modernity, the laws do not change meaning. Natural law, common law, customary law, and traditional law are older than the U.S. government and the U.S. Constitution. While the current Navajo Nation government is fairly young, the Fundamental Laws the people live by and follow do not change with time. Modernity has altered how Diné people think today but it has not altered the Fundamental Laws. The people will live by the Fundamental Laws as long as the earth is alive. That has not changed and it will remain. Diné people can realize this; and conceivably, this realization will lead to a place where the Navajo Nation as a whole will live, govern, and follow the Fundamental Laws as their ancestors did in the past.

NOTES

1. See *Wagner v. Tsosie*.
2. See Powell and Curley (2008).
3. See Navajo Nation Council (2009, July 23).
4. Read Fundamental Laws of the Diné (Navajo Nation Code, 2002).
5. Read Fundamental Laws of the Diné (Navajo Nation Code, 2002).
6. Read Fundamental Laws of the Diné (Navajo Nation Code, 2002).
7. See Shebala (2009, November 12).
8. See Shebala (2009, October 29).
9. See Shebala (2009, November 12).
10. Read Fundamental Laws of the Diné (Navajo Nation Code, 2002).
11. See Amnesty International USA, *Maze of Injustice: The Failure to Protect Indigenous Women from Sexual Violence in the USA*.[[Au: the details not listed in the reference list]]
12. See Wagner and Randazzo (2008, March 28).
13. Read Fundamental Laws of the Diné (Navajo Nation Code, 2002).
14. See Donovan (2009, November 5).

REFERENCES

Donovan, B. (2009, November 5). A first good year for Fire Rock. *The Navajo Times*, pp. A–51, A–55.
Navajo Nation Code. (2002). *Fundamental Laws of the Diné.* Window Rock, AZ: Author.
Navajo Nation Council. (2009, July 23). Navajo Nation Council completes final day of 2009 summer session. News release.

O'Brien, S. (1993). *American Indian Tribal Governments*. Norman, OK: University of Oklahoma Press.

Powell, D. E., & Curley, A. (2008). K'e, Hozhó, and non-governmental politics on the Navajo Nation: Ontologies of difference manifest in environmental activism. *Anthropological Quarterly, 81*, 17–58.

Shebala, M. (2009, October 29). Ethics panel kills subpoena for discretionary funds records. *The Navajo Times*, p. A–54.

Shebala, M. (2009, November 12). Slush funds total over $35 million. The *Navajo Times*, pp. A–51, A–53.

Wagner, D., & Randazzo, R. (2008, March 28). Navajos set to tap power of the wind. *The Arizona Republic*.

Wagner v. Tsosie. (2007). Navajo Nation Supreme Court No. SC-CV-01–07.

Wilkins, D. E. (2003). *The Navajo Political Experience*. Lanham, MD: Rowman & Littlefield.

SECTION IV

Indigenous Knowledge, Education and Science: Beyond the Formal Curriculum

As already noted, until quite recently, the implications of Indigenous knowledges and philosophies for schooling and education in Euro-American contexts have largely been ignored or under-explored. Yet such knowledges have important educative value for learners. Therefore, how can we read such knowledges politically, practically and pedagogically to envision new and different forms of schooling and education for youth? What are the lessons Indigenous knowledges can offer for transforming our current school systems? Is there a link between Indigenous knowledge and science education? How can we conceptualize Indigenous Knowledge as Indigenous Science for teaching about science, health, culture, arts and technology? What contributions can local cultural resource knowledge bring to re-visioning genuine educational options for youth? And, what are the pedagogic, instructional and communicative relevance of Indigenous philosophies, including story forms, oral and communicative practices? These are some of the tough questions that this section addresses. We do not presume to have any easy answers to these questions. What we do know is that there is an urgency for an intellectual politics of disengaging from a colonial educational legacy. The colonial paradigm of the production, interrogation, validation and dissemination of knowledge needs to be replaced. The focus on Indigenous knowledge has a politics that envisions a system of education in Indigenous traditions and philosophies at par with mainstream education. Indigenous perspectives are founded upon and express thoughts about the ways of life, traditions and cultures of local peoples. All learners can, and do, benefit from such knowledge.

All communities have their own active knowledge base, rooted in their local histories, cultures, cultural memories, identities, languages, cosmologies, and epistemologies which actively nourish and inform social awareness and collective existence. We must revision schooling and education in ways that provide learners with the means to maintain, deepen, renew and expand the frontiers of their own knowledge rooted in history, language, culture identity and politics. For example, the knowledge, awareness, consciousness one's language, culture, traditions, and history can be empowering in healing the words of Eurocentricity. As already noted in Section Two the education of today's learner must recognize the existence of Indigenous knowledge as an epistemology, a way of knowing and a set of discursive practices that not only challenge dominant knowledge systems but offer specific forms of knowledge production in themselves. Teaching about Indigenous knowledge requires paying attention to such issues as pluralities and multiplicities of knowledges and the recognition of the contested representations of such knowledge systems.

In the search for knowledge synthesis in school systems there are some questions for us to ponder over: How do we embrace multiple knowledges through an anti-colonial approach to theorizing colonial and re-colonial relations and what are the implications of imperial structures on processes of knowledge production, interrogation, validation and dissemination, as well as the critical understanding of Indigeneity and the pursuit of agency, resistance and subjective politics? How does a critical anti-colonial discursive lens center the complex ways colonial and re-colonial relations and projects manifesting themselves in variegated ways, forms and context in contemporary contexts (e.g., schools)? There are long standing legitimate Indigenous claims that Western systems of knowledge (e.g., intellectual property rights) do not adequately provide for the protection of Indigenous culture, heritage and art, so: What would be an appropriate anti-colonial education involving effective classroom pedagogies and instruction grounded in Indigenous ways of knowing and social practice in a way that protects the ownership and integrity of the knowledges? In what ways can we harmonize Western and Indigenous knowledge systems to maintain the integrity of different knowledge systems, especially respecting the traditions and local cultural resource base of Indigenous peoples? How do we move toward a critical dialogue of knowledge systems and the creation of space for mutual engagement between Indigenous and other knowledge traditions in the context of asymmetrical power relations?

In his paper, "Bringing the Experience of Indigenous Peoples into Schools" Gregory Smith rightly argues that formal education has not paid adequate attention to the knowledge systems and cultural practices of Indigenous peoples. Formal school systems as central tools of colonization have subtly and sometimes brutally stripped learners' experience of their natal/home cultures. This problem has in large measure accounted for the rejection of mainstream schooling and its lessons by Indigenous children. This rejection has manifested itself in the rising dropout rates for Indigenous learners higher than for other groups in the United States general population. Fortunately, the last decades have seen efforts to redress and reverse the trend. Educators in Alaska, Arizona, and Hawaii have been experimenting with approaches that dilute the colonizing message of schools by bringing Indigenous knowledge systems and cultures into the classroom. These approaches are giving young Indigenous learners service and leadership opportunities aimed at drawing them into a sense of social affiliation and efficacy. As a result students in these schools are demonstrating higher levels of academic engagement, achievement, and connection to their communities. Equally important is that there are reciprocal benefits to local communities from which these young learners come from.

Judy Iseke and Brennus BMJK's chapter on "Learning Life Lessons from Indigenous Storytelling with Tom McCallum" examines how oral storytelling can be pedagogical tools for learning about one's life through critical interpretation and engagement in the storytelling process. Tom McCallum, a Métis Elder and a Sun Dance lodge keeper, tells three stories: first, *Falling Through the Ice and the Sun Dance Tree* and its second part *Sun Dance Story about the Meaning of Life;* and two humorous stories, *Humorous Horse Story* and *Dancing Dog Story.* The pedagogic, instructional and communication relevance and implications of these stories are highlighted. The authors discuss the epistemology informing the research methodology, the importance of Elders as keepers and teachers of knowledge, and the respectful protocol for research with Elders are discussed. It is noted that Tom and other important Elders have agreed to have their stories and the wisdom from these stories taped and shared so that their knowledge is not lost and is passed on for others of their community to learn and grow as people and community. Stories are real learning tools. By examining the pedagogy of stories from not only the writers' perspectives but from many perspectives we can better interpret our lives.

Chin, et als. paper "*Ua Lele Ka Manu*; The Bird Has Flown: A Search for Hawaiian Indigenous/Local Inquiry Methods," notes that although Indigenous Hawaiian students are the majority in many rural schools where farming, fishing, and hunting continue to update and augment traditional ecological knowledge they are persistently underrepresented in college preparatory science courses. The students have few role models in science, technology, engineering, and mathematics careers. The problem is that public schools follow Western science models that have historically marginalized Indigenous inquiry perspectives and practices. The paper discusses how ten educators, 8 Indigenous Hawaiian, sought a shared understanding of Indigenous inquiry methods in order to apply them in professional development programs. They share their own Indigenous inquiry endeavors in community and school settings and how they employed Indigenous knowledge as a foundation for student inquiry. Five themes emerged, four supporting and one impeding Indigenous inquiry in mainstream educational settings. Indigenous narratives, identity, sense of place, and ability to connect science to Indigenous practices supported Indigenous inquiry, but school schedules/policies and teachers' lack of knowledge of Indigenous culture and inquiry methods presented barriers to school implementation. It is argued that Indigenous inquiry as a "cultural template" is characterized by 4 cultural elements: 1) Indigenous sense of place, 2) *mālama*, caring for a familiar place; 3) *kuleana*, recognizing that rights to resources entail responsibility; and 4) conducting inquiry with appropriate protocols. The authors conclude with a call to reestablish *Mālama I Ka 'Āina*, Sustainability as a science content standard that recognizes the historical, place-based development of Indigenous inquiry and supports systems thinking, problem solving, and civic action.

Njoki Wane in her paper, "*The Kenyan Herbalist Ruptures the Status Quo in Health and Healing*" looks at Indigenous healing in the context of rural Kenya. Through qualitative interviews with healers/herbalists and lay people she highlight specific practices and epistemological underpinnings of African Indigenous healing and its contribution to contemporary healing knowledge in Kenya. The analysis is located in African philosophical principles which speak to local beliefs systems, values, signs and symbols of traditional healing practice. It is argued that in order to make sense of African healing practices one needs to understand the worldview of African peoples and the complex interplay of society, culture and nature. Traditional African healing knowledge is acquired through intuition, practice, spiritual guidance and apprenticeship. Healing traditions are passed from one generation to the next through visions, stories and dreams and healing practices rely on observation and experience. These ways of knowledge and knowledge transmission constitute Indigenous systems of knowing of local communities.

In "'Glocalising' Indigenous Knowledges for the Classroom" Ocean Ripeka Mercier focuses on the pedagogy of Indigenous Knowledge. *MAOR317: Science and Indigenous Knowledge* is a Victoria University of Wellington Māori Studies course that introduces students to narratives and literatures on or related to Indigenous Knowledge (IK). It also presents students with the challenge of exploring the interface between 'Indigenous' and 'Western' knowledge and science through various classroom activities and assignments. Mercier reflects on the ideological challenges of designing and teaching a University course labelled "Indigenous Knowledge," in light of cautions against taking

IK out of context, generalising it and attempting to define it. She presents 'glo-**c**-alising' as an alternative to generalising. Glocalising acknowledges the local perspective of the generaliser, but also anticipates that generalisation is done in order to better understand a local context. The author then discusses examples of "our classroom glocalisations" where she has synthesised, reorganised and systematised features of different local IK systems, and as a way to then reapply those glocalisations to better understand local cases. It is noted that a glocalising approach helps to mediate the limitations of the 'Western' academy as a space for teaching IK. The paper concludes with some comments on what the students and the teacher (don't) get from learning about IK in the university.

Lyn Carter's paper, "The Challenges of Science Education and Indigenous Knowledge" notes that globalisation and its attendant acknowledgment of diversity have meant that Indigenous knowledges have become increasingly prominent in many educational disciplines including that of science education. Consequently, questions about the ways in which science should be conceptualised and represented within science education not only invite debate about the epistemological parity between Western science and other non-Western sciences and Indigenous knowledges, but also, promote reflection on moral and value imperatives. Too often though, science education, like Western modern science (WMS), continues to portray itself as universal, value free and objective even as it attempts to include some Indigenous knowledges within its field. The paper traces the cultural diversity scholarship within science education that includes issues of Indigenous knowledge, suggesting that we must be vigilant to avoid new forms of colonization that may flow from how Indigenous knowledge is appropriated and represented. The author goes further to utilize the newer theorisations on postcolonialism and epistemological diversity to see how they may contribute to the development of a truly decolonising science education.

CHAPTER FIFTEEN

Bringing the Experience of Indigenous People into Alaska Rural Systematic Initiative/Alaska Native Knowledge Network

GREGORY SMITH

Schools in the United States have been notably unsuccessful in their effort to educate Native American students. Graduation rates for young people indigenous to this continent and the Hawaiian Islands are lower than for any other population group—50 percent compared to 76 percent for Asian Americans, 75 per cent for White students, 55 percent for Hispanic, and 51 percent for African Americans (Alliance for Excellent Education, 2009). These numbers are often interpreted as a sign of individual failure or of deficits associated with poverty or cultural background. Only rarely do educators or the general public grasp the possibility that these statistics might instead be indicative of a more active decision on the part of students to reject the knowledge and skills they encounter in school.

Researchers such as John Ogbu (1978) and Paul Willis (1981) have observed similar responses on the part of groups denied full participation in society because of their race or social class as well as prior defeat by a colonizing group. Never deeply questioning the purpose or nature of formal schooling, however, Ogbu and, to a lesser extent, Willis tend to see this rejection as more self-defeating than empowering, a form of false consciousness that hurts resistant students more than it helps them. Such was not the case two and a half centuries ago when a group of Native American leaders declined an invitation to send their young people to the College of William and Mary in Virginia:

> Several of our young people were formerly brought up at the Colleges . . .; but, when they came back to us, they were bad Runners, ignorant of every means of living in the Woods, unable to bear either Cold or Hunger, knew neither how to build a Cabin, take a Deer, or kill an Enemy, spoke our Language imperfectly,. . .were totally good for nothing. . . .(Smyth, 1907, pp. 98–99)

Such is not the case, as well, with contemporary Yup'ik educator Oscar Kawagley who observes that

> By not teaching the Yupiaq youngsters their own language and way of doing things, the classroom teachers are telling them that their language, knowledge and skills are of little importance. The students begin to think of themselves as being less than other people. After all, they are expected to learn through a language other than their own, to learn values that are in conflict with their own, and to learn a "better" way of seeing and doing things. They are taught the "American Dream" which, in their case, is largely unattainable without leaving behind who they are. (Kawagley, 1999, pp. 18–19)

For Kawagley, a more appropriate response can be found in the creation of another kind of education (see below), one that affirms the wholeness and competence of Indigenous students while enhancing the relationship they experience with their natal community and place on the planet. Such an education would support rather than deny the cultural experiences of Indigenous students.

In their 2001 volume, *Power and Place: Indian Education in America,* Vine Deloria and Peter Wildcat suggest that affirming Indigenous students' wholeness and competence may also require identifying the way mainstream American culture and education violate a number of principles encountered in Native American societies. The preoccupation with individual competition and mobility in typical U.S. classrooms, for example, runs counter to the way that personality in Indigenous societies is tied to membership in a specific community and the responsibilities associated with this membership. In addition, the focus on universal principles in most schools and the assumption that these principles are applicable in all places stands in opposition to the Indigenous understanding that the world is extraordinarily diverse—geographically, historically, and biologically. Instead of thinking that there is only one way to do things, it makes more sense to encourage a multiversity of responses. Such responses, furthermore, are more likely to be appropriate when human beings develop a finely tuned attentiveness to the natural and social environments in which they live their lives, an attentiveness cultivated through direct experience rather than an experience of the world mediated through books and visual media encountered in most classrooms. For Deloria and Wildcat, Indigenous education should aim to

> . . . expand the ability of children to experience the world—the world they are a part of as their home, an environment or refuge of happiness (with hard work) and love (with respect). We can and must educate a generation of children who find home in the landscape and ecologies they inhabit. (p. 70)

An education that leads Indigenous students to feel at home in the world rather than alienated from it seems more likely to be embraced than rejected; this is an education, however, that runs contrary to the kind of schooling commonly found in the United States that diminishes for all students a sense of relationship to any community or place in the interest of preparing them to join a competitive market society.

In his article, "The Best of Both Worlds: A Critical Pedagogy of Place," educator David Gruenewald (2003) suggests a way that Kawagley's concern about cultural restoration can be conjoined with a Deloria and Wildcat's critique of mainstream American values and perspectives. There he argues that an education grounded in local culture and issues—an approach to teaching and learning called place- and community-based education—can be linked to efforts to help students understand their capacity to challenge generally unquestioned social norms and to shape their cultural experiences in ways that will be more beneficial for themselves and their communities. Embarking on that process, especially for Indigenous students, will require a process of decolonization. Decolonization involves confronting elements in one's social life that are oppressive and restrictive, naming these, and then taking steps to alter them. Paulo Freire (1993) used the term conscientization to describe what it means to grasp and then make use of one's power as a culture shaper. In addition to critiquing oppressive aspects of social life, altering those conditions requires what Gruenewald calls reinhabitation—an active effort to conserve, restore, and create relationships with people and place that support the health of human and natural communities. For Gruenewald, and for me, this dual approach has relevance for all students, not only those from historically oppressed communities. In some respects, all population groups in the United States have been inducted into an economic and political system that restricts their life options and diminishes their relationship to particular communities and places. Place- and community-based educational approaches, however, are especially relevant to Indigenous students who have been the victims of more explicit forms of colonization.

During the past two to three decades, Indigenous peoples in some parts of the United States and elsewhere have been regaining authority over the process by which their children are being educated. Sometimes on their own, sometimes in conjunction with Euro-American colleagues, they have been either remaking or establishing schools to better meet the needs of their own children. In doing so, they have integrated elements of Indigenous culture into school settings in ways that are challenging the dominance of conventional curricular and pedagogical models. Although not necessarily informed by Gruenewald's perspectives about decolonization and reinhabitation, their work demonstrates how both of these elements of a more humane and place-centered educational approach can be implemented.

In what follows, I will describe in more detail four initiatives of different scope that I have become familiar with through conversations with educators involved in these reforms, school visits, or research tied into writing projects about place- and community-based education, the central focus of my own scholarly agenda. My selection of these examples is a result more of serendipity than a systematic review of literature, but each demonstrates in different ways possibilities that have significant promise for Indigenous students growing up at the beginning of the 21st century.

Alaska Rural Systemic Initiative/Alaska Native Knowledge Network

For the decade between 1995 and 2005, Alaska was the site of a multi-million dollar effort to address the experience of rejection by far too many Alaska Native students enrolled in the state's educational system. Co-led by Oscar Kawagley (mentioned earlier) and Ray Barnhardt, educators at the University of Alaska-Fairbanks, the Alaska Rural Systemic Initiative (AKRSI) supported by the National Science Foundation and the Annenberg Rural Challenge-funded Alaska Native Knowledge Network (ANKN) sought to improve the academic performance of Alaska Native students and to attract more of them into scientific vocations by diminishing the division that existed between students' lives outside of school and what they encountered within the classroom. These dual initiatives were implemented in 20 rural school districts that enrolled approximately 19,000 students. Ninety percent of the students in these districts are Alaska Native with the remaining 10 percent made up of White, Asian, and Black students (Hill, Kawagley, & Barnhardt, 2006).

Specific reform efforts associated with AKRSI and the ANKN grew out of conversations with Alaska Native communities throughout the state. Serious attention was directed to the fact that Indigenous peoples in Alaska come from diverse tribal and cultural backgrounds. Regardless of these significant differences, participants were able to craft a set of standards for "culturally responsive schools." Subsequently adopted by the Alaska Department of Education, these standards have served as a foundation for much of the work that has emerged from this reform process. The standards were articulated for students, educators, schools, curricula, and communities. Standards for teachers include the following broad categories:

A. Culturally-responsive educators incorporate local ways of knowing and teaching in their work.
B. Culturally-responsive educators use the local environment and community resources on a regular basis to link what they are teaching to the everyday lives of the students.
C. Culturally-responsive educators participate in community events and activities in an appropriate and supportive way.
D. Culturally-responsive educators work closely with parents to achieve a high level of complementary educational expectations between home and school.
E. Culturally-responsive educators recognize the full educational potential of each student and provide the challenges necessary for them to achieve that potential. (Assembly of Alaska Native Educators, 1998).

These standards were aimed at encouraging teachers to move away from simply teaching about cultural heritage as a subject in the curriculum to using local culture as the basis for their educational decisions and activities.

As the authors of the standards write, "It is intended that all forms of knowledge, ways of knowing and world views be recognized as equally valid, adaptable and complementary to one another in mutually beneficial ways" (Assembly of Alaska Native Educators, 1998, p. 3). Such a position challenges the often unquestioned assumption that the ways of knowing and worldview associated with Western civilization are superior to the ways of knowing and worldviews encountered among other cultural groups. The process of decolonization demands the willingness to take this step.

A range of projects and activities has helped educators translate this ambitious goal into classroom practice. Central to the work of the Alaska Rural Systemic Initiative and the Alaska Native Knowledge Network has been the creation of lesson plans that demonstrate how to incorporate aspects of students' outside-of-school lives into the teaching of the conventional curriculum. *Village Math* (Dick, 2003) and *Village Science* (Dick, 1997) are two of the volumes written as part of this reform effort. With regard to mathematics, for example, students are asked to use algebra to determine how much oil per gallon should be used in a two-cycle engine if the suggested ratio is 20:1, 50:1, or 100:1; another problem requires them to figure out how much it costs to run different common household appliances such as a coffee maker or skill saw. Lessons like these demonstrate to young people that there is a place for them and the lives they and their families lead within the context of the curriculum.

Lessons from *Village Science* build on extended conversations with Alaska Native elders about traditional knowledge regarding the local landscape and its resources and are categorized under the following broad topics:

- Skills, tools, and craftsmanship
- Shelters
- Ways and means of travel

(Dick, *Village Science*, retrieved from http://ankn.uaf.edu/publications/VS/ on January 4, 2010)

Among the topics included under "shelters" are insulation and vapor barriers. A vapor barrier in the form of a properly installed sheet of visquine can make the difference between a well-insulated and long-lasting house and one that is chilly and rots quickly. Grasping why a vapor barrier is important involves understanding the relationship between wood, oxygen, water, heat, and the effect of bacteria on wood fibers. In addition to learning how contemporary people use visquine to create a vapor barrier, students also learn how traditional sod roofs can achieve the same result. Two learning activities from this unit include:

- While in a warm house, close the cover on a jar. Bring the jar outside or put it in a freezer. Is there condensation inside the jar when it is cooled? Bring the jar into the warm house again. What happens?
- How are winter shoe packs with felt liners like a wall without a vapor barrier? What happens in very cold weather when you try to take the liners out of the boots after wearing them all day? Why does this happen? Can you think of a way of preventing this?

(Dick, *Village Science,* retrieved at http://ankn.uaf.edu/publications/VS/insulation.html on January 4, 2010)

Through activities like these, students are able to see the relationship between formal academic learning and the requirements of life in rural Alaska.

The lessons found in *Village Math* and *Village Science* and other curricular materials developed by AKRSI and ANKN grew out several "Academies of Elders." During these Academies, Elders and scientists would share their knowledge of some element of the local environment with teachers who would then translate what they had learned into lessons or units. Their work would then be checked for accuracy with the Elders and the scientists and later field tested with students (Hill, Kawagley, Barnhardt, 2006, p. 7). Units developed in this way focused on many thematic areas: among these were weather forecasting, animal behavior, navigation skills, observations, pattern recognition, food preservation and preparation of plants, star knowledge, waste disposal, and counting systems.

With regard to the humanities, teachers were encouraged to engage their students in the creation of "cultural atlases." This task requires students to engage in inquiry activities related to a wide variety of topics including " . . . life histories, genealogies, place-names, language documentation, uses of local flora and fauna, subsistence practices, community histories, traditional arts and crafts, mapping projects, and weather knowledge" (Barnhardt, 2008, pp. 125–126). Frequently, materials collected by students would be made available on the Internet. For example, eighth graders in the Yup'ik village of Kasigluk in southwest Alaska created a website that presented information about their school, the Yup'ik Studies Program there, and their community. They collected information and photographs and then learned how to make use of a multimedia lab at the school to post this information on-line. The website, still available at http://www.ankn.uaf.edu/NPE/CulturalAtlases/Yupiaq/Akula/firstpage.html, was written in both the Yup'ik language and English and features information about Eskimo dancing, Yup'ik values, demographics, subsistence, and religion. Scott Christian, an Annenberg research associate who helped coordinate this program observed:

> It was a rare moment to see a student working alone during the week. Typically, there would be two, three, or four students huddled around a computer, or pile of writing or photos. I didn't realize until I talked to John (teacher in the school), that there were mainstreamed special education students in the room, and students with very low proficiency in English. Through the process, students were continually asking each

other's opinions. Many of these conversations were in Yup'ik although they occasionally spoke in English also. We were all amazed with how quickly the students mastered the software: Page Mill and Photoshop. Even though they had never used the software, by the end of the first day, they were experimenting, and teaching me new applications of the programs. (Rural Challenge Research and Evaluation Program, 1999, p. 106).

Collaborative projects such as this one at the Akula School are much more in keeping with the less formal and more personal interactions of Alaska Native communities, something that AKRSI and ANKN also highlighted in their work with teachers and schools. In addition to project-based learning, teachers were encouraged to provide many opportunities for students to learn by doing or observing, again affirming the value of local Indigenous cultures and educational practices. At the Effie Kokrine School, a charter secondary school in Fairbanks that grew out of these initiatives, students have the opportunity to engage in subsistence activities with Elders as part of their academic program and participate in traditional arts and crafts as well as subsistence activities in the field; at the same time, students can gain high school and college credit by taking courses at the local community college or university. Underlying these Alaskan initiatives is a deep commitment to helping students learn how to walk in both worlds, mastering knowledge and skills needed to live successfully in communities committed to the preservation of traditional lifeways and understandings as well as in the classrooms and offices of mainstream institutions.

The final report for these initiatives submitted to the National Science Foundation in 2006 indicates that work to that point had resulted in improved school performance as well as improved academic trajectories for students in participating districts. Although the gap between the performance of Alaska Native students and their White counterparts had not closed in standardized tests of mathematical and reading abilities, students given the opportunity to experience a more culturally responsive education made significant gains (Hill, Kawagley, Barnhardt, 2006). More important is the way these initiatives reduced the inclination of Alaska Native students to reject the kinds of education they encountered in schools that in the past reflected little about the places and the communities they knew as home. By creating a curriculum that includes snowshoe races and the building of fires in the PE curriculum, beading or wood carving in the art classroom, or Alaska Native weather prediction or food preservation practices in science lessons, educators say to students that the school contains a place for their lives and experiences. Students embrace the kind of education they encounter at the Effie Kokrine Charter School, and so do their families. As the grandmother of one of the young men enrolled at the school noted:

> You know, you hear this term, No Child Left Behind. This is the first school that this child has been in that, yes, he has never been left behind. He has always been included in things. He has been taught to enhance his study skills, to enhance his listening skills, the values that our Native people look for: to listen, to learn, and to go out there and be a productive member of the community. And I can actually say that my grandson has accomplished all of those things. ("About Our School: Effie Kokrine Charter School" retrieved at http://ekc.k12northstar.org/about-our-school on February 18, 2010)

This is the true test of whether a school is meeting the needs of the community it serves. Educators in Alaska are demonstrating that it is possible to construct school experiences that build on rather than deny the unique characteristics of students' cultures and communities and by doing so successfully invite more Indigenous children and youth into the demands and opportunities of formal learning. With luck and careful stewardship, this is a lesson that will not be forgotten quickly.

The STAR School, Arizona

I learned of the STAR School from Ray Barnhardt, the aforementioned co-director of the Alaska Rural Systemic Initiative. He had visited the Little Singer School on the Navajo Reservation during his tenure as a board member of the Annenberg Rural Challenge. The principal of the Little Singer School, Mark Sorensen, had also written a successful Rural Challenge grant, and Barnhardt had told me about how impressed he was with educational innovations there. By the time I contacted Sorensen, he and his wife, Kate, had started a new charter school just off the southwest corner of the Navajo Reservation about 30 miles from Flagstaff. I was able to spend a week there in the spring of 2005 and have remained in touch with Sorensen since that time.

Sorensen had come to the Navajo Reservation as a young man and never left. At the time, he was writing a dissertation about the educational experiences of Black and Native American students in the post-American Civil War period. He had intended to spend only a summer in Arizona to gather more first-hand knowledge of the Navajos but instead found his life work there. He taught and then became a school leader, holding positions at a number of reservation schools, including the Rough Rock Community School. Well respected by the Navajos, he was asked a number of years ago to become a community peacemaker.

The STAR School embodies many of the educational reforms started in the 1970s at the Rough Rock Community School. The Rough Rock Community School was one of the first K-12 tribally controlled educational institutions in the United States (McCarty, 2002). It began the process of collecting, selecting, and then integrating the cultural knowledge of Indigenous peoples into the curriculum that inspired the work in Alaska described in the preceding section. Rough Rock also served as a testing ground for the applicability in a Navajo setting of the work of educator Roland Tharp, who with educators Kathryn Au, Cathie Jordan, and Lynn Vogt had developed culturally responsive educational approaches for Native Hawai'ian students at the Kamehameha Schools in Honolulu (see Au, 1980; Jordan, 1985; Tharp, 1989). This effort contributed to the formation of the Center for Research on Education, Diversity, and Excellence (CREDE), now at the University of California-Berkeley, which has served to disseminate Tharp's and others' work, oftentimes with students from Indigenous communities. During my visit to the STAR School, teachers were involved in a long-term effort to help them integrate CREDE-developed approaches into their own classrooms. These approaches will be described in more detail in what follows.

Founded in 2001, the STAR School currently enrolls approximately 120 students, the majority of whom are Navajo. Much of the education young people encounter there is predicated on the Navajo value of *k'e*. The term, *k'e*, denotes clan membership or kinship, referring not only to one's blood relationships but one's relationship to all people and beings. This sense of relatedness permeates the school. Located on 40 brush- and juniper-covered acres on the main road between Flagstaff and the reservation, the school can be identified by a blue tarp that covers an outdoor area behind its brown adobe-like buildings. When Sorensen initially showed me around the school, he explained that the tarp is the school's effort to replicate the traditional Navajo shade house, a simple pole structure roofed with loose branches that provides cover from the sun. This outdoor classroom serves to signal to students that the school is connected to architectural structures with which they are familiar. From a child's first sight of the school, he or she can see its relationship to Navajo communities, a relationship aimed at affirming and working with the strengths of Indigenous communities rather than dominating them through the imposition of values associated with mainstream American society.

Sorensen went on to say that the school property was previously owned by a gentleman who had allowed it to become covered with old machinery and refuse. Children and teachers at the school now strive to make it a place of both beauty and thoughtful stewardship. Pointing out the small junipers that dot the land, Sorensen noted that buildings and paths have been sited to avoid taking out any trees. Later, students in a K-2 class described to me the way they have cared for a juniper on the property that was not thriving. Clearly influenced by the school's concern about vegetation, they had placed recycled cardboard on the ground around its trunk to increase the amount of moisture available to its roots.

Working with a Navajo master gardener skilled in permacultural techniques, students have also shaped gardens to make the best use of the Southwest's limited rainfall and establish an approach to food production that requires few external inputs. By coupling this innovative technique with traditional Navajo water collection strategies, the STAR School is opening up possibilities for agriculture that could potentially increase the range of vegetables available to people in this drought-prone region and enhance their food security. With regard to land use and agriculture, the STAR School is modeling a variety of activities that demonstrate ways that traditional knowledge can be married to Western knowledge to better preserve natural resources and at the same time meet human needs. In this it parallels the educational work in Alaska described in the preceding section.

The STAR School is also experimenting with alternative sources of energy. Surprisingly to an outsider, this region of Arizona is not served by electrical utilities. People either live without electricity or produce their own. Sorensen and his family have lived for a number of years on a small ranch five miles from the school. They have become knowledgeable about the use of solar and wind power and have brought their expertise to the school. A sizeable array of photovoltaic cells has been built just south of the school's gardens. This array produces all of the school's electricity, which is stored in a collection of batteries for days when the sun is not shining. The school has recently installed windmills to supplement solar power. These technologies provide valuable learning opportunities for students and also demonstrate for the broader community the possibility of introducing similar systems for homes that are off the grid.

In addition to its attention to environmental issues, the STAR School—whose acronym stands for Service To All Relations—strives to affirm students' relationship with their own communities, integrating into its curriculum multiple opportunities for students to serve others. Earlier in the year before my visit, middle school students had visited the homes of elders on the reservation where they distributed baked goods and helped with household chores. In the spring, K-2 students had taken offshoots of spider plants they had been cultivating, potted them, and then distributed the fledgling plants to other "grandmas" and "grandpas."

One of the most striking examples of this service ethic I was able to observe involved the development of a plan to address litter in Leupp, a reservation community 17 miles away that is home to many of the school's students. Relentless wind the previous two days had strewn loose trash in brush throughout the village. When asked by their teacher how they could help Mother Earth, the children developed a plan to deal with the problem. One girl, whose grandmother regularly took her and her sisters to serve food at the Chapter House—Leupp's equivalent to a city council—thought that it might be possible for students to get on the agenda for an upcoming meeting. With this in mind, they then participated in a "Think, Pair, Share" activity during which they discussed the question: "How can we help Leupp deal with the trash problem?" For two minutes students paired up and considered possibilities. When a timer buzzed, they quickly redirected their attention to the center of the room and contributed ideas about enlisting the aid of students at a school in Leupp to go door to door to encourage people to help pick up trash, telling stories about Old Leupp to show why the community is worth caring for and approaching a reporter from the *Navajo-Hopi Observer* to write an article about the issue. The discussion led to small group work later in the day during which students composed a letter to the school's principal requesting permission to attend a Chapter House meeting and a 10-step proposal for addressing the trash problem. Activities like these demonstrate to children that their ideas and voices are important—a message rarely encountered in schools that seek to colonize more than empower. Such activities also encourage students to think about how they can contribute to the betterment of their communities, a central aspect of Gruenewald's concept of reinhabitation.

The CREDE staff development activities mentioned earlier encourage teachers to design this kind of learning experience. CREDE emphasizes the value of creating educational settings in which the relationship building so central to the experience of *k'e* is the norm. Three of CREDE's five instructional standards provide students with opportunities to form meaningful ties with one another in the context of the school's academic program: learning through teachers' and students' joint productive activity, connecting school to students' lives, and teaching through conversation.[1] All of these standards are in evidence in the classroom activities described above. What is surprising is how infrequent this kind of teaching and learning is in many conventional classrooms where teacher-centered talk dominates and student conversation is discouraged. It is not uncommon, especially in secondary schools, for students to be unaware of the names of other students in their classes. In such circumstances, the initiation and sustenance of relationships are given little consideration.

Also evident at the school is the frequent use of study centers. Because class sizes are small, students often learn in the company of three or four others either at stations that allow for independent work or close interaction between a teacher or aide and a small group of children. When students are working at a station with no adult present, they turn to one another when they have questions or need assistance. At stations with an adult, they receive direct guidance with skills related to literacy or numeracy. Both exemplify joint productive activity and teaching through conversation. At the STAR School, little instruction involves teachers lecturing or presenting information to an audience of passive children. Conversation and interaction are ongoing, exactly the kind of social experience that forms the basis for sustained relationships.

One final aspect of the STAR School contributes to the cultivation of *k'e*. Parents are more visible here than they are in many schools. To begin with, a half dozen of the school's faculty and staff members are the parents of students. They include a teacher, an aide, the school's secretary, cooks, and janitor. For them, the school has become a vital part of the community, providing both employment and education. Furthermore, other parents and community members frequently visit the school. One teacher observed that in places where he had previously taught, the school was disconnected from the community. "Here, it's almost like teaching on stage. The parents, they are always here. They are always looking at how you do things. They always have comments to make to you about it. It's a discussion; it's very open. It's not like the teacher is over here with the kids, and the parents are somewhere else. They are here." For a number of generations, Native American parents have been denied this kind of access to schools and teachers. Relationships between Indigenous families and teachers who served as agents of a contrasting culture were virtually non-existent or adversarial. At the STAR School, parents are co-partners in the education of their children, a situation that allows them to be part of the broad circle of relationships the school is attempting to describe. Here, service truly is to "all" relations, including the critical relationship students experience with their parents and extended families.

From a school climate characterized by interpersonal warmth to service learning projects that link children to their community, from instructional activities that encourage relationship building to the accessibility of teachers and principal to parents, the STAR School embodies educational practices that underline students' connections to people both inside and outside the school. Rather than functioning as an institution that isolates children from their natal community and its values in ways that can diminish their sense of personal value and efficacy, the STAR School helps to integrate its students into the broad kinship networks that link them to all people, beings, and things, affirming their power to do good work and to make a difference in their own lives and the lives of others.

Hawai'ian Studies (Wai'anae High School) and PRISM (Aka'ula School) Programs

The final programs I'll discuss work primarily with Native Hawai'ian and Polynesian students on the islands of O'ahu and Moloka'i. Neither has ties to the other, but both have created learning and service opportunities for students that are grounded in their home communities. Each, as well, provides opportunities for students to engage in projects that have value beyond the classroom, demonstrating to them that the work they are doing in school has social as well as individual meaning.

The Hawai'ian Studies Program (HSP) at Wai'anae High School on the leeward side of O'ahu was started in the 1996 by three teachers concerned about the limited engagement, low academic performance, and high dropout rates of their primarily Indigenous students. Working initially with a local non-profit organization, Ka'ala Farm, they hoped to create a set of academic offerings for 11th and 12th graders that would give them an opportunity to learn more about Hawai'ian culture and language as well as engage in weekly field experiences situated in the local environment or human service organizations. Approximately 60–100 students participated in the HSP in a typical year. When Wai'anae High School went through a restructuring process in 2005, the Hawai'ian Studies Program was folded into a Natural Resources Academy where students continue to be involved with activities related to those encountered during the program's early years. Nearly all of the research that is available about the HSP is from the period prior to 2005. Although the program has continued to evolve and change since then, the learning experiences provided by teachers and local non-profit organizations for the students who participated at that time demonstrate the value of linking school learning to important community values and issues.

The central goal of the HSP has been "to empower students to become self-sufficient, productive, contributing members of their own community and of the global community, caring for the land and natural resources that make life possible" (Hawai'ian Studies Program, 1997). As happened with the Alaska Rural Systemic Initiative, teachers in the HSP sought to do this by integrating Hawai'ian values and culture with the formal study of science, social studies, and the humanities. This integration was able to build on weekly field experiences at different sites around the Wai'anae Coast (Yamauchi, 2003). Some students were involved in archaeological excavations at different locations in the Wai'anae Valley. Information they helped surface was used in legal hearings about the potential commercial development of sites of cultural and historical significance to Native Hawai'ians. Other students conducted water quality tests of Wai'anae and Makaha streams and participated in long-standing efforts to reduce the amount of water diverted from local streams to the regional water supply, a practice that was diminishing the amount of water available for the semi-arid Wai'anae Valley, itself. Both projects demonstrate the way that decolonization—challenging practices that disadvantage or oppress the original inhabitants of a place—and reinhabitation—the restoration of social and natural communities—can be addressed with Indigenous adolescents. A third regular field study site was the Wai'anae Coast Comprehensive Health Center, where students were able to gain experience with the health care industry and become involved in projects like investigating the nutritional content of fast foods sold in local restaurants or writing pamphlets about different topics for the center. In all of these instances, work in the field was tied to the development of academic skills such as writing, mapmaking, public speaking, and scientific analysis.

Local topics were also brought into the classroom. One year in social studies, for example, students investigated the distribution of funding for public schools in Hawai'i (Yamauchi, Wyatt, & Carroll, 2005). The teacher began the unit by asking students to brainstorm how their own school was deteriorating. Together they came up with a list that included "peeling paint, large amounts of trash on the ground, graffiti, and lack of toilet tissue in the bathrooms" (Yamauchi et al., 2005, p. 235). The teacher then had them read about schools that had received funding from the state legislature the previous year. Although state dollars are supposed to be allocated first to repairs needed to insure health and safety, less than a fifth of the projects that received funding met this requirement. Instead, state dollars were spent on an all-weather track at the University of Hawai'i and extending another school's parking lot. Students went on to explore the location of funded projects and the fact that most were in schools that served higher income communities. The lesson finished with students writing letters to their representatives about conditions at their own school and the lack of consistency between stated requirements and the way dollars had in fact been allocated, an activity that demonstrated to them their ability to potentially influence public decision-making.

As at the STAR School, teachers in the Hawai'ian Studies Program had adopted the five standards for effective pedagogy promoted by the Center for Research in Education, Diversity, and Excellence (CREDE). Especially significant in the HSP were efforts to contextualize instruction, to provide opportunities for students and teachers to become involved in collaborative projects, and to take on challenging tasks. The result of these experiences was much higher levels of academic engagement on the part of students. More than their peers at Wai'anae High School, students in the HSP demonstrated good attendance, were less likely to drop out, and more frequently enrolled in community colleges or universities after graduating. Their grades improved, and interviews with them indicated that—more than other students at Wai'anae High School not enrolled in the HSP—they saw themselves as people who were already making a difference in their community, believed that they were valued by their peers and adults, expressed interest in Hawai'ian history and culture, and were more likely to have thought about what they hoped to accomplish as adults (Yamauchi et al., 2005). Clearly, something about the educational experiences they encountered in the HSP had caught the attention of students and led them to see the relationship between formal learning and the development of skills and competencies they could contribute to the welfare of their own community. As in Alaska and Arizona, teachers in the HSP are providing learning experiences that are embraced rather than rejected by students.

At about the same time that the Hawai'ian Studies Program was created, two teachers in a K-8 school on Moloka'i were inspired to establish a program with a similar focus on local community and environmental issues. The program is called Promoting Resolutions with Integrity for a Sustainable Moloka'i (PRISM). As at Wai'anae High School, the great majority of students at the school are of Native Hawai'ian or Polynesian ancestry. Moloka'i, an island with fewer than 10,000 residents, was beginning to encounter the development pressures that had already transformed most of the other islands in the state. Teachers Vicki Newberry and Dara Lukonen felt that their students needed to become aware of decisions that could affect the quality of their lives as adults and given the opportunity to become players in rather than merely observers of community life.

Unlike the other programs discussed to this point, their intent had less to do with students' cultural identities than their relationship to the land. The results in terms of student engagement in academic work and a deepening connection to their community, however, have been similar. Drawing upon an approach to exploring potentially controversial natural resource issues called Investigating and Evaluating Environmental Issues and Actions (IEEIA) developed by educators at the University of Southern Illinois (Ramsey, Hungerford, & Volk, 2005), they invite their students to participate in extensive inquiry projects about local environmental concerns that culminate in day-long symposiums for the community. Over the years students have investigated issues such as the environmental impact of an airport runway extension and planned ecotourism projects, the restoration of traditional Hawai'ian fishponds, emergency preparedness on Moloka'i, the relationship between ballast water releases and exotic marine species, the creation of a school- and then island-wide solid waste recycling program, the effect of ungulates on island ecology, and the pros and cons of the seed corn business.

The IEEIA process requires students to develop a deep and comprehensive knowledge about the perspectives of multiple players with a stake in the issues they are investigating. This means that students often need to read material significantly beyond their own reading levels—something they accomplish by questioning one another about refining the meaning they take from difficult texts. They must also develop interview skills and the willingness to interact with adults outside the school. Over time, their presentations have gained the respect of island adults, and this has led students to want to do their best in what they say or write. The consequence has been enhanced abilities as readers, writers, and speakers (Volk & Cheak, 2003). The action component of IEEIA has also led students to develop and implement a recycling plan for the school, write a measure to recycle bottles that was passed by the Hawai'i State Legislature, participate in fish pond restoration, design stormwater controls, and gain the agreement of local businesses to market alternatives to polystyrene, a non-biodegradable material. These students are truly contributing to the wise use and preservation of local resources.

An unexpected benefit of PRISM has been the impact that students' work has had on adult involvement in island decision-making and involvement. As one parent commented, "Other parents that I know who have kids in PRISM, it's not only their children who have learned or that have had their eyes opened to what is going on, but it is as if their whole families went through the PRISM process" (Cheak, Volk, & Hungerford, 2002, p. 37). Sometimes, students' engagement with learning activities can motivate their parents to become involved in ways they might never have expected. An aunt described the shift she saw in her niece's mother: "We would come down and listen to how the research turned out and stuff like that. . . . Her mom—who never got involved in community things—is now one of the Enterprise Community Board and volunteered to be on the waste management project" (in Cheak, Volk, & Hungerford, 2002, p. 37). In this instance, a school-based program has become a stimulus for community regeneration and pride.

Over the years that the PRISM Program has been in existence, it has been the recipient of significant recognition from elected officials. In 2002, a news release from the website of Hawai'i's second district Congressman, Ed Case, included his announcement of an award to the program from the U.S. Environmental Protection Agency and his reflection about its significance. "All of us in the Second Congressional District and throughout our Hawai'i can be so very proud of the students who have made this amazing program a model of success and sustainability" (Case, 2003). Then in 2007,

Hawai'i Governor Linda Lingle issued a proclamation in which she praised the PRISM program for creating a "community of critical thinkers who are able to investigate and take informed action on social, cultural, and environmental issues" (retrieved at http://Hawai'i.gov/gov/news/events/2007/Akaula on December 31, 2008). Students also gain recognition from adults at conferences such as the annual North American Association for Environmental Education meeting in Portland, Oregon, where in the fall of 2009 they made formal presentations about their work.

Students in both the Hawai'ian Studies Program and the PRISM Program are provided with the opportunity to integrate their experience as Native Hawai'ians and inhabitants of their ancestral homes into their formal education. In doing so, they are able to enact a central value of traditional Hawai'ian culture—m~lama I ka'~ina—caring for the land, a critical element in the process of reinhabitation. They are furthermore provided with the chance to do work that brings with it positive recognition from their communities and the broader world, work that demonstrates to them their value and their capacity to make important contributions to the welfare of the Earth and other people. Too often, formal education has told Indigenous students that they and their communities are inadequate. What students in both of these programs encounter time and again is exactly the opposite message. They are shown that what they say and do matters, that their cultures have value, and that the people around them are willing to listen to what they have to share.

Conclusion

Indigenous students whose ancestral communities have been the victims of colonization have good reason to reject the lessons of conventional schools. As Oscar Kawagley notes, success in the eyes of these schools is equated with the loss of students' identities as members of distinct social groups associated with particular places. Doing well in school will in most instances ill-prepare children for the demands of life in what are often rural or remote locales. Furthermore, few of the skills mastered in school are likely to match available employment opportunities. Investigating a primarily white fishing village in Nova Scotia, Michael Corbett (2007) discovered that in this setting, as well, schools primarily help students learn how to leave their communities rather than invest their lives in the social and environmental networks into which they were born. The notion that children must leave home to become successful is a social fabrication encountered primarily in modern industrial civilizations. It is an assumption that undercuts the long-term sustainability of population groups that have not bought into the widely shared belief that there is no alternative to the economic, cultural, and political institutions that now dominate our lives. This is a dilemma for all population groups, but especially those for whom participation in mainstream society has been blocked because of historical patterns of oppression and exclusion.

Overcoming these patterns within the context of an institution created to induct children into the opportunity structures and demands of industrial civilization is no easy matter. As Seymour Sarason (1996) observed almost forty years ago, the "behavioral and programmatic regularities" encountered in schools tend to resist change. The innovations described in the body of this chapter challenge those regularities. Whether they will have the staying power needed to shift the direction of education in the schools where they are now in evidence remains an open question. One factor in their favor is the widespread concern about the low academic performance of traditionally underserved groups demonstrated by the National Science Foundation, other philanthropic organizations, and the U.S. Department of Education. Although the standards movement and No Child Left Behind possess serious flaws, each has raised the profile of Indigenous students as well as other students of color in the United States in ways that could be beneficial, especially if a door to experiments like those discussed here remains open.

What seems especially strong in the efforts encountered in Alaska and at the schools in Arizona and Hawaii is the way that the hegemony of the dominant worldview and values of American society is being diluted through the recognition that other cultural or political alternatives in fact have merit. In each of these initiatives, assets inherent in local communities, traditional culture bearers, or the students themselves are being recognized and given a place in the formal curriculum. The kind of uprooting that has tended to characterize the schooling of Indigenous children and youth is not so evident in these examples, and one of the results is that students have become more willing to invest themselves in their educations. The examples offered here vary in the degree to which traditional cultural perspectives are highlighted, but in each instance the value of students' relationship to specific communities and a specific place is clearly pivotal to the way teachers approach their work. Also striking about these educational experiments is how the schools where they are being enacted seek to bridge differences between life in industrial societies and life in Indigenous communities. By balancing instruction in subsistence activities with participation in college classes at the Effie Kokrine School in Alaska, exposure to traditional water conservation strategies with the use of solar panels in Arizona, or the restoration of traditional fishponds with participation in the political process in Hawai'i, Indigenous students are learning how to negotiate the demands and possibilities of these two worlds. Judging by their enhanced educational performance, this process appears to be resulting in increased participation, commitment, and confidence. This can only be good for both the students in these schools and their communities.

Expanding such initiatives to other schools, however, is not something that will happen automatically. Schools remain a colonizing institution, and only few seem likely to readily adopt the kinds of approaches described here. Those that do will have administrators and teachers who are willing to step out of their comfort zone to embrace more experiential and potentially controversial educational approaches. The communities in which these schools exist must furthermore demonstrate a willingness to identify the kinds of knowledge and learning experiences they believe their children require to grow into whole and contributing adults, and make sure that a changing guard of school teachers and administrators truly teach in ways that honor the perspectives, knowledge, and values of the local community and its culture bearers. All of this will be fraught with challenge.

What these examples demonstrate, however, is that change is possible. The dehumanization and oppression that have too often characterized the educational experience of Indigenous students can be replaced with other approaches that are more in harmony with the needs of their communities and their places, and more likely to prepare children to gain the knowledge and skills required by mainstream political and economic institutions. A starting place for this change is the rejection of the belief that the culture of Western industrial societies is superior to all others and that the beliefs and patterns of behavior associated with this culture provide the only route to success for young people in the 21st century. Taking this step invites the introduction of other perspectives and other ways of doing things. Educators in the schools described in the preceding pages are showing what this kind of shift both entails and can accomplish. Their work with Indigenous students could potentially serve as exemplars for teachers of students from any group who are interested in drawing young people into deeper and more responsible relationships with their own communities and the land, the kinds of relationships that conventional schools have tended to disrupt but that may be essential for us all as humanity confronts the environmental and social challenges of the coming decades.

Note

1. The remaining two standards involve developing language and literacy across the curriculum and teaching complex thinking.

References

Alliance for Excellent Education. (2009a and b) Understanding high school graduation rates. Washington, DC: Author. Retrieved at http://www.all4ed.org/files/Alaska_wc.pdf and http://www.all4ed.org/files/National_wc.pdf on January 2, 2010.

Assembly of Alaska Native Educators. (1998). *Alaska standards for culturally responsive schools.* Fairbanks, AK: Alaska Native Knowledge Network.

Au, K. H. (1980, Summer). Participation structures in a reading lesson with Hawai'ian children: Analysis of a culturally appropriate instructional event. *Anthropology and Education Quarterly, 11*(2), 91–115.

Barnhardt, R. (2008). Creating a place for indigenous knowledge in education: The Alaska Native Knowledge Network. In D. Gruenewald and G. Smith (editors), *Place-based education in the global age: Local diversity*, pp. 113–136. Mahwah, NJ: Erlbaum.

Case, Ed. (2003). Kualapu'u school PRISM program is a model for Earth Day April 22nd: The Moloka'i school's PRISM program wins national award for environmental work. Retrieved on December 20, 2005 at http://wwwc.house.gov/case/press_releases/200334.html

Cheak, M. Volk, T., & Hungerford, H. (2002). *Moloka'i: An investment in children, the community, and the environment.* Carbondale, IL: The Center for Instruction, Staff Development, and Evaluation.

Corbett, M. (2007). *Learning to leave: The irony of schooling in a coastal community.* Toronto: Fernwood.

Deloria, V. & Wildcat, D. (2001). *Power and place: Indian education in America.* Golden, CO: Fulcrum.

Dick. A. (2003). *Village math.* Retrieved at http://ankn.uaf.edu/publications/VillageMath/on January 2, 2010.

Dick, A (1997). *Village science.* Retrieved at http://ankn.uaf.edu/publications/VS/ on January2, 2010.

Freire, P. (1993). *Pedagogy of the oppressed.* New York: Continuum. (Original work published in 1970).

Gruenewald, D. (2003). The best of both worlds: A critical pedagogy of place. *Educational Researcher*, 32:4, pp. 3–12.Hawai'ian Studies Program. (1997). Mission statement. Wai'anae, HI: Author.

Hill, F., Kawagley, O., & Barnhardt. R. (2006). *Alaska Rural Systemic Initiative: Final report phase II; 2000–2005.* Fairbanks, AK: Authors.

Jordan, C. (1985). Translating culture: From ethnographic information to educational program. *Anthropology and Education Quarterly, 16*:2 (Summer), 104–123.

Kawagley, O. (1999). Alaskan Native education: History and adaptation in the new millennium. *Journal of American Education,* 39:1 (Fall). Retrieved at http://jaie.asu.edu/v39/V39I1A3.pdf on December 28, 2009.

McCarty, T. (2002). *A place to be Navajo: Rough Rock and the struggle for self-determination in Indigenous schooling.* New York: Routledge.

Obgu, J. (1978). *Minority education and caste: The American system in cross-cultural perspective.* New York: Academic Press.

Ramsey, J., Hungerford, H., & Volk, T (2005). A technique for analyzing environmental issues. In H. Hungerford, W. Bluhm, T. Volk, & J. Ramsey (editors), *Essential readings in environmental education* (3rd edition), pp. 191–196. Champaign, IL: Stipes.

Rural Challenge Research and Evaluation Program. (1999). *Lessons from the field.* Cambridge, MA: Harvard Graduate School of Education.

Sarason, S. (1996). *Revisiting "the culture of schools and the problem of change.* New York: Teachers College Press.

Smyth, A. (1907/1784). *The writings of Benjamin Franklin, Volume X, 1789–1790.* New York: The Macmillan Company.

Tharp, R. G. (1989). Psycho-cultural variables and constants: Effects on teaching and learning in schools. *American Psychologist, 44*:2, 349–359.

Volk, T. & Cheak. M. (2003). The effects of an environmental education program on students, parents, and community. *Journal of Environmental Education, 34:*4, 12–25.

Willis, P. (1981). *Learning to labor: How working class kids get working class jobs.* New York: Columbia University.

Yamauchi, L. (2003). Making school relevant for at-risk students: The Wai'anae High School Hawai'ian Studies Program. *Journal of Education for Students Placed at Risk, 8:*4, 379–390.

Yamauchi, L., Wyatt, T., and Carroll, J. (2005). Enacting the five standards for effective pedagogy in a culturally relevant high school program. In A Maynard and M. Martini (editors), *Learning in context: Family, peers, and school*, pp. 227–245. New York: Springer.

CHAPTER SIXTEEN

Learning Life Lessons from Indigenous Storytelling with Tom McCallum

JUDY ISEKE & BRENNUS BMJK

Indigenous Elders are the educators of our children, youth, adults, and communities, and storytellers and historians of our communities. Their stories and histories, shared through Indigenous pedagogies, educate communities and aid in sustaining our cultures. The contributions of Métis Elders help Métis communities understand the contributions of Métis peoples, past and present, to our provinces and Nations. Métis Elders' knowledge helps us understand Indigenous pedagogies in Indigenous education and the ways these can inform the education of children, youth, and Indigenous and non-Indigenous communities.

We explore the storytelling of Tom McCallum, White Standing Buffalo, a Métis Elder who explains the power of stories shared in communities. Through his stories we come to better understand Indigenous pedagogies and practices in storytelling. Tom's first story is in two sections entitled *Falling through the Ice and the Sun Dance Tree* and its continuation in *Sun Dance Story about the Meaning of Life*. These explain Tom's youthful experience and how it sets a pattern for his learning the meaning of his life. His subsequent two stories, *Humorous Horse Story* and *Dancing Dog Story* share understandings about community storytelling and the role humor plays in teaching lessons.

We begin by introducing the authors, and the epistemological underpinnings that inform the research method and approach.[1] We discuss meanings of Tom McCallum's storytelling and learn how Indigenous pedagogies use stories as an approach to share understandings. Through interpreting Tom's stories, we learn valuable lessons about the role of storytelling and ways that storytelling can influence one's life journey.

INTRODUCING THE AUTHORS

I am Judy Iseke, a Métis woman, researcher, and scholar from St. Albert, Alberta, which was once a strong Métis community, but it has changed over the years into a mixed urban center. I am a descendant of the Métis families that founded this community. In my academic work I have been working with Métis Elders to explore storytelling traditions. I teach academic courses at the graduate level on Indigenous Education in the Faculty of Education, Lakehead University. I have spent many years working in Ontario and Alberta learning about my own beliefs about Indigenous traditions and storytelling. I consider myself a beginner in these practices and defer to the Elders as the experienced ones. I have heard many stories and am interested in the power of storytelling that is the focus of my research program.

What I have learned in my personal experiences of storytelling is that it is a powerful pedagogic tool in which the old ones tell us stories from which we are to draw our own understandings and conclusions. The stories teach by showing us various ways to look at a problem and help us to consider different viewpoints that might expand our understandings of how to live or how to solve a problem. The stories are situated in a cultural, family, and communal context that provides the backdrop to stories and to which the stories are tied. As such the stories have greater meaning to those within the contexts from which the stories are told than to those who do not share these understandings. But other Indigenous peoples who come to our community and hear the stories can relate to our stories as there are similar stories in their own contexts—stories of love, of family, of trouble, of making do when times were tough, of strength of family and friendship ties that keep us strong, and stories that tie us to the land and to spiritual practices that we are to continue in order to keep the land clean and the people that walk on it healthy. The stories teach us respect for ourselves, for our families, our Elders, our communities, our neighbors and respect for all life. They are powerful teachings that aid us in knowing who we are.

I find myself now, as a mother, teaching my children by telling them stories. They often ask me about some time long ago or some event, and I find myself telling them stories of their ancestors, of their relations, of the lands and communities I and their family came from or stories from my life that can help them understand the complexity of the world. The stories just seem to flow from me as they listen and learn. I find myself, as a university professor, teaching in this way as well. I rarely explicitly lecture on a topic or issue but rather prefer to tell a story from which students are asked to build connections and understandings.

As a Canada Research Chair, I decided to undertake work with the old ones from our communities and to understand the many lessons they teach in their lives and their work as storytellers, educators, healers, and community leaders. I wanted to understand the power of storytelling not just from my personal experiences of hearing and telling stories but from those who had far greater experiences than I did in this important tradition. My research program has brought me into contact with storytellers beyond those in my own immediate family and community. It is a great honor to have the opportunity to work with these knowledgeable people. They have taught me a great deal and continue to teach me as our relationships continue through the research process and beyond.

I am Brennus and I am of Northern Irish and Canadian heritage. I am a freelance writer and researcher. Being of Irish descent, there was always one of my uncles telling an Irish traditional story full of humor and life lessons. I understand well how the old stories of Irish legends like Brian Boru and Cu' Chulainn have shaped Irish culture and tradition and my understanding of what it means to be Irish—long before St. Patrick brought Christianity to Ireland. Sadly, I cannot speak Gaelic. However, I am an *Outsider* when it comes to Indigenous oral storytelling. As part of my undergraduate and more particularly, my master's research (Brennus, 2005) I was involved in studying with the Oneida Nation Educators and Elders, concerned with themes of cultural, environmental, and language erasure and recovery. Storytelling was also an important theme.

For this research and chapter, I have been involved with understanding and interpreting the meaning of Tom McCallum's stories in regard to my own understandings of my own traditions, in regard to that I had come to know in some way in the Oneida Nation, and in regard to my learned experiences and interactions with Indigenous educators and students, and non-Indigenous students at University of Toronto. I come to this research with my humble thoughts and ideas, of which it is an honor to work with these Indigenous individuals, educators, and communities.

EPISTEMOLOGY INFORMING THE RESEARCH METHODOLOGY

Kovach (2005), a Nèhiÿaw and Saulteaux researcher, cautions that conceptions of research are "so entangled with haughty theories of what is truth" (p. 32) that we may forget that research is truly "about learning and so is a way of finding out things" (Hampton, 1995, p. 48). Smith (1999) suggests "researching back," like "talking back" as a form of "recovery of ourselves, an analysis of colonialism, and a struggle for self-determination" (p. 7). Research that engages in this resistance, recovery, and renewal is central to Indigenous peoples as it supports our lives and work in communities and in academic settings.

Elders are important in this process of recovery and resistance, and in reinsertion of the importance of remembering our past and remaking our futures. Elders mentor and provide support and have systematically gathered wisdom, histories, skills, and expertise in cultural knowledge (Smith, 1999). Their role as Elders is based on their knowledge and the way they use their knowledge for the collective good (Smith, 1999).

The research methodology in working with Elders must be based on respectful relations. Lassiter (2000) explains the importance of dialogic and collaborative texts produced within Indigenous communities that are based on human relationships which "produce deeper dialogues about culture" and "engender moral and ethical commitments" (p. 610) between collaborative participants in research.

Being ready to hear the stories when the tellers are ready to tell them calls the researcher into the relationship of listener and reflects the holistic process of both parties and asks the researcher to remember that deep respect is required in a storytelling approach to research:

> In an oral culture, story lives, develops, and is imbued with the energy of the dynamic relationship between teller and listener. The story can only exist within an interdependent relationship of the narrator and audience. Writing story becomes a concession of the Indigenous researcher (Kovach, 2009, p. 101).

Both Winona Stevenson (1999) and Shawn Wilson (2008) explain the complexity of putting oral stories into written texts. They both use a style of writing that shifts quite deliberately between a narrative style of experiences and more analytical style of discourse reflecting the stories. This chapter follows this style.

Kovach (2009) explains that there are two forms of stories—the ones with "mythical elements, such as creation and teaching stories" and then there are the personal stories of "place, happenings, and experiences" that are shared with the next generation through oral traditions (p. 95). Tom McCallum explains in a discussion in regard to this chapter that the name for the mythical kind of stories to which Kovach alludes are called "Atayohkiwina" in Cree. "These are not made up but come from the spirits. There are certain spirits known as Atayohkan," thus the name for the mythical elements but "these are not stories per se, but have been given to us as a people." Tom further explains that the stories that Kovach called personal stories are called "Acimona" and are "stories about human life and events . . . observations and things you may have heard from someone else—kind of like news." Tom further notes that "Atayohkiwina don't change, just Acimona" change. Telling stories is a practice in Indigenous cultures that has long sustained us (Castellano, 2000).

A RESEARCH APPROACH

"Research, like life, is about relationships" (Kovach, 2005, p. 30). The cultural context, just as in storytelling, positions the participants in research including the one we might typically think of as the researcher (Bishop, 1998). Research in such a context becomes a collaborative venture whose effect is the shared development of new storylines (Bishop, 1998, p. 207). Kovach (2005), drawing on King (2003), suggests that "each story is alive with the nuances and wisdom of the storyteller" (p. 27) or in this case the multiple storytellers involved in the process, including the researchers who also tell the story of the research. This research story includes the focus to work with Métis Elders as collaborators to examine stories, histories, and pedagogies shared by Métis Elders in storytelling sessions. The objective was to undertake a collaborative analysis with Elders in order to understand the stories and histories of Métis peoples and the role of storytelling in the sharing of Indigenous knowledges—past and present. The intentions of the research were (1) to respond to the need for Indigenous interpretations and representations of culture, history, pedagogy, and curriculum, (2) to provide increased research opportunities and publicize the work of Indigenous Elders, and (3) generate better understandings of the relationships between Métis peoples' knowledges and mainstream education and research practices.

In this research program Elders were contacted by Iseke based on their previous involvement with a research program with Métis Elders. Gifts of tobacco and cloth were given by Iseke to ask the Elders to participate in the discussions:

> The exchange of tobacco signified that what was spoken was truth as each person knew it. There was a further recognition that the person's story would become a part of the social and historical fabric of the people, a historical truth, through their honour. It requires belief in another's integrity, that there is a mutual understanding that speaking untruths will upset the relational balance (Kovach, 2009, p. 103).

For Iseke and the Elders the tobacco also signified their relationship and the responsibility of the researcher to respect that relationship with the Elders and the knowledge that they shared. It suggested the responsibility to the integrity of the stories told and to respect and honor the Elders throughout the research process. It also was a commitment to continue to work with the Elders in representing their stories.

These Elders had worked with numerous organizations that conducted research including the Métis Center, National Aboriginal Health Organization (NAHO) in Ottawa. Elders were given an information letter about the research and asked to sign a consent form indicating they consented to the research as this research was being conducted in conjunction with a university and the university ethics committee wanted to see forms signed.

The Elders were given a sheet of paper with research questions that would guide and focus discussions. They were then free to respond in whatever way they saw fit. A talking circle format was used to encourage discussion and to ensure opportunities for full participation of each Elder. Elders were audio and video recorded while sitting in circle. All Elder discussions were transcribed and roughly sorted into topics. Film scripts, papers, and chapters were written based on the transcripts. Iseke visited Elders in their homes in Northern Alberta and at Sun Dance ceremony and local visits in British Columbia to discuss the films, papers, and chapters. Ongoing dialogue via e-mail and telephone conversation has helped to ensure that the research continues to be respectful of the ideas Elders shared. Three films have been produced and one is in production that draws together some of the ideas that Elders shared. Versions of the films have been provided to Elders for ongoing comment and feedback.

This kind of filmmaking and research is as much about the process of community relationships as it is about the development of film products and research outcomes. The Elders wanted to see their stories on film and wanted to ensure their ideas were shared with the next generation and these films are welcomed as ways to do this within Indigenous communities. Elders also understood that their ideas would be shared in academic papers. The researcher has been in contact with the Elders and shared a version of the chapter and sought feedback from the Elders.

To ensure we had a good research time together, Elders held a pipe ceremony. They were asked with tobacco to do this ceremony. All present were included in the ceremony. The ceremony was held in the research space where the ongoing work of producing film and papers would continue. A closing ceremony was provided by the Elders in giving thanks for this opportunity together. The closing allowed us all to be a part of a complete cycle of ceremony over these 9 days.

INTRODUCING TOM MCCALLUM

This chapter draws upon stories from one of the Elders in the research, Tom McCallum, who was born and raised in Ile à la Crosse, Saskatchewan, and is fluent in Cree and Michif—a unique language to the Métis peoples composed of an Indigenous language with French and/or English language words used. Tom has a passion for the Cree language and promotes its use as he explains the way the language has shaped his way of seeing the world. Tom grew up on the land and has a close relationship with it and in working with medicines. Tom uses traditional teachings to work with inmates, youth, men's healing circles, and in cross-cultural workshops. Tom shares stories in this text and has reviewed this text prior to its submission to make any changes he saw fit. Tom's stories are in italics. We have edited Tom's stories in the interest of space.

Tom McCallum explains that

> Stories are a history of our people from many lifetimes and the stories are real. Storytelling was used in communities as a form of entertainment . . . because we have what we call a holistic approach. We include a lot of things in storytelling that we leave for the other person to be able to interpret themselves. It gets their mind going. It puts their experience together and validates them as a person who has the ability to be able to draw from that storytelling and relate it to their own lives.

Carabi (1994) similarly suggests that stories are ways we create ourselves, and they are what we are made of. Our understanding of these stories combined with our lived experiences help us mold and create who we are. Taylor (1996) suggests that we reach deep into ourselves and connect our own understandings to those in the story. Smith (1998) suggests that stories do not have a single meaning but have a plurality of meanings based on our own interpretations of the story. The stories allow us to "pose new questions and in doing so challenge us to imagine new possibilities, to 'expand the limits of where we can go'" (Gross, 2009, p. 78). Tom teaches us through stories so that we can interpret and come to understand meanings in our own lives through the stories.

Vaserstein (2001), drawing on Allen Ryan's book *Humour and Irony in Contemporary Native Art,* wrote that stories entertained and educated and provided adventure for generations of Indigenous people. These encouraged "curiosity, ingenuity, playfulness, earthiness, irreverence, and resilience" as well as an understanding of "self-identity of Native people and their place in the world" (Vaserstein, 2001, p. 309). Tom believes that it is up to the listener to find the appropriate meaning for themselves within these stories from the particular perspective in their lives.

TOM'S *FALLING THROUGH THE ICE AND THE SUN DANCE TREE*

> At 13 years old, this one fall, the ice was just starting to freeze and people were skating along the shore because the ice was already thick around the shore. . . . And there were four of us. We thought we would go across the lake. People said "No. Don't go. You'll fall through. It's not thick enough." But we were kids. We thought we could do it. So we took off, started skating across, heading for this island we called big island. And there was a crack that ran across from one point to the other, and I stepped over that crack and the others guys stepped over also and we went to big island and skated there most of the day. It started getting dark and I told those guys I said "we better get back, better get home" and they said "okay." We came to that crack and they asked me, "how are we going to get across" and I said "well, we'll get across the same way we came. We'll step over it." So they all did. They all stepped over the crack, except me. I told them "I'm going to jump over that crack, you know, we stepped over before. I'm going to try jumping over it." So I skated back and took a run at it, when I came close I jumped over the crack. Made it, it was easy to jump over, but when I hit the ice on the other side I went right through. . . . And I went underneath and I looked up and it was pitch black all over. I looked up and there was a little hole there of light. And I thought, that must be where I came through so I started swimming, and I came up through that hole, and the water pushed me up, the pressure of the waters. . . . So I got on top of the ice and it would bend and I would go back again . . . there was nothing to hold on to. . . . The biggest guy in our group, and he tried to come close and every time he'd come close the ice would crack and he'd jump back. . . . I was starting to sink. And what went through my mind was these poplar trees that we see outside, trembling aspen. In the springtime their leaves dance in the wind, beautiful, beautiful sight. That's the thought that came in my head—I thought I'll never see those trees again. And a big lump formed in my throat. Tears came down my eyes. And I wondered why, I mean to this day I wonder why I didn't think of my mom, I didn't think of anyone else, except for that tree. That tree is what I thought about. And at that time I thought well, I can't let go, I've gotta try once more. So I kicked once more and I pulled myself up. And I went like this (reaches out) and there was a hole in that ice where there wasn't before. And that's where I hung on. It's impossible for a hole to be in the ice in the fall time. There is no reason for it but it was there, and I hung on until that guy came. When he came close enough I told him to throw me his jacket and that's how he pulled me out.

> It went out of my mind until 1985. I gave tobacco to this medicine woman and told her this story. And I asked her what does that mean? And she prayed with that tobacco and she told me, "That tree saved your life. That is the center pole of the Sun Dance tree. It has given you back your life. Someday you will have to go back and repay that tree." And in my mind I thought "Well, I guess I'll go to a Sun Dance." And I did. The following year I went to a Sun Dance. I didn't dance, I went and looked, observed, helped out. Something was calling me. So the following year I started Sun Dancing.

Taylor (1996), in a discussion of oral tradition and storytelling as it relates to Native Theatre in Canada, explains that storytelling is a form of creativity and passing on Indigenous knowledge and experiences that involves "taking your audience on a journey" (p. 29). Tom takes the audience on the journey of falling through the ice and the understanding that much later is explained—that he is to thank the Sun Dance tree for saving his life. Taylor further explains that storytelling relates the history of community and explains human nature. Taylor (1996) explains that in storytelling each teller is involved in a "process of reaching deep inside yourself to find that nugget that is your grounding, your earth, the essence of who you are. It was a way of explaining human nature" (p. 30). That nugget for Tom was the tree and the connection to the Sun Dance.

In Tom's story he tells us, although he does not understand at the time, that the poplar tree appeared to him, that he did not think about his mom or family. Vizenor (1992) explains that "the awareness of coincidence in personal stories is much more sophisticated in tribal cultures" (p. 227). It takes Tom some time to truly understand the coincidence or synchronicity of the poplar tree and the Sun Dance. Tom explains that we do not allow for coincidence in our world. He suggests we replace the word coincidence with the term synchronicity—a term shared with him by Claide Abins—A Métis ceremonialist who has shared his teachings with Tom. Gross (2007) adds that natural elements are part of the story. Wilson (1996) further adds to this idea, that life histories reflect human stories as well as non-human elements. In Tom's case the image of the tree is powerful and as Phelan (1996) suggests "I still don't know why it was a coyote that appeared that day. . . . As I thought about what coyote taught me" (p. 131). Tom thought it very strange at the time that it was the poplar tree that appeared at this moment. He did not understand fully the meaning of the tree for many years, but he understood it would become important.

Schwenniger (1995) reiterates that in non-human nature we can find spiritual power. He gives the example of a boy who finds a chipmunk is a tree stump. "The chipmunk turns out to be a human boy. . . . The stump from which he emerges turns out to be the chipmunk boy's wise old grandfather who delivers an oration about who the human boy will become" (p. 149). In Tom's story we see the interconnections of the poplar tree that foreshadows who Tom will become—a Sun Dance lodge keeper.

TOM CONTINUES *THE SUN DANCE STORY ABOUT THE MEANING OF LIFE*

In 1994 I went to a Sun Dance. I had been dancing a number of years since then, but I went to Kehewin [reserve]. I brought some tobacco. . . . I got a really, really long print . . . to thank the tree for saving my life. . . . It was dark blue, beautiful blue color. I went to this one man, I said "I have come to pay this tree back" and I told him the story, and he said "I know just the man you need to talk to." He led me to this Elder, and told that Elder the story, and what my intentions were. He said "Ok, come with me." So he had blanket offerings, and that flag was tied to that tree, that long flag. So the tree sat like this. . . . And they got ropes on it. And all these Elders stood over here, and I was standing there with them. And they said "Ok!" and they pulled up the tree, and as they pulled up the tree all these Elders there started crying. And tears just jumped from my eyes too, I don't know why, until that tree was up, and that pfft, it was gone. We all stopped crying.

On the second day of that Sun Dance, I was dancing, danced all day, and then . . . four o'clock in the morning these people come to wake me up. They said "you better take your wife to the hospital she's going to have a baby." . . . I took her to the hospital in Bonneville, that's where my daughter was born. So I gave her the name Kehew because of the Kehewin reserve. And that was in July, and the second name I gave her was Nepin, which means summer. Kehew Nepin is her name. It means Eagle Summer.

> . . . I went back to the Sun Dance and they were dancing already, it was about 8–8:30, in the morning. I crawled in the tent with my son and I immediately fell asleep. I was just sleeping real nice, when somebody shook my foot. I looked up and it was that Elder. He said . . . "are you going to go and finish?" I said "no I have to stay here with my son." I didn't want to go. He said, "Never mind that," he said, "I got lots of daughters, lots of granddaughters here, they'll take care of him. He said, "you go and finish."
>
> So I went back to the Sun Dance, they were dancing, and I started dancing. Then we went down, and I heard him coming, and he stopped everything. And had me stand up and he announced the birth of my daughter. And all the whistles started, and drums and they broke into a song and started singing. And that Sun Dance lodge started to spin around. Like this. . . . And all of the colors of the rainbow were there because of the cloth that was there. And I started to raise up. I started to raise up like this and I flew away. I came to this place with this beautiful green grass all over. And people . . . there is little paths like this, people were walking and talking in very, very gentle tones. Gentle voices and laughing. Everybody seemed so happy. And I stayed there. I could hear the drums, I could hear people talking, I could still hear the whistles. But I was not there I was somewhere else. All day I was in that place, I didn't want to come back. I never felt any sensation of dancing at all. I was just hovering in the air. Than I heard the Sun Dance chief say this would be our last set, we're going to shut down. And in my mind I was thinking "No, No. Don't shut it down. Please. I wanna stay here, I don't wanna go back." And I was thinking, "I wonder if there is another Sun Dance somewhere so I can go back to this place." But my understanding of that is that, that poplar, white poplar tree, had granted me a life, giving me another chance at life to finish what I need to do on this earth. And when I acknowledged that, when my daughter was born, again that tree took me somewhere and showed me what life is about, what's real. What we're all about.

Kroeber (2004) documents that storytelling creates "imaginable impossibilities" and "liberates our imaginations" to create possibilities (p. 76). In particular, in regard to this story, storytellers in Indigenous populations are fully connected and "in tune" with the natural world around them. Tom, in Kehewin, at Sun Dance, learns from the poplar tree lessons that are shaping his life. These lessons are partially learned in the spirit world (Carabi, 1994).

Smith (1998) explains that stories have a plurality of meanings rather than a single meaning. The person listening to the story has to listen and interpret the story, finding meaning in the story from their own experiences. There are many meanings that one could draw from a story, depending on what the listener hears, highlights, and emphasizes and ultimately what they interpret. Smith writes that listeners "are invited to construct their own meaning, to enter into liberative conversation[s]" (p. 532). Gross (2009) writes that "the power of the story comes from our reaction to it. . . . So the whole process is very organic . . . a storytelling tradition [is] to mutually enrich each other" especially to encourage the listener to make connections (pp. 76–77). Storytellers can therefore create new questions and possibilities to imagine and to expand understandings and the limits we place on imagination. Tom creates possibilities for us to think about our own lives and to draw meaning from past experiences and events in order to have clarity and focus.

In this process "old stories change; [and] new stories emerge. . . . They encourage us to become members of a community engaged in telling, hearing, retelling, contradicting, and reweaving, rather than in simply receiving" (Smith, 1998, p. 532). Often the communities are made up of families and extended families, as in the case of Tom's Sun Dance story in which the Elder has daughters and granddaughters to look after Tom's son. Gross (2009) suggests that "Families are one of the blessings. . . . Living without family would be like trying to live without air and water" (p. 72). Tom affirms the importance of his family and community in the Sun Dance.

In regard to this paragraph, Tom reflected on his own journey and added in regard to old stories changing to new stories that

> I understand this to be a part of my journey on this earth. . . . A pact so to speak that I had made with the Creator before I came to this earth . . . I am a part of an unfolding of this journey toward wholeness and although it seems new to me, my spirit already knows about it. . . . As a human being it may seem it has changed and a new story unfolded, but in fact it is a continuation of the same story, just a new chapter so to speak (T. McCallum, personal communication, April 5, 2010).

Tom's story of falling through the ice and being saved by the Sun Dance tree demonstrates the connecting of an old story—the Sun Dance, with a new story—Tom's experiences of seeing the Sun Dance tree when in the water. Gerald Vizenor (1992) explains that stories in the oral tradition "are the remembered landscapes" (p. 226). In the case of Tom's story there is the landscape of the space in Ile à la Crosse and the lake and the ice. There is also the landscape of the spiritual world in which Tom's story of the Sun Dance takes place. Vizenor (1992) contends that "the landscapes of tribal memories are heard, read, and remembered as personal and new ceremonial stories. The natural world is created in personal stories" (pp. 226–227). In this case the way of living as boys in another era in another place is witnessed in Tom's story. This is a new personal and ceremonial story that creates the natural world. Carabi (1994) contends that "natural elements, and members of the natural world by extension, have their own story to tell and so engage in the dialogic process as well" (p. 47). The poplar tree is a main character in this story, teaching Tom about the cycle of life.

McAvoy (2002) contends that "Cultural/symbolic meaning is where a place creates a sense of emotional symbolic, historic, spiritual and cultural significance for a whole group. It often involves spiritual connections to nature" (p. 390). In the case of Tom's story the place of the Sun Dance creates this significant location. Tom's story about falling through the ice suggests that "a heightened sense of place or connection to the land is the result of the importance placed on the human/nature relationship and a long historical tie to the land" (McAvoy, 2002, p. 391). Tom's history of living on the land/territory creates this set of relations and connections. His story of seeing the Sun Dance tree further suggests the Tom's relationship to the land and the spiritual aspects of life (McAvoy, 2002).

Tom speaks of the Sun Dance ceremony which Smith (1998) explains "is a sacred rite of transformation, . . . a way to change his life" (p. 528). "The sun dance, . . . held in a circular lodge built from fresh cut poplars, covered with brush . . . , involves singing, drumming, dancing and prayer" to the Creator as well as giving thanks (Jenish, 1999, p. 27). Morgan (1999) writes the Sun Dance is four days and

> a time of celebration and plenty. It starts with a tall tree being ritually cut and carried to where the ceremony will take place. There, the cut end is buried securely. That part that stands above ground is draped with cloth banners honoring the four directions. . . . Thus decorated, the tree is considered an umbilicus, connecting the tribe to the earth (p. 10).

Further Smith (1998) contends that "the Sun Dance marks a communal coming home" (p. 520).

We see this in Tom's story about going to the Sun Dance and entering into a sacred community of dancers, into the sacred world in which he is transformed, and into the sacred circle of life. Tom's life is changed by the Sun Dance and by thanking the tree.

In editing this chapter Tom further explains his understandings of the Sun Dance: "My understanding of the Sun Dance is that we go there to sacrifice ourselves for the duration so that other people may live" (T. McCallum, personal communication, April 5, 2010). He further explains his understandings of the Sun Dance tree:

> The trees were made before us human beings and are closer to the Creator than we are so it has agreed to give up its life so we may continue to live. The trees were the first children of Mother earth and as such they are our grandfathers and they give up their lives for us. It goes through four stages and has 4 names till it reaches Creator—4 days after the end of the Sun Dance.
>
> The cloth that we use to decorate the tree represents clothes. We are clothing the tree—beyond the 4 directions it includes the whole universe—and the colors are representative of the sacred vibrations each color vibrates at.
>
> . . . In my Sun Dance we carve the tree on the north and south sides. On the north is the lightning representing the Thunder beings and on the south the buffalo. The connection that we have with the tree is to the Creator. The earth provides the nourishment for the tree and we feed the tree berries before we stand it up.
>
> It has been told to me that the Sun Dance is the closest any human will ever be to the Creator on this earth. It is a very profound event or ceremony that will be described from many dimensions. Some people will obviously encounter more than others due to their journey and how much work they have done on themselves. It is hard to describe as it is an experience and words cannot do justice to what it is about. When one is connected to the tree via the ropes through piercing one starts to understand to some limited degree what this is about. . . . It seems that like all other ceremonies, that you can only describe it based on your experience with the ceremony and it will vary with everyone. (T. McCallum, personal communication, April 5, 2010).

Tom's telling helps us understand how he learns the full lesson of his life. Hernandez-Avilla (2002) explains that

> "language is story." Through these stories, the past and the future come together in the present conscious situationality/relationality. . . ."stories are, in a sense, maps." Maps to deep truth(s), maps that help us to know the lay of the land and of our bodies, of our points of origin/emergence, of our hearts and spirits, of the universe, of our minds, of the planet we call home, we call Earth. These story maps allow us movement between the past and the future: looking back, we look forward, looking forward, we look back, always conscious of how the present moment at once holds both past and future (p. xi).

In Tom's story we see a mapping of his life, connecting of past, present, and future in his own life and also in the lives of his family and the community members, all connected in ceremony and in life. As Hernandez-Avilla (2002) suggests "the stories are given back and forth, shared and cherished. They are sustained by humans, by relations in the natural world, by those in the spirit world, by the earth herself. The spirit(s) speak(s) in stories" (p. xi). In Tom's story he connected to the spirit world in the Sun Dance ceremony as he is shown his connection to all of creation again as he was when he saw the Sun Dance tree as a youth. In sharing this story, Tom "can (re)connect through the land, through memory, through spirit" (Hernandez-Avilla, 2002. p. xvii). As Wilson (1996) explains "my connection to land and place is solidified with each telling of the story" (p. 12) as is the case with Tom.

Tom shares the story of his daughter's birth while he was at the Sun Dance at Kehewin—the place of eagles—and also the name of a reserve in Northern Alberta. Thorton (1997) clarifies that

> place names tell us something not only about the structure and content of the physical environment itself but also how people perceive, conceptualize, classify, and utilize that environment. . . . The context of nar-

ratives, songs, and everyday speech, provide valuable insights into the ways humans experience the world and appropriate images of the landscape to interpret and communicate their experiences. . . . Place names also convey a great deal of information about the social environment (p. 209).

In this case the name of the place where this child was born becomes the name of the child and reflects the cycle of life in which she becomes a part of the story and "the mutual influence of the earth and its inhabitants upon each other" (Thorton, 1997, p. 210) as "the ties between the people and the land are close" (p. 218).

Tom's daughter's identity is associated with the location of her birth and the story in which it unfolds. As Karr (2000) explains, Indigenous peoples "often see themselves, a part of the environment they inhabit, drawing a defining notion of who they are, an identity, from their surroundings" (p. 383). Jenish (1999) explains that all things we do have purpose and that children are often named in ceremonies such as the naming ceremony but in this case this was done at the Sun Dance.

In Tom's story he falls through the ice and the water surrounds him. He is drawn into that water and when he emerges from it he sees that tree. In these early experiences he is already "making connection with mother earth and the spirits. . . . The preparation is mental, social, and spiritual" (Tollefson & Abbott, 1993, p. 216) toward his eventual journey as a Sun Dance lodge keeper. In this process "the land manifests soul: its own . . . stories give identity to a place. . . . That's how you know you belong" (Cochran, 1995, p. 70). Within this connection "the spirit inspires imagination that creates a world of spirit, the land inspires stories that create an identity for the land" (Cochran, 1995, p. 71). Tom's identity is reflected in the stories in how much this has meant to him and his journey.

SWITCHING FOCUS TO HUMOROUS STORIES

Tom further explains about storytelling. "Storytelling has so much in it, it's not only something that is serious, but it's very beautiful stories, very serious, or very romantic. There is also a lot of humor in it." Garrett, Garrett, Torres-Rivera, Wilbur, and Roberts-Wilbur (2005) explain that "stories, anecdotes, witty one-liners, these are all examples of an expression of the spirit of Native people in a tradition that is unique to every tribal nation but shares the same power across tribes" (p. 194). They further suggest that "stories and anecdotes are but one means of reinforcing and reminding in-group members of the cultural values and unspoken rules by which they live" (Garrett, Garrett, Torres-Rivera, Wibur, & Roberts-Wilbur, 2005, p. 198). They also suggest that "oral traditions emphasize the important life lessons through the subtle humor expressed in stories" (Garrett, Garrett, Torres-Rivera, Wibur, & Roberts-Wilbur, 2005, p. 196).

TOM'S HUMOROUS HORSE STORY

I wanna share a short little story about people sitting around camp fires and drinking tea and just sharing stories, sharing laughter. . . . Where I come from we have a lake and there are 4 rivers that empty into that lake and people live in different areas. . . . The method of travel long time ago . . . used horses . . . so whenever they went hunting they would try and take a horse in the event that they would kill a moose. And . . . a one horse sleigh. . . . This was in spring time. . . . It was a beautiful sunny day and the guy was going hunting. . . . The sun was beating down and the snow was starting to melt so it was easy going. . . . Towards the evening it started to get cold and . . . that snow that melted turned into ice. Very slippery. . . . When the

> horse slipped the sleigh would slide, . . . hit the back of the horse, and he would get scared so the horse would kick and he starting kicking that sleigh and the sleigh started to break into pieces . . . by the time he got home there was nothing left of the sleigh just 2 runners and that's what he was riding on all the way home.
>
> And this other guy . . . sitting there said "oh yeah I know that happened to me this one time . . . but for me my horse is a little smarter . . . and he figured it out. . . . There was a clump of ice here and a clump of snow there so he would go on the clump of snow there and he would ski to the next clump of snow and that's the way he got me home . . . and so I got my sleigh home 'cause that horse is really smart."
>
> So that's the kind of stories that there are too. It's just to make people laugh, whether it happened or not. . . . It's like a cartoon almost. So, those lighten up the atmosphere. They used to have competitions like that, where they'd have a big can of tobacco, somebody would win that. Who could come up with the best story. And that's just the part of the people coming together and gathering and sharing after they haven't seen each other for a long time.

Vine Deloria (1969) explains that Indigenous people "are brought together by sharing humour of the past. They are retold over and over again wherever Indians gather" (pp. 147, 152). Carabi (1994), in an interview with poet Joy Harjo quotes her words that "Indian people have one of the most developed senses of humor I've ever heard" (p. 46) that "in the middle of all the tension and destruction, there is a laughter of absolute sanity" (p. 47).

Stories have "a high tolerance for disorder, seeking out the unfamiliar, embracing physical existence" (Gross, 2009, p. 67). Tom's horse story deals with the harsh reality of physical existence in a humorous tone. In this story, Tom is also interested in the real connections between humans and animals. Vizenor (1995) explains that "animals are imagined in nature and literature, translated, and compared in memories, narratives, and cultural contexts" (p. 662). Through stories and understandings of animals we can sometimes "trace our presence in animals" (Vizenor, 1995, p. 662). Tom's story relates horse behavior to human behavior, showing us how the horse is stumbling around just as humans sometimes do. Humans sometimes cause destruction in the process as does the horse, breaking the sleigh. This relationship of human stories to animal stories is repeated in Tom's dancing dog story.

TOM'S DANCING DOG STORY

> I'll give an example of how storytelling connects the past to today, and how it may impact the future. . . . So when the creator was making everything, everything had a gift, and it seemed like there was something, like in the story of Adam and Eve, they were forbidden to eat of that one tree. They couldn't eat that fruit. Well that's kind of like what happened. Take for instance dogs. Dogs were able to talk to people, all animals had the ability to talk to people. They still have that ability, it is us as people who do not have that ability to be able to listen to them anymore. It was mentioned here that listening . . . is very, very important. The art of listening, we seem to have lost that, or put it away somewhere.
>
> So these dogs loved to dance, oh they just loved dancing. But they were forbidden to dance. For some reason the creator said "no you can't dance." There's a reason why for that, but I'm not sure what it is. But they were forbidden to dance. But they loved to dance, and they wanted to dance, it was inside of them, they just couldn't get it out. . . . But there were certain things in the physical body of these animals that the creator could hone in on and know what they were doing, and it happened to be the rectum. . . . So they had a council meeting, they wanted to have a dance, but how could they have a dance without the creator knowing? So they said, well we got to find some way of taking that rectum out, or whatever is in that rectum and

putting it somewhere else, so that the creator won't know we're dancing. So they did. They devised a way. So they had this great big clearing where they all gathered, it only had one entrance, and they all gathered there and as they went in they took their rectum off and put it at the door. And they all gathered in there and they danced, and they danced, and they danced. All night they danced. They were so happy. And there was one dog standing on a hill watching for the creator to come. Early in the morning the creator was coming and hollered at the other dogs and they all ran out. And on their way out they grabbed a rectum and stuck it on there. But of course it wasn't theirs, because they were in such a hurry they didn't have time to look for their own. So they just grabbed one and stuck it on there. So today when you see two dogs meeting each other right away they go like that, they sniff each other, they're still looking for their rectum.

Tom speaks about *when the creator was making everything, everything had a gift, . . . all animals had the gift to talk to people.* Andrews (1998) writes that Indigenous stories "frequently include animals that act as creators, messengers, protectors, guardians, and advisors. They were often thought to possess human qualities and had the ability to speak, think, and act like humans" (p. 197). Tom's story then subtly suggests the strict roles given by the Creator to dogs per se, and mentions about forgetting to listen. Tom's very humorous and elaborate story shows what happens when dogs go against the rules.

Taylor (1996) furthers this by stating how animal stories can relate to the human community. "It was a way of explaining human nature" (p. 29). How is this done in Tom's Dancing Dog story? Gross (2007) writes that "humor 'gives reason to play' and humor 'sustains reflection'" (p. 71). In Tom's story the dogs are playfully dancing and there is a reflection about their not following the rules. Stories allow one to "be able to see him or herself in a frank and open manner [and] to recognize the shortcomings of his or her character" (Gross, 2007, p. 72) in this case the shortcomings of the dogs following Creator's rules. Tom's story emphasizes physical and slapstick comedy with anal humor which is common in Indigenous storytelling (Gross, 2007, 2009). In Tom's story the dogs are in a rush to escape the Creator so they pick up any anus whether it is theirs or not and attach it. This story explains the peculiar behavior of dogs sniffing each others' behinds.

"There are stories about dogs. . . .We're kind of tough on dogs." (Gross, 2009). In fact, Garrett, Garrett, Torres-Rivera, Wibur, and Roverts-Wilbur (2005) have another version of Tom's story of why dogs sniff each other's behinds: "I nominate that dog for president who smells good underneath his tail" (Garrett, Garrett, Torres-Rivera, Wibur, & Roverts-Wilbur, 2005, p. 194) after the dogs cannot find an appropriate leader amongst the fast runners, good hunters, and other characteristics. Vizenor (1995) goes further in his ridicule of the dog, "and remember, dogs don't like ghosts or witches....For instance, has created a wild and comic scene of two dogs stuck together in a natural sexual dance" (p. 673). However, the relationship between humans and dogs also includes respect of learning from dogs in Tom's story. Vizenor (1995) states "Indians and dogs go together. . . . It's an ancient, honorable alliance" (p. 663). Tom illustrated this idea in his story of how our behavior can be understood via the humorous behavior of the dogs. Here we see the influence of dogs and humans learning from each other and the strong relationship of dogs and humans in the humorous stories.

CONCLUSION

Tom explains that stories are real. We can understand them as true pedagogic spaces. In stories we create meaning. Through Tom's pedagogy he is teaching us to look at a story from many perspectives and find key elements of our own lives that give us purpose and meaning. Enriched by these pedagogic experiences we can create lives that are powerful and meaningful. In this process of hearing stories we are challenged to understand Indigenous knowledges not just as stories told by an Elder, but as stories in our own lives that help us reinterpret our own lives and the meanings we make within them, as is the case with Tom's story of ceremony.

Ceremony is a pedagogical location in which Tom learns lessons about the importance of family, community, and the cycle of life. Through vision and spiritual awareness Tom understands himself, his role in life as a Sun Dance lodge keeper, and his place in the community and the cycle of life. When Tom shares these stories with listeners he takes us on his and our own journey to help us imagine and understand the connections he is making while we make new connections within our lives.

Nature is also a teacher in Tom's stories. The landscape helps us understand the connections to place. The tree is a main character that foreshadows Tom's future role in life. It is also the way that Tom connects to the spirit world through the Sun Dance ceremony and here the tree affirms its and Tom's spiritual power. We are challenged to consider our own spiritual journeys and the process of developing our own spiritual power.

In the emergence of Tom's story from an incident as a youth to a full realization of its meanings as an adult, we see the pedagogical growth and development of understanding through the process of life and storytelling. The journey of learning is a process of "reweaving rather than in simply receiving" (Smith, 1998, p. 532). Tom's story becomes woven into the fabric of the family and community through his telling of it. This is part of the pedagogic power that storytelling has in communities when stories are told and retold.

In the act of remembering, reading, and hearing ceremonial stories we create personal connections to the natural and spiritual worlds. Tom's stories create imaginative landscapes in which we can understand our own stories. The stories have the potential to create "emotional, symbolic, historic, spiritual and cultural significance for a whole group" (McAvoy, 2002, p. 390). Tom's stories of the Sun Dance ceremony also explain the sacred rite of transformation. The sacred community of dancers and sacred circle of life are central to Tom's transformation and in learning the lessons of life that enable him to take up his role as a Sun Dance lodge keeper. Tom is connecting past and future as he tells the story in the present, connecting through land, memory, and spirit, using the story to affirm his place in the cycle of life, ceremony, and community. He reaffirms his place each time he tells the story. As listeners to these connections, we are challenged to understand, accept, acknowledge, and honor the connections that Tom is making in his story. We are called upon through this pedagogic practice to understand ourselves in new connections.

Spirit inspires connecting landscape to Tom's own life journey and finding meaning in the connections, like the Sun Dance tree and how it plays a major role in Tom's life. It inspires us to consider the role of stories in understanding identity, life journeys, and in creating and making meaning within pedagogical moments created in stories.

Humorous stories inspire connecting to community and reaffirming relationships and connections. They suggest ways to find humor in the harshness of the physical reality of life. Hunting can be a very challenging undertaking but there is humor in the telling of this hunting story. The stories also show us the parallels between animal behavior and human behavior, learning about resilience in the horse story, learning to laugh at the struggles, and learning that we are also fallible. In the dog story we learn about the consequences of not following the natural order and disobeying the Creator with humorous consequences in the story. Both stories are a reflection through animals of our own behavior. Humor sustains reflection and allows us to be frank about our own shortcomings (Taylor, 1996). While storytellers make fun of animals they also honor them (Vizenor, 1995). They help us learn to honor the alliances and interrelationships between human beings and animals and the many lessons to learn from these interrelationships which is a valuable pedagogic practice in which to engage students and listeners.

Tom's personal and historical stories help us understand that youthful accidents can lead to understanding one's responsibilities as community storyteller and Elder. They suggest that the many stories inherent in our own lives may take on greater meanings as their lessons become evident later in life. These are powerful pedagogical moments.

Tom's stories educate communities and aid listeners in understanding, in a personal way, one's place on the land, and in the community, culture, and spiritual world. This is powerful teaching that needs to be shared in broader educational circles. His pedagogy emphasizes that listeners have a responsibility to be active participants in the story, to interpret meanings, and make connections to their own lives. This is important in the development and understandings of children and youth. Through this type of pedagogy, listeners are encouraged to develop a 360-degree viewpoint that allows them to see any problem from multiple perspectives and to consider multiple solutions to problems so that they are better prepared to encounter, learn from, and deal with problems in life.

Indigenous pedagogy encourages a broader understanding of identity in relation to the cycle of life, the natural world, the community, and the Nation. This kind of community education enriches the lives of community members, including children, youth, and adults. It creates a sense of interconnectedness and engagement within the spiritual and communal lives in Indigenous culture.

As educators, we are challenged to consider Indigenous pedagogies and their power in aiding students/listeners in challenging their own assumptions and narrow viewpoints. We are challenged to reconsider Indigenous epistemologies and pedagogies in our classrooms, our homes, our communities, our workplaces, and our cultural settings and ways these can inform educational practices and decision making. Students/listeners must understand that Indigenous pedagogies disrupt our taken-for-granted assumptions about what education is and should be. They challenge us to consider how we live storied lives and how the stories we tell and believe partially dictate the decisions we make and the way we live our lives. By telling/living/believing new stories we broaden our understandings and find new ways to make our lives meaningful and can find new meanings in the lives we live.

As educators we are also challenged to consider pedagogic practices that go beyond telling stories to explain facts but rather as a practice to expand one's ability to think about, understand, consider, reconsider, and challenge the very ideas we assume we know. Storytelling, while often assumed to be a process one uses with young children, is a powerful form of teaching that gives us knowledge and skills that can put us in a powerful and thoughtful place for our entire lives. It is a practice that we benefit from as children, grow deeper understandings of as we grow, and if we remain open to storytelling, it remains a practice in which we can learn for a lifetime. This would appear to be a wonderful and powerful undertaking and a worthy pedagogic practice from which all educators could learn lessons and in which all communities could develop understandings. Perhaps the greatest task for education in today's practices is the development of the next generation of storytellers who can practice the skills, develop the knowledge, encounter and become the 360 degree perspective, and master the ability to understand the complexity of life. In these stories we are challenged to reach inside ourselves to find our own interpretations and meanings in the stories and to connect these to our lives in multiple ways with each new telling.

Storytelling is a powerful practice even if it appears simplistic from the outside. The most powerful stories take a great understanding and a complex mindfulness to comprehend. These most complex and powerful stories cannot be reproduced here as the reader/listener to stories must develop the ability to comprehend and understand the stories. These stories and lessons have been left for another telling by a powerful storyteller when the listener has reached the developmental stage to understand them. Until then we can learn a great deal from initial stories that help us develop the skills and knowledge to get us ready to hear more complex stories.

NOTE

1. This research was supported in part by the Social Sciences and Humanities Research Council, Canada Research Chairs Program, and Canadian Foundation for Innovation Fund as well as Lakehead University, and Confederation College Broadcast Program. A similar section to the one entitled "A Research Approach" in this chapter is included in a journal article "Importance of Indigenous Spirituality in Healing Communities" under review by the *Canadian Journal of Native Education*.

REFERENCES

Andrews, T. J. (1998). Share in the Light: Native American Stories of Creation. *World and I, 13*(7), 196–203.

Bishop, R. (1998). Freeing ourselves from neo-colonial domination in research: A Maori approach to creating knowledge. *Qualitative Studies in Education*, 11(2), pp. 199–219.

Brennus, B. (2005) *My Self-in-Relation-to Learning Oneida/On^yote'a:ka Language/Culture via the English Language. De-colonizing, Problems, Difficulties and Language Erasure: Oneida/ On^yote'a:ka Nation—A Case Study.* (Master's thesis). Toronto, University of Toronto.

Carabi, A. (1994). Interview with Joy Harjo. *Belles Lettres, 9*(4), 46–49.

Castellano, M. B. (2000). Updating Indigenous Traditions of Knowledge. In G. J. S. Dei, B. L. Hall, & D. G. Rosenberg (Eds.), *Indigenous Knowledges in Global Contexts: Multiple Readings of Our World* (pp. 21–36). Toronto: University of Toronto.

Cochran, S. (1995). The Ethnic Implications of Stories, Spirits and the Land in Native American Pueblo and Aztlan. *MELUS, 20*(2), 69–91.

Deloria, V. (1969). *Custer Died for Your Sins: An Indian Manifesto*. Norman, OK: University of Oklahoma Press.

Garrett, M.T., Garrett, J., Torres-Rivera, E., Wilbur, M., & Roberts-Wilbur, J. (2005). Laughing It Up: Native American Humor as Spiritual Tradition. *Journal of Multicultural Counseling and Development, 33*(4), 194–204.

Gross, L W. (2007). Silence as the Root of American Indian Humor: Further Meditations on the Comic Vision of Anishinaabe Culture and Religion. *American Indian Culture Research Journal, 31*(2), 69–85.

Gross, L. W. (2009, Spring). Humor and Healing in the Nonfiction Works of Jim Northrup. *Wicazo Sa Review, 24*(1), 65–87.

Hampton, E. (1995). Towards a Redefinition of Indian Education. In M. Battiste & J. Barman (Eds.), *First Nations Education in Canada: The Circle Unfolds* (pp. 5–46). Vancouver: UBC.

Hernandez-Avilla, I. (2002) Introduction. *Frontiers, 23*(2), ix–xviii.

Jenish, D. (1999, August 16). Rekindling the Spiritual Life. *Maclean's, 112*(33), 26–27.

Karr, S. M. (2000). Water We Believed Could Never Belong to Anyone. *The American Indian Quarterly, 24*(3), 381–399.

King, T. (2003). The Truth About Stories: A Native Narrative. Toronto: House of Anansi Press.

Kovach, M. (2005). Emerging from the Margins: Indigenous Knowledge. In L. Brown & S. Strega (Eds.), *Research as Resistance: Critical, Indigenous and Anti-Oppressive Approaches* (pp. 19–36). Toronto: Canadian Scholars.

Kovach, M. (2009). *Indigenous Methodologies: Characteristics, Conversations, and Contexts*. Toronto: University of Toronto Press.

Kroeber, K. ed. (2004). *Native American Storytelling: A Reader of Myths and Legends*. Malden, MA: Blackwell.

Lassiter, L. E. (2000). Authoritative Texts, Collaborative Ethnography, and Native American Studies. *American Indian Quarterly, 24*(4), 601–614.

McAvoy, L. (2002). American Indians, Place Meaning and the Old/New West. *Journal of Leisure Research, 34*(4), 383–396.

Morgan, R. (1999, March). Near the Cross. *The Other Side, 35*(2), 10.

Phelan, S. (1996, Summer). Coyote Politics: Trickster Tales and Feminists. *Hypatia, 11*(3), 130–149.

Schwenniger, L. (1995, Summer). Nature Power: In the Spirit of an Okanagan Storyteller. *Melus, 20*(2), 149–151.

Smith, C. (1998, Summer). Coyote, Contingency, and Community: Thomas King's Green Grass, Running Water and Postmodern Trickster. *The American Indian Quarterly, 21*(3), 515–534.

Smith, L. T. (1999). *Decolonizing Methodologies: Research and Indigenous Peoples*. London: Zed.

Stevenson, W. (1999). Colonialism and First Nations Women in Canada. In E. Dua & A. Robertson (Eds.), *Scratching the Surface: Canadian Anti-racist Feminist Thought* (pp. 49–80). Toronto: Women's Press.

Taylor, D. H. (1996). Alive and Well: Native Theatre in Canada. *Journal of Canadian Studies, 31*(3), 29–37.

Thorton, T. F. (1997). Anthropological Studies of Native American Place Naming. *The American Indian Quarterly, 21*(2), 209–228.

Tollefson, K. D., & Abbott, M. L. (1993, Spring). From Fish Weir to Waterfall. *The American Indian Quarterly, 17*(2), 209–225.

Vaserstein, T. (2001). The Trickster Shift. *Humor: International Journal of Humor Research, 14*(3), 308–311.

Vizenor, G. (1992). North American Indian Literature: Critical Metaphors of the Ghost Dance. *World Literature Today, 66*(2), 223–227.

Vizenor, G. (1995). Authored Animals: Creature Tropes in Native American Fiction. *Social Research, 62*(3), 661–683.

Wilson, A. C. (1996, Winter). Grandmother to Granddaughter: Generations of Oral History in a Dakota family. *The American Indian Quarterly, 20*(1), 7–13.

Wilson, S. (2008). *Research Is Ceremony: Indigenous Research Methods*. Halifax: Fernwood.

CHAPTER SEVENTEEN

Ua Lele Ka Manu; The Bird Has Flown

A Search for Indigenous/Local Inquiry Methods

Pauline Chinn, Isabella Aiona Abbott, Michelle Kapana-Baird, Mahina Hou Ross, Lila Lelepali, Ka'umealani Walker, Sabra Kauka, Napua Barrows, Moana Lee, & Huihui Kanahele-Mossman

More than one-fourth of students in Hawai'i's public schools self-identifies as Native Hawaiian. They are the majority in 17% of public schools, but 52% of these schools versus 12% of those in which they are a minority are "planning for restructuring" or being "restructured" under No Child Left Behind (Kekahio, 2007). Many of these schools serve rural communities in which farming, fishing, and hunting contribute to extensive knowledge of land, ocean, and sky. Meyer's (1998) interviews with Hawaiian elders revealed the critical roles of place, practice, and culture in learning for Indigenous youth. But this informal knowledge seldom connects to formal science learning. Differing views on what Native Hawaiian students should be learning, how they should be taught, and how learning should be assessed have led to culture-based programs, charter, and language immersion schools.

This chapter explores this educational issue in the area of Indigenous/local inquiry in science, emphasizing from the outset that in Hawaiian, there are no words that convey the Western meanings of science, nature, or physical universe. We include local perspectives as for over 200 years Hawai'i has been a multicultural, multilingual society. We are personally concerned with this issue as science educators seeking to understand the role of culture in instruction of Indigenous students. The question on Indigenous/local inquiry and methods will thus cast a wide net. What we find will help to define Indigenous/local inquiry methods and contribute to discussions on its relevance for science teacher education, curriculum design, and pedagogy. (Note: For brevity, the word Indigenous appears alone but includes local in subsequent use.)

We are Isabella Aiona Abbott, scientist; Michelle Kapana-Baird, Polynesian Voyaging Program teacher; Mahina Hou Ross and Lila Lelepali, Hawaiian immersion science teachers; Ka'umealani Walk, Hawaiian immersion geography teacher; Sabra Kauka and Napua Barrows, Hawaiian studies/science teachers; Moana Lee, archeologist/educator; Huihui Kanahele-Mossman, science teacher/administrator and doctoral student; and Pauline Chinn, Hawai'i-born, Chinese American teacher educator and former secondary science teacher. Pauline is the "I" narrating the chapter. Our chapter includes our reflections about the ways *kanaka maoli*, those of Native Hawaiian descent, and long-time/Hawai'i-born residents, *kama'āina*, engage in inquiry: observing, accumulating, analyzing, sharing, and developing knowledge informing decisions and action in the world.

First I discuss the title then provide a brief overview of major curricular ideologies that reflect mainstream, middle-class American culture and influence policies and practices in U.S. schools. These are discussed in the context of sociocultural theories of learning that view cultural patterns as shaping psychological processes and ways of being in the world. Next I introduce Indigenous Hawaiian ways of viewing and acting in the world and contrast them with dominant American ideologies. Then we present our thoughts and experiences with Indigenous science inquiry. We conclude with reflections on the title, implications for teacher education and curriculum development, and close with a call for *Mālama I Ka 'Āina (Sustainability)* as a Hawai'i State science content standard informed by Indigenous practices and perspectives and relevant to current concerns over sustainability.

Meaning of Title: Ua Lele Ka Manu, the Bird Has Flown

Dr. Isabella Aiona Abbott, the first Indigenous Hawaiian to receive a doctorate in natural science, contributed the title "*Ua Lele Ka Manu*; the Bird Has Flown." She said she often heard her mother saying it as she searched for something missing, possibly still present but overlooked or not recognized. As we talked about meanings, she said birds might be a metaphor for youth growing up ignorant right under our noses. I thought of the day I saw a small banana plant in a bucket in her laboratory. I was surprised as Dr. Abbott is renowned for her studies of marine algae. It was shortly before a NOAA (National Oceanic and Atmospheric Administration) research cruise to the North West Hawaiian Islands with Sabra Kauka and other science educators. The captain had approved Dr. Abbott's request to present it as an offering, symbolizing *Kanaloa*, god of the sea to notify the *akua*, gods, and *aumakua*, ancestral gods, associated with these places of the arrival of visitors. It was the appropriate cultural protocol, the proper thing to do; Sabra presented the offering as the ship approached the islands.

The title *Ua Lele Ka Manu* inquires if the bird of Indigenous inquiry has flown or is still here, under our noses. What is its current form and, like the banana plant shimmering between different meaning systems, can it be recognized? If so, can Indigenous Hawaiian inquiry methods inform science education? This chapter owes much to Dr. Abbott's insights and experiences as a member of Hawaiian, scientific, and educational communities.

TRENDS IN CURRICULUM IDEOLOGIES IN AMERICAN SCHOOLS

Educational ideologies that reflect mid-20th-century assembly-line economics and American culture continue to shape educational policies that focus on test scores as measures of successful learning. Schiro (2008) views US education as guided by four major Western ideologies that influence educational goals, actions, and aims: *scholar academic* focused on acquisition of disciplinary knowledge; *social efficiency* focused on efficient preparation of learners to be productive members of society; *learner centered* focused on experience-based preparation for the future; and *social reconstruction* focused on problem finding and problem solving in an imperfect world. Educational systems employing high-stakes testing tend to follow *scholar academic* and *social efficiency* ideologies more appropriate to 20th-century models of resource-intensive, individualistic consumption, and competition. They reflect American cultural ideas, everyday practices, and artifacts that value competitive behaviors leading to recognition of individual achievement. Markus and Hamedani (2007) observe that:

> North American psychological tendencies have in many significant ways been created, fostered, and maintained by widely distributed ideas—such as the importance of individual achievement—and have been reinforced and instituted by dense networks of everyday practices—such as complimenting and praising one another for individual performance by a frequent distribution of awards and honors in classrooms and workplaces (p. 6).

Sternberg's (2003) research showed that educational ideologies centered on mastery of disciplinary content and preparation for urban, consumer-driven economies had two undesirable outcomes. They favored the success of middle class, mainstream students, thus perpetuating the underrepresentation of marginalized minorities, and produced what he called *pseudo-experts* lacking practical, place-based experiences needed to develop critical thinking and real world problem-solving skills.

In contrast, *learner-centered* and *social reconstruction* ideologies reflect sociocultural views of learning as "engagement, or a coming together, an encounter, of a person making sense of a world replete with meaning, objects, and practices" (Markus & Hamedani, 2007, p. 8). These ideologies recognize the need to prepare learners for rapid technological and cultural change during a 21st-century transition to sustainability (Adams & Jeanrenaud, 2008; National Research Council, 1999). Collaborations of educators, scientists, and the business community agree that school knowledge and skills should be aligned with the integrative, process-oriented knowledge and skills reflective of a rapidly changing, complex, globally interconnected world (www.21stcenturyskills.org/). These include critical and systems thinking, problem solving, creativity, and intellectual curiosity; collaboration and self-direction; global awareness; and civic literacy.

This transdisciplinary and transformative vision expects students to engage, evaluate, create, and effect changes in their lives and communities. It asks teachers to apply instructional approaches that address individual, cultural, and geographical diversity. Teachers' roles shift from that of curriculum deliverers to curriculum developers able to connect students' diverse experiences to meaningful, active learning about real world issues such as climate change and conservation that have both local and global impacts. Viewing learning as authentic engagement requires teachers to establish working relationships with members of a range of discourse communities each having its own expectations and ways of communicating, behaving, and thinking.

Education that enables students to understand their placing between the local and the global is guided by sociocultural views of learning as developing through situated, context-rich, social interactions (Lave & Wenger, 1991). Gee, Hull, and Lankshear (1996) observed that "language, literacy, and learning can only be understood when situated in their social and cultural setting" (p. 1). Fairclough (1999/2006) holds that "people need resources to examine their placing . . . between the global and the local . . . and need from education a range of resources for living within socially and culturally diverse societies" (p. 151). Engaging learners in place- and community-based discourse communities develops "common pools of knowledge—the knowledge commons—over which members of these communities labor to produce new knowledge" (Waters, 2006, p. 161).

SOCIOCULTURAL APPROACHES TO LEARNING: PLACE AND INQUIRY–BASED PROGRAMS

Gruenewald (2008) provides a sociocultural, social reconstruction framework for designing place- and inquiry-based science curricula: "What needs to be transformed, conserved, restored, or created in this place . . . [could] provide a local focus for socioecological inquiry and action that, because of interrelated cultural and ecological systems, is potentially global in reach" (p. 149). A human-in-ecosystem view recognizes interconnected social and natural systems as "complex adaptive systems where social and biophysical agents are interacting at multiple temporal and spatial scales" (Janssen & Ostrom, 2006, p. 1465). Woodhouse and Knapp's (2000) review of place-based North American school programs identified five "essential characteristics" that establish each program's unique, local nature: (1) natural and historical-cultural content specific to place; (2) multidisciplinary approaches; (3) experiential and/or service learning; (4) broader focus than preparation for a technological and consumer-oriented society; and (5) understanding of place, self, and community as part of a social-ecological system. They conclude that place-based learning provides students with "knowledge and experiences needed to actively participate in the democratic process". Current educational views encourage preparation for multiple literacies, critical thinking, and awareness that individual actions have both local and global dimensions. Indigenous Hawaiians already understood humans as part of a social-ecosystem in which actions had both societal and ecological consequences. Hall's (2004) review of global adult environmental education programs yielded seven characteristics relevant to Hawai'i: (1) a sense of place; (2) valuing of biodiversity; (3) connection with nature; (4) revitalization of traditional and Indigenous knowledge and practices; (5) building of social networks; (6) understanding of power-knowledge relationships; and (7) valuing learning from elders.

In self-sustaining societies such as Hawai'i's, close observation, analysis, and thoughtful action based on evidence and knowledge gained over generations of living in a place informed a Hawaiian sense of place associated with a worldview, values, and practices oriented to sustainability of socioecosystems.

HISTORICAL DEVELOPMENT OF INDIGENOUS HAWAIIAN SOCIETY

Kirch (1996), Abbott (1992), and Beckwith (1970) present linguistic, archeological, botanical, and oral history as evidence for Indigenous Hawaiians' connections with Tahiti, Marquesas, Cook Islands, New Zealand, Samoa, and Tonga. Kirch (1996) divides Hawaiian cultural history into four periods: "1) Colonization, 300–500 C.E., likely from the Marquesas or Society Islands; 2) Developmental, 600–1100 C.E., appearance of uniquely Hawaiian culture; 3) Expansion, 1100–1650 C.E., *kapu* and *ahupua'a* management systems develop, oral narratives suggest transpacific voyages cease; and 4) Proto-Historic, 1650–1795 C.E., system of chiefs, priests (*papa kahuna pule*), occupational specialists (*kahuna*), and commoners . . . held together by the equally elaborated *kapu* system" (p. 6). Kamakau (1991) describes the range of expertise: *papa kahuna pule*, priests for chiefly class; *papa kāula*, prophets; *papa hulihonua*, land experts; *papa kuhikuhi pu'uone*, locators of sites; *papa kilokilo lani,* readers of sky omens; *kilo hōkū*, star experts; *kilo 'ōpua*, readers of cloud omens; *kilo honua,* readers of earth signs; *papa ku'ialua*, experts in *lua* (martial arts); *papa lonomakaihe*, experts in spear throwing (pp. 7–8).

During the Expansion period, population growth, development of fishpond and farming systems, and cultural stratification led to the *ahupua'a* system of socioecological organization (Kirch, 1996). Abbott (1992) notes that "Hawaiians did not belong to a village but rather to an *ahupua'a*, a land division extending from the mountain heights to the sea" (p. 11) including at least one valley, its ridges, fresh water, and the sea to the depth of a man's chest or edge of the reef. Hawaiians lived, married, and sustained themselves within *ahupua'a*. Highly variable topography, soils, and microclimates led to hundreds of named cultivars of the staple crops, taro and sweet potatoes. People living upland, *mauka*, exchanged products with those living *makai*, seaward.

According to Maly (2001):

> Hawaiian customs and practices demonstrate the belief that all portions of the land and environment are related, like members of an extended family. . . . Just as place names tell us that areas are of cultural importance, the occurrence of a Hawaiian nomenclature for environmental zones also tells us that there was an intimate relationship between Hawaiians and their environment. (pp. 2–3)

Pukui, Elbert, and Mookini (1974) and Clark's (2002) collections of thousands of place names and their stories illustrate a Hawaiian sense of place, a valuing and cultural connectedness to specific places. A storied landscape enabled Hawaiian myths and nature gods to enter "into all the affairs of daily life" (Beckwith, 1970, p. 2). *Mauka-makai* interdependence within *ahupua'a* may have supported "an organized conception of form . . . where from lower forms of life emerge offspring on a higher scale and water forms of life are paired with land forms" (Beckwith, 1970, p. 3). The land-sea connection is seen in the names of organisms and the linking of land and sea events in everyday sayings. For example, pigs, *pua'a*, (*Sus scrofa*) and triggerfish, *humuhumunukunukuapua'a (Rhinecanthus rectangulus*) are linked by similarities in snouts and the flowering of a native tree is associated with increased danger from shark attacks. Hawaiians employed binary nomenclature similar to the Linnaean system: all triggerfish are *humuhumu*; the second name identifies a distinguishing feature.

KAPU, MO'OLELO, 'ŌLELO NO'EAU: INDICATORS OF INDIGENOUS INQUIRY

Beckwith (1970) notes that *mo'olelo*, legends, relating to the gods of fishing (*Kū'ula*) identify "authentic fishing grounds and stations for fishermen in island waters" (p. 20) and describe ways of establishing fish aggregation and spawning sites. *Mo'olelo* about the *'elepaio*, (*Chasiempis sandwichensis*), suggest close observation of the behavior of an insect-eating bird worshiped by canoe makers as the *kinolau*, bodily form, a goddess. The *kahuna kalai wa'a*, priest of canoe-making, declared a tree free of boring insects if the bird explored the trunk but did not stop to peck and probe for insects. Abbott (1992) notes this as a rare case of men taking guidance from a goddess. She suggests that *kapu* that forbade women from contact or consumption of foods that were *kinolau* of the major gods *Ku* (coconut), *Lono* (pork), *Kāne* (taro), and *Kanaloa* (banana) likely contributed to gendered knowledge.

Pre- and post-Western contact stories about migratory *kōlea*, golden plover (*Pluvialis fulva*), a lesser god, scout, and carrier of messages connect conservation ethics, practices, and sense of place. The first is from Beckwith(1970):

Kumu-hana, a bird hunter, recklessly slaughters the plover even when he does not need them to eat. His neighbor, who worships the plover god *Kumu-kahi* and has been made ill by contact with the smoke from *Kumu-hana*'s oven, warns him against this sacrilege. *Kumu-hana* disregards the warning and is overwhelmed by a flock of plover, who enter his house and peck and scratch him to death. The place where he lived is called *Ai-a-kōlea* to this day (pp. 137–138).

After European contact, a new *'ōlelo no'eau*: "*Haole ki kōlea!* Plover-shooting *haole*!" (No. 477, Pukui, 1983) disapproves of Caucasian (*haole*) values and behavior. Hawaiians netted sleeping birds at night, taking only what they needed.

Chiefly and godly edicts were associated with fresh water, *wai*, a precious, life-giving resource that determined worth and value, *waiwai*. *Konohiki*, resource managers, supervised irrigation ditches, *auwai*, and equitable distribution of water: "A spirit of mutual dependence and helpfulness prevailed, alike among the high and the low, with respect to the use of the water" (in the work cited Perry, 1912, p. 95; Franco, 1995, p. 28). Place names and *'ōlelo no'eau*, proverbs or sayings, convey the importance of water associated with *Kāne*, "the great life-giver" (Abbott, 1992, p. 15), god of procreation, ancestor of chiefs and commoners, embodied in fresh water, sunlight, taro, sugarcane, and bamboo (Handy, Handy, & Pukui, 1972). The saying "*Hahai no ka ua ka ulula'au*; Rains always follow the forest" (No. 405, Pukui, 1983) suggests Hawaiians knew forests protected the watershed, thus cut trees only as needed.

Hawaiians did not abandon chants and *mo'olelo* learned "from their mothers or grandmother or aunties, or, less often, from certain exceptional and strange poetic-minded men" (Pukui & Korn, 1983, p. xii) after the *kapu* system was dismantled in 1819. Hawaiians also retained ancestral gods, *'aumakua*, that took the forms of sharks, owls, mud hens, geckos, turtles, or deities such as Pele, goddess of volcanoes, who did not require sacrifices.

Oral narratives, *mo'olelo*, are considered by Hawaiians to relate historical events (Beckwith, 1970). The myth of Pele who searches for a volcanic home after voyaging from her ancestral homeland of Kahiki (Emerson, 1915) holds clues to Indigenous inquiry. Pele begins her search for a home in an active volcano on the eroded remnants of long-extinct volcanoes northwest of the main Hawaiian Islands. She plunges her *o'o*, digging stick, into each island, and disappointed, proceeds down the chain of increasingly younger volcanic islands until she arrives on the largest, youngest island of Hawai'i where she finds a home in Kilauea, an active volcano. J. Tuzo Wilson's Hotspot Theory of the formation of the Hawaiian Islands may be viewed as a Western science version of Pele's journey (http://en.wikipedia.org/wiki/Hawaii_hotspot).

INDIGENOUS INQUIRY METHODS AS SUSTAINABILITY SCIENCE: RESTORING KAHO'OLAWE ISLAND

Native Hawaiians and *kama'āina*, (Hawai'i-born, literally, child of the land) create modern *'ōlelo no'eau* conveying traditional values of sustainability. "The ocean is our refrigerator" cautions against taking more than needed. Growing awareness that "ecological and resource management issues . . . necessitate an approach that does not fit well with the conventional mechanistic, linear science of the Age of Enlightenment" (Dudgeon & Berkes, 2003, p. 84) leads to new appreciation for traditional ecological knowledge (TEK). Based on "detailed observation of the dynamics of the natural environment, feedback learning, social system/ecological system linkages, and resilience-enhancing practices," the hope is that TEK can contribute to a new science of sustainability (Dudgeon & Berkes, 2003, p. 85).

Cajete (2000) suggests that Indigenous and Western trained scientists collaborate in participatory research oriented to sustainability. In 1999, the National Research Council identified three research and five action priorities for sustainability science. The following are relevant to Indigenous inquiry in Hawai'i (National Research Council, 1999, pp. 10–13):

- *Research Priority 1.* Develop a research framework that integrates global and local perspectives to shape a "place-based" understanding of the interactions between environment and society.
- *Research Priority 3.* Promote better utilization of existing tools and processes for linking knowledge to action in pursuit of a sustainability transition.
- *Action Priority 5.* Restore degraded ecosystems while conserving biodiversity elsewhere.

Until 2005, Hawai'i's Hawaiian content standard *Mālama I Ka 'Āina (Sustainability)* supported culturally responsive, place- and problem-based curriculum and pedagogy (Chinn, 2006, 2008; Kaneshiro et al, 2005). Kanahele's (1986) explanation of the standard's cultural, spiritual, and socioecological significance resonates with Hall's (2004) findings from global adult environmental programs and National Research Council's research and action priorities cited above:

> If we are to be truly consistent with traditional Hawaiian thought, no one really owned the land in the past. . . . The relationship was the other way around: a person belonged to the land. . . . We are but stewards of the *'āina* and *kai,* trusted to take care of these islands on behalf of the gods, our ancestors, ourselves, and our children (Kanahele, 1986, pp. 208–209).

Reinstating a sustainability science standard incorporating Hawaiian cultural perspectives would be timely in light of local and global concerns over sustainability.

Hawaiian Traditional Ecological Knowledge oriented to sustainability and *'ōlelo no'eau* such as "*He ali'i ka 'āina he kauwā ke kanaka*; The land is a chief, man is its servant" (No. 531, Pukui, 1983) expressed the conservation ethic of active care (*mālama 'āina*), responsibility (*kuleana*) and respect/love (*aloha 'āina*) for the land that sustained life. A *kapu* system regulating human behavior may have developed as population growth intensified agricultural activities on marginal lands and reduced fallow periods (Franco, 1995). Dry-land cultivation of Kaho'olawe, an island that lies in Maui's rain shadow, led to loss of native vegetation and soil erosion so severe that the interior was abandoned around 1700. In the 19th and 20th centuries, Kaho'olawe served as a penal colony, a ranch, a forest reserve, and a bombing range. In 1993, the U.S. government returned it to the State of Hawai'i as Kaho'olawe Island Reserve, a status requiring that Kaho'olawe and the surrounding two miles of ocean (http://www.kahoolawe.org/history.html) be dedicated solely to:

1. Preservation and practice of all rights customarily and traditionally exercised by the native Hawaiians for cultural, spiritual, and subsistence purposes.
2. Preservation and protection of its archaeological, historical, and environmental resources.
3. Rehabilitation, revegetation, habitat restoration, and preservation.
4. Education.

The Kaho'olawe Island Reserve Commission (KIRC) decided to adopt Indigenous knowledge and practices for rehabilitation, revegetation, habitat restoration, and preservation. Sam Gon, III (2003) describes the research that guided the planning process: "A review of Hawaiian traditional ecological knowledge and land management practices was undertaken . . . all stemming from chants and recorded practices of Hawaiians. It becomes clear that traditional approaches have much to offer the modern restoration effort" (p. 5). Looking to the past and acknowledging sources of learning yields a genealogy of knowledge analogous to citations in a science publication (Chinn & Hanaʻike, 2010). Charles Kauluwehi Maxwell, Sr. notes that the saying, "*Nānā I ke kumu,* Look to the source" has a dual meaning, to seek the wisdom of elders (*kūpuna*) and the ancestral elder, nature: "One must study nature itself with all its wisdom that is portrayed in the forest and streams, the ocean with all its life and the air that keeps it alive" (http://www.moolelo.com/nana.html).

KIRC researchers fluent in Hawaiian and knowledgeable in cultural protocols interviewed elders, traditional practitioners, and reviewed the literature. There was little on restoration and propagation except for valued species. "For wild-collected plants the rule was: Take some, but leave some: don't take all. For those plants that could be propagated readily the rule was to replant when you harvest wild items" (Pukui, Lee, & Haertg, 1972, p. 16).

Notably, researchers found Hawaiian and Western culture differed in views of humans and nature in six ways (Gon, 2003) that delineate relationships, practices, artifacts, and values relevant to Indigenous inquiry:

- Relationship between humans and natural objects or living things (e.g., *ʻaumakua*).
- Rights and responsibilities apply to all things in the natural world.
- Consciousness of the natural world and its elements.
- Humans may speak directly to those elements of interest.
- Environmental ethics include asking permission for resources.
- Giving something when taking anything of significance.

KIRC's plan for the restoration and reinhabiting of Kahoʻolawe includes maintaining special advisors in the role of *kuhikuhipuʻuone* (land experts), applying land practices known in other arid areas, applying traditional planting practices and protocols, developing *kapu* and protocol specific for Kahoʻolawe, and reestablishing *kinolau*. Gon (2003) pointed out that "some [*kinolau*] of great significance to modern Hawaiians (e.g., the *pueo*), should not be treated "merely" as biological elements, but with appropriate cultural protocol (p. 9). The plan suggests adaptive resource management, an iterative process of "learning by doing" connecting research, practice, and decision-making "in the face of uncertainty with an aim to reducing uncertainty over time via system monitoring (http://en.wikipedia.org/wiki/Adaptive_management).

A team of scientists and researchers developed KIRC's framework for Indigenous inquiry grounded in cultural knowledge and practices. Would a similar framework be found in K12 school–and community-based programs that specifically integrate culture with science?

INDIGENOUS INQUIRY AND METHODS: PERSPECTIVES FROM EDUCATORS IN HAWAIʻI

Over the course of several months, in preparation for a 2010 place- and culture-based professional development program, science teachers and an archeologist/educator exchanged ideas on Hawaiian Indigenous inquiry and its methods. The intent was to learn from our own knowledge and experiences with place, culture, and science, a "making sense of a world replete with meaning, objects, and practices" (Markus & Hamedani, 2007, p. 8). Conversations were digitally recorded over the course of a two-day meeting in February; other sources were informal interviews, telephone interviews, and e-mails spanning November 2009 through April 2010. I transcribed recordings, reviewed notes from interviews, and organized the writing into themes brought up multiple times by different individuals across data collection formats. Everyone reviewed drafts and was invited to comment. Quotes were edited for brevity and clarity but retain their conversational quality expressive of individual voices.

Five major themes related to Indigenous inquiry methods and K12 science education emerged. Each of the following themes is discussed separately in the remainder of this section.

1. Role of hula, chants, ʻōlelo noʻeau, and moʻolelo.
2. Role of Indigenous identity and cultural expectations.
3. Role of place in Indigenous inquiry practices.
4. Role of Indigenous knowledge and practices in Indigenous inquiry.
5. Institutional, cultural, and societal barriers to Indigenous inquiry.

Role of Hula, Chants, ʻŌlelo Noʻeau, and Moʻolelo

Sabra, Moana, Huihui, and Kaʻumealani describe how cultural narratives provide a genealogy of place-based information able to trigger emotions as well as inquiry and action.

> Sabra: Legends inherited from our ancestors hold clues to our purpose and place in this world. Perhaps the most important is that of *Haloa*, the first-born *kalo* plant. When I teach the parts of the *kalo* those words carry meanings that go beyond the plant: *ohā*, the offshoot of the main corm, forms the word *ʻohana*, or family. The *hā*, or stalk, also means breath as in the word *aloha*, to be in the presence of the breath of life, or love. The ultimate lesson: if we take care of *Hāloa* as the elder sibling, it will take care of us; we will have food in perpetuity. Once we lose that plant, we, too, will be gone.

Moana describes her sense of loss when plants and landscapes described in a hula no longer exist. Huihui, a doctoral student researching cultural narratives as a source of science inquiry responds and elaborates:

> Moana: *Moʻolelo* kept alive through hula are so much a part of Indigenous research methods. There's a red flower in a hula I was learning, and my auntie had to explain it to me because I'd never seen that explosion of red and the picture that language brings to your mind. That's something I'd know intellectually, but never emotionally. What a loss that we still have our language but not the land to tie it to.

> Huihui: That is the difference between scientists and Hawaiian practitioners—you both hear the song, but when we cannot see what is being referred to, it hurts us because our chants are also our genealogies. We hear songs about a certain kind of white *kolea* that does not exist anymore. We know a detailed list of living things from the *Kumulipo*, but half of those organisms no longer exist. Our sources of research are these living things in our songs and stories, as books, journal articles and research studies are sources of information for western scientists. Our sources of research are disappearing. Stories communicate past happenings. In the *Pele* and *Hiʻiaka* chant, *Polihua* is a beach on Lanai and *hua* is an egg, so this beach is probably a nesting site for *honu* (green sea turtles). So in this small section of a chant you learn the location of a beach that had a turtle's nest and therefore know the characteristics of this beach. Information in the hula tells us why it is an important place to observe.

Stories are important in teaching. When we were growing up we would only listen when my mother told stories. She is a *kamaʻāina* so her stories were accurate. We learned about fishing holes and hammerhead sharks, things that would be different for people growing up in Hilo and Maui. When we go out and see these things and hear stories about them, we start thinking and begin to theorize. In the Pele and Hiʻiaka story, at Panewa (near Hilo) a woman uses her skirt to fight a giant *moʻo* (mythical water lizard). If you just tell that part to children from that area, they like it. They know all the place names and the weather, because that story is about the rain and *moʻo* are found where it is wet.

Ka'umealani discusses an Indigenous geography program she is piloting with her immersion students.

I'm teaching geography as Indigenous geography so our students feel good about looking through the lens of being Native Hawaiian. This is new, our school has never heard about Indigenous geography. We want to take our students out and to apply Indigenous ways of knowing. We've chosen water quality, so when we revitalize a *loʻi kalo* (taro pond field) we'll have questions, "What do we need to do today, what did they do back then, how do we know we've done a good job, who do we answer to?" Those simple questions take us back to an Indigenous methodology: who we answer to in order to maintain the integrity.

We really have to look at *ʻōlelo noʻeau* as coded messages from the past: "*Ma ka hana ka ʻike*; In working one learns." We recognize different forms of knowledge, *ʻike*, spiritual as well as intellectual/temporal *ʻike*, and to be Indigenous both have to be present. When we begin to see through that lens, we begin to see the full understanding of science.

For example, I'm not a scientist, but I love science. So you know how our people believed everything is alive, everything has a spirit. People talk about energy and cycles. You can take a rock, that solid mass, and put it back in the *loʻi*, and it's going to turn into a different form. So systems on land coordinated with systems in ocean, they were coordinated with the lunar systems, and so forth. So that's the science. It comes with *kuleana* (responsibility); and that *ʻike* transferred from one generation to the next allowed us to have the *ʻōlelo noʻeau* in the *ʻāina*, waiting for us to recognize our *kuleana*, to carry on. I don't think western science understands the pivotal understanding that both must be present.

Role of Indigenous Identity and Cultural Expectations

Sabra, Moana, and Napua described how growing up in Hawaiian families shaped views and approaches to Indigenous inquiry and research:

Sabra: Inquiry, asking questions whether they are silent or asked aloud, is a natural process. In Hawaiian culture it is often considered rude to ask questions. It is very cultural to observe, observe, observe, actually, *not* ask questions until you're ready. Being raised in a Hawaiian family I was always taught to *hamau*, to be quiet, and *nānā*, to observe. We were called *niele*, or nosy, if we asked a lot of questions. "Be patient and wait," my *kupuna* (grandparent, member of grandparent's generation) would tell me. "The answer will be revealed to you when you are ready to understand." There was and still is the belief that the answers to all of our questions will be revealed to us when we are ready to understand them. To this day I try to look, watch and observe before I ask a question. Scan the environment first before asking a question that could be answered already. It took me a long time to figure out what they meant. I understand now and I am ready and many of the answers are being revealed.

Moana: I was not that person. My *tutu* (grandfather) had a favorite saying that carried over to my father, "If I tell you, will you understand?" And I didn't know how Hawaiian that is. It is something I eventually learned.

Napua Barrows, a teacher in the Hawaiian Studies *Kupuna* Program on Maui, describes how cultural identity and expectations during an alien seaweed-removal workshop shaped her thoughts and actions:

> Coconut Island is where I found my niche—at that workshop when we removed alien *limu* and I thought it should be restored. I work with *limu* restoring, replanting, since the area I live on Maui is where my *tutu* is from and I learned the family *moʻolelo*. She took me around, showed me all the lands and gave me the *kuleana* to take care of this family land—little did I know that it covered the whole area.
>
> What I take care of at Waiheʻe has extended to all of Maui and connected with other islands. I felt it was necessary for us to expand with our Hawaiian Studies Program. It has generated a lot of excitement—we work with the communities, get the kids involved. Now we're really trying to connect with the teachers, because in the Hawaiian Studies Program we're always separated even though we have tried to work with them. So we're trying to connect up, bridge that gap. It helps to reinforce our position in the schools and help teachers to recognize our *kūpuna* and make use of them.
>
> So it's been exciting as we *kupuna* network together to see what is happening with *limu* restoration. Of course, science has always been something that has always been way beyond, but we take it step by step. Now the young ones that come into the program are learning Hawaiian and Hawaiian culture. They see the science and how it works and see that elders are very supportive in what we're doing. They see that we are making that bridge and yet the culture is still so strong. The beauty of it is it helps to connect with the teachers and administrators, too, despite schedules and budget cuts. *Mahalo* (thank you) to everyone—it's exciting to go to all these different places to see what everyone else is doing. That has helped generate the desire to do something.
>
> If someone had said this before, I would have said, "NO!" You just can't even imagine it, not until it bites you. When we get out to the land and start working it, it starts coming back. We were raised with some of it and we're ready to get back. And I can hear my grandmother. That's where the knowledge is, waiting there for us if we open that door. Then you have to go with it after that, you just can't drop it.

Role of Place in Indigenous Inquiry Practices

Interaction with and knowledge of place are culturally inseparable from responsibility, *kuleana*, and active care, *mālama*. For two decades Sabra Kauka and Moana Lee have worked to monitor and restore Nuʻalolo Kai, a culturally significant site that "shows the longest continuous sequence of occupation on Kauaʻi" (Abbott, 1992, p. 10). In 2006 several teachers and I cleared a small spring, counted goats, and surveyed plants. We submitted a plan to restrict goats, protect key native plants, and develop a plant nursery watered by the spring:

> Sabra: Nuʻalolo Kai chose us; in 1992 we took back our first re-interment as a result of the Native American Graves Repatriation Act (NAGRPA). These *iwi* (bones) came home and we took them back to their place of origin. The trail was only a goat trail, so overgrown you couldn't see very far, so the *kupuna* led us there. We realized that we needed to begin to *mālama* that special *ʻāina*, we had to clean and clear. State Parks archeologists led the early work teams to clean, clear and map the extensive rockwork. They were at the tip of the spear to poke it through the system, the bureaucracy.
>
> Moana: The foundations and rocks are already there. What will be restored next is truly the restoration/recreation. The part I find interesting—other places are restored and people go there, learn things and there are caretakers, but you don't have the idea of it as having once being settled. But Nuʻalolo Kai, maybe because we spend so much time there, you feel that you are walking in someone else's shoes, and this is why we return. Perhaps as we use it we evolve into who we are.
>
> Sabra: Nuʻalolo Kai is still dynamic. We are studying it hoping to once again to live that place, and bring

others in to live that place, even if for a short period at a time. This work is deeply satisfying and a great deal of fun. Ancient sites like Nu'alolo Kai have something to teach us. The extensive rock-work, the rope ladder up the cliff that led to a trail to the next valley called Nu'alolo 'Āina where *kalo* and *'uala*, or sweet potato, grew are evidence of people who worked hard. The *kahua*, or main ceremonial complex, is designed so that a person chanting on any of the five levels can be heard far away.

We've had some incredible partnerships. They put up an electric fence at the top of the cliffs but goats found another route and there are 175 in there. We only fenced off 1/6 of an acre plot of native plants and they are beautiful, but there are many more acres we want to restore. But the good news is that state parks, state forestry and the community worked together to devise a plan, and that's a first. During the 2009 summer field season a botanical restoration demonstration garden was established with Hawai'i Tourism Authority funding. Leading this effort is the National Tropical Botanical Garden and many community volunteers. This spring my hula students are learning an ancient hula celebrating *Nu'alolo Kai* to perform at that special place. An important part of place-based studies is taking students to see for themselves the beauty of our island and earth.

Michelle's alien *limu* removal program began in 2004 in Maunalua Bay where her students apply what they learn in her Polynesian Voyaging Program.

Before I only took my class, then I thought, "What if they don't want to go—what if they all have sports one day?" So for the first time we invited kids from the leadership classes because guaranteed they're going to show up because they have to make their service learning quota. Then the marine science students, because they need to learn to take care of our island, too, and not just live in the lab. I lectured to the class and I took samples and they started squeezing the samples. So I scolded them, "There's not going to be anything left for 4th period." Then 70 kids came out, and my husband said, "Who's going to watch these kids!?" And I thought one time *pau* (finished). Then the kids started asking, "Hey Miss, when's the next one?" They started spreading the word, the basketball team started to come, then I talked to the Environmental Club. I said in one hour we cleared 3,850 lbs—and so the kids said, "OK, we'll come." It's getting to be more pleasurable and my kids don't feel overttaxed.

Role of Indigenous Knowledge and Practices in Indigenous Inquiry

Michelle, Mahina Hou, Huihui, and Lila describe the ways they apply Indigenous knowledge and practices in their secondary science programs. Michelle Kapana-Baird describes how she teaches an Indigenous method of locating sites in Maunalua Bay:

Recently our students were in charge of invasive algae cleanup. A member of the community organization came that day to help us. She asked, "What are your GPS markings?" I said, "I don't have one today." "So how do you know it's accurate? I knew she wanted to know how wide my area was that I cleared, what are the markings of my site, what are the points, how you do it, how you triangulate it. These things, it's all the science.

So I told my student, "Mele, Hawaiians didn't have GPS. This is what Ka'au told me when we use to sail into Kualoa. This is what I learned how to sail into the harbor. You'd find a high land mark and a low land mark." And I know the lady is listening to me. "How do you line it up and how will you see something that you will remember? What is a good landmark and what makes sense to you?" So I asked her to line it up with the *hālau* (canoe house), a coconut tree, the Norfolk tree and the mountain. "Can you line that up with that little bump up there? So that's your top landmark. And on the other side, do you see the water tower at the top of the mountain" "And what is down at the ocean level?" "The white mansion with the pillars." "And what is the top of the mountain? So Mele, you have the *hālau* and the trees and the mountain on this side and on the other side the dome and the mansion." The lady came to me and said, "You triangulated your sights. I know you know what you're doing."

Mahina Hou Ross teaches science through Indigenous inquiry methods in a Hawaiian language immersion program on Molokaʻi, an island in which Indigenous Hawaiians who maintain subsistence lifestyles are the majority.

> We have four sites we visit each quarter, Moʻomomi Bay and 3 fishponds. The kids actually see the health of the different parts of Molokaʻi, more invasive *limu* along the south shore. The reef is not too healthy compared to Moʻomomi and further east. Today we were at a fishpond. Main focus, look at the organisms using the latest technology. We have the underwater camera and they're pretty good doing PowerPoints, I-movies, using Final Cut Pro software. They're going to do web pages. We take students into the water, look at the fish and check what they've been eating. Like *kole* (*Ctenochaetus strigosus*), cut them open to check. They might look so similar but they taste different. To get the cycles and seasons for spawning, what time of the year, you've got to cut them open to find out. Then you've got to eat them, so we fried them up.

> We have various scientists as resources, but I think the most important people are the teachers who have developed the program and made the connections with the community. Books are good to match what we catch, get the vocabulary. Drawings show the different parts; have the kids match them. But you've got to catch the fish. And the standards are going to be there, so show the learning is standards-based. Main thing is build the relationships with the students—they see the relevance of the curriculum when they go hunting, fishing, diving.

> Uncle Mac Poepoe of Moʻomomi says, "My generation, no can teach us, we're the one that took the fish. If you can teach the kids what the *kupuna* taught us, we have a chance." So we've developed a traditional lunar calendar.

Huihui discusses how ancestral knowledge can be applied to Indigenous place-based curriculum design and explains to Michelle how she can apply it to her Maunalua Bay setting:

> If you look in the *Kumulipo* there are three different facets of science. *Papahulilani*, what's above, rain, stars sun, moon, wind, clouds, measurement of vertical and horizontal spaces; *Papahulihonua*, the earth, ocean, caves, the study of natural earth, ocean, development, transformations and evolution by natural causes; and *Papahanaumoku*, things that are born, regenerate and procreate. There were schools and *kahuna* for these three things so we are looking at three different divisions of scientists. We just did a workshop on *Kanaloa*—there are different *Kanaloa*, clouds, moons, and jellyfish in the ocean. Then you have *keala Kanaloa*, the corridor our sun moves in between the meridian and the solstice.

> *Noho papa* refers to something that has been in one place for generations (ordered and arranged like a feather lei), it means you start with the knowledge of the place and apply it to everything else. We recently did something for Hilo. Since social studies teachers are asked to do a place-based lesson, we know the information that Hilo surprised us with and how we can connect that information to other things—*Papahulilani*, the hilo moon, star, winds; Papahulihonua, the Wailuku River itself, people are familiar with its dangers. Nehu fish (Hawaiian anchovy) congregate in Hilo Bay and nehu season starts the rain.

Huihui answers Michelle's question about applying this approach to Maunalua Bay:

> What you have asked has to do with landmarks just of your place, specific to your place. What does *Papahulilani* have to do with Maunalua, its stars, wind, rain? *Papahulihonua*—what is it about the coastline, what do breakers look like there on a north swell? Where do we get our fresh water? What are the names of the springs? For *Papahānaumoku*, the birthing cycle of flora and fauna, where are the mempachi (*ʻuʻu*, *Myripristis berndti*) holes, where are the *mano* (sharks), what about the birds? All this has to do with knowing your place.

Lila describes how Indigenous inquiry methods develop cultural knowledge, sense of place, and questions needing further study:

> Today we took our students to Punalu'u Valley to be taught on an ancestral *'āina* by the *kupuna* who was born and raised there. It was an initial stage for our research in Punalu'u, to feel the *'āina*. The *kupuna* taught them native Hawaiian plant identification and cultural practices in *la'au lapa'au* (herbal medicine). The students did land surveying and mapping and service learning. It was productive and the students showed they were capable of completing several tasks. We learned that Punalu'u Beach was a source for *limu kohu* (*Asparagopsis taxiformis*) but none can be found today. *Honu* (green sea turtle) come into the bay seasonally. The *kupuna*'s father fed the fish out on the *papa* (reef flat). Next month we will do science and geography research.

Institutional, Cultural, and Societal Barriers to Indigenous Inquiry

Educators expressed frustration with a number of barriers to place-based, Indigenous methods of inquiry. In addition to familiar issues of school schedules and high-stakes testing that interfere with fieldtrips and projects, several obstacles relevant to Indigenous inquiry are noted below: distrust and rejection of Western science by some Hawaiians, degradation of familiar places, urban lifestyles disconnected from outdoor experiences, and the challenge of developing transdisciplinary curricula:

> Moana: I started out as a scientist. About 25 years ago I was at a public meeting. One of the things being rejected by the Hawaiian community was science. Scientists are no good. Science was outright rejected because it had nothing to do with culture. I remember standing up. I was there to say something, as they were all rejecting science. My grandmother was a nurse, a healer. And you guys don't like science, but my grandmother was a scientist, she observed, she asked questions. She came to her conclusions out of her observations. If you think science is not Hawaiian, you're wrong. We would still be in the dark ages, we wouldn't even know how to sail the ocean. I was very unpopular.

> Michelle: My son will never go to Kapena Falls and swing on the rope into the water because of the *leptospirosis*. So many things our kids will never do; so many things kids should do as science. When I was growing up and my dad said you're going Makapu'u!? I wanted to go there because the water's cleaner than Sandy Beach (site of a sewage outfall). It just passed on to another generation. Those kids in Kalihi never went to the beach. Their parents were always working, so the beach they knew was Sand Island Beach, all broken coral. There are some we have to give that experience.

> Pauline: Many teachers are not from the place where they teach. Or maybe then haven't done place-based lessons or considered asking their students about their lives and communities. So they bring in outside experts. Teachers need to gain an understanding of the place in the sense that we've been talking about—from the people and land as key resources even if it is uncomfortable to move away from prepared curricula. What do I know of my place that I can bring to learning? The main thing is that teachers can help kids to connect to land and community as resources for learning.

> Sabra: Another challenge is combining science, education and culture. The Canoe Plants Project (plants brought to Hawai'i by Polynesian voyagers) took about two years and required the expertise of three different people. An NSF fellow, provided scientific knowledge, a GK-12 graduate student wrote the lesson plans, and I provided the cultural component.

DISCUSSION

Ua Lele Ka Manu as a Search for a "Cultural Template"

Ua lele ka manu. Has the bird of Indigenous inquiry flown or is it present but seen only by some? How can it be recognized? Moana, the archeologist/educator, thought Indigenous inquiry might be a form of "cultural template." Central to the notion of such a template is a Hawaiian sense of place actively connecting people to inhabited, storied landscapes from ancestral times to the present and future:

> We keep track of landmarks because they can tell us something about the fishing spots in traditional times that can be brought into modern times. I'd like to say we're still doing it in the same way, like in *auana* (modern hula) we're still talking about the place. We recognize it is our template and we find ourselves within this template. This is what we're trying to provide to our students in an authentic way. We go to our *kupuna* to talk to them and do the sciencing but the students are collecting the data and they themselves have the *'ike* and they themselves are determining what to do with it.

Our study suggests a cultural framework for Indigenous inquiry and methods can be found in the ways groups led by Indigenous individuals like Michelle, Napua, and Sabra care for their chosen places. It can also be found in the State's restoration of Kahoʻolawe Island. But Indigenous inquiry methods, even when known, are applied by relatively few science educators due to challenges noted earlier regarding developing a transdisciplinary knowledge base, establishing community relationships, and implementing lessons that do not fit neatly into Western science curricula and school schedules.

But even more significant barriers may exist in the differences between the ideologies of mainstream American schools and those of Indigenous cultures oriented to sustainability. A sociocultural view of learning suggests that the way Western school science portrays, evaluates, and acts in the natural world, as understandable through experiments leading to laws that are universally applicable, thus placeless, impersonal, and without meaningful cultural contexts, is alien to Indigenous Hawaiian sensibilities, values, and practices. This suggests Indigenous ways of thinking about, inquiring, and acting in the world should be part of science teacher education. This would provide culturally informed practices and understandings as resources for working more effectively with Indigenous students in Hawaiʻi's public schools.

Implications for Teacher Education and Curriculum Design

Hawaiʻi-based research (Chinn, 2006, 2007, 2008, 2010) finds place- and culture-based professional development has the potential to support teacher agency by linking Indigenous cultural roles to relevant science content and practices. A resource manager role informed by the roles and responsibilities of traditional *konohiki* or *papa hulihonua* could be reoccupied by teachers guided by core Indigenous values of *kuleana*, responsibility, and *Mālama I Ka ʻĀina*, care for the land that feeds. As Bandura (2006) notes, "humans can create visualized futures that act on the present; construct, evaluate, and modify alternative courses of action to secure valued outcomes. . . . To be an agent is to influence intentionally one's functioning and life circumstances" (p. 164). Sabra's comments express agency informed by Indigenous inquiry and sense of place:

> The survival of life on earth, let alone Hawaiian culture, depends on understanding how the natural world works. We have to heed the teachings of our ancestors and *mālama*, or take care of, the earth. If we do it

will take care of us and future generations. If we don't it will be the end of us. We get people from all over the world at Nuʻalolo Kai. I tell them start where you are.

Our study of Indigenous inquiry suggests a framework that can be applied to science education with four process elements: (1) developing a Hawaiian sense of place through learning its stories and interacting with it, (2) *mālama*, caring for/monitoring/restoring this storied place; (3) *kuleana*, recognizing that the right to use resources comes with responsibility for that place; and (4) conducting inquiry with appropriate protocols respectful of Indigenous knowledge, values, and practices of that place. We encourage Hawaiʻi's science teachers to develop place-based science lessons incorporating Indigenous inquiry methods connecting learning to students' places and elder knowledge. We encourage teachers to become familiar with local science-related resources, histories, places, and place names and to view these as primary resources and venues for learning. Teachers with culture-science networks extending into the community increase the ways to engage diverse students' interests and enable them to act as researchers contributing to a growing body of new knowledge. Secondary sourced, text- and classroom-based learning shifts to primary sourced, community-based learning relevant to students' present and future lives.

Resources for teachers interested in Indigenous research include groups caring for public places and courses providing relevant science content and professional development. The revitalization of Hawaiian language and culture and Hawaiʻi's importance in biological, earth, ocean, and astronomy research support an extensive body of place-based scholarship. Reprints of works by Hawaiian scholars, translations of Hawaiian language newspapers, and Web sites relevant to culture- and place-based science provide resources for curriculum development. The use of Hawaiian for street and place names, laws informed by Indigenous practices related to ocean access and water rights, restoration of significant places (*wahi pana*), and use of traditional land divisions present an Indigenous, storied, cultural landscape to educators ready to learn and teach from Indigenous perspectives.

CONCLUSION

We conclude that *Ua lele ka manu* is an appropriate metaphor for Indigenous inquiry methods. It can be found more often in Hawaiʻi's communities than in its schools, where it has been largely displaced. Despite the rhetoric of active learning, inquiry, and critical thinking Indigenous inquiry and its methods will continue to be rare in school science as long as policies reflect Western ideologies of individualism, competition, production, and consumption. Western science now recognizes that eco-centric Indigenous inquiry methods can play an important role in adaptive resource management and sustainability science. *ʻAʻohe pau ka ʻike i ka hālau hoʻokahi,* All knowledge is not taught in the same school (No. 201, Pukui, 1983) means that one can learn from many sources. Re-establishing *Mālama I Ka ʻĀina (Sustainability)* as a Hawaiian science content standard would return Indigenous inquiry methods to K-12 science education and support a transition to sustainability through systems-thinking, problem-solving, and civic engagement.

REFERENCES

Abbott, I. A. (1992). *Laʻau Hawaiʻi: Traditional Hawaiian Uses of Plants.* Honolulu: Bishop Museum Press.
Adams, W. M., & Jeanrenaud, S. J. (2008). *Transition to Sustainability: Towards a Humane and Diverse World.* Gland, Switzerland: International Union for Conservation and Nature.

Adaptive Management. Retrieved September 1, 2010 from http://en.wikipedia.org/wiki/Adaptive_management.
Bandura, A. (2006). Toward a Psychology of Human Agency. *Perspectives on Psychological Science.* 1: 164–180.
Beckwith, M. (1970). *Hawaiian Mythology.* Honolulu: University of Hawai'i Press.
Beckwith, M. (1972). *The Kumulipo: A Hawaiian Creation Chant.* Honolulu: University of Hawai'i Press.
Cajete, G. (2000). *Native Science: Natural Laws of Interdependence.* Santa Fe: Clear Light.
Chinn, P. (2006). Preparing science teachers for culturally diverse students: Developing cultural literacy through cultural immersion, cultural translators and communities of practice. *Cultural Studies of Science Education, 1,* 367–402.
Chinn, P. (2007). Decolonizing methodologies and Indigenous knowledge: The role of culture, place and personal experience in professional development. *Journal of Research in Science Teaching, 44*(9), 1247–1268.
Chinn, P. (2008). Connecting traditional ecological knowledge and Western science: the role of Native Hawaiian teachers in sustainability science. In A. Rodriguez, (Ed.), *The Multiple Faces of Agency: Innovative Strategies for Effecting Change in Urban School Contexts* (pp. 1–27). Rotterdam: Sense.
Chinn, P. (2010). Science, culture, education and social-ecological systems: A study of transdisciplinary literacies in student discourse in a place- and culture-based Polynesian Voyaging Program. In A. Sumi, A. Hiramatsu, & K. Fukushi, (Eds.), *Adaptation and Mitigation Strategies for Climate Change* (pp. 249–265). New York: Springer.
Chinn, P. & Hana'ike D. (2010). A case study of David, a Native Hawaiian Science Teacher: Cultural Historical Activity Theory and implications for teacher education. *Cultural Studies of Science Education.* 3(2), 229-246
Clark, J. R. K. (2002). *Hawai'i Place Names: Shores, Beaches, and Surf Sites.* Honolulu: University of Hawai'i Press.
Dudgeon, R. C., & Berkes, F. (2003). Local understandings of the land: Traditional ecological knowledge and Indigenous knowledge. In H. Selin (Ed.), *Nature across Cultures: Views of Nature and the Environment in Non-Western Cultures* (pp. 75–96). New York: Kluwer Academic.
Emerson, N. B. (1915). *Pele and Hiiaka: A Myth from Hawaii.* Honolulu: Star-Bulletin.
Fairclough, N. (1999/2006). Global capitalism and critical awareness of language. In A. Jaworski & N. Coupland (Eds.), *The Discourse Reader,* 2nd edition (pp. 146–157). New York: Routledge.
Framework for 21st Century Learning, A. Retrieved September 1, 2010 from http://www.21stcenturyskills.org/.
Franco, R. (1995). Water: Its meaning and management in pre-contact Hawaii. Project Report PR-96–02. Water Resources Research Center. University of Hawai'i at Mānoa.
Gee, J., Hull, G., & Lankshear, C. (1996). *The New Work Order: Behind the Language of the New Capitalism.* Boulder, CO: Westview.
Gon III, S. M. (2003). Application of traditional ecological knowledge and practices of Indigenous Hawaiians to the revegetation of Kaho'olawe. *Ethnobotany Research and Applications. 1,* 5–20.
Gruenewald, D. A. (2008). Place-based education: Grounding culturally responsive teaching in geographical diversity. In D. A. Gruenewald & G. A. Smith (Eds.), *Place-Based Education in the Global Age: Local Diversity* (pp. 137–154). New York: Lawrence Erlbaum.
Hall, B. (2004). Towards transformative environmental adult education: Lessons from global social movement contexts. In D. E. Clover (Ed.), *Global Perspectives in Environmental Adult Education* (pp. 169–191). New York: Peter Lang.
Handy, E. S. C., Handy, E.G., & Pukui, M. K. (1972). *Native Planters in Old Hawaii: Their Life, Lore, and Environment.* Honolulu: Bishop Museum Press.
Janssen, M., & Ostrom, E. (2006). Governing social-ecological systems. In L. Tesfatsio & K. L. Judd (Eds.), *Handbook of Computational Economics,* Vol. 2: Agent-Based Computational Economics (pp. 1465–1509). New York: Elsevier.
Kahoolawe. Retrieved September 1, 2010 from http://www.kahoolawe.info/history.html.
Kamakau, S. M. (1991). *Ka po'e kahiko: The People of Old.* Bernice P. Bishop Museum Special Publication 51. Honolulu: Bishop Museum Press.
Kanahele, G. H. (1986). *Ku Kanaka Stand Tall: A Search for Hawaiian Values.* Honolulu: University of Hawai'i Press.
Kaneshiro, K., Chinn, P., Duin, K., Hood, A., Maly, K., & Wilcox, B. (2005). Hawai'i's mountain-to-sea ecosystems:

social-ecological microcosms for sustainability science and practice. Profile in *EcoHealth* special issue, Emerging Infections Disease and Social-Ecological Systems, *2*(4), 349–360.

Kekahio, W. (2007). Native Hawaiians in public schools: implications of AYP Status in predominantly Native Hawaiian schools. Public Education Brief Series, May. Kamehameha Schools Research & Evaluation Division. Retrieved March 11, 2010, from http://www.ksbe.edu/spi/PDFS/Reports/K-12/ayp_200705.pdf

Kirch, P. V. (1996). *Legacy of the Landscape: An Illustrated Guide to Hawaiian Archeological Sites*. Honolulu: University of Hawai'i Press.

Lave, J., & Wenger, E. (1991). *Situated Learning: Legitimate Peripheral Participation.* Cambridge, UK: Cambridge University Press.

Maly, K. (2001). *Mālama pono i ka 'āina*—an overview of the Hawaiian cultural landscape. Retrieved March 2, 2010, from http://www.kumupono.com/Hawaiian%20Cultural%20Landscape.pdf

Markus, H. R., & Hamedani, M. G. (2007). Sociocultural psychology: The dynamic interdependence among self-systems and social systems. In S. Kitayama & D. Cohen (Eds.), *Handbook of Cultural Psychology* (pp. 3–39). New York: Cambridge University Press.

Maxwell, C. K., Sr. *Nana I Ke Kumu*—'Look to the Source,' published in Maui Inc. Magazine. Retrieved September 1, 2010 from http://www.moolelo.com/nana.html.

Meyer, M. (1998). Native Hawaiian epistemology: Contemporary narratives. Doctoral dissertation, Harvard University. Cambridge, MA.

National Research Council. (1999). *Our Common Journey: A Transition Towards Sustainability.* Washington, D.C.: National Academies Press.

Perry, A. (1912). Hawaiian water rights. In T.G. Thrum (Ed.), *Hawaiian Almanac and Annual for 1913*, pp. 90–95. Honolulu.

Pukui, M. K. (1983). *'Ōlelo No'eau: Hawaiian proverbs and poetical sayings*. Honolulu: Bishop Museum Press.

Pukui, M. K., Elbert, S., & Esther Mookini, E. (1974). *Place Names of Hawaii*. Honolulu: University of Hawai'i Press.

Pukui, M. K., & Korn, A. L. (1983). The echo of our song: Chants and poems of the Hawaiians. Honolulu: University of Hawai'i Press.

Pukui, M. K., Lee, C. A., & Haertg, E. W. (1972). *Nānā i ke kumu*. Honolulu: Queen Liliuokalani Children's Center.

Sternberg, R. (2003). What is an "Expert Student?" *Educational Researcher, 32*(8), 5–9.

Schiro, M. S. (2008). *Curriculum theory: Conflicting visions and enduring concerns*. Thousand Oaks, CA: Sage Publications, Inc.

Waters, D. J. (2006). Preserving the knowledge commons. In E. Ostrom & C. Hess, (Eds.), *Understanding Knowledge as a Commons: From Theory to Practice* (pp. 145–168). Cambridge: MIT Press. Retrieved February 27, 2010, from www.section108.gov/docs/PreservingtheKnowledgeCommons.doc

Woodhouse, J. L., & Knapp, C. E. (2000). Place-based curriculum and instruction: outdoor and environmental education approaches. Retrieved March 13, 2010, from http://www.ericdigests.org/2001-3/place.htm.

CHAPTER EIGHTEEN

The Kenyan Herbalist Ruptures the Status Quo in Health and Healing

NJOKI WANE

This chapter investigates Indigenous healing in rural Kenya through qualitative interviews with healers/herbalists and lay people. The central objective of study was to examine the practices and epistemological underpinnings of African Indigenous healing and its contribution to contemporary healing knowledge and practices in Kenya. The intent of this chapter and research project is not to produce recipes for healing but rather to make an important contribution to ongoing, albeit limited, debates and discussions of African Indigenous healing. This is in keeping with Aime Césaire's (2000) call to return to the source. Although Cesaire's idea was a symbolic call for all Black people to rally together in relation to their common origin, Cesaire's notion of returning to one's history, culture, etc., speaks of the idea of embracing and reclaiming African Indigenous knowledges and in this particular case, healing practices. There is a substantive amount of scholarship on alternative healing in North and South America, New Zealand and Australia; however, this chapter focuses specifically on scholarship that is related to African Indigenous healing.

My analysis is situated in a perspective that examines the total human experience grounded in African philosophical principles which underlie belief systems, values, signs and symbols. In addition, the chapter tries to address the following questions: What is healing? What is traditional African healing? What is Indigenous healing? What is the major difference between Indigenous and contemporary healing? Before addressing these questions I will provide a brief overview on Kenya's population, health provisions, the debates on Indigenous and contemporary healing practices, as well as the health challenges currently facing Kenyans. In addition, I will provide details of the methodology employed, recruitment strategies, and information on the seven participants whose narratives form the basis for my analysis.

I write this chapter with lots of emotions, especially having gone through a neo-colonial education that made sure, whether consciously or unconsciously, that I should distance myself from my traditions and move as far away as possible from what was familiar to me; from what my parents tried desperately to remind me of on a daily basis when I would come home from colonial schools.

These memories are painful because after all my struggles to achieve what I thought was ultimate success (see Wane, 2006), I realized my whole being was a vacuum and that what I had despised growing up (my traditions, healing herbs, Indigenous ways of knowing) was what I needed in order to establish firm grounds from which to anchor my life and work. It was this realization that made me focus on researching Indigenous knowledges, African Indigenous health systems, African philosophical thought in education, and African systems of thought.

My research projects showcase just a few examples of what happens at a micro-level in Kenya. The colonial government in Kenya, despite their emphasis on colonial education, did not succeed in uprooting the Indigenous ways of knowing, nor did the neo-colonial government succeed in masking the philosophical foundation of these knowledges. The ordinary citizens and their local Indigenous sage formed formidable invisible walls of resiliency and forms of resistance that were evident during my conversations with the research participants in rural Kenya.

In the last four decades of neo-colonial rule, the majority of Kenyans have relied on their Indigenous knowledge base for their health and economic survival. They have negotiated spaces in between the Western forms of knowledge and Indigeneity. Many Kenyans are dissatisfied with government systems, in particular health services, and most of them have decided to take responsibility for their well-being into their own hands and have reverted to Indigenous traditions instead of waiting for outsiders to come and rescue them. In my conversations with the participants, I was asked: What went wrong with all the promises of a better life, good health, and prosperity after the acquisition of Western education? In order to make sense of what happened, I will provide a brief overview of anti-colonial thought.

INDIGENOUS KNOWLEDGES: AN ANTI-COLONIAL THEORETICAL FRAMEWORK

In confronting the concepts and conditions of colonial and neo-colonial health systems in Africa, it is important to move beyond the internal conflicts or decaying social structures of neo-colonial governments and examine the psychological impact of colonialism. The essence of anti-colonial thought is to challenge ideas or ideologies that are presented in unworkable abstracts or in idealistic forms which are more damaging to the psyche than the visibilities of the original colonial rule. It is crucial to employ a holistic approach when interrogating colonial and neo-colonial issues of Indigenous health practices. This is because the narratives of colonial knowledge and colonial powers cannot simply be assembled in neat piles of conquest or different forms of resistance but must be explored within the histories of economic exploitation, political coercion, or military conquest.

The agency of anti-colonial thought is to search for ways of dismantling colonialism and neo-colonialism, visible and invisible, as well as finding ways of dealing with psychological traumas that have no name. It is necessary for us to go back to the source and ask ourselves how has colonialism as a theory, a project, praxis, and discourse, managed to produce and reproduce itself—politically, socially, culturally, materially, and ideologically? As proponents of anti-colonial theory one might find themselves at crossroads. What is the purpose of our discourses in the anti-colonial project?

Nyamnjoh (2004) has expressed his reservation about the Western construct of valid knowledge especially when compared to the popular and traditional epistemologies of the African continent. Nyamnjoh centered his criticism on the basis that the Western construct of valid knowledge tends to limit the definition of reality to "anything whose existence has, or can be, established in a rational, objective manner, with universal laws operating in perceived space and time" (2004, p. 163). In this case, any form of knowing that cannot be expressed in Cartesian or behaviorist terms is discarded as unreal, metaphysical, and irrationally subjective and in some cases primitive.

African systems of thought have been constructed to validate and legitimize "the dualism of knowing" and to show there are multiple ways of seeing the world such as: physical and metaphysical; real and unreal; rational and irrational; objective and subjective; natural and spiritual; and finally science and superstition. The celebration of this oxymoronic process of constructing Indigenous knowledges is grounded on the ontological, axiological, and epistemological foundations of Indigenous knowings. Intuitions, dreams, visions, proverbs, oral narratives, songs, fables, myths, and superstitions are all validated as legitimate means of knowing. In reality, Indigenous knowledges do not restrict the arena of production, validation, and distribution of knowledge to any specific areas as noted in Western/conventional ways of knowing. Indigenous knowledges are produced in homes, communities, and environments. Among rural Kenyan healers, the healing practices are sites of theorizing pedagogies while participating in keeping anti-colonial work alive.

Unfortunately, these ways of knowing and sites being produced are not counted as valid and legitimate means of knowing in the conventional/Western classroom of learning. Elsewhere (Wane, 2005a) I have observed that Western discourse has served the purpose of justifying the neo-colonial agenda which remains deeply embedded in systems of education that influence current educational approaches at local, national and international levels. Colonialism began, I believe, as an imaginary idea that later translated into a philosophy, a creed and a way of life. This imagination meant that people's land, physical, and mental capacities should be taken away from them through forced/persuaded indoctrination that would catalyze this exploitative agenda. In a different context, Smith (1999) posited:

> The globalization of knowledge and Western culture constantly reaffirms the West's view of itself as the centre of legitimate knowledge, the arbiters of what counts as knowledge and the source of 'civilized' knowledge. This form of global knowledge is generally referred to as 'universal' knowledge, available to all and not really 'owned' by anyone, that is, until non-Western scholars make claims to it. When claims like that are made history is revised (again) so that the story of civilization remains the story of the West. For this purpose, the Mediterranean world, the basin of Arabic culture and the lands east of Constantinople are conveniently appropriated as part of the story of Western civilization, Western philosophy and Western knowledge. Through imperialism, however, these cultures, people, and their nation states were repositioned as 'oriental' or 'outsider' in order to legitimate the imposition of colonial rule. For indigenous people from other places, the real lesson to be learned is that we have no claim whatsoever to civilization. It is something, which has been introduced from the West, by the West, to indigenous peoples, for our benefit and for which we should be duly grateful (1999, pp. 63–64).

Similarly, Semali and Kincheloe (1999) have argued that the tyranny of Western epistemology decrees that the reality worth talking about in centers of knowledge production should be constructed only through Cartesian-Newtonian ways of seeing. Knowledge constructed is centralized and limits the power to produce knowledge in the hands of a limited power bloc. Such situations set Western ways of knowing as the benchmark through which the productions of non-Western civilization are measured. This process influenced Europeans in the late seventeenth century to increasingly become condescending toward the "primitive" knowledges of other cultures. Such perceived primitivism justified the civilizing efforts of the White man's burden and the pedagogical dynamics embedded in the concepts of domination and exploitation (Dei, 1994).

According to Semali and Kincheloe (1999) the term "Indigenous" and the concept "Indigenous knowledges" have often been associated with Western understanding of primitive, wild, and fetishization. After observing one of the traditional healing rituals by a Maasai healer in Kenya, I could not help but imagine how any one witnessing these unfamiliar ritual practices would easily classify them as primitive and "uncivilized." However, the notion of constructing other knowledges as primitive, fetishization, and uncivilized because one does not understand or is not familiar ought to be contested. It is important for readers to understand that I am not centering my argument on the premise that Indigenous knowledges should not be interrogated by other knowledges. In fact, I endorse the notion of various knowledges interrogating one another to arrive at solid knowledge relevant for human growth and development. All that I am stating is that there is a need for centering African research on African Indigenous systems of thought as a way of privileging and documenting that which has been decentered in the Western discourse.

Ivan Sertima (1984) eloquently writes in *Black Women in Antiquity* that, there is a need for Africans to unearth the knowledges buried beneath the massive years of oppression under colonial and neo-colonial rule. There is a need for us to revisit, glorify, and acknowledge these ancestral knowledges in order to correct the distorted imaging, identities, and histories of African people. African civilizations were like diamonds that were shattered. We need to ask ourselves how we can begin to piece these diamonds back together. Reclaiming Indigenous knowledges as alternative frameworks of historically denied values and worldviews is another way of doing so. The reclamation and recognition of traditional healing practices is an attempt to recapture and legitimize a form of knowledge that is embedded in the cultural psychology and psycho-ecology of a community. It is not enough to identify the health challenges of a community; it is important to explain what causes them and how they can be eradicated. One must understand and appreciate the beliefs, values, symbols, myths, and the social-cultural components that are associated with healing practices. This is because in many cases aspects of Indigenous practices are appropriated without acknowledgment through written text or media, and in the process their authenticity is lost.

In order to rupture the complexities of Indigenous practice in Kenya a brief description of the research setting and the methodology used to collect the data is provided in the next section.

RESEARCH SETTING

The research for this project took place in seven Provinces of Kenya. Kenya is situated on the eastern side of the African continent astride the equatorial latitude and is bordered by Tanzania, Uganda, Sudan, Ethiopia, Somalia, and the Indian Ocean. It has a relief that stretches from sea level on the east coast to 5199 feet at the peak of Mt. Kenya. In spite of the two rainy seasons (March to May and October to November), Kenya is deficient in rainfall, so that drought is a recurrent concern. The drought situation has been made worse by lack of land resources, deforestation, and irrigation farm projects owned by multinational companies. This state of affairs has affected the availability of herbs for traditional healers and their healing abilities.

Kenya, a country of 35 million people, attained its political independence from Britain in 1963. However, this political move brought with it colonial structures of health care, education, and social and economic institutions. Forty-six years later, there is very little evidence that the country has moved away from the above inherited governance structure. However, what is not obvious is how Indigenous institutions of learning, knowledge formation, dissemination, and storage that had been suppressed during colonial times have survived colonial rule and have continued to thrive, although not as part of mainstream structures. Every successive government since independence has promised that they will revert to traditional institutions that had held different communities together and that worked as blueprints for educating the youth to take up their responsibilities in their various communities. Every government signed all kinds of treaties forging relationships either with the old colonial masters or new powers that wanted to get a stronghold on the African continent. Efforts to improve health services have been difficult because of the cost of contemporary medicine as well as new forms of health problems that Kenyans did not have several decades ago such as HIV/AIDS.

RESEARCH METHODS

The research was qualitative in nature, consisting of non-structured interviews using guided questions. Extending over a 6-month period, the study used both primary and secondary research methods. The study had two broad research goals: to examine African Indigenous healing practices, in particular, herbal healing practices among several Kenyan communities, and to assess the contribution of herbal healing practices to contemporary heath care in Kenya.

The study consisted of loosely structured interviews with open-ended, strategic guiding questions. The central focus of the interviews was on exploring how participants understood Indigenous healing, how they acquired this knowledge, what relationship they saw between Indigenous and contemporary healing and the types and methods of treatment they provided. A total of 56 herbalists (32 men and 24 women) and 30 laypeople (19 women and 11 men) were interviewed in seven Kenyan provinces (Nairobi, Rift Valley, Western, Nyanza, Eastern, Central, and Coast). The North Eastern province was excluded due to time restrictions and access constraints. Participants were recruited through random sampling, word of mouth, and snowballing. However, it is important to note that the research assistants from each province knew most of the herbalists and they assisted us in compiling lists of all the known herbalists. The herbalists to be visited were randomly selected from the list. Although I initially planned to record the interviews on audio tape, few participants would consent to this and subsequently most interviews were hand recorded. Both herbalists and laypeople were asked to respond to a numbers of questions.

Although 56 people were interviewed, I will base my analysis for this chapter on seven narratives. The seven participants represent the diversity of those interviewed in terms of gender, experience, age, knowledge of healing practices, and level of education. Most of the herbalists and the lay people who participated did not have a university degree, but they were all very conversant with Indigenous knowledges. **Beki, 61,** was a lay male who knew different herbs that could treat minor ailments for various members of his family as well as his livestock. He only had a grade eight education. **Mene**, an 82-year-old woman, had practiced Indigenous healing for more than 50 years. Mene did not have formal schooling and could not read or write. However, she was one of the few participants who knew the necessary plants, roots, rocks to treat most of the diseases. She knew the history of her community and provided good background on how her community has been fragmented by diseases that were alien to her community. She attributed this fragmentation to the acquisition of Western-type education that distanced people from their roots. She learnt her Indigenous healing skills from her grandfather. She was a knowledgeable healer who had assisted many people with what she termed as incurable diseases such as HIV/AIDS or arthritis. **Njeri,** a 25-year-old undergraduate female student, was keen to learn more about Indigenous Healing practices and read widely on Indigenous

African knowledges. **Daktari,** 58, a male herbalist owned several clinics in the country. He had a high school diploma and was a self-motivated, self-educated person. He has traveled to different countries in Africa in search of Indigenous healing knowledges. **Mutia,** a 60-year-old male herbalist, was well known for treating backaches and skin diseases and had been practicing healing since he was a young man. **Lemi,** is a 65-year-old male herbalist and teaches at one of universities in Kenya. Although he does not have a university degree, he is well respected because of his vast knowledge of Indigenous healing practices, herbs, plants, and roots. He has a herbal clinic where he trains high school graduates to be herbalists. **Jeffy,** a 45-year-old male, indicated that he grew up in a home where no one was taken to hospital. His parents knew what remedies to give them whenever they complained of any form of ailment. Although he was not a practicing herbalist, he knew the names of herbs, roots, and how to prepare them to treat members of his family. He indicated that this knowledge was very valuable because the high cost of living made it very difficult to afford medical treatment in government or even private hospitals.

The research team comprised of seven research assistants and two professors assistants (they were all students at a local university where I was a visiting scholar in 2006). The seven assistants came from the seven Provinces and spoke the local dialects. Each of them was familiar with particular traditional protocols required when approaching an elder or a traditional healer. In order to establish uniformity and consistency, each researcher was requested to familiarize themselves with all the components of the research project under the following major questions: (1) How do the healers conceptualize Indigenous healing? (2) What is their understanding of healing in relation to Indigenous knowledges? (3) What are some of the philosophical principles of healing knowledge? (4) Could they describe the various methods that they employ in their healing practices? (5) What are some of the pedagogical and instructional implications of this research? Before setting out to carry out the research, I had a briefing with all the researchers. During the briefing, they were able to seek clarification of what the five major themes entailed and their relevance to Indigenous knowledges. What follows, therefore, is a discussion of the research findings, highlighting some of the conversations that the research team had with the herbalists and the lay people, organized around the five questions.

CONCEPTUALIZING INDIGENOUS HEAlING PRACTICES IN THE BROADER AFRICAN CONTEXT

All the research assistants had a vast knowledge of my research project and had shown interest in participating in data collection. They all had taken a course on Indigenous cultures and as a result were conversant with the conceptual framework of this project. They were aware of the tensions that existed between Western epistemologies and Indigenous knowledges.

African healing practices are unique because all physical, mental, and spiritual phenomena were studied, understood, and practiced and taught to the whole community (Afrika, 2004). Afrika explains that ancient African Indigenous practitioners taught their patients about herbs and healing. Using this mode of knowledge dissemination, almost all families acquired basic knowledge of health and healing. For instance among the Luos in Kenya, Geissler et al. explain how "13 year-old children . . . know most commonly used herbs for the treatment of common illness . . . and often use herbal medicines without adult consultation . . . by school leaving age they have acquired knowledge of most plant remedies that their mothers know and use" (2000, p. 41). This quote emphasizes Malidoma Some's (1999) statement that healing practices were well known among members of a family or community. He further explains that this was due to the fact that traditional healing has always been central among African peoples, because our ancestors learned very early that human beings are vulnerable to physiological and biological breakdown and, when this happens, it affects all aspects of their existence (p. 21). This is echoed by Beki who stated

> *Among many African societies, traditional healing is not a new phenomenon. The knowledge was acquired through experimentation and observation; some of the knowledge may be obtained through dreams—that is the information is given through dreams on the various plants that may be used to treat certain diseases* (Beki, Interview: 2006).

Indigenous healing is one of the oldest forms of structured medicine, that is, a medicine that has an underlying philosophy and set of principles by which it is practiced. This argument is supported by Mene who said

> *African Indigenous healing is a form of health care or healing systems that have been used by Indigenous Africans for thousands of years before the coming of contemporary medicine . . . [and] this information is usually passed—if very specialized—to only a selected few who are given the names of herbs, roots, or leaves that are medicinal* (Mene, Interview: 2006).

There were, and of course still are, some regional differences between the principles and philosophy of traditional healing although there are also many fundamental similarities which are shared by all traditional healing practices; these arise from the profound knowledge of natural laws and the understanding of how these influence living things,. This claim also was eloquently articulated by one of the participants (Njeri, Interview: 2006) who stated

> *African healing practice is unique to a particular community but shares some commonalities with other communities. For instance, I am a Luyia; however, what we practice is unique to our group, but you can find some elements of this among other groups in Kenya, such as Luos, Kikuyu or Kipsigisi. These practices have been passed down generation after generation. However, these practices are not static and keep changing according to the needs of the community or the challenges facing the community—e.g., the HIV/AIDS epidemic—and they are guided by traditional principles, norms or values.*

AFRICAN INDIGENOUS KNOWLEDGE PRACTICES

According to Daktari

> . . . healing is making yourself well . . . mentally, physically and environmentally, cleaning my compound . . . healing that does not involve the medical philosophy of drug administration . . . boiling my drinking water and eating these types of food (pointing to some green Indigenous vegetables that had been served for lunch by his wife).

Daktari's words are echoed by O'Dea who stated: "To regain your balance, you must turn inward to touch the deep wellsprings of compassion and energy that source your being, and then reach out with discernment and knowledge until you find wisdom" (O'Dea, 2004, p. xiii).

Although Daktari and O'Dea come from two different communities, they seem to agree that healing is creating or having balance in one's life. Ancient healers concentrated on delivering healing that is holistic, that treats the body as a whole and not as fragmented body segments (Arewa, 2000). They delivered their healing by using what the environment provided for them. They provided balanced healing. "Balanced healing enables a patient to choose and use the methods that are best suited to their particular needs so that they can achieve a true balance in their lives and in their health" (Altshuler, 2004, p. xvii). One of the challenges with advances in medical treatment is the fragmentation of treatment. Modern medicine views a person's body as a collection of parts and not as an entity.

Being healed, according to Carlson and Shield (1990), means living in peace, which emphasizes both individual and community health. This point is taken up by Jungerius (1998), whose work explores the relationship between the healers and the ecosystem in the Keiyo District of Kenya. Through his study, Jungerius found that herbalists are well versed with Indigenous knowledge and how that knowledge speaks to the climate, geology, water, soil, vegetation, and fauna. In other words, disrespecting the natural world leads to the disruption of the health of the community, which then has an impact on the health of the people. This is confirmed by the study carried out by Geissler et al. (2002) among the Luos of Kenya who describe how the social, family, and cultural structures facilitate dissemination of traditional healing knowledge and in particular herbal remedies found within the natural environment. Tuck (2004) describes healing as a transformative process which occurs during illness in addition to the efforts made to treat or eradicate disease. Further, traditional healing works to heal the individual as a whole, focusing on the person rather than the illness.

Healing has been defined as a process of cure, restoration, a journey of recovery, or a process of bringing order. Healing may also mean having a clear mind or a spiritual way of thinking and it could be freedom from rage, anger, and hurt and believing in the Creator and in yourself as well as other people. For complete healing to take place, any society has to pay attention to their community and search for various ways of healing it at all levels. In other words, healing is a developmental process aimed at achieving balance within oneself, within human relationships, and between human beings and the natural and spiritual worlds. Healing also could be defined as a form of intervention, and this could be in the form of bodywork, massage, trance, or rituals. Hammond-Tooke (1989) argues that healing is conceptualized as constituted through a culture's worldview (p. 32). Both Constantine, Myers, Kindaichi, & Moore (2004) and Helms and Cook (1999) understand Indigenous healing practices as those helping beliefs and strategies that originate within a culture or society and are designed for treating members of a given cultural group. Further, they argue that every society has designated individuals or groups of people known as healers. Malidoma Some (1999) argues that healing is central for African peoples because of the vulnerability of human beings to physiological and mental breakdown. The principles and philosophy of traditional healing practices focus on natural laws, as these govern all organisms and the natural environment. Nature is the foundation of Indigenous life; without reference to nature, the concepts of community, purpose and healing would be meaningless (Altshuler, 2004). Nature, according to Malidoma Some (1999), is the foundation of healing; nature provides the materials for healing and healing is dependent on relationships with nature. Overwhelmingly, African Indigenous healing emphasizes interconnectedness and the importance of harmony within the body, the community, and the natural environment (Afrika, 2004).

PHILOSOPHICAL PRINCIPLES OF INDIGENOUS HEALING KNOWLEDGE

To begin to make sense of healing practices in Africa one needs to understand the worldview of African peoples and the complex make up of each culture. Every community has their unique ways of sensing when the community is falling apart, when one of the members is out of balance or when misfortune has struck. The term "traditional healer" refers to a person involved in a broad range of practices including herbalism and spiritualism. Traditional healers may include diviners (shaman, priests, or priestess—oracle, spirit medium, ceremonial specialist), herbalists, or religion-based healers. Among many African Indigenous peoples, healing practices do not entail written instructions or lengthy periods of study at formal institutions. Rather, knowledge is acquired through intuition, practice, spiritual guidance, and apprenticeship. In most instances, healing traditions are passed from one generation to the next through visions, stories, and dreams and healing practices rely on observation and experience. It is vital to note that African traditional healers use their experiences and insight in their healing practices. Thus, healer's practices may vary enormously and be both geographically and temporally bound (Altshuler, 2004). Malidoma Some (1999) provides an excellent discussion of traditional healing practices. He suggests

> Methods of healing must take into account the energetic or spiritual condition that is in turmoil, thereby affecting the physical condition. If you focus only on the physical translation of the underlying energetic disorder, then you are ignoring the source of the physical illness. If you address only the physical problem, then you end up perhaps with a cure which fixes the physical condition, providing a momentary sense of victory over debilitation. This act denies the needs of the energy, the adjustment of the spirit needed to make the cure last. Sooner or later, this disordered energy will figure out a new way to affect the physical body often in a new and more virulent manner than it did originally. If you instead address the energy of the mind and spirit, whose status is infected, the physical body . . . [is]likely to heal. . . . Hence, in the wisdom of indigenous concepts of healing, all healing must begin by first addressing the energetic problems (Some, 1999, p. 30).

Some emphasizes the urgency of a holistic approach to healing as well as the importance of contextualizing physical manifestations of ill health within broader spiritual, environmental and community contexts. In discussing African Indigenous healing philosophy and practices, it is necessary to name the devastating effects of colonialism on the longevity and legitimacy afforded to this long-standing system of healing. McClintock (1995) explains how European settlers envisioned the "Dark Continent" as empty and devoid of civilized people. In this process, both Indigenous peoples' healing practices and knowledge were demonized and both formally and informally suppressed (Some, 1994). Subsequently medical knowledge and practices informed by Western values and thought and practiced by European practitioners and practitioners were legitimized and normalized through colonization.

At this moment, with a renewed pharmacological interest in African medicinal plants, it is vital to frame and understand Indigenous healing knowledge and practice while remaining cognizant of devastating colonial legacies. Through this anti-colonial investigation of Indigenous healing, attempts are made to negotiate the "legitimacy" lent to Indigenous healing by pharmaceutical and scientific research and the potential risks of profiteering by pharmaceutical industries and continued appropriation of Indigenous knowledges.

The principles and philosophy of traditional healing practices always deal with natural laws, because all life is subject to them and ill-health is usually due to an abnormal imbalance, either within an organism, or of the organism with its environment (Arewa, 2000; Some, 1999). Therefore traditional healing practices do not only involve work that only corrects the internal imbalances through which disease can manifest in an individual but emphasizes re-establishing an individual's harmony with their environment and their relationship with the natural cycles to which all life is subject to (Some, 1999). Nature is the foundation of Indigenous life and without it, concepts of community, purpose, and healing would be meaningless. People's relationship to the natural world and its laws determines whether or not they are healed. Nature, according to Malidoma Some (1999), is the foundation of healing, and hence the importance of the natural world around us. Malidoma Some is making reference to the trees, hills, mountains, rocks, that is, everything that was here before humankind. This means, we can find all the materials needed for healing within nature. These views were reflected in some of the participants' conversations. For instance, Mene stated

> Healing herbs are everywhere , . . . but you need to know which ones they are . . . sometimes I use tools such as feathers or horns when seeking guidance on a particular sickness—the people who come to seek help must have trust in my work and what I use . . . African indigenous healing is important because even contemporary drugs are a mixture of the same substances as those used in indigenous healing only they are packaged.

This is echoed by Daktari who stated

> . . .these healing practices may not be necessarily ancient but what I give my clients does not have artificial substance . . . the medicines have not been altered . . . or their properties split . . . and . . . the advantage of what we give is their ability to cure many diseases at once.

Traditional healing sees the universe as operating according to natural laws that manifest according to specific rules. Among African Indigenous peoples, there is a strong belief that the purpose of life and the nature of disease cannot be understood without knowledge of these laws and their correspondences. Many Indigenous communities know that the natural world is an integral part of their world. It is therefore important to begin healing by reconnecting with the natural world, because nature is "our first home, the foundation of our community, the dwelling place of the spirits who watch over us and long to be reconnected with us" (Some, 1999, p. 57).

From the interviews, it is clear that African Indigenous healing refers to a health care system that has been in place for thousands of years and has numerous holistic, dynamic, complex, and community-specific healing practices. Traditional healing operates from the understanding that there is no separation of body, mind, and spirit and thus employs practices which are holistic in nature. Sickness, whether manifesting itself through physical, mental, or emotional symptoms, cannot be treated as an isolated "problem."

In the last 100 years we have advanced tremendously in every aspect of life. Modern medicine has offered us great knowledge and understanding of diseases and their cures. As Altshuler (2004) comments: "surgeons routinely replace damaged body parts with donor organs or mechanical devices" (p. xvii) something that was unthinkable 100 years ago. However, Altshuler explains that this remarkable progress in modern medicine has come with cost or risks, because: " . . . many of modern medicine's remedies often give us as many problems as benefits" (p. xvii). Also, modern medicine concentrates on healing parts of the body instead of treating the body as a whole, while traditional healing emphasizes restoration of the natural harmony of the body through an integrated and holistic manner. It is therefore imperative to remember that treating the body's ailment is more than treating the separate parts. This is eloquently stated by Geissler et al. (2002) while reporting their findings on traditional healing practices among the Luos of Kenya: "The body is a container full of power and potential, but also contains unknown weaknesses and dangers; . . . There is no victory over disease in this . . . practice, only balance, a truce, or at times the possibility to move an ailment" (p. 45) from one element to another. Although there is a need to create a balance in the form of treatment that a patient is given, Geissler et al. (2002) found that, among the Luos, plant remedies are just a part of the healing process and are not expected to solve the patient's medical problem but initiate a process of total recovery and wholeness. Interestingly, until the advent of medicine as a scientific discipline, the role of the healer was to restore wholeness. However, advancement in modern medicine distances us from the concept of wholeness, a component that is very essential in healing.

DISCUSSION OF RESULTS

Overwhelmingly, participants emphasized the long history of Indigenous healing practices. There is also an emphasis on Indigenous healing practices and philosophy that predate colonialism and continue to be used alongside contemporary medicine. It is vital to note the geographic and cultural specificity of Indigenous healing practices; participants repeatedly emphasized how healing was community specific and adaptable to community health needs. Additionally, in defining Indigenous healing, participants hinted at the methods of knowledge acquisition and training in Indigenous healing.

Training/Knowledge

Although Indigenous healers' training varies by culture and type of healing; this research revealed that some healers undergo rigorous training and education in order to achieve their positions. This training is often transmitted, learned, and remembered in an oral, non-literate tradition. More than half of the participants reported having acquired this knowledge from older members of their communities while others named family members or friends as their source for training. A small number of participants indicated that they obtained their knowledge through their interactions with known herbalists and from contemporary reading on herbal medicine. Herbalists acquire their training in myriad ways. For example, Lemi learnt through observation from *"those other herbalists . . . that's how I became a herbalist. In addition, I took courses in herbal healing and I have a diploma in this area."* He indicated that his main reason for devoting his life to learning more about herbal medicine was *"due to frustrations of diseases that were resisting contemporary medicine and seeing patients die in large numbers in hospitals where I was practicing as a clinical officer"*.

Daktari said

> I was intrigued by the way my father used to use herbs to treat his family members and his animals. I got interested and wanted to know more and I started to follow old men as they went to the forest to hunt for roots. I would ask them the names of different plants, and their purpose. I then researched in books and when I completed high school, I continued with this search.

He (Daktari) continued to explain

> since I wanted to make sure what I was doing was not going to kill people, I used to take any herbal medicine that I would prepare to KFRI (Kenya Forest Research Institute) for verifications. I would then consult more books in order to know what to mix with what and what dosage to administer.

Daktari, whose family has herbal clinics over all country, was trained by his great grandfather and his father. He describes his main reason for his interest in herbal treatment:

there are many new untreatable diseases in Kenya, and modern medicine has failed to find a cure. Many people come to us, and we feel helpless sometimes, however, this helplessness had made us to carry out more research and to come up with cures for these diseases.

Mene, who acquired her knowledge from her grandparents, attributes her acquisition of Indigenous healing to her interest in medicine:

my interest in herbal medicine propelled me to be in the company of my grandparents and especially my grandfather. I learnt the names of herbs and what they could cure. After high school, I started attending seminars and went to places where they were teaching herbal medicine. In addition, I joined Ameru Herbalist Organization that exposed me to herbal practitioners who know different ways of treating various ailments. It was through this organization that I got my license to practice.

One man acquired his information from farmers through his work as an agricultural officer. In addition, he decided to search for books that would provide more knowledge in this area. Mutia acquired Indigenous healing knowledge from his father who was also a herbalist. He said

As we went grazing our cattle, my father would uproot some plants and tell me to chew, while others were taken home and added to chicken soups and everyone in the house was made to drink the soup. This made me interested in finding out more about the medicinal value of plants

Mutia goes on to state

I acquired this knowledge from my father when I was young. I feel it is my responsibility to pass this knowledge to my children. I usually take my children to the forest when I go in search of medicinal plants.

From the participants' reflections, it is clear that the processes of training and means of acquiring knowledge on Indigenous healing are incredibly varied. It is evident that family and elders in the community play a central role in passing on knowledge and skills. However, from the participants' responses, it is also necessary to note the commitment to other forms of training, including reading and research, professional affiliations and formal training. It is worthwhile to note that these various forms of training and knowledge acquisition work conjunctively to prepare herbalists for their work in the community. The following section provides examples of healing some of the most common disease in rural Kenya—malaria.

Malaria

Participants discussed numerous ailments and healing strategies; however, there was considerable hesitation on participants' behalf to sharing information about the preparation and methods of healing. Participants did share substantial information in relation to malaria. Many participants named malaria as a serious health concern and common disease amongst most Kenyan communities. I focus on malaria because of its prevalence as a health concern for Kenyan communities; however, it should not be read as the sole or necessarily most central focus of the work of all herbalists. Rather, this discussion of malaria should be seen as but one example of Indigenous healing.

According to participants, malaria is a tropical disease and has claimed many lives. It is caused by a plasmodium or a protozoan which is transmitted by a female anopheles mosquito usually through puncturing of the skin. Mosquitoes are found in cool and wet areas where there is stagnant water, such as swamps or where there are overgrown shrubs or bushes. Participants named high fever, joint pain, headaches, dizziness, vomiting, and diarrhea as symptoms of malaria.

Most laypeople named the Mwarubaini or the Neem tree as a treatment for malaria; its leaves, bark, and roots are medicinal (the Neem tree is used to treat over 40 diseases). The treatment may involve boiling leaves or pieces of bark for 5 to 10 minutes, sieving the mixture and cooling it (in some cases, the solution may be taken while warm). The mixture is very bitter and honey is often added. This mixture is given three times a day after meals (one glass for adults, one-fourth of a glass for children) until an ailing person feels better. Also, once the leaves or the bark of the Neem is boiled, the sick person may be covered with a blanket for 10 to 15 minutes under the container with the boiled leaves or bark so that they can inhale the steam to facilitate sweating. In addition, the patient is bathed in some of the water. The process of inhaling and bathing may be repeated twice a day until the patient feels better. It is believed that when the person inhales the steam, the malaria is healed from inside as well as outside the body.

Aloe Vera[1] was also suggested as a treatment for malaria. According to most participants, the preparation is similar to that of the Neem tree; however, the Aloe Vera is added to water once it has already boiled. It is then left to sit for 2 hours and the water will change to a green hue. Adults should be given a glass of the solution three times a day and children one-fourth of a glass three times a day. Both Neem and Aloe Vera are very bitter solutions, and it is suggested that one should add honey before taking them.

In terms of preventative measures, participants indicated that the Mutaa (midnight queen) tree is described as a naturally occurring plant with a strong, sweet scent which drives mosquitoes away. Families that do not have the plant are encouraged to plant it around their homes to keep mosquitoes away. Beki described how Akambas families are advised to plant the midnight queen bush. Other preventative measures that communities are encouraged to follow are to clear all overgrown shrubs within the vicinity, to burn all used up metal and plastic containers, fill up all open pits and to pour kerosene in all stagnant waters.

Indigenous healing emphasizes community-specific practices for treating disease. For example, Jeffy explained to us how malaria was treated in his community. According to him, "*some community members used tripes of a goat to treat malaria.*" He continued to explain:

> a goat is slaughtered and the tripe with all its content boiled and the patient given to drink twice a day. The tripes of a goat are believed to contain all kinds of medicinal herbs. Most people will not believe that tripe can cure malaria, but I have seen it work.

Jeffy added that in addition to tripe, there was another method where a patient was given a drink prepared from the roots of Omobeno tree. This drink caused diarrhea which was meant to remove the malaria protozoa from the stomach, thus facilitating the healing of the patient. An additional method was the boiling of the leaves of the Omoutakiebo tree; this was then given, twice a day, to the patient to drink, causing them to vomit. In inducing vomiting, it was believed the malaria parasites were expelled from the body and would relieve the patient of their sickness.

Among the Maasai, malaria was treated by boiling Msanduku and the patient made to inhale the steam. The treatment also involved boiling leaves or a piece of bark, and then the mixture is sieved and left to cool. This bitter medicine, often sweetened with honey, is given three times a day, until the person feels better. Malaria may also be treated using grapefruit, which is believed to contain quinine, a known anti-malarial. The grapefruit would be boiled, mashed, and strained and the liquid given to the patient three times a day for 5 days. If the patient is experiencing nausea or vomiting, he or she may be given a mixture of salt and lemon to lick. Another method for treating malaria among the Maasai is using Entipilikua plant; it was boiled for 30 minutes to 1 hour until water turns a reddish-brown; when the solution has cooled, half a glass is given to the patient twice a day. Olg'osua thorns may also be boiled and the patient is made to breathe the vapor while covered with a blanket. This encourages the patient to sweat and relieves the running nose. Following this, the patient bathes in the solution.

What is clear from the descriptions of healing provided by participants is the use of myriad methods, the treatment of illness and symptoms, and the emphasis on prevention. It is worth noting that many of these treatments are described from the perspectives of laypeople, rather than herbalists, many of whom were hesitant to detail their treatment practices during interviews. However, the knowledge that laypeople possess about malaria treatment indicates that healing knowledge, although not readily reported to interviewers, is shared with community members. Further, from the descriptions of laypeople, we can see how these practices reflect Indigenous healing philosophy. By focusing on holistic healing and community prevention, healing practices operate from the position that malaria is not an individual illness, but a community issue.

Listening to detailed explanations on how to cure malaria, one could not avoid reflecting on the differences between Indigenous healing and contemporary healing. The following section highlights some of the major conceived differences.

Differences between Contemporary and Indigenous Healing

Some respondents said that in the past, people used to fear herbalists as they were referred to as witchdoctors. However, these days, people have started accepting them because there are many well-known herbalists who have clinics all over the country. As Beki commented: *"Herbalists have opened up these clinics in good time when lots of diseases cannot be treated with modern medicine . . . some herbalists even counsel and teach the patients on how to keep their environment clean . . . they teach patients how to stay healthy."* Daktari thinks that those who have knowledge of herbal medicine can share it with contemporary practitioners. He felt there was a need to enrich each other's profession. He explained that most of the herbalists do not have equipment for packaging their powdered medicine or even X-ray machines; if the two professions work together, they can provide support to each other. He gave examples of some hospitals that referred patients to him or even called him to visit patients in hospital wards. He recommended that herbal medicine should be regularized and standardized so that the patients are given similar treatments all over the country.

Daktari and Mene believe that the two types of medicine can complement one another. For example, Mene wishes at times that she could know exactly what a patient is suffering from and imagines that if she did, it would be easy to administer the right herb. She emphasized the need for laboratory tests for her patients. She explained that, she always sent her patients to a medical doctor for tests or stitching of open wounds if that was required. While Daktari longed "for that day when we can sit around the same table with medical doctors and discuss some of the common diseases that are killing our people . . . these practices should be exposed to as many people and communities as possible."

From our observation, most herbalists do not have any particular way of knowing how much to give a patient. They do not have the necessary equipment to prepare the medicine. However, on reflection of what the herbalists were saying, there was consensus that contemporary medicine has some side effects which most of the doctors do not tell the patients, while herbal medicine offers mainly minerals, vitamins. Contemporary practices have different ways of diagnosing the sickness; while some herbalists try to guess what a person is suffering from and sometimes this could result in giving the wrong treatment. This does not mean that contemporary practices do not make mistakes—on the contrary there is a lot of malpractice within the health industry. Some of the other major differences are the forms of sterilization—herbal practices use lemon, salt, garlic, charcoal, while contemporary practices have sterilization equipment. With contemporary medicine, there are laboratories where samples of blood, urine are sent for diagnosis, while traditional practices rely on the results brought from the hospital—hence the lack of facilities interferes with their work. Both Indigenous healing practices and contemporary healing practices do have roles to play in every community in Kenya. What is required is to find ways of working together. The following text provides some examples of how the two can complement each other's practice.

In order to rupture the status quo of contemporary medicine experienced and community renowned herbalists should be allowed to teach in teaching hospitals. In addition, the government of Kenya should assist them in their practices by funding research and the necessary equipment. The complementary role was well articulated by Lemi who said

> *Most of us have helped patients who have suffered for many years even after going to hospitals, so if the government recognized the work we are doing, and provided laboratory services for us, they would enable us to advance our work. . . .Most patients that come to see me mainly because the hospitals have failed to cure their illness. I, however, send patients to hospitals to carry out laboratory tests, and once I confirm their sickness, I start treating them. I cannot treat patients without their medical history from their doctors or from hospitals where they have been attended to.*

While Daktari noted

> *Both types of practices can be used; for example, use of plasters for broken bones is good . . .we do not have the equivalent of that in herbal medicine. These practices should be encouraged for both young and old people because people of all kinds come to our clinics . . .the government should find ways to make us assist each other in our work together. The two practices should be married together as each has its strong points and they both complement each other.*

Lemi argues that

> *Contemporary healing is more advanced; however, this healing is sometimes not effective at all. I think Indigenous practices are better in some aspects and contemporary practices have their strong points as well. Indigenous practices should be encouraged and recommended as complementary to contemporary practices. This is because both practices are used by all people, poor, rich, etc. Unfortunately today to be attended by a good herbal doctor, it has become very expensive. I try to keep my fees low; however, because getting the herbs can be very expensive in terms of travel in search for the right herbs, it becomes difficult to not charge high fees. For example to treat arthritis—which has become very common in Kenya, it never used to be there, I charge ksh15,000 ($250 CND). This amount is too much money, for most people; as a result, I usually have different fees for people who are unemployed or some of the elders in our community.*

Most herbalists indicated that they never sent away patients who came to see them and have no money. They always treated them.

PEDAGOGICAL AND INSTRUCTIONAL IMPLICATIONS TO EDUCATION

The participants' narratives reveal that there is tension between Indigenous ways of treating illnesses and Western practices, and this tension has been internalized. The herbalists clearly articulate their frustration with how their practices are viewed despite the fact that different herbs have been known to cure "incurable" diseases in Kenya. The Western-trained doctors in Kenya have indicated that there is very little room for negotiating with Indigenous healers who are not adequately trained because they lack the Eurocentric training. There is a feeling among most doctors that if the set-up is altered, it will contaminate their Western model that has given them a particular privilege in society.

In Kenya, the British colonizers established a hierarchical social structure that was based on race, gender, and class. What will therefore be some of the pedagogical implications if traditional doctors have to share spaces in hospitals or in medical training schools? Indigenous healers in post-independent Kenya continue to be invisible due to class-based stratification that dominates the social, economic, and political spheres. The social inequities between those who have a Western mode of education and those who do not are among the continuing legacies of the colonial era. Although my research clearly demonstrates that Indigenous healers are contributing to the well-being of Kenyans, they constitute an unrecognized body that is bereft of any decision-making power to advance their positions in the health industry. The work of Indigenous healers is marginalized and unacknowledged.

Elsewhere (Solom & Wane, 2005), I have argued that colonial encounter had disrupted the Indigenous ways of knowing, learning, and teaching for most Indigenous people in the world. Such disruption affected how Indigenous educators came to understand how knowledge should be produced and what space is appropriate for imparting knowledges. The effect is that both custodians of Indigenous knowledges and learners came to devalue and depreciate knowledges that were exchanged in the process of interactions. As pointed elsewhere (Wane, 2005a), when Edward Said (1994) talked about the colonizer "doing something" about Indigenous people in order to get their land and property, they were invariably talking about devaluing and debasing their knowledges and cultural beliefs till the colonized lose interest in acquiring and/or sharing them. As a result, many colonized subjects struggle daily to maintain their own traditional and cultural heritage. Accordingly, George Lamming (1995) rightly argued, we can change our laws overnight and we can even reshape the images of our feelings, but to dislodge the myth of the intrinsic superiority of Western knowledge is nothing less than a Herculean task.

Currently, I work as a researcher and a professor in a renowned university in the West and try to bring into my work elements of my ways of knowing. Considering all aspects of Western colonial mechanism that Africans found seductive, the most irresistible of them all was formal Western education. Africans acquiring literacy in English or French were quick to realize that a university education opened up prospects for economic advancement, individual attainment, and dignity that ultimately provided keys to political power and self-government or self-advancement (Wane, 2005b). Similarly, Dei (2004) in his research in Ghana confirmed through the responses from participants that many Ghanaian students acknowledged and adored the cultural asset colonial education brings to individuals and therefore do not want any educational reform, current or future, to jeopardize their opportunity of attaining colonial education. Yet, these privileges come at a great price, that is, loss of one's local culture, values, knowledges, and anything that an Indigenous person holds dear during their upbringing in their community. Like Some (1994) I have come to realize that our lives have been taken away from us because during the years I spent in this colonial education, the colonial institution assumed that its goal was my goal. The result is the slow death of our identity and everything I held dear as a woman of African ancestry.

My study also shed light on the connections and the gaps between traditional and Western healing practices. It is my hope that this chapter contributes to the growing body of literature on Indigenous knowledge, traditional healing and the tension between Western mode of healing and traditional healing practices. By carrying out this research, I was able to acknowledge verbally and on paper the Indigenous healers' knowledge and skills—which for too long have been unacknowledged and unrecorded.

Traditional health systems, when compared to Western ones are viewed as a distinctly different ones that have a different model of diseases and that operate within a different world view. In the Western healing model, the healing process is initiated when the doctor gives the patient some medication to deal with the sickness. In traditional healing practices, both the patient and the traditional doctor exchange news about family, weather, politics, seasons, food, etc., after which the patient talks about their illness. The patient is prescribed some herbs to take. However, in addition to that, the healer provides prescriptions for healing the root cause of the sickness. In the analysis of the illness in contemporary times, there is an assumption that the patient's sickness is a separate entity from the domains such as social, economic, or cultural structures. Among the traditional healing rituals, there are implicit questions such as: What has disrupted the circles of balance in one's life? What will it take to bring harmony and flow of energy back to its acceptable body or environmental normative? What type of preparation is necessary for complete healing? Although these questions were not on the interview guide, they were answered very eloquently by five herbalists who indicated that in addition to healing the particular sickness, it was important to establish the root cause of the disease. For instance, if the patient was suffering from malaria, the herbalist would advise his client to go and clear the bushes around the home and if possible to buy a mosquito net. If the patient was suffering from bilharzias, or any waterborne diseases, they would be told to treat the water or to find ways of getting clean water for home consumption or they would be advised to wash their hands, vegetables, and utensils thoroughly. If it was something to do with any form of cancer, the herbalist explained to the patient what caused the disease, etc. As a result, the patient was fully aware of what was being treated and how they could avoid recurrence of that sickness in the future. How then do we collapse the divide and complement the two practices?

CONCLUSION

This study explored the knowledge base of practicing herbalists and laypeople in Kenya. From the narratives of various participants, Indigenous healing is very much part of everyday experiences of most Kenyans. However, there is a tension between the contemporary health practitioners' model and Indigenous healing practices. It is also clear that the Indigenous practitioners are willing to work with Western-trained doctors to complement each others' work. I strongly believe that the government should step in and help in the conservation of medicinal plants, in addition to regularizing how herbalists operate in the country. This would legitimate their work. This chapter examined the tension between tradition healing and contemporary Western mode of healing and its pedagogical implication. As I come to the end of this chapter, some of the big questions that I have been trying to wrestle with are: How can we as educators bring Indigenous healing knowledge to Kenyan medical schools? Where should the conversation begin, is it with officials at the Ministry of Health or should this be done by the Ministry of Education? Should academics working in cultural knowledge departments initiate this conversation? I can still remember when I presented my work to medical students in Kenya, and their reactions to my research findings. From their reaction, it was clear that, they did not have too much space for Indigenous healing practices. As seen, traditional healing practices are alive and well in Kenya despite the continuing impact of colonialism and neo-colonialism. In many cases traditional healers are able to help people who either do not have easy access to modern medicine or cannot find cures through it. There are still many challenges in terms of making traditional healing practices better known, recognized and more acceptable to the mainstream and to Western-trained medical professionals. It is my hope that this chapter will be a contribution toward achieving that objective.

NOTE

1. There are numerous other plants which were named as possible treatments for malaria, including: Mukambura, Mufa, Njeru Warurii, Mucuthi, Thuthiga, Mwiria (Rosaceae or Prunus Africana), Muvuti, Mugoran (Rhamus prinoldes), Muguucwa (Zenthoxylus asiatica), Mucharage (Olea Capensis), Mujuthi (Caeslpiniaceae), Munganga, Kirurite (Lamiaceae), Muchani, Murao, Mukinduri, Muthiamura, Scena, Periodic, Muthiga, and Cinchona.

REFERENCES

Afrika, L. O. (2004). *African Holistic Health*. Brooklyn, N.Y.: A & B.

Altshuler, L. (2004). *Balanced Healing: Combining Modern Medicine with Safe & Effective Alternative Therapies*. Washington: Harbor.

Arewa, C. S. (2000). *Opening to Spirit: Contacting the Healing Power of the Chakras and Honouring African Spirituality*. London: Thorsons.

Carlson, R., & Shield, B. (eds.). (1990). *Healers on Healing*. New York: Tarcher.

Césaire, A. (2000). *Discourse on Colonialism*. New York: Monthly Review.

Constantine, M. G., Myers, L. J., Kindaichi, M., & Moore, J. L. III (2004). Exploring Indigenous Mental Health Practices: The roles of Healers and Helpers in Promoting Well-Being in People of Color. *Counseling and Values, 48*(2), 110–125.

Dei, G. J. S. (1994). Afrocentricity: A Cornerstone of Pedagogy. *Anthropology and Education Quarterly, 25*(1), 3–28.

Dei, G. J. S. (2004). *Schooling and Education in Africa: The Case of Ghana*. Trenton, N.J.: Africa World Press.

Geissler, P. W, Harris S. A., Prince R. J., Olsen, A., Odhiambo R. A., Oketch-Rabah, H., & Mølgaard, P. (2002). Medicinal Plants Used by Luo mothers and Children in Bondo District, Kenya. *Journal of Ethnopharmacology. 83*, 39–54.

Hammond-Tooke, W. D. (1989). *Rituals and Medicines*. Johannesburg: A.D. Donker.

Helms, J. E., & Cook, D. A. (1999). *Using Race and Culture in Counseling and Psychotherapy: Theory and Process*. Boston: Allyn & Bacon.

Jungerius, P. D. (1998). Indigenous Knowledge of Landscape-Ecological Zones Among Traditional Herbalists: A Case Study in Keiyo District, Kenya. *GeoJournal, 44*(1), 51–60.

Lamming, G (1995). The Occasion for Speaking. In B. Ashcroft, G. Griffiths, & H. Tiffin (eds.), *The Post-colonial Studies Reader* (pp. 12–17). London: Routledge.

McClintock, A. (1995). *Imperial Leather: Race, Gender and Sexuality in the Colonial Contest*. New York: Routledge.

Nyamnjoh, F. B. (2004). A Relevant Education for African Development—Some Epistemological Considerations. *Africa Development, XXIX*(1), 161–184.

O'Dea, James, (2004). Foreword in: Larry Altshuler's book *Balanced Healing: Combining Modern Medicine with Safe & Effective Alternative Therapies*. Washington: Harbor Press.

Said, E. (1994). *Culture and Imperialism*, New York : Vintage Books.
Semali, L. M., & Kincheloe, J. L. (eds.). (1999). *What Is Indigenous Knowledge? Voices from the Academy*. New York & London: Falmer.
Sertima, I. V (1984). *Black Women in Antiquity*. New Brunswick, NJ: Transaction.
Smith, L. T. (1999). *Decolonizing Methodologies: Research and Indigenous Peoples*. London: Zed.
Solom, A. & Wane, N. (2005). Indigenous Healers & Healing in a Modern World. In R. Moodely & W. West (eds). *Integrating Traditional Healing Practices into Counseling and Psychotherapy* (pp. 52–60). London. Sage.
Some, M. (1994). *Of Water and Spirit: Ritual, Magic, and Initiation in the Life of an African Shaman*. New York: Tarcher/Putnam.
Some, M. (1999). *The Healing Wisdom of Africa: Finding Life Purpose through Nature, Ritual, and Community*. New York: Tarcher/Putnam.
Tuck, I. (2004). Development of a Spirituality Intervention to Promote Healing. *Journal of Theory Construction and Testing, 8*(2), 67–71.
Wane, N. N. (2004) (summer) Black Canadian Feminism Thought: Tensions and Possibilities. *Canadian Women's Journal*. Vol 23. No.2. pp. 145-153 Wane, N.N. (2005a) Black Canadian Women and the Question of Black Feminisms *Canadian Journal of Women Studies*.
Wane, N. N. (2005b). Claiming, Writing, Storing, Sharing African Indigenous Knowledge. *Journal of Thought,* 40(2), Summer, 27–46.
Wane, N. N. (2006). Is Declonization Possible? In G. J. S. Dei, and A. Kempf (eds.), *Anti-colonialism and Education: The Politics of Resistance* (pp.87–107). Rotterdam/Taipei: Sense.

CHAPTER NINETEEN

'Glocalising' Indigenous Knowledges for the Classroom

OCEAN RIPEKA MERCIER

In the universities of Aotearoa New Zealand, teaching about Indigenous people used to be the domain of anthropology, and Māori academics have been involved in this discipline for decades (Buck, 1938). The seedlings of both Māori Studies and Indigenous knowledge (IK) were wards of this discipline up until 30 years ago (Mead, 1997a). Since the pioneering move to an independent school by founding professor Hirini Moko Mead, Māori Studies has become a thriving area of enquiry, with schools in all eight of Aotearoa New Zealand's Universities. In the last two decades, whare wānanga, or tribal tertiary institutions (Mead, 1997b), have radically changed the Indigenous teaching landscape. Academics in Māori Studies have also long been interested in the experiences of other Indigenous peoples: our narratives have resonance, our struggles with colonial powers are similar and we share similar values. The institutionalising of activity related to Indigenous knowledge—seen, for example, in the re-naming of certain schools of Māori Studies to Māori and Indigenous Studies[1]—is a reflection of the extent to which Māori Studies staff engage with other Indigenous academics and their discourses. Māori Studies has become the place within the academy to nurture Indigenous knowledge as an area of enquiry (rather than anthropology or history; Hereniko, 2000).

In spite of occupying an arguably more marginal space in the university, Indigenous ways of knowing are being held in higher esteem across our academies. The global anxiety about our planet's welfare has resulted in interest amongst the natural sciences for what are seen as the sustainable practices of Indigenous knowledge (Warren, Liebenstein, & Slikkerveer, 1993). Nakata argues that this 'partial' interest in relation to Indigenous knowledge is fed by capitalist, 'record and capture,' 'mine and extract' and political motives (Nakata, 2007b). This selective valuing of Indigenous knowledge by Western forms of knowledge is dangerous to Indigenous knowledge systems, particularly if processed and fed back to Indigenous peoples as their own. What is heartening to see is postmodernism's Western scholars, the thin end of the wedge, opening the table to discussion from modernism's 'others' (Denzin, Smith, & Lincoln, 2008; Pettman, 2001), and increasingly, Indigenous people themselves who are speaking and writing their discourses, theories and models into the libraries of the academy.

When I moved from Physics to Māori Studies in 2004, I came with little more than matter-related theories in physics to teach 'MAOR124: Māori Science' for Te Kawa a Māui (the School of Māori Studies). Year after year I confronted many of my own prejudices about 'other' ways of knowing. I believe that as a Western-trained scientist those prejudices were learned, that they can be unlearned, but that we do not necessarily know when the unlearning has ended. It was from my background reading for the teaching of Māori Science that I learnt about the history and philosophy of Western science (WS), came to appreciate the breadth and reach of mātauranga Māori (Māori knowledge) and felt myself being constructed and engineered into a bridge between them (Callaghan, 2009, p. 106). In my reading I began to encounter an area well-staked by Indigenous and non-Indigenous scholars alike. I also came to realise a need for university students to strip themselves of a positivist perspective (as I attempt to) if they were to be able to respect and engage with IK. And yet, for myself, it was impossible to do this unlearning without first understanding the mechanics of the 'Western' science machine. In the teaching of 'Māori Science' within the university, it is still necessary to discuss 'Western science,' and use this understanding to unpack any assumptions that will limit a student's understanding of Māori science.

In 2006, I visited the University of Alaska, Fairbanks, to meet Ray Barnhardt and Oscar Kawagley, and to learn more about their work with the Alaska Native Knowledge Network in recording and revitalising traditional and Indigenous knowledge and science. I also met with Marie Battiste and Glen Aikenhead at the University of Saskatchewan, Canada, and enjoyed stimulating discussions with them around exploring the spaces occupied by science and Indigenous knowledge. Those initial connections gave rise to others, and conversations with Sakej Youngblood Henderson, Yvonne Vizina, Leroy Little Bear, Sean Topkok, Beth Leonard, Hajo Eicken, Matt Druckenmiller and Lolly Carpluk have all in some way influenced the design of the collaborative classroom space discussed here.

'MAOR317: Indigenous Knowledge and Science' came from these connections. Its intent was to explore Indigenous knowledge in different contexts and some of the manifestations of its burgeoning relationship with 'Western' science. We first offered MAOR317 in 2007, and nine students enrolled. In 2009, 24 students enrolled in the course. The course provided a follow-on option for students who had completed 'MAOR124: Māori Science,' although MAOR124 was not a prerequisite. MAOR317 course content was heavily influenced by North American scholarship related to the interface between Western science and Indigenous knowledge.

The adage 'think global, act local' has been thought to give rise to the term 'glocalisation,' in use since the 1980s. While the term 'glocal' has been used in a variety of contexts, mostly relating to economic, political, social (Robertson, 1992) and cultural, in this chapter I propose a postmodern understanding in relation to IK. The early part of MAOR317 is concerned with generalising or 'globalising' some of the common features of Indigenous oral histories and traditional ecological knowledge. Near the end of the course, students embark on their own 'local knowledge project,' and in doing so 'localise' (or re-'localise') those 'global' frameworks to their own contexts. This 'glo-**c**-alising' approach can then be understood as one that seeks commonalities from a global community it assumes membership of, and guidance from that global network of wisdom, in order to effect positive local change. The 'glo**c**alising' approach aims to synthesise the global (in all of its diversity of contexts) from a specific local perspective, primarily for the purpose of local, not global understanding. As the word '**g**local' retains the 'local,' a 'glocal understanding' overtly retains the local perspective from whence the 'globalising' (or generalising) has come. Glocalisation then, may be an approach that, knows its limits and lays no claims to universalities or 'globalisms,' respects local variations and counter-narratives, and allows for unique interpretations for each student and classroom. For instance, a glocal framework for IK in one context's classroom will be different to that devised for another. In this interpretation, our proposed understanding of 'glocal' is a significant departure from previous uses.

The first section of this chapter defines 'science' as used in MAOR317. It then explores the dynamics of interaction between Indigenous and Western knowledge and science and the space between, or interface. The chapter then describes in detail specific teaching activities and assessment outcomes that illustrate 'glocalisation.' It concludes by discussing the challenges, lessons and limitations of teaching Indigenous knowledge within the university classroom.

THE ELEPHANT OUTSIDE THE CLASSROOM: RE-FRAMING 'WESTERN' SCIENCE

For this course, I posit that science is a multitudinous set of self-consistent knowledge producing practices. It also has a 'plurality of origins' (Kawagley, Norris-Tull, & Norris-Tull, 1998, p. 134) and the sciences may be performed differently depending on how the practitioner is influenced by those origins. Naturalistic science is distinct from creation science in the choices available to the overarching theory or assumption that underpins each: one must not accept supernatural influence and the other must. If a science is practiced in a self-consistent and repeated way to produce knowledge, questions such as 'Is the phenomenon observable, measurable, repeatable and independently verifiable?' become somewhat redundant.

The anthropologists of the early 20th century, whose practice was infused with these very tenets, saw curiosity and preservation value in Indigenous oral histories. They certainly did not see Indigenous science (IS)—or if they did, it was considered 'rude' and 'barbaric,' reflecting to them only what their own race's knowledge producing practices once had been. Their modernist outlook/inlook overlooked those aspects of Indigenous knowledge, that built it into a self-consistent set of practices. Critical theorists and Indigenous scholars have long been critiquing these works (Churchill, 1998; Deloria, 1997; Nakata, 2007b; Smith, 1999; Walker, 1992) and I will add nothing further here.

In a section of MAOR317 that is designed to turn the gaze back on the modernist and his impact on our thinking in motional mechanics, we reveal the myth behind a well-known set of physics principles. These are

1. Time flows at a constant rate.
2. Space and time are independent variables.

The Newtonian principles above have been, and continue to be, not just foundations of science, but of our mundane and everyday movements in the world. These principles were once taken as foundational and immutable. However, Einstein's notions of relativity make the first statement an approximation at best, and the second untrue altogether. Nonetheless, these (mis-)conceptions of space and time are so pervasive, that even though Einstein's relativity has superseded Newtonian conceptions of space and time by a century, the myths survive in our collective consciousness.

Our metaphysical experience of time is related to something experiential, not just physically quantifiable. Certain events disconnect us from a conscious awareness of the passage of time. Being asleep is one such activity, but then so is being in good company or being engaged in a favourite pastime. Time can often drag—when spent in limbo or waiting, for instance. Durie speaks of this metaphysical fluidity of time in relation to the marae (Durie, 1999). Indeed, Einstein paved a way to descriptions through mathematical formalism of different rates of time flow between spaces. The passing of 10 seconds in one frame of reference may be equivalent to 6 seconds in another. That 'time flows at a constant rate' is groundless when stated in light of our experience, and modern physics is in agreement.

Einstein also paved a way to understanding that space and time are actually interdependent, cannot exist in isolation of each other, and fold in and around each other in some circumstances. David Suzuki states that 'as a fact of pure experience, there is no space without time, no time without space; they are interpenetrating' (2003). This opens up the possibility of time travel. Imagine that space and time are NOT independent, that how time unfolds has an influence on the space around. We can then entertain the possibility that we may experience a particular space not just at the present time but simultaneously at times past and times future. Complementarily, a specific time can connect different, maybe distant spaces. David F. Peat explains how spaces huge distances apart can be spanned in a moment, by particles of light called photons:

> Einstein's theory of relativity tells us, that with respect to the light ray, the time taken for the journey from star to eye is zero—no time at all. Suppose that you were to travel along a similar path and to measure the journey by your watch. The faster you go the more your watch would slow down until, at the speed of light, the watch would not tick at all, thus the time that you would measure for this vast journey would be 'no time' . . . as far as the photon is concerned, the distant star and the eye-consciousness of the Mayan astronomer are in intimate contact (Peat, 2002, p. 211).

David F. Peat also argues that Indigenous thought was in many ways akin to modern physics, and thus arguably more advanced than Western thought of the time. While this contention carries the whiff of one-upmanship, his juxtaposition of the different ideas is interesting and stimulating.

Overall, this teaching exercise is designed to point out the irony of a system that labels IK and other knowledge systems myth and yet is silent on the perpetuation of 17th century Newtonian half-truths in the public mind. We must all acknowledge that we believe in myths, sceptic or not, and resist the indulgence of our mean-spirited urges to debunk other ways of knowing.

AN ELEPHANT IN THE CLASSROOM: DISCOMFIT AND COMPROMISE AT THE 'INTERFACE'

In spite of our redefining of science to open our minds to IK and IS, the elephant outside of the room, not party to those discussions, still retains the beliefs and nature of an elephant. Confronted with Western science and its self-assured sense of its value- and myth-free nature, how does IK engage?

The interface, described as the place where Western science meets Indigenous knowledge, has been conceptualised in various ways. It has been seen as the central space along a continuum, emphasising its position as one in between the extreme features of various knowledge systems (Durie, 2005b): for Western science, quantifiable data, objectivity, naturalism and Indigenous knowledge values are intertwined through recourse to the supernatural. However, this 'sterile dichotomy between Indigenous and Western' (Agrawal, 1995, p. 5) is seen by many as unhelpful, though the emphasis of difference does serve to highlight uniqueness (Roberts, 1996). The interface has been described as the intersection of knowledge systems, with an emphasis on the 'common ground' between them (Barnhardt & Kawagley, 2005; Mercier, 2007; Roberts, 1996; Simon, 2002). It has been described as a meeting place for the different holders of different worldviews and value systems, with Nakata calling it a cultural interface (Nakata, 2007a), and Smith et al. (2008) referring to a 'negotiated space' in which local decisions are made based upon goals shared and identified amongst the community involved.

With the humanity of endeavours across worldviews and knowledge systems in mind, Durie has devised a framework and four guidelines for interface research (Durie, 2005a): that activity should be embarked upon with mutual respect, and with shared benefits, human dignity and discovery in mind. These guidelines enable us to examine the motivations of the metaphorical elephant of 'Western science'. (*discussed in Section 2.*) participating in interface projects and critique their aims in light of Indigenous principles: namely, that research should be decolonising (Smith, 1999), empowering and emancipating (Rigney, 1999), and should take for granted and affirm our Indigenous identities (Smith, 1997). In the space of our classroom, then, we address the imbalance of power by consciously putting Indigenous interests on an equal footing or ahead of those of Western science.

As an assignment, students chose an interface project as a case study and interrogated it with checklist based on these values. A short list of case studies was provided—including Te Whata Kura Ahupūngao (2008), the UNESCO LINKS resources (Nakashima & Nilsson, 2003) and the Alaska Native Knowledge Network (http://www.ankn.uaf.edu) repository—but about half of the class sought and found other projects to report on, including Victoria University of Wellington's Allan Wilson Centre tuatara (a large lizard native to Aotearoa New Zealand) restoration project (Ramstad et al., 2007) and a case where tikanga Māori (protocols) were developed for the neuroscience laboratory (Cheung, Gibbons, Dragunow, & Faull, 2007). Students submitted a report that assessed the project under Durie's interface criteria. They could estimate the balance of power between WS and IK practitioners in the partnership. On consideration of all of the students' work on 20 distinct projects, having each apply these checks and measures, it became evident that if the project was Indigenous-led, it had a much better chance (but no guarantee) of realising a partnership of equity. By examining projects in light of key Indigenous 'principles for interface research' students were able to evaluate not only the appropriateness of the research for the Indigenous groups involved but the usefulness of the guidelines themselves.

ELEPHANTS ASIDE: COMMUNITY KNOWLEDGE BUILDING THROUGH GLOCALISING

One of the pedagogical tools that allows us to retain, make sense of and recall information is to generalise and systematise diverse and perhaps disparate data into themes, and it is a technique that I have come to understand as 'glocalisation' in our specific space. As a mostly Indigenous class of students local to Aotearoa, the presentation of some of our own IK alongside that of peoples all over the world, is a glocalising action. The lens through which we see other Indigenous narratives is our own, and our framework and interpretation can never be 'global' or objective. It can only be glocal, as such carrying with it a perspective that is marked with the ray path of our perception. In this section I discuss two examples of this 'glocalisation.' We then discuss other class assessments and activities, and comment overall on their usefulness to us in learning about IK.

Indigenous Knowledge—Oral Histories

There has been much discussion in this book regarding what constitutes IK and I won't go into detail here. We regularly used other variations on the term in the classroom, such as 'local knowledge,' and 'traditional knowledge,' inflecting the knowledge with location and antiquity respectively. While IK is generally used to refer to the knowledge and wisdom of Indigenous peoples, debate surrounds the nature of the 'knowledge' itself. For instance, mātauranga Māori—Māori knowledge related to 'experiences, worldviews and lifeways' (Royal, 2009, p. 2)—has been argued to be created in common and everyday experience but also emerges from the relationship between atua (sources of spiritual power) and tohunga (conduits of spiritual power). Indigenous ways of living in nature (IWLN) is a recent suggestion (Aikenhead & Ogawa, 2007) that was designed to convey the applied functionality of much of what is understood to be IK. However, in all of this discussion we must be mindful of Battiste and Henderson's critique of what they see as a Eurocentric predilection for defining 'other' knowledges. Room must remain for a diversity of understandings of what IK is.

Through this literature, we seek windows, or perhaps binoculars, into other Indigenous realities and experiences. The objects of our gaze take the form of various literatures, through the watching of contemporary and older videos filmed in and around Indigenous peoples and through discussions online and via videoconference with Indigenous students in Alaska (discussed later in this section). In our examination of various oral histories and examples of contemporary and traditional ecological knowledge, we rely on glocal frameworks to order features of Indigenous knowledge. While there is a danger in global frameworks having a homogenising effect on the knowledge (Agrawal, 1995), glocal frameworks allow us our perspective on others, and an exploration of how glocalisation creates a culture 'more homogeneous in some aspects and more heterogeneous in others' (Damm, 2001, p. 70). Frameworks aid students in four ways: as a way to organise and systematise diverse offerings of information, as a memory device, as a way to understand local knowledge in comparison with other Indigenous knowledges and finally (but not), as a description that may have local usefulness to the MAOR317 classroom.

One of the class's first activities is to examine some written accounts of selected 'myths' of different Indigenous peoples and look for commonalities. 'Embedded in the stories are themes and myth-messages that provide precedents, models and social prescriptions for human behaviour' (Walker, 1992, p. 182). Walker further states that the traditions are 'logically arranged' and designed to perform 'explanatory functions.' The oral traditions selected for the class discussion included creation histories from Tahiti, Ghana, Aotearoa New Zealand, Canada and the United States. The oral histories were distributed amongst small groups of students who read through each one and found some or all of the following features, informed by Elder and Wong's discussion (1994):

1. *The participation of human characters in creation.* Paoa was a migrant ancestor of the East Coast tribes of New Zealand who was building a canoe. He found a tall tree far inland, and felled it. By urinating he created a great waterway, by which his log was conveyed to the sea (McConnell, 2002, pp. 18–22). The existence of human or human-like creatures in the days of creation is a feature of several other oral histories examined here also.

2. *Existence in nature of 'residual power' from creation.* Māori people speak of *mauri*, which is the life force or essence that flows through all material things, whether rock-forms, waterways or animate beings. Other Indigenous peoples speak of the spirit that pervades all things. In the Tahitian account of creation as told in Tangaroa, maker of all things (Elder & Wong, 1994, pp. 40–41), this residue of creation is embodied by fragments of Tangaroa's, the Creator, shell that exist in all beings and in all physical things.

3. *Counter-balanced primal forces.* In a Mohawk telling of creation (Elder & Wong, 1994, pp. 32–39), the daughter of the Great Spirit had two children: the elder a good spirit and the younger an evil spirit, to whom she died giving birth. The two spirits set about creating the entities and beings of the natural world, their different contributions to creation balancing each other out. To Māori people these primal forces are tapu (sacred, of the gods) and noa (common, everyday). The binary appears in other forms too, such as the male and female primal parents.

4. *Local geography and environment become keys in narrative.* In the Origin of the Sun and the Moon (MacDonald, 2000, p. 277) the Nunamiut people remember certain everyday implements and artefacts. A brother who had violated his sister was riven with sorrow, and sought to apologise to her and atone for his wrongdoing. She had by this time fled; taken an Inuit lamp and begun to rise into the air. He took his tool bag and followed her. She, with her lamp, became the Sun. The brother became the Moon, his tool bag visible in the dark patches on the lunar face. He is doomed to chase her forever, and to be ever overshadowed by her. Their physical character reminds us of the brother's wrongdoing but also the relative value yet complementarity of local artefacts.

5. *Local to audience and local in time.* While certain basic principles are embedded in narratives, the telling of stories is adapted to the learning needs of the audience, and to any one story can be added layers of complexity that resonate with adults, as well as children, or vice versa. The way a tradition is told also reflects particular times, socialisations and environments.

6. *The importance of narrative and humour.* The dynamic creativity and humour in narratives, amongst other things, helps people to remember the narratives and then retell them, thereby keeping the knowledge alive. The punctuation of stories by specific emotions—shame, excitement, fear, anger, amusement, love—ensures that the library of knowledge can be drawn upon in situations when most needed, in times when these emotions are at the fore of our experience.

7. *The importance of a 'Trickster' character.* Anansi owns all tales that are told. (Elder & Wong 1994, pp. 195–197) retell a Ghanaian history of creation. Anansi, the spider, coveted the stories of the Sky God, who owned all tales at that time. The Sky God agreed to trade with Anansi—some tales, for some of the creatures of the Earth: hornets, a python and a leopard. Through his resourcefulness and trickery, Anansi was able to capture all three of these dangerous creatures and earn for himself all stories and knowledge. This 'trickster' character, so common to Indigenous oral stories, acts as a catalyst for change. They often break protocols in order to do so but in doing so show us that sometimes the ends justifies the means.

8. *Interconnectivity between all beings.* This feature is connected with the residual power that inhabits and connects all beings and things. The combination of this interconnectivity and

channelling of a residual power can result in the shape-shifting of one creature to another. In Māori narratives, Tāne Mahuta, the god of the forests, was able to turn himself into a bird, and also to embody the form of kauri trees.

9. *A 'moral of the story.'* A system of values underpins any narrative, but oral histories are designed to reveal specific values, morals, precepts and ethics. For instance, in Thunder and Lightning (MacDonald, 2000), Manelaq of the Netsilik tells of a brother and sister who were orphans. Being uncared for, they were left behind one day by their community. They debated amongst themselves what they might become, and after considering and naming all natural Earth-bound possibilities, they decided to become thunder and lightning. In doing so, they took retribution on the community who had abandoned them. They continue to exist today—acting as a reminder for us to care for the bereaved.

When each of the small groups presents their findings on their particular oral history, other groups and the class as a whole are able to connect certain commonalities from one oral history to another. This glocal set of nine features provides a starting point from which we can ponder how Indigenous oral histories might differ or be similar to our own. Our privileging and framing of these similarities are based on glocal choices and are such that they inform us better on the meanings of our own histories.

Traditional Ecological Knowledge

While traditional ecological knowledge (TEK) can be understood as a 'Western construct' (McGregor, 2000) and a globalising framework (reflecting the attempt to corral a set of practices under a single umbrella), we can nonetheless be edified by examining environment-related knowledge in IK in a glocal way. Indigenous ways are seen as having a low impact upon the environment, and Indigenous people who live by ancestral ways as enacting TEK. We can examine some of these traditions for similarities in features. A four-element glocal framework (under the global umbrella of TEK) was developed for the class activities in reference to Battiste and Henderson's work with Emery (1997) and specific examples of Indigenous ecological management in Māori traditions.

Traditional ecological knowledge is

1. Cumulative, dynamic (Emery, 1997) and local;
2. Empirical, tested, systematised;
3. Respect for historical contracts/relationships contributes to balance in the ecosystem (Battiste & Henderson, 2000); and
4. Values contribute to sustainable management of the ecosystem.

As an activity, students are asked to test this framework against other local examples of what might be globally classified as TEK. Specifically, students watched a video called *Wild South: Tracks of the Hunter* (Fairley, 2002). In this documentary, an Aboriginal man from Arnhem land named Datjing Burrawanga takes Larry Gray, a 'whitefella,' on a journey into the outback. There they rely on Datjing's hunting and survival practices. Datjing's bush knowledge is not simply 'man-vs-wild' style subsistence but betrays a deep appreciation of the spirit and voices of the land and its inhabitants. In watching this, students note for themselves how practices and their attendant values can be positioned within the TEK four-element glocal framework. For instance, Datjing's respect for the historical contract between man and crocodile is evident in his painting of it upon his kayak. This, thus, becomes an exercise in a generalised framework being reapplied to understand another local context, whether Indigenous or non-Indigenous.

Local Knowledge Project

In this assignment, students were encouraged to engage the principles of Indigenous knowledge recording within a local space of their own choosing. In their course prescription they were asked to engage their choice of media as a means of documenting local knowledge specific to their own community, defined in a number of ways, for example, whānau (family), hapū (subtribe), students, common interest group. Suggestions given for the form of the project included a journal, a media scrapbook, a short film, an educational resource, a cultural atlas using Google Earth and a Facebook page. Ideas included reviews of Māori and Indigenous films at the International Film Festival, charting the impact of scientific and technological advancements (e.g., the 60 wind turbines in the West Wind Farm built along the South-West coast of Wellington, Aotearoa) on local landscapes and giving an audio commentary on family home movie footage. The students drew upon these ideas and came up with media and topics appropriate to their own local communities.

Students were encouraged to work with people close to them on a project that would directly benefit those people. Although the project was graded, students had the option of withholding personal information from assessment. The information in the projects was not for the university or any publication, besides publication in the chosen medium for the chosen community. Students were expected to offer informed consent and the right of withdrawal to their participants but no consent forms were required.

Students reported feeling highly motivated by the opportunity to do research in a context that enabled some benefit to flow back to the community of their choosing. They also reported various challenges, especially around the recording of perspectives, from family members, for example. In some cases, accounts of a single event differed. In others, the sharing of those perspectives stood to alienate community members from each other. Students were able to read these experiences in light of Leanne Simpson's cautions around 'capturing' local knowledge (2004). They reported that the excuse to speak to their community, sometimes elders in their families, about issues of relevance to them created new bonds but also new expectations in that community. Within the bounds of the assignment students had limited time, were restricted by the geographic spread of their communities and the volume of potential work, but they did become aware first-hand of issues involved in recording; considering what knowledge can and should be recorded in light of how it will be disseminated.

UAF-VUW Forum and Videoconference

In this activity, students in MAOR317 at Victoria University of Wellington met online with students enrolled at the University of Alaska Fairbanks in 'CCS601: Documenting Indigenous Knowledge.' They discussed two readings: a chapter from *Kaupapa Maori Science* (Stewart, 2007) and the article 'Deg Xinag Oral Traditions' (Leonard, 2009). The students, through their forum conversations, discussed student-devised questions relating to Indigenous knowledge. Seven of the Aotearoa New Zealand students went on to prepare a conference presentation with Ocean Mercier and Beth Leonard, and shared this at the 2010 Ngā Pae o te Māramatanga 4th Traditional Knowledge Conference.

Through these assignments, students take up as a tool the 'glocal look' at IK that has been developed through the course, and interact with other IK systems with confidence. They then apply it to the local context they have chosen. Through this process, they negotiate for themselves a space between the global 'learnings' and the local 'doings' of the course.

CONCLUSION

The key messages of MAOR317 are two. First, through a critique of Western science and redefining the term science, I seek to ameliorate the surgical impact of a positivistic and naturalistic Western institution—thus paving the way to teach IK with a more open mind. Secondly, I've sought to develop a safe pedagogical tool that gives students licence to analyse literature-based IK and makes its concepts meaningful to their own contexts, without the tyranny of claiming that generalisation works in any context but that of our local one.

We could argue that what we don't get from the course is anything to do with Indigenous knowledge. Our financial limitations and time constraints do not enable us to bring non-Māori Indigenous guest speakers to the students, let alone have students visit other Indigenous contexts. We are restricted to discussing Indigenous knowledge in the English language. We are constrained by the norms of Western academia, which requires written assessment of student work. We do not practice IK, let alone live it (McGregor, 2005). MAOR317 is literature-based.

However, a key component of the assessment consisted of 'field work' in and with students' own families and/or communities. Through this, students are reminded that Indigenous knowledge is local, but that their glocal Indigenous knowledge frameworks can be reapplied in the local contexts, because they've drawn on other IK from a local lens. Glocal understanding eschews the imperialism of universalisms because in the term is an explicit acknowledgment of the observer.

What we do get from the course are seriously engaged students. In end-of-course evaluations two students reported that they spent 20 hours per week (5 hours above that expected and probably 10 hours above the average) on the course, yet one wrote 'I was motivated to work hard.' Students in the course have asked for postgraduate level courses and are exploring interface topics for their honours (400-level) research essays. Seven of the students who took part in the exchange presented a panel discussion in the aforementioned 2010 Traditional Knowledge Conference. Their meeting with Beth Leonard, an Athabascan woman from Shageluk, effected a transformation of global spaces to a local one at the conference centre that brought their experiences and dialog together. Furthermore, we observed the meeting of two distinct glocal understandings of IK and the negotiation of a new shared understanding at this interface.

Through this discussion, I have argued that a glocal view of IK allows us to systematise IK's features in a way that acknowledges our local perspective, prejudices and biases but through doing so enables us to place and understand our local IK in a global context.

ACKNOWLEDGMENTS

A version of this chapter was first presented at the APSTS Conference in Brisbane 2009, and I acknowledge APSTS travel support to get to the conference. I am grateful to the Royal Society of New Zealand for ISAT linkages funding for two visits to the University of Alaska Fairbanks, United States, and the University of Saskatchewan, Canada (ISATA06–39 and ISATA07–42). The classes of MAOR317 have made the teaching of the course a stimulating experience, and to them I am grateful. Conference expenses for myself and students of MAOR317 were met by Te Kawa a Māui and the Office of the Pro-Vice Chancellor (Māori) at Victoria University of Wellington.

NOTE

1. In 2009, Victoria University approved a name change for the School of Māori Studies, to the School of Māori and Indigenous Studies.

REFERENCES

Agrawal, A. (1995). Indigenous and Scientific knowledge: some critical comments. *Indigenous Knowledge and Development Monitor, 3*(3), 1–9.

Ahupūngao, T. W. K. (2008). The New Zealand Physics Teachers' Resource Bank Retrieved May 4, 2010, from http://www.vuw.ac.nz/scps-demos/TeReoResources.htm

Aikenhead, G., & Ogawa, M. (2007). Indigenous Knowledge and Science Revisited. *Cultural Studies of Science Education, 2*(3), 539–620.

Barnhardt, R., & Kawagley, A. O. (2005). Indigenous Knowledge Systems and Alaska Native Ways of Knowing. *Anthropological and Education Quarterly, 36*(1), 8–23.

Battiste, M., & Henderson, S. J. Y. (2000). *Protecting Indigenous Knowledge and Heritage. A Global Challenge*. Canada: Purich.

Buck, P. H. (1938). *Vikings of the Sunrise*. New York: Stokes.

Callaghan, P. (2009). *Wool to WETA: Transforming New Zealand's Culture & Economy*. Auckland: Auckland University Press.

Cheung, M. J., Gibbons, H. M., Dragunow, M., & Faull, R. L. M. (2007). Tikanga in the Laboratory: Engaging Safe Practice. *MAI Review, 1*(1), 1–7.

Churchill, W. (1998). *Fantasies of the Master Race: Literature, Cinema and the Colonization of American Indians*. San Francisco: City Lights.

Damm, J. (2001). The WorldWide Web in China and Taiwan: The Effects of Heterogenization and Homogenization in a Glocal Discourse. *Berliner China-Hefte, 20*, 66–78.

Deloria, V. (1997). *Red Earth White Lies. Native Americans and the Myth of Scientific Fact*. Colorado: Fulcrum.

Denzin, N. K., Smith, L. T., & Lincoln, Y. (2008). *Handbook of Critical and Indigenous Methodologies*. Los Angeles: Sage.

Durie, M. (1999). Marae and Implications for a Modern Maori Psychology. *Journal of the Polynesian Society, 8*(31), 351–366.

Durie, M. (2005a). Indigenous Knowledge Within a Global Knowledge System. *Higher Education Policy, 18*, 301–312.

Durie, M. (2005b). Pūtaiao: Tides of Discovery *Ngā Tai Matatū: Tides of Māori Endurance*. Melbourne: Oxford University Press.

Elder, J., & Wong, H. D. (1994). *Family of Earth and Sky: Indigenous Tales of Nature from Around the World*. Boston: Beacon.

Emery, A. R. (1997). *Guidelines for Environmental Assessments and Traditional Knowledge*. Ottawa: Centre for Traditional Knowledge.

Fairley, W. (Writer) (2002). *Wild South: Tracks of the Hunter*. In M. O'Malley (Producer). New Zealand: Natural History New Zealand.

Hereniko, V. (2000). Indigenous Knowledge and Academic Imperialism. In R. Borofsky (Ed.), *Remembrance of Pacific Pasts: An Invitation to Remake History* (pp. 78–91). Honolulu: University of Hawaii Press.

Kawagley, A. O., Norris-Tull, D., & Norris-Tull, R. A. (1998). The Indigenous Worldview of Yupiaq Culture: Its Scientific Nature and Relevance to the Practice and Teaching of Science *Journal of Research in Science Teaching, 35*(2), 133–144.

Leonard, B. (2009). Deg Xinag Oral Traditions: Reconnecting Indigenous Language and Education Through Traditional Narratives. In M. Williams (Ed.), *The Alaska Native Reader: History, Culture, Politics* (pp. 123–144). Durham, N.C.: Duke University Press.

MacDonald, J. (2000). *The Arctic Sky: Inuit Astronomy, Star Lore and Legend*. Toronto: Royal Ontario Museum and Nunavut Research Institute.

McConnell, B. (2002). *He Taonga Ano: More Ngati Porou Stories from the East Cape*. Auckland: Reed.

McGregor, D. (2000). The State of Traditional Ecological Knowledge Research in Canada: A Critique of Current Theory and Practice. In R. F. Laliberte, P. Settee, J. B. Waldram, R. Innes, B. McDougall, L. McBain & F. L. Barron (Eds.), *Expressions in Canadian Native Studies*. Saskatoon: University of Saskatchewan, University Extension Press.

McGregor, D. (2005). Traditional Ecological Knowledge: An Anishnabe Woman's Perspective. *Atlantis, 29*(2), 103–109.

Mead, S. M. (1997a). Maori Studies in the Universities: Te Kaupapa Maori i nga Whare Wananga. In S. M. Mead (Ed.), *Landmarks, Bridges and Visions: Aspects of Maori Culture* (pp. 42–47). Wellington: Victoria University Press.

Mead, S. M. (1997b). New Initiatives for Maori at Tertiary Level Institutions. In S. M. Mead (Ed.), *Landmarks, Bridges and Visions: Aspects of Maori Culture* (pp. 54–63). Wellington: Victoria University Press.

Mercier, O. R. (2007). Indigenous Knowledge and Science. A New Representation of the Interface between Indigenous and Eurocentric ways of Knowing. *He Pukenga Korero, 8*(2), 20–28.

Nakashima, D., & Nilsson, A. (2003). Beginnings: Local and Indigenous Knowledge Systems (LInKS) Project Retrieved May 4, 2010, from http://portal.unesco.org/science/en/ev.php-URL_ID=4856&URL_DO=DO_TOPIC&URL_SECTION=201.html

Nakata, M. (2007a). The Cultural Interface. *The Australian Journal of Indigenous Education, 36*(Supplementary), 7–14.

Nakata, M. (2007b). *Disciplining the Savages: Savaging the Disciplines*. Canberra: Aboriginal Studies.

Peat, F. D. (2002). *Blackfoot Physics*. Boston: Weiser.

Pettman, R. (2001). *World Politics: Rationalism and Beyond*. New York: Palgrave.

Ramstad, K. M., Nelson, N. J., Paine, G., Beech, D., Paul, A., Paul, P., et al. (2007). Species and Cultural Conservation in New Zealand: Maori Traditional Ecological Knowledge of Tuatara. *Conservation Biology, 21*(2), 455–464.

Rigney, L. (1999). Internationalisation of an Indigenous Anticolonial Cultural Critique of Research Methodologies. *Wicazo Sa Review, 14*(2), 109–121.

Roberts, M. (1996). *Indigenous Knowledge and Western Science: Perspectives from the Pacific*. Paper presented at the Science and Technology, Education and Ethnicity: An Aotearoa/New Zealand perspective.

Robertson, R. (1992). *Globalization: Social Theory and Global Culture*. London: Sage.

Royal, T. A. C. (2009). *Te Kaimānga: Towards a New Vision for Mātauranga Māori*. Paper presented at the Macmillan Brown Lecture Series. Macmillan Brown Centre for Pacific Studies, University of Canterbury.

Simon, K. H. (2002). *Searching for Synergy: Maori/Indigenous and Scientific Conservatory Values. Reconciling Affinity and Difference?* Paper presented at the Victoria Law School 19th Annual Law and Society Conference. Wellington.

Simpson, L. R. (2004). Anticolonial Strategies for the Recovery and Maintenance of Indigenous Knowledge. *American Indian Quarterly, 28*(3&4), 373–384.

Smith, G. (1997). *The Development of Kaupapa Maori: theory and praxis*. University of Auckland, Auckland.

Smith, L. T. (1999). *Decolonizing Methodologies: Research and Indigenous Peoples*. London: Zed.

Smith, L., Tiakiwai, S.-J., Hemi, M., Hudson, M., Joseph, R., Barrett, A., et al. (2008). *Negotiating Space: Creating Environments to Realise Vision Matauranga*. Paper presented at the Running Hot! conference. Interconnection in the 21st Century. Te Papa, Wellington.

Stewart, G. (2007). *Kaupapa Maori Science*. University of Waikato, Hamilton.
Suzuki, D. (Writer) (2003). *The Web of Life*. Canada: Avanti.
Walker, R. (1992). The Relevance of Maori Myth and Tradition. In M. King (Ed.), *Te Ao Hurihuri: Aspects of Maoritanga* (pp. 170–182). Auckland: Reed.
Warren, M., Liebenstein, G. V., & Slikkerveer, L. (1993). Networking for Indigenous Knowledge. *Indigenous Knowledge and Development Monitor, 1*(1), 1–4.

CHAPTER TWENTY

The Challenges of Science Education and Indigenous Knowledge

LYN CARTER

As a field, science education is vast, diverse, and ambiguous, having developed its own areas of interest and groups of practitioners distinct from the concerns of academic scientists, general educational researchers or science teachers, only since the curriculum reforms of the early 1960s. It is formulated from, and represents, the multiple positionalities of educational theory and practice, and the heterogeneous assemblages that we call Western modern science (WMS). Its interests range from classroom-based teaching and learning, curriculum, teacher education, student-related factors, measurement and evaluation, historical perspectives and so on, to policy development and implementation, and to the more theoretical concerns of epistemology, philosophy and sociocultural critiques of the nature of WMS itself. While these areas are formulated predominately in normative terms, the literature also contains a small but influential collection of more critical perspectives usually identified as the oppositional and marginal discourses (see, for example, the work of Calabrese Barton, 2003; Kyle, 2001).

Recent times have seen a rise in sociocultural perspectives within science education that are a testament to the wholly transforming and increasing complexities of globalisation. While not explicitly acknowledged within the science education literature (for exceptions see Bencze, 2001; Carter 2008, 2005), globalisation has meant on the one hand, the geo-political spread of the market orthodoxy while on the other, increasing diversity, plurality and hybridity as the world's peoples rub more closely together. Lemke (2001) suggests that the encounter between normative science education and cultural and linguistic diversity has been an important focus. This growing preoccupation with diversity that includes Indigenous knowledge can be regarded as a consequence of the newly inter-civilisational encounters of our rapidly globalising world. Consequently, questions about the ways in which science should be conceptualised and represented within science education not only invite debate about the epistemological parity between WMS and other non-Western sciences and Indigenous knowledges,[1] but also promote reflection on moral and value imperatives that seek a decolonising science education.

In this chapter then, I explore the current challenges of science education and Indigenous knowledges. I begin with an overview of science education and then focus in on the cultural diversity scholarship within science education that includes issues of Indigenous knowledge. This also requires a brief look at postcolonial theory. The final section of the chapter argues for the utilisation of the newer theorisations on postcolonialism and epistemological diversity to see how they may contribute to the development of a truly decolonising science education.

I write here with the perspective of a Western white female academic. As a non-Indigenous woman, I am only too aware of the fraught nature and potential colonisation of Western academic projects like this text. However, I believe Walter Mignolo when he suggests, that Western academics can assist in fracturing open the colonial hegemony of Western knowledges like science education (Mignolo, 2007). Walter Mignolo is one of the foremost scholars in the history and theory of colonialism, cosmopolitanism and Latin American studies. Along with Arturo Escobar, he is the founder of the modernity/coloniality project at Duke University which "locates its own inquiry in the very borders of systems of thought and reaches towards the possibility of non-Eurocentric modes of thinking" (Escobar, 2007, p. 180).

A critical consciousness leads me to be a part of this broader project of non-Eurocentrism in science education that for too long has been blind to its perpetuation of hegemonic models of both science and education.

AN OVERVIEW OF SCIENCE EDUCATION

Conceptualising science education requires a consideration of previous science education reforms in a field that many believe has been in reform one way or another since its emergence (Gallagher, 2000). In a well-regarded overview, Fensham (1992) describes the myopic 1960s science education reforms of Britain and America contextualised within the political and economic agendas of the Cold War, and an unbridled confidence in the social benefits and utility of WMS. These reforms focussed on the development of 'teacher proof' curriculum materials, built around theories of teaching and learning derived from psychocognitive experimental studies, and the nature of WMS as a process of inquiry. There was little, if any, representation from non-Western science knowledge or Indigenous knowledge. Countries such as Australia adopted these packages, either importing them intact or developing local versions. At the primary (elementary) level, they privileged WMS processes over content and emphasised Piagetian ideas of concrete, 'hands-on' experience that still have currency today. At the secondary level, sequential assumptions about scientific knowledge, and learning and curriculum processes meant well-established WMS topics were conceptually and theoretically updated and revised to fit with approaches used at university. The resultant fragmented bodies of knowledge recapitulated WMS as objective truth seeking within a unified view of reality. These reforms were explicitly aimed at training vocational scientists and engineers despite only a minority of students at the time going on to senior secondary education.

As evidence of the failures of these reforms began accumulating during the 1970s, science education came to be seen as more complex, and with competing interests vying for ascendancy. Fensham (1997) suggests that constructivist views of conceptual learning where learners construct their own knowledge within collaborative social frameworks became one major imperative. He goes on to argue suggest that these Western-centric theories of cognitive and conceptual learning have helped to perpetuate the 'legacy' science curriculum of canonical WMS topics that are still apparent today. Fensham (1992) also describes the emergence of conflicting goals of science education. The highly abstract science programme geared for a vocational elite was in tension with a more general education required by the diverse learners staying on longer at school. 'Science for all' became the catchcry of further curricula reforms during the 1980s and 1990s, some based on science-technology-society approaches that promoted scientific literacy as an essential characteristic for a world increasingly shaped by science and technoscience.

From this time on, scientific literacy gained wide currency as the goal of science education probably because of its potential to accommodate a large range of interests (De Boar, 2000). It was variously interpreted as preparation in the WMS disciplinary base sufficient for vocational and consequently economic development in Northern and Southern countries,[2] the production of a knowledgeable public sympathetic to the goals of WMS, the understanding of WMS's constitutive cultural and social role, and the ability to follow scientific issues appearing in the media. Some indication of the extent to which it has grown to become the overall goal of science education comes from its inclusion as one of three domains (the others are reading and mathematical literacy), deemed essential for life in the 21st century by the OECD/PISA programme (Harlen, 2001). It was the focus of major international testing in the year 2006.

CONTEMPORARY SCIENCE EDUCATION AGENDAS

Within more contemporary science education agendas, two major themes have become apparent reflective of the broader discourses and complex transformations of our rapidly globalising world. Firstly, science education is the subject of (yet more) reform agendas, modelled this time on neoliberal ideas of education that advance the extension of the enterprise form. In general, these reforms promote mastery of WMS concepts and changed teaching practices, that while described in the 'science for all' rhetoric of equity, diversity and scientific literacy, are replete with the inequities of centralised testing regimes, the slicing and dicing of knowledge as standards, the construction of sanctioned teacher and student subjectivities, authorised pedagogies and cults of accountability.[3] For those supporting these changes nothing short of the universal reinscription of science teachers and their students will actually do. For example, taking a non-critical and somewhat celebratory stance, Anderson (2001) suggests we need to change "our science education system on a massive scale . . . we want to change what students learn as well as how teachers teach. We want to change not just what students know but how they think" (p. 629).[4]

The second theme within science education coheres around sociocultural perspectives reflective of the cultural turn in social science theory more generally.[5] This shift has included, suggests Lemke (2001), the social-interactional, the historical, the linguistic, the political and the sociological that for Wong (2001), together with postmodern and feminist thinking, are part of enlightened contemporary science education discourse. Other sociocultural work foregrounds critical, feminist and poststructuralist theories that explore access to science knowledge, education and power through the intersections of race, gender and class (for example, Calabrese Barton & Osborne, 1998; Cobern, 1996; Ogawa, 1996). Within this perspective can be found the issues of other knowledges including Indigenous knowledge, informed largely it must be said, by scholarship from the normative educational literatures on cultural diversity, multiculturalism and comparative studies.

Over the last decade, three special journal editions from the premier science education journals and a number of one-off studies (for example, Brandt, 2008; Chinn, 2007; Roth, 2008) are testament to the growing interest and concern being expressed about consequences of cultural diversity within science education. These include a *Science Education* issue edited by Aikenhead and Lewis (2001) focussed on multiculturalism and science education, while the *Journal of Research in Science Teaching (JRST)* devoted one issue introduced by Lee (2001) to language and cultural diversity, and another edited by Calabrese Barton and Tobin (2001) to science education in urban settings where linguistically and culturally diverse students concentrate. Those articles dedicated specifically to the issues of Indigenous knowledge, however, are less frequent. Key word searches using *Indigenous knowledge, Indigenous science, traditional knowledge* and *traditional ecological knowledge* as it is sometimes called, yielded only a handful of responses for the last decade in each of the world's top science education journals: *International Journal of Science Education (IJSE), Research in Science Education (RISE), Science Education* and *JRST*. Considering the enormous oeuvre of science education, it is marginal representation at best. The literature seems to use more generic terms like cultural diversity or multiculturalism to encompass the issues of Indigenous knowledge whether explicitly stated as such, or indeed, whether it is appropriate or not. Cultural diversity has become a type of script that can at times, be read as Indigenous knowledge. Hence, in order to discuss the science education scholarship on Indigenous knowledge, in this chapter, I am to some extent reduced to following suit.

Taken as a whole then, the scholarship on cultural diversity and other knowledges including Indigenous knowledge, displays a number of related and interpenetrative tendencies that seem to draw together around two main positions: one focussed on the identities/subjectivities of those learning WMS, that is, the culturally diverse students themselves, and the second, on considerations of science as culturally located WMS and non-Western knowledge systems. There are a number of other approaches I would group together for convenience into a third category, not relevant to the discussion here. In the sections to follow, I will summarise the normative positions on cultural diversity found within science education scholarship and give some sense of a critique of the same derived from postcolonial theory. Postcolonial analysis is especially important when considering issues of Indigenous knowledge because it facilitates Indigenous peoples' reworking of the historical ruins of colonisation in ways that foreground the complexities of recuperation and the restoration of knowledges, identities and cultures. As needed, I pause briefly to describe some of the main tenets of postcolonialism before continuing the discussion on cultural diversity and science education.

POSTCOLONIALISM

With its origins in Commonwealth literatures, literary and cultural studies, and social theory, postcolonialism is a heterogeneous field that stretches across different historical periods, cultural activities and geographical regions. It draws from, in Northern academic and disciplinary terms, cultural studies, anthropology, international relations, economics, history, politics and literary studies, resourced by the critical practices of poststructuralism, feminism, Marxism, psychoanalysis and linguistics. For Young (2001) and others, it is an elastic and highly contested notion that simultaneously includes, firstly, postcolonialism as epoch that acknowledges post–World War II international decolonisation, not only commemorating resistance over colonial powers but also describing 'postcoloniality' as the contemporary condition of existence. Secondly, postcolonialism describes the development of new aesthetic and cultural formations responding to these changed historical circumstances. Thirdly, postcolonialism as methodology draws from poststructuralism and deconstruction as the theoretical method of postmodernism. In this vein, earlier Fanonian-inspired (Fanon, 1961) and Marxist projects of resistance have given way to the more poststructurally driven theorisations of identity, difference, hybridity and ambivalence prominent in the work of those like Bhabha (1994) and Appadurai (1996). Lastly, postcolonialism refers to an ethical and political project resisting hegemonic power and seeking redistributive justice at the local and everyday level as sites of intervention and renewed action.

Despite postcolonialism's broad but essential heterogeneity, many theorists have suggested significant clusters of ideas useful for considering the postcolonial. These ideas, while differing in scope and emphasis, inevitably include the constructs of cultural translation and representation, difference, multiculturalism, hybridity, localism, boundaries and borders, fragmentation, and pluralism in ways that reshape the categories of culture, identity and difference. Postcolonial analysis usually proceeds around a critique of embedded binary representations of the Other, the hegemony of some forms of knowledge and delegitimation or epistemicide of others, the spread of modernity with its normative humanist rhetoric of universalism, the role of the economic-political, as well as developing capacity for Southern agency. Quayson (2000) argues that all these forms of postcolonial critique should be important to many domains of knowledge as part of a larger project interested in differential experiences and social redress. As much of science education's scholarship on cultural diversity articulates an interest in such concerns, it follows that postcolonial perspectives should be indispensable to science education.

Mignolo (2007) is one amongst a growing number of scholars and analysts who interrogates the postcolonial work of those like Bhabha (1994) and makes the distinction between his view of decolonisation and anti-colonialism discourse, and postcolonialism. For Mignolo (2007), postcolonialism is derivative of Northern scholarship, particularly the poststructuralists like Derrida, Lacan and Foucault, who were not overly concerned with the issues of Indigenous knowledge. Mignolo (2007) argues that true decolonial scholarship has its origins in the experiences and ideas from those of the South, particularly utilising his own context in Latin America's strong traditions of liberation philosophy, dependency theory, and participatory action research.[6] http://Hawai'i.gov/gov/news/events/2007/Akaula.[7] Those who need assistance, Cobern's (1996) worldview theory suggests, include non-Western and Indigenous students whose culture interferes with learning WMS as well as Western students whose prior knowledge, gender and/or class make science equally foreign. Snively and Corsiglia (2001) applaud these culturally sensitive perspectives and suggest science education has begun to explore what it means to prepare students for a culturally diverse world.

Postcolonial analyses would suggest, however, that these normative perspectives actually work against the learners, emphasising their need to shift within a frame that at best makes diversity/Indigeneity problematic, at worst pathologised. The representation of WMS as a discrete and unitary knowledge system engages in binary practices of Othering that render culturally diverse students the Other, such that intercultural exchanges like border crossing become indispensable. Some scholars do recognise that the inevitable absorption of broader Western epistemological templates attendant to the learning of WMS includes a potential to diminish students' Indigenous identities and culture (for example, Stanley & Brickhouse, 2001). What is generally not recognised within these literatures are the students' abilities to simultaneously occupy several identity-inducing categories. Usually, analyses proceed in one type of identity category only (for example, gender versus ethnicity, class) reflecting Lemke (2001) argues, deep-seated ethnocentric assumptions on the part of even the most empathetic science education advocates and researchers.

Moreover, in practice border crossing strategies propel predominantly monocultural teachers into roles of 'cultural brokers' with the view that once they have mastered new vocabularies of Indigenous knowledges and strategies, they will be effective teachers of diversity (McKinley, 2001). In other words, learning the Other's knowledges will make teachers effective in their role as cultural brokers. From a postcolonial perspective, such approaches not only employ conceptualisations of culture that perpetuate the binary processes of Othering, they do little, McKinley (2001) argues, to help teachers shift their perceptions of Indigeneity or acknowledge their difficulties. Rather, they deflect attention away from potentially better solutions like systemic initiatives to diversify the teaching population. Perhaps the emphasis on border crossing strategies and teachers as effective cultural brokers is not surprising, as it represents a more manageable option than undertaking the difficult work of decolonisation and re-examination of Western knowledge production that taking seriously the various identities of students would require.

Multicultural Approaches to Science

The second tendency in the cultural diversity literature clusters around science as Western and non-Western knowledge systems including Indigenous knowledge that problematises WMS, acknowledges its Eurocentrism and the contributions of the other Indigenous and civilisational knowledge. In particular, it raises questions about the place of the Other's knowledge in school science (Stanley & Brickhouse, 2001), with those like Snively and Corsiglia (2001) arguing for the inclusion of Indigenous and traditional science knowledge (see also Arellano, Barcenal, Bilbao, Castellano, Nichols & Tippins, 2001; Cajete, 1999). While much of this discussion emanates from the North, there is an increasing contribution from Southern contexts struggling with the tensions of multiple knowledge systems that see cultural, religious and political imperatives compel the maintenance of traditional/Indigenous knowledge, and development priorities demand the expansion of Western technoscientific knowledge (see Aikman, 1997; Semali, 1999).

Perhaps not surprisingly, there are difficulties juxtaposing or meshing Western and Indigenous knowledge in science education, despite the apparent invitation to openness. Postcolonial analyses of this position indicate that while the inclusion of Indigenous science as the affirmation of cultural diversity has the potential to challenge the dominance of WMS within school science, this normative orientation of cultural diversity paradoxically works to make power relations invisible and keep dominant norms in place. Postcolonial readings highlight the continuing Eurocentric nature of comparison with its assumptions of universalism and the bounded and homogeneous nature of contexts, cultures, identities, and knowledges (Huggan, 2001). While it aims to recognise pluralism and difference in corrective attempts at social redress, Huggan (2001) argues that it actually superimposes the dominant perspective by fixing and essentialising stereotypical characteristics of various groups. Consequently, Otherness is configured as alternative forms of the sameness that can only be appreciated as cultural diversity by the dominant group in whose cultural forms the difference has been constructed and represented. Hence, despite intentions to the contrary, this approach to cultural diversity becomes a mechanism of control that domesticates the Other, emphasising their inferiority against the dominant norm (in this case Indigenous knowledge against WMS), and further compartmentalises within reasserting borders. Under a veneer of acceptance, the Indigenous knowledge is translated into familiar cultural forms in ways that construct it as possessing knowable characteristics able to be apprehended and controlled. This occurs when science education scholars attempt to map Indigenous knowledge/science against WMS as a way of making WMS concepts more approachable for Indigenous students.[8] Examples of this include Aikenhead (2001, 2002) and Glasson, Mhango, Phiri and Lanier (2010).

As these unconscious processes of Othering work at preserving the integrity of WMS, the inclusion of the Indigenous science in school curricula risks an empty form of pluralism implicated in restorationist and neoconservative/neoliberal agendas to reassert Eurocentric cultural control (McCarthy & Dimitriadis, 2000). It is naïve to see these cultural diversity approaches, McKinley (2001) argues, as anything other than pedagogical moments that are 'managed' or 'simply technical' (p. 74), as they do not substantially challenge relations between dominant and subordinate groups marked by histories of oppression. For McKinley (2001) culturally diverse science education should be a decolonising education interested in social change that disrupts hegemonic ways of seeing rather than attempting pluralism and inclusivity.

THE CHALLENGES OF INDIGENOUS KNOWLEDGE FOR SCIENCE EDUCATION

Of what then, would a decolonising science education that took seriously delegitimated knowledges such as Indigenous knowledge consist? I suggest here two of many possibilities. Firstly, I believe that science education should include postcolonial theory within its approaches despite its reticence to engage with it up to now. Some prominent exceptions include Carter (2006, 2004), Gough (2007), McKinley (2007, 2001) and Ninnes (2001). This seems like an oversight because, as already noted, postcolonial perspectives can offer science education at once political analysis, cultural critique and philosophical insight to disrupt the continuing Eurocentrism of normative assumptions of cultural diversity. These assumptions are bound to stable and unitary ideas of nation, culture, identity, comparison and difference that, though now outdated, remain embedded within much of science education's take on cultural diversity. Postcolonial perspectives can help science education develop more appropriate and complex conceptualisations that include cultural translation and representation, difference, hybridity, localism, boundaries and borders, fragmentation, and pluralism in ways that reshape the categories of culture, identity and difference better suited to contemporary global culture. They can also expose some of the new forms of imperialism being entrenched within globalised approaches to science education reform outlined above.

More specifically, postcolonialism as one of science education's approaches, can offer the unique methodological insights that come from deconstructive or oppositional reading practice, which while prominent elsewhere have yet to be explored within science education. Such tasks are only just beginning to be thought about and most of this work is still to be done, as it is profoundly challenging. Nonetheless, the significance of postcolonialism for science education lies in its willingness to look beyond science education's conventional categories of analyses and to help revise its philosophical frameworks in the face of an overwhelming, uncertain and rapidly reconfiguring world. Such a critique is necessary to move science education beyond its conventional categories of analysis, exemplified here in the cultural diversity scholarship as it has been previously, as inward looking, self-referencing and repetitive of colonial coordinates that linger in the cultural unconscious (Coombes & Brah, 2000).

Secondly, science education would benefit from engagement with some of the newer approaches to negotiating multiple epistemologies which are just beginning to appear within the literature (see, for example, Bang & Medin, in press; Roth, 2008; Van Eijck & Roth, 2007). One such approach comes from Boaventura de Sousa Santos' reading of epistemological diversity. For Santos (2007a), epistemological diversity or the ecology of knowledges[9] springs from the South's resistance to the hegemony of Northern knowledges and the epistemicide committed upon Indigenous knowledges deemed unable to meet modern scientific standards of truth. At its most basic, epistemological diversity postulates the plurality of knowledges and within a frame of the reciprocity of knowledge and social and cultural life, or what Stengers (2000) sees as the "irreducible link between the production of knowledge and the production of existence" (p. 148). While many complex factors influence the creation of knowledge, it cannot proceed outside the social context and cultural assumptions of the people producing it, owing all to how they interpret their existence (Turnbull, 2000). Conversely, knowledge and its artefacts shape the way social and cultural life can develop. Hence, multiple knowledges exist as a consequence of multiple existences.

Santos (2007b) has developed several ideas for theorising epistemological diversity that arise from outside Eurocentrism and are, he believes, differentiated from the more conventional approaches (see also Santos, Nunes & Meneses, 2007). To that end, Santos argues that science studies have challenged WMS as knowledge's pre-eminent arbiter, exposing it instead as a local, contingent, situated and partial knowledge like any other. These critiques have opened the door to the recognition of plural heterogeneous knowledges (one of which is WMS), and their sustained and dynamic interconnections. Here, I have conflated and reinterpreted Santos' ideas here into a number of interrelated points or axioms. Santos' term of choice is, in fact, *axiom*, and I will adopt its use despite what could be perceived as its potential inadequacy.[10]

Different Human Communities Produce Diverse Forms of Viewing the World

This axiom argues that comprehending the world requires more than Northern knowledges, enabling a much broader vision of what we do and do not know. Vast non-Western understandings and derivative hybrid formulations of Northern and Southern knowledge ensure there is almost an inexhaustible diversity of potential knowledge. More importantly, this axiom conceives of knowledges as interventions enabled in the real world. No single type of knowledge can account for all possible interventions in the world. Knowledge-*as-intervention*-in-reality becomes the measure of realism, not knowledge-as-*a-representation*-of-reality. The credibility of knowledge can be judged by the type of intervention in the world that it affords, and where choices are to be made, the ethical-political domain is considered along with the cognitive. Hence, diverse Indigenous knowledges must not be temporalised or historicised against Eurocentric timelines of development and knowledge types, but regarded like all knowledge, as contemporary, partial and situated.

The Epistemological Privilege of WMS Is a Complex Phenomenon That Cannot Be Explained in Purely Epistemological Terms

This axiom recognises WMS's co-articulation with colonialism and capitalism under modernity that gave it the power to define all other Indigenous knowledge as local and inferior. It postulates that not only is the coloniality of power, now as always, inextricable from the coloniality of knowledge, but equitable distribution of scientific knowledges and products in the contemporary world is impossible without the decolonisation of power and reform of exploitative capitalism. This axiom is a central tenet of science studies and much debated in the *Science Wars*. Zammito (2004) is one theorist who discusses these ideas at length.

WMS Is Part of the Ecology of Knowledges:

This axiom identifies WMS as one amongst many knowledges that is partial, situated and incomplete. That it is a robust, reliable and useful knowledge system that has enabled much human flourishing is acknowledged. It is also acknowledged that enmeshed as it is in the global capitalist progress paradigm, WMS has also been coproductive of hegemonic interests resulting in many unintended consequences, not least of which is the global environmental crisis with which we are all faced. Indeed Beck's (1992) seminal book, *Risk Society*, famously documented, amongst others, this very unintended consequence.

There Are Natural Hierarchies and Pragmatics within the Ecology of Knowledges

This axiom assesses the worth of 'interventions in reality' that different knowledges can offer. It acknowledges that natural hierarchies are generated between knowledges, circumventing the accusations of relativism often used against formulations of plural knowledges. This axiom argues for context-dependent hierarchies of alternative real-world interventions rather than a single universal scientific hierarchy that became dominant under Eurocentric modernity. Likewise, Code (2000) argues for "a *mitigated epistemological relativism*" (p. 69, her italics), which recognises "that knowledge construction is always constrained by the resistance of material and human-social realities" (p. 69). The benefit of Code's (2000) view is that relativism is avoided as many representations of reality are necessarily and pre-emptively ruled out by our tangible experiences or interventions in the world. Santos (2007b) goes on to argue from his first axiom that choosing between different knowledge systems' real-world interventions also requires an ethical-political principle of precaution where "preference must be given to the form of knowledge that guarantees the greatest level of participation to the social groups involved in its design, execution, and control and in the benefits of the intervention" (n.p.). It is also Harding's (2000) point that some knowledges are better for getting rocket ships to the moon, while others are better for assessing the worth of such an enterprise, and still others for living sustainably on the planet we all share.

I would argue that any worthwhile science curriculum should include all of these knowledges though not everyone would agree. There is a similarity here with the intention of the axiom 'there can be no global social justice without global cognitive justice,' discussed later, and a privileging of a science studies approach to science education that reflects the real messiness of our ways of knowing.

Intercultural Translation Is Necessary with the Ecology of Knowledges

As a consequence of Eurocentrism's epistemicide of other Indigenous knowledges, this axiom privileges intercultural translation as a means of recognition, attempting to move past the incommensurability, incompatibility or reciprocal unintelligibility that impedes intercultural dialogue. The hegemony of Northern knowledges has meant that they have been the usual starting and reference points for these dialogues, and as such, are limited in what they can achieve. By contrast, intercultural translation resides in Southern knowledges, and counter-hegemonic and ethical-political resistances, and their local/global articulation. These become the new sites for the development of fresh and hopefully more effective conversations.

There Can Be no Global Social Justice without Global Cognitive Justice

This axiom replaces modernity's knowledge-*as-regulation* bordering functions with knowledge-*as-liberation*. Knowledge-as-liberation recasts a counter-hegemonic, ethical-political purpose for science, historically frustrated by its epistemological exclusiveness. "(S)cience ceases to be a metonymy of knowledge and becomes one of its constituents . . . within the constellation of knowledges aiming at social (liberation)" (Santos, Nunes & Meneses, 2007, p. li). Science is liberated and now able to utilise its internal limits to promote alternative scientific practices and its external limits to encourage interdependence between scientific and non-scientific knowledges. Although this is admittedly a problematic call, and one still highly contentious under *Science Wars*, I believe it has the potential to open the way for the intercultural translation and discussion that is essential to global justice of all types, including within our field. Visvanathan (2006) also has a discussion on other axioms for alternative knowledges that aim towards global cognitive justice. His argument includes the idea of a commons of knowledge as resources available to all and sustained by careful use.

Taken together Santos (2007b) axioms attempt to reset, as it were, the fundamental cartographies and purposes of modern knowledge, that includes Indigenous knowledge within its purview, developing what he identifies an 'epistemology of the South,' that is, a means of working towards global justice. For Santos (2007a) then, the ecology of knowledges/epistemology of the South/epistemological diversity are destabilizing epistemologies that engages the politics of the possible without yielding to an impossible politics. However, Santos (2007b) is not Pollyannaish about the prospects, viewing its enactment as no easy task. "The critical task ahead cannot be limited to generating alternatives. Indeed, it requires an alternative thinking of alternatives" (n.p.).[11] This is already occurring, if somewhat embryonically, Santos (2007a) argues, within the initiatives, networks, organisations and movements that constitute counter-hegemonic globalisation.[12]

Clearly if science education wishes to move beyond its current normative approach to cultural diversity and truly engage with the issues of Indigenous knowledge in a transformational way, then it needs to explore decolonising approaches such as those suggested by the tenets of postcolonialism and Santos' epistemological diversity. As Santos (2007b) notes, we are only beginning this task, and true cognitive justice and epistemological diversity will take the intellectual resources and best will of generations to come. Certainly for science educators, these perspectives offer profound challenges not only to our research agendas but also ultimately for how Indigenous knowledge will become part of everyday schooling for all students. All educators will need to think much more carefully about ways we do our work. My perspective here would not be surprising to Lemke (2001) who fears the traditional backgrounds of most science educators leaves them ill-equipped for the practical and theoretical work of this type. He also calls for greater engagement by science educators with cultural studies, politics and so on, to which I add postcolonialism and epistemological diversity, in order to help revise science education's philosophical frameworks and classroom practices in the face of a rapidly globalisng world and advance it as discipline. Only then will Indigenous knowledge find a place within contemporary science classrooms.

SUMMARY

In this chapter, I have argued that science education's engagement with Indigenous knowledge has proceeded largely from a normative base, much of it embedded within the two broad conceptualisations of cultural diversity, one focussed around the culturally diverse students themselves and the second, on different types on Western and non-Western sciences including Indigenous knowledge, known as multicultural approach to science education. Within the former, such normative perspectives unintentionally but frequently cast the cultural resources of the Indigenous students themselves as deficit and in need of cultural brokers to facilitate their border crossing into WMS. The latter reasserts the dominance of WMS even as it tries to be plural and inclusive. All of this proceeds within an overall science education context that is being reformed by neoliberal and market-based ideology. Like McKinley (2001), I believe more radical approaches to science education are necessary to avoid entrenched but unconscious colonial coordinates lingering in its philosophical approaches if we are to truly pursue decolonising education interested in social change. To this end, I argue that science education needs to engage with the newer theorisations of postcolonialism and epistemology diversity. These become the challenges for science education for the foreseeable future.

When it comes to a discussion on science, definitional dilemmas readily arise and many terms such as science, modern science, Western science, Eurocentric science and so on are in common use. These are all indicative of science's ambiguous and political complexity. Other difficulties can be attached to the terms 'technology,' 'technoscience' and other intersections between science and technology including the naming of scientific research in its 'pure,' or 'blue sky' compared with its 'applied' forms also known as 'commodified,' and 'intensified' science. Further definitional dilemmas arise with naming 'ethnoscience,' 'Indigenous science,' 'local knowledge,' 'traditional ecological knowledge' and 'civilisational' knowledges, all terms that have some currency in the various literatures that concern themselves with Indigenous knowledge issues. Harding (1998) points out the term 'science' has been conceptualised to contrast with earlier European and non-European/Indigenous knowledge practices and is hence, an advance of Eurocentrism/Occidentalism. But there is a sense amongst some scholars that a general definition of 'science' as a movement of knowledge should not be identified only with the practices and applications of its normative form that abounds in the West. Along these lines, Harding (1998) and Paty (1999) prefer a more inclusive view of science that sees it as any systematic attempt to produce knowledge about the natural world. Under this view, as Indigenous knowledges or Indigenous sciences concern themselves to some extent with understanding the natural world, then they are indeed 'science.'

In this chapter I follow Harding (1998), and also Gough (1998) who view the term Western modern science (WMS) to mean anywhere that follows Enlightenment science which traces its trajectory back to 17th-century Western Europe. When a more inclusive view of science is necessary, I will name it as such. However, I choose not to define the terms any further in order to convey some of these conceptual difficulties, seeing this stance as deliberately reflecting the ambiguity, contingency and changing nature of the (re)construct(ion) of science.

The appropriateness of terms used to describe contemporary asymmetrical economic political and social world relations are much debated within the literature. For example, the *First* and *Third Worlds, developed* and *developing* nations, the *West, East* and *Middle East* which only make geographical sense if one is situated in Europe or America, are imbued with the semiotics of coloniality. Here, I adopt the use of *Southern* which encodes a colonial past and continuing disadvantage within the hegemony of globalisation, and *Northern,* which Harding (2006) suggests refers to the origins and beneficiaries of the dominant knowledges, criteria, choices and actions. The *South* and *North* have both geographical and metaphorical immanence.

Although reform is the core of many government reports, policy documents and educational policy analyses on science education, there is interestingly only a small research literature concerned with exploring these reforms. Some examples include the discussion of standards-based curricula in various Australian states (Cross, 1997; Ninnes, 2001), within Canada (McNay, 2000), America (Eisenhart, Finkel & Marion, 1996), and in England and Wales (Donnelly, 2001), comparative international testing (Harlen, 2001), and the devolution and macro systems-level reforms (Drori, 2000). Beyond these studies, the reforms in the science education literature are considered almost in passing, their antecedents glossed over, as they act as a raison d'être to whatever aspect of science education is being elaborated in the particular publication at the time. Gallagher and Richmond's (1999) view that "(s)ignificantly, interest in such reforms emerged virtually simultaneously around the globe, and its language is now part of prominent rhetoric used by scientists, educators, and policy makers in many parts of the world" (p. 753), typifies the apparent lack of interest in exploring the reform movements.

The recent tendencies identified by De Boar (2000) and Laugksch (2000) to conflate scientific literacy with the mastery of standards and measurable outcomes refigures scientific literacy as a shorthand for the sedimentation of the reform agendas. It shifts the broad conceptualisation of scientific literacy with the potential to meet learners' diverse needs including those of Indigenous students, to a narrow and instrumental construct, able to be implemented and tested. As a case in point, by arguing that 'science for all' demands equity issues be addressed so as "all students (can) achieve high academic standards" (p. 499), Lee (2001) gives as much currency to the standards agenda as she does to the cultural and Indigenous equity issues upon which her article is focussed.

The recent critiques from science studies have been especially influential in the rise of science education's sociocultural perspectives. Science studies (see Jasanoff, Markle, Peterson & Pinch, 1995) is the heterogeneous intellectual critique of science that argues we can only know nature through culturally constituted conceptual or epistemological frameworks, enabled and limited by discursive practices, institutional structures, interests, values, cultural norms, and so on. Harding (1998) organises science studies into the two schools of post-Kuhnian and postcolonial. The former focuses on the construction of scientific knowledge within Western-style scientific institutions revealing it to be characterised by the same messy and conflicting individual values, tacit knowledge, social negotiation and cultural constructions as any other knowledge field. Postcolonial science studies moves beyond Kuhn's focus on WMS, to Indigenous and localised perspectives emerging from belated acknowledgement of other knowledges. Both schools of science studies argue the claimed universalism of science to be a particularised universalism, a nexus of interacting people, agencies, materials, interests, technologies and histories (Turnbull, 2000), coexisting with other various and multiple particular/local versions of science. These critiques of science have resulted in the so-called *Science Wars* (Ross, 1996), with scientists like Gross & Levitt (1994) and Nanda (1997) during the heated debates of the 1990s, along with Zammito (2004) more recently, arguing the inadequacies of social and cultural critiques of WMS. None-the-less, science studies have offered discourses of critique capable of interfering with science education's normative scripts of WMS and make space for Indigenous knowledge and practices, privileging local, diverse, and plural perspectives characteristic of the globalisation dialectic. While no doubt the *Science Wars* will rage on and on (as will their influence on science education), those like Roberts & Mackenzie (2006, p. 157) see the more important questions pertinent here as "(w)hat kinds of movements between science and other knowledges are possible or desirable?" (also Visvanathan, 2006).

NOTES

1. When it comes to a discussion on science, definitional dilemmas readily arise, and many terms such as science, modern science, Western science, Eurocentric science and so on are in common use. These are all indicative of science's ambiguous and political complexity. Other difficulties can be attached to the terms 'technology,' 'technoscience' and other intersections between science and technology including the naming of scientific research in its 'pure,' or 'blue sky' compared with its 'applied' forms also known as 'commodified,' and 'intensified' science. Further definitional dilemmas arise with naming 'ethnoscience,' 'indigenous science,' 'local knowledge, 'traditional ecological knowledge' and 'civilisational' knowledges, all terms that have some currency in the various literatures that concern themselves with Indigenous knowledge issues. Harding (1998) points out the term 'science' has been conceptualised to contrast with earlier European and non-European/Indigenous knowledge practices and is hence, an advance of Eurocentrism/Occidentalism. But there is a sense amongst some scholars that a general definition of 'science' as a movement of knowledge should not be identified only with the practices and applications of its normative form that abounds in the West. Along these lines, Harding (1998) and Paty (1999) prefer a more inclusive view of science that sees it as any systematic attempt to produce knowledge about the natural world. Under this view, as Indigenous knowledges or Indigenous sciences concern themselves to some extent with understanding the natural world, then they are indeed 'science.'

2. The appropriateness of terms used to describe contemporary asymmetrical economic political and social world relations are much debated within the literature. For example, the *first* and *third worlds*, *developed* and *developing* nations, the *West*, *East* and *Middle East,* which only make geographical sense if one is situated in Europe or America, are imbued with the semiotics of coloniality. Here, I adopt the use of *Southern,* which encodes a colonial past and continuing disadvantage within the hegemony of globalisation, and *Northern,* which Harding (2006) suggests refers to the origins and beneficiaries of the dominant knowledges, criteria, choices and actions. The *South* and *North* have both geographical and metaphorical immanence.

3. Although reform is the core of many government reports, policy documents and educational policy analysis on science education, there is interestingly only a small research literature concerned with exploring these reforms. Some examples include the discussion of standards-based curricula in various Australian states (Cross, 1997; Ninnes, 2001), within Canada (McNay, 2000), America (Eisenhart, Finkel & Marion, 1996), and in England and Wales (Donnelly, 2001); comparative international testing (Harlen, 2001), and the devolution and macro-system–level reforms (Drori, 2000). Beyond these studies, the reforms in the science education literature are considered almost in passing, their antecedents glossed over, as they act as a *raison d'être* to whatever aspect of science education is being elaborated in the particular publication at the time. Gallagher and Richmond's (1999) view that "(s)ignificantly, interest in such reforms emerged virtually simultaneously around the globe, and its language is now part of prominent rhetoric used by scientists, educators, and policy makers in many parts of the world" (p. 753), typifies the apparent lack of interest in exploring the reform movements.

4. The recent tendencies identified by De Boar (2000) and Laugksch (2000) to conflate scientific literacy with the mastery of standards and measurable outcomes refigure scientific literacy as a shorthand for the sedimentation of the reform agendas. It shifts the broad conceptualisation of scientific literacy with the potential to meet learners' diverse needs including those of Indigenous students, to a narrow and instrumental construct, able to be implemented and tested. As a case in point, by arguing that 'science for all' demands equity issues be addressed so that "all students [can] achieve high academic standards" (p. 499), Lee (2001) gives as much currency to the standards agenda as she does to the cultural and Indigenous equity issues upon which her article is focussed.

5. The recent critiques from science studies have been especially influential in the rise of science education's sociocultural perspectives. Science studies (see Jasanoff, Markle, Peterson & Pinch, 1995) is the heterogeneous intellectual critique of science that argues we can only know nature through culturally constituted conceptual or epistemological frameworks, enabled and limited by discursive practices, institutional structures, interests, values, cultural norms and so on. Harding (1998) organises science studies into the two schools of post-Kuhnian

and postcolonial. The former focuses on the construction of scientific knowledge within Western-style scientific institutions, revealing it to be characterised by the same messy and conflicting individual values, tacit knowledge, social negotiation and cultural constructions as any other knowledge field. Postcolonial science studies moves beyond Kuhn's focus on WMS, to Indigenous and localised perspectives emerging from belated acknowledgment of other knowledges. Both schools of science studies argue the claimed universalism of science to be a particularised universalism, a nexus of interacting people, agencies, materials, interests, technologies and histories (Turnbull, 2000), coexisting with other various and multiple particular/local versions of science. These critiques of science have resulted in the so-called Science Wars (Ross, 1996), with scientists like Gross & Levitt (1994) and Nanda (1997) during the heated debates of the 1990s, along with Zammito (2004) more recently, arguing the inadequacies of social and cultural critiques of WMS. Nonetheless, science studies have offered discourses of critique capable of interfering with science education's normative scripts of WMS and make space for Indigenous knowledge and practices, privileging local, diverse and plural perspectives characteristic of the globalisation dialectic. While no doubt the 'Science Wars' will rage on and on (as will their influence on science education), those like Roberts & Mackenzie (2006, p.157) see the more important questions pertinent here as "(w)hat kinds of movements between science and other knowledges are possible or desirable?" (also Visvanathan, 2006).

6. For another decolonial perspective, see the work of Linda Tuhiwai Smith with a focus on Maori (Tuhiwai Smith, 1999).
7. Glen Aikenhead and others (see Aikenhead, 1996, 1997, 2001; Aikenhead & Jegede; 1999 and Jegede & Aikenhead, 1999; Lee & Fradd, 1998) have developed a number of tenets about borders, their characteristics and functions, and their 'crossing' that include:

    (1) Western science is a cultural entity itself, one of many subcultures of Euro-American society; (2) people live and coexist within many subcultures identified by, for example, language, ethnicity, gender, social class, occupation, religion and geographic location; (3) people move from one subculture to another, a process called *'cultural border crossing';* (6) most students experience a change in culture when moving from their life-worlds into the world of school science; therefore, (7) learning science is a cross-cultural event for these students; (8) students are more successful if they receive help negotiating their *cultural border crossings;* and (9) this help can come from a teacher (a culture broker) who identifies the *cultural borders* to be crossed, who guides students *back and forth across those borders,* who gets students to make sense out of cultural conflicts that might arise (Aikenhead, 2001, p. 340, my italics).

    In Aikenhead's terms, borders can be identified and crossed, and guides (usually the teacher) can facilitate the passage and help negotiate any cultural conflicts that might arise; in short, clear borders exist between different Indigenous subcultures and WMS. An effective culture-broker would be highly skilled in identifying "the cultures in which students' personal ideas are contextualized" and able to introduce "another cultural point of view, that is, the culture of Western science, in the context of Aboriginal knowledge" (Aikenhead, 2001, p. 340). Aikenhead's (2001) constructs of 'cultural border' and 'cultural border crossing' have become a taken-for-granted commencement point within science education scholarship on cultural diversity and Indigenous knowledges in recent years.
8. This argument has been developed more fully in Carter (2004).
9. Santos (2007a, 2007b) and Santos, Nunes and Meneses, (2007) use the terms *epistemological diversity, the ecology of knowledge(s)* and *epistemological* and *cognitive justice* somewhat interchangeably. Goonatilake (2006) clearly prefers the 'ecology of knowledges' as for him, knowledges have historical " . . . lineages stretching back millennia or centuries or shorter periods. . . ." (p. 170) meaning knowledges must be ecological.
10. An 'axiom' is a statement or proposition that is regarded as being established, accepted or self-evidently true (*Oxford Dictionary of English*, 2nd Ed) The use of this term is then clearly problematic as it appears to embody the very modern truth standards which epistemological diversity seeks to challenge. It could be that Santos' (2007a, 2007b) use here is ironic. It should also be noted that in law, one of Santos' primary fields of interest, axioms (like maxims) are often used as conceptual points of departure illustrative of a moral, legal or policy standpoints underlying a broader analysis. They are not so much 'truths' as 'perspectives' that are them-

selves informed by a corpus of literature and its attendant intertextualities.
11. Readers interested in following Santos' (2007) [[Au: please specify "2007a" or "2007b"]]work further are directed towards his edited books *Another Knowledge Is Possible: Beyond Northern Epistemologies*; *Cognitive Justice in a Global World: Prudent Knowledge for a Decent Life*; *Democratizing Democracy: Beyond the Liberal Democratic Canon* and *Another Production is Possible: Beyond the Capitalist Canon*.
12. See Santos (2001) for a fuller discussion on movements that constitute counter-hegemonic globalization.

REFERENCE

Aikenhead, G. (1996). Science education: border crossing into the subculture of science. *Studies in Science Education, 27*, 1–52.

Aikenhead, G. (1997). Towards a First Nations cross-cultural science and technology curriculum. *Science Education, 81*, 217–238.

Aikenhead, G. (2001). Integrating Western and Aboriginal sciences: Cross-cultural science teaching. *Research in Science Education, 31*(3), 337–355.

Aikenhead, G. (2002). Cross-cultural science teaching: Rekindling traditions for Aboriginal students. *Canadian Journal of Science, Mathematics and Technology Education, 2*(3), 287–304.

Aikenhead, G., & Jegede, O. (1999). Cross-cultural science education: a cognitive explanation for a cultural phenomenon. *Journal of Research in Science Teaching, 36*(3), 269–287.

Aikenhead, G., & Lewis, B. (2001). Introduction: Shifting perspectives from universalism to cross-culturalism. *Science Education, 85*, 3–5.

Aikman, S. (1997). Interculturality and intercultural education: A challenge for democracy. In V. Masemann & A. Welch (Eds.), *Tradition, Modernity and Post-Modernity in Comparative Education* (pp. 463–480). Hamburg: Kluwer Academic.

Anderson, C. (2001). Systemic reform, inquiry, and the personal sense-making. *Journal of Research in Science Teaching, 38*(6), 629–630.

Appadurai, A. (1996). *Modernity at Large: Cultural Dimensions of Globalization*. Minneapolis: University of Minnesota Press.

Arellano, E. L., Barcenal, T. L., Bilbao, P. P., Castellano, M. A., Nichols, S., & Tippins, D. J. (2001). Case-based pedagogy as a context for collaborative inquiry in the Philippines. *Journal of Research in Science Teaching, 38*(5), 502–528.

Bang, M., & Medin, D. (in press). Cultural processes in science education: Supporting the navigation of multiple epistemologies. *Science Education*.

Beck, U. (1992). *Risk Society: Towards a New Modernity* (M. Ritter, Trans.). London: Sage.

Bencze, J. (2001). Subverting corporatism in school science. *Canadian Journal of Science, Mathematics and Technology Education, 1*(3), 349–355.

Bhabha, H. (1994). *The Location of Culture*. London: Routledge.

Brandt, C. (2008). Discursive geographies in science: Space, identity, and scientific discourse among Indigenous women in higher education. *Cultural Studies of Science Education, 3*(3), 703–730.

Carter, L. (2004). Thinking differently about cultural diversity: using postcolonial theory to (re)read science education. *Science Education, 88*(6), 819–836.

Carter, L. (2005). Globalisation and science education: Rethinking science education reforms. *Journal of Research in Science Teaching 42*(5), 561–580.

Carter, L. (2006). The challenges of postcolonialism to science education. *Educational Philosophy and Theory, 38*(5), 677–692.

Carter, L. (2008). Globalisation and science education: The implications for science in the new economy. *Journal of Research in Science Teaching 45*(5), 617–633.

Cajete, G. (1999). *Igniting the Sparkle: An* Indigenous *Science Education Model*. Skyand: Kivaki.

Calabrese Barton, A. (2003). *Teaching Science for Social Justice*. New York: Teachers College.

Calabrese Barton, A., & Osborne, M. (1998). Marginalized discourses and pedagogies: Constructively confronting science for all. *Journal of Research in Science Teaching, 35*(4), 339–340.

Calabrese Barton, A., & Tobin, K. (2001). Urban science education. *Journal of Research in Science Teaching, 38*(8), 843–846.

Carter, L. (2004). Thinking differently about cultural diversity: using postcolonial theory to (re)read science education. *Science Education* 88 (6) pp 819–836.

Carter, L. (2006). The challenges of postcolonialism to science education. *Educational Philosophy and Theory*, 38(5), 677–692.

Chinn, P. (2007). Decolonizing methodologies and Indigenous knowledge: the role of culture, place and personal experience in professional development. *Journal of Research in Science Teaching. 44*(9), 1247–1268.

Cobern, W. (1996). Worldview theory and conceptual change in science education. *Science Education, 80*, 579–610.

Code, L. (2000). How to think globally: Stretching the limits of imagination. In U. Narayan & S. Harding (Eds.), *Decentering the Centre: Philosophy for a Multicultural, Postcolonial, and Feminist World* (pp. 67–79). Bloomington, IN: Indiana University Press.

Coombes, A., & Brah, A. (2000). *Hybridity and Its Discontents. Politics, Science, and Culture*. London: Routledge.

Cross, R. T. (1997). 'Back to the future': The sixties come to school—science in Victorian schools. *Melbourne Studies in Education, 38*(2), 103–113.

De Boar, G. (2000). Scientific literacy: Another look at its historical and contemporary meanings and its relationship to science education reform. *Journal of Research in Science Teaching, 37*(6), 582–601.

Donnelly, J. F. (2001). Contested terrain or unified project? 'The nature of science' in national curriculum for England and Wales. *International Journal of Science Education, 23*(2), 181–195.

Drori, G. (2000). Science education and economic development: Trends, relationships, and research agenda. *Studies in Science Education, 35*, 27–58.

Eisenhart, M., Finkel, E., & Marion, S. (1996). Creating the conditions for scientific literacy: A re-examination. *American Educational Research Journal, 33*(2), 261–295.

Escobar, A. (2007). Worlds and knowledges otherwise. *Cultural Studies, 21*(2–3), 179–210.

Fanon, F. (1961). *The Wretched of the Earth*. (2004 Edition) New York: Grove.

Fensham, P. (1992). Science and technology. In P. W. Jackson (Ed.), *Handbook of Research on Curriculum* (pp. 789–829). New York: Macmillan.

Fensham, P. (1997). School science and its problems with scientific literacy. In R. Levinson & J. Thomas (Eds.), *Science Today: Problem or Crisis*. London: Routledge.

Gallagher, J. (2000). Meeting challenges inherent in reform of science teaching and learning. *Journal of Research in Science Teaching, 37*(5), 399–400.

Gallagher, J., & Richmond, G. (1999). Stimulating discourse on science education reform: An editorial and call for papers. *Journal of Research in Science Teaching, 36*(7), 753–754.

Glasson, G., Mhango, N., Phiri, A., & Lanier, M. (2010). Sustainability science education in Africa: Negotiating Indigenous ways of living with nature in the third space. *International Journal of Science Education, 32*(1), 125–141.

Goonatilake, S. (2006). Knowledge as an ecology. *Theory, Culture & Society, 23*(2–3), 170–172.

Gough, N. (1998). All around the world: Science education, constructivism, and globalization. *Educational Policy, 12*(5), 507–524.

Gough, N. (2007). Geophilosophy, rhizomes and mosquitoes: Becoming nomadic in global, science education research. In B. Atweh, M. Borba, A.Calabrese Barton, D. Clark, N. Gough, C. Keitel, C. Vistro-Yu & R. Vithal (Eds.), *Internationalisation and Globalisation in Mathematics and Science Education* (pp. 57–94). Dordrecht, The Netherlands: Springer.

Gross, P., & Levitt, N. (1994). *Higher Superstition: The Academic Left and Its Quarrel with Science*. Baltimore: Johns Hopkins University Press.

Harding, S. (1998). *Is Science Multicultural? Postcolonialisms, Feminisms and Epistemologies*. Bloomington, IN: Indiana University Press.

Harding, S. (2000). Gender, development, and the post-Enlightenment philosophies of science. In U. Narayan & S.

Harding (Eds.), *Decentering the Centre: Philosophy for a Multicultural, Postcolonial, and Feminist World* (pp. 240–261). Bloomington, IN: Indiana University Press.

Harding, S. (2006). *Science and Social Inequality: Feminist and Postcolonial Issues.* Chicago: University of Illinois Press.

Harlen, W. (2001). The assessment of scientific literacy in the OECD/PISA project. *Studies in Science Education, 36,* 79–90.

Huggan, G. (2001). *The Postcolonial Exotic.* London: Routledge.

Jasanoff, S., Markle, G., Peterson, J., & Pinch, T. (Eds.). (1995). *Handbook of Science and Technology Studies.* Thousand Oaks, CA: Sage.

Jegede, O., & Aikenhead, G. (1999). Transcending cultural borders: Implications for science teaching. *Journal for Science and Technology Education, 17,* 45–66.

Kyle, W. (2001). Towards a political philosophy of science education. In A. Calabrese Barton & M. Osborne (Eds.), *Teaching Science in Diverse Settings: Marginalized Discourses & Classroom Practice* (pp. xi–xvii). New York: Peter Lang.

Laugksch, R. (2000). Scientific literacy: A conceptual overview. *Science Education, 84,* 71–94.

Lee, O. (2001). Culture and language in science education: What do we know and what do we need to know? *Journal of Research in Science Teaching, 38*(5), 499–501.

Lee, O., & Fradd, S. (1998). Science for all, including students from non-English-language backgrounds. *Educational Researcher, 27*(4), 12–21.

Lemke, J. L. (2001). Articulating communities: Sociocultural perspectives on science education. *Journal of Research in Science Teaching, 38*(3), 296–316.

McCarthy, C., & Dimitriades, G. (2000). Globalizing pedagogies: power, resentment, and the re-narration of difference. In N. Burbules & C. Torres (Eds.), *Globalization and Education: Critical Perspectives* (pp. 187–204). New York: Routledge.

McKinley, E. (2001). Cultural diversity: Masking power with innocence. *Science Education,* 85, 74–76.

McKinley, E. (2007). Locating the global: Culture, language and science education for Indigenous students. *International Journal of Science Education. 27*(2), 227–241.

McNay, M. (2000). The conservative political agenda in curriculum: Ontario's recent experience in science education. *Journal of Curriculum Studies, 32*(6), 749–756.

Mignolo, W., (2007). DeLinking: The rhetoric of modernity, the logic of coloniality and the grammar of de-coloniality. *Cultural Studies, 21*(2–3), 449–514.

Nanda, M. (1997). The science wars in India. *Dissent, 44*(1), 1–6.

Ninnes, P. (2001). Representations of ways of knowing in junior high school science texts used in Australia. *Discourse, 22*(1), 81–94

Ogawa, M. (1996). Four-eyed fish: The ideal for non-Western graduates of Western science education graduate programs. *Science Education, 80,* 107–110.

Paty, M. (1999). Comparative history of modern science and the context of dependency. *Science, Technology & Society, 4*(2), 171–203.

Quayson, A. (2000). *Postcolonialism. Theory, Practice or Process?* Cambridge: Polity.

Roberts, C., & Mackenzie, A. (2006). *Science, Theory, Culture & Society, 23*(2–3), 157–163.

Ross, A. (Ed.). (1996). *Science Wars.* Durham, NC: Duke University Press.

Roth, W. M. (2008). Bricolage, métissage, hybridity, heterogeneity, diaspora: Concepts for thinking science education in the 21st century. *Cultural Studies of Science Education, 3* (4), 891–916.

Santos, B. (2001). *Nuestra America:* Reinventing a subaltern paradigm of recognition and redistribution. *Theory into Practice, 18*(2–3), 185–217.

Santos, B. (2007a). Beyond abyssal thinking: from global lines to ecologies of knowledges. Retrieved 15/08/2009: http://www.ces.uc.pt/bss/documentos/AbyssalThinking.pdf

Santos, B. (Ed) (2007b). *Cognitive Justice in a Global World: Prudent Knowledge for a Decent Life.* Lanham: Lexington.

Santos, B., Nunes, J., & Meneses, M. (2007). Introduction: opening up the canon of knowledge and recognition of difference. In B. Santos (Ed.). *Another Knowledge Is Possible. Beyond Northern Epistemologies* (pp. xx–lxii). London: Verso.

Semali, L. (1999). Community as classroom: Dilemmas of valuing African Indigenous literacy in education. In L. King (Ed.), *Learning, Knowledge and Cultural Context* (pp. 302–319). Hamburg: UNESCO Institute for Education & Kluwer Academic.

Snively, G., & Corsiglia, J. (2001). Discovering Indigenous science: Implications for science education. *Science Education, 85*, 6–34.

Stanley, W., & Brickhouse, N. (2001). Teaching sciences: the multicultural question revisited. *Science Education, 85*, 35–49.

Stengers, I. (2000). *The Invention of Modern Science*. Minneapolis: University of Minnesota Press.

Tuhiwai Smith, L. (1999). *Decolonizing Methodologies: Research and Indigenous Peoples*. London: Zed.

Turnbull, D. (2000). *Masons, Tricksters and Cartographers*. Amsterdam: Harwood Academic.

Van Eijck, M., & Roth, W. M. (2007). Keeping the local local: recalibrating the status of science and traditional ecological knowledge (TEK) in education. *Science Education, 91*(6), 926–947.

Visvanathan, S. (2006). Alternative science. *Theory, Culture & Society, 23*(2–3), 164–169.

Wong, D. (2001). Perspectives on learning. *Journal of Research in Science Teaching, 38*(3), 279–281.

Young, R. (2001). *Postcolonialism: An Historical Introduction*. Oxford: Blackwell.

Zammito, J. (2004). *A Nice Derangement of Epistemes: Post-positivism in a Study of Science from Quine to Latour.* Chicago: University of Chicago Press.

SECTION V

Future Challenges: Centering Spirituality and Spiritual Ways of Knowing and the Discourse of Indigeneity in the Academy

To transform oneself and social existence is to embody knowledge for change. In seeking to transform our social setting we must place the spirit on the axis (as a substructure) on which we understand material, political, and cultural forces of change. Decolonizing dominant knowings requires that we nurture and uphold the strengths and vitality of spiritually centered ways of knowing. We offer a central place for spirituality and Indigeneity given that Indigenous knowings are largely misrepresented and demonized in Eurocentric discourses and public imaginations about what is valid and invalid in the hierarchy of knowing. In Western academies many of us are struggling with issues of disembodiment in the learning process. The call for re-embodiment is a recognition that learners go into schools as embodied subjects. Apart from the negation of the fact of "embodied subjects/learners" in claims of the universal student (as one without race, class, gender, sexual identities, etc.) many learners are constantly dealing with the effects of dismemberment. This plays out in the tensions of "community" and the politics of fracturing communities. It is through spiritual resistance and working with the "notion of repair" that oppressed and Indigenous learners survive the everydayness of spiritual wounding and mental bondage.

In arguing for engaging spirituality as a theory of practice of decolonizing the academy, we are insisting on spirituality as embodied, that is, seeing learners as embodied beings. We are also asking to challenge the possibilities of "spiritual death" from Eurocentric mimicry. We need to challenge the hegemonic discourses and practices of Euro-American education system (e.g., the power of neoliberalism, compensatory, and remedial approaches to education; see Porfilio & Malott, 2008). A critical and decolonized education should be about building spiritually, politically, and materially sustainable communities. The politics of radical scholarship requires that we develop the spiritual courage and moral fortitude to challenge the dominance of particular ways of knowing and begin to work with the "pedagogy of hope" so as to creating community of learners or to see "schooling as community" (Dei, 2010).

The key elements of Indigenous spirituality that help transform established ways of knowing include the acceptance of a cosmologically anchored worldviews as powerful base of knowledge. Knowledges must be seen as circular with no beginnings nor ends. All knowledges are interdependent and connected. The core aspect of knowledge is community which is connected to the past, present, and future. There is the power of the spoken word. Orality is not only a key component of Indigenous knowledges and spiritualities, but also Indigenous forms of communication (language, oral expressions, folkloric productions, etc.) allow for passing down inter-generationally and through a sacred medium respect, trust, responsibility, and acceptance. The spirit informs the body, mind, and soul as inextricably interconnected and interdependent in contrast to Cartesian ideas of depersonalizing bodies and an individualized model which privileges the mind and fragments the body and soul.

It is without saying that the assertion of Indigenous knowledge is part of the intellectual politics of transforming our academies. By helping us work with subjugated and oppositional knowledges, Indigenous knowledges point to significant lessons in the pursuit of educational change. It has been argued in preceding chapters how Indigenous knowledges as spiritually centered ways of knowing engage emotions and intuition to constitute valid and legitimate ways of knowing. There are challenges and possibilities of engaging with spiritually centered ways of knowing. Given the resistance to such ways of knowing in the academy it behooves critical educators to strategize for the promotion of multi-centric knowledges in the academy. We must find ways to address the resistance to such knowledges and employ our respective discursive agencies through classroom pedagogies, instruction, texts, and other communicative practices to create spaces for such knowledges to exist in their own right.

Today, there is the reassertion of Indigenous identities. The maintenance of cultural autonomy has been a "powerful resource in providing the ideological context in which [Indigenous people] are framing their 'new' world" (Nash, 1999, p. 33). Indigenous struggles cannot be understood exclusively as questions about identity and subjectivity but must be viewed as part of a vast network of connections. Economic, political, symbolic, and spiritual considerations need to be taken into account in order to move beyond Eurocentric interpretations of Indigenousness. By simultaneously emphasizing the issues of culture, identity, history, and politics we can begin to understand why and how Indigenous peoples continue to be subjects and actors of social change. One of the biggest challenges facing Indigenous peoples globally is the violation of their rights to land, cultures, and the spiritual realms within their own communities. This violation has been part of state genocidal policies—policies that have caused the loss of territorial autonomy and extreme poverty in many Indigenous communities.

So we attempt to end where we began. The re-creation of Indigenousness and Indigeneity is linked to the possession of space and land. In the face of insurmountable threat to their existence, Indigenous peoples have managed to change in ways that continue to preserve their cultural integrity. They are generating innovative solutions to daily problems, looking to their cultures, traditional norms, and notions of spirituality. An adherence to a dynamic relation between nature, culture and society, the sanctity of life, as well as sacredness of local environment have been powerful forces in the preservation of local/Indigenous cultures. Rather than listen to misguided calls to abandon old traditions, values and customs, Indigenous peoples have devised pragmatic ways of allowing these customs and traditions to serve contemporary political, cultural, and social interests as well as territorial/sovereignty and claims. They rely on both real and fictive/imagined/putative representations of an authentic Indigenous identity to deal with the unprecedented pace of global change (see also Nash, 1999). The Indigenous peoples' struggles provide significant lessons in the search for a global moral community with a more "egalitarian redistribution" (Nash, 1999, p. 35) of resource, power, and knowledge. The reassertion of such identity by Indigenous movements cannot also simply be reduced to class relations. There is cultural context for varied Indigenous political and economic struggles. Indigenousness emerges out of a particular/specific historical context and forces that are "simultaneously structural and cultural" (Nash, 1999, p. 36). In effect, the reassertion of Indigenous identities cannot be separated from economic and material conditions that give rise to ethnic revitalization/revivalism.

Cynthia Dillard and Charlotte Bell's chapter "Endarkened Feminism and Sacred Praxis: Troubling (Auto)Ethnography through Critical Engagements with African Indigenous Knowledges" deals with the centrality of spirituality in African-centered Indigenous knowledges. The chapter highlights the way in which engagements with Indigenous knowledges through endarkened epistemologies is deeply sacred work, often troubling the very Western discourses, cultural frameworks, and methodologies that we have used to think ourselves in our research and academic lives as teachers and scholars. Using the Ghanaian context as a base for discussion, and particularly, highlighting their experiences in the Cape Coast slave dungeons, the authors put forth the notion of *nkwaethnography* (sacred ethnography) as an endarkened feminist methodology that seeks to enact and embrace spirituality and sacred praxis in education. The chapter shows the relevance for decolonizing dominant research methodologies using an Indigenous frame of reference.

Kimine Mayuzumi's "Re/membering In-Between 'Japan' and 'the West': A Decolonizing Journey through the Indigenous Knowledge Framework" unpacks the author's "decolonizing" journey that begun during her doctoral research studies applying the Indigenous knowledge framework. In the discussion she centers an autoethnographical account of her exploration as a female graduate student in the Western academy, born and raised in rural Japan, who conducted a life history interview with a female rural Japanese elder. By engaging in the four different stages of calligraphy as metaphor in this writing (which strengthened and maintained the "re/membering" effect not only through mind, body, and spirit), she enunciates significant steps in the decolonizing journey: moving to the West, awakening, from *obasan*'s story to her own, and why the Indigenous knowledge framework? This chapter posits that the Indigenous knowledge framework provides possibilities to decolonize the dominant ways of thinking in the academy as well as the misrepresentation of minoritized groups in transnational contexts. To the author the reflexive text in autoethnography with the Indigenous knowledge framework has allowed her to go through "re/membering" actions. There needs to be more space for dialogue around the Indigenous knowledge framework in various educational settings. She concludes with the hope that those who feel fragmented in the Western academy, including diasporas and international scholars, will be inspired to cultivate their own reflexive journey and re/member their own sacred faces.

Riyad Shahjahan and Kimberly Haverkos' chapter on: "Revealing the Secular Fence of Knowledge: Towards Reimagining Spiritual Ways of Knowing and Being in the Academy" offers an anti-colonial lens to uncover the tools of dominance inherent in the European secular epistemological vision, as well as resistances to it, over three corresponding time periods. Using the fence metaphor, the authors demonstrate how dominant theories and ideologies emerge within the secular epistemological vision, while displacing and negating spiritual epistemologies and Indigenous cosmologies. The discussion foregrounds the sites of resistance in which such colonial secular discourses have been contested/contingent or proven not to be absolute given the context. It is argued that this historical backdrop is essential to understanding how the secular epistemological vision (the secular fence of knowledge) is a Eurocentric discourse that is colonial in nature and has implications toward determining what knowledges are considered legitimate and represented in the academy. The chapter concludes by pointing to steps to begin the process of decolonizing the academy using spiritual epistemologies as resistant and resisting knowledges.

Soenke Biermann's chapter "Knowledge, Power, and Decolonization: Implications for Non-Indigenous Scholars, Researchers, and Educators" draws on Dei's (2010) notion of epistemological equity and Connell's (2007) call for engagement with "southern" theory, to highlight some of the key challenges for the project of intellectually decolonizing the academy. Informed by European as well as Indigenous anti-colonial critiques, and with a particular focus on Australia and other "settler" states such as Aotearoa/New Zealand, Canada and the United States, the writer carefully examines how Indigenous philosophies are situated by, and within, colonial higher education structures and discourses. The author also analyzes the relationship between knowledge, power, and colonialism in creating and maintaining hierarchies of power/knowledge. The chapter is relevant given the critical epistemological challenges Indigenous philosophies pose to dominant Western conceptions of pedagogy, curriculum, and academic research. The question is: What are the possibilities for the future? The author explores how non-Indigenous scholars, researchers, and educators, in particular, need to come to terms with their own role in this process and consider their practice in relation to questions of Eurocentrism, decolonization, and ethical engagement with Indigenous peoples and philosophies.

Together with the ubiquitous agents evocateurs, Pat O'Riley and Peter Cole in their chapter, "Coyote and Raven Chat about Protecting Indigenous Intellectual Property" engage trickster discourse and narrative shapeshifting as they share research protocols and community conversations based on their research with the four Lower Stl'atl'imx communities (Xa'xtsa, N'Quat'qua, Skatin, and Samahquam First Nations) of British Columbia, Canada, in their efforts toward language and cultural regeneration, community sustainability, and self-determination. The unique and creative narrative and conversational style highlights some of the important dilemmas and tensions as we seek to decolonize knowledge and work with Indigenous knowledges from an anti-colonial stance grounding Indigenous representation and constructions of self, history, identity, place, and land.

Eric Ritske's chapter "Indigenous Spirituality and Decolonization: Methodology for the Classroom" offers critical educational insights, reflections, and directions to engaging Indigenous knowledge as a decolonizing project in the academy. He sees Indigenous spirituality as an integral part of the transformative learning process, provided such knowledge is connected to the communities from which they emerge. There can be that dissonance of knowledge when we bring an active and embodied Indigenous spirituality into the Western academy in ways that fragments and disconnects knowledge. Classroom and pedagogic practices that seek to transform spaces and our learning communities must be constant communication "with the community." It is pointed out that this connection of Indigenous spirituality and the community is complex and dynamic, and the future of education for social change lies in interdependence of the classroom and the community in knowledge production.

Zahra Murad's chapter "Beyond Deconstruction: Evolving the Ties between Indigenous Knowledges and Post-Foundational Anti-Racism" asks the question: Are all anti-racisms necessarily anti-colonial? As she searches for a holistic framework through which to organize her intellectual work, nourish the self, community, and continue to resist structures of domination, the author finds herself perplexed by a love of post-foundationalism and its "generative uncertainty." The author looks at the implications of utilizing post-foundationalism as the primary lens through which to theorize resistance. She examines and reflects on the goals of such anti-racism, and its inadvertently re-colonizing possibilities. In looking at post-foundational anti-racism as one way of knowing and a way of resisting, the chapter gestures toward enriching possibilities for knowing and acting based on a recentering of Indigenous knowledges within anti-racist thinking.

Priscilla Settee's chapter "Indigenous Knowledge: Multiple Approaches" makes a case for the inclusion of Indigenous knowledge into the educational experience. The author describes her formal and informal education journey from the early 1970s as a student in Canada's first Native studies department forward to her life as a senior academic in a prairie university. It also includes the author's experience in making sense of the personal and community disruption that has taken place as a result of Canada's colonial relationship with First Nations and Indigenous peoples. Drawing on scholarship by early critical theorists and through to contemporary Indigenous authors, Settee looks at Indigenous knowledge within her home community, the academy, as well as internationally. Settee's international research and her grounding in the academic and teaching world makes her contribution to Indigenous knowledge scholarship timely and relevant.

REFERENCES

Connell, R. (2007). *Southern Theory: The Global Dynamics of Knowledge in Social Science*. Crows Nest: Allen &Unwin.

Dei, G. J. S. (2010). *Teaching Africa: Towards a Transgressive Pedagogy*. New York: Springer.

Nash, J. (1999) The Reassertion of Indigenous Identity: Mayan Responses to State Intervention in Chiapas. *Latin American Research Review, 30* (3), 7–41.

Porfilio, B., & Malott, C. (Eds.) (2008). *International Examination of Urban Education: The Destructive Path of Neoliberalism*. Rotterdam: Sense.

CHAPTER TWENTY-ONE

Endarkened Feminism and Sacred Praxis

Troubling (Auto) Ethnography through Critical Engagements with African Indigenous Knowledges

Cynthia B. Dillard and Charlotte Bell

JOURNEYING BACK TO GO FORWARD

This chapter focuses on the centrality of spirituality in African-centered Indigenous knowledges. More particularly, this work is about the ways that engagements with Indigenous knowledges is deeply sacred work, often troubling the very Western discourses, cultural frameworks, and methodologies that we have used to think ourselves in our research and academic lives as teachers and scholars (Dillard, 2006; Dillard & Okpalaoka, in press; Smith, 1999). Many African ascendant[1] scholars (Asante, 1988; Cruse, 1967; Dillard & Okpalaoka, in press; Hilliard, 1995; hooks & West, 1991; King, 2005) suggest that there is fundamental crisis that goes far beyond the biographical situatedness of the researcher and the research project for African ascendant scholars. The crisis we speak of here is the difficulty of working within and against the hegemonic structures that have traditionally and historically negated and impeded the intellectual, social, and cultural contributions of African (and African feminist) knowledge. These are structures that have also negated the *spiritual* contributions of African ascendant people, Indigenous knowledges that would not only contribute to our cultural and intellectual understandings, but that might ultimately save our lives (Alexander, 2005; Dillard, 2008; Nnaemeka, 1998; Walker, 2006).

As African *American* women from the United States, a Western standpoint would posit that our orientation to the world began when our ancestors were sold into slavery, physically isolated us from our place of belonging in the world. The prevailing discourses have situated African American personhood historically as *freed slave*, a personhood that began on this (U.S.) side of the water and involving degradation beyond measure. Such a position denies the very existence and certainly the value of Indigenous African knowledges, epistemologies, ontologies, and cosmologies prior to the trans-Atlantic slave trade and to the institution of slavery in the United States and throughout the world. For many of African ascent, a fundamental question becomes: How do we understand ourselves as *African* Americans? In our encounters with African-centered knowledges and culture, what is it that many African Americans can "feel better than we can explain," between/within us as African ascendant people (Du Bois, 1903/1970)?

Part of what we feel is a *spiritual* connection. And we believe that spirituality must be recognized as the center of the thought and discourse for African ascendant people such that we can see our work as both about engagements with Indigenous knowledges and about healing the very epistemological and methodological tools we've traditionally used to engage research (King, 2005). This is *healing* work. Dillard (2008) speaks of healing methodologies as situated, sacred, and spiritual work that happens in multiple spaces and places where African ascendants and other Indigenous peoples find ourselves.[2] She further suggests that healing methodologies from an endarkened feminist framework also involve several critical engagements:

1. A person must be drawn into and present in a spiritual homeland.
2. A person must be engaged with/in the rituals, people, places in intimate, authentic [and humble] ways
3. A person must be open to being transformed by all that is encountered and recognize those encounters as purposeful and expansive, as healing methodologies. (Dillard, 2008, p. 287).

Such engagements also guide this chapter, in examining our return to a sacred place for African people, a place implicated in our complex relationships to the past and present, that has the possibility to both center the spirit and to shift the epistemological and cultural location of our thought and action in the world. For this inquiry, we engaged in a pilgrimage that was simultaneously sacred, secular, and spiritual (Busia, 1989; Dillard, 2008; Marshall, 1984) that is, to the slave dungeons in Ghana, West Africa. As Busia (1989) describes in her analysis of Paule Marshall's landmark book *Praisesong for the Widow*, we hoped to engage our journey

> in the same active process of recognizing and reassembling cultural signs of a past littered along our roads of doubtful progress. The challenge therefore is not to look at this [journey] as abstraction, but as a concrete aspect of our lives where our meaning—our story—becomes what we can read and what we can no longer, or never could, read about ourselves and others (Busia, 1989, pp. 197–198).

But as in *Praisesong*, the journey's "end" was not the shores of the United States: Our journey's end was *Africa . . ."*symbolically reversing the diasporic journey and recross[ing] . . ." (Busia, 1989, p. 199), symbolically and physically going *back* through the door of no return. We theorize how this movement to/in West Africa also necessitated an examination of our positionality in the world (physically, intellectually, and spiritually) and about the implications and transformations—the healings—of thought and methodologies that can arise with such engagements.

It is important to note that we each began engaging this work as *auto*ethnographers, each writing and studying ourselves and this sacred place of African memory. But how did being on/in the sacred grounds in the slave dungeons in Ghana *necessitate* a more complex, multiple, contested, spiritual movement and understanding for us, movements that troubled and transformed the very meaning (and the doing) of *auto*ethnography for us as well?

MONDAY'S CHILDREN ARE NOT ALONE: SACRED SPACES AND THE WORK OF THE SPIRIT

In divinity (and maybe irony), we made our pilgrimage to the Cape Coast slave dungeon on a Monday. We were both born on Monday, too. In Ghana, our given name is Adjoa, meaning "a girl born on a Monday." The relationship between the day a person is born into a culture and a given name represents one of many instances we can point to that may describe our orientation to the world. Girl children born on Monday, a part of sacred practice of membership within African culture, a legacy that has persisted yesterday, today, tomorrow, tomorrow's tomorrow. This process of naming was always present in the history of African people, a part of our spiritual and cultural knowings, a way that we anchored our personhood and spirit to its rightful place on this earth. However, through the trans-Atlantic slave trade, the process of disregarding and changing the names of captured African people was also an attempt to colonize the African spirit. But what we recognized on that day was that *the attempt had failed*: Our day names endured, made even more apparent by the day of our visit to the dungeons. There was a deeper meaning to our names and a divine order that they represented that created a decolonizing encounter for both of us on this day.

One hardly knows that you've reached the slave dungeon in Cape Coast. It is nestled among kiosks, busy with craftsmen selling their goods, standing in contrast to commercial banks and neighboring buildings. Our bus pulled up to a small parking space alongside a white wall. At first glance, we are taken aback by the very image of the dungeon, a stunningly beautiful, rather stark building, dazzlingly white against the blue sky and equally blue sea. We could hear the waves crash and we could feel the tears well up in our eyes. We are sure that our ancestors did not see beauty in this place.

We purchased our tickets and met our tour guide, a young Ghanaian man named Patrick.[3] He took us first to an open and airy room on the very top floor of the dungeons that was formerly the market, the room reserved for the auctioning of captured Africans to various slave traders—from Holland, from England, and from "the New World" as the United States is often rather affectionately called. The irony this Monday? The space was filled with contemporary paintings that a Ghanaian artist was attempting to sell. We wrestled with the commercialization of the space and the economic needs of the brother to make a living. The contrast was just too great: We were weighted down by this reappropriation of the space, the heaviness of the ironies, and the realities and the heat of the sun.

In this room, Patrick shared with us an overall history of the slave dungeon. That it was initially built by the Swedish in 1654 as a small fortress, and it changed hands several times among competing "Western" nations and their interests. It settled into the hands of the British in 1665, who developed it from a small fort into a castle. It took more than 200 years of additions and demolitions for the castle to be constructed as it stands today (with mostly African labor, of course). Hearing that the castle itself was over 345 years old situated slavery as a real and protracted historical event for us as we stood within the walls of this dungeon, itself a historical site, so symbolic of capitalism and imperialism. Something about this moment, the depth of this reality was "new," deeper, *real*.

In elementary school, the study of slavery was very brief for both of us. We learned that our ancestors, Black people, were slaves brought from Africa to pick cotton and serve White people. None of the pictures were real photographs, but sketches. None of the pictures included the place where we now stood. But the sights and feelings swirling around us moved beyond the sketchy nature of our social studies textbooks and their pitiful and inaccurate depictions of our people. Slavery was just a part of a long stretch of time that involved many people: White men from then "developing" Western nations, African chiefs, some in search of opportunities for their people and others in search of trinkets, drink, and material goods for themselves. But the bottom line? It remained in place for hundreds of years because it was a *profitable* business based in the trade of human beings, of *human cargo*. And the Cape Coast Castle/Dungeon was one of three slave castles and seventeen forts in Ghana alone, built by the British, Dutch, Swedish, and Portuguese, who came to Ghana because of the profitable trade in gold, diamonds, and ivory. But in that space, we learned how the sale of human beings was part of a larger, longer capitalistic system that not only forever changed Ghana and other African nations but forever *changed the relationship between African people*. Not only did African kingdoms (within and beyond Ghana) lose a significant portion of future generations through slavery, but major companies that continue to reproduce wealth today in the United States have their very history and roots in the slave trade. We asked ourselves: How could an ethical and moral line shift in human beings from the sale of objects to the sale of humans? These are the questions that arise in your mind from the moment you step onto these grounds. And emotionally, they created feelings beyond pain that became heavier and heavier as we continued through the tour. A feeling that the heart was breaking wide open. A feeling that brought uncontrollably weeping for one, and tears that were unable to fall for the other.

Europeans came to spread the Gospel. As African American women with roots and personal histories in the Christian church, we tried to fathom the complexities—and the tensions—of capitalism and spirituality. Throughout the journey, a very troubling relationship between slavery and spirituality confronted us. For example, next to the church that the English built as their place of worship within the castle (and which was directly atop the male slave dungeon) was a spy hole. As White people went to pray, they could literally both listen to and look down upon male slaves in the dungeons below. What must that have felt like? What was the overall *condition of the spirit* in the slave dungeon, the spiritual consciousness of those who existed in the castle, both free and captive? We learned that many of the slave ships were painted with names such as "Jesus," "God is Great," and "Santa Maria." While it was tempting to demonize those engaged in the slave trade, I think there are more meaningful complexities to consider. We wrestled with the spiritual nature of their choices, and the spiritual conditions that allowed human slavery to exist, the capacities humans carry that may push us to engage in the trade of other human beings.

While we visited both the male and the female slave dungeons, the female dungeons resonated most strongly with our bodies, minds, and spirits as Black women. We entered these dungeons and descended down a dark and uneven ramp, grasping at the brick wall for balance, or holding on to others to steady ourselves, both physically and emotionally. Going from the bright, sunny day down into this dark, dank place, the very *nature* of the air changed, becoming putrid and fetid. Our breathing changed too, short and rapid and anxious. The longer we were in the female dungeons, the more uneasy and faint we felt. Our bodies and spirits seemed to have a mind of their own: Cynthia's legs and body shook, almost uncontrollably; Charlotte's stomach churned. In this small space, over 120 female slaves would be held, Patrick shared. Women forced to urinate, defecate, vomit, menstruate in the same place where they had to lay their heads. *In the same place* where we now stood. . . . In excavating the floors, the chains, vomit, feces, and blood found on the floor surface was more than eight inches thick in places. In the same place *where we now stood* . . . We tried to imagine the daily existence for the female slaves. No, we tried to imagine the daily existence for our *sisters*, the darkness and smells mixing up the past, present, future. When we closed our eyes, we could see Black sister faces in agony, in this overcrowded and inhumane place, uncertain and not knowing what we/they had done to receive this punishment. Their/our voices wailed and moaned, as if to ask that question on that day. The physicality of the experience was overwhelming, beyond our ability to describe it adequately in words here. But what we know is that time and place changed in that moment in those dungeons. Where our personhood stopped and our sisters' personhood began became blurry, unclear to us. Where is the sound coming from? Is it my voice or my sisters' who wail and moan here? This dirge was coming from *our* bodies, collectively and uncontrollably, a spiritual response, a reflex of memory.

And, here we stood, facing the past in the present as African ascendant women. Living the past of our ancestors in these dungeons, the present of our rememberings as "free" African Americans, the future of those who will read this story and maybe even make a pilgrimage to the slave dungeons themselves. It is difficult to find the right tense to write in. To use past tense assumes that the effects of slavery and experiences of the slave dungeons do not impact the present. To use present tense means to ponder the past as present, to literally feel one's understanding and knowledge of the long and deep history of slavery grow bigger, wider, to include the complexities of human slavery in mind, body, and spirit.

Our final place in the dungeons was a location and fixture common to all of the dungeons that dot the Western coast of Africa: The door of no return. Patrick shared that once a captured African went through these doors, they lost all contact with Africa. The trans-Atlantic slave trade lasted 500 years. Five hundred years of captives through this door of no return. The estimate is that over two million slaves passed through Cape Coast slave dungeons, about one-third of whom did not survive the inhuman conditions within the dungeons. To really re-member this number hurts to the soul even now as we write and remember again. We can see our ancestors as they walked, often crawled through this door, the hard sand and rocks beneath their feet, grinding into their knees. Cannons stood facing the sea, looking out over the ocean like big black binoculars, seemingly watching the waves. How could something so beautiful represent so inhumane a history as the carrying of millions of humans away from their homeland? Patrick, our guide, says that outside the slave dungeons, visitors are met with the beautiful stature of the castle. Yet inside, a very different reality exists. Complexity emerges—beauty on the exterior, yet beneath the layers of it, fundamental questions of what makes us human. Questions that turns our gaze inward, both to the spirit, and to the inner workings of the spirit of human slavery that are deeply fragmented and vaguely understood, maybe incomprehensible.

Africans were dispersed widely in the slave trade: About one-third to South America and Brazil, the West Indies and Caribbean receiving the second largest number, and North America receiving the least. But standing in the courtyard of these dungeons, the Diaspora became real, understandable. Prior to this experience, many African Americans struggle to connect (both consciously and unconsciously) to the African continent, to explore the deeper meanings of the African in the American of our identities. Slavery, as we're taught, seemed something that happened a long time ago, a thin thread of a distant African heritage, mysterious and fuzzy. In this moment, we could not only feel but see and experience: We are part of the African body throughout the trans-Atlantic world. Through the door of no return, our ancestors were taken with the ancestors of many Africans *from one soil, from one homeland* to many different parts of the world. Being an African American connects us to others in the world beyond the United States. Whatever doubts concerning our place and relationship to African ascendants globally were dismissed that day. Here, in the slave dungeons, we stood in a place that allowed us to see our African heritage and our connection as Indigenous persons in the African Diaspora. Our spirits reoriented themselves to the world, metaphorically turned those slave ships around. Walking through the door of no return and then turning around to walk back through the same door was symbolic of a return that generations after slavery was **not** suppose to happen. Yes, the name of that door embodied the desires of the slave traders. But nothing can keep people from their home *forever*. On that day, we gave thanks, embodied in the letter below, one that carries the profound new vision we have of our work and our lives as *African* American women scholars:

> Dear and wonderous Ancestors,
> We come before you on this day,
> in deep gratitude,
> To honor you,
> upon whose underground cells
> we sit,
> the sun on our shoulders,
> free to look out over the blue sea,
> free to make decisions about our work,
> our purpose,
> our bodies and how they will move in the world.
> We come to you today,
> grateful for your sacrifices,
> the lack of liberty and freedom you suffered,
> the injustices you were dealt,
> that have enabled us, Monday's children of Africa,
> to be in this place on this day,
> to be educated,
> to be able to work,
> for the very things that were *taken* from you.
> We render ourselves humble
> for your lives,
> and we recommit ourselves
> to the hard work
> Of justice
> Of freedom
> Of the human right
> to become more fully *human*.
> We are reminded today
> of our privilege, Dear Ones,
> received only through your
> *choice*
> to survive.
> We pledge to our Creator today
> and to you, our Dear Guides,
> to continue Your work
> *Our* work,
> With renewed vigor,
> With wonder and awe,
> With a joyful heart.
> Ayeeko!
> Amen.[4]

NOT ALONE AND NOT THE SAME: TRANSFORMING AUTOETHNOGRAPHY TO NKWAETHNOGRAPHY (SACRED OR LIFE ETHNOGRAPHY)

This narrative of our engagements as African American women with/in the slave dungeons in Ghana raises interesting connections and challenges between the complex—and persistent—notions of spirituality, African Indigenous knowledge and research. As we see in this narrative, although the attempt was made to colonize the African spirit, it did not succeed. Whether in our encounter with the structure, our very desire for pilgrimage to the African continent, in our bodies, minds, and spirits and the spirits encountered in the dungeons, the African spirit survived. Hence, there is a need in our teaching and research encounters to recognize and understand the deeper meanings of these spiritual knowledges in our epistemologies, our educational contexts, and in our ways of engaging inquiry.

Before leaving for Ghana, we framed our project as reflexive autoethnography (Ellis, 2004). As co-researchers traveling to Ghana, West Africa, we sought to consider how our experiences with Ghanaian people, Indigenous knowledges, and culture would influence our standpoints, particularly as they relate to autoethnography (Jackson & Mazzei, 2008). We separately and often together took copious notes, photographs, and video recordings. We posed questions that each of us answered, sometimes individually, sometimes together, and often in dialogue with one another. We sought a more critical and complex engagement with the concept of authoethnography, drawing upon transnational Black feminist thought, acknowledging differences in how reality (and consequent commitments) are constructed differently when centered upon a different—and Black—epistemological understandings of knowledge and reality (Collins, 2000; Dillard, 2008; Dillard & Okpalaoka, in press). But given the profundity of our experience within the slave dungeons, autoethnography as described by Jackson and Mazzei (2008) and Ellis (2004) still seemed somehow limited, not quite big enough for the gravity of the task at hand.[5]

What we needed was a kind of ethnography that truly honored the complexities of the Indigenous and the "modern" that we'd experienced in our bodies, minds, and spirits. Something both dialogical and multiple. Both spiritual and sacred. Something both historical and cultural. Something that honored the fluidity of time and space, of the material and spiritual world. Mostly, we needed an ethnography that acknowledged both the joy and pain of location, dislocation, and the transformation of both in our stories: African women are not stories of a singular self but are stories of *we*, collective stories deeply embedded in African women's wisdom and Indigenous knowledges.

Dillard & Okpalaoka (in press) suggest that whatever the research methodology, for African-centered work such frameworks need to be *transnational* in nature. They are methodologies (in our case, arising out of Black or endarkened feminist epistemologies) that are beyond or through (*trans*) the boundaries of nations. They further suggest that engaging such theories of the globe also brings to bear a greater possibility of a *change* in our viewpoints given the multiple backdrops against which we could theorize experience, using multiple lenses, the kind we advocated at the beginning of this chapter.

Such an endarkened feminist epistemology is also an approach to research that honors the spirituality, wisdom, and critical interventions of transnational Black woman's ways of knowing and being in research, with the sacred serving as a way to describe the doing of it, the way that we *approach* the work (Dillard, 2006). Dillard and Okpalaoka (in press) make a distinction between spirituality and the sacred that may be useful here. They define *spirituality* as having a consciousness of the realm of the spirit in one's work and the recognition that such critical consciousness is a transformative force in research and teaching (Alexander, 2005; Dillard, 2006; Dillard, Tyson, & Abdur-Rashid, 2000; Fernandes, 2003; hooks, 1993; Hull, 2001; Moraga & Anzalda, 1981; Ryan, 2005; Wade-Gayles, 1995). However, when they speak of the *sacred* in endarkened feminist research, they are referring to *the way the work is honored and embraced as it carried out*. Said another way, work that is sacred is worthy of being held with *reverence* as it is done.

The idea here is that, as we considered the meanings of our experiences in the slave dungeons in Cape Coast, we knew that the work must also embody and engage spirituality and be carried out in sacred ways. Mostly, we are suggesting that both spirituality and the sacred are embedded fundamentally in the very ground of our inquiry, in the knowledge and cultural production of Black women's lives and experiences and that it is this understanding that helps us to understand Black feminism transnationally, our experience in the dungeons, and their implications for a *different* ethnography, what Madison (2005) refers to as more dangerous one. We want here to attempt to render *visible* the work of research as *sacred* work, centered in spiritual notions constructed by Black women on the continent and in the diaspora and our *intersubjectivity* in the dungeons. We want to explore further the profound question—and the equally profound response—put forth by M. Jacqui Alexander (2005) in her ground-breaking work *Pedagogies of Crossing: Meditations on Feminism, Sexual Politics, Memory, and the Sacred*:

> What would taking the Sacred seriously mean for transnational feminism and related radical projects beyond an institutionalized use value of theorizing marginalization? *It would mean wrestling with the praxis of the Sacred* (p. 326, emphasis ours).

What might be the sacred praxis (the thought and action) required here, given the complexities of our experiences in the Cape Coast dungeons? We believe it begins with acknowledging that any African-centered epistemology of ethnography must center in the notion of "we-ness": We can only understand ourselves as individuals through our culture, communities, and symbols, even given the various visions and versions of being an African ascendant. So *there can be no **auto**-ethnography from an endarkened feminist framework*. What is needed is a different ethnography, beyond the prefix "auto" or singular version of ethnography to gesture toward the prefix "trans" or beyond the singular, multiple by nature. We put forth here the possibilities of *nkwaethnography*, an ethnography that embraces "nkwa," a Twi word meaning sacred or life affirming. It is important here to note that thinking about the ways that our approaches to research might be made more sacred is **not** a departure from endarkened or Black feminist thought, which is deeply embedded with and draws attention to the nature and importance of the spiritual within a Black feminist framework (Collins, 2000; hooks, 1993; Dillard, 2006). Our attempt here is to draw attention not only to the central place of spirituality in endarkened feminist frameworks but to also point to the importance of seeing and approaching our teaching and research as sacred, as worthy of reverence as well. Our analysis here can be thought of as an example of what Dillard and Okpalaoka (in press) have put forth as tenets of a transnational and endarkened feminist research. We seek to engage these tenets *operationally*, articulating how a sacred and spiritual endarkened feminist framework assisted us in rethinking our original methodologies, analysis, and representations in ways that embrace nkwaethnography, a sacred and life-affirming ethnography.

First, *nkwaethnography* recognizes the fluidity in time and space, spanning the spiritual and the material conditions of its "subjects." As co-researchers, we certainly acknowledge "the multiple meanings of Black womanhood and the shared legacy of oppressions both on the continent of Africa, the continent of North America and the diaspora of African women" (Dillard & Okpalaoka, in press). Our experience in the slave dungeons "raised up" in a very visceral and spiritual way, the interrelated nature of oppressions for Black women, implicating and connecting us, as researchers and Black women to the long legacy of slave trading in Ghana and slavery in the United States (and beyond), one that created the very reality of the two of us being able to return through the door of no return, to stand in that place in contemporary times as ascendants of the very people who were taken from their homeland. Yes, the degrees of oppressions between those who were in the dungeons, those who chose to survive the Middle Passage and the degrading institution of slavery, and those of us who are the ascendants of these strong African people are different and need not be compared. We are all marked by enslavement, colonization, slavery, across temporal and geographic boundaries. But what we know now is that this fluidity of time and space is indeed real because we could feel them—in our bodies, minds, **and** spirits. And as Bob Marley says: "Who feels it knows it all" (Marley & Wailers, 1999). This is what we attempted to represent in the narrative, through our thick descriptions, theorizing the interconnected, and intersubjective nature of our experiences. Even in the writing, we eventually had to write one story from what we'd originally thought were "separate" field notes. While Cynthia had visited the dungeons several times, this was Charlotte's initial visit. However, as we examined Cynthia's first visit to the dungeons from fifteen years ago (and even her experiences during this visit) the notes from the field (the spiritual, physical, and emotional experience) were nearly identical. This suggests that nkwaethnography must recognizes such fluidity in time and space, the spiritual and the material conditions of its "subjects" in all aspects of the re-search and see the conceptions of time and space as not only present, but past and future, as embodied, and spiritual.

Second, nkwaethnography fundamentally, systematically and symbolically shifts one's understanding and experience of personhood: It is sacred because it re-centers, allowing the recovery of one's humanity and one's spirit.

At the core of Black feminism (Collins, 2000; Steady, 1981) and endarkened feminism (Dillard, 2006) is the recognition of the expertise that Black women acquire through our lived experiences and specific to our lived conditions. An approach to endarkened transnational feminist research is one in which the researcher and the researched are engaged in a mutually *humbling* experience, where each understands our limitations in speaking *for* the other. An endarkened transnational feminist epistemology and methodology recognizes that there are multiple experiences outside of one's own—but as Black women there is a connection to one another—past, present, and future. The power of the experiences of being in the slave dungeons, like so many others, is one that will never be forgotten and from which we were able to re-member, a collective re-memory: This is its transformative power. But it is important to recognize that the shift in our perspectives was not just about how we physically shifted locations from the United States to West Africa. It is the way that being in those dungeons specifically and in connection with Indigenous knowledges more generally fundamentally, systematically, and symbolically *reversed the diasporic journey* for us, as African ascendant people (Busia, 1989; Marshall, 1983). Drawn into and present in our spiritual homeland, engaged with/in the rituals, people, places of Ghana in authentic and intimate ways, we were shown a way to look at our present without seeing the past as valueless, and to see the hopefulness of the future as well. This is an important knowing that moves beyond simple intellectual knowledge for the African ascendant, whose history with/in the United States and the continent itself has been and continues to be a colonized one, as Achebe (1989), Fanon (1967), Steady (1981), and others remind us. Nkwaethnography, thirdly, embraces community and the idea of a common destiny.

Here, the South African concept of Ubuntu ("I am because we are") and the Ghanaian (Akan) proverbial ideal of Funtummireku-denkyemmireku ("We have a common destiny") embody the need to recognize the powerful and omnipresent role of community from an endarkened transnational perspective. Contrary to Western thought that seeks to elevate the individual above the community, we were committed to an endarkened transnational feminist praxis—and open to the sacred work of transformation—in those slave dungeons. As re-searchers, we were committed to seeing our encounter as one that had purpose as Black women in relation to both our scholarly lives and our lives beyond the academy. From this standpoint, our work as researchers has as part of its purpose understanding our historical conditions as Black people and recognizing the "specifics" of the oppressions within and amongst African ascendant women as *our* collective reality, a struggle that we all must engage for freedom from oppression and full humanhood. Nkwaethnography re-cognizes—made us think *again*—of the long and collective struggle for liberation, and in this case, provided additional understanding of the specifics of the conditions of Black women historically held in those dungeons. Most profoundly it is the life-altering recognition that "there but for the grace of God go I": There would be no African *Americans* without the sacrifices of those who were in the dungeons, who survived the Middle Passage, who endured slavery in the New World, and those of us still involved in the struggle for liberation, freedom, and full personhood. This is not our legacy solely as African Americans: This is our legacy as African people.

Finally, nkwaethnography recognizes that body, mind, and spirit must all be engaged in the process of research.

Given our experiences, there had to be space for mind, body, and spirit to be a part of the entire re-search endeavor. We wanted to invite our whole persons as researchers and the whole persons of the "researched" into the work, knowing that the mind, body, and spirit are intertwined in their functions of maintaining the well-being of the individual and community. The place of the sacred in endarkened and transnational feminisms requires a radical openness, especially on the part of the researcher, who understands deeply that her/his humanity is linked with that of the people s/he studies *with*. In this case, we sought to engage all of our senses and our spirits. We prayed and meditated. We wrote and wrote and wrote through our feelings and often through our tears. We listened deeply, allowing ourselves to feel the sounds, the environment, the very air that we breathed. We believe that such acts of radical openness, of hearing the voices of those who have been silenced and marginalized and being changed by those voices is a spiritual act, one which must come with a deep sense of humility and desire for intimacy. Further, a sense of reciprocity is fundamental from this epistemological and methodological space, a sense that the researcher and the "researched" are both changed in the process of mutual teaching and learning the world together. From a spiritual perspective, it also means that the intersubjectivity that is possible in a reciprocal relationship is experienced and embodied as the collective "heart" of memory, important to the re-search process.

FINAL THOUGHTS ON NKWAETHNOGRAPHY: RECOGNIZING AND REMEMBERING

Through this work, one thing has become very clear: Qualitative re-search can be a spiritual re-search, a place both physical and spiritual that can also position the qualitative researcher as a narrator of memory, both her/his own and the collective memory of our hearts and souls. That is what we've shared here in the chapter. However, for the Black or endarkened feminist researcher, whose work is often deliberately situated in Indigenous spaces, places, and knowledge production (such as in the slave dungeons in Ghana), this is not simply the narration of a story: It is the *deliberate* work of engaging and *preserving* these stories, both of the "thing" itself and our engagements and experiences with it. But, from an African Indigenous space it is also our *duty*—our responsibility—to *remember*. We are those who can bear witness to our African "past," "present," and "future." That is fundamental to what it means to be in community, to be in the spirit in African time. Spirituality and recognitions of the sacred nature of life and work are part and parcel of what Booth (2006) describes as *enduringness*, the central ways that spirit structures understandings of our place within Indigenous community. For the African ascendant person, having the opportunity to think and experience through an endarkened spirituality within our schools and systems of education might lead to what Palmer (1983) suggests is an authentic spirituality in education that:

> wants to open us to truth, whatever truth may be, wherever truth might take us. Such a spirituality does not dictate where we must go, but trusts that any path walked with integrity will take us to a place of knowledge (p. xi).

This is our responsibility: To remember African Indigenous spiritual truths and to bear witness to them in our thought and actions, as our praxis. Let it be so.

NOTES

1. In the spirit of the epistemic nature and power of language discussed by Asante (1988), Kohain Hahlevi, a Hebrew Israelite rabbi uses the term African ascendant to describe people of African heritage. In contrast to the commonly used term "descendent," he argues that African ascendant more accurately describes the upward and forward moving nature of African people throughout the diaspora as well as on the African continent herself. We subscribe to this notion.
2. Questions are often raised about authenticity and definitions of Indigenous, who belongs and who does not. In that spirit, Indigeneity describes the knowledge, values, and practices of Indigenous groups, particularly those with contemporary roots in African culture that are honored, nurtured, and valued in contemporary times. We lean on Hilliard (1995) who defined African Indigenous teachers/scholars as "selfless healer[s], intent on inspiring, transforming and propelling students to a higher spiritual level" (pp. 69–70).
3. The name Patrick is a pseudonym.
4. This meditation is adapted from "Slave Dungeons II," an unpublished manuscript by Dillard, C. B., entitled *Living Africa: A Book of Meditations*.
5. In Dillard and Okpalaoka (in press), the authors contend that experience has and continues to be a space of contestation, particularly for post-structural scholars. As example, Jackson & Mazzei (2008) argue for the need for experience in autoethnography "that acknowledges the constraints of 'one' telling, that theorizes the ethics of such tellings, and that works the limits of the narrative 'I'" (p. 299), seeking instead a deconstructive autoethnography that puts experience under deconstruction, that confronts experience as questionable, incomplete, problematic "rather than as a foundation for truth" (p. 304). They further speak to the need, in a deconstructive autoethnography, to engage "a critique of the *relations of power* in the production of meaning from experience" (p. 304, emphasis theirs). In this need to critique the relations of power, Dillard and Okpalaoka (in press) see Jackson and Mazzei's (2008) call for a different sort of autoethnography (and by extension, qualitative research generally) as useful and important. However, even in their call for a critique of power, the framing of experience remains something that is strikingly singular and somewhat personal (even in their notion

of a performative versus narrative "I"). This is counter to African-centered understandings of experience as *collective*, sacredly imbued with a connected spirituality to all that exists past, present, and future. As Dillard (2006) suggests, we remain in agreement with Lubiano's (1991) notion that an African feminist "post" position must "be politically nuanced in a radical way, focusing on such differences' implications especially in moments of oppositional transgressions" (p. 160). Dillard goes on to suggest that one way that the African American presence in postmodernism can offer a critique is to engage in an alternative cultural discourse in keeping with the spirit of an African ethos. Hence, we argue here for a sense of experience that is more deeply complex and centered in the African notions of the collective.

REFERENCES

Alexander, M. J. (2005). *Pedagogies of Crossing: Meditations on Feminism, Sexual Politics, Memory, and the Sacred*. Durham: Duke University Press.

Asante, M. K. (1988). *Afrocentricity*. Trenton, NJ: Africa World.

Booth, W.J. (2006). Communities of memory: On witness, identity, and justice. Ithaca, NY: Cornell University Press.

Busia, A. P. A. (1989). What is your nation? Reconnecting Africa and her diaspora through Paule Marshall's *Praisesong for the Widow*. In C. A. Wall (Ed.), *Changing our Own Worlds* (pp. 196–212). New Brunswick: Rutgers University Press.

Collins, P. H. (2000). *Black Feminist Thought : Knowledge, Consciousness, and the Politics of Empowerment*. New York: Routledge.

Cruse, H. (1967). *The Crisis of the Negro Intellectual*. New York: Morrow.

Dillard, C. B. (2006). *On Spiritual Strivings : Transforming an African American Woman's Academic Life*. Albany: State University of New York Press.

Dillard, C. B. (2008). When the ground is Black, the ground is fertile: Exploring endarkened feminist epistemology and healing methodologies in the spirit. In N. K. Denzin, Y. S. Lincoln, & L. T. Smith (Eds.), *Handbook of Critical and Indigenous Methodologies* (pp. 277–292). Thousand Oaks: Sage.

Dillard, C. B., & Okpalaoka, C. (in press). The sacred and spiritual nature of endarkened transnational feminist praxis in qualitative research. In N. K. Denzin & Y. S. Lincoln (Eds.), *Handbook of Qualitative Research* (4th ed.). Thousand Oaks: Sage.

Dillard, C.B., Saleem, D., & Tyson, C.A. (2000). My soul is a witness: Engaging pedagogy of the spirit. *International Journal of Qualitative Studies in Education*, 13(5), 447–462.

Du Bois, W. E. B. (1903/1970). *W.E.B. Du Bois: A Reader*. New York: Harper & Row.

Ellis, C. (2004). *The Ethnographic I : A Methodological Novel about Autoethnography*. Walnut Creek, CA: AltaMira.

Fanon, F. (1967). *Black Skin, White Masks*. New York: Grove.

Fernandes, L. (2003). *Transforming Feminist Practice: Non-violence, Social Justice and the Possibilities of a Spiritualized Feminism*. San Francisco: Aunt Lute.

Hilliard, A. G. (1995). *The Maroon within Us: Selected Essays on African American Community Socialization*. Baltimore: Black Classic.

hooks, b. (1993). *Sisters of the Yam: Black Women and Recovery*. Cambridge: South End.

hooks, b. & West, C. (1991). *Breaking Bread: Insurgent Black Intellectual Life*. Cambridge, MA: South End.

Hull, G. T., Bell-Scott, P., & Smith, B. (1982). *All the Women Are White, All the Blacks Are Men, but Some of Us Are Brave : Black Women's Studies*. Old Westbury, NY: Feminist.

Hull, A. G. (2001). *Soul Talk: The New Spirituality of African American Women*. Rochester, VT: Inner Traditions.

Jackson, A. Y., & Mazzei, L. (2008). Experience and "I" in autoethnography: A deconstruction. *International Journal of Qualitative Studies in Education*, 1(3), 299–318.

King, J. E. (2005). *Liberating Metholodology: Activist Research in the Spirit of Jemima*. Paper presented at the First Qualitative Inquiry Congress, Urbana-Champaign, IL.

Lubiano, W. (1991). Shuckin' off the African-American native other: What's "po-mo" got to do with it? *Cultural Critique, 18*, 149–186.

Madison, S. D. (2005). *Critical Ethnography : Method, Ethics, and Performance*. Thousand Oaks: Sage.

Marley, B., & the Wailers. (1999). Track: Running away. On *Songs of Freedom* (CD, Disc 3). Island Records.

Marshall, Paule (1984). *Praisesong for the widow*. New York: Dutton.

Moraga, C., & Anzalda, G. (1981). *This Bridge Called My Back : Writings by Radical Women of Color*. Watertown: Persephone.

Moyers, B. D. & Pellett, G. (Producers) (1988). *Chinue Achebe*. New York: Public Affairs Television WNET.

Nnaemeka, O. (1998). *Sisterhood, Feminisms, and Power : From Africa to the Diaspora*, Trenton, NJ: Africa World.

Palmer, P. (1983). *To Know as We Are Known: Education as a Spiritual Journey*. San Francisco: Harper.

Ryan, J. S. (2005). *Spirituality as Ideology in Black Women's Film and Literature*. Charlottesville: University of Virginia Press.

Smith, L. T. (1999). *Decolonizing Methodologies : Research and Indigenous Peoples*. London: Zed.

Steady, F.C. (1981) The Black woman cross-culturally: An overview. In F. C. Steady (Ed.). *The Black Woman Cross-Culturally*. Cambridge, MA: Schenkman.

Wade-Gayles, G. (Ed.) (1995). *My Soul Is a Witness: African-American Women's Spirituality*. Boston: Beacon.

Walker, A. (2006). *We Are the Ones We Have Been Waiting For: Inner Light in a Time of Darkness*. New York: New.

CHAPTER TWENTY-TWO

Re/Membering In-Between "Japan" and "the West"

A Decolonizing Journey through the Indigenous Knowledge Framework

KIMINE MAYUZUMI

もくもくと雪に絵の具を散りばめて染みこんでいく夢を見るかな

This chapter begins with my calligraphy. I wrote the poem above on a quiet Saturday morning while sitting in a straight posture with my calligraphy brush. I wrote the poem in the Japanese *tanka* style as an instinctive expression of my feelings toward the academy within which I resided and later read it in front of my "Women in Higher Education" class. More recently, rewriting the poem in calligraphy enabled me to (re)embody the meaning that I intended to convey at the time it was created and reconnect to the *hiragana* (Japanese-based characters) and *kanji* (Chinese-based characters), which allow me to convey a heightened level of expression compared to the English alphabets.

To this (re)embodiment experience through my *tanka* in calligraphy style, I wish to apply the notion of "re/membering," which Jeong-eun Rhee (2006) effectively applied to her decolonizing text. It refers to

> [T]he double acts of remembering (recalling) and re-membering (becoming a member again). 'Remembering' brings the silenced history and the voice of the marginalized back to [one's] mind and 're-membering' continuously affirms [one's] solidarity or belonging to the voice of the displaced (p. 597).

By foregrounding this experience of writing the poem in calligraphy using *hiragana* and *katakana*, I remember or recall my connection to the cultural knowledge that I had forgotten since my move to the West and re-member or once again become a member of the group that reclaims such cultural knowledge as a legitimate way of knowing.

The poem can be translated as: "Intently spreading watercolor on the snow, which gradually dissolved the ice, [I] dreamt of. . . ." The white snowy scenery metaphorically describes the academy, which I wish to transform into other colors. In this image, the snow covers everything and turns other colors into one dominant color—white. The power of the snow and its colonial nature in the academy are recognized in the poem, yet a sense of resistance is also expressed. Through the "re/membering" experience in the action of calligraphy, (re)writing this poem became even more "anti-colonial," which centers the agency of the colonized and signifies Indigenous knowledge as a tool to resist "coloniality" that is the epistemic logic of domination, control, and exploitation (Dei, 2006; Mignolo, 2005; Shahjahan, 2005).

This chapter extends from my poetic interpretation of the academy in my decolonizing journey, begun during my doctoral studies, where I began applying the Indigenous knowledge framework in my scholarship. In the following autoethnographical account, I further explore my re/membering journey by discussing my experience as a female graduate student, born and raised in rural Japan, who conducted a life history interview with a female elder from rural Japan. This chapter posits that the Indigenous knowledge framework provides possibilities to decolonize the dominant ways of thinking in the academy as well as the misrepresentation of minoritized groups in the transnational context as it has allowed me to go through re/membering actions such as writing this text.

First, I will discuss the Indigenous knowledge framework, which I learned and later applied in my doctoral research. Second, I will elucidate autoethnography as a methodology and situate myself within the Indigenous knowledge framework in a transnational context, more specifically between "Japan" and "the West."[1] I will also explain the use of metaphor as a method of inquiry in my writing. Third, I will describe my "decolonizing" journey by reflecting on my move to "the West" (i.e., North America), my awakening experience, and the process of reclaiming my Indigenous knowledge during periodical visits to my hometown in Japan and through an interview with *obasan* (grandma's sister) on her life history. Fourth, I will discuss the relevance of the Indigenous knowledge framework in the context of my case study. Lastly, I will discuss the implications of my decolonizing journey through the Indigenous knowledge framework and the relevance to other populations beyond the Japanese context.

INDIGENOUS KNOWLEDGES

The concept of Indigenous knowledge is based on the notion that there are diverse ways of knowing (Battiste & Henderson, 2000; Dei, 2000; Semali & Kincheloe, 1999; Shiva, 1997). It ruptures the dominance of certain knowledge that is often universalized and assumed to be the only legitimate way of knowing. By reclaiming the legitimacy of other ways of knowing, the concept of Indigenous knowledge seeks to create space for those who have been silenced. The process of silencing may occur because people are excluded from the dominant group whose knowledge has been legitimized in a given social context. Moving subjugated knowledge from the margin to the center unfolds new anti-colonial possibilities for rebalancing power in society.

Indigenous knowledge is any body of knowledge that has been accumulated and developed in a local area and has been central to the long-term survival of a community as it is locally appropriate (Millat-e-Mustafa, 2000; Purcell, 1998). In other words, a body of Indigenous knowledge is rooted in a specific context and history (Battiste & Henderson, 2000; Dei, 2000; Semali & Kincheloe; 1999). It is physically and metaphysically embedded in people's everyday lives. It also resides in the holistic and relational realm of people's lives (Cajete, 1994; Castellano, 2000; Dei, 2000) wherein spirituality, intuition, and dreams are valid epistemologies (Duran, 2001; Shahjahan, 2005; Tisdell, 2003). It is also transmitted from generation to generation, though some changes occur over time as no tradition is static (Linnekin, 1992; Wong, 2002).

I use the term "Indigenous" with a capital "I" throughout this chapter in order to distinguish it from the frequently used term "indigenous," which refers to populations such as Aboriginal peoples. The capitalized term "Indigenous" indicates the notion discussed above and "signals the power relations and dynamics embedded in the production, interrogation and validation of such knowledges" (Dei, 2000, p. 114). Dei elaborates on the notion of "Indigenous," stating that it "recognizes the multiple and collective origins as well as collaborative dimensions of knowledge and affirms that the interpretation or analysis of social reality is subject to differing and sometimes oppositional perspectives" (p. 114).

There is also a political agenda underlying the notion of Indigenous knowledge, which I refer to as "decolonization." "Decolonization" is interpreted here as a political act whereby I attempt to center the concerns and worldviews of the marginal communities with whom I identify. This is done with the goal of understanding theory from their own perspective and employing it for their own purposes, rather than "reading [their] 'difference' in contrast to Western 'sameness'" (Rhee, 2006, p. 597). This process is essential in resisting the hegemony of ideas and images that are imposed on non-dominant groups by others (Alfred, 1999; Smith, 1999). The process of decolonization implies reclaiming their own subjectivity of the marginalized (Graveline, 1998) through "rediscovering [their] history and recovering [their] culture, language, identity and so on" (Laenui, 2000, p. 153). I engage this decolonizing process in an effort to counterbalance my complicity in social and historical hierarchies of knowledge production through a form of "strategic essentialism" that allows the marginalized as a heterogeneous group to collaborate and achieve their goal of decolonization (Spivak, 1993).

METHODOLOGY

This chapter centers me as a writer, researcher, and activist within a larger transnational context. I apply the methodology of autoethnography, which foregrounds the personal as a political subject who analyzes her/himself as an object located in a social dynamic and has the goal of social change (Holman Jones, 2005). It does not seek a single truth but a truth among many in "the social world from the perspective of the interacting individual" (Denzin, 1997, p. xv). Through this lens, it examines the sociohistorical implications and places the author's subjectivity at the center (see Peshkin, 1988). It is not intended as a self-indulgent exercise nor is it meant solely for individualistic learning or growth. Instead, it aims to inspire the readers to cultivate their own self-reflexive mode of learning and become active agents of change (Mayuzumi, 2009; Spry, 2001). In this light, my own reflexive stories situated within the Indigenous knowledge framework shape this autoethnographical text.

I am a heterosexual able-bodied female graduate student in a Western academic institution who was born and raised in the Gunma prefecture of rural Japan. In this chapter, I attempt to illustrate how the Indigenous knowledge framework has played a role in decolonizing my mind through my journey from Japan to the West. In doing so, I reflect on my experiences before and after encountering the Indigenous knowledge framework. I focus on the metaphysical embodied knowledge embedded in my everyday life, most of which I gained through my upbringing in rural Japan. Despite the fluidity of my identity, I evoke the knowledge that speaks to my heart and body in the deepest manner with respect to my origins. It is also this knowledge that has been subjugated in the discussions on "Japanese women" as a homogenized group and "rural Japan" as being commodified or commercialized on this global capitalistic terrain (Mayuzumi, 2009). When I discuss "my communities" in this chapter, I refer to multiple communities that associate my metaphysical knowledges with Indigenous knowledge. The question of authenticity and hybridity is important in the discussion of colonization; however, I assert the importance of speaking with my voice from my social location, knowing that I am privileged in the Western academy and possess certain cultural capital. My reflections show that I am also a product of hybridity. Ang (2001) emphasizes hybridity as a basis for cultural politics:

> Hybridity . . . should not be dismissed pejoratively as the merely contingent and ephemeral, equated with lack of commitment and political resoluteness, but should be valued, in James Clifford's words, as 'a pragmatic response, making the best of given (often bad) situations . . . in limited historical conjunctures' (p. 3).

I also speak out of the fear that third parties may speak for me and my communities (including Japanese women and rural Japan) and perpetuate the misrepresentation of the marginalized communities. I do not purport to represent all Japanese women or rural Japanese communities, or even my village, but rather to explicate my story from the perspective of an individual in a given social context.

Moreover, I am very much aware that the colonized can also occupy the role of colonizer. Evidently, Japan is historically implicated in the colonization of the Indigenous lands and peoples such as the Ainu, as well as neighboring countries in Asia and the Pacific. Applying the Indigenous knowledge framework in this discussion may demonstrate how it can be a lens for other contexts, including the issues of Japanese internal colonization as well as the relationships between Japan and other regions/countries.

In this chapter, I also include my experience of informally interviewing an elderly rural Japanese woman, my father's aunt, whom I called *obasan* (aunty). In summer of 2005, I had an opportunity to interview this *obasan* about her life history by visiting her house and having tea together with my mother. Interestingly I needed my mother to mediate between the *obasan* and myself, although we were all speaking the same language, as my mother had much better knowledge of the *obasan*'s life and the sociocultural context. More importantly, my mother was much more acquainted with the *obasan* than I was. Even though this "research" was methodologically limited in the sense of how I, as researcher, could access the knowledge of the informant, I include this experience because it truly inspired me to "re/member" my own experiential knowledges and the voice of the silenced submerged in my colonized mind.

I also wish to embrace what Tisdell, Tolliver, and Villa (2001) state regarding cultural identity:

> In order for social transformation to happen both individuals and cultural groups need to explore the mechanisms imposed by cultural hegemony and colonialism that have impacted their four faces: the personal face, the historical face, the political face, and the sacred face. Furthermore individuals and cultural groups need to, in reclaiming these four faces, incorporate other ways of knowing grounded in cultural and spiritual experience, such as through music, art, and poetry grounded in their cultural identity (p. 2).

Therefore, in this chapter, I also use metaphor, which gives life to my voice through my imagined action of calligraphy. In this chapter, my writing progresses as if I am going through the four steps of Japanese calligraphy, providing a guide for this writing journey as a method of inquiry (see Mayuzumi, 2006; Richardson & St. Pierre, 2005). Imagining myself doing calligraphy helps me not only to perform autoethnography within my own mode of experiential knowledge but also to concentrate on "the body as the site from which the story [knowledge] is generated" and "[begin] the methodological praxis of reintegrating my body and mind into my scholarship" (Spry, 2001, p. 708).

A DECOLONIZING JOURNEY

(The first stage of calligraphy)

> In a quiet room, I sit on my knees at a floor table in a straight posture. To make black ink, I scrape an ink bar on a suzuri (stone dish). Holding the ink bar, my hand moves back and forth slowly and carefully with a rhythmic sound. I smell the ink and, as it flows, I also begin to feel its thickness. My entire body is focussed on the ink in the suzuri. No thinking is required and my mind is empty.

MOVING TO THE WEST

My North American experience started in the third year of my undergraduate degree, when I moved to the United States as an international student. Now, after almost a decade of residence in North America, I am able to navigate through and interrogate the "lived West" and gain perspective on the "imagined West" I envisioned before my move (see He, 2002). The term "the West" does not only refer to the geographical dimension of Western nation-states but also refers to the power and privilege imbued in historical and contemporary coloniality. Therefore, my moving to "the West" was not an innocent act, but had conscious or unconscious mind that was aiming for certain power that I had learned through my social and educational upbringing. Part of my original vision before moving to the West was to gain social mobility by becoming fluent in English and getting a degree from an American academic institution.[2] In the 1980s, just before my move to the United States, the Japanese media and government began to discuss what "internationalization" meant and what it meant to become an "international" person (Ehara, 1992; Habu, 2000). During the 1980s and early 1990s, the U.S. universities also invested in Japan to recruit Japanese students for American higher education institutions, partly as a means of rectifying trade imbalance between Japan and the United States (Habu, 2000). In this context, I knew I wanted to be "international," which seemingly meant being close to or part of the West in my colonized definition, and started developing my English language skills by first going to an English conversation school and then to a second school to enhance my TOEFL scores.[3]

Once I moved to the United States to pursue higher education, I began discussing and thinking more about "Japan" and myself as a "Japanese woman" or how I might be perceived as a Japanese woman by non-Japanese people in the West. Whether it was conscious or not, I attempted to fit the image of "Japanese." At the same time, I also tried to absorb the white-dominant Western cultural capital as much as I could by being assimilated into dominant ways of thinking and knowing. Whether I conformed to the West or remained "Japanese," either interpretation of my identity was simply a different side of the same coin, which was to please the white North Americans who resided at the top of the cultural hierarchy in my colonized mind.

I undertook my undergraduate degree in Anthropology at a Midwestern university in the United

States. The lectures focused on different theorists who were seen to be important in the history of Anthropology, such as Radcliffe-Brown, Malinowski, Boaz, and Lévi-Strauss. I observed that many of these theorists developed the field of Anthropology by examining cultures and "Other" bodies through a white male lens. I also took a course on North American Archeology, taught by a white male instructor, where we learned about different native peoples who formerly occupied the land. I never questioned the colonial nature and history of the field and was even eager to adopt the mainstream analytic lens by overlooking the on-going issues of colonization of indigenous people in the land as well as putting my subjectivity aside. After returning to Japan with my bachelor's degree, I had difficulty adjusting back to my former life. I began criticizing the way my parents interacted with each other, discounting their community events and unwritten rules and missing the "civilized" way of life I learned in the United States. I even made my mother regret having let me go to the United States and become "Americanized." I also observed that my "teachers" of English conversation and American literature at a local community college were mostly white males at the time, who were seen to be respectable figures that were represented in the media and through the dominant knowledge I was exposed to in Japan. Given these circumstances, I found it was time to pursue further studies in the West.

In the early stages of my higher education experience in North America, one of my biggest challenges was my limited proficiency in English, which affected not only my ability to communicate with people, but also my self-esteem to a large extent. Most notably, I felt excluded from conversations, including class discussions (Mayuzumi, Motobayashi, Nagayama, & Takeuchi, 2007). Moreover, I had bought into the colonial discourse on the English language, by asserting that English is an "international" language. I was also interested in acquiring "proper" English pronunciation, without an accent. Behind this concept of accent, there was a misconception about English proficiency, which determines not only one's "official" language level but also the quality and quantity of one's knowledge, intelligence, or credibility (see Lippi-Green, 1997). I was hardly aware of language as "the substantive technology through which social exclusion is built around power and hegemony" (Dei, 2006, p. 16). I regularly asked my white peers to correct my English pronunciation whenever they found "mistakes" in my English. I was also reproducing the colonial measurement through my desires, motivations, and goal-orientedness as I attempted to find my place in the West.

(The second stage of calligraphy)

> The ink texture and colour are ready to be used in the act of writing. I place a white sheet on the table in front of me. I prepare to write by dipping the brush in the ink and soaking it until it becomes soft and holds the right amount of ink. I trust my body, which knows what the brush should feel like. I straighten my posture once more and now my attention is on the blank piece of paper, which reflects my mind, made empty during the meditation on ink preparation.

AWAKENING

Despite my desire to gain social mobility by adhering more and more to dominant cultural norms, I realized at some point that I would never be perceived as being part of a dominant group in the West. Instead, I would be depicted as non-Western and non-white—an Asian woman in the West (see Ang, 2001). Seeing myself through such a colonial lens hindered the growth of my spirit, body, and mind and gave rise to my fragmented self by devaluing my knowledge and experience, where I was coming from (e.g., my ancestors, family, and communities), and even who I was with (e.g., my community members). My self-esteem diminished and I began blaming myself in situations where I felt excluded from the dominant groups in discussions. This began to widen yet disguise the gap between my spiritual subjectivity and what I was forced to be. The "model minority" stereotypes of quietness and gentleness directed at me as a Japanese/Asian woman held me in an unquestioned colonized position for a long period of time. The model minority stereotype was not only directed at me as an Asian, but also as a Japanese person. For example, I was sometimes compared with other minority groups, such as the Chinese, a comparison that had hierarchical and cultural connotations.

Having been raised in rural Japan, it was challenging to understand what I was imagined to be by others in the West. The high-tech, cosmopolitan, secularized image of "modern" Japan was not even close to what I grew up with. Stereotyped images of "traditional" Japan, often represented by the *samurai, geisha,* or *sumo,* did not reflect my origins either. Furthermore, much of the feminist scholarly work on Japanese women focused on educated, urban middle-class women who supposedly suffered under patriarchy (Mayuzumi, 2009). While I was interested in women's experiences, once I started my graduate studies in Canada I did not feel that I belonged to the mainstream white middle-class liberal feminism that dominated the feminist discourse inside and outside the academy (see also hooks, 1984; Kim, 2009). In the search for where to belong, I have come to understand that it is fluid and I can belong to more than one community depending on the moment. I have come to recognize how my metaphysical knowledge had been rejected in the academic domain, leading me to almost forget such an important part of myself and my community.

Despite the humility I embodied through my upbringing, I quickly learned the importance of asserting one's own achievement and success in the Western academic environment (see Rhee, 2006). It was not easy for me to jump into classroom discussions in the Western context, where louder voices were paid more attention (see Arisaka, 2000; Zhou, Knoke, & Sakamoto, 2005). It has been a challenge to discuss myself and my work, as I was taught during childhood to be humble rather than boast. From an epistemological perspective, visibility and conceptual analysis are dominant in the Western paradigms (Bai & Scott, 2009). Bai and Scott (2009) point out that the field of philosophy should go beyond "the singularity of analytic, rational, logical, and conceptual" to acknowledge Asian philosophies grounded in other forms of consciousness.

A number of key incidents and people were influential in my understanding of how I was represented as a Japanese woman in the West. For example, I came across more than a couple of men (both white and non-white) who were happy to tell me that Japanese women are the best wives in the world. These kinds of comments triggered me to look into the literature discussing the eroticization of Asian women through both historical and contemporary representation (see Mayuzumi, 2006, 2009). Loti's description of Japanese women dating back to 1920 as a "tiny personage with narrow eyes and no brains" (as cited in Hsia & Scanzoni, 1996, p. 309) remains a powerful image for me. I began asking questions such as: Whose knowledge is this? How does it make an impact on the representation of Japanese women, including myself, as social being? This led me to question the dominance of white male power shaping the discourses on Japanese women beginning in the colonial era (see Marchetti, 1993; Prasso, 2005).

There are a number of scholars who assert that "what is considered theory in the dominant academic community is not necessarily what counts as theory for women of color" (as cited in Scheurich & Young, 2002, p. 57). As Mohanty (2003) advocates, " . . . theory is a deepening of the political, not a moving away from it: a distillation of experience, and an intensification of the personal" (p.

191). Various feminist thinkers claim different theoretical spaces based on their own epistemologies (e.g., Bannerji, 1991; Carty, 1991; Collins, 2000; Elabor-Idemudia, 2001; Garry & Pearsall, 1996; Harding, 1998; Wane, Deliovsky, & Lawson, 2002; Webber, 2005). Many scholars (e.g., Alexander, 2005; Ang, 2001; Arisaka, 2000; Asher, 2009; Dillard, 2006; hooks, 1994; Mohanty, 2003) who search to represent their subjective locations in the academy inspired me to look at my own histories/stories through my scholarship.

Moreover, my encounter with the concept of Indigenous knowledge was pivotal in that it further pushed me to center my subjectivity and experience in my thinking about my identity, knowledge, and representation. A few of the graduate courses that I took in my doctoral program that were grounded in the Indigenous knowledge framework provided me with a space to bring in my subjectivity. In one course, I did a presentation with a Mayan colleague in a dialogue format whereby we exchanged our spiritual knowledges through rituals. It was a powerful moment in a sense that we came up with both convergence and divergence in our colonized locations. In another course on Indigenous knowledges, I employed autoethnography as a methodology for the first time to center my subjectivity in my final chapter, which was converted to an article published in a prestigious peer-reviewed journal (i.e., Mayuzumi, 2009). Some literature (e.g., Battiste & Henderson, 2000; Dei, Hall, & Rosenberg, 2000; Semali & Kincheloe, 1999; Smith, 1999) also inspired me to further look into the concept of Indigenous knowledges especially in the academic context. Overall, I contend that the Indigenous knowledge framework has been empowering for me as a tool with which to theorize my epistemologies. More specifically, this concept of Indigenous knowledge has provided me with: (1) a conceptual framework whereby I can better articulate the subjugated knowledge that is closely linked to my lived experience, (2) a space where I can center my Indigenous knowledge and my communities rather than leaving them in the periphery, (3) a sense of courage and confidence to bring up my subjectivity and be legitimized in the academy, and (4) an opportunity to interrogate local and global systems that create and reflect the power dynamics in knowledge production (Mayuzumi, 2009). As a result, I have become more explicit in my political agenda, which is to decolonize what has been colonized, including myself and others searching for justice and healing from colonization. The awakening experience described above was a beginning stage where I began to comprehend the Indigenous knowledge framework and question the hierarchy of knowledge in my own mind.

(The third step of calligraphy)

> I gently guide the brush to the surface of the white sheet and allow my hand to glide the way my body wants it to. My whole body is concentrated on my hand movements and my eyes focus on how the brush makes strokes, pauses, and moves off the paper. I am able to situate myself in relation to "nothingness" through the writing process and aim to discover a new experience.

FROM *OBASAN'S* STORY TO MY OWN: EXPLORING MY SACRED FACE

In summer of 2005, after encountering the concept of Indigenous knowledge in my graduate program, I had a chance to interview my grandmother (more specifically, my father's aunt, here referred to as *obasan*) about her life history. She shared the hardships that she experienced in her childhood, youth, and early adulthood. Her hardships seemed to have mostly been derived from her having been adopted by a family when she was small and their lack of material resources in general. She even expressed how fortunate young people are nowadays in this technologically advanced and materially well-off era. I asked her if she wished she had been born much later. After a small pause, she said, "No way. Nowadays there are too many crimes and killings." At first I thought that this contradicted her comment about people these days being fortunate. But after reflecting on what she had mentioned throughout the interview, I felt I understood in my way why she was not envious of contemporary young people. In her discussion of her hardships, she expressed her gratitude toward the people who came to aid her and her family. For example, during the Second World War, *obasan,* her husband, and their small children escaped from a city to the village without any material resources. One expression she uttered remains clear in my mind: "*Watashi wa makenaiyo*" (I won't be beaten and I won't back down). Although her voice was soft, I could sense strength, pride, and confidence in every phrase she uttered.

I asked *obasan* what she thinks of while taking her morning walk. She said, "Nothing negative." She simply appreciates the air she feels in the moment. This reminds me of how Thich Nhat Hanh (1991) describes being mindful at the present moment in one's life and the notion of "nothingness" (Nakagawa, 2000; Nishitani, 1982). During the initial stages of my doctoral studies, I did not think as conceptually as I do now. I recognize that I have been trained in the Western academy to conceptualize social phenomena and support my arguments with specific examples (see Bai & Scott, 2009). Nowadays, I tend to focus solely on conceptualization. Once a year, I return to my hometown to visit my family. Being surrounded by the mountains I grew up with and few artificial sounds helps me slow down. Though many things have changed over the past decade, there are things that still remain the way they used to be. It is partly because I am visiting my family for my vacation, but my whole body also begins to feel relaxed as I rediscover the energy and air of rural Japan. It is not only a nostalgic sense, but also embodied knowledge of the local that allows me to feel grounded in the land (see Somé, 1994). It is such a small part of the world. Yet, it was my whole world for a long time during my childhood.

I also asked *obasan* what rituals and custom she still practices throughout the year. At first, she was not responsive to the terms I used, perhaps because she doesn't name her everyday practices as rituals or customs as they are just part of her daily life. It was only when my mother, who acted as interpreter between the two of us, mentioned *yashiki matsuri,* that *obasan* began to elaborate. *Yashiki matsuri* is a house celebration that takes place in mid-December when people offer food to a stone altar behind their house and pray to the house spirit. As *obasan* noted its importance, I began to recall when I was a child and played with my cousins around my other grandmother's house. We sometimes came across a little stone altar for house protection behind the house in the dark shade of the bamboo trees. There I was reminded that some kind of spirit dwelled there and I felt I had to behave well in that space.

Another concept that was shared by my *obasan* was *mottainai,* which is often translated as "what a waste" in English. She used the line to express regret that a member of the family had bought a very expensive watch. Reflecting on the meaning and usage of the line, I came to understand that it was not only a material way of thinking about wasting resources but also spiritual way of thinking about material objects. In the context of the cultural use of the expression, its spiritual implications may have been eroded over time as Japanese society has become more secularized. This *mottainai* mindset rescued people from the poverty in Japan in the past although it was partly promoted as a national propaganda message, especially during World War II. It was developed and practiced though both material hardship and the people's belief in spirits living in materials, as the term originates from Buddhist philosophy. This conceptualization applies to the context of natural resources such as food, water, energy, and even time. It is interesting that once the Kenyan environmentalist Wangari

Maathai, who was awarded the Nobel Peace Prize in 2004, recognized the importance of the Japanese *mottainai* concept, the media and the public began to use the term, although it had been transmitted from generation to generation in Japan. Even a research paper on ecology now refers to *mottainai* as a concept that Maathai introduced and explained to the public (i.e., Fujii, 2006). What is disturbing is that the *mottainai* concept and "ecology" seem to be treated as if they are recently adopted just because some authorities started talking about them. They have actually been practiced as Indigenous knowledge for a long time. There was rarely scientific discussion of "ecology" but the *mottainai* practice was contributing to the "ecology" that we now conceptualize in this era. My mother explained to me some of the environmental practices that were simply taken for granted in her day, for example, that people used to reuse the paper used for sliding doors to blow their nose as well as to clean themselves after their bowel movement. They would roll the old paper taken off the door and keep it for further use. Furthermore, I was told by my parents and elders that you should not leave any grain of rice in your bowl because each grain contains the farmers' sweat, a metaphor for hard work.

Through these lessons, my "sacred face," or metaphysical knowledge, was developed during my upbringing in rural Japan. Certain local phrases reflect the sacredness which I am referring to, for example, "*Bachiga ataru*," which means "to be cursed." This was often used by my parents and grandparents who tried to discipline their children or grandchildren. When a child acted disrespectfully toward the elderly, symbols of deities, foods, or nature, an adult would say "*Bachiga ataruyo*." This meant, "[If you do so], you will be cursed [by some kind of supernatural force]." The other expression is *okagesama*, which is used when one has success or even appreciates the way one can live a decent life. It refers to grateful and humble feelings for the circumstance one was given. One can use the term in reference to all beings that are part of the creation of the environment in some way or another. In other words, *okagesama* is based on a belief in that certain relations influence one's success and achievements. This usage originated in Buddhist thanksgiving to the supernatural. The main Japanese worldviews influenced by Buddhism are that each human being is made up of body, mind, and spirit and that human being exists all in circulation and in connection (Shirahama & Inoue, 2001). As Shirahama and Inoue (2001) point out, "vertical spiritual care is directed toward ancestors and spirits (gods of nature), and horizontal spiritual care is directed toward all others of the society (Seken)" (p. 69). The tea ceremony and calligraphy are examples of my spiritual practices, which enable me to slow down and feel the interconnections with my environment. The water in the tea ceremony represents the purification of the soul and the slow, rhythmic movement of the ink bar in calligraphy allows me to meditate as a ritual. For me, these practices are healing, and entail cleansing my body and spirit, which are connected to my mind (see Mayuzumi, 2006).

(The fourth stage of calligraphy)

> After writing the whole sentence, I slowly place the brush aside. I observe the letters I have written on the paper and focus on how each letter is related to each other in composing a whole sentence. As I view it, life emerges from each letter and then from the entire sentence. This life is given through both my writing and my observation of the letters and gives rise to meaning and emotion.

WHY THE INDIGENOUS KNOWLEDGE FRAMEWORK?

How does the concept of Indigenous knowledge work as an interpretive framework as I travel between the West and rural Japan? There have been different events and situations, other than those I described earlier in my decolonizing journey, where I have felt I needed the Indigenous knowledge framework to counteract the colonial forces emerging from the hegemony of certain knowledges in the transnational context. For instance, I have been fortunate enough to be able to go visit my family in rural Japan once a year. The aunties and uncles in the same town I knew in my childhood are getting old. I see certain things changing over time, such as the scenery and lifestyles influenced by capitalism, secularism, and individualism which had begun to penetrate rural Japan. Over the past few decades, I have observed changes in my hometown in terms of landscape, community events, and lifestyles. For example, people have started going to large supermarkets in which sell things at lower prices and, as a result, many small family-owned stores have closed down. The funerals and anniversaries of deaths, which used to take place at the house of the dead, have been institutionalized and taken over by private companies. There is now a golf course behind the hills of my hometown. Related to the increase in nuclear families, there is now a nursing home near my parents' house. The golf course and the nursing home developed in the village are becoming major landmarks of the neighborhood. "Christmas" decorations can now be seen in front of many rural homes during the month of December. Traditional community events and activities have been simplified and sometimes not celebrated at all. Despite all these changes over a couple of decades, I still encounter community members who remind me of where I came from. My parents are still active in community governance and participate in local events. My bowing practice comes back to my body automatically when I am in Japan. I don't deny that things change as I recognize that traditions are not static. But, I do feel some kind of force that plays a role in redirecting our community and I wonder if there is any resistance to this change. If there is, I would argue that the Indigenous knowledge framework contributes to opening possibilities of resistance through a discussion of knowledges and power dynamics in the transnational context of global capitalism. With a parallel to what Sandy Grande (2004) advocates, the Indigenous knowledge framework "does not aim to reproduce an essentialist or romanticized view of 'tradition'" (Grande, 2004, p. 166). Rather, tradition "is expressed as a *commitment* to the future sustainability of the group" for "an intellectual, social and political movement" (Grande, 2004, p. 166) against such a hegemonic force that dominates and universalizes the globe.

I recently felt the need to bring forward the Indigenous knowledge perspective in my academic work, when I read an article by a Japanese scholar describing and analyzing his experience of Japanese calligraphy (Yoshida, 2005). In his chapter, Yoshida explores how Rudolf Steiner's Waldorf education model can be applied to Japanese education. He conveys his spiritual and transformative experience of writing a Chinese character, *kawa* (river), using a form of Japanese calligraphy and explicates that it was Rudolf Steiner's insights that helped him understand this transformative experience. Yoshida says, "As the experience with the river and calligraphy has shown, I appreciate Steiner's insight in helping me to understand my experience [of the calligraphy]" (p. 134). Reading his insights, I could relate to the spiritual side of his experience. However, what made me uncomfortable in Yoshida's account was that he identified the colonial nature of Steiner's text as a source of his awakening about his own experience with Japanese calligraphy, and he thus foregrounds Steiner's theory throughout his chapter envisioning holistic education in Japan. For example, Yoshida cites Steiner (1919/1943) as follows:

> The Eastern view is exactly the opposite. The Oriental remains, in a sense, at the level of childhood, not allowing his astral body and ego to plunge down into the physical and etheric bodies although at the present epoch it is fore-ordained that humanity should do so (as cited in Yoshida, 2005, p. 134).

Steiner's narrative reminds me of the term "noble savage" (Grande, 2004, p. 64), which describes the Other through an Orientalist lens (see also Said, 1979). More specifically, it is colonial in the sense that: (1) This white Austrian man essentializes Eastern philosophical meanings; (2) this perspective dichotomizes views of the West/East as the civilized/developed versus the uncivilized/untamed; (3) he labels the "Eastern" as "the Oriental," which is an Othering term; and moreover (4) he speaks *for* the Other and has positioned himself as a kind of "authority" on "Oriental" philosophy.

Above all, what is most disturbing is that Yoshida (2005) does not question the colonial text but corresponds to what Steiner says above: "It is true that ego (or I) in the East (or at least in Japan) is very unique, we might say weak, but I am not sure that we should say it is at the level of childhood" (p. 134). Even though Yoshida does not agree with all the points Steiner made, he actually supports Steiner's main point by providing further examples of the weak nature of ego in the Japanese language and relationships/interactions in a Japanese context without questioning the colonial nature of Steiner's text. Although Yoshida attempts to support the Japanese (or "Eastern") Indigenous way of knowing in holistic education while questioning the effect of modernization in Japan that attempted to catch up with "Western civilization," he still nevertheless internalizes Steiner's colonial discourse in order to understand his own cultural experience. Bai and Scott (2009) raise the issue of Japanese scholars placing much emphasis on Western paradigms, even in the field of philosophy. In describing an "international" philosophy of education conference held in Japan, they state:

> It turned out there was hardly anyone (except one panel presentation that was poorly attended) who talked seriously about non-Western philosophies, including the hosting Japanese scholars! It was also apparent that the pride of scholarship for our hosting Japanese philosophers of education lay not in their knowledge of Asian philosophies, but in their knowledge of Western philosophy.... What we are critical of is the privileging of the Western philosophy over non-Western philosophies. This is precisely the legacy of colonialism, and it is very much alive today in Philosophy of Education. In fact, the veritable sign of colonial subjectivity is that *the colonized firmly believe that Western ideas and philosophy are superior to non-Western ones* (p. 5; emphasis added).

This Western (white) superiority in Japanese academia can be traced back to the Meiji period when Japanese intellectuals were encouraged to learn Western ideologies through Western education due to their sense of cultural and racial inferiority to Western "civilization." (Kawano, 2010). What appears to be needed through both the narratives above is an anti-colonial account of the Indigenous knowledge framework. One must recognize the epistemological differences among different knowledge systems and question the hegemony in knowledge production and dissemination globally. Who serves the hegemonic knowledge system? Who or which body is considered to be the authority? What makes Japanese scholars place so much emphasis on Western hegemonic knowledges? I am very much implicated in the imbalance of power relations in knowledge systems. Why did I want to go to the United States in the first place? Why did I want to be fluent in English? Why did I want to obtain Western academic credentials? The answers to these questions are varied and complex. However, I do admit and regret that my mind was colonized by the social world, which I problematized in this discussion of knowledge production. For clarification, I am not trying to construct a dichotomy between West and East. I am aware of the danger of rigid categorization as another form of colonization, which imposes a fixed meaning on something or somebody. I am not arguing that we shy away from dominant Western knowledges. I am aware that both "Eastern" and "Western" knowledge systems influence each other and that there are different ways of thinking among Western knowledge systems as well. I have had the privilege to engage in oppositional knowledge production and scholarship because of my stay in the Western academy yet not without compromising to some extent my access to Indigenous knowledges from my own background. I am not promoting romanticization of Indigenous knowledges, which would allow any disempowerment or the non-static nature of tradition within the community to be obscured. The Indigenous knowledge framework is not about preserving a culture the way it was, since "the culture's reality has already been superseded by the 'fashionable' modernity" (Somé, 1994, p. 4). It is about the *survival* of a culture, of knowledge, and of the community in one form or another (Dei, 2009; Dirlik, 1997; Grande, 2004; Somé, 1994). I wish to emphasize the imbalance of power in knowledges and to seek possibilities in this concept of Indigenous knowledges to counter-balance the existing and prevailing power relations that result in the disempowerment and misrepresentation of the marginalized population. This is what is called "decolonizing the mind" (see Thiong'o, 1986), which I wish to advocate as a collective act through more scholarship.

CONCLUDING REMARKS

This reflexive text through autoethnography has allowed me to engage the Indigenous knowledge framework mentioned above. It inspired me to center my subjectivity and examine how I am implicated in the colonial relations of knowledge production, as I have written about elsewhere (e.g., Mayuzumi, 2006, 2009). The Indigenous knowledge framework also makes me question, "What if I did not have this awakening experience through the framework?" I might have continued disguising my sacred face, which has played an important role in my self-identification and epistemology; I might have looked at or interacted with my community people, including *obasan* and my mother, differently; and I might have perpetuated colonial aspects of academic work through hegemonic lenses. Instead, writing this chapter became a decolonizing exercise, which allowed me to embrace the re/membering process through different aspects of the writing journey. I intended to disrupt an exclusively cognitive method of academic writing by engaging in the four different stages of calligraphy, which actually strengthened and maintained the re/membering effect not only through my mind but also through my body and spirit. My interview with *obasan* also reminded me of both my limitations in accessing local knowledges due to my colonial/colonized location and the possibilities in (re)connecting to the wisdom of local knowledge holders. It is ironic that I had to learn the importance of decolonization from the theoretical framework and not from my mother, who I believe held wisdom through her way of living. While I do recognize the power of academic discourses in society, in my view the academy holds a responsibility to work toward justice and equity, especially in knowledge production. The main motivation for my scholarship comes from the feelings expressed in the poem I introduced at the beginning of this chapter. It may be too much snow that has been piled up over time to dismantle it. Yet, if nothing is done, more snow will accumulate. In order to embody the process of decolonization and re/member where I am coming from, I want to metaphorically relearn how to use a calligraphy brush by rethinking my standpoints as they have been influenced by the Indigenous knowledge framework. Through the brushstrokes in the four different stages of calligraphy, I may better speak to who I am as a researcher and what I wish to accomplish through my work.

An analysis of the significance of the Indigenous knowledge framework in my autoethnography reveals some implications for the broader structural dimensions of education. There needs to be more space for such dialogue (i.e., the Indigenous knowledge framework) in the classroom, workshops, conferences, and international student offices to encourage an expression of one's sense of fragmentation in knowledge hierarchy and embrace one's own Indigenous way of knowing. The Indigenous knowledge framework helps one to critically interrogate the normalized daily conversations that come along with material privileges as well as normalized structural forces. In educational settings, it is crucial to recognize the voice of the silenced as a form of resistance against the colonial regime of education, with the Indigenous knowledge framework as an entry point for decolonization. Educators and administrators who are in positions of authority and leadership should take an initiative to open this anti-colonial space rather than celebrating superficial "multiculturalism" that ignores ideological and material power relations embedded in educational settings. Moreover, in the context of global capitalism, the profit-oriented commodification of higher education underlines international students more than ever before in advancing the knowledge economy (Rizvi, 2000; Sidhu, 2006). As a former international student who now travels back and forth between "Japan" and "the West," I believe that autoethnographical exploration through the Indigenous knowledge framework is an important step for many to decolonize themselves and bring forward their own agency. I end this chapter with the hope that those who feel fragmented in the Western academy, including diasporas and international scholars, will be inspired to cultivate their own reflexive journey and re/member their own sacred faces.

Notes

1. In this chapter, rather than trying to fix the meaning of the terms "Japan" and "the West," I employ them as broad geographical, social, and historical categorizations.
2. As some authors find complex layers of motivations for Asian women to come to the West (e.g., Habu, 2000; Ichimoto, 2004; Rhee, 2006), I am also aware of different elements of power that pushed and pulled me to the United States.
3. In their study, Piller and Takahashi (2006) illustrate that Japanese women's desire to learn English has been, more or less, promoted by the English language industry and media discourse that created a romanticized notion of the West, implying romance with white men, who "are often associated with sophistication, sensitivity, and refinement, . . . not so different from the ways in which Hollywood starts and Western musicians are represented in the same media" (p. 66).

REFERENCES

Alexander, M. J. (2005). *Pedagogies of Crossing: Meditations on Feminism, Sexual Politics, Memory, and the Sacred*. Durham, NC: Duke University Press.
Alfred, T. (1999). *Peace, Power, Righteousness: An Indigenous Manifesto*. Don Mills, Ontario: Oxford University Press.
Ang, I. (2001). *On Not Speaking Chinese: Living between Asia and the West*. London: Routledge.
Arisaka, Y. (2000). Asian women: invisibility, locations, and claims to philosophy. In N. Zack (Ed.), *Women of Color and Philosophy: A Critical Reader* (pp. 219–223). New York Blackwell.
Asher, N. (2009). Decolonization and education: locating pedagogy and self at the interstices in global times. In R. S. Coloma (Ed.), *Postcolonial Challenges in Education* (pp. 67–77). New York: Peter Lang.
Bai, H., & Scott, C. (2009). Asian philosophies and the primacy of consciousness in epistemology: Implications for education. Unpublished work. Simon Fraser University.
Bannerji, H. (1991). But who speaks for us? Experience and agency in conventional feminist paradigms. In H. Bannerji, L. Carty, K. Dehli, S. Heald, & K. McKenna (Eds.), *Unsettling relations: The university as a site of feminist struggles* (pp. 67–107). Toronto: Women's Press.

Battiste, M., & Henderson, J. Y. (2000). *Protecting Indigenous Knowledge and Heritage: A Global Challenge.* Saskatoon, Saskatchewan: Purich.

Cajete, G. (1994). *Look to the Mountain: An Ecology of Indigenous Education.* Skyland, NC: Kivaki.

Carty, L. (1991). Black women in academia: a statement from the periphery. In H. Bannerji, L. Carty, K. Dehli, S. Heald, & K. McKenna (Eds.), *Unsettling Relations: The University as a Site of Feminist Struggles* (pp. 13–44). Toronto: Women's.

Castellano, M. B. (2000). Updating aboriginal traditions of knowledge. In G. J. S. Dei, B. L. Hall, & D. G. Rosenberg (Eds.), *Indigenous Knowledges in Global Contexts: Multiple Readings of Our World* (pp. 21–36). Toronto: University of Toronto Press.

Collins, P. H. (2000). *Black Feminist Thought: Knowledge, Consciousness, and the Politics of Empowerment.* New York: Routledge.

Dei, G. J. S. (2000). Rethinking the role of Indigenous knowledge in the academy. *International Journal of Inclusive Education, 4*(2), 111–132.

Dei, G. J. S. (2006). Introduction: mapping the terrain—towards a new politics of resistance. In G. J. S. Dei & A. Kempf (Eds.), *Anti-colonialism and Education: The Politics of Resistance* (pp. 1–23). Rotterdam: Sense.

Dei, G. J. S. (2009). Afterword: The anticolonial theory and the question of survival and responsibility. In A. Kempf (Ed.), *Breaching the Colonial Contract: Anti-colonialism in the US and Canada* (pp. 251–257). Dordrecht, The Netherlands: Springer.

Dei, G. J. S., Hall, B., & Goldin Rosenberg, D. (Eds.). (2000). *Indigenous Knowledges in Global Contexts: Multiple Readings of Our World.* Toronto: University of Toronto Press.

Denzin, N. K. (1997). *Interpretive Ethnography: Ethnographic Practices for the 21st Century.* London: Sage.

Dillard, C. B. (2006). When the music changes, so should the dance: Cultural and spiritual considerations in paradigm "proliferation." *International Journal of Qualitative Studies in Education, 19*(1), 59–76.

Dirlik, A. (1997). *The Postcolonial aura: Third World Criticism in the Age of Global Capitalism.* Boulder, CO: Westview.

Duran, J. (2001). *Worlds of Knowing: Global Feminist Epistemologies.* New York & London: Routledge.

Ehara, T. (1992). The internationalization of education. In G. D. Hook & M. A. Weiner (Eds.), *The Internationalization of Japan* (pp. 269–283). London: RoutledgeCurzon.

Elabor-Idemudia, P. (2001). Equity issues in the academy: an Afro-Canadian woman's perspective. *The Journal of Negro Education, 70*(3), 192–203.

Fujii, S. (2006). Environmental concern, attitude toward frugality, and ease of behavior as determinants of pro-environmental behavior intentions. *Journal of Environmental Psychology, 26*(4), 262–268.

Garry, A., & Pearsall, M. (Eds.). (1996). *Women, Knowledge, and Reality: Explorations in Feminist Philosophy.* New York & London: Routledge.

Grande, S. (2004). *Red Pedagogy: Native American Social and Political Thought.* Lanham, MD: Rowman & Littlefield.

Graveline, F. J. (1998). *Circle Works: Transforming Eurocentric Consciousness.* Halifax: Fernwood.

Habu, T. (2000). The irony of globalization: the experience of Japanese women in British higher education. *Higher Education, 39*, 43–66.

Hanh, T. N. (1991). *Peace Is Every Step: The Path of Mindfulness in Everyday Life.* New York: Bantam.

Harding, S. (1998). *Is Science Multicultural? Postcolonialisms, Feminisms, and Epistemologies.* Bloomington, IN: Indiana University Press.

He, M. F. (2002). A narrative inquiry of cross-cultural lives: Lives in Canada. *Journal of Curriculum Studies, 34*(3), 323–342.

Holman Jones, S. (2005). Autoethnography: Making the personal political. In N. K. Denzin & Y. S. Lincoln (Eds.), *The Sage Handbook of Qualitative Research: Third Edition* (pp. 763–791). Thousand Oaks, CA: Sage.

hooks, b. (1984). *Feminist Theory: From Margin to Center.* Boston, MA: South End.

hooks, b. (1994). *Teaching to Transgress: Education as the Practice of Freedom.* New York & London: Routledge.

Hsia, H. -C., & Scanzoni, J. H. (1996). Rethinking the roles of Japanese women. *Journal of Comparative Family Studies, 27*(2), 309–329.

Ichimoto, T. (2004). Ambivalent "selves" in transition: A case study of Japanese women studying in Australian universities. *Journal of Intercultual Studies, 25*(3), 247–269.

Kawano, Y. (2010). Fanon's psychology of the mind, the "yellow" colonizer and the racialized minoritized in Japan. In G. J. S. Dei (Ed.), *Fanon and the Counterinsurgency of Education* (pp. 157–175). Rotterdam, The Netherlands: Sense.

Kim, L. M. (2009). "I was [so] busy fighting racism that I didn't even know I was being oppressed as a woman!": challenges, changes, and empowerment in teaching about women of color. In R. D. Crabtree, D. A. Sapp, & A. C. Licona (Eds.), *Feminist Pedagogy: Looking Back to Move Forward* (pp. 195–208). Baltimore: The Johns Hopkins University Press.

Laenui, P. (2000). Processes of decolonization. In M. Battiste (Ed.), *Reclaiming Indigenous Voice and Vision* (pp. 150–160). Vancouver: UBC.

Linnekin, J. (1992). On the theory and politics of cultural construction in the Pacific. *Oceania, 62*, 249–262.

Lippi-Green, R. (1997). *English with an Accent: Language, Ideology, and Discrimination in the United States*. London: Routledge.

Marchetti, G. (1993). *Romance and the "Yellow Peril": Race, Sex, and Discursive Strategies in Hollywood Fiction*. Berkeley & Los Angeles, CA: University of California Press.

Mayuzumi, K. (2006). The tea ceremony as a decolonizing epistemology: Healing and Japanese women. *Journal of Transformative Education, 4*(1), 8–26.

Mayuzumi, K. (2009). Unfolding possibilities through a decolonizing project: Indigenous knowledges and rural Japanese women. *International Journal of Qualitative Studies in Education, 22*(5), 507–526.

Mayuzumi, K., Motobayashi, K., Nagayama, C., & Takeuchi, M. (2007). Transforming diversity in Canadian higher education: a dialogue of Japanese women graduate students. *Teaching in Higher Education, 12*(5–6), 581–592.

Mignolo, W. D. (2005). *The Idea of Latin America*. Malden, MA: Blackwell.

Millat-e-Mustafa, M. (2000). Towards an understanding of indigenous knowledge. In P. Sillitoe (Ed.), *Indigenous Knowledge Development in Bangladesh: Present and Future* (pp. 27–30). London: Intermediate Technology.

Mohanty, C. T. (2003). *Feminism without Borders: Decolonizing Theory, Practicing Solidarity*. London: Duke University Press.

Nakagawa, Y. (2000). *Education for Awakening: An Eastern Approach to Holistic Education*. Brandon, Vermont: Foundation for Educational Renewal.

Nishitani, K. (1982). *Religion and Nothingness*. Berkeley: University of California Press.

Peshkin, A. (1988). In search of subjectivity—one's own. *Educational Researcher, 17*(7), 17–21.

Piller, I., & Takahashi, K. (2006). A passion for English: desire and the language market. In A. Pavlenko (Ed.), *Bilingual Minds: Emotional Experience, Expression and Representation* (pp. 59–83). Bristol: Multilingual Matters.

Prasso, S. (2005). *The Asian Mystique: Dragon Ladies, Geisha Girls, & Our Fantasies of the Exotic Orient*. New York: Public Affairs.

Purcell, T. W. (1998). Indigenous knowledge and applied anthropology: questions of definition and direction. *Human Organization, 57*(3), 258–272.

Rhee, J. (2006). Re/membering (to) shifting alignments: Korean women's transnational narratives in US higher education. *International Journal of Qualitative Studies in Education, 19*(5), 595–615.

Richardson, L., & St. Pierre, E. A. (2005). Writing: a method of inquiry. In N. K. Denzin & Y. S. Lincoln (Eds.), *The Sage Handbook of Qualitative Research* (3rd ed., pp. 959–978). Thousand Oaks, CA: Sage.

Rizvi, F. (2000). International education and the production of global imagination. In N. C. Burbules & C. A. Torres (Eds.), *Globalization and Education: Critical Perspectives* (pp. 205–225). New York: Routledge.

Said, E. (1979). *Orientalism*. New York: Vintage.

Scheurich, J. J., & Young, M. D. (2002). Coloring epistemology: are our research epistemologies racially biased? In J. J. Scheurich (Ed.), *Anti-Racist Scholarship: an Advocacy* (pp. 51–73). Albany, NY: SUNY.

Semali, L. M., & Kincheloe, J. L. (1999). Introduction: what is indigenous knowledge and why should we study it? In L. M. Semali & J. L. Kincheloe (Eds.), *What Is Indigenous Knowledge? Voices from the Academy* (pp.

3–57). New York & London: Falmer.

Shahjahan, R. A. (2005). Spirituality in the academy: reclaiming from the margins and evoking a transformative way of knowing the world. *International Journal of Qualitative Studies in Education, 18*(6), 685–711.

Shirahama, K., & Inoue, E. M. (2001). Spirituality in nursing from a Japanese perspective. *Holisitc Nursing Practice, 15*(3), 63–72.

Shiva, V. (1997). Western science and its destruction of local knowledge. In M. Rahnema (Ed.), *The Post-Development Reader* (pp. 161–167). London: Zed.

Sidhu, R. K. (2006). *Universities and Globalization: To Market, to Market.* Mahwah, NJ: Lawrence Erlbaum.

Smith, L. T. (1999). *Decolonizing Methodologies: Research and Indigenous Peoples.* London: Zed.

Somé, M. P. (1994). *Of Water and the Spirit: Ritual, Magic, and Initiation in the Life of an African Shaman.* New York: Penguin Compass.

Spivak, G. C. (1993). *Outside in the Teaching Machine.* New York & London: Routledge.

Spry, T. (2001). Performing autoethnography: an embodied methodological praxis. *Qualitative Inquiry, 7*(6), 706–732.

Thiong'o, N. w. (1986). *Decolonizing the Mind: The Politics of Language in African Literature.* Oxford, UK: James Currey.

Tisdell, E. J. (2003). *Exploring Spirituality and Culture in Adult and Higher Education.* San Francisco: Jossey-Bass.

Tisdell, E. J., Tolliver, D., & Villa, S. (2001). Toward a culturally relevant and spiritually grounded theory of teaching for social transformation and transformational learning. Retrieved March 16, 2004, from http://www.edst.educ.ubc.ca/aerc/2001/2001tisdell.htm

Wane, N. N., Deliovsky, K., & Lawson, E. (Eds.). (2002). *Back to the Drawing Board: African-Canadian Feminism.* Toronto, Ontario: Sumach.

Webber, M. (2005). "Don't be so feminist": exploring student resistance to feminist approaches in a Canadian university. *Women's Studies International Forum, 28*, 181–194.

Wong, Y.-L. R. (2002). Reclaiming Chinese women's subjectivities: Indigenizing "social work with women" in China through postcolonial ethnography. *Women's Studies International Forum, 25*(1), 67–77.

Yoshida, A. (2005). Interface of holistic changes in Japanese schools and Waldorf education. In J. P. Miller, S. Karsten, D. Denton, D. Orr, & I. C. Kates (Eds.), *Holistic Learning and Spirituality in Education: Breaking New Ground* (pp. 129–135). Albany, NY: State University of New York Press.

Zhou, Y., Knoke, D., & Sakamoto, I. (2005). Rethinking silence in the classroom: Chinese students' experiences of sharing indigenous knowledges. *International Journal of Inclusive Education, 9*(3), 287–311.

CHAPTER TWENTY-THREE

Revealing the Secular Fence of Knowledge

Towards Reimagining Spiritual Ways of
Knowing and Being in the Academy

RIYAD SHAHJAHAN & KIMBERLY HAVERKOS

WHAT IS A FENCE?

A fence is a structure that directs movement by restricting and preventing passage across a boundary. It both excludes and contains, while simultaneously demarcating space. It is considered a safety and security device for property owners as it prevents trespassers, wanderers, and predators from entering. It also limits the view from both inside and outside. In this chapter, the metaphor of the fence is used to illustrate the construction and maintenance of dominant forms of knowledge production in Western academia. In its quest to maintain control over the production of knowledge, the academy has erected a secular "fence of knowledge" which permits the entry of certain epistemologies and ways of being while leaving others outside the "gates" of the academy.

By the term "academy," we are referring to universities and colleges and not to K-12 schools, because we want to situate our discussion in the context of the "highest" centers of learning located in the West—those spaces where the "fence" is strongly guarded. A secular epistemological vision does not simply insist that religious practice and belief be confined to a space where it cannot threaten political stability or the liberties of "free-thinking" citizens, but it builds on a particular conception of the world ("natural" and "social") and of the problems generated by that world (Asad, 2003, p. 191). Within the academy, the secular fence of knowledge concentrates the effects of a secular epistemology by privileging certain knowledge forms (e.g., empiricism, rationalism, objectivism, reductionism, instrumentalism, anthropocentrism, and humanism). These ideas inform most curricula, research grants, administrative practices, and the overall purpose of higher education (see Caanan & Shumar, 2008; Olssen & Peters, 2005).

In the present-day context, the commodification of knowledge and the colonization of the mind have been accelerated within the academy to serve global capital (Olssen & Peters, 2005). These trends have made it more challenging to represent different ways of knowing in the academy. The knowledge economy has reinforced the secular fence in the academy, which results in the subjugation of spiritual epistemologies. However, the history of the dominance of the secular epistemological vision provides a backdrop to understand the range of challenges in the contemporary context of academia. We argue that this secular epistemological fence perpetuates a domestication project that restricts the place for Indigenous epistemologies that are spiritually grounded. We posit that this fence is neither neutral nor inevitable and has roots in colonial history. With respect to Indigenous epistemologies, Rauna Kuokkanen (2007) asserts the importance of tracing colonial influences in the origins of the academy:

> The academy must recognize its colonial history and acknowledge that its structures perpetuate the practices and discourses of exclusion and foreclosure. In other words, the academy must acknowledge and address its ongoing denial of and studied ignorance about indigenous epistemes. To this end, it will have to examine its own institutional and individual beliefs, biases and assumptions and achieve some understanding of how these developed and became naturalized in the course of history (p. 150).

Through an anti-colonial lens, scholars have begun to interrogate the normalized beliefs, assumptions, and biases prevalent in the academy by historicizing it in colonial relations (Kuokkanen, 2007; Smith, 1999). Such histories of knowledge production are often left untold and do not form part of our dominant histories shared in the academy. Furthermore, secular ideas are used as progressive signifiers in the academy and are thus rarely critically historicized (Jakobsen & Pellegrini, 2008). In this chapter we use an anti-colonial lens (Dei, 2000; Mignolo, 2005; Smith, 1999) to illustrate how history is alive in our contemporary everyday relations in the academy in terms of classroom discourse, scholarships, student learning, and rewards structures. From an anti-colonial lens, history is viewed as a narrative of struggle, where we observe the imposition of and resistance to dominant knowledge systems (Kempf, 2006). From this perspective, the logics of domination are transhistorical and not fixed in the past (Mignolo, 2005).

Writing this chapter is neither an apolitical nor a neutral endeavor for us. I (Riyad) am a South Asian Canadian Muslim, heterosexual, able-bodied male who grew up in different parts of the world. Born in the United Kingdom, I grew up in Kuwait with my parents of Bangladesh origin. Currently, I am a privileged scholar in a Western academy who enjoys the opportunity to speak and be heard. This chapter is part of a broader decolonizing project for me, which foregrounds the question of spiritual ways of being and knowing in the academy by centering spirituality in my own scholarly writings and opening up other spaces where Indigenous knowledges can be discussed and embodied within the higher education context. I (Kimberly) am a White, able-bodied heterosexual female, born and raised inside the borders of the United States. As a science educator in the Midwest, I began to question the narratives that are provided to students, parents, teachers, and administrators about education. I returned to higher education, where, as a doctoral student, I am now learning to challenge the discourses of Eurocentric knowledge production and science. In short, we bring our common/distinct past experiences, different standpoints, positions of privilege/oppression, to writing this chapter. In so doing, we hope to reimagine the challenges and possibilities for Indigenous knowledges in the academy that stem from the secular fence of knowledge.

We structure this chapter into two major parts. Using an anti-colonial lens, in the first part, we begin to uncover the tools of dominance inherent in the European secular epistemological vision, as well as resistances to it, over three corresponding time periods: (1) Greek origins to scientific revolution in the 18th century; (2) 18th-century liberalism to 19th-century colonialism; and (3) 19th- to

21st-century global economy. In the second part of this chapter, we discuss some steps to begin the process of decolonizing the academy by examining the ways in which the secular fence of knowledge metaphor operates and how it can be resisted using spiritual epistemologies. We finally conclude with some seeds of thought.

REVEALING THE SECULAR FENCE OF KNOWLEDGE

In this section, we demonstrate how dominant theories and ideologies emerge within the secular epistemological vision, while at the same time displacing and negating spiritual epistemologies and certain aspects of Indigenous cosmologies. Within this historical account, we also foreground the sites of resistance in which such colonial secular discourses have been contested/contingent or proven not to be absolute given the context.[1] By the term "resistance" we are referring to forms of subversion and opposition (armed/non-violent protest/struggle) against epistemic and material forms of domination and oppression (Jefferess, 2008). We sometimes use the term "resistance" and "struggle" interchangeably to refer to collective movements that work toward reconstituting social relations and/or affirming subjugated knowledges/experiences (Jefferess, 2008). We now turn to the origins of the secular fence of knowledge.[2]

DEMARCATING SECULAR WAYS OF BEING AND KNOWING FROM THE REST

At some point between the lifetime of Homer and that of Plato, a sharp break occurred in Greek epistemology so as to turn it away from a participatory consciousness and ontology of interconnection to the gradual disappearance of spiritual animism (Berman, 1981). Scholars such as Thales, Pherecydes, and, above all, Anaximander, sought to explain the origin of the cosmos in natural rather than supernatural terms (Falk, 2002). Their effort was continued by Pythagoras. This secular epistemology was then developed by later Greek playwrights who constantly ridiculed Greek gods and spiritual traditions. Their reduction of gods to fools led to the end of Greek belief in their religion, which lost its power and its meaning. Finally the Greeks espoused secularism. It was during this classical Greek philosophical period that the secular epistemological vision adopted the idea of relationships based on humanistic explanations rather than a naturalistic explanation which linked nature and life (Smith, 1999). This new secular humanistic vision separated people out from the world around them, and placed humanity on a higher plane, with their superiority attributed to characteristics such as language and reason (Smith, 1999). Socrates, Plato, and Aristotle were the founders of this humanistic tradition. Thus, through the Greek tradition, the demarcation of human beings and human knowledge as different or separate from the natural world was part of a process that undermined the spiritual epistemologies of early societies. However, this process was not without resistance. Spiritual cults, such as the Egyptian-based cult of Isis, rose to prominence in Greece and what is today Italy (Heyob, 1975). Often emerging from and attracting large numbers of followers in the lower classes, these spiritual cults often gained political power, only to lose it again at the hands of the elite through political and legal maneuvering (Heyob, 1975). The Celtic religions in Northern Europe and on the British Isles continued to worship nature in a way that brought humanity and nature together (Thompson, 1996).

During the medieval period, Europeans constructed knowledge through a participatory consciousness (Berman, 1981), where the cosmos "was a place of belonging" and a "member of this cosmos was not an alienated observer of it but a direct participant in its drama" (p. 16). This worldview was drastically altered once the Europeans encountered the Americas. This encounter became significant in the rise of Europe as an economic power and the rise of capitalism soon after the first contact in 1492 (when Columbus was discovered by the Americas!). The year 1492 demarcated a significant history for the rise of secular epistemological vision in Europe, as it was the first time in history where a world-circuit of trade was constructed in which the trade circuits in the Mediterranean, Asia, and Africa were connected to Atlantic trade routes (Blaut, 1993). Within Europe, during this same time period, spiritual ways of knowing tied to women's bodies and alchemists were undermined (Berman, 1981; Federici, 2004).

From the 14th to 16th century, tied to the colonization of the Americas, European thought saw many changes leading to the control of knowledge through a rise in objectivist epistemology (Mignolo, 1995) and the further establishment of secular epistemology. Mignolo (1995) described how the celebration of "the letter" laid the foundation for an objective epistemology that aided in the colonization and exploitation of the Indigenous population in the Americas in the 15th and 16th centuries. This new form of literacy, available to the Renaissance man, was used to develop a power differential based on these systems of representation and communication. Among the European educated elite, there was a need to quickly and accurately portray results, experiences, and observations in order to support their newly "discovered" claims, and the letter became essential in this process. Indigenous oral and pictorial forms of knowledge representation were considered primitive and not useful for systematic knowledge production needed for imperial purpose—they were removed from the space demarcated earlier and placed outside the secular fence of knowledge. As letters, numbers, and language converged to create a language of science, it became a powerful political tool in the conquest, colonization, and capitalistic ventures of the late Renaissance. The languages and epistemologies of the other (i.e., Indigenous) ways of knowing, which included oral traditions and pictorials, were systemically displaced. For example, before Spanish and Portuguese colonialism around the 16th century, the "New" World was named by its Indigenous people—Tawantinsuyu in the Andes, Anáhuac (modern-day Mexico), and Abya-Yala (today's Panama) (Mignolo, 2005). Mignolo (1995) argues that, while there was an almost "universal" desire among Europeans and Indigenous peoples to gain and pass on knowledge, it was the European methods of knowledge dissemination that became *the* way of knowing and filtered what constituted valid knowledge in history, literature, geography, and science.

From then on, the secular epistemological vision permeated and formed the Eurocentric intellectual legacy down to Descartes and Bacon, who represented, in the 17th century, the two poles of epistemology—rationalism and empiricism (Berman, 1981, p. 27). Influenced by the Cartesian idea of mechanism, this period marked the displacement of the centrality of the hermetic principles of interconnectedness, reverence for existence, and symbiotic reciprocity between male and female (Stewart-Harawira, 2005). By the middle of the 17th century, formal and informal colonialism continued on a massive scale in the Americas and around the coasts of Africa and Asia. Through this colonial expansion, the European bourgeoisie bolstered their class privilege. This allowed an emerging capitalist-class community to mobilize state power for its benefit, such that the entire society contributed to the encouragement of colonial adventures and to the preparation of infrastructure such as cities and roads, while the state's police and military power could now be mobilized to force people off the land and into wage work. However, these processes were not unidirectional but also grew in proportion as they faced much peasant resistance from heretical movements within Europe, such as the vegetarian and anti-war Cathars of southern France, the anti-nobility Taborites of Bohemia, and women's leadership in peasant movements (Federici, 2004). But as time went on, ruling class strategy specifically shifted to targeting female community leaders for a "witch hunt," in order to destroy diverse female practices, collective relations, and systems of knowledge that had been the foundation of European women's power and resistance in the medieval period (Federici, 2004). Within this social context, through the scientific revolution, empiricism, and rationalism came together further, first through the works of Newton and Galileo. Through the scientific revolution, the "how" became increasingly important and the "why" increasingly irrelevant (Berman, 1981, p. 28). The rise of this mechanized thinking allowed for the manipulation of both nature and people.

The modern science that was developed in Europe during the 17th century spread in subsequent centuries to the rest of the world and began to occupy a dominant epistemological position (Goonatilake, 1993). European colonial powers relied on "machines as the measure of men" and civilization (Baber, 1996, p. 17). According to dominant colonial discourse, the perceived lack of modern science and technology in other societies represented societal immaturity and a lack of social responsibility. The colonizers adopted the responsibility of "fixing" the situation, which also provided them with the ideological justification for the preservation of empire (Baber, 1996). Colonial production of knowledge included a clash with and a marginalization of the knowledge and belief systems of those who were conquered (Smith, 1999). Essentially, the transition from traditional holism to the rationalist empiricism and Cartesian dualism of modernity also legitimated the negation of Indigenous epistemologies and cosmologies (Stewart-Harawira, 2005, p. 62). However, these forces of the secular epistemology were resisted. For instance, as early as 1777, a Cherokee named Old Tasse commented about Eurocentric thought:

> Much has been said of the want of what you term "Civilization" among the Indians. Many proposals have been made to us to adopt your law, your religion, your manners and customs. We do not see the propriety of such a reformation (cited in Battiste & Henderson, 2000, p. 105).

The rise of an "objective lens" within Eurocentric modern science legitimated Eurocentric ideas of power over others. This was (and continues to be) deeply implicated in the construction of racist and sexist ways of thinking about human beings and the differences between them (Gould, 1981; Shiva, 1989). From the mid-18th century onward, science came to articulate Europe's contacts with the imperial frontier and to be articulated by them (Pratt, 1992). As the only "rational" beings, Western European males became the only legitimate source of knowledge production. Secular epistemologies were immediately gendered and racialized due to the socially constructed dualisms between science/nature; man/woman; civilized/uncivilized; objectivity/subjectivity; rationality/emotionality. The continued progression of the construction of a link between woman/nature and savage/nature through the objective and rational use of science allowed for the continued justification of imperial and colonial oppressions (de Sousa Santos, 2007).

In summary, the secular fence of knowledge first demarcates space by disconnecting human ways of being from the rest of the universe. Interconnected with the greed for material and social capital, it further sets apart a secular way of being by isolating rational, empirical, and literate ways of knowing from other epistemologies in order to construct a certain type of "civilized human-being." Finally, a hierarchy of knowledge was constructed to legitimize this secular way of being and consolidate the suppression of multiple ways of being tied to spiritual epistemologies. We next discuss how the posts of the secular fence of knowledge are set throughout the 18th century.

SETTING THE POSTS: INDIVIDUALISTIC IMPERIALISM AND COLONIZATION OF THE OTHER

The secular epistemological vision that originally derived its humanistic tradition from the Greeks grew more anthropocentric and humanistic through the notion of individualism in classical liberal philosophy of the 18th century (Majid, 2000). In challenging the traditional, social, moral, and philosophical authority of the church, European intellectuals during the 18th century, influenced by Protestant thought, sought to establish a framework for society that avoided the religious conflicts of the previous centuries (DeRoover, 2004). The solution, outlined most notably by philosophers such as John Locke and Immanuel Kant, was to place the religious in the private sphere of life—to clearly separate it from the public realms of politics, science, and philosophy (Carrette & King, 2005, pp. 2–3). Religion, as a result, was demarcated and redefined as individual choice, belief, and private states of mind. Hence, secularism, as we know it today, is a European construct that grew out of a conflicting Christian history. It is also important to note that, "the idea of 'religion' as a universal category of human experience" did not "precede the Enlightenment, but is, instead, an Enlightenment project" (Jakobsen & Pellegrini, 2008, p. 7). In other words, the secular epistemological vision did not lead to disappearance of "religion," but actually defined and narrowed it to forms of institutionalized religion (Baird, 2008, p. 165).

According to DeRoover (2004), the Protestant doctrine remained "the implicit background of the contemporary political theories of liberal toleration in the West." He continues:

> It takes the conceptual schemes of Christian theology—more specifically, its division of the world into a spiritual religious sphere and a temporal political sphere—as though these correspond to the universal structure of human societies. Moreover, secularism suggests that plural societies will fall apart, if they fail to adopt the Protestant norm of the religious and the political (DeRoover, 2004, "A Modern Christian Value" section, para. 7).

As a result of this influence, in the contemporary era, North American society championed the Jeffersonian idea that there should be a separation between church and state. In short, by restricting religion to the private sphere, the secular epistemological vision constructs religion as a private enterprise which should not influence politics or the public space. Furthermore, the secular fence masks the origination of secularism in Eurocentric and Christian "religious particularities" and passes it "as a universal secular" idea (p. 3). Furthermore, this idea was then imposed or internalized throughout the colonial world as a universal idea (Keddie, 2003).

Displacing the grasp of Christianity, but appropriating some of its assumptions, the secular epistemological vision took up and nurtured a new understanding of human beings through the philosophy of human individualism. Locke's rationalism provided this basis. Individuals were now endowed with natural rights that extended to the ownership of private property and were propelled to maximize their self-interest and enter into all sorts of contracts (Stewart-Harawira, 2005). This ontology of individualism reconfigured human morality to reform it into a new social order and further excluded traditional religious commitments by rendering them as irrational (Majid, 2000, p. 2). This trend toward the privatization of the self in Europe was in stark contrast with the more communal social structures evident in the majority of societies globally (Green, 2007; Some, 1994).

This philosophy of individualism was further bolstered through its connections with capitalism and imperialism. During the 18th century, the global economy was constructed around Enlightenment notions of luxury, consumption, and commercial society. David Hume, a Scottish Enlightenment philosopher, advocated for a human ontology based on the need for consumption (Stewart-Harawira, 2005). He argued that the social benefits of consumption were the driving force behind the development of the rational self. Luxury, in this new materialistic ontology, was considered as a tool to accumulation and a moral discourse that would civilize people, which would in turn transform them from being passion-driven to needs-driven. In short, Hume's ideas influenced the capitalist need for territorial expansion, which resulted in the pillaging and stealing of Indigenous people's lands and destruction of their social and political structures (Stewart-Harawira, 2005).

It is important to note that Enlightenment philosophers were involved in colonial projects which had significant influences on their theories about human nature, freedom, and social contracts. For instance, Hume's ideas were a product of a time in which Europe was changing from agricultural states to nation states with imperial ambitions (Morton, 2002). An important aspect of Hume's era was the transatlantic slave trade. Similarly, Locke invested a large sum in the Royal African Company, an enterprise specifically devoted to trading in slaves for sale to the plantations in the Americas (Bernal, 1993). Furthermore, "the slave trade and slavery were the economic basis for the French revolution, as all the industries in France during this period had their origin in goods and or commodities destined either for the coast of Guinea or for the Americas" (Said James, cited in Blaut, 1993, p. 204). These examples demonstrate that the secular epistemological vision was a significant product of an imperial project that involved the dehumanization and enslavement of the "other," and the consolidation of material wealth and power. This is not to say that this dehumanization process was without resistance. The slave revolution in Haiti resulted in the only nation-state that was born out of a slave revolt (Young, 2001), and slave resistances also occurred in the Americas—from learning to read and write, performing banned Indigenous ritual celebrations, from non-compliance to escape from slavery, were some ways that subversion/opposition against the imperial logic occurred (Collins, 2003). In these instances, we see how alternative ways of knowing and being struggled against being corralled by the secular fence of knowledge.

The secular epistemological vision, already endowed with capitalist and imperial components, was further fuelled in its materialistic pursuits through the concept of sovereignty, heavily influenced by British political theorists such as Thomas Hobbes, whose absolutist notions were expressed in Western political thought. Hobbes believed that, we, as human beings, were naturally self-absorbed and had an innate desire for self-preservation. Based on this belief, Hobbes argued that human beings needed to form social contracts, or else we would kill each other (Brannigan, 2004). Furthermore, as part of this change, there was an increase in the secularization of political theory, which now put a stronger emphasis on the idea that a human being's existence had neither ultimate objectives nor absolute goals—his/her role was interpreted as that which was in the highest interest of the state (Masseri, 1994). From the 18th century onward, the strength and wealth of the state thus became the driving force for all human activity. People were now conceived of as resources to be used to ensure the development and viability of the state (Stewart-Harawira, 2005, p. 71). While expansion through colonization by countries such as Spain, Portugal, and Britain had begun two centuries earlier, the doctrine of absolute sovereignty became a rationalist justification for further expansionist imperialism (Stewart-Harawira, 2005, p. 73). With this growing hegemony of materialistic philosophies, ethics became synonymous with benefit and enjoyment, and the purpose of life was to find this benefit and enjoyment as well as to increase production and profit. Ethics began to be derived from utilitarian philosophies based on scientific laws and mathematical calculations of utility (Masseri, 1994).

In summary, the posts of the secular fence of knowledge were set throughout the 18th century through the tenets of anthropocentric "possessive individualism," state sovereignty, and the logic of "private property" (McClintock, 1995, p. 23). Furthermore, the secular fence of knowledge constructs the boundaries of "religion" and claims that the ideology of secularism is "in fact, universal and fully separate from Christianity" (Jakobsen & Pellegrini, 2008, p. 3). In the following section, we demonstrate how the posts of secular fence are further solidified throughout the 19th to the 21st century.

CEMENTING THE POSTS INTO PLACE: THE 19TH TO THE 21ST CENTURY

Critical scholars have pointed to how the secular epistemological vision continued to invade and subjugate the world in the 19th and 20th centuries through the powers of colonialism, the concept of nation-state, "developmental" initiatives, capitalism, and a new form of imperialism—globalization (de Sousa Santos, 2007; Shiva, 1989; Stewart-Harawira, 2005). Colonial racialized and gendered oppressions were further bolstered through the scientific discoveries of the 19th century.

In the late 19th century, a transnationalist elite network emerged, committed to economic liberal ideas and imperialist aspirations that were rationalized by Darwinist ideologies (Stewart-Harawira, 2005, pp. 74–75). United States manifest destiny also spread their economic agenda of market capitalism and political superiority across the globe. Furthermore, during the 19th and 20th centuries, economic liberalism became the driving force behind the race for possession of the remaining lands and resources of the world. This race was coupled with the re-emergence of discourses that recast Indigenous peoples as naïve and dependent, which legitimated their role as the "wards of the imperial powers" (Stewart-Harawira, 2005, p. 75). Furthermore, philanthropy linked with industrial development created and constructed human commodities as workers in a new division of labor which was informed by ideologies of civilization and Christianity (Stewart-Harawira, 2005).

Throughout the expansionist period of imperialism, securing access to native-owned land for development by settler colonies and for the establishment of capitalism was one of the strongest agendas of colonizing governments (Stewart-Harawira, 2005). The primary goal of native policy in colonized territories and the primary agenda in provision of colonial education for natives was the acquisition of land and labor as resources to be exploited for the expansion of capitalism. The colonization of the native minds and the disciplining of populations were integral to the success of this mission. Next to genocide and assimilation, the undermining of the ontologies and cosmologies of the natives was the most important strategy of the first wave of colonization. Colonial violence includes an epistemic aspect, specifically an attack on the culture, ideas, and value systems of the colonized peoples (Nandy, 1991; wa Thiongo, 1986). This colonial violence can be seen with respect to spiritual traditions not only in the context of White settler societies such as Canada, United States, Australia, and New Zealand, but also in other colonized regions of the world such as Africa, India, Asia, and Latin America (see Baber, 1996; Donaldson & Pui-Lan, 2002; Mayuzumi, 2009). Many colonial and racist beliefs created the need to abolish spiritual teachings in North America and around the world (see Grande, 2004; Stewart-Harawira, 2005). Many of these bans and conversions took place because Indigenous epistemologies were considered weapons of resistance that led to collective gathering in efforts to dismantle colonial authority. However, the banning of Indigenous spiritual traditions and the imposition of Western spirituality were resisted by the colonized throughout the world. For instance, Christian penetration linked to imperial expansion provoked anti-Christian resistance as in the Maji Maji rebellion in East Africa (1905–1907), the Boxer Uprising, and Islamic revivals in Malaya, Dutch East Indies, India, and Algeria (Bush, 2006).

The idea of developing a secular nation-state, a product of the secular epistemological vision, was practiced by the colonizers and their native intellectuals throughout the world (Keddie, 2003), which resulted in the displacement of many different spiritual ontologies and epistemologies. Furthermore, as mentioned earlier, colonial Christian missionaries played an important role in the spiritual conversion and displacement of native spiritual traditions in Africa, Asia, and the Americas (see Battiste & Henderson, 2000; Donaldson & Pui-Lan, 2002; Mazama, 2002). The institutionalization of the nation-state and the spread of "developmental" initiatives from North to South continued the imperialistic violence in the 20th century. These two projects perpetuated epistemic aggression against other cultures that shared the communal traditions of kinship and honor (Majid, 2000). For instance, informed by a spiritual epistemology, Mohandas K. Gandhi resisted the zeal of the secular epistemological vision by advocating for a spiritualized self-determination of the people in India. He argued that the modernist project of development would undermine communal and spiritual ways of being and lead to the exploitation and suffering of the working class (Gandhi, 1990).

Throughout the mid-20th century and onward, development projects and initiatives, based on a materialistic economic paradigm and the idea of progress (Mehmet, 1999), were used around the globe to "develop" and bring "progress" by preaching the values of the secular epistemological vision, while at the same time undermining Indigenous ways of being and knowing based on spiritual traditions (Shiva, 1989; Stewart-Harawira, 2005). Based on Eurocentrism, the earlier rhetoric of "savage" and "primitive" of the earlier colonial era, has been replaced in the late 20th century by new signifiers such as "underdeveloped" and "backward." But more importantly, developmentalism, based on the ideals of economic progress, saw spiritual ways of knowing and being as obstacles that required cultural transformation or eradication (Stewart-Harawira, 2005). However, these discourses of developmentalism and its associated projects have been contested and resisted by Indigenous peoples and the colonized around the globe. For instance, Sami women played a significant role in the resistance to the building of the hydroelectric dam in Northern Norway during the early 1970s and 1980s, and continue to work on projects of revitalization of Sami language and cultural heritage (Green, 2007).

At the end of the 20th century, new secular philosophies have been born: neoliberalism and the knowledge economy. This neoliberal philosophy, a version of neo-classical economics, has become effective and dominant throughout the globe through the sponsorship of super-power Western nation-states (Olssen & Peters, 2005). Carrying similar ideas of liberalism from the 18th century, neoliberalism continues to promote the worldview of a "self-interested individual." Unlike liberalism, the state has a positive function in the role of market. As a result, there has been an increase in the forces of standardization, accountability, and privatization in public services throughout the globe. Based on global trade infrastructures built through the World Trade Organization (WTO), new trade initiatives have been instituted, such as General Agreement of Trade in Goods (GATT), General Agreement of Trade in Services (GATS), and Trade Related Intellectual Property Rights (TRIPS), to liberalize trade across borders and to add new commodities in the global market (Spring, 2009).

Moving away from a goods and services economy and facilitated by GATS and TRIPS, the world has also entered a new economy entitled the "knowledge economy" (Olssen & Peters, 2005; Spring, 2009; Stewart-Harawira, 2005). This is the most significant addition in the secular epistemological vision in the 21st century—knowledge has been turned into capital. As a result of this secular epistemological vision, the world economy has now entered a "global skills race" or "knowledge wars" (Brown, Lauder, & Ashton, 2008, p. 4), where knowledge has been turned from a public enterprise to a private good which allows the owners of intellectual property to reap the profit of creating new knowledge. According to Stewart-Harawira (2005), "Underpinning this [secular idea] is a mixture of Hegelian utilitarian rationalism that allocates ownership by viewing ideas as an extension of their creator and Lockean ideologies that allocate ownership on the basis of transformation of an object through the action of labor upon it" (p. 214).

Transnational corporations are major benefactors of this economy, whereby intellectual property rights have been extended from inanimate goods to include animate matter such as genes, microorganisms, plants, and animals (de Sousa Santos, 2007). Unlike previous commodities that were viewed to be finite, knowledge is considered to be an exponentially growing product that can be exchanged in the market (Olssen & Peters, 2005). In this secular vision, schools and universities are being turned into new plantation systems to harvest, produce, and utilize intellectual labor and produce intellectual products (Stewart-Harawira, 2005). To this end, universities have become the new engines of the economy (Olssen & Peters, 2005). Furthermore, the knowledge economy has had drastic effects on minoritized people and their traditional knowledge systems, including Indigenous peoples around the world as they experience biopiracy and intellectual theft (Stewart-Harawira, 2005).

In short, today, through neoliberalism and the knowledge economy, the hegemony of the secular epistemological vision continues to be bolstered. In the process, living organisms from the molecular level to human beings, from spiritual ways of knowing to sacred spaces, are either turned into a utility to be invaded, re-packaged, and sold in the free market, or devalued and made extinct (Carrette & King, 2005). However, this packaging of the sacred is being resisted. Many court cases and collective struggles have been initiated by Indigenous peoples to resist the commodification of their scared healing sites (Battiste & Henderson, 2000). For instance, in the Oka struggle in 1990, the Mohawks in Canada fought to maintain sacred burial grounds that were being claimed for a golf course (Smith & Ward, 2000). By disconnecting Indigenous spiritual practices from their land bases, dominant society continues to undermine Indigenous peoples' claim to the protection of the land base as an integral part of their survival as Indigenous peoples (Smith, 2005). Indigenous peoples around the globe insist that their enjoyment of spiritual and cultural integrity take priority over commercial and recreational use of wildlife by others (Smith, 2005). Due to the social-materialistic forces that gave rise to the secular epistemological vision in the first place, such as Eurocentrism, imperialism, sexism, and racism, these same forces continue to nurture the spread of the secular epistemological vision, while undermining others' ways of knowing and being in the world.

Numerous minoritized groups around the globe have resisted the colonization of their lives and knowledges. Notable examples include the Zapatista struggle against neoliberal policies in Mexico, the U'wa people's legal challenge to American oil companies in Colombia, the Innus struggle against mineral companies in Canada, and the Mirrar people's resistance toward Jabiluka uranium mine in Australia (Banerjee, 2000; de Sousa Santos, 2007; Smith & Ward, 2000). It is important to remember that these fights for land rights are often also struggles over symbols and meaning which are rooted in spirituality. Beyond these spiritual struggles for land, Walter Mignolo (2005), for instance, reminds us how Afro-Andeans and Indigenous groups are resisting the secular epistemological vision by reappropriating and redefining themselves through language, the power of naming, and the creation of "an-other" way of thinking and being.

In summary, from the 19th century to the present day, the secular fence of knowledge has increasingly directed the control of knowing, meaning, and being toward human utility and material profit. However, this fence is not inevitable but continues to face deconstruction and spiritual resistance. We explore these topics next.

TOWARD UNDERMINING THE SECULAR FENCE: RECLAIMING SPIRITUAL EPISTEMOLOGIES

The most radical struggles in the 21st century will take place on the battlefield of knowledge and reasoning (Mignolo, 2005, p. 100).

Walter Mignolo eloquently summarizes the topic of this chapter. Our historical testimony articulates how the control of meaning (i.e., knowing) informs and is shaped by the control of being (way of being) which are both intertwined with the question of the political economy. Through our historical sections, we witnessed how systematically, the secular epistemological vision through demarcating human beings from the rest of the universe, separates people from the land, from one another, and from their spirit, and are intertwined with historical realities within social, economic, and political forces that continue with us today. We next employ the fence as a strategic metaphor to help us visualize how imposition and domination occur in knowledge production that continues with us today.

STRATEGIES OF EXCLUSION AND MARGINALIZATION OF SPIRITUAL EPISTEMOLOGIES

In this section, we will argue that the secular fence of knowledge is informed by and perpetuates a domestication project on Indigenous ways of knowing and being. We refer to domestication as the "process of hereditary reorganization of" non-humans "into new forms according to human interests," which also entails "a form of control whose subject" undergoes "profound behavorial" and "morphological changes" (Anderson, 2008, p. 477). Our intention here is to think through the lens of a fence and understand it as an agent of domestication, civility, and a boundary marker in order to highlight the trends and tensions within secular knowledge production.

On a structural level, the secular fence of knowledge operates by preventing other ways of knowing from entering the consigned spaces of valid knowledge. In the secular epistemological vision, rationality, anthropocentrism, and empiricism are lauded over many other ways of knowing (e.g., emotions, intuition, metaphysical, and ancestral connections). Various forms of marginalization have taken root in the knowledge production driven by the secular epistemological vision through the construction of epistemological yardsticks used to validate certain ways of knowing, while rendering other ways of knowing invisible. For example, in the Renaissance period, the letter and number became dominant epistemological tools to systematize knowledge for an imperial project used then to undermine oral traditions and visual ways of knowing. Here the fence of knowledge operates like a fence for domesticated livestock that prevents the "wild" from harming or eating the "tamed" animals used for human consumption.

By attributing particular concepts of "animality" (animals are nothing more than their biology and instincts) (Anderson, 2008, p. 479) to particular ways of knowing (interconnected with particular groups), certain knowledges were considered non-human and bestial. This notion of "animality" is a historical product of Western human societies, where classical ideas about animal differences and human uniqueness were historically constructed and connected with notions of culture and nature and more precisely, "cultivating the wild" (Anderson, 2008, p. 487). In this secular vision, undomesticated plants were "weeds," nondomesticated animals were "wild," and non-Western Indigenous peoples were "savage" as they remained undomesticated (Ibid., p. 489). Similarly, the secular epistemological vision, informed by this animality narrative, uses such a fence to demarcate what is "tamed" and "wild" knowledge. It functions to separate tamed/civilized epistemologies from "wild" knowledge such as spiritual/Indigenous epistemologies. The dominance of the secular fence of knowledge has been made possible "because of its power in the subalternization of knowledge located outside the parameters of modern conceptions of reason and rationality" (Mignolo, 2000, p. 67). The fence is erected so that knowledge systems are not allowed to coexist, that is, the tamed and wild knowledges should not mix due to a fear that the tamed knowledge systems, which are considered valuable, will be consumed by the wild or be lost.

As our historical testimony reflects, the practice of refining knowledge systems and life forms (e.g., non-humans and people) was glorified by the secular fence as a marker for a "civilized" human being. Embedded within this domesticating process is a set of ideas which includes "control . . . and 'improvement' of wildness (into service and products)" (Anderson, 2008, p. 487). It also "entailed intrusive interventions in the circumstances of other life-forms" and groups of people where their "'wildness' is brought into a fold" (Anderson, 2008, p. 493). For instance, many Indigenous peoples and colonized peoples around the world were herded to missionary schools where their behavioral futures were strictly regulated (Anderson, 2008; Grande, 2004; Smith, 1999). The idea was to selectively "breed" secular ways of being for material exploitation and profit. Similarly today, the academy has become a predominant space for herding and selectively breeding the elite and future workers for the global economy (Spring, 2009).

Historically, the secular epistemological vision has facilitated the hierarchization and stratification of groups of people through creating binaristic hierarchies of knowledge, such as rational/irrational, text/oral traditions, and empirical/intuition. Wild knowledges are considered those that are supernatural and spiritually based. By determining who and what knowledge is a "trespasser," the secular epistemological vision limits and directs the movement of capital, materials, knowledges, and bodies. Through such knowledge validation processes, the secular fence isolates and selectively reproduces a secular way of being that is "disembodied, universal, and mobile" (Berg, 2004, p. 556).

Tied to the domestication project, our historical narrative of the secular epistemological vision also highlights how certain secular colonial ways of knowing have fenced in the lands and bodies of others. For instance, during the expansionist period of imperialism, as native-owned land was secured, the Indigenous populations' bodies and minds were colonized and their spiritual teachings displaced. Furthermore, in a physical sense, English land was being fenced in through enclosure processes of the commons in a move to privatize land (Wordie, 1983). The compartmentalization of material space ran parallel to the beginnings of secular fencing in/out knowledge. As a European construction, fences were imposed on physical land, unlike Indigenous demarcation strategies that used objects of nature to demarcate land and were a means to construct land-based identities and reciprocal connections with nature. This artificial secular fence of knowledge is continually imposed on people's land, bodies, and minds, with the power to dispossess them of their spiritual identities and knowledge systems.

Beyond the domestication narrative, the secular fence of knowledge nurtures the feeling of satisfaction, security, and privacy for those who own the fence as it limits trespassers from entering or challenging the status quo. Historically, this sense of satisfaction and security among colonizers was perpetuated through the discourses of developmentalism, missionary zeal, and secular salvation via scientism. The fence acts as a *do not enter* sign for trespassers, unless they have permission to do so, lest they face certain consequences. Throughout our historical account, we demonstrated how certain ways of knowing become the gates through which to filter out certain ways of being (e.g., women,

Indigenous peoples, peasants, non-Christians, and non-White bodies), by the secular fence of knowledge through the discourse of a "civilized human being." These minoritized bodies may only enter if they act and assimilate the discourses of secular salvation. Similarly, this "do not enter sign" is experienced in the contemporary academy, with regards to spiritual epistemologies, as Dillard, Abdur-Rashid, & Tyson (2000) aptly point out:

> Given the reward structure and cultural milieu of the academy, spiritually-minded academicians have often received the implicit message to hang their spirituality outside the doors of the university and to pick it up again (if they are still inclined to do so) on the way out (p. 449).

A fence is a display and a means of protection of wealth that is seductive to those outside of the fence. It reinforces the feeling of ownership and validation among those who own the secular dominant discourses and feel protected by this fence of knowledge.

The presence of a fence is not only physically experienced but can become normalized into belief systems to the extent that its presence is forgotten. In other words, a secular fence of knowledge operates as an invisible boundary marker that "depersonalizes[s] power," perpetuates "implicit or explicit norms," and marks boundaries which are "visible or invisible, physical or symbolic" (Newman & Paasi, 1998, p. 194). In this sense, the physical secular fence is invisible until it is transgressed, at which point its physical and symbolic effects can be measured. For instance, while minoritized students and faculty are encouraged to bring different ways of knowing into the academy they continue to face material repercussions when they transgress the secular fence of knowledge during tenure evaluations, publication processes, and their dissertation process. Secular colonial schooling disciplines our minds to uncritically accept these fences of knowledge, in turn enclosing ourselves in these fences and limiting our views and ways of being in the world. The secular fence of knowledge is thus used to cage those of us whose minds have been culturally assimilated into secular discourse via the production of native intellectuals. As Jakobsen and Pellegrini (2008) state: "Secularism with its promise of universal reason is widely hailed by both the right and the left as the most powerful protection from the dangers of fundamentalism" (p. 2). We, in the academy, rarely question how these secular ideals are an incarnation of Eurocentrism, particularly ideas within the Protestant worldview, that is fundamentally tied to present day free market ideologies. For instance, we rarely question how the "secular calendar remains tied to Christianity" (Jakobsen & Pellegrini, 2008, p. 3).

From a social perspective, dominant secular discourses distort the organic nature of the world, and our functions and roles as human beings. For instance, in the 18th and 19th centuries, as a possessive individualism was being privileged, a moral discourse emerged that considered transforming human beings from being passion-driven toward needs-driven. This transformation was essential for the development of the rational self, while liberatory for some, was at the expense of other ways of being. In contemporary times, the secular fence of knowledge confines our ways of being and knowing to utilitarian notions of neoliberal subjectivity. As David Hume imagined it, people are conceptualized in this view as individual beings that are only connected to their own desires and are predominantly subject to the whims to the nation-state, and more recently to transnational capital. For instance, middle-class youth entering higher education are currently attempting to "'colonize' their futures within the neoliberal order" and buy into the competition for "'psychological capital' necessary for successful enterprise" (Demerath & Lynch, 2008, p. 189). Similarly, faculty in the academy are increasingly pressured and seduced into the lure of transnational capital in terms of research agendas, branding themselves and their institutions, and teaching for profit (Caanan & Shumar, 2008; Giroux, 2002).

Finally, this fence of knowledge was informed by and sustained through its interconnection with capital. In other words, the secular fence of knowledge can be seen "as the product of both a political economy and a cultural politics of knowledge production" that were intimately interconnected (Berg, 2004, p. 556). To this end, we are reminded of Kim's brothers' experiences of working for a fence construction company. Forty to fifty hours a week they constructed fences, bounding property lines and setting up gates in the places the property owners wanted. They also repaired fences that had weakened—whether the wood had rotted, the nails had rusted, a gate had broken, or an animal had dug beneath the fence. Kim's brothers' experiences highlight for us how the maintenance of a secular fence similarly takes a lot of labor and material effort to hold its ground. Similarly, today the global knowledge economy and transnational corporations maintain and materially support the secular fence of knowledge. However, the resistances to this fence are numerous. In the following section, we discuss the question of resistance and the role of spiritual epistemologies in the academy.

STRATEGIES OF RESISTANCE AND ITS RELEVANCE FOR THE ACADEMY TODAY

"There is a crack in everything. That's how the light gets in" (Leonard Cohen, cited in Luke, in press)

The secular fence of knowledge does not remain impenetrable, nor is it monolithic. As Anderson (2008) reminds us, just like some species, such as gazelles, that fled from human efforts to confine them during the domestication process, people find that the secular fence of knowledge continues to be full of cracks. Throughout history, as we have demonstrated, this fence has been challenged from its inception (Cooper & Stoler, 1997; Mignolo, 1995; wa Thiongo, 1986). Colonial agents often had conflicting visions of the role of Western culture in colonial societies: some wished to preserve tradition, others to modernize (Bush, 2006). Imperial languages also stimulated cultural resistance in revivals of Indigenous languages and the creation of Creole languages. Such resistance also embraced the subversion of dominant cultural codes through mimicry that utilizes the tools of the dominant, in non-standard forms (Bush, 2006, p. 133). For instance, in the contemporary context, Indigenous communities are mobilizing their self-determination struggles globally through the use of internet, film, video, and other forms of expressive media (Smith & Ward, 2000).

Historically, "trespassers" such as women, people of color, and Indigenous peoples have challenged these boundaries and made a concerted effort to undermine them using both top-down and bottom-up approaches. Through these efforts, "tunnels" have been dug to weaken the ground upon which a fence stands, for example, by integrating oral traditions, narrative, and subjectivity into curricula and scholarship. As Smith (1999) points out, testimonies, storytelling, remembering, and celebrating survival (as opposed to demise) are ways that Indigenous knowledges can aid in recovery and healing of marginalized identities and communities. Spiritual epistemologies offer a site through which we can decolonize the academy by offering a means to climb over the fence. For instance, Brayboy, Castagno, and Maughan (2008), based on ethnographic data, describe how two Indigenous students use secular colonial tools such as Ivy League credentials and negotiation and research skills for the survival and self-determination of their tribal communities. Nevertheless, what allowed these students to persist so that they can give back to the community and challenge the neoliberal forces, were their Indigenous epistemologies of reciprocity and responsibility. As Brayboy, Castagno, and Maughan. (2008) state: "At the heart of Indigenous epistemologies are notions of community and its concomitant survival," where "the survival of the community is more important than any individual" (p. 175).

To undermine and dismantle this fence, different ways of knowing need to be incorporated, which are intimately connected with multiple ways of being. There is a sharp disconnection between how spiritual ways of knowing are learned in their communities and the learning models used in colonial university classrooms. For instance, Andrea Smith shares how within her Cherokee community, an elder said, "If you want to learn, be quiet and pay attention. Only through being part of the community over a period of time and developing trust does the knowledge come to you—very slowly" (Smith, 2005, p. 134). However, we can begin this incorporation by building relationships. Indigenous epistemologies will be centered if we start reclaiming interconnected subjectivities, that is, we are not individualistic social beings, but spiritual beings who are interconnected with others, including non–human beings.

Incorporating spiritual epistemologies is about slowing down, performing rituals, and reconceptualizing and resisting secular notions of time (Some, 1993) that increasingly strip people of their spiritual interconnectedness and instead align their spirits with the functions of the global economy. For many Indigenous peoples, and the colonized around the world, spiritual ways of knowing are central to healing, reclaiming ontologies of political governance, and maintaining connections with their ancestors and their land (Grande, 2004; Stewart-Harawira, 2005). Before colonization, in many regions of the world, women were at the forefront of spiritual practices. Through the subjugation of spiritual epistemologies, we also see the subjugation of women's role in knowledge production and social structures (see Green, 2007). Spiritual epistemologies offer alternative models of being in the world (Stewart-Harawira, 2005).

We need to return the world, not to a naïve place, but to a more holistic "reintegration of that which was 'rent by objectivist proclivities'" (Stewart-Harawira, 2005, p. 49). We would argue that Indigenous philosophies grounded in spiritual realities need to be recognized as valid knowledge forms, as they serve as practical knowledge forms that are needed for the preservation, healing, and agency of colonized peoples along the lines of race, gender, class, sexuality, and ability, in terms of students, faculty, administrators, and general staff. Andrea Smith has reminded us how the negation of the body as sacred being had led to internalized self-hatred among minoritized bodies which, in turn, causes a belief that sexual and other types of violence are warranted within the community (Smith, 2005). Indigenous epistemologies will only be incorporated as we center the questions of relevance and reciprocity (i.e., resources, recruitment, and retention of diverse bodies who embody different ways of being) and institute policy, programs and practices that are informed by spiritual epistemologies in the academy (Pidgeon, 2010).

The introduction of Indigenous epistemologies is about understanding and interrogating the various ontologies that shape the knowledge systems that we assimilate, transmit, or validate in universities and colleges. It is fundamentally asking the question of what is higher education for and whom does it serve. It helps us move beyond secular human capital models of education (Spring, 2009), where knowledge and human learning is seen as tools of material capital and profit. They also help us interrogate the kinds of secular practices we have in the world, for example, anthropocentrism and the commodification of knowledge and diverse modes of being. Spiritual epistemologies grounded in Indigenous knowledges are important for reminding us about multiple ways of knowing that are connected to land, ancestors, and metaphysical realities, and the values of reciprocity, community, and connection. In other words, it is about legitimizing ways of knowing that include intuition, emotion, oral traditions, language systems, body, and the interconnection of human and non-human, seen and unseen spirit. These knowledge systems will help us in deconstruction, subversion, and transformation.

Spiritual epistemologies remind us that these material relations are informed by a set of epistemologies that have constructed these fences of knowledge which, while imaginary, also have material power, but are also contingent on being circulated and narrated in our everyday practices. During a time when the dominance of English language continues, we are also witnessing the disappearance of Indigenous languages throughout the world. The lack of protection for minority languages continues as we fail to use them in an instructional setting (Spring, 2009, p. 193). Indigenous epistemologies offer us a vital resource to resist the standardization of knowledge and monocultures of the mind.

BUILDING CONNECTIONS: FINAL SEEDS OF THOUGHTS

In summary, spiritual epistemologies, not reliant on building fences, but instead on building connections across diversity, act as a reminder of how the non-material world and material world are interconnected, and it is this connecting thread, not fence building, that should be at the center of working toward a just global order. As Stewart-Harawira (2005) states:

> [W]ithout a fuller understanding of the interrelationships between the material and spiritual worlds and between the human and ecological spheres, and without an embedding of these understandings at the heart of our socio-politico-economic structures, efforts at just models of governance are doomed to failure. The development of a just political and economic framework for global well-being involves matching the outward exploration of existence with an inward exploration of meaning of being, of the nature of being human and of the purpose of existence. . . . It involves coming to terms with the spiritual reality of our collective existence (p. 252).

Extending from the works of Mignolo (2005) and Stewart-Harawira (2005) we would contend that centering spiritual epistemologies is about "delinking," thinking otherwise as a necessary and possible process which can only occur through the creation of an institution of higher education that implements unity through diverse ways of knowing and being that can conflict and coexist at the same time. We are not advocating for replacing the secular fence of knowledge with a spiritual one. Instead, we are suggesting that there should be equity in knowledge production, and to this end, the hegemonic and universal role of secular discourses needs to be questioned. We need to ask: what world does the secular fence of knowledge imagine? What ways of being does it construct and breed? What kind of universalism does it put in place? And what are alternative ways of being? (See Jakobsen & Pellegrini, 2008.) Centering spiritual epistemologies is about making connections across the fences of knowledge, so that marginalized communities have the epistemic rights and the ability to use Western and Indigenous cosmologies to free themselves from coloniality and "lead to a pluricultural state with more than one valid cosmology" (Mignolo, 2005, p. 120). To this end, spiritual epistemologies are necessary for the survival, growth, and nurturance of multiple ways of being, but more importantly for revealing the secular fence of knowledge that needs to be dismantled. Spiritual epistemologies offer us the cracks in the secular fence of knowledge so that multiple ways of being can enter and thrive in the academy.

Notes

1. Of note, we had a difficult time documenting sites of resistance to these colonial secular forms of knowledge in the periods before the 19th century, as the literature mostly focused on the questions of resistance after this period. This also highlights how an oppressive consciousness pervades the literature, and the question of agency in colonial knowledge production received very little attention.
2. Our intention is not to search for ultimate origins. We are aware that history is partly constituted in the present by our interpretations of past events (Anderson, 2008).

REFERENCES

Anderson, K. (2008). A walk on the wild: A critical geography of domestication. In H. Bauder & S. Engel-di Mauro (Eds.), *Critical Geographies: A Collection of Readings* (pp. 476–506). Kelowna: Praxis.

Asad, T. (2003). *Formations of the Secular: Christianity, Islam, Modernity*. Stanford: Stanford University Press.

Baber, Z. (1996). *The Science of Empire: Scientific Knowledge, Civilization and Colonial Rule in India*. Albany: State University of New York Press.

Baird, R. (2008). Late secularism. In J. Jakobsen & A. Pellegrini (Eds.), *Secularisms* (pp. 162–177). Durham: Duke University Press.

Banerjee, S. B. (2000). Whose land is it anyway? National interest, indigenous stakeholders and colonial discourses: The case of the Jabiluka uranium mine. *Organization & Environment, 13* (1), 3–38.

Battiste, M., & Henderson, J. (2000). *Protecting Indigenous Knowledge and Heritage: A Global Challenge*. Saskatoon: Purich.

Berg, L. D., (2004). Scaling knowledge: Towards a critical geography of critical geographies. *Geoforum* 35, 553–558.

Berman, M. (1981). *The Reenchantment of the World*. Ithaca: Cornell University Press.

Bernal, M. (1993). Black Athena: Hostilities to Egypt in the eighteenth century. In S. Harding (Ed.), *The "Racial" Economy of Science: Toward a Democratic Future* (pp. 47–63). Bloomington: Indiana University Press.

Blaut, J. M. (1993). *The Colonizer's Model of the World: Geographical Diffusionism and Eurocentric History*. New York: Guilford.

Brannigan, M. C. (2004). *Ethics Across Cultures*. New York: McGraw-Hill.

Brayboy, B., Castagno, A., & Maughan, E. (2008). Indigenous epistemologies and the neoliberal view of higher education. In J. Canaan & W. Shumar (Eds.), *Structure and Agency in the Neoliberal University* (pp. 172–192). New York: Routledge.

Brown, P., Lauder, H., & Ashton, D. (2008). *Education, Globalization and the Knowledge Economy*. London: Teaching and Learning Research Programme.

Bush, B. (2006). *Imperialism and Postcolonialism*. Harlow, England: Pearson Longman.

Canaan, J., & Shumar, W. (Eds.). (2008). *Structure and Agency in the Neoliberal university*. New York: Routledge.

Carrette, J., & King, R. (2005). *Selling Spirituality: The Silent Takeover of Religion*. New York: Routledge.

Collins, G. (2003). *America's Women: Four Hundred Years of Dolls, Drudges, Helpmates, and Heroines*. New York: HarperCollins.

Cooper, F., & Stoler, A. (Eds.). (1997). *Tensions of Empire: Colonial Cultures in a Bourgeois World*. Berkeley, CA: University of California Press.

Dei, G. J. S. (2000). Rethinking the role of indigenous knowledges in the academy. *International Journal of Inclusive Education, 4*(2), 111–132.

Demerath, P., & Lynch, J. (2008). Identities for neoliberal times: Constructing enterprising selves in an American suburb. In N. Dolby & F. Rizvi (Eds.), *Youth Moves: Identities in Global Perspective* (pp. 179–193). New York: Routledge.

DeRoover, J. (2004). Secularism, colonialism and the Indian intellectuals. *India-Forum*. Retrieved October 10, 2006, from http://www.india-forum.com/articles/72/1/Secularism,-Colonialism-and-The-Indian-Intellectuals

de Sousa Santos, B., (Ed.). (2007). *Another Knowledge Is Possible: Beyond Northern Epistemologies*. London: Verso.

Dillard, C. B., Abdur-Rashid, D., & Tyson, C. A. (2000). My soul is a witness: Affirming pedagogies of the spirit. *International Journal of Qualitative Studies in Education, 13*(5), 447–462.

Donaldson, L. E., & Pui-Lan, K. (Eds.). (2002). *Postcolonialism, Feminism & Religious Discourse*. New York: Routledge.

Falk, G. (2002). *Man's Ascent to Reason: The Secularization of Western Culture*. Lewiston: Edwin Mellen.

Federici, S. (2004). *Caliban and the Witch: Women, the Body and Primitive Accumulation*. Brooklyn: Autonomedia.

Gandhi, M. (1990). *The Essential Gandhi*. New York: Vintage.

Giroux, H. (2002). Neoliberalism, corporate culture, and the promise of higher education: The university as a democratic public sphere. *Harvard Educational Review, 72*(4), 425–463.

Goonatilake, S. (1993). Modern science and the periphery: The characteristics of dependent knowledge. In S. Harding (Ed.), *The "Racial" Economy of Science: Toward a Democratic Future* (pp. 259–267). Bloomington: Indiana University Press.

Gould, S. J. (1981). *The Mismeasure of Man*. New York: W.W. Norton.

Grande, S. (2004). *Red Pedagogy: Native American Social and Political Thought*. Lanham: Rowman & Littlefield Publishers.

Green, J. (Ed.). (2007). *Making Space for Indigenous Feminism*. Halifax: Fernwood.

Heyob, S. (1975). *The Cult of Isis among Women in the Graeco-Roman World*. Leiden, Netherlands: E. J. Brill.

Jakobsen, J., & Pellegrini, A. (Eds.). (2008). *Secularisms*. Durham: Duke University Press.

Jefferess, D. (2008). *Postcolonial Resistance: Culture, Liberation and Transformation*. Toronto: University of Toronto Press.

Keddie, N. (2003). Secularism and its discontents. *Daedalus, 132*(3), 14–30.

Kempf, A. (2006). Anti-colonial historiography: Interrogating colonial education. In G. Dei, & A. Kempf (Eds.), *Anti-colonialism and Education: The Politics of Resistance* (pp. 129–158). Rotterdam: Sense.

Kuokkanen, R. (2007). *Reshaping the University: Responsibility, Indigenous Epistemes, and the Logic of Gift*. Vancouver: UBC.

Luke, A. (in press). On this writing: An autotheoretic account. In D. Nunan & J. Choi, (Eds.), *Culture and Identity in Language Learning and Use: A Microethnographic Approach*. London: Routledge.

Majid, A. (2000). *Unveiling Traditions: Postcolonial Islam in a Polycentric World*. Durham: Duke University Press.

Masseri, A. (1994). The imperialistic epistemological vision. *American Journal of Islamic Social Sciences, 11*(3), 403–415.

Mayuzumi, K. (2009). Unfolding possibilities through a decolonizing project: Indigenous knowledges and rural Japanese women. *International Journal of Qualitative Studies in Education, 22*(5), 507–526.

Mazama, M. A. (2002). Afrocentricity and African spirituality. *Journal of Black Studies, 33*(2), 218–234.

McClintock, A. (1995). *Imperial Leather: Race, Gender and Sexuality in the Colonial Contest*. New York: Routledge.

Mehmet, O. (1999). *Westernizing the Third World: The Eurocentricity of Economic Development Theories*. New York: Routledge.

Mignolo, W. D. (1995). *The Darker Side of the Renaissance*. Ann Arbor, MI: The University of Michigan Press.

Mignolo, W. (2000). *Local Histories/Global Designs: Coloniality, Subaltern Knowledges, and Border Thinking*. Princeton: Princeton University Press.

Mignolo, W. (2005). *The Idea of Latin America*. Oxford: Blackwell.

Morton, E. (2002). Race and racism in the works of David Hume. *Journal of African Philosophy 1(1)*. Retrieved September 3, 2006, from http://www.africanphilosophy.com/vol1.1/morton.html

Nandy, A. (Ed.). (1991). *Science, Hegemony and Violence: A Requiem of Modernity*. Delhi: Oxford University Press.

Newman, D., & Paasi, A. (1998). Fences and neighbors in the postmodern world: Boundary narratives in political geography. *Progress in Human Geography, 22*(2), 186–207.

Olssen, M., & Peters, M. (2005). Neoliberalism, higher education and the knowledge economy: From the free market to knowledge capitalism. *Journal of Education Policy, 20* (3), 313–345.

Pidgeon, M. (2010). *Our Collective Responsibility and Accountability to Indigenous Higher Education*. Paper presented at the Annual Meeting of the American Educational Research Association (AERA), May 2, Denver, Colorado.

Pratt, M. L. (1992). *Imperial Eyes: Travel Writing and Transculturation*. London: Routledge.

Shahjahan, R. A. (2005). Spirituality in the academy: Reclaiming from the margins and evoking a transformative way of knowing the world. *International Journal of Qualitative Studies in Education, 18*(6), 685–711.

Shiva, V. (1989). *Staying Alive: Women, Ecology and Development*. London: Zed.

Smith, L. T. (1999). *Decolonizing Methodologies: Research and Indigenous Peoples*. London: Zed.

Smith, A. (2005). *Conquest: Sexual Violence and American Indian Genocide*. Cambridge: South End.

Smith, C., & Ward, G. (2000). *Indigenous Cultures in an Interconnected World*. Vancouver: UBC.

Some, M. (1993). *Ritual: Power, Healing, and Community*. New York: Penguin Compass.

Some, M. (1994). *Of Water and Spirit: Ritual, Magic, and Initiation in the Life of an African Shaman*. New York: Tarcher/Putnam.

Spring, J. (2009). *Globalization of Education: An Introduction*. New York: Routledge.

Stewart-Harawira, M. (2005). *The New Imperial Order: Indigenous Responses to Globalization*. London: Zed.

Thompson, J. (1996). *Women in Celtic Law and Culture*. Lewiston, NY: Edwin Mellen.

wa Thiongo, N. (1986). *Decolonising the Mind: The Politics of Language in African Literature*. London: James Currey.

Wordie, J. (1983). The chronology of English enclosure, 1500–1914. *Economic History Review, 36* (4), 483–505.

Young, R. (2001). *Postcolonialism: An Historical Introduction*. Oxford: Blackwell.

CHAPTER TWENTY-FOUR

Knowledge, Power and Decolonization

Implication for Non-Indigenous Scholars, Researchers and Educators

SOENKE BIERMANN

Across the world, Indigenous people are challenging monolithic, monocultural, and mono-epistemological academic traditions to respond to and engage with other philosophical standpoints, intellectual traditions, and worldviews. Linda Tuhiwai Smith's (1999) seminal work, *Decolonizing Methodologies*, encouraged Indigenous intellectuals to continue resisting dominant approaches to academic knowledge production and to develop their own methodologies based on anti-colonial paradigms. Research methodologies, in particular, have been the focus of much recent work in Australia (Arbon, 2008; Martin, 2006; Rigney, 1997; Wilson, 2004), spelling out Indigenous methodologies, protocols, and obligations for researchers working with Indigenous communities. In their different ways, these Indigenous thinkers and scholars have articulated and translated longstanding Indigenous intellectual traditions into the arena of higher education research practice and theory, thereby both providing alternatives for researchers looking for more ethical methodologies as well as drawing lines in the sand that communities can point to in their negotiations with researchers operating within dominant paradigms. This intellectually pioneering work involves a constant battle to legitimate and validate Indigenous philosophies within a dominant colonial paradigm that demands their articulation into already-defined categories of knowledge. With such an uneven playing field, this process is about more than difference and cross-cultural communication, difficult enough though they are, but about struggling against mutually constitutive frameworks of power and knowledge that naturalize certain approaches to knowledge and define others as intellectually *other*.

While research methodologies have become a highly contested and emergent domain of intellectual resistance, the field of higher education pedagogy has received comparatively little attention in this regard (Biermann & Townsend-Cross, 2008). The role of Indigenous philosophies, practices, and processes in the areas of curriculum design and pedagogy at universities is perhaps more complex in light of institutional demands and surveillance of teachers but no less pressing. However, what also adds to the problematic is a general under-theorization of the concept of pedagogy. In his famous article "Why Pedagogy," Lusted (1986) laments the misunderstanding of and disinterest in this concept but affirms its central importance to questions of knowledge production:

> Why is pedagogy important? It is important since, as a concept, it draws attention to the process through which knowledge is produced. Pedagogy addresses the 'how' questions involved not only in the transmission of knowledge but also in its production. Indeed, it enables us to question the validity of separating these activities so easily by asking under what conditions and through what means we 'come to know' (pp. 2–3).

Lusted thus draws our attention to the fact that questions of pedagogy go to the heart not only of practical or procedural matters of teaching style but of the basic ontological and epistemological assumptions that underpin our academic system of knowledge production. In light of this insight, the question of pedagogy should sit at the centre of any attempt to fundamentally reshape and open up universities to multiple philosophical and intellectual traditions. For many of us, the question of decolonization within the contemporary Western Academy is thus of a multifarious and challenging nature. While Indigenous peoples are perhaps pursuing decolonization as a means to resist colonizing and assimilatory educational agendas and restore Indigenous philosophies, knowledges, and processes to their rightful and valued place (Arbon, 2008), why should this concern non-Indigenous people, particularly within modern "settler" states such as Australia, Aotearoa/New Zealand, Canada, and the United States where they constitute a majority of the population?

To me, this question goes to the heart of how those who are privileged by colonialism deal with the inequalities it (re)produces—in the Academy and beyond. As a white middle-class male working in a university, how can I possibly reconcile my privileged position with principles such as fairness, equity, and social justice? As a migrant in a "settler" state slowly establishing a sense of belonging, how do I benefit from and therefore relate to the inequalities and disparities produced by colonialism and its aftermath? To me, there exist at least three compelling reasons to decolonize. Firstly, there is a concern rooted in principles of solidarity and social justice, recognizing the injustices of colonial oppression and, as a fellow human being, doing all within one's power to dismantle unequal and unjust structures that produce privilege and disadvantage. Secondly, there is the realization that colonial systems of oppression diminish everyone's humanity, including and especially the oppressor's, necessitating resistance by those who are systematically *privileged*, for example, by whiteness. Finally, there is the concern of mutual benefit—how might engagement with Indigenous philosophies, knowledges, and processes facilitate greater understanding of many contemporary challenges and questions about the human condition?

Recognizing the way in which the Academy has historically been implicated in the process of colonization required me to take another look at intellectual traditions I had previously thought of as forces for social justice and emancipation. Through my engagement with the works of a range of Indigenous thinkers and scholars, I have come to realize that this represented a Eurocentric view suspended and sheltered from the realities of the colonial encounter. This has prompted me to re-evaluate my own epistemological assumption and to realize how inextricably academic knowledge production is tied up with the maintenance of unequal power relations. Despite some epistemological and methodological openings created by pioneering Indigenous scholars, the Academy remains very much a neo-colonial Western institution in "settler states" such as Australia, Aotearoa/New Zealand, and Canada. It lacks a decisive commitment to inclusiveness, cultural diversity, and epistemological pluralism in its institutional structures, processes, and practices. This situation, then, necessitates the kind of multi-faceted anti-colonial work that deconstructs colonial power relation, engages with other intellectual and epistemological traditions, and proposes new models for facilitating "epistemological equity" (Dei, 2008, p. 8). Although it shares some of the concerns and methods of post-colonialism, anti-colonialism goes beyond primarily discursive analyses based on Eurocentric theoretical referents to include an emphasis on subjugated Indigenous voices, knowledges, and philosophies, a focus on the material dimensions of colonialism, and a political commitment to resistance and anti-oppressive practices (Dei, 2006).

Informed by these concerns, this chapter will explore the relationship between Indigenous philosophies and academic systems of knowledge production, legitimization, and dissemination in "settler" states from the vantage point of a non-Indigenous scholar attempting to come to terms with his own implicatedness in colonial structures. The first part of this chapter will explore colonialism in its relation to the "settler" state and the way in which the "event" of invasion and dispossession of Indigenous peoples is made into a permanent underlying feature of the state via structural, psychological, and discursive mechanisms. Secondly, I will discuss how "settler" colonialism (re)produces power/knowledge hierarchies in educational institutions and thus situates Indigenous philosophies as *other* than, and outside of, legitimate academic epistemologies. Conversely, Indigenous philosophies and intellectual decolonization pose inherent challenges to the normative, taken-for-granted process of academic knowledge production, legitimization, and dissemination. Finally, I will discuss what I consider to be the pertinent challenges for non-Indigenous scholars wanting to come to terms with their own relation to the process of decolonization.

COLONIZATION AND "SETTLER" STATE

Colonialism as a "structured relationship of domination and subordination" (Barrerra, 1979, p. 193) establishes and maintains racialised hierarchies of power/knowledge that legitimate, serve, and naturalize the interests of the dominant group. Osterhammel (2005) offers three key points that distinguish colonialism from other forms of domination: its manipulation and transformation of an entire society; its emphasis on hierarchical cultural dissimilarity between colonizer and colonized, with a distinct antipathy toward intellectual exchange and counter-acculturation; and finally, that colonialism is not only a structural relationship "but also a particular *interpretation* of this relationship" (Osterhammel, 2005, p. 16).

For many years, the impacts of colonialism have predominantly been examined, discussed and understood in their political, economic, and social dimensions. This is particularly true for "settler" colonies, which operate differently from other types such as exploitation colonies or maritime enclaves by virtue of their European presence and permanence, as the original act of invasion is legally structured into a lasting unequal encounter. Before discussing this further, it is important to note that the term "settler" is of course highly problematic, as "it evacuates the word 'colonialism' of any implication of an encounter between peoples, or of conquest and domination" (Loomba, 1998, p. 2). Rather, it aims to erase memories of prior occupation as part of a process of selective amnesia and, as Garbutt (2007) has so convincingly shown, seeks to establish a kind of "New World" white autochthony which generates a strong sense of exclusivist belonging. We should therefore use this term with major qualifications and awareness of its genocidal baggage. In "settler states," colonization did not end with the formation of a new nation (Ferro, 1997). Instead of heralding an era of decolonization, "movements for colonist-independence" by white or Creole settlers in Australia, South America, North America, and elsewhere can be understood as "the most advanced stage of white colonial expansion" (Ferro, 1997, p. 211), since they involved a proclamation of national sovereignty on behalf of the descendants of the original invaders while leaving Indigenous peoples disenfranchised in the creation of the new state.

As to their nominal independence, Osterhammel argues that while settler states managed to attain self-government quite early on, "[t]hese societies were [. . .] not 'decolonized' by stripping the power of the colonists and driving them out, as was the case in Algeria." Instead, they either seceded abruptly by means of a colonist revolution (United States) or "by gradual dissociation on basically good terms (Canada, Australia) from the European center of the empire" (Osterhammel, 2005, p. 17). Because these movements for independence were driven by white "settlers," the underlying colonial relationship to Indigenous peoples did not change. Post independence, settler states maintained what Barrerra terms "internal colonialism" in which "the dominant and subordinate populations are intermingled, so that there is no geographically distinct 'metropole' separate from the 'colony'" (Barrerra, 1979, p. 194). An understanding of this type of ongoing internal or endo-colonialism is critical in order to appreciate both the inability of "settler" societies to re-imagine and remake themselves as independent *and* anti-colonial, and the ongoing nature of the colonial experience for Indigenous peoples. Today, while many Indigenous people in "settler" states would undoubtedly consider themselves to be living under conditions structured by ongoing colonialism, few "settler" descendants would think of their own nations and their institutions as colonial.

However, colonialism also operates in nuanced manner and there are several dimensions one needs to consider in order to understand this multifaceted concept, including its structural, psychological, and discursive elements. Osterhammel (2005) reminds us that,

> [t]he history of colonialisms is [. . .] not only—perhaps not even chiefly—a history of conquest, acquisition, and flag-hoisting. It is a history of the gradual emergence of state structures and societal forms and their geographic expansion or contraction within nominally claimed regions (p. 28).

In this context, it is most instructive to follow Patrick Wolfe's lead and conceive of the settler-colonial encounter not as an event but primarily as a structure. As Wolfe (1999) states in relation to Australia, the institutionalization of settler colonialism as a national framework ensured that "[t]he determination 'settler-colonial state' is [. . .] society's primary structural characteristic rather than merely a statement about its origins" and that, therefore, "invasion is a structure not an event" (p. 163). The structure of invasion and colonialism is thus foundational to and remains embedded in national cultures, landscapes, and systems of governance, law, and education. As national systems of governance, law, and education were developed, they were largely compatible with British imperial interests and therefore even "the effect of institutional and political change was to reinforce the British connections and the dependent conditions" (Denoon, 1983, pp. 223–234). Drawing on Wolfe's ideas, Elkins and Pedersen (2005) state that,

> . . . settler colonialism cannot be seen as an essentially fleeting stage but must be understood as the persistent defining characteristic, even *the condition of possibility*, of . . . [a] new settler society. [. . .] Settler colonialism, then, is not the past—a violent but thankfully brief period of conquest and domination—but rather the foundational governing ethic of [a] 'new world' state (pp. 2–3 [my emphasis]).

This key insight moves the focus on colonialism from a temporal to a spatial dimension, to how colonization has shaped a particular landscape, institution, or place. Recognizing institutionalized longevity even in the face of separation of formal ties with the original colonizer, Elkins and

Pedersen (2005) remark that "settler projects and practices [. . .] have their ghostly afterlife in postcolonial regimes" (p. 16). As will be discussed later on, educational institutions are particularly important nodes in the network of structural colonialism, as they are key sites for hegemonic struggles over *collective* understandings within the settler state. The state's power, however, is derived from the interplay with other important factors, such as psychological and discursive ones.

In addition to structures which have institutionalized colonial ontologies and epistemologies, and rendered them invisible (and thus powerful), psychological colonialism has shaped people's *individual* conception of what is right, true, just, and desirable. In this context, Nandy speaks of two forms of colonization: while the first had as its sphere of projection the human body and works through physical-material domination and subordination, the second targets the mind and operates in a more hegemonic fashion, thus altering cultural priorities and even becoming seen by the colonized as the prerequisite for their own liberation (Nandy, 2005, p. viii). As a result, Nandy (2005) argues, this form of colonization:

> helps generalize the concept of the modern West from a geographical and temporal entity to a psychological category. The West is now everywhere, within the West and outside; in structures and in minds . . . [it is] a colonialism which survives the demise of empires (p. vii).

Reinforcing the structural and material practices as well as the underlying psychological assumptions of colonialism is thus a discourse of Otherness. Edward Said (1993) even goes so far as to say that colonialism should be regarded *principally* as an "ideological formation" (p. 9). Osterhammel (2005) also stresses the "spirit of colonialism" which sustained and animated unequal power structures (p. 16). This idea builds on Foucault's notion of the interrelatedness of power and knowledge whereby the truth of a matter is determined by the prevalence of particular discourses or the fields of power/knowledge that produce it (Foucault, 1980). Analyzing discourse, then, is not the same as studying representation, but examining the conditions for its production. Loomba (1998) concurs that the "study of colonial discourse ought to lead us to a fuller understanding of colonial institutions rather than direct us away from them" (p. 97). Just how has colonialism shaped the modern Western Academy, then? And how has it situated Indigenous knowledges and philosophies vis-à-vis dominant epistemologies and with what consequences?

COLONIALISM, UNIVERSITIES AND INDIGENOUS PHILOSOPHIES

Similar to its connection with international law, colonialism's historical association with academia is characterized by a mutually dependent relationship that resulted in the establishment and development of bodies of knowledge to describe, regulate, and order the Indigenous Other based on European frames of reference. Functioning as part of the state apparatus that provided internal legitimacy and technical support to the process of colonization, learned institutions delivered the intellectual goods by providing pseudo-scientific justifications of racial superiority and civilizing missions as well as more practical support in terms of naval engineering and cartography. Simultaneously, encounters with societies vastly different to their own precipitated attempts by Europeans to explain these differences within a familiar linear hierarchical framework of human development and technological progress, giving birth to such disciplines as anthropology, history, and sociology. In other words, "[c]olonialism thus refracted the production of knowledge and structured the conditions for its dissemination and reception" (Loomba, 1998, p. 69).

By way of illustration, Osterhammel (2005) discusses the colonial practice of separating Indigenous and non-Indigenous population in response to prominent scholarly thinking at the time:

> This separation resulted in part from a well-calculated ruling technique, partly from the projection of new western criteria of ethnicity onto societies, the study of which now became the task of ethnologists and anthropologists. Whatever scholarship had distinguished on the basis of linguistic and social science criteria was now to be divided in practice as well. British indirect rule in the theoretical form it acquired at the turn of the century by Sir Frederick Lugard and the segregationist 'politique des races' of some of his French contemporaries had this type of ethnological underpinning (Osterhammel, 2005, p. 90).

Yet colonialism's influence wasn't limited to those new disciplines—on the contrary, Loomba (1998) claims that it "reshaped existing structures of human knowledge. No branch of learning was left untouched by the colonial experience. The process was somewhat like the functioning of ideology itself, simultaneously a misrepresentation of reality and its reordering" (p. 57). At the same time, the disciplines, via their methodologies and theoretical canons, began to re-inscribe colonial knowledges into existing power relations, thus at the same time justifying, aiding, and profiting from colonialism by having access to new fields and objects of study. In other words, metropolitan colonial discourses on distant peoples, their lands, and their cultures began to exert their influence in the houses, classrooms, and hospital wards of the colonies. This is what Abdul Jan Mohamed (1985) identified as "a profound symbiotic relationship between the discursive and material practices of imperialism" (p. 64).

While many of us like to think of their transformative potential, education systems also act as agents of colonialism by maintaining dominant standards and norms, acculturating and assimilating students into desired ontological, epistemological, and axiological frameworks, and circumscribing visions of a life worth living. Osterhammel (2005) reminds us that, all other things being equal, "[t]he colonial state had two functions: to secure control over the subjugated peoples and to create a framework for the economic utilization of the colony" (p. 57). One important element in this structure of order and control is what is often referred to as "'communication imperialism': the systematic collection, processing, and dissemination of information about the colonized society by centralized institutions" (Osterhammel, 2005, p. 64). According to Osterhammel (2005), what distinguished modern European colonialism in a pedagogical sense was the pronounced unwillingness of colonizers to engage with Indigenous intellectual and philosophical traditions in a process of counter-acculturation (pp. 15–16). While the colonized were expected to acculturate to the values and customs of Europe, "established colonial pedagogy was invariably disdainful of [I]ndigenous cultures" and did not seek to produce any kind of cultural synthesis (Osterhammel, 2005, p. 102). In the languages of Christian missionaries and Social Darwinists alike, Indigenous peoples were seen as outside of civilization and humankind, destined to either eternal damnation or salvation through assimilation to Western culture.

When considering the role of universities as that of generating, legitimating, and disseminating knowledge, the question as to what kind of and whose knowledge seems as pertinent today as it did in the eighteenth or nineteenth century. This is even more so in "settler states" with significant Indigenous populations and a whole raft of contemporary social, political, and environmental problems and challenges. As Marie Battiste (citing Blaut) states so clearly, "[a]s an imaginative and institutional context, Eurocentrism is the dominant consciousness and order of contemporary life"

(Battiste, 2009, p. 183). As such, Indigenous knowledges and philosophies, despite lip-service to their inherent worth and value, are all too often still positioned by the Academy as Other, alien and outside the scope of academic knowledge.

While being able to provide different perspectives and conceptual starting points, Indigenous philosophies do not receive the same recognition and appreciation as other knowledge systems. On the one hand, this problem is rooted in colonial attitudes of superiority and scientific racism which classified Indigenous peoples as inferior human beings and their knowledges as superstitious and irrelevant to the modern world. In recent years, however, the problem has also been compounded by non-Indigenous *and* Indigenous people emphasizing the value of Indigenous cultures at the expense of other ways of conceiving of Indigenous systems of knowledge. This has also been true in academia, where, as long as researchers speak of *cultures*, *ways of learning*, or *worldviews*, there exists, perhaps an inherent unspoken assumption that these concepts are less rigorous, complex, or accessible than nominally academic or intellectual pursuits. Battiste (2002) puts it succinctly:

> Postmodernist scholars have noted that culture is often viewed as what the inferior 'other' has. While some peoples have civilizations, philosophies, romance languages, or cultured societies; other peoples have cultures, dialects, worldviews, and tribal knowledge. Peoples with 'civilizations' are regarded as inherently superior to peoples with 'cultures' (p. 16).

Reflecting on comparative approaches to philosophy, Indigenous Australian philosopher Errol West found that the intellectual dimension of Indigenous reality often lacked an overt facet and was thus practically unrecognized by Indigenous and non-Indigenous publics alike. West (1998) explains that,

> Western epistemology differs from Indigenous epistemology in that we Koori peoples already know the origin, nature, methods and limits of our knowledge systems, what we unlike westerners seem to lack is the capacity to flaunt that knowledge as a badge of our intellect and cultural integrity, in a very public sense.

The issue of putting Indigenous philosophies on an equal footing with other intellectual traditions within our universities goes to the core of power relations and intellectual sovereignty in modern "settler states." The legacies of colonialism weigh heavily on the contemporary Academy which, rather than a place of enlightenment and liberation, is seen by many Indigenous people as an oppressive agent of colonialism. This is especially apparent whenever it really matters: when theses are examined, journal articles reviewed and research grants distributed. Here, the status quo asserts itself most strongly and forcefully defines and defends what counts as legitimate knowledge.

According to Ferro (1997), "institutional and bureaucratic standardization has gone hand in hand with the development of the state" (pp. 353–354), thus widening authority through a Foucauldian capillary form of power and extending the social distance between the centre and the periphery. Through colonialism and globalization, one consequence of the Westernization of the world in a capitalist mold has been the standardization of institutions (Ferro, 1997, p. 354). In higher education, this process of standardization can be observed in a number of areas, including in the fields of curriculum design and pedagogy, research, governance, quality control, and the use of English as an academic lingua franca.

As a result of this dual process of expansion and conflation, Indigenous knowledges are often usurped within the canon of established disciplines, but in the process are dismembered and then reconfigured to fit into a European paradigmatic mold. This tokenistic and appropriative engagement with other knowledges is what Polly Walker calls "structural violence." According to Walker (2003), processes of Western education in general and of the Academy in particular are "structurally violent" since they,

> seek to bring about the inclusion of non-Europeans and/or non-European achievements in canonical subject matters, while leaving the methodological and conceptual parameters of the canon itself essentially intact (p. 37).

The challenge posed by a substantive engagement with Indigenous philosophies is thus about the rejection of a hierarchical colonial epistemological paradigm and the meaningful integration of multiple ways of knowing. Indigenous philosophies do not just amount to additional or different content-knowledge within a European canon but encapsulate different kinds of process-knowledge. As McNally (2004) notes, this is important in terms of engagement:

> What makes Indigenous theories of culture distinctive is in part that they are less a matter of theory than of process, and thus we cannot just enumerate the content of the theories more effectively; we must engage their dynamism in creative ways (p. 604).

Having a different understanding of the *process* of knowledge generation, legitimization, and dissemination, rather than just additional perspectives that can easily be slotted into existing paradigms, is thus a major challenge to the institutional mechanisms of curriculum design, pedagogy, and assessment. Martin Nakata's (2007) book *Disciplining the Savages, Savaging the Disciplines* clearly shows how one of the key concerns of the contemporary Academy needs to be whether and how to position Indigenous knowledges and epistemologies within a dominant Western university system. Underpinning this approach is a process of intellectual decolonization that challenges disciplinary boundaries, established epistemological traditions, and normative assumptions.

DECOLONIZATION

Like colonialism, decolonization has predominantly been viewed though a Eurocentric framework and expressed in historical, political, and legal terms as the "fall" of empires and the "loss" of overseas possessions. However, "settler states" such as Australia face a particular decolonization dilemma. Caught in the middle of a "double-bind" of external and internal colonial relationships, the state is formally independent of the original colonial power. However, internally these nation-states are a case of colonists that never left and, for Indigenous peoples, colonialism that never ended. The settlers brought and developed traditions, systems, and structures which have since become the basis of the independent state. Meanwhile Indigenous peoples have been relegated to minority positions in their own countries with varying degrees of guaranteed rights yet in no demographic position to politically challenge the power of "settler" descendants. This means that decolonization in "settler states" is primarily concerned with continuing assertions of Indigenous sovereignty and rights, the reclamation of Indigenous philosophies and knowledges as well as the exposition and dismantling of hidden structures, ongoing processes, and unquestioned traditions of colonial governance within the formally independent nation-state.

Because of this contradistinction, the decolonization process has to entail addressing colonial *practices* as much as structures, theories, and institutions. Decolonization implies more than "making up" or "getting along," but a serious re-consideration of the totality of relationships to other people and the land we live with. Rather than understanding decolonization solely as empowerment of Indigenous peoples, it also has to entail the deflation of white power (Watson, 2007) as well as dominant society's responsibility to question its own advantage in light of how this position inhibits non-hierarchical engagements with others. Turning the tables on the supposed advantages of dominance means viewing colonialism itself through a deficit prism and bringing to light that whatever the short-term benefits supremacy bestows over others, oppression ultimately works to diminish and dehumanize everyone, including and especially the oppressor (Cesaire, 2000). As Rose (2004) suggests, being perhaps the first generation of "settler"/invader descendants to appreciate the magnitude of devastation caused by the onslaught of colonialism, the question for many non-Indigenous people surely also ought to be: how do whitefellas decolonize? (p. 6)

Stephen Muecke (2004) states that "[d]ecolonisation [. . .] cannot be about the removal of one kind of state power; it is about the creation of a new assemblage" (p. 48). Indeed, we might understand decolonization as the active unraveling of assumed certainties and the re-imagining and re-negotiating of common futures. Importantly, this has to occur from a position of equality, not dominance, and thus involves a reflective peeling back of various layers of privilege and the ignorance that comes with it. Speaking to this fundamental quality, Chandra Mohanty (2003, pp. 7–8) argues that "decolonization involves profound transformations of self, community and governance structures. It can only be achieved through active withdrawal of consent and resistance to structures of psychic and social domination." Speaking about a decolonizing approach rooted in the Indigenous humanities, Findlay (2003) points out that, "[i]n working together across difference, the Indigenous humanities acknowledge that we all have a stake in dismantling colonial structures and oppressive singularities while reimagining and rebuilding practices and institutions and telling stories otherwise" (p. 4).

What, then, can those non-Indigenous people who understand the damage colonialism causes and who do not want to be complicit in perpetuating unjust and unequal colonial relations do to deconstruct and reconstruct themselves? The answer to this question is inextricably tied up with a recognition and dismantling of privilege as well as access to, and willingness to honestly consider, other philosophical traditions. Being exposed to and respecting and engaging with Indigenous philosophies is a crucial element to not only recognize and reaffirm the sovereignty of Indigenous peoples but to generate the decolonizing conditions for the creation of shared knowledges, processes, and relationships. Importantly, this cannot occur in an unreflective way that disregards questions of power, so any conversation and negotiation about decolonization needs to be steeped in discourses of sovereignty, human rights, and social justice. This is particularly pertinent in the field of higher education through which the state generates, legitimates, and disseminates officially sanctioned knowledges. In order to do theory and practice in a globally inclusive way (Connell, 2007), then, I would argue that there are three key challenges that non-Indigenous academics need to respond to: deconstructing colonial privilege, engaging with Indigenous and majority-world theories and practices, and, in conversation with Indigenous scholars and thinkers, developing models that facilitate "epistemological equity" (Dei, 2008, p. 8) inside and outside of the classroom.

The first challenge, deconstructing colonial privilege, must involve an active process of conscientisation (Freire, 1972). It means interrogating the role of both structures and discourses in creating and maintaining systems of colonial domination within which we operate and by which we are located. While this is hardly a new idea and has been successfully practiced as an anti-colonial strategy for quite some time, it is important to realize that this process is equally important whether the position we occupy within a structure or discourse is one of disadvantage or of *privilege*. Indeed, Choules' (2007) argument has convincingly shown how attention to privilege can be a powerful tool in engaging members of the dominant culture in struggles for social justice. As a multi-dimensional concept that includes economic, social, and cultural aspects, deconstructing privilege involves asking self-reflective questions such as "how am I positioned and advantaged by current structures and discourses," such as whiteness, gender, and class. By opening up the discussion as to how systemic injustices and inequalities are produced and reproduced, the process of deconstructing colonial privilege challenges the false meritocratic narrative one is invited to draw on to justify a position of relative privilege and instead focuses on the unearned structural advantages one might enjoy.

Here, the deconstructive potential of critical pedagogy is significant in bringing about this kind of awareness. Based on the work of Paulo Freire (1972) and a range of later writers such as Shor (1987), Giroux (1988, 1997), Weiler and Mitchell (1992), McLaren (1995), and Kincheloe (2005), critical pedagogy is a tool for "understanding and deconstructing the operations of power and social practices that maintain dominant, marginalizing views of the world and limit possibilities for the recognition of difference" (Austin & Hickey, 2008, p. 135). I would argue, however, that this kind of deconstructive work needs to be placed explicitly within a colonial context and pay attention not only to the material circumstances but especially to the ongoing structural, psychological, and discursive consequences of colonialism, such as the production of epistemological privilege. This heeds Coloma, Means, and Kim's (2009) reminder that analyses of colonialism and imperialism should play a much more prominent part in educational praxis. Finally, it is important for non-Indigenous scholars not only to engage with and consider Indigenous theories of decolonization such as those developed by Laenui (2000), but also to articulate, think through, and theorize the process of their own non-Indigenous intellectual decolonization.

The second challenge, engaging with Indigenous and majority-world theories and practices, is closely related to the first and crucial if we wish to broaden our intellectual horizons and break out of self-perpetuating colonial paradigms. However, if done in isolation without also attending to the critical deconstruction of colonial privilege, this engagement can easily become unreflective and appropriative, as it does not grasp the underlying issues of power that are inseparable from the knowledge that is generated, legitimated, and disseminated. In her book *Southern Theory,* Connell (2007) confronts the paradigm blindness of sociology which is built on a dominant *northern* (i.e., Western, industrialized) theoretical framework deaf to *southern* (i.e., Indigenous and majority-world, rural, colonized) voices other than as objects of research or contexts for the application of northern theory.

As scholars, we need to be asking ourselves who is served by the dominance of a limited range of accessible perspectives and epistemologies, and who misses out because of this. Are Indigenous people disenfranchised not only by a lack of application of diverse epistemological traditions in places of higher education, but also by a lack of awareness that they even exist? Does *everyone* miss out due to a dominant ethnocentric view that considers Indigenous and majority-world peoples as objects or context of study, not producers of knowledge which is valuable, relevant, and interesting for everyone (Dasen & Akkari, 2009, p. 8)? On a personal level, what theories and epistemological frameworks do you draw on to inform your practice as an educator, scholar, and researcher? Battiste (2009) challenges us to consider that "Indigenous knowledge is compatible and relevant to contemporary education systems, and requires a process of respectful dialogue and the development of postcolonial strategies" (p. 169).

The third challenge, finally, draws our attention to the necessity of developing such strategies, frameworks, and ethical processes by which to facilitate what Dei has termed "epistemological equity" (2008, p. 8) in our classrooms and in our scholarship. In fact, Dei sees this as the key issue confronting the Academy today: "One of the biggest challenges of anti-colonial education is the search for synthesis of multiple knowledges" (Dei, 2008, p. 11). This process includes bringing not only different knowledges and perspectives into a conversation but different ontologies and epistemologies. It is an immensely challenging task, especially in light of the asymmetric power relations that are a result of the colonial encounter, which must be undertaken with a keen awareness of and heightened sensitivity toward issues of power/knowledge.

Importantly, this is not about developing a neat linear progression, but an open-ended, messy, and unpredictable process determined by the crucial principle of respectful, equal dialogue. However, rather than these being restrictive or negative attributes, they relate to Connie North's (2009, p. 574) claims about anti-oppressive teaching strategies invariably involving "unpredictability, partiality, and contradictions." In a similar vein, Dei (2008) speaks of the importance of a "humility of knowing," the "uncertainty of knowledge," and the search for "[d]iscursive synthesis [which] is at the heart of claims of multicentric knowing" (p. 12). Battiste (2009), finally, points out that this process must begin "with Indigenous peoples providing the standards and protections that accompany the centering of Indigenous knowledge" (p. 191).

CONCLUSION

Having surveyed the enormous impact of colonialism and its ongoing structural, psychological, and discursive dimensions, one might be forgiven for feeling overwhelmed by the enormity of the challenge of institutional, theoretical, and practical change. However, retreating to the false comfort of a one-dimensional epistemological space will no longer suffice in a twenty-first century characterized by strong anti-colonial education movements, calls for substantive curricular equity within the Academy and global crises that require collaborative solutions. The challenge for non-Indigenous educators, scholars, and researchers in their various disciplines, particularly in "settler states" that have never substantively decolonized their institutions, is to think through what the process of intellectual decolonization has to offer in terms of social justice, ethical engagement, and the development of more democratic forms of interaction.

Where, then, can those non-Indigenous educators, scholars, and researchers keen to face the challenge of intellectual decolonization start on a personal level? I would suggest that any engagement has to start with a rethink of how we organize curricula, run our classes, and conceive of the role of the teacher-learner relationship. Indigenous knowledges and philosophies need to be afforded the kind of conceptual and methodological autonomy that allows them to be judged according to their own standards and by their own internal criteria of validity. For non-Indigenous educators, this requires a process of *un*learning one's own assumptions, valuing the complexity of considering a variety of knowledges, and engaging with the trail-blazing theoretical work of Indigenous scholars and thinkers as well as the complex lived realities of local Indigenous communities. We might also have to rethink our conceptions of pedagogy within the institution and experiment with taking students outside of the classroom and into the community. Thus, Eurocentric conceptions of who is a "qualified expert" need to be revisited when we engage with Indigenous teachers, guest lecturers, and knowledge holders. In all of this, I concur with Connell (2007, p. 48) about its importance in contemporary social justice-oriented scholarship when she says that "[w]e really have no choice but to face the difficulties of doing theory [and practice] in a globally inclusive way."

REFERENCES

Arbon, V. (2008). *Arlathirnda ngurkarnda ityirnda/Being-Knowing Doing: De-colonising Indigenous Tertiary Education*. Teneriffe, Qld.: Post Pressed.

Austin, J., & Hickey, A. (2008). Critical Pedagogical Practice through Cultural Studies. *International Journal of the Humanities, 6*(1), 133–139.

Barrerra, M. (1979). *Race and Class in the South-West: A Theory of Racial Inequality*. Notre Dame: University of Notre Dame Press.

Battiste, M. (2002). *Indigenous Knowledge and Pedagogy in First Nations Education: A Literature Review with Recommendations*. Retrieved June 26, 2007, from http: www.ainc-inac.gc.ca/pr/pub/krw/ikp_e.pdf.

Battiste, M. (2009). The Decolonization of Aboriginal Education: Dialogue, Reflection, and Action in Canada. In P.R. Dasen & A. Akkari (Eds.), *Educational Theories and Practices from the Majority World* (pp. 168–195). New Delhi: Sage.

Biermann, S. & Townsend-Cross, M. (2008). Indigenous Pedagogy as a Force for Change. *The Australian Journal of Indigenous Education, 37*(S), 146–154.

Cesaire, A. (2000). *Discourse on Colonialism*. (J. Pinkham, Transl.). New York: Monthly Review.

Choules, K. (2007). The Shifting Sands of Social Justice Discourse: From Situating the Problem with "Them," to Situating It with "Us." *The Review of Education, Pedagogy, and Cultural Studies, 29*, 461–481.

Coloma, R. S., Means, A., & Kim, A. (2009). Palimpset Histories and Catachrestic Interventions. In R.S. Coloma (Ed.), *Postcolonial Challenges in Education* (pp. 3–22). New York: Peter Lang.

Connell, R. (2007). *Southern Theory: The Global Dynamics of Knowledge in Social Science*. Crows Nest: Allen & Unwin.

Dasen, P. R., & Akkari, A. (2009). Introduction: Ethnocentrism in Education and How to Overcome It. In P.R. Dasen & A. Akkari (Eds.), *Educational Theories and Practices from the Majority World* (pp. 7–22). New Delhi: Sage.

Dei, G. J. S. (2006). Introduction: Mapping the Terrain—Towards a New Politics of Resistance. In G.J.S. Dei & A. Kempf (Eds.), *Anti-Colonialism and Education: The Politics of Resistance* (pp. 1–24). Rotterdam: Sense.

Dei, G.J.S. (2008). Indigenous Knowledge Studies and the Next Generation: Pedagogical Possibilities for Anti-Colonial Education. *The Australian Journal of Indigenous Education, 37*(S), 5–13.

Denoon, D. (1983). *Settler Capitalism: The Dynamics of Dependent Development in the Southern Hemisphere*. Oxford: Clarendon.

Elkins, C., & Pedersen, S. (2005). Settler Colonialism: A Concept and Its Uses. In C. Elkins & S. Pedersen (Eds.), *Settler Colonialism in the Twentieth Century: Projects, Practices, Legacies* (pp. 1–20). New York: Routledge.

Ferro, M. (1997). *Colonization: A Global History*. (K. D. Prithipaul, Trans.). London: Routledge.

Findlay, I. (2003). Working for Postcolonial Legal Studies: Working with the Indigenous Humanities. *Law, Social Justice, and Global Development Journal*. Retrieved November 1, 2009, from http://www2.warwick.ac.uk/fac/soc/law/elg/lgd/2003_1/findlay.

Foucault, M. (1980). In Gordon. (Ed.), *Power-Knowledge: Selected Interviews and Other Writings, 1972–1977*. (C. Gordon, L. Marshall, J Mepham, & K. Soper , Trans.). Brighton: Harvester.

Freire, P. (1972). *Pedagogy of the Oppressed*. (M. Bergman Ramos, Trans.). Harmondsworth: Penguin.

Garbutt, R. (2007). "Locals Only"? Identity and Place in Australian Settler Society. PhD Thesis, Southern Cross University.

Giroux, H. A. (1988). *Teachers as Intellectuals: Toward a Critical Pedagogy of Learning*. New York: Bergin & Garvey.

Giroux, H.A. (1997). *Pedagogy and the Politics of Hope: Theory, Culture, and Schooling*. Boulder, CO: Westview.

Jan Mohamed, A. R. (1985). The Economy of Manichean Allegory: The Function of Racial Difference in Colonialist Literature. *Critical Inquiry, 12*(1), 58–87.

Kincheloe, J. (2005). *Critical Pedagogy Primer*. New York: Peter Lang.

Laenui, P. (2000). Processes of Decolonization. In M. Battiste (Ed.), *Reclaiming Indigenous Voice and Vision* (pp. 150–160). Vancouver: UBC.

Loomba, A. (1998). *Colonialism/Postcolonialism*. London: Routledge.

Lusted, D. (1986). Why Pedagogy? *Screen, 27*(5), 2–14.

Martin, K. (2006). Please Knock Before You Enter: An Investigation of How Rainforest Aboriginal People Regulate Outsiders and the Implications for Western Research and Researchers. PhD Thesis, James Cook University (4745).

McLaren, P. (1995) *Critical Pedagogy and Predatory Culture: Oppositional Politics in a Postmodern Era*. London: Routledge.

McNally, M. D. (2004). Indigenous Pedagogy in the Classroom: A Service Learning Model for Discussion. *American Indian Quarterly*, 28, 604–617.

Mohanty, C.T. (2003). *Feminism without Borders: Decolonizing Theory, Practicing Solidarity*. Durham: Duke University Press.

Muecke, S. (2004). *Ancient and Modern: Time, Culture and Indigenous Philosophy*. Sydney: UNSW.

Nakata, M. (2007). *Disciplining the Savages: Savaging the Disciplines*. Canberra: Aboriginal Studies.

Nandy, A. (2005). The Intimate Enemy: Loss and Recovery of Self under Colonialism. In A. Nandy, *Exiled at Home*. New Delhi: Oxford University Press.

North, C. (2009). The Promise and Perils of Developing Democratic Literacy for Social Justice. *Curriculum Inquiry*, 39(4), 555–579.

Osterhammel, J. (2005). *Colonialism: A Theoretical Overview*. 2nd ed. (S. Frisch, Transl.). Princeton: Markus Wiener.

Rigney, L.-I. (1997). Internationalisation of an Indigenous Anti-Colonial Cultural Critique of Research Methodologies: A Guide to Indigenist Research Methodology and Its Principles. *Journal for Native American Studies*, 14(2), 109–122.

Rose, D. B. (2004). *Reports from a Wild Country: Ethics for Decolonisation*. Sydney: UNSW.

Said, E. (1993). *Culture and Imperialism*. London: Chatto & Windus.

Shor, I. (1987) *Critical Teaching and Everyday Life*. Chicago: Chicago University Press.

Smith, L.T. (1999). *Decolonizing Methodologies*. Dunedin: University of Otago Press.

Walker, P. (2003) Colonising Research: Academia's Structured Violence Towards Indigenous Peoples. *Social Alternatives*, 22(3), 37–40.

Watson, I. (2007). Settled and Unsettled Spaces: Are We Free to Roam? In A. Moreton-Robinson (Ed.), *Sovereign Subjects: Indigenous Sovereignty Matters* (pp. 15–32). Crows Nest, NSW: Allen & Unwin.

Weiler, K., & Mitchell, C. (Eds.). (1992). *What Schools Can Do: Critical Pedagogy and Practice*. Albany, NY: State University of New York Press.

West, E. (1998). Speaking Towards an Aboriginal Philosophy. Paper presented at the *First Conference on Indigenous Philosophy*. "Linga Longa" Philosophy Farm, NSW.

Wilson, S. (2004). Research as Ceremony: Articulating an Indigenous Research Paradigm. PhD Thesis, Monash University.

Wolfe, P. (1999). *Settler Colonialism and the Transformation of Anthropology*. London: Cassell.

CHAPTER TWENTY-FIVE

Coyote and Raven Chat about Protecting Indigenous Intellectual Property

PAT O'RILEY & PETER COLE

Voice over...if humankind had not invented the eyed needle (or at least mimicked nature's processes of weaving knitting and darning) would there be a haystack in which to lose so many things and are places of formal education the right places for growing minds and bodies to learn how to do things in a good way...and does "a good way" matter

Voice beside...if language had not been taken so seriously would human beings still be part of nature and would it make any difference

Voice under...who is in charge of thinking and regulating thinking and assigning merit and is digging for answers the same as digging a well...it's there somewhere we just need to know something about something in order to do something context matters unless of course we are totally intuitive about everything and what about the witching stick...speaking with the forest

Voice from the Bush [salal] *kalan7wi samas*...raven and coyote have been having tea with some archaeologists following a conference and as longtime residents of the western hemisphere they have their own ideas about research done on the first peoples of the *americas* and their ancestors including after the fact and despite the "fact/s"

raven begins...*ama7 sqit ama7 s7atsxen tumulhana muta7*...*takem swat, tsitmusam ats7*

coyote intervenes and the seesawing begins *sek:on...cwis mitsaq lti zenka...kalanmints tsina sqweqwel* says coyote...we would like to acknowledge the first peoples whose traditional territory we are on within these pages electronic or composed from deceased forest dwellers from the tree nations howsoever formatted situated or exhibited...thinking on my own forebears my mind drifts to the *onkwehonwe* to my french and irish foregoers and their journeys and lives on the land...wherever we travel wherever we live and work in the world the ancestors are with us beside around by as about and withal *cwis mitsaq lti zenka* circles of joined hands *wraaaakk* everyone in archaeology land was sort of okay with the accuracy of the archaeological methods and methodologies and the prehistoric situatedness of human beings living in long ago and primitive mexico but not open to it being such a mind boggling long time ago...and lo' this caused a (d)rift to grow between geology and archaeology because the latter could not accept any of the former's dating techniques which though they confluenced with the clovis timelines as measured by bones mixed in aggregate with geocontext...they also showed how inordinately (and cardinally) long ago first peoples have lived in the "new" world since before they were in "the old country" insofar (and near) as acceptable evidence goes...bulletin: more stones more people found everywhere

Vox ex voce...trigrammaton am i...*in arcadia ego* but it was a long time ago and I'm not sure anymore...the written words affect my memories...the translations confuse me

Voice from the Waters [backeddy]...oh for a muse of fire

Voice from the Cloud [nimbo-stratus] kalan7wi samas...we are most of us in visitor mode most of the time most of the space it is those selfsame stewards of the land I wish to acknowledge *aho!* they have looked after the land not by owning exploiting and undermining it but by acting according to their original instructions each of us on this earth this air these waters was given original instructions by the creator a manifesto telling us our responsibilities and protocols...with respect to the rest of creation

nia:wen...ancestors...descendants...coming generations...time out of mind caretakers and guardians of the land...land which was never empty...no matter how many papal and other intercessor bulls and decrees deemed it so the land was never merely occupied...it was embraced embracing...the people and land as one becoming

Voice from the Earth [semi aridity mixed with aridity]...*ama7 s7atsxen tumulhana muta7...kwe kwe...shcan o nie onkwe hunkwe se:kon mino kij igan...dammecin queam ico oa*

sfx:...sound of siren...dogs barking...ravens cawing thrrrt thrrrt click clack cat snarling...coyotes howling...bison thundering...people yelling partying ya ya far out...go for it man...horses wooohahahahahahah wipeout!! (Surfaris, 1963) screech of brakes sudden SILENCE

hold it everybody hold it...hold it listen...I...can turn the blue skies grey...I can make it snow whenever I feel that way...oh I can turn a castle into a single grain of sand I can make a flood with a simple twist of my hand but my life is incomplete and I'm so rued (Whitfield & Strong, 1969)

HEEEY!...says norm hey says barrett you stole that song...you stole that song from us and then you changed it...disjunctive hybridity is so not fair...*boooo!*...that is our intellectual property...our words...written our way...our way written using our words

I really want to......see you...I really want to...be with you I really want to see you lord...but it takes so long, my lord (Harrison, 1970) uhn uhn uuuhn I did not steal or otherwise pilfer it...any more than george stole that song from ronald mack and the chiffons...or shakespeare stole themes and whole speeches from kit marley hollingshead...the bible and aemilia bassano lanyer

stole is stole is stole is [goes on singing "stole is" to the tune of my sweet lord]......it's the provenance that matters...the state of the genealogical record keeping *whakapapa* who was in the canoe when where and in what circumstances

noo noo noo noo noo noo noo [to the melody of "my sweet lord"]
I did not steal one bar...one hemidemisemiquaver...one chord progression

I found it...in the public realm...right over there in *hmv*......in this cd case
and I made it my own...I personalized it...now it's a hybrid song......*this segment of my talk brought to you by hmv* I'd have preferred sam the record man but he's gone now
it's our song...and you stole it...*[à la beatles] ya ya ya...ya ya ya yaaa* (McCartney & Lennon, 1964)
sing the temptations barry gordy michael jackson and stevie wonder
don't let it bother you...I'll look after it like it was my own...but mark you [and they did] I don't own it I don't claim to own it...I would never say it's MY intellectual property look at it more as a life long life wide lease...it's more of a topographical domain...something to make something so that we can trade or sell that for accommodation...shelter and cover for our bodies...we all buy we all sell even if it is just a signature or our silent assent...it's about risk and opportunity how much risk for how much reward
hmm the public domain into which all things indigenous seem to seep...if you are not laying claim to it then what's that C with a circle around it...you copyrighted it
(singing to tune of O Canada!) from C to shining C......to shining C to
C C rider well now see...see what you have done (Leadbelly, 1999)...no no no no that is not a copyright sign...it's my circle c brand I've got a big ranch...you see...don't mean nothin' in fact...*I was hangin' round town just a spendin' my time out of a job and not earnin' a dime...a fellah steps up and he says* (Fletcher, 1959)
but I wrote that song with my very own hand...and now you've put on your own brand it's lyrical piracy piratical lyricism...since when has democracy upstaged capitalism?
your life is incomplete and you're so blue (Whitfield & Strong, 1969)
that will do raven!
gentlemen ladies...infants don't get into a funk *just be cool...everything's all right yes everything's cool and I want you to sleep well tonight close your eyes...close your eyes and relax think of nothing...be cool* (Rice & Webber, 1971)
heeey...I wrote that song says sir tim rice knight bachelor way back when
yes...says sir lord andrew lloyd webber and that's my music...my tune what is this larceny central
nooo timmy tim tim and andy oops that song is universal...it just condensed from the universe right into my mind sublimations for the generations and I wrote it down distilled it from the collective unconscious...what year do you think you wrote it because I'm sure it crystallized into my mind long before...perhaps even before I was born...I was quite precocious...gifted...it was a gift from the beyond
no no no no say tim and andrew...that's not the way it happened...you condensed it from the radio...from frostwire from a cd...from an mp3 file it's our IP and no amount of doubletalk jabberwocky malarkey will change that...our solicitor will be in touch
just calm down boys says the voiceover...*sleep and I shall soothe you calm you and disjoint you...fleece for your cold forehead oh...don't you know* (Rice & Webber, 1971)
it's my song!   no matter how much you change the words and try to doubletalk your way out of having stolen it
transition music [women's warrior song] (Pierre, n.d.)
hey hey yukki ya...yukki ya a a hey hey yukki ya...
narrator:...ah a *stl'atl'imx* generated song from martina pierre's dream
coyote and raven have been hanging around *stl'atl'imx* people for a very long time in fact.........they were part of their stories before there were any forests or rivers or discernible geographic features in what is now british columbia
that's a cute trick...says the anthropologist examining raven's beak with a laser powered magnify-

ing glass......seems to me there's always been those things forests and rivers and such
sure thing says coyote...but h₂o got in the way...of there being any rivers or forests...dihydrogen oxide did the big number...*water water everywhere...nor any drop to drink* (Coleridge, 1917)
[different voice] hey that sounds familiar I think I wrote that says samuel t's ghost
be cool...be cool sammy t......or *all the boards will shrink...all in a hot and copper sky the bloody sun at noon* (Coleridge, 1917) just relax or you'll get heat exhaustion I was there on the boat with sammy...so not to worry
sounds like coyote ratiocination to me says anthro...you said there was too much water for there to be rivers?...how can that be? are you saying the rivers were overflowing their banks that they were present in the form of lakes and were lakine rather than riverine or brookine
actually the water was in the form of crystals...ice crystals
snow way!...*nieve jamais non ti credo*
yes...packed snow and ice...get out yer scrapers...yer snowshoes...yer broomball shoes...yer crampons...yer pitons and yer mammoth stalkers...*so get ready so get ready 'cause here I come* (Robinson, 1966)
the ice ages.......you're trying to tell me there were indians hereabouts before the ice ages?...sounds like somebody added a couple of handfuls of quartz crystals to that tale...or maybe that's just the percussion section...by my accounting the indians were still on the far side of beringia back then *beringia...feringia be bo...hortingia* (Ellis & Chase, 1964)...or maybe they/we/I were still in africa awaiting exit visas...or maybe they/we/I hadn't branched off into the *homo corvax canis* branch yet...still swinging free...*wimoweh wimoweh wimoweh wimoweh wimoweh wimoweh   ooo ooooo...ooo...ooo* (Linda, 1939)...another voice: the ice ages were actually brought on...and I say this from first paw experience not by hortense pretense or post tense...but by a *stl'atl'imx* medicine person...of the female variety...who got tired of the *tsilhqoten* stealing our women all the time for exogenic procreative centromeric metaphase purposes...divide and rule the glaciers were only supposed to extend as far as the edges of *tsilhqoten* territory sounds to me like your anthrotale is walking on wobbly stilts
so says anthro where is the evidence for all this geo malarkey...about pre ice age indians
I'll bet it's all been scraped away by retreating glaciers how convenient! *glacier ex machina*
more like *machina sub glaciato*...we are in fact the evidence...overproof
events did get a little out of hand...says raven...pushing the magnifying glass away...you see...that *stl'atl'imx* spell caster lost a lot of credibility when most of the province became covered with the white stuff...it wasn't supposed to happen that way...even the stratosphere got co-opted into the deep freeze...*And I wonder...I wah wah wah wah wonder...why why why why why why they ran away...*(Shannon & Crook, 1961)...*tsilhqoten runaway* and if mr del shannon is in the audience...I'd like to say thank you *for the music...the songs I'm singing*
runaway is right   I guess he/she/it...didn't have a spell...checker [nobody laughs...or even snickers...some eye rolling lip pointing]
coyote...you were talking about us being longtime friends of the *stl'atl'imx* people...do you think that makes us experts on them after all these millennia...could we maybe have enough knowledge to write a book an article...or get in a newspaper story about them a play an ethnography maybe we could scrape away some dna while we're having tea or boiling fishheads...get some epithelial cheek samples...or stories...we could collect their stories...that's a good trick!
what does any of this have to do with research anyway says anthro...that's what you're supposed to

be talking about up here in front of all these people...
PEOPLE!? says coyote putting down her san pellegrino...whooo well will you lookee that...(coifs herself)...an audience of spectators eyes and ears and hilled hulled hoed and everything
research? says raven...whooo...haven't heard that word for a while......hmmm closest I've heard has been "investigative reporting"..."in depth reporting"...hmm research—makes me want to put on my asbestos thinking cap...slick up my pompadour...and don my dusky geiger counter watch
geiger counter watch?
why sure...we decided a couple of generations back to shoot radio isotopes at our stories just so's we could identify them as ours......now they emit alpha particles...beta rays gamma globulin...omega watches and apple pie the whole 8 meters...you know...like those telemetry collars they put on grizzly bears...now we can locate our stories using gieger counters...but now they have half-lives rather than whole ones so we'll have to remedy that and the emerging stories are causing transgenerational haploid mutations
coyote and raven yuck it up for a while until they are brought back to "the task at hand" by anthro......who says...that research is not a dirty word...despite reports to the contrary it is a good word...it is what has brought us to the state we are currently in
research helps to civilize it helps to move us all forward...together says anthro
cough cough cough forward...hmm...says raven...seems to me...that the forwarder we move together the behinder we get as informants coresearchers and mentions on the acknowledgments page...must be something in that breakfast cereal the indian agents made us eat...or the backward pills they fed us with retro juice...precolumbian coffee and "together"?...did you say we were moving forward together?
excuse me says coyote...I'm feeling a bit off
could a bin the whisky......might a bin the sin...could a bin the 3 or 4 snowpacks
I don't know...but look at the province I'm in (Paxton, 1981)
get serious
satellite radio for the masses...especially useful for indians living in remote employment equity excluded mountainous areas who cannot pick up normal radio waves and other perturbations of the ether with the galvanic current operating between silver-mercury fillings now that they've got broadband...trouble is few have jobs but they can buy...oh they don't have any money...which complicates things...and most of the reserves don't have stores they're not on the provincial telephone or electricity grid and cell phones don't work but if you can afford a few thousand for a satellite or radio phone system...well you're one of the few with disposable income
raven says anthro...I'm here to help you and coyote and the indians
help us?...hey coyote...do we need want did we ask for...help
not sure...I'll ask the indians (asks audience) hey do you guys need anymore anthros...archaeos linguos...(shakes head to audience and says with them) NOOOOO!
wheww consensus big time did you hear the chorus...sounds like they're doing okay without the researchers...anything else before I dispense with the suspension of disbelief
hey says anthro...who's going to help the indians get their research grants so they can learn about themselves and move forward in a scholarly way...who's going to be on the *sshrc nsir cihr cfi*...grant committees to move their grants forward
if not for me winter would have no spring couldn't hear the robin sing (Dylan, 2000)
move forward well mother may I?...are you saying that aboriginal people are not already moving forward HEY are you guys doing the bunny hop down there or what? sorry anthro they're danc-

ing but they're going in a circle does that count as moving forward?
research is a serious topic...it's what is keeping indigenous cultures alive
whoo...wouldn't know about that...it's mostly the people who come and ask us questions who end up being hired at universities as researchers and professors...so it seems to be helping them a lot...it's mostly the phds from the *nct*'s—the newcomer tribes—who are the primary investigators of *fnrp*'s
pardon me?
first nations research projects...*fnrp*!...the indians are in the out and out
research projects!...*sniff sniff*...smells like rhodes scholars
sniff sniff smells more like rhodes s/kill indians getting in the rhodes of authenticity in the rhodes of progress oops detour shutdown nogo...highway 99 to pemberton lillooet port douglas...hello...international olympic committee...I need a pass to get back home...call the vanoc hi vanoc...I travel 99 mostly in the early morning so as to avoid the traffic...ooh it's closed in the morning but we've lived there for millennia oh I see no exceptions "just be patient" CLICK
it's okay raven...the shoulders on highway 99 are pretty narrow anyhow...not worth the risk...and pretty cold...especially if you get on the wrong side...of the scapula......so how come the *nct*'s are the *pi*'s of the *fnrp*'s...have they run out of white stuff to investigate they've done snow ivory clouds washed gravel and snowshoe rabbits
doesn't seem to be much to their cultures...I guess newcomer tribes have also been diagnosed to death including autopsied or maybe they ran out of outlaw motorcycle gangs...prisoners homeless people to research...maybe the settler researchers could do a bit more research on the rcmp...indian affairs...government corruption doping in sports corruption on wall street bay street...that would keep them going for a while...and while they're at it they could have another go at the ioc and vanoc which brings us back to whistler and land claims and indians...funny how it always comes back to us and we always end up as the last story and only if there's room
and what's with those settler anthros sociologists linguistics et al all referencing one other and hardly any indians being mentioned...*habeus corpus* being the dead indian languages cited where did they get their data from...indian expert 1 cites indian expert 2 cites indian expert 3 and so on down the line which pretty much incites all the indians because none of it is accurate or culturally sensitive or frankly any of their business
but they've passed university ethics...filled in the forms...gotten "informed consent"......somebody's signed them off on ethical research protocols...it's been on the up and up
fed...yes but the indians are more on the outskirts than ever of successville......no we're not called informants anymore...what are we now coresearchers but you know what? most of us don't even have a cv where we can put that down but hey! we keep appearing on the acknowledgements page whooee!...tell it to the t & p committee...tell it to the hiring committee tell it to the bank on royalties day "appeared on the acknowledgements page" 63 times
it's a long process says anthro takes time
gentlemen please!...yes but I always thought people moved faster than glaciers...most of the funding allocated for first nations research projects still goes to non–first nations researchers...what if most of the funding earmarked for feminist research went to men...or gay or lesbian funding went to straights or black funding went to non-blacks...somehow indians always end up being fiduciated...right out of the ball park...home run...run home do not pass go and please remember to tip the indian agent
anthro interjects...indigenous people don't have the requisite skills or experience to be primary

investigators that's why indian research projects are run by qualified outsiders

the deficit model of indianness strikes again look out! are there any qualified indians out there?...do I see any hands...yes...robert warrior and elizabeth cook lynn...jace weaver...presence duly noted...donna house...ines talamantez...ada deer gerald vizenor

how about north of the border?...lots of hands going up...bonita lawrence...taiaiake alfred...eldon yellowhorn...deb mcgregor quite a few more hands at the back

and it seems that there aren't enough aboriginal people in canada even for the aboriginal canada research chairs because most of them are being offered to non-aboriginal people...how is that happening?...oversight? another spectrum disorder?...refractive shortcoming?

we're disqualified says raven not because we lack perquisite qualifications but because we are not in places of power...it is not aboriginal communities and aboriginal scholars who are in charge of deciding which *fnrp*'s will be funded it is mainstream settler canada...aboriginal communities are not even close to being the main beneficiaries of so-called "aboriginal" research projects

you don't expect white and other settlerly professors who are hugely invested in objectifying and otherwise fiduciating aboriginal people to allow that kind of academic freedom and ethical principles...says coyote...the outcry would be unbelievable seems to me...there are no crosswalks on the academic road...no flashing ambers just flashing reds...do not enter...detour...that's why the indians are either mostly all on one side of the road scholarship...the downside curbside

so...says anthro that's what academic rigor is all about what are you going to do about it...besides complain and talk about the past

the past hmm...in my language the past exists in and is spoken about using the present tense the past impacts the present the past impacts the future and it's all happening right now in the present tense as we............spoke

when is the last time an indian word *gained entrée* into the english language

there's lots of them says anthro...*tipi...toboggan igloo...mocassin the tomahawk and the bow and knife cherokee nation...cherokee tribe* (Loudermilk, 1971)...are you going to talk about noninclusion now it *is* the english language after all...how many foreign expressions do you want...we have translated the bible into aboriginal languages what more do you want? you should be grateful we have created such a beautiful language...so what if you can't speak your own languages you've got english the zenith of linguistic development

we can say stuff in english they never even had a word for in indian languages

mmm...says coyote reflectively...like clearcut genocide biocide oil spills and diet coke

coyote what were we thinking...you wanting your *howls and yips*...and me my *wracckkks...and...thrrrrrmmmps*...when we've got english...why don't we just translate everything into english and get rid of the original languages and sounds and rhythms

after all pete seeger copyrighted the words and music of solomon linda's song *mbube* calling it *wimomweh*...a mishearing of the chorus *uyi mbube* [you're a lion] followed many other pretenders...weiss...peretti and creatore reworked it and called it "the lion sleeps tonight" it was only in 1960 when mariam makeba came to the US and recorded the song as *mbube* 20 years later that linda received credit for the song...interesting genealogy follow the money (hands on hips)

whatever! let's get back to research says anthro...what has language got to do with research does it matter what language the research is done in or which language is saved or extinguished...isn't extinction the natural end of languages and most other things

I am not quite at that point yet...worrying about what language it would be done in...I was still at the point of the assumption of "the right to research"...how about "the right not to be researched" what

is it about academia that presumes "the right to peer at other cultures"
without research indigenous people would have lost their languages and cultures long ago
oh?...lost? *oops hey herman alma kaykay I think I lost my language must have left it on the bus my culture too* are you saying that aboriginal people have not always worked to retain their languages and knowledges?...and if some are not in the process of language or cultural recovery where did that come from?...who or what do you think might be responsible for aboriginal language loss in the first place?
okay let's say I want to enter the faculty of environmental studies take a master's degree or phd...how do I get knowledge relating to coyotes from a primary source?...where do I get primary sources for us as a tribe without the knowledge going through my own human subjectivity?...who are the coyote experts and how does anyone know whether or not they know what they're talking about? have they lived in our dens birthed and looked after our little ones...enacted our rites rituals protocols...do they understand our languages?
well says anthro problem is there aren't enough coyotes in academia right now who have the qualifications to do research on coyotes or who possess *cek* (coyote environmental knowledge)
cek!
and are able to put it forward using an academic shape coyote substance itself doesn't matter...it has to be understood translated standardized otherwise there would be chaos
doesn't being a coyote qualify me within the academy in the area of coyote traditional knowledge?...isn't being aboriginal itself a qualification for teaching aboriginal education? isn't it a pre-requisite and speaking of chaos what about entropy isn't it part of the foundation of western science and western thinking laws and axioms...coyote is coyote is coyote...ask wild bill *hic hoc hominem coeli*
you wouldn't even make it into the parking lot coyote...there's a bounty on you...you wouldn't be taken seriously in front of a classroom or in a research situation except as something to be dissected and raven...people would throw stones at you
which is where shapeshifting comes in handy......*poof*...oscar wilde appears complete with cravat and pomade *Most people are other people. Their thoughts are someone else's opinions, their lives a mimicry, their passions a quotation* (Wilde, 1996, p. 11)
we stand on the shoulders of sasquatches as my grandmother used to say
then let us cite the sasquatches rather than comment on the view...I'm sure someone famous must have said that
what existed before research? asks the narrator...during a nano lull in the dialogue...while the ergs were building nests inside the quarks
that "before" still exists says coyote...many aboriginal individuals have not been researched directly though their intellectual property has doubtless been copyrighted and otherwise purloined by some non-aboriginal scholar
I object!
-ify......to what?...on what grounds?...or I should say whose?
academics need to follow the same rules as the rest of us in terms of ethical guidelines and ethical practice
researchers are in a special category
they sure are *non–compos mentis in hoc nomine* especially the voyeurs who keep coming to my community demanding answers they talk about informed consent HA!
ha! what?...why do you scoff at informed consent

informed?...how do you inform a community in which everyone suffers from post traumatic stress and in many cases it's not even post...the stress is there right now...caused by events taking place in the present tense or the past progressive...the majority of the people in my community up home are functionally illiterate...when the majority of a community is high on drugs or alcohol or depressed and starving most of the time when are they in a state to be informed? what is their level of awareness and understanding with respect to academic discourses when most suffer from some form of fetal alcohol spectrum disorder and syndromes associated with violence including against self...how can there be informed...consent when the educational system is standardized to essentialize indianness and to hide the genocidal policies and practices of the newcomers...what can people in the community learn about themselves in educational institutions...provincial curriculum is the new bible mr anthro...where in the history curriculum do schoolchildren learn about the treaties signed under extreme duress when the people were starving to death or freezing to death or under attack from enemies or within other coercive contexts...and this after generations of poor treatment by canada britain or france with whom they had been valuable military allies they are offered a meager bundle of cash a coat a blanket a temporary respite from hopelessness and oblivion promises of medical care and education agreeing to give the canadian state the land they wanted and accepting in return the poorest land...where do they learn about the residential schooling...the 60s scoop taking aboriginal children from their families and communities so that they might be assimilated into the settler society...where do they learn about the government acting in contravention to its own laws this is not what the first peoples have agreed to...pavlovian experimentation...instrumental investigation action research stations...but hey how about auction research

sounds good raven...let's sell off an aboriginal research site with bones and everything......how about an *ishkin*...a pithouse site together with *in situ* artifacts unopened...guaranteed to be at least 12–14 thousand years old...let's have an auction research!

okay where do you want to start on this beauty on the block this afternoon *ishkin* bo bishkin banana panna wa bishkin fee fi (Ellis & Chase, 1964) *ishkin* do I hear an opening bid of one hundred and fifty thousand one a one a one over there with the bulge in his silk suit jacket do I hear two one and a half now 75 will you go two...two with the fedora do I hear three three three three woman with the microsoft ball cap now four up front with the sacred bundle...of cash...no halves now we're on roll whattayawannabid whattayawannabid waddabid waddabid now do I hear five five a five a five a woman with the xerox earrings go half...five and a half now six and now...a half to the man with the red bolo tie

there's a reserve bid on this folks...reservation for those of you from south of the border......and we're not even close to it do I hear a million...and now two two two two...and a half now three in the *trenchcoat badge out laid off said he's got a bad cough...wants to get it paid off!* (Dylan, 2000) will you go four 4 million one from the phone now 4 and a half do I hear 5 and a half now 6...6 million one hundred eighty eighty eighty come on folks this is one of a kind merchandise let's get serious *this is where the people lived and did their stuff* six one ninety in the front row with the corporate smile and now a half one a one a one and one ninety five woman in the pinstripe and now let's go 6 two whattabid whattabid whattabid comeonnow folks 6 million two...woman with the dead mammal collar and now fifteen up there with the environmentally unfriendly lincoln suv keychain and twenty wannabid wannabid wannabid now six million 225 do I hear 30 wheredoyawannago wheredago wheredago now bid fifty...250 now come on folks this is a one of a kind opportunity to purchase an authentic pit house...a what's it called again...*ishkin*...you won't find one in any retail outlet anytime soon and we'll throw in a stainless steel shovel 10,000 name tags and a whisk brush...6 million 250

250 250 250...*stop! in the name of research*...let's go folks and now 50 55 60 now 65 and 70...75 now 80 will you go 5 and now 6 million 300 thousand wheredo you wanna go wheretogo wheretogo 200 now 250 275 now 3 and a half on the phone now 6 million 350 thousand will you go 6 and a half ladies and gentlemen this is a bargain at ten times the price...gentleman with the west vancouver golf club blazer and now a half will you go 6 six six six...seven and now eight 825 35 40 now 850...now 75...now 900 bid 950...whatabid whatabid now 7 million wheredoyawanna go wheretago wheretago sir are you bidding please...this is no place to be doing calisthenics there's a yoga studio down the street and a ymca a couple blocks over...*young man! there's no need to feel down I said young man pick yourself off the ground...I said young man 'cause you're in a new town...There's no need to unhappy...it's fun to stay at the YMCA It's fun to stay at the YMCA* (Belolo, Morali, & Willis, 1978)...thank you have a nice day...lady with the lady with the lady with the linda lundstrom jacket will you go 7 one and now two and now 3 hundred thousand let's go on this one let's go let's go and now 7 four...now 5 6 and now 7 7 7 7 will you go half......7 million two and a half and now 3 and now 4......I might as well put this microphone down and open up a kiosk at the ferry terminal...come on folks get out your fingers and hands...whatabid whatabid whatabid will you go half and now 450 from the phone fromthephone fromthephone fromthephone now a half will you go 5 we got a phone war going now oooh and now phone...email......internet...war...chatroom bids...listserv bids facebook...twitter...tweeter daffy duck...let's go now 550 now 60 65 70 75 now 80 coca cola pepsi bo bepsi hee haw olà (Ellis & Chase, 1964) back to line 1 and now 85 line 3......yes ma'am that's you you're three and now in back with the dark glasses cigarette holder high heels...yes sir you...7 million...six fifty bid now do I hear 75 now 80 please sir go across the street if you want to stretch *Young man are you listening to me...I said, young man, what do you want to be, I said young man, you can make real your dreams, but you've got to know this one thing* (Belolo, Morali, & Willis, 1978)—I'm trying to run a business here...do I hear 80 80 80 80 that's it folks six eighty...just getting started gottago gottago gottago 680 now 90 with the dollar sign tattoo...back to you with the chinchilla coat 700 and now 50 50 50 50 whatabid now 50 with the sealskin boots...whattabid whattabid whattabid let's go now now do I hear 60 65 now 70...thank you......ladies and gentleman this is an authentic first nations abode where people lived before contact...what's that...and after.........and during......do I hear 780 we've got a long night ahead if we're gonna move this slow gotta move gotta move gotta move now do I hear 785 and now 800...7 million 800 thousand...ladies and gentleman this is from the collection of a wellknown westcoast collector a great...what was she? a great captain of industry and indiana collector *cascadia* collector a great supporter of deceased indigenous people...what's that?...she didn't like them...well let's move it out of her collection right now do I hear 825 now 30 930 gotta go now...going once...going twice sold to the woman with the 6 high-tech devices attached to her coming up next on the block the faculty of medicine university of xxx where do you want to start with this 75 million all right goodtogo goodtogo goodtogo now 80 80 co weighty bo beighty ba beighty bonana pana eighty now eighty five

how often do they have these auctions...queries narrator

oh depends sometimes it's an estate sale sometimes a collector wants to move into something different they get tired of a particular indigenous site that the public is feeling protective of...you know...like stanley park...kitsilano...the ubc endowment lands

so what about the research you're doing right now

oh...well...we have a three year grant to work with the stl'atl'imx community says raven...in particular those south of the duffy lake road but not exclusive of those further to the north...coyote pipes up...why do you want to know...are you doing research on us?

uh...no no I was just curious

our research is about language and cultural revitalization...in particular it's about community and individual self empowerment...and renaming and reclaiming the parts of the territory

we are working with the community to collect stories related to the "history" of the stl'atl'imx community before and since and during...contact...these stories are being collected for the most part by other community members who are coresearchers

we spent a lot of time with those living on- and off-reserve to set up protocols at meetings in all and each of the communities...using robert charlie's rules of order and a lot of drumming and singing...we have an elders research council that oversees every aspect of the project...including determining what research needs to be done by whom with whom where...ensuring that *stl'atl'imx* philosophies knowings methodologies and protocols guide the project ensuring that the community has collective control over our intellectual and cultural property...and that the *stl'atl'imx* are the principal beneficiaries of the research

the hereditary chief of tenas lake of samahquam is our key research assistant......*kakilah* clarke smith...the one and only

the youth work with the elders to collect data in the *ucwalmicwts* language and in english the stories are to be shared **as** a book and we hope the beginning of an animated film about our flood story everybody's got a flood story...everybody needs one water is the final reclaimer

*thrrrrp......click click......*well...gotta go...says raven

me too says coyote......we gotta get back to the real world of nonacademia

I'm starting to forget how to howl

oh I'm an expert on that...says raven...just put your head back...right...it opens up your throat...and...whooooosh raven steals coyote's supper

hey says coyote...lucky I tied a string to it

exit raven with coyote's supper...string dangling

hmm I guess I forgot to tie it to anything...oh well I guess there's always next time

kukwstum

nia:wen

REFERENCES

Belolo, H., Morali, J., & Willis, V. (1978). *YMCA* [Recorded by The Village People]. On Village People [LP]. New York: Sigma Sound Studios.

Coleridge, S. T. (1917). The Rime of the Ancient Mariner. In *The Rime of the Ancient Mariner and Other Poems* (pp. 5–22). London: Humphrey Milford/Oxford University Press.

Dylan, B. (2000). *If Not for You*. On New Morning [CD]. New York: Columbia.

Ellis, S., & Chase, L. (1964). *The Name Game* [2001]. On Shirley Ellis—The Complete Congress Recordings [CD]. London: Connoisseur Collections.

Fletcher, C. (1959). *The Strawberry Roan*. [Recorded by Marty Robbins]. On Gunfighter Ballad and Trail Songs [LP]. New York: Columbia Records.

Harrison. G. (1970). *My Sweet Lord*. On All Things Must Pass [LP]. London: EMI Records.

Leadbelly. (1999). *C. C. Rider* [CD]. UK: Cat Fish Records.

Linda, S. (1939). *Mbube*. Recorded by Evening Birds. South Africa: Gallo Record.

Loudermilk, J. D. (1971). *Indian Reservation (The Lament of the Cherokee Reservation Indian)* [Recorded by the Raiders]. On The Legend of Paul Revere. New York: Columbia Records.

McCartney, P., & Lennon, J. (1964). *She Loves You* [Recorded by The Beatles]. On The Beatles Second Album. [LP]. Los Angeles: Capital Records.

Paxton, T. (1988). *Wasn't That a Party*. On the Very Best of Tom Paxton [CD].

Pierre, M. (n.d.). *Women's Warrior Song*.

Rice, T., & Weber, A. L. (1971). *Everything Is Alright*. On Jesus Christ Superstar [LP]. New York: Decca/MCA/Decca Broadway.

Robinson, S. (1966). *Get Ready*. On Greatest Hits. [Recorded by the Temptations]. Detroit: Motown Records.

Shannon, D., & Crook, M. (1961). *Runaway*. On Runaway with Del Shannon [LP]. New York: Big Top Records.

Surfaris. (1963). *Wipe Out*. On The Sufaris Play Wipe Out. [LP]. Los Angeles, CA: Capital Records. Big Top.

Wilde, O. (1996). *De Profundis*. Minneola, NY: Dover.

Whitfield N., & Strong, B. (1969). *Can't Get Next to You*. [Recorded by The Temptations]. [45 RPM]. Detroit, MI: Motown Records.

CHAPTER TWENTY-SIX

Indigenous Spirituality and Decolonization

Methodology for the Classroom

ERIC RITSKES

Much of the writing on Indigenous knowledges operating within the Western academy emphasizes the importance of engagement, embodied learning, and not "sitting in pristine fashion" outside of other knowledge, but choosing instead to actively engage with multiple ways of knowing (Dei, 2000). Indigenous spirituality is seen as a vital aspect of Indigenous knowledges and yet, too often, it is left unpacked in terms of engagement with the Western academy. Both Indigenous knowledges and spirituality stem from lived experiences of the individual and the community and yet little time has been spent on how these oppositional ways of knowing can both resist and exist within the Western academy, a site of hegemonic power that seeks to posit itself as the sole provider and authenticator of knowledge. Indigenous spirituality weaves its way inextricably through all aspects of life so how can it be brought to a Western academy that seeks to fragment and compartmentalize knowledge as a method of control and containment? How can a sense of community and connection be brought into a space that alienates and distances people from their connections and their whole selves? These are some of the questions that this chapter will seek to explore.

In examining the links between Indigenous spirituality and the Western classroom, this chapter seeks to explore the connection between community and classroom and how both are vital sites of knowledge production which cannot work or exist apart from each other. This chapter recognizes that the term "community" has too often been co-opted within Western discourses to act as a sort of "Trojan horse," hiding within its vague promises of participation and equal involvement a universalizing Western project of domination which seeks to devalue other ways of knowing and subjugate "Other" bodies. This chapter seeks to deconstruct the ways that "community" has been used in an attempt to reveal positive ways that the community can be integrated within classrooms. This chapter will argue that, for communities to be valued as partners in knowledge production, Indigenous spirituality needs to be seen as active and embodied. Indigenous spirituality is vital to understanding the web of relationships and connections that make up both the community and the classroom and in understanding how these two sites are connected. Through Indigenous spirituality multiple ways of knowing can be affirmed, diversity can be seen as empowering rather than disabling and knowledge production can shift from a one-way flow from academy to community, instead working in reciprocity to strengthen both sites to resist Western discourses of colonialism and domination.

This chapter seeks to provide some new avenues to explore in terms of schooling and Indigenous knowledges, always being mindful of those who have gone before and those who have initiated the conversations—those to whom this chapter is in great debt to. I approach the topic of Indigenous spirituality with great humility and echo Hanohano (1999) in stating, "[I am] begging your compassion as I stumble on" (p. 210). The intent of this chapter is both an invitation to join in the discussion and provocation to act because, as Howard (2006) so aptly questions, how can we discuss anti-oppression without having any action-oriented implications for anyone? In fact, this detached sense of impartiality only furthers the Western project of colonialism which for so long has posited itself as scientific and reasonable. It is because of this that this chapter seeks to go beyond the theoretical ponderings and ground itself in actionable, embodied learning, seeking to examine Indigenous spirituality as methodology within the academy.

THEORETICAL FRAMEWORK

As a white male who has grown up in Canada, there is no escaping my explicit implication with the very systems of domination and colonialism that this chapter seeks to resist. Also, in writing about Indigenous spirituality I am also aware of my position as a Western Christian, stuck squarely within a system of power that fought so diligently to dehumanize and denigrate Indigenous spirituality as primitive, barbaric, pagan, and heathen. Too often white Canadians have attempted to distance themselves from any implication in colonial violence, choosing instead to begin their history when it suits them best; I choose instead to locate myself within this history, in a nation built on "the cumulative hurt of others" (Brand, 2001, p. 82) and to recognize the inextricability of this position—as Memmi (1969) states: "the European living in a colony but having no privileges . . . does not exist" (p. 10). As someone who writes about pedagogy and education I am also keenly aware how the academy has been constructed as a space of disempowerment for all except a small, privileged group which I am a part of.

While I cannot change my whiteness or my gender, I feel the need to contribute to the demise of these discourses, working to undermine the positions that privilege me while still being accountable and aware of how they position me. Nabavi (2006) states that we are all part of the relationship between domination and resistance and I want my work to both recognize the complexity of this relationship and to find ways to enact resistance, rather than oppression. It is this desire to resist oppression that informs this chapter and allows me to choose to use an anticolonial discursive framework. I posit the "colonial" not as something necessarily foreign or alien but, rather, as "dominating" and "imposing" (Dei & Asgharzadeh, 2001). An anticolonial framework grounds itself in the histories of the subjugated, centering multiple ways of knowing in an effort to resist and disrupt Eurocentric ways of knowing which posit themselves as exclusive and universal.

The anticolonial discursive is centered on the power of Indigenous knowledges and, as such, it is vital to attempt to define what is meant by Indigenous knowledges. This chapter refuses to place a totalizing definition on what is seen as a necessarily fluid term and recognizes that, "the quest for universal definitions ignores the diversity of the people of the earth and their views of themselves" (Battiste & Henderson, 2000, p. 36). Instead, a "working definition" is sought, one that allows for the vitality and fluidity of Indigenous knowledges as it constantly creates and re-creates itself in the face of new challenges and situations. In resisting a set definition, there is also the recognition that for too long Indigenous bodies and knowledges have been constructed and defined from outside in order to contain and dominate them. Dei, Hall, & Rosenberg (2000) locate Indigenous knowledge in relationship to a long-term occupancy of a particular place as well as "the sum of the experience and knowledge of a given social group [that] forms the bases of decision making in the face of challenges both familiar and unfamiliar" (p. 6). Indigenous knowledges are not a desperate reach into a static, romanticized past but a realization that, through history and embodied experience the present and the future can be informed and transformed; Indigenous knowledges are dynamic and fluid.

"Indigenous" obviously encompasses a wide, diverse group, and there is the need to be careful not to homogenize or suppress diverse experiences or ways of knowing. Instead, "anti-colonialism calls for connecting discussions among the local, marginalised and Indigenous experiences" (Dei, 2006; p. 15). The anticolonial does not ignore or leave unattended issues of diversity but explicitly seeks to use them to interrogate relationships and connections, to understand power dynamics and to use the power of diversity in resistance. Not only is there the recognition of diversity of experiences through location but also through gender, race, ability, and class. Experiences of colonialism are not uniform and affect each individual differently, yet, it is in this diversity that common experiences can be found to strengthen resistance. Spirituality is one of the key connectors between individuals and groups, and this is why it is important to interrogate its role in Indigenous knowledges and anticolonial resistance.

INDIGENOUS SPIRITUALITY

What is meant by Indigenous spirituality? It is the recognition of the connectedness of all things, both animate and inanimate, from past through the present and into the future. It is the realization of a common essence within us that is constantly being shaped and re-shaped in response to the multitude of connections and relationships that constantly affect us, a realization that we as humans are only one link in a grand chain of existence. It is this understanding of ourselves as part of a greater schema that informs our desire to work for peace with one another, to work for good relationships that do not seek to damage others and to live in balance and respect with others.

This is in direct opposition to a Western conceptualization of spirituality which not only posits the individual as the sole "locus for selectivity and determination of belief" (York, 2001, p. 366) but which emphasizes an individualized spirituality that fits into a commodified, Western liberal framework. The Western conceptualization of spirituality is shaped by an inward movement which seeks to prioritize the individual, as Rendon (2000) states, "I can make a difference for others only if I make a difference for me" (p. 11). This spiritual solipsism renders itself sterile in the fight for empowerment and justice by refusing to recognize individuals as inextricably marked and connected through their environments and relationships. Indigenous spirituality resists the hegemony of "me," as Dei (2002b) argues, and destroys the self/other dichotomy, "rendering the self as not autonomous but connecting to a larger collective" (p. 7). Indigenous spirituality is not a negation of the self but a refusal to center it at the expense of others and a refusal to ignore the vitality and importance of connections. Indigenous spirituality, through this emphasis on connection, is grounded in the lived realities of the community; as Kinchloe (2006) argues, "A human being simply can't exist outside the inscription of community with its processes of relationship, differentiation, interaction, and subjectivity" (p. 192).

COMMUNITY AND INDIGENOUS SPIRITUALITY

Central to this discussion on Indigenous spirituality is an understanding of what is encompassed within the term "community." Too often this term is bandied about as a covering mechanism to obscure Western agendas or to validate Western knowledge about the "Other," a stamp of authenticity on a project, report, or proposal with little regard for who the community actually is. Gujit and Shah (1998) show how community involvement became the by-word of the Western development agenda in the 1990s, seeking to add local voices to Western-driven projects. They argue that too often the community was viewed naively as "a harmonious and internally equitable collective" (Gujit & Shah, 1998, p. 1) which only served to obscure the power dynamics and differences that operated within the communities. Too often the community was seen as bounded and static, obscured the voices of women and others with little power to speak, and ignored the dynamic realities of people and power transfer (Daniels, 2009; Gujit & Shah, 1998; Maguire, 1996). Too often, as Young (1990) states, "community" privileges unity over diversity and acts as an arbiter between authentic and inauthentic social relationships.

In an attempt to navigate these dissonances, too often the response has been to fall back on Benedict Arnold's conceptualization of "imagined communities." As Dei & Asgharzadeh (2001) point out, the idea of community, despite it necessarily being fluid and dynamic, is very real in its meaning and evocation and has profound consequences for Indigenous and colonized peoples. It is the community, both as a whole and as a unit made up of individuals, which embodies Indigenous spirituality and knowledge: "Indigenous knowledge is so much a part of clan, band, or community, or even the individual, that it cannot be separated from the bearer to be codified into a definition. Those who have the knowledge use it routinely, perhaps every day, and because of this, it becomes something that is a part of them and unidentifiable except in personal context"(Battiste & Henderson, 2000, p. 36). Indigenous spirituality is embodied through the connections of the community, through their everyday actions, and through their very "breath." It is in the "personal context" that Indigenous spirituality is realized as the dynamic force that it is. It is through lived experiences that Indigenous spirituality and knowledge is created and re-created on a daily basis through connections and relationships. Again, it needs to be re-emphasized that this emphasis on connections does not privilege the community over the individual or vice versa but recognizes the inextricability of the two, the inter-dependence of the individual and the community.

For Indigenous peoples, community involves not only the people in the immediate location but relationships with the environment/whole earth, relationships with the ancestors who have gone before, and relationships with those who are to come: "community means the living, the unborn, the dead, and nature as a whole" (Wangoola, 2000, p. 271). Spirituality weaves these three connections together and allows for a community that is broad and dynamic. Dei (1993) explores how nature, the spirits, and the ancestors are connected through a spiritual understanding of the earth which is not only imbued with spirits but also acts as a bridge between the living and the dead. Mazama (2002) states, "There can be no dichotomy between so-called natural and supernatural worlds" (p. 221). Each individual is connected in different ways but they are still part of this greater "web" and have the rights and responsibilities that are imbued by the community.

What does Indigenous spirituality look like inside of the Western academy? The goal of Indigenous knowledges within the academy is to resist and disrupt Eurocentric, colonial ways of thinking which seek to dominate, and Indigenous spirituality, as a vital aspect of Indigenous knowledges, has an important role to play in this resistance. The emphasis placed on connections and lived experiences oppose a Western worldview that values individualism and rational, scientific thinking. Indigenous spirituality is embodied and active, and the challenge then becomes: How do you bring a spiritual, holistic, embodied learning into an academy that is built on Western rationalism, fragmentation of knowledge, and disembodied learning? If the goal of Indigenous spirituality is to break down borders and dichotomies, how can it be brought into and contained within a course syllabus and the walls of a classroom?

Dei & Doyle-Wood (2006) argue that Indigenous spirituality cannot simply be an aesthetic undertaking but one of activity and of resistance. Anticolonial writers such as Memmi (1969), Fanon (1963), and Said (1993) emphasize that colonial power never "gives anything away out of goodwill" (Said, 1993, p. 207), that the colonial situation can only be broken through sustained resistance. Dei & Asgharzadeh (2001) assert that to emphasize the "Indigenous" is to exist in a state of perpetual confrontation with the colonial order that seeks to negate all opposition. In spite of the inherency of resistance within discourses of the "Indigenous," there must be a willingness to interrogate this resistance and recognize the vast complexities involved in these power relationships; as Lila Abu-Lughod (1990) emphasizes in her work, resistance is too often romanticized and enshrined as inherently beneficial. In enacting resistance there needs to be caution demonstrated as not to replicate the very dichotomies and systems that we are seeking to bring down; all too often the "Indigenous" is set up in a dichotomy with "Western" where the Indigenous is good and the Western is evil. This good/evil narrative is the very thing that has been co-opted by society to exclude Indigenous spirituality and label it evil, pagan and not relative to modern society.

The resistance that Indigenous spirituality seeks to enact is one that emphasizes the power of creation. It is not simply a reactionary, defensive stance to Western hegemony but a constructive force that speaks through inclusivity and transformation. Through the exploration of community and connection, Indigenous spirituality seeks to empower individuals and groups to enact social change. This resistance is not some vague, universalizing "we are all one" project but one that willingly and forcefully interrogates difference and dynamics of power in the hope that this informed resistance will bring about people who can recognize and identify their own lived experiences and how they connect to others' experiences, connect to society and communities, and how they fit into the relationships between oppression and resistance. Resistance is embedded in the day-to-day; through gestures, choices, and actions, both by individuals and the collective, Indigenous spirituality is able to resist discourses that seek to silence it. It is not some grand, romanticized narrative of resistance that Indigenous spirituality seeks to enact but one that is embodied in the people and their desire to construct something new.

INDIGENOUS SPIRITUALITY, COMMUNITY, AND THE CLASSROOM

How can Indigenous spirituality and the community be integrated into the classroom? This question is a key undertaking if ideas of Indigenous spirituality are to move beyond theorizing and to maintain their position as active and embodied. We cannot simply talk about or learn about Indigenous knowledges or spirituality; they must be enacted, lived, and used. In failing to push the "Indigenous" beyond theory there is a sense of hesitation found in most writings, a hesitation to "prescribe," or perhaps inscribe, a method or technique onto something that is so dynamic and localized. In interrogating how Indigenous spirituality can be used in the classroom, this chapter also looks to avoid such prescriptive measures. Yet, there is the need to move forward and explore Indigenous spirituality not purely as method but as methodology. Within this methodology there will ultimately be a multitude of interpretations and implementations, but these issues of activity must be engaged with in an effort to utilize the power and resistance that is embedded in Indigenous spirituality.

Part of the reticence in discussing methods or methodology is the history of past failed experiments in integrating the community, Indigenous knowledge and spirituality. Too often "community engagement" or "participatory learning" has been a cover-up for continued colonial relations. McNally (2004) looks at ways to bring Indigenous pedagogy to the classroom and arrives at a "service learning model" which originates from the idea that "knowledge is used in service of community" and results in students going to Indigenous communities to serve and, ultimately, learn. While it is hard to fault his starting position, the service learning model leaves questions of power uninterrogated. The community is seen as a location rather than a dynamic body capable of producing knowledge; they are a "proving ground" for privileged others, a place to gain experiences without serious engagement. It is a learning model directed, managed, and evaluated by Western bodies, a sort of educational tourism which only benefits the privileged "tourist" and only further engrains us/them dichotomies and the one-way flow of knowledge and service from the academy to the communities.

Instead, we need to imagine new ways to bring the community and Indigenous spirituality into conversation with the Western academy. Ways in which the community is not merely a receptacle for Western knowledge or a place to be "developed." Ways in which to de-center the Western academy as the sole producer of knowledge and recognize the community as producers of knowledge rather than merely consumers. Ways that recognize the power dynamics between privileged bodies and the dominated. To do this, learning and education need to begin with the community rather than the academy. Edwards and Hewitson (2008), in their interrogation of Indigenous education programs in Australia, forcefully state that the primary consideration of education needs to be: is it meaningful to the community? Dei (2002a) also clearly states, "It is important to start by defining how learning proceeds in the community" (p. 354). Wangoola (2000) sees the academy as a place for the community to sow, cultivate, and harvest knowledge, as an integrated tool of the community rather than outside of it. The flow of knowledge needs to be reversed so that the community is valued and so that the academy cannot escape into its lofty theoretical grandiose without grounding itself in reality. If schooling is to begin with the community and their conceptualizations of education and spirituality, how can we conceptualize this?

This chapter will broach two broad areas in which Indigenous spirituality and ideas of community can be brought into the Western classroom: valuing emotional and spiritual knowledge and affirming collaborative learning. Out of necessity they are broad categories and undoubtedly given too little space in this short chapter but, heuristically, they are hopefully useful in inviting discussion and provoking action.

VALUING EMOTIONAL AND SPIRITUAL KNOWLEDGE

Castellano (2000), in his three aspects of Indigenous knowledge, includes revealed knowledge which is provided by dreams, revelation, and intuition. It is this aspect of knowledge that has been constantly derided by science and Western society as lacking rational basis. Because it speaks to subjective experiences and cannot be verified by "facts" it is discredited as knowledge. It is a problem of what is considered "evidence," a problem exacerbated by the Western privileging of what can be seen over what is experienced by the other senses, including what is commonly called the "sixth sense." It is this intuitive knowledge which is part and parcel of the spiritual knowledge that Wangoola (2000) argues forms the basis for Indigenous social and political life and which is mediated through connections with the elders, ancestors, and with nature. The community and individuals recognize connections to what cannot be seen but only experienced. This type of knowledge is very much in line with what Cooper (1997) calls "emotional intelligence" which "provides a deeper, more fully formed understanding of oneself and those around us" (p. 13). It is a knowledge grounded in experience and informed by cultural customs. This spiritual knowledge is about being able to apply and use the power of intuition and emotions to provide a holistic education.

In the Western academy there is currently no use for this kind of knowledge which flies in the face of everything that it stands for. Spirituality and emotions are shied away from as childish and unable to conform to the academy's fascination with "objectivity." This is not to say that there haven't been attempts at integrating spiritual knowledge within the classroom environment, but many of these fail to recognize that spirituality cannot be contained with a syllabus but are embodied. In attempting to integrate Indigenous spirituality into the academy, there needs to be a concerted effort to not only value spiritual knowledge but to use spiritual knowledge to challenge and resist the Eurocentric discourses that discredit it. Shahjahan (2006) reveals how one of the underlying discourses of the academy is the Baconian ideal of "control"; researchers and those in power must show that they are in control not only of what they study but of themselves. Spiritual knowledge disrupts this and recognizes the value of being vulnerable and open. It challenges ideals of objectivity by valuing personal experience and emotion.

Within a classroom this can mean allowing students to bring their whole selves into the academic discussion rather than sequestering or discrediting aspects that seem irrational or unobjective. Spiritual knowledge can be utilized to provide depth to discussions and to connect students to knowledge production and to other learners in new ways. By recognizing spiritual knowledge, issues of agency and power are recognized. No longer are students seen as "deficient" or devoid of knowledge and in need of "filling up"; instead, they are recognized as full of experiences and able to access a vast storeroom of knowledge that already exists. Students become agents, spiritual subjects, and creators in their own education.

AFFIRMING COLLABORATIVE LEARNING

By recognizing students as already existent knowledge vessels, the roles of the teacher, the curriculum, and the classroom shift. There is the recognition of a shift in roles for the educators; no longer is their role to impart knowledge but to provide a space and a vocabulary which allows students to explore their spiritual knowledge and to explore their vast connections to each other, to their communities and to larger power dynamics. To do this requires educators to have an explicit understanding of the power dynamics within a classroom as well as to understand their own positioning, location, and connections. There needs to be a conscious effort to break down the student/teacher dichotomy in a way that allows everyone to bring their selves and experiences into the knowledge production process in transformative ways. There must be a commitment to co-production of knowledge and co-learning with and among students. Instead of presenting learning as a competitive, individual endeavor leading to personal gain, education needs to be viewed as a path to uncover and understand our connections, to understand how they shape who we are, and how we can create resistance through connectedness. As hooks (2003) argues, "conventional education teaches us that disconnection is organic to being" (p. 180). A connected spirituality ruptures the conventional classroom. Spirituality creates community and shared experiences through humility, empowerment, and dialogue, opening up a space for learners to belong to knowledge production.

In doing this, the classroom moves from being an abstract location that is divorced from the messy realities of students' experiences to a space where students feel free to engage and explore their connections and identities. The classroom no longer conforms to a Western standard of objectivity and rational distancing from emotions, lived experiences, and spirituality but instead recognizes and works with the power of spirituality and personal experience to create a fluid and dynamic source of knowledge production. Knowledge is recognized as fluid and intrinsically tied to personal beliefs and experiences rather than being distant and impersonal. In recognizing student's individual spirituality, the classroom becomes a space to learn about individual stories and daily resistances, showing us the complexities of daily changing power structures (Abu-Lughod, 1990).

Not only is collaborative learning essential for allowing students to learn from each other and to recognize their role in knowledge production, but it is also essential in helping them recognize the role of the communities in the classroom. Knowledge is no longer divorced from their connections but alive and actively being produced in their homes, places of worship, and communities; knowledge production must be relevant to the students and their communities. There needs to be an explicit goal to position the classroom in a reciprocal relationship with the communities and connections of the students, allowing for the community to fully permeate the classroom. Again, this has been a problematic relationship as bringing the community to the classroom has often meant token visits from town or spiritual leaders or perhaps something in line with service learning projects. The community must be seen as collaborators in the knowledge productions, there can be no inside/outside dichotomy in this regards. Knowledge needs to be seen as flowing in both directions—from the classroom to the community and from the community to the classroom.

To make collaborative learning a possibility there has to be recognition of the diversity of connections and individuals. Much like in a community, the classroom is not always made up of people with common ideas or shared values; it is diverse and dynamic. How can educators navigate this diversity and bring each student to draw from their spiritual knowledge and contribute to a shared project of knowledge production? It begins with seeing learners beyond the construction of "students" and recognizing how their identities have been refracted through various lenses such as race, gender, sexuality, and ability. This project of diversity is one which is closely tied to the ideas of inclusive education; as Dei (2005) states, "A school is inclusive to the extent that every student is able to identify and connect with her/his social environment, culture, population and history" (p. 268). It is about connecting the learner to both the particularities of their personal experience and also to the broader community and spiritual contexts. Difference is often something that is perceived as a liability, but instead it needs to be recognized as a force of resistance to the homogenizing Western discourses that seek to universalize knowledge and spirituality.

Collaborative learning is recognition of the personal aspect of relationship as emphasized in Indigenous spirituality, the recognition that knowledge and its impartation is based in personal experiences. Interactions are valued as furthering community and spiritual connections. Knowledge production becomes a gathering of individuals to a place where they are affirmed and where they can create new connections and knowledges. The classroom is the space which allows these connections to flourish and grow; the educator becomes a facilitator. This is the intersection of resistance and creation, in the sharing of personal experiences and working together to explore connections not only to one another but also to the larger historical, political, and spiritual connections. The classroom is connected, through each of the students, to a larger community and framework.

CONCLUSION

This chapter is a call to resistance through a spiritually centered pedagogy that puts learners and their connections and communities at the center of the discourse. It explores the possibilities and challenges in integrating Indigenous spirituality into the Western academy which seeks to devalue spiritual and community knowledges. Cajete (1994) believes that the vision for Indigenous spirituality and education comes from "the Centering Place" or "the Asking" which is a place of questioning where questions are the beginning for dialogue and this chapter also seeks to begin with the Asking. How can we connect learners in ways that value their spiritual knowledge and in ways that creates spaces for students to affirm their connections and work toward using them for resistance to dominant norms? How can the community be integrated into the classroom space as co-producers of knowledge through the use of Indigenous spirituality?

Bringing Indigenous spirituality into the classroom is never an easy task it has to negotiate the tensions of the academy, seeking to resist and all the while recognizing the potential danger of replicating dominant discourses within itself. Still, it is a necessary task if we seek transformative education which energizes and empowers students to engage with their communities. This project is vital in the project to create resistance that is creative rather than merely responsive. Indigenous spirituality cannot be contained in a set of readings or curriculum but cuts across knowledges through emphasizing connections and the embodied, personal nature of knowledge.

Indigenous spirituality is full of possibilities. This chapter presents no definitive answers or strategies but, hopefully, rather connections and possibilities to be explored further by teachers, administrators, and educators. A connected spirituality encourages the spirit of exploration as we seek to uncover the relationships that shape who we are and how we can positively work within these relationships, resisting those that seek to dominate and encouraging those that seek to promote peace and openness. The classroom is a vital space in working toward spiritual understanding and in giving individuals a place to safely explore the many connections that they bring to the community. We need to embrace the complexity of these connections and struggle to create safe spaces for exploring these complexities; this is the goal for educators concerned with a transformative education process that includes the whole learner. This chapter is both a discussion and provocation to take a step on the journey toward this type of transformative education.

REFERENCES

Abu-Lughod, L. (1990). The romance of resistance: Tracing transformations of power through Bedouin women. *American Ethnologist, 17*(1), 41–55.

Battiste, M. Y. & Henderson, J. (2000). What is indigenous knowledge? In *Protecting indigenous knowledge and heritage,* (pp. 35–56). Saskatoon: Purich.

Brand, D. (2001). *A Map to the Door of No Return: Notes to Belonging*. Toronto: Vintage Canada.

Cajete, G. (1994). For life's sake—the spiritual ecology of American Indian education. In *Look at the Mountain: An Ecology of Indigenous Education* (pp. 42–73). Durango, CO: Kivaki.

Castellano, M. B. (2000). Updating Aboriginal traditions of knowledge. In G. J. S. Dei, B. L. Hall, & D. G. Rosenberg (Eds.), *Indigenous Knowledges in Global Contexts: Multiple Readings of Our World* (pp. 21–36). Toronto: University of Toronto Press.

Cooper, R.K. (1997). *Executive EQ: Emotional Intelligence in Leadership and Organizations.* New York: AIT & Essi Systems.

Daniels, D. (2009). Community history as a male-constructed space: Challenging gendered memories among South African Muslim women. *Diaspora, Indigenous, and Minority Education,* 3(2), 81–95.

Dei, G.J.S. (1993). Indigenous African knowledge systems: Local traditions of sustainable forestry. *Singapore Journal of Tropical Geography,* 14(1), 28–41.

Dei, G. J. S. (2000). Rethinking the role of indigenous knowledges in the academy. *International Journal of Inclusive Education,* 4(2), 111–132.

Dei, G. J. S. (2002a). Learning culture, spirituality and local knowledge: Implications for African schooling. *International Review of Education,* 48(5), 335–360.

Dei, G. J. S. (2002b). Spiritual knowing and transformative learning. *The Research Network for New Approaches to Lifelong Learning,* 4–16.

Dei, G. J. S. (2005). Social difference and the politics of schooling in Africa: A Ghanaian case study. *Compare,* 35(3), 227–245.

Dei, G. J. S. (2006). Introduction: mapping the terrain—towards a new politics of resistance. In G. J .S. Dei & A. Kempf (Eds.), *Anti-colonialism and Education: The Politics of Resistance* (pp. 1–23). Rotterdam: Sense.

Dei, G. J. S., & Asgharzadeh, A. (2001). The power of social theory: The anti-colonial discursive framework. *Journal of Educational Thought,* 35(3), 297–323.

Dei, G. J. S., & Doyle-Wood, S. (2006). 'Is we who haffi ride di staam': Critical knowledge/multiple knowings—possibilities, challenges, and resistance in curriculum/cultural contexts. In Y. Kanu (Ed.), *Curriculum as Cultural Practice: Postcolonial Imaginations* (pp. 151–180). Toronto: University of Toronto Press.

Dei, G .J. S., Hall, B. & Rosenberg, D. (2000). *Indigenous knowledges in global contexts: Multiple readings of our world.* Toronto: University of Toronto Press.

Edwards, S., & Hewitson, K. (2008). Indigenous epistemologies in tertiary education. *The Australian Journal of Indigenous Education,* Supplement, 96–102.

Fanon, F. (1963). *The Wretched of the Earth.* New York: Grove.

Gujit, I., & Shah, M. K. (1998). Waking up to power, conflict and process. In I. Gujit & M.K. Shah (Eds.), *The Myth of Community: Gender Issues in Participatory Development* (pp. 1–23). London: Intermediate Technology.

Hanohano, P. (1999). The spiritual imperative of Native epistemology: restoring harmony and balance to education. *Canadian Journal of Native Education,* 23(2), 206–226.

hooks, b. (2003). *Teaching Community: A Pedagogy of Hope.* New York: Routledge.

Howard, P. S. S. (2006). On silence and dominant accountability: A critical anticolonial investigation of the antiracism classroom. In G. J. S. Dei & A. Kempf (Eds.), *Anti-colonialism and Education: The Politics of Resistance* (pp. 43–63). Rotterdam: Sense.

Kincheloe, J. L. (2006). "Critical ontology and Indigenous ways of being: Forging a postcolonial curriculum." In Y. Kanu (Ed.), *Curriculum as cultural practice: Postcolonial imaginations.* Toronto: University of Toronto Press, pp. 181–202.

Maguire, P. (1996). Proposing a more feminist participatory research: knowing and being embraced openly. In K. de Konig & M. Martin (Eds.), *Participatory Research in Health: Issues and Experiences,* (pp. 27–39). London: Zed.

Mazama, M. A. (2002). Afrocentricity and African spirituality. *Journal of Black Studies,* 33(2), 218–234.

Memmi, A. (1969). *The Colonizer and the Colonized.* Boston: Beacon.

Nabavi, M. (2006). The power of oral tradition: critically resisting the colonial footprint. In G. J. S. Dei & A. Kempf (Eds.), *Anti-colonialism and Education: The Politics of Resistance* (pp. 175–192). Rotterdam: Sense.

McNally, M.D. (2004). Indigenous pedagogy in the classroom: A service learning model for discussion. *American Indian Quarterly,* 28(3&4), 604–617.

Rendon, L. (2000). Academics of the heart: Reconnecting the scientific mind with the spirit's artistry. *The Review of Higher Education,* 24(1), 1–13.

Said, E. (1993). *Culture and Imperialism*. New York: Vintage.

Shahjahan, R. (2006). Spirituality in the academy: Reclaiming from the margins and evoking a transformative way of knowing the world. *International Journal of Qualitative Studies in Education, 18*(6), 1–23.

Wangoola, P. (2000). Mpambo, the African multiversity: A philosophy to rekindle the African spirit. In G. J. S. Dei, B. L. Hall, & D. G. Rosenberg (Eds.), *Indigenous Knowledges in Global Contexts: Multiple Readings of Our World* (pp. 265–277). Toronto: University of Toronto Press.

York, M. (2001). New Age commodification and appropriation of spirituality. *Journal of Contemporary Religion, 16*(3), 361–372.

Young, I. M. (1990). The idea of community and the politics of difference. In L. Nicholson (Ed.), *Feminism/Postmodernism*, (300–323). London: Routledge.

CHAPTER TWENTY-SEVEN

Beyond Deconstruction

Evolving the Ties between Indigenous Knowledges and Post-Foundational Anti-Racism

ZAHRA MURAD

Anti-racism has been my activism, my lens of critique, and my source of strength for almost a decade. I have built my academic and personal life around it, striving to hold myself and the people important to me accountable to one another and to its principles. And, I have always assumed that anti-racism can, and does, function coherently with anti-colonialism. I am beginning to learn that it is naïve to assume this of all anti-racisms, that this assumption is perhaps a product of my own privilege as a settler on Turtle Island and my perspective as a displaced person, rather than a reflection of a truth.[1] Despite some very clearly delineated theorizing within the Academy with regards to what anti-racism may or may not be, it has been my experience that anti-racism is as diverse in its practices as it is in its adherents. Although I have looked on this diversity as a strength, I must acknowledge that, like all mechanisms that attempt to govern the impact of social interactions, anti-racism is flawed, contextual, and not at all perfect.

This chapter is a reflection of my experiences in specific communities and movements with a particular form of post-foundationalist anti-racism, and of the re-colonizing implications of utilizing post-foundationalism as the primary lens through which to theorize resistance. Post-foundational anti-racist theorizing in the Academy is often productive and subversive, challenging dominant structures of colonization and racialization. Rather than reflecting on post-foundational anti-racism as it is theorized in text, however, I look at the ways in which I and other activist-academics, with whom I have worked, take up its concepts. I refer to this anti-racism as post-foundationalist throughout this piece, and it should not be conflated with the many other anti-racisms already existent which draw on different narratives and logical systems to exist.

Through an overview of some of the moments and processes in which I have engaged with post-foundational approaches to anti-racism and its resultant relationships to Indigenous knowledges taken up in communities and movements, I examine and reflect on the goals of such anti-racism, and its inadvertently re-colonizing possibilities. Decentering post-foundational anti-racism as one way of knowing and, subsequently, one way of resisting, this chapter gestures toward enriching possibilities for knowing and acting based on a recentering of Indigenous knowledges within anti-racist thinking in activist pedagogies. This chapter focuses its latter half on beginning an exploration of some of these generative possibilities.

I came to anti-racist communities struggling to find ways to articulate my experiences of racialization and displacement on stolen land. These communities have quite often stood in place of culture, religion, and family for those of us who have lived within them. Through my early adulthood, Indigenous and displaced peoples who also struggle to make themselves coherent in this age of obscured colonialism and imperialism have helped me to speak my uncertainty and pain with pride from the margins. For me, this is what anti-racism and anti-racist community have been about—active resistance to hegemonies of white hetero-patriarchy and a search for an inevitably incomplete coherency in patchwork communities of people with partial histories, interrupted memories, and dreams full of monsters.

But even as I reflect on the very real relationships of nurturing I have been engaged in as an anti-racist, I am aware of an ever-growing sense of ongoing loss and restlessness. As an anti-racist, I have actively engaged post-foundationalism to help me make sense of my incoherence in a world that worships linear structure. Yet, this particular form of anti-racism, as I have experienced it in my communities and as I have practiced it as an educator, has not filled the empty spaces carved out by colonialism and imperialism. As I come to realize this, I begin to ask myself: Why have I been asked consistently to leave my spiritual self at the door, not only in State-sponsored institutions but in anti-racist spaces as well? Why have I so often felt that the pitfalls and pain that render activists unproductive every now and then have been things I must experience and deal with alone? What feeds this deep dissonance that keeps Indigenous people and displaced migrant peoples separated and often incoherent to one another, even when we work to resist the common root of our oppression?

The anti-racism I have known and lived has grown out of Eurocentric foundationalist and post-foundationalist thinking.[2] And it can be, in so many ways I am now coming to see, a tool of re-colonization. My anti-racism, inspired by European rather than Indigenous knowledges, works within the logical frameworks of that knowledge.

I am an anti-racist, but I am learning that I cannot feel whole within an ideology that does not center Indigenous knowledges and ways of knowing as paramount in the project of decolonization. In an effort to move in more nourishing directions, I hope to challenge the centrality of the deep ties my anti-racism has with foundationalist and post-foundationalist systems of thought.

TO WHOM DO I OWE THE SYMBOLS OF MY SURVIVAL?
(AUDRE LORDE, 1982)

Today is Himani Bannerji's retirement conference. I have never met her before, but her academic, artistic, and activist work as a fierce and intelligent woman of color has been pivotal to the construction of my personal frameworks. Her work, though not explicitly post-foundational, has been valuable and inspirational to the communities of anti-racists I have been a part of. Today, I am sitting in a large room at York University in Toronto that has somehow managed to merge the aesthetic and atmospheric elements of a high school gym and a South Asian wedding. The room is packed with students and professors. This is an historic moment, for me and for the hundreds of other young anti-racists here today—especially first- and second-generation South Asian women. Despite this, I feel strange and out of place, even as I listen to my academic elders speak about the challenges and triumphs for Marxist and post-modernist anti-racism in academia over the last two decades. The women who sit at the front of the room are those whose works have created some of the only discursive spaces in which I have ever felt at home. Their prominence has given me power and their struggles have given me strength. There should be no place in academia where I feel I belong more than right here, sitting across the room from women who, though they may not know it, have been my mentors and teachers. My theoretical mind has grown up on a marriage of Marxist and Foucauldian thought by Turtle Island anti-racist scholars. But as they speak, I feel a separation between myself and the theory, and between the theory and my experience of its praxis. The growing dissonance, discomfort, and disillusionment of the last five years I have spent in anti-racist organizing crash together in my head. I am suddenly able to articulate a suspicion I have harbored and ignored for too long; perhaps, sometimes, anti-racism and anti-colonialism are not the same thing.

I learned my anti-racism the way that many others did—under siege. As a new immigrant, I quickly apprehended the lesson that my Eurocentric education back home had been trying hard to teach me: that in order to be right, I had to be white. I needed to embody the values of whiteness, and speak within traditions of knowledge which made sense to Eurocentric frameworks of discourse and epistemology. In the west lies progress and freedom; to the west I must turn for learning and resistance. At Trent University in Peterborough, Ontario, where I completed my undergrad, there was not much room for activist or academic thought that challenged the white-centered 1960s-inspired frame of mind that pervaded politically minded communities. Trying to fight against the combined prejudices and racisms of my professors, classmates, and friends, I turned to the work of Iris Marion Young, Sherene Razack, Himani Bannerji, Michel Foucault, and other Marxists and post-foundationalists to assist me. I used their incisive challenges to foundationalist mores of absolutism and certainty of knowledge to break through the myths the people around me had internalized about people like me. I used the cultural capital granted by the ability to mobilize post-foundationalist language effectively to validate my ideas and ensure my words carried weight. I learned that refusing to play the theoretical games laid out for us in academia would get me nowhere. I had to play them and I had to play them better than my white colleagues, deconstructing their interpretations of key texts and turning their meaning to my advantage. In doing so, I moved away from ways of knowing that were rooted in generative knowledges. I was not alone in this; there was a derision of Indigenous knowledges and ways of speaking and knowing that lurked beneath the surface of the activist-academic spaces I inhabited. This derision seemed to me to be rooted in the ways post-foundational and Marxist work were taken up. As a member of these spaces, I was looking to gain legitimacy in the academic world, and so I internalized the need to lay claim to post-foundationalism in order to bring anti-racism into my scholarship.

It is important to note that the tentative critique I am drawing here is *not* about the work of Marxist and post-foundational anti-racist scholars like Sherene Razack and Himani Bannerji. Nor am I insinuating that post-foundationalist thinking has nothing to offer, or is broken in all its forms. It is, rather, the ways in which I have seen this work taken up, and the ways in which I myself have taken it up that I seek to problematize. Post-foundationalism is not often located as one part of a multifaceted movement against racism and imperialism that might include both western *and* Indigenous knowledges. I have more frequently seen it used, intentionally or not, as a means by which to silence Indigenous voices and further marginalize Indigenous ways of knowing. This, I believe, is a symptom of one of the unanswered questions I have felt deep in my anti-racist skin: what am I fighting *for*, rather than what am I fighting against. In resisting and subverting oppressive power, we cannot simply seek to position ourselves as wielders of that same power. By its very nature, the power we are fighting to gain entry to is exclusive and unsustainable. It requires an oppressed mass in order to exist (Smith, 1999). Yet, this is just what many of us who fight against racism in the Academy perpetuate.

In seeking legitimacy through positioning ourselves as authorities, we create a hierarchy of knowledge that can only reinforce the oppression we experience. In attempting this, I began on a path of self-harm that very nearly broke my ability to resist, in a way that guns or batons never could. Sitting in a large room at York University, listening to the brown women who taught me it was possible to be brown and a woman, and fierce and a human being on Turtle Island, I felt tired and hopeless. As I listened to some of the presenters argue playfully about whether to call themselves and each other Marxists or Foucauldians, I wondered in what tradition of thought *I* would feel at home. Do I have choices outside of our European pantheon? Must I always tie my sinking boat to dead white men in hopes of survival?

Ziauddin Sardar (1999) clearly and with amazing precision articulates the treacherous elements of post-foundationalism. In his article, "Development and Locations of Eurocentrism," he articulates the mess of confusion and emotion I felt as I fretted through my complicated and fraught relationship both to European and to Indigenous knowledges.[3] Like Sardar, who complicates the exclusive use of post-foundationalism in creating change, I felt the power of western domination and Eurocentricity encroaching, even in spaces where we stood to resist. As education scholars, or theorists of discourse, or activists against oppressive domination, many of us challenge what we have been taught is worth knowing. Some of us even question how we are taught to know things. Why, then, is it commensurable in our logical systems to teach ourselves to know, imagine, and build our futures based primarily or even solely on theories grown out of the knowledges of those who have oppressed us?

THE FUTURE IS DEFINED IN THE IMAGE OF THE WEST
(ZIAUDDIN SARDAR, 1999)

What happens in our communities when we build anti-racism primarily around, out of, and in response to post-foundationalism? Sardar peels away the layers of inaccessible rhetoric that often serve to shroud post-modernism from critique and the exposure of its systems of logic as a sophisticated move beyond modernity in the quest for a stable Eurocentricity. He argues that, particularly in the case of development, post-modernity is used to create a spatial and temporal map of the world dominated by the west and Eurocentric forms of knowledge. Allowing us to challenge space as an absolute concept, post-modernity succeeds in dispersing Europe throughout the world. Spiritual challenges to modernist conceptions of space and place trouble timelines and borders in many different ways, offering notions of connection (between people and places), repetition (of time and life), and simultaneity of place. These challenges have the power to debunk both modernist notions of space and post-modernist notions of agency and the subject (Shah, 1964).

Unlike the spatial challenges of different spiritualities, post-foundationalism troubles space in a way that breaks down political and narrative borders that may serve to protect marginalized people but do not push the intellectual, spiritual, and physical boundaries that protect Christian/Atheist

Europe. Post-modernism narratively situates itself as a "next step" in development. Although its own logics dispute the neat teleological formulation of time that starts at point A and goes to point B and can start nowhere else and go nowhere else, it actually recreates this structure. Sardar argues that this creates a developmental outlook that situates the non-west always in the west's past, and the west always in the non-west's future. Using post-modernism's attack of teleology, post-foundationalism has effectively colonized the future.

Arguing in and around these points anti-racists, including myself, have in some ways devised a system of thought that is very similar to that which Sardar criticizes in post-modernist understandings of, and contributions to, development. Arguing for a marriage of Marxist and Foucauldian thought (one did, after all, grow out of the other) as a means by which to know ourselves, we argue for historicization and a deconstruction of discourse. But in locating these ways of knowing as our starting points for speaking ourselves out of the margins we do two things. First, we ignore the knowledges already existent in Indigenous praxes that accomplish the same work as historical materialism and discourse analysis, but which do so in different ways, subverting the colonialism of historical materialism and discourse analysis. And second, through this we once again place the source of resistance and revolution in the hands of white men. We historicize only our oppression, not our knowledge. What do we lose in this process? How does this teach us to imagine?

One of the ways in which I have seen Indigenous ways of knowing locked out of my communities is through a continuous fracturing of collectivism and a stolid denial or negation of blood memory and spirit injury. I have generally found, for example, that when I use terminology like "we" people around me respond with distrust, suspicion, sometimes anger. In many ways, I can understand this; the fracturing of the homes, communities, and spirits of colonized people has not left traditions of collective strength untouched. Many colonized people have felt further marginalized and abused in the very communities they have hoped to call safe (Smith, 1999). Tellingly, however, I have rarely encountered the same suspicion and wariness around use of the term "they," particularly in Eurocentric academic spaces. Quite aside from issues around cycles of abuse within colonized communities, there seems to be a connection made between speaking of a "we" and ideas of pure and true modernist authenticity. In the process of rejecting this concept, so many anti-racist communities (or collections of people) have rejected our own Indigenous knowledges, ideas of collectivism, and indeed the term community itself.

Sardar's arguments around post-foundationalism illustrate well the kind of temporal understanding that allows a question about the erasure of Indigenous knowledges to become an issue of purity and authenticity. Indigenous knowledges in this understanding are located in the past—and not *simply* in the past as they were in modernist notions of time, but more *complicatedly* outdated. In post-modernist conceptions, Indigenous knowledges are rooted in the past because in order to be Indigenous they must not be western (Alcoff, 2000). Therefore, they must attain a level of purity and isolation that is simply not possible—if it ever was—in a globalizing world. Claims to or calls for Indigenous knowledges are "modernist" in that they invoke ideas of essentialism, authenticity, and purity. They are also pre-modern, because they call upon faulty systems of identification that assume homogenous "in" groups and absolute "out" groups (Alcoff, 2000). Post-modernity, however, is viewed as the future, as the missing link between Indigenous knowledges and the ability to work effectively in the world. It is the only way in which anti-oppression can be, because Indigenous knowledges are also viewed as being always male, cis-gendered, and heterosexual.

Theorists working in Indigenous studies and researching within Indigenous knowledges have pointed out repeatedly that to employ Indigenous knowledges is to employ a different way of knowing that is neither static nor mutually exclusive to western knowledge frameworks (Dei, 2000a; Wane, 2008). Yet, post-modernity consistently takes up the question of the absence of Indigenous knowledges absence in the same way. In a post-colonial world, a decolonization that centers Indigeneity is not an attainable end-goal. Instead, in this bright western future, colonized people must use Eurocentric post-foundationalism or systems of foundationalist thought such as Marxism in order to challenge the continued supremacy of whiteness. In this way, an anti-racism is born that, while it claims to be occupied with issues of colonialism, cannot truly address any of the deep issues of ongoing colonialism and re-colonialism. This anti-racism, inspired by Eurocentric foundationalist and post-foundationalist thought, rather than Indigenous knowledges and systems of knowing, seeks to debunk the colonial myth of the essential "native" or "colored." However, in rejecting all essence, and in leaving out spirituality, emotion, and our bodies (as physical beings rather than concepts to theorize), this anti-racism positions Eurocentricity as the only approach to humanity. The goal of this anti-racism is equity, not decolonization. And equity can happen, ostensibly, within western Eurocentric perspectives on the world.

In my experiences with anti-racist activism, the partial use of post-foundationalism to inform praxis has perpetuated rather than challenged spirit injury and fragmentation. The location of Indigenous knowledges in the past and their framing as pure and authentic (which post-modernism critiques but rarely moves beyond) is taken up in personal and individual ways. People in my community talk about culture as though it has an expiration date. Non-western culture or cultural knowledge is allowable only if a person experiences it and knows it in childhood and if it is an uninterrupted part of that person's being throughout their lives. Any contamination—immigration, displacement, mixing—is often seen as "westernization," and people are asked to own up to their "western privilege." Simultaneously, culture is located spatially—over there, and not over here. People long for the real, soul-nourishing experience of non-western culture, which they believe can only exist away from the west, further erasing Indigenous ways of knowing and living that belong to the geographic west. Conversations about our cultural knowledges so often turn into tests of authenticity. Who has the correct source? Who can speak from most immediate experience? Who really has the right to lay claim to this or that culture or element of culture? In striving to locate Indigenous cultural knowledges and memories on an absolute grid of privilege and oppression, we trivialize our knowledges. We also preclude the possibility for Other ways of knowing to subvert the ongoing colonization of knowledge and imagination, turning access to non-dominant ways of thinking into a game of authenticity.

In these communities, we feel that our experiences of displacement have moored us in a post-modernist limbo, unable to access non-western ways of knowing and living, yet not accepted into the west. This locates non-western and/or Indigenous ways of knowing and living firmly in the past of most peoples' lives; it situates them as instinctive, as part of early childhood learning, and as something that can only survive with careful protection. Hence, non-western ways of knowing are once again understood as essential and static, and as geographically anchored.[4] And, as Sardar points out, this simultaneously locates the west as the inevitable future, unburdened by spatial specificity. In an often good faith attempt to deal with this future and not be guilty of appropriation, issues of spirituality, land, bodily knowledge, and non-western ways of knowing and dreaming are tacitly ignored or purposefully excluded from people's thinking.

TO PRODUCE KNOWLEDGE, YOU NEED TO HAVE AUTHORITY; YOU HAVE TO BE ABLE TO SEE WHAT THE NATIVES THEMSELVES CANNOT SEE (EDWARD SAID, 1994)

In his introduction to *Indigenous Knowledges in Global Contexts: Multiple Readings of Our World*, George Dei (2000a) defines Indigenous knowledges as being those that stem from one geographic location, in which they have evolved over time. Dei further defines them as forms of knowledge that have not inserted themselves into any place by force but rather have grown out of learning shared between people and the land they inhabit, and between people and others they encounter, in a spirit of exchange rather than conquest. Unlike the post-foundationalist anchoring of Indigenous knowledges to land, Dei's definition of Indigenous knowledges ties them to the land in a way that underscores the intimacy between knowledges and the environments in which they are developed. Because of this link, Dei argues that Indigenous knowledges are multicentric, tied to place and time and aware that there are other ways of knowing. This definition challenges the west's claim—through modernism as well as post-modernism—to universality both spatially and temporally. It separates colonizing western knowledge from its omnipresence and replaces it into cultural particularity.

By virtue of its colonizing imperatives and lack of close ties to specific places, western knowledges cannot be called Indigenous. They are, however, one world of many, one way of knowing. This assertion challenges the west's modernist claims to sole ownership of absolute truths in a way that also challenges post-foundationalism's perhaps-unconscious reconstruction of a meta-narrative, of a truth which decrees that there can be no truth.

The challenge this articulation of knowledge poses to post-foundationalist thought and to the approaches to pedagogy and knowing that I have worked within has not been easy for me to digest. Although post-foundationalism rejects absolutism, it is nonetheless constructed as the one true way of knowing. It is not a knowledge that allows for a multiplicity of thought, and although it argues that we are all socially constructed beings, it resents being situated as a European or western way of knowing.

The implications of decentering (but not by any means removing) post-foundationalism (and Marxism) from radical academia are many. For me, one of the most prominent and promising strategies is to question the primacy of Judeo-Christian secularism and atheism in all public and academic spaces to which foundationalism and post-foundationalism both adhere.[5] It is, perhaps, through this decentering of atheism and the deep and pervasive paradigm shifts that this would entail that migrant people and Indigenous people on this land can begin to build understandings and solidarities.

It has been my experience that while most anti-racist initiatives focusing on migrant people of color and our experiences are situated as secular (if not explicitly atheist), spirituality is an important element of Indigenous resistance to the ongoing colonization of Turtle Island. Unlike Eurocentric knowledge, many Indigenous peoples the world over rely on the maintenance of individual and collective spiritualities to keep knowledges alive. However, if anti-racist movements, based in secular foundationalist or post-foundationalist thinking refuse to seriously engage spirituality in any form, we lose important parts of our own diverse migrant knowledges and also alienate Turtle Island Indigenous communities from our organizing praxes.

It has only been recently that I have begun to understand some of the reasons behind the very real rift between anti-racist activists in Toronto and Indigenous people. In part, it is the fact that we very rarely discuss Indigeneity—including our own Indigeneity—in ways that are not sidelining, dismissive, or in footnotes. Connected to this is also the fact that post-foundational anti-racism can easily function as the next discursive step to colonialism (Sardar, 1999).

RESISTING MEANS ASSURING ONESELF OF THE HEART'S HEALTH (MOHMOUD DARWISH)

In "Centering Spirituality in the Academy: Toward a Transformative Way of Teaching and Learning," Riyad Shahjahan (2004) argues for the need to allow students and teachers to reflect on their lives and experiences in a holistic way. This, for Shahjahan, means making spirituality a meaningful part of the ways we learn and teach. Shahjahan's desire to bring spirituality into the classroom challenges foundationalism and post-foundationalism in direct, urgent, and unavoidable ways. While post-foundationalism and some kinds of foundationalist logic might argue creditably against Sardar's astute accusations, it seems impossible for either system of thought to adequately respond to Shahjahan's call. Spirituality is simply a part of the way in which Indigenous knowledges know. If Shahjahan's call is to be heeded, this would necessitate the inevitable incorporation of Indigenous knowledges into Eurocentric thought, on their own terms. Although Shahjahan is not alone in this wish, the resistance with which politically aware embodiments of spiritualities are met in academia speaks to the threat they can pose to dominant ways of knowing.

The basis of anti-colonial spiritually minded learning and teaching practices challenge the core value of Enlightenment rationality and objectivism: that all things can be quantified and known, and that with effort we as human beings may know, understand, and control everything including each other (Shahjahan, 2004). In posing a threat to the continued dominance of western knowledge, the incorporation of Indigenous spiritualities in academia in a central and undeniable way offers us many hopeful possibilities. In *The Revolution Will Not Be Funded: Beyond the Non-profit Industrial Complex* (INCITE! Women of Colour Against Violence, 2007), several anti-colonial scholars and activists argue that the money- and product-oriented bureaucracy of non-profit–based activism has stripped such organizing of its real, radical change-making potential. Madonna Thunder Hawk argues eloquently in her essay, "Native Organizing before the Non-profit Industrial Complex" against the trappings of careerist activism. At the center of her argument is the principle that as human beings and as communities we must continue to ensure that we are held accountable to one another, to the environment we live in, and to ourselves (Thunder Hawk, 2007). Andrea Smith echoes this sentiment in her introduction, arguing that state-sponsorship of activism fosters a competitive environment in which solidarity is unwelcome. She adds that when we remove our hearts, bodies, and spirits from our organizing, we create unsustainable and bureaucratic movements (Smith, 2007). If we imagine education's institutions, including the Academy, as an industry like the non-profit sector whose funding is guaranteed only insofar as it functions to serve the interests of the state, we see important parallels between Smith's, Thunder Hawk's, and Shahjahan's arguments. The centering of spirituality is a disruption of Eurocentric compartmentalization of space and time. It has the potential to generatively restructure the conversations we have with ourselves as colonized people, perhaps healing some of the fragmentation and spirit injury that keeps us from feeling meaningfully connected to our ancestors, to our allies, and to our selves. Through this, the centering of many critical, anti-colonial spiritualities has the power to disrupt the state-sponsorship of academic activism—knowledge productions which seek to deconstruct and subvert dominant discourses. It encourages instead the production as well as the *recollection* of knowledge, and situates the work of this knowledge firmly in communities; the work of activism in the Academy must not be to study Indigenous peoples, but to work to challenge and resist the continuing destruction of non-European knowledges and the environments from which they grow.

The centering of anti-colonial spiritualities also has generative implications for the ways we learn to teach and know ourselves, as people beyond units of labor in the battle against oppression. As an anti-racist activist, I have come to understand the discursive and narrative mechanisms of racialization as necessitating, in part, a certain confused ignorance on the part of dominant peoples. The individualistic culture that European colonialism has worked to create functions in concert with a publicly enforced ahistoricism that allows people attached to dominant identities the luxury of this ignorance. Education has always been a part of my activism, but the urgency with which grassroots anti-racist pedagogy seeks to convert people to its way of thinking has by turns exhausted and concerned me. What would the incorporation of my spirituality into my pedagogical practice do for my practice and for my self? Could its inclusion help me fight the reliance on Enlightenment rationality, control, and compartmentalization that I have learned to seek and enforce in my own educational practices?

In the past, when I have thought about spirituality in the classroom, I have come up against modalities which do little for marginalized students and are constructed on a foundation of what has looked like European humanism, one that centers a multicultural notion of forgiveness and threatens to end in total annihilation. As I turn away from western conceptions of both spirituality and the classroom, I come to some of the same ideas that Shahjahan (2004) draws on in his article and that mystics and teachers such as Jalaluddin Rumi have woven into their work. If we as anti-racist and anti-colonial activists and educators center spirituality, not as a superficial solution to the pain of oppression, but as an essential element of our resistance, it is possible to re/turn to a space in which anger, forgiveness, healing, and change co-exist. There is a potential to arrive at a way of knowing that is humanizing in ways that western ways of knowing are generally not. Trapped only within Eurocentric ways of knowing, colonized peoples can never be human—the basis of Eurocentric thought is the construction of subjugated peoples as property, as sub-human. If I consider forgiveness and resistance as a spiritual *as well as* a political act, I open up the possibility of caring for myself and my communities as a human being, of healing myself consistently in ways that do not allow my anger to tear me apart.

I am an educator. Education is not simply my profession, but rather, I think, in some inner part of my self it is through educating that I learn and grow and feel challenged and nourished. In many ways, I think education is about telling stories, and so to me, saying that I am an educator comes very close to saying that I am human. I came to curriculum studies because I wanted to make a difference in the world as an educator and in the way in which we learn to teach and the stories we tell when we do. I had believed that the only system of thought within education studies that offered a substantial critique to systems of education—that challenged the entirety of the paradigm within which we are taught what, how, and why to know—was anti-racist education. The kind of anti-racist thinking I am acquainted with is based on the same post-modernist anti-racism I described above. It is born and grows up outside the Academy, in anti-racist movements and communities but is articulated through academic scholarship occasionally as hopeful, radical pedagogy. Its pedagogy focuses on using education as a tool to reassign social power, to unlearn or to learn differently, and to erase or at least critique discourses of social oppression often perpetuated through the hidden curriculum

(Lopes & Thomas, 2006). Yet I never found, as an educator who focused on anti-racism and anti-oppression from a post-foundationalist perspective, that my conversations with students were complete. Anti-racist education should, and in some of its formulations can, very definitely challenge the roots of dominant ways in which we learn to know (Dei, 1996). But in many of its formulations, it does little more than repeat the same processes on which colonial foundationalist thinking is based (Anner, 1996; Arnold, Burke, James, Martin, & Thomas, 1991; Bishop, 2001; Curry-Stevens, 2003). Further to Sardar's (1999) critique is the reality that although post-foundational anti-racism does not set itself up explicitly as purely oppositional, most of the work done under its banner is a deconstruction of European systems of power. While this is both important and necessary, the question Paul Gilroy (2000) posed a decade ago remains relevant—what are anti-racists for? As adept as anti-racist scholars are at discourse analysis and deconstruction, post-foundationalism has offered us little in the way of actually creating anything (Wright, 2003). Can a pedagogy that is concerned mainly with mapping power-relations as a means to a political end function generatively in classrooms? What is the world we are dreaming of?

When using post-foundationalist anti-racism as pedagogy I constantly came up against barriers erected by anti-racist ideology that make classroom pedagogy a battle, with the odds stacked against me. Other teachers and students who ascribe to this philosophy within my work as a community educator have told me that it is not our job to educate privileged people. I have also been told that white people, straight people, middle- or upper-class people should not be allowed to take up classroom time and space to work through their guilt, or their ignorance. As an anti-racist, there have been times when I have been perfectly able to understand this. I am, even now, not entirely in disagreement with it. If we allow classrooms to become spaces in which issues of power are worked through in ways that center the learning of dominant bodies over the healing of marginalized peoples, we replicate the power dynamics we are seeking to fight. As an educator, however, I have never understood how this idea can effectively be worked into pedagogy. The perennial problem of education persists: how can we as educators build a classroom space to which *all* students can contribute and from which *all* students can benefit? It is undeniable that what students can give and what they need will be at least in part determined by their social positioning. Yet, it is also possible that Shahjahan and others who argue for the necessity of making space for spirituality in the classroom can offer educators more effective ways of dealing with this problem, ones which allow us to acknowledge social positioning without reducing our entire beings to it. This is not to imply that anti-colonial approaches will have the magical effect of decolonizing pedagogy quickly, efficiently, and without problems. However, it might return to us a piece of the pedagogical puzzle that I have found anti-racism often misses. It might allow us to work toward social change through a humanization that challenges practices of domination rather than through the mapping of identities and actions on to an uncompromising and inflexible grid. In this way, we might be able to re-think the anti-racism that tells us immigrant or naturalized people of color have no right to access their Indigenous knowledges as part of a diaspora. We might be able to move beyond our inability or unwillingness to understand knowledges constructed outside of Eurocentric paradigms. In so doing, we may address the centering of western masculinist thought that positions Indigenous knowledges in the Academy as absent or as parts of the opening ceremony but never the real discussion. Perhaps it is through the creation of pedagogy centered around a holistic understanding of teacher and student, and the very important position that spirituality has in the beings of many teachers and students, that we can move toward multicentric classrooms in which we learn to create as well as critique.

TOWARD A PARTIAL BEGINNING

I am aware that I am in grave danger of setting up (if I have not already done so) a binary that is at least partially false. It is not my intention to imply that when we center Indigenous knowledges, then community, forgiveness, and authentic self-growth will come easily. Nor do I mean to insinuate that European knowledges have nothing to offer us, and that decolonization can only be achieved through their obliteration. It is important to remember that the work of decentering dominant discourses, bodies, and practices should not be synonymous with their devaluation or their annihilation. However, in challenging Eurocentricity, we do open possibilities for creation. Post-foundationalist anti-racism is not a holistic system of thought; it does not offer the resources we need to live as human beings, only some of those we might require in our attempts at resistance. Without our hearts, bodies, and spirits, we can only understand ourselves and each other as partial beings.

Having journeyed with post-foundationalist anti-racism for years, I arrive here disillusioned, isolated even from myself, and bone tired. This kind of anti-racism, searching for equity but not decolonization, gives nothing back to those who engage with it seriously. It burned up my anger, sapped my strength, and yet gave me no tools to create spaces of comfort and no refuge. Many of us who have traveled this path stand at the end of it feeling dehumanized and broken apart, alienated from those parts of our being that nurture and weary of seeing ourselves and our bodies as units of labor and resistance but nothing more. Looking for a way to build a partial new beginning, I have to believe that putting the pieces of myself that I have learned to keep apart back together might be a fertile space to start.

NOTES

1. The land I refer to is known in colonial terms as "Canada" or "North America." I refer to "North America" through this chapter as Turtle Island, a term used by anti-colonialists to recognize Indigenous peoples and their claims to this land.
2. The term "post-foundational" is used here as an umbrella term referring to all the "posties"—post-modernism, post-structuralism, post-colonialism, post-functionalism, and so on that, while sharing a common epistemic basis (anti-Enlightenment), have different foci. (Definition courtesy of Dr. Ayaz Naseem.)
3. My own Indigenous knowledges and other peoples'.
4. I am aware that most non-western knowledges are tied to the land. However, in conjunction with other notions of such knowledges as static, rigid, and fragile, the addition of an uncritical binding of knowledges to the land does not allow for possibilities of migrant-Indigenous knowledges, knowledge sharing, and the growth of Indigenous knowledges through geographic movement, rather than their obliteration through displacement.
5. I refer to the notions and practices of secularism and atheism as Judeo-Christian to underscore their spatial, cultural, and temporal specificity and logical framework (for example, secularism's reliance on compartmentalization of religion as private and community as public or atheism's location as a denial of a specific form of colonizing, compartmentalizing, reductionist spirituality). It is not my intent to situate either as invalid but to point out their specificity.

REFERENCES

Alcoff, L. M. (2000). Who is afraid of identity politics? In P. M. L. Moya, & M. R. Hames-García (Eds.), *Reclaiming Identity: Realist Theory and the Predicament of Postmodernism* (pp. 312–344). Berkeley: University of California Press.

Anner, J. (1996). *Beyond Identity Politics: Emerging Social Justice Movements in Communities of Colour*. Boston: South End.

Arnold, R., Burke, B., James, C., Martin, D., & Thomas, B. (1991). *Educating for a Change*. Toronto: Between the Lines.

Bannerji, H. (1995). *Thinking Through: Essays on Feminism, Marxism and Anti-racism*. Toronto: Women's.

Bishop, A. (2001). *On Becoming an Ally: Breaking the Cycle of Oppression in People*. (2nd ed.). London: Zed.

Curry-Stevens, A. (2003). *An Educator's Guide for Changing the World: Methods, Models and Materials for Anti-oppression and Social Justice Workshops*. Toronto: CSJ Foundation.

Darwish, Mahmoud. (2010). Under Siege. *Palestine Chronicle*. Retrieved from http://palestinechronicle.com/view_article_details.php?id=14055

Dei, G. J. S. (1996). *Anti-racism Education: Theory and Practice*. Halifax: Fernwood.

Dei, G. J. S. (2000a). *Indigenous Knowledges in Global Contexts: Multiple Readings of Our World*. Toronto: University of Toronto Press.

Dei, G. J. S. (2000b). Re-thinking the role of indigenous knowledges in the academy. *International Journal of Inclusive Education, 4*(2), 111–132.

Gilroy, P. (2000). *Against Race: Imagining Political Culture Beyond the Colour Line*. Cambridge: Harvard UP.

INCITE! Women of Colour Against Violence. (Eds.). (2007). *The Revolution Will Not Be Funded: Beyond the Non-profit Industrial Complex*. New York: South End.

Lopes, T., & Thomas, B. (2006). *Dancing on Live Embers: Challenging Racism in Organizations*. Toronto: Between the Lines.

Lorde, A. (1982). *Zami: A New Spelling of My Name*. Berkeley: Crossing.

Said, E. (1994). *Orientalism*. Toronto: Random House.

Sardar, Z. (1999). Development and the location of Eurocentrism. In R. Munck & D. O'Hearn (Eds.), *Critical Development Theory: Contributions to the New Paradigm* (pp. 66–61). London: Zed.

Shah, I. (1964). *The Sufis*. London: Octagon.

Shahjahan, R. (2004). Centering spirituality in the academy: Toward a transformative way of teaching and learning. *Journal of Transformative Education, 2*(4), 294–312.

Smith, A. (2007). Introduction: The revolution will not be funded. In INCITE! Women of Colour Against Violence (Eds.), *The Revolution Will Not Be Funded: Beyond the Non-profit Industrial Complex* (pp. 1–18). New York: South End.

Smith, L. (1999). *Decolonizing Methodologies: Research and Indigenous Peoples*. New York: Zed.

Thunder Hawk, M. (2007) Native organizing before the non-profit industrial complex. In INCITE! Women of Colour Against Violence (Eds.), *The Revolution Will Not Be Funded: Beyond the Non-profit Industrial Complex* (pp. 101–106). New York: South End.

Wane, N. (2008). Indigenous education and cultural resistance: A decolonizing project. *Curriculum Inquiry, 39*(1), 159–178.

Wright, H. (2003). An endarkened feminist epistemology? Identity, difference and the politics of representation in educational research. *Qualitative Studies in Education, 16*(2), 197–214.

CHAPTER TWENTY-EIGHT

Indigenous Knowledge

Multiple Approaches

PRISCILLA SETTEE

As a First Nations Swampy Cree woman,[1] I am proud of my heritage. My ancestral lands were located in the boreal landscape of northern Saskatchewan. The region was once an intact forest ecosystem that contained an undulating patchwork of slow-growing evergreen forests. It still shares weathered outcrops of granite and innumerable lakes, marshes, bogs, and other wetlands that are typically found along the Canadian Shield. This magnificent shield sweeps in a broad arc through northern Alberta and Saskatchewan. I first became interested in Indigenous Knowledge Systems because of my roots in this resource-rich community. As a second-generation urban First Nations person, it was the self-sufficiency, beauty, and knowledge of northern and land-based communities that spoke to me. Teaching in the North in the mid-1970s, I witnessed a transformation. Communities, which were self-sufficient, were being negatively impacted by development in the form of clear-cuts, forestry, and mining. In 1967, the Squaw Rapids Dam, later named the E. B. Campbell Dam, was completed. The disruption of the natural water flow had a negative impact on the area's natural resources. Economically, it was catastrophic for those who earned their livelihood as fishers and trappers.

Over time, many people were forced to move to cities in search of work or languish with destroyed local economies and ways of life. I noticed the commonality of Western developmental impact on the majority of Indigenous communities in my province and throughout Canada. The human cost of development was immeasurable.

During the early 1970s, my studies at Trent University afforded me another opportunity to hear first hand how the Cree were being displaced, both geographically and culturally, by the construction of large dams in the James Bay area of Quebec. In my undergraduate classes, I developed a critical consciousness of the oppression of Indigenous peoples in other parts of the world. I became a voracious reader of Paulo Freire. The concept of *conscientization*, or critical awareness, is foundational to the work of Paulo Freire (1970). Critical awareness is made possible through praxis, which

Freire defines as " . . . reflection and action upon the world in order to transform it" (Freire, 1970, p. 33). He connects reflection and action together as part of the process in the recognition and transformation of social, economic, and political contradictions. The readings of Paulo Freire (1970) resonate with the critical rereading of my people in Saskatchewan, whose quality of life and living was and remains substandard. In terms of our schooling, Indigenous peoples inherited a colonial system that did not critique our circumstances, pose solutions to community problems, or consider our organic Indigenous experience. As a First Nations woman, I learned that critical consciousness allows us to question the nature of our historical and social situation and to read the world with the goal of acting as subjects in the creation of our own democratic society. Paulo Freire's methodologies spoke to me in ways that none of my formal schooling did. I was intrigued by the educational transformation he described in places like Guinea Bissau and Brazil. Later I would read works by Henry Giroux (1983), a disciple of Freire, who used the terminology of radical pedagogy: "Its spirit is rooted in an aversion to all forms of domination, and its challenge centers around the need to develop modes of critique fashioned in a theoretical discourse that mediates the possibility for social action and emancipatory transformation" (p. 2). Later, I would read Antonio Gramsci (1971) whose writings contextualized my situation and that of my community within a broader analysis, one that explained hegemony and cultural domination.

My activism today results from grappling with both intellectual reflection and my immediate personal experience. In academic institutions, I found that legitimated discourses of power privilege what books may be read by students, validate what instructional methods may be utilized, and authorize what belief systems and views of achievement may be taught. In so doing, power discourses undermine the cultural interpretations of language, establishing one correct reading that implants a particular hegemonic message into the consciousness of Indigenous readers. As I look back at the process of becoming a professor and researcher, questions about how gains are made in the world of academia have challenged me. Through this process, I gained a new understanding of the relationship of power to knowledge, particularly concerning those who are privileged and oppress and those who are powerless. Initial efforts involved negotiating and wresting power away from public education agencies to establish Indigenous schools in Winnipeg (Children of the Earth High School) and Saskatoon (Joe Duquette High School). These alternative schools inspired thriving community-based programs that presently serve the educational, cultural, and spiritual needs of urban Aboriginal students. Indigenous-led schools verified the possibility of improving the academic learning of students from Indigenous backgrounds through the use of culturally responsive instructional theory, that is, instruction reflecting the values and practices similar to their traditional roots. I have been instrumental in leading both parent/community councils in both schools during a time when most if not all mainstream schools were failing Indigenous students.

I approached the activism in my intellectual life as theory in the making—unfinished and open-ended—as I pondered what differences could be made in education. I began contemplating with a historical glance to those who have theorized and pondered the dilemmas of Indigenous intellectual life. As I reread my own history, stories of my own family's suffering emerged. My father, Henry McKay Settee, a trapper and hunter, served in the First World War and was subsequently deemed "civilized" after the war. Under the Indian Act, he was forced to move from his reserve community. This statute was the rule of law for people who gave service during the war. The act of removing and disenfranchising people from their communities was a very clear statement that Indigenous communities—and all they represented—were devalued. Henry McKay Settee's removal from his home community meant more than simply a geographical removal. It was a symbolic removal of a man and his family from his spiritual and physical ties to the land, and it was the removal of the knowledge and way of life embodied in that land. He died in urban poverty as a victim of the system that had marginalized him, a man who had served his country like many others. In much of my writing today I use the stories of similar people displaced from the land, whose lives have been forever transformed by circumstances and disruptions beyond their control. Their stories have important contributions to make in understanding Indigenous knowledge. The layered truths embedded in their stories are essential to cultural continuity (King, 2003). It is my hope and that of many of my contemporary colleagues that our stories can have a greater influence in the educational process and that they be recognized as legitimate knowledge. Stories have taught Indigenous peoples how to conduct themselves in a good way for the good of the community. In so doing, I utilize storytelling as a methodology to represent the essence of what it is to be an Indigenous person and to focus on our layers of knowledge. My beliefs are that these stories, and many others yet unheard, rich sources of Indigenous knowledge, must transform the academy; and, in the spirit of Freire, they will lead to social and cultural transformation as well as to our own survival (1970).

Extensive travels for teaching and researching since the late 1970s demonstrate that, at present, Indigenous people worldwide share common beliefs, practices, and similarities of knowledge including the experience of the tension of Western development. In many cases, the issues of land, power, disenfranchisement, and genocide of Indigenous peoples keep surfacing. In the Indigenous worldview, the concept of power takes on a different meaning particularly in relation to the natural world as Armstrong states

> It seems to go back to the idea that human beings, and specifically human beings from the colonizing culture, are elevated above the rest of the natural world and that they have a prior right to use everything around them. It is a fundamental split in ideology that requires aggression. It advocates aggression as a principle of power and achievement. It is an ideology that advocates accumulation as a part of power and is central to the idea that the measurement of a person's worth is their economic and oppressive power. The consequences of that ideology, both internally and externally to all life forms, is very frightening (cited in Jensen, 2002, p. 287).

The destruction of the natural environment has had a great impact on the knowledge base of Indigenous peoples. It has only been by reconnecting to their traditional lands through the restoration of ceremonies and practices that they have begun to heal. The knowledge that has sustained Indigenous communities for millennia has more recently been referred to as *Indigenous knowledge systems*. This inherited knowledge included the traditional forms of knowledge developed by parents and other elders in relation to ways of knowing, relationships/codes of conduct, and information that helped in daily living. Personal experience defines an individual's worldview. As a person deeply involved in the cultural, educational, and political events in my community, I have expanded my own definition of Indigenous knowledge to include women's knowledge and other aspects of community knowledge. Throughout my academic development, my definition has been enhanced by the knowledge of my extended community of global colleagues who were describing the need to challenge Western knowledge and strengthen the Indigenous knowledge emanating from their communities. It was necessary during my documentation of Indigenous Knowledge Systems to develop a critical theoretical framework that would encourage, allow, and support those systems.

A central component to what it means to be Indigenous is to have a relationship and close ties to the land and all that lives on the land. That relationship is so deep and tied to natural laws that many

Indigenous peoples have names that are derived from connections to the land, such as *people of the earth* or *people of the land*. When our Indigenous knowledge is under threat, we have no choice but to become activists and identify the goals of activist scholarship/action. This threat is evidenced by the rapid disappearance of Indigenous languages, plant and animal species, and the degradation of Indigenous homelands, which threatens the very survival of Indigenous peoples. Along with the land degradation comes the disappearance of traditional foods resulting in extreme health problems for Indigenous peoples. Peoples' health is linked to the health of the land and the food harvested from that land. This situation of extinction and degradation of Indigenous Knowledge Systems and what it means in its entirety is something that urgently needs to be analyzed through a critical framework and addressed, "It calls for a discourse that acknowledges as a central concern the categories of history, sociology, and depth psychology" (Giroux, 1983, p.2).

It was also during the 1970s that I became familiar with the writings of Frantz Fanon (1963), Eldridge Cleaver (1968), Angela Davis (1974), and Albert Memmi (1974). Advocates for equality and basic human rights like freedom, their writings stress that intellectuals must always remain connected with the struggles of the land and home communities. These writers helped me understand the impact of racism, cultural and political hegemony, and the domination of peoples of color and women. Later, I read bell hooks (1984), Howard Adams (1975), Gloria Anzaldúa (1999), and many others whose work were either influenced by or had similar experiences to the writer Antonio Gramsci (1971) but saw power and domination through a race analysis. Gramsci wrote extensively from his prison cell about the deep layers of state domination over oppressed groups. This domination was so entrenched in all levels of society—including education, literature, church, government, and the legal system—that it impacted every aspect of humanity. He wrote prolifically during a time when he faced personal persecution, which included being jailed for challenging oppressive regimes. Many of the writers Gramsci influenced made the link between class, race, and gender; and they described the deep impact of colonialism, racism, and hegemony. As an Indigenous scholar and a follower of Gramsci, Freire, Giroux, and others, I feel the importance of challenging the hegemony of Western knowledge. It is my goal to ensure that Indigenous Knowledge Systems take their rightful place within the academy as legitimate knowledge. As Indigenous scholars, we have an important role that we inherit from our culture. It is also an intellectual role in defining, challenging, and working to eradicate oppression. This is the role of intellectual sovereignty:

> Indigenous intellectuals in the United States and Canada are living at the center of the global empire, and we are the best-placed people in the world to counter the ongoing production of imperial attitudes and to defy its pretensions. It is our responsibility to reorient our own values and our ways of being away from cooptation into the imperial system. (Alfred, 2004, p.97)

TRADITIONAL VALUES

Collectivity is central to Indigenous being and the collectivity of Indigenous knowledge is reflected in many of the ceremonies, teachings, and cultural expressions. Aboriginal people have described Indigenous knowledge with words, which reflect ancient knowledge for community life, well-being, and sharing of values. In the Cree language this is called *pimatisiwin*. It is taken from the root word *pimatisi*, "to be alive." Another core value is *miyo-wichihtowin,* which means "having good relations." Individually and collectively people have, since time immemorial, been instructed by their teachings to strive and conduct themselves in ways that create positive relationships with our extended community. In many ways the concept of collectivity which is central to Indigenous knowledge runs counter to the concept of individualism which is promoted by formal schooling systems. The concept of extended community and family is fundamental in Indigenous communities. Aunts, uncles, and grandparents are surrogate parents. The community is an extension of the family and many community members have family ties. This relationship is extended to the animals and the natural environment. These are ones who cannot speak for themselves, but whose existence is essential to human survival. The extended community takes in all relationships, human and nonhuman, and is reflected in our interdependence. My people, the Cree, begin each day by smudging with sage, which helps us to purify our thoughts, actions, and deeds. Smudging insures that our actions will be done with a good heart, a good mind, and gratitude for the gift of living another day. This ritual also reminds us to perform our duties for the betterment of humanity. Reference is made to the concept of all my relations, which means that all of humanity and living things are related and must be cared for by one other. A Western capitalist system which promotes educational individualism and moving ahead of fellow human beings undermines what is at the heart of the concept of *wakohtowin*, the betterment of all our relations and our communities. Ceremonies, such as the Sweat Lodge Ceremony and others, represent Indigenous knowledge ways of purifying oneself and renewing commitment to community. The most sacred and important ceremony of plains tribes is the annual Sun Dance that renews the allegiance, loyalty, fidelity, spirituality, and unity of First Nations people. Another value is the important role that hard work had in community; however, some lament that hard work today has slipped by the wayside for some.

WAKOHTOWIN

For my people, the Cree, relationship values are embedded in natural laws called *wakohtowin*. Our symbol of the circle reflects the equality of all people and their capability to care for, nurture, protect, and heal the people and the land.

In the past, living and survival was an art that required skills, knowledge, and values to integrate many spheres. Some knowledge is timeless, such as, the knowledge that gives communities the values and roles for worthy human behavior. Some values—such as sharing, caring for, and interdependence with fellow human beings and the environment—have not changed, but a capitalist society driven by monetary interests now creates tension in present human interactions. Cree Elder Emma Minde recalls:

> That is what the Whites call cooperation, I will say it in English again, sharing as they call it, that is what Crees used to do long ago. When they had a surplus of something, they used to give it to one another. This also is not well understood, I guess, as money is the general obsession now and you only try to make money from everything (Ahenakew, 1987, p. 89).

In the Cree teachings, essential human values are represented by the thirteen poles of the tipi: respect, humility, happiness, love, faith, kinship, obedience, cleanliness, thankfulness, sharing, strength, hope, and good child rearing (Saskatchewan Indian Cultural Center poster). The top binding that holds the tipi together represents relationships, and the fourteen pins keeping the tipi canvass intact represent the family. One value that is common to all Indigenous peoples is the value of working for the betterment of the community, which means putting community before individual gain. Mohawks refer to this as *Rotinohshonni Kaienerekowa*, or "the Great Law of Peace." Its philosophy is simple and promotes unity among individuals, nations, families, and clans while upholding the diversity of Indigenous cultures.

According to Mohawk scholar Taiaiake Alfred (1999), who quotes the *Kaienerekowa*, "the Great Law of Peace":

> You shall be a good person, and you shall be kind to all of the people, not differentiating among them, the people who are wealthy, and the poor ones, and the good natured ones, and the evil ones who sin readily; all of them you shall treat kindly, and you shall not differentiate among them. As to your own fireside, never consider only yourself, you must always remember them, the old people, and the young people, and the children, and those still in the earth, yet unborn, and always you will take into account everyone's well-being, that of the on-going families, so that they may continue to survive, your grandchildren (p. 97).

Similarly, Athabascan values and worldviews resemble those of the Cree, by having a focus on self-sufficiency, hard work, care and provision for the family, good family relations, unity, humor, honesty, fairness, and love for children. Athabascan values also include sharing, caring, village cooperation, responsibility to village, respect for elders and others, and knowledge. Wisdom from life experiences, respect for the land, respect for nature, practice of traditions, honoring ancestors, and spirituality round out the worldview of Athabascans (Alaska Native Knowledge Network poster, n.d.). In times of conflict, or when mistakes were made, the emphasis within the Indigenous world was on reconciliation, healing, and fitting back in, rather than on punishment and isolation:

> Even when a person had made mistakes in life, there were people that would counsel them. There was a process of reconciliation. It was done through the oral language. It was done through the elders. There they talked about that person getting back into a balanced life and were made aware of how [to] focus [on] what was important in life. And if that person had listened and took the appropriate guidance from those kinds of people and they would get back into a balance and be able to help them, to learn from these things (Cardinal & Hildebrandt, 2000, p.16).

Indigenous Knowledge Systems do not encompass a singular body of knowledge but reflect many layers of being, knowing, and methods of expression. Indigenous Knowledge Systems include knowledge about economics, politics, music, leadership, transportation, building, astronomy, women's unique contributions, art, literature/stories, humor, and community values. Expressions of Indigenous Knowledge Systems are interconnected; hence, Indigenous science knowledge is not separate from Indigenous artistic knowledge. Songs and legends that reflect Indigenous knowledge strengthen community and predate recorded history. Anzaldúa (1999) states, "In the ethno-poetics and performance of the shaman, my people, the Indians, did not split the artistic from the functional, the sacred from the secular, arts from everyday life" (p. 88). The exquisite silver grey birch bark basket that has been constructed and dyed embodies a knowledge of science, including engineering for strength and botanical knowledge of plant dyes. Similarly, the ancient pot, made from the clays of the Missinipe River in northern Saskatchewan, is one that has the scientific basis to endure the most extreme heat and cold, and it is lovely to behold. That being said, Indigenous Knowledge Systems are not something frozen in time.

Indigenous knowledge is dynamic and continually adapting to reflect the dramatic changes occurring within Indigenous communities today. Some communities are in a state of disruption; they are devastated by Western encroachment. Communities—which have been exploited for their natural wealth and beauty with activities like mining, deforestation, dams, and tourism—are now the least productive for hunting and gathering societies whose knowledge depended on these natural resources. I have identified these conditions and believe they must be considered when engendering a critical role of Indigenous Knowledge Systems. Worldwide, land is central to Indigenous being and contains the power to heal humanity. Meyer and Aluli (2004) of Hawaii note:

> We will heal and we will be educated by aina (land). This is key. We will, once again, be "fed" by the tides, rains and stories of a place and people made buoyant because this is how culture survives. This is how children learn best. This is how we will survive. We will survive because excellence of being is found in the practice of aloha and that, believe it or not, is an epistemological point. So, let us shape our school lessons by this ideal and let us shape our lives accordingly. (p. 57)

These values and worldviews are currently under threat for multiple reasons. The very communities and homelands that gave life to these values and worldviews are being undermined. Historical events such as colonialism, imposed dominant systems of governance, economics, and schooling have created near genocidal conditions. The history of residential schools, which gravely impacted cultural practices and created human rights abuses, nearly eradicated Indigenous languages and cultures. Simply put colonialism and hegemony make it virtually impossible for Indigenous cultures, including their worldview and values, to endure. Indigenous peoples' way of life and values are under threat by many layers of dominant forces represented by mainstream culture, economics, and systems of governance. Our communities have historically provided the raw materials for the creation of wealth elsewhere, leaving many of our communities underdeveloped, disrupted, and marginalized. My father, Henry McKay Settee, was an unfortunate example of this disruption. If we are to survive as Indigenous peoples it will mean being able to analyze and challenge these all-encompassing, dominant forces. We are not the only people impacted by forces of domination, and every day the numbers grow. We can take lessons from, and share strategies with, similarly impacted groups. Our history and our cultures join the list of global peoples who have been oppressed by Western development and practices that marginalize and claim more victims among once-rich cultures. To counteract the impact and combat oppression and effect a rebirth, we can create a deeper understanding and hone our skills for survival. Once again we can rebuild strong nations by sharing our stories that reflect our culture and current realities. Ours is an uphill battle because we work within the larger framework of educational traditionalism that ignores the problem, choosing to focus on individualism or serving dominant masters (Giroux, 1983, p. 3).

My work in researching Indigenous Knowledge Systems has taken me to South Africa and other regions of the world to examine the universality of such systems. This international experience, which has spanned over three decades, has enhanced my definition of Indigenous Knowledge Systems and added a new dimension to my extended community. My extended community has grown to include colleagues in the academy in Canada and other parts of the globe in Africa, Vanuatu, and Hawaii, adding people that I share no cultural ties with. The work that I do in the academy has the potential to influence the direction of formal education. I desire to share my Indigenous knowledge with my extended academic community through course development, organization of symposiums and conferences.

In South Africa, Indigenous scholars have defined Indigenous Knowledge Systems as local knowledge that is unique to a culture or society and is outside the formal educational system. Indigenous Knowledge Systems allow communities to survive and are the basis for decision making in health, agriculture, food preparation, natural resource management, and education. In keeping with traditional practices, communities rather than individuals hold Indigenous knowledge. It is embedded in community practices, rituals and relationships making it difficult to codify. Indigenous knowledge is part of everyday life (Snyman, SCECSAL Editor, 2002, p. 101). South Africans have critiqued the theoretical base of colonialism and its inherent cultural and intellectual domination that has been the force leading the African Renaissance and the rebirth of ubuntu.

SCHOLARSHIP, INDIGENOUS KNOWLEDGE, AND ACTIVISM

My desire is to locate Indigenous knowledge as a scholarly discourse in the academy because there is a critical need for its inclusion. Working at a university means having an opportunity to create knowledge with a critical perspective. At an early age, I became both a feminist and an environmentalist. This gave me a stance wherefrom to critically position what was happening with Indigenous peoples, women, the land, health, and well-being of community. As land continues to deteriorate globally, so do people's well-being; Mander and Tauli-Corpuz (2005) claim that this is attributable to unsustainable Western development. Under these conditions Indigenous peoples' knowledge has no place. Women existing under the influence of male domination in many Indigenous communities, as well as others, are beaten and killed. The treatment of Indigenous peoples is a metaphor for the treatment of our Mother Earth. The courts and jails are filled with Indigenous peoples. These human conditions need to be critically interrogated to reveal the underlying social and economic origins and to develop possible solutions. Identifying Indigenous knowledge as a valid knowledge source raises the challenge of sharing the privilege, space, and power to adapt and change higher learning institutions. The global governance systems that fuel and promote such extinction are seldom on scholarly radar. I believe that any definition of Indigenous Knowledge Systems must include this very critical aspect.

Hegemony, the dominance of one group over another, is another important concept for scholars to be well versed in—to understand how their scholarship, writing, and ways of knowing are either included or excluded. Giroux (1983) describes hegemony as not simply referring to the content found, for instance, in the formal curriculum of schools. It is that and much more; it also refers to the way such knowledge is structured. Additionally, hegemony refers to the routines and practices embedded in different social relationships; and, finally, it points to the notion of social structures as natural configurations that both embody and sustain forms of ideological hegemony (Giroux, 1983, p. 197).

We have many jobs, like the warriors' dual work of challenging hegemony and creating respectful protocols to give a free rein to Indigenous knowledge, which has the potential to build a better world. Both efforts will help large numbers of youth live with a sense of history and future built on dignity and human rights.

There are many reasons why Indigenous Knowledge Systems need to be fully explored within higher learning and make a contribution toward community well-being. I believe that a lot of thoughtful consideration is needed to create institutional change by integrating Indigenous Knowledge Systems that honor our ancestors, develop a critical consciousness among Indigenous and non-Indigenous learners alike in order to create a positive future for our children.

My vast network of international scholars has helped me to query how Indigenous Knowledge Systems will improve the quality of life and learning within our extended communities and institutions of higher learning. Our collaborative conversations became an exchange and reformulation of ideas and reflective questions. By sustaining and extending these conversations, it helped identify and understand our stories of learning as we explored our place in communities and the academy.

I believe we can learn a lot from the scholarly writings produced by schools of thought such as the New African Renaissance. In the post-apartheid ideology of the New African Renaissance, writing serves as a political tool that is essential in critiquing the dominant political and social systems. Writing in fact, is vital to cultural and racial survival because it is not just to communicate, writing is for discovering oneself. South African scholars have written extensively on Indigenous Knowledge Systems in an attempt to define for themselves who they are and who they should become. *Indigenous Knowledge and the Integration of Knowledge Systems, Towards a Philosophy of Articulation*, by Dr. Catherine Odora Hoppers (2002) contains articles that describe integrating Indigenous Knowledge Systems into higher learning. Odora Hoppers' work is a response to a call from the Parliamentary Portfolio Committee on Arts, Culture, Language, Science, and Technology for the Heads of South African Science Councils. Her book explores the role of the social and natural sciences in supporting the development of Indigenous Knowledge Systems. Odora Hoppers (2002) explains her thoughts on the contributions of Indigenous Knowledge Systems:

> At the philosophical or methodological level, one finds the harrowing legacy of epistemological silencing and the concerted strategies that have combined to pre-empt any possibility for co-existence, fruitful exchange of methods, or even dialogue around heuristic methods. At the level of application is found the arrogance of practice, which is still rife in formal institutions that are confidently, and without qualms, determined to continue with the monochrome logic of Western epistemology (p. vii).

Like other African scholars, Odora Hoppers states the need to instill Indigenous Knowledge Systems as a tool that will rebuild democratic values, ethics, sustainable development, and, ultimately, human liberation free from all forms of discrimination. Higher learning in South Africa was largely driven by white intelligentsia, which took the lead in creating apartheid-enforced identities in knowledge production. Black scholars such as hooks (1984), Davis (1974), and Dei (1999) claim that only when intellectual production is de-racialized and black intelligentsia fueled by African values will an African Renaissance truly take place. These are thoughts that can be useful to Aboriginal scholars in other parts of the world. In addition to intellectual production being de-racialized, it must also be de-hegemonized. Affording Indigenous knowledge the same value as the dominant knowledge can do this.

One attempt at teaching and learning Aboriginal knowledge, including history and contemporary issues, has been the establishment of Native studies departments at mainstream universities (Couture, 1999; Kulchyski, McCaskill, & Newhouse, 1999; Lawrence cited in Anderson & Lawrence, 2003; Mihesuah, 2003). The first department of Native studies was established in 1969 at Trent University in Peterborough, Ontario. The goal was to create a cadre of leaders and allies who would work over the course of their lifetimes to create new realities for Aboriginal peoples in this country and elsewhere. Initially, this course of study provided students with a foundation in Aboriginal history and politics, and in Haudenosaunee and Anishnaabe culture, tradition and language. Since then, others have been developed including my own Department of Native Studies at the University of Saskatchewan that was established in the mid-1980s. The discipline of Native studies has faced many challenges such as being on an uncertain footing in the academy. The uncertainty stems from a lack of commitment, under-resourcing, and a lack of understanding of the department by the university administration. Because Native studies is more recent in comparison to other departments, it suffers from reduced financial contributions enjoyed by larger more established departments. Most university administrators and few faculty were ever required to take Native studies in order to expand their understanding or knowledge of who we are. Native studies is interdisciplinary because of the immensity and complexity of the discipline, which encompasses anthropology, history, political studies, economics, sociology, health, education, and the arts. Aboriginal peoples are in the process of dramatic change, which is a direct result of their colonial past, and by the fact that they represent many diverse groups not only here in Canada but throughout the world.

The establishment of Native studies departments is not a simple solution to including Indigenous knowledge in academia or Indigenizing the academy. Couture (1999) describes the tension between Native studies and the university. He claims that what is needed by the university is an open position and willingness to find complementary means of learning, understanding, and interpreting the traditions of others. Like others, he describes the elitism that plagues universities and its neutral values as inappropriate to Native studies. Native studies has to be more than just adding courses to address vacuums of knowledge in regards to Aboriginal communities. It must also examine methodologies (Kovach, 2009, p. 58) and ways of learning, challenge mainstream pedagogies, and crack the structurally racist hiring practices and policies for which universities are renowned.

When describing what would be some agreed principles for Indigenizing the academy, from the textbook of the same name, Tyeeme Clark states:

> First, everyone here agrees, at least for now, that to decolonize what currently is widely accepted as knowledge about "Indians" is crucial. Second, a consensus emerges in these pages around the need to theorize, conceptualize, and represent Indigenous sovereignty so that our people may live well into the foreseeable future. Third, contributors to this volume argue for the necessities of producing indigenous knowledges for Indigenous peoples rather than primarily as subjects for non-Indigenous curiosity (Clark, 2004, p. 219).

I feel that we produce knowledges for both Indigenous peoples and others and not necessarily for their curiosity but in the hope that such knowledges will make them better human beings and create the desperately required social change for Indigenous peoples and all peoples in a world that is increasingly becoming bereft of human values.

When I and my other colleagues have taught a critical perspective of Canadian and First Nations relations, we have often been taunted and challenged by the "ball cap" crew (The young men who sit at the back of the class and mutter insults under their breath, especially if they are taking a required Native studies class). This aggressive attitude finds its roots in the complacency or lack of critical awareness that pervades other university courses from other disciplines. If critical awareness was standard across all disciplines, it would make our job somewhat simpler because the entire faculty would be critiquing the many forms of domination and subjugated knowledge. The lack of a critical mass of Native studies graduate students, which could help develop a Native studies profile, is partially due to the fact that Native students don't bring many financial resources to their academic learning experience. With few or no resources many of these students do not aspire to graduate, even where universities might offer graduate Native studies courses. What is lost is a growing pool of potential Indigenous faculty members who could populate both Native studies and other departments.

While I believe that Native studies departments are not the only answer to the browning of the academy, there are actions that empathetic colleagues can take to help. I believe there is a role that non-Indigenous colleagues can play within the broader university community to become involved in the Indigenization of learning. Our colleagues who are not Indigenous have tremendous opportunities to use their places of authority to influence decision-makers in creating spaces for Indigenization. They can insist that new hiring be filled by Indigenous candidates. And just so they are not just scooping up Indigenous candidates, or "vacuuming Indigenous colleges" as it has been referred to, they can help produce and strengthen the pool. Our colleagues can do this by using their experience to work with junior faculty members and graduate students to provide opportunities for advancement and to seek out funding. Inversely, academics can stop applying for research dollars that are clearly designated for Indigenous research. They can examine their own paternalism. Our colleagues can insist on equity on committees where important decisions are made. They can insist that funding decisions reflect diversity goals. They can use their influence to convince their colleagues who may be less than convinced about equity. They can talk, and preferably listen, to marginalized people and take courses and learn about experience from marginalized perspectives. They can take risks and get involved with grassroots communities. They can demand answers to the reasons for the high attrition rate of Indigenous students. While they may never be marginalized and should not speak for Indigenous communities, they can begin the slow journey to appreciating who the "other" is. If universities do not have vision statements that espouse commitment to creating Indigenous spaces, they can collaborate with Indigenous colleagues to create such statements. They can ensure that universities live up to written statements of commitment. They can also get involved in academic life and begin to understand other forms of domination faced by women faculty and others who face discrimination within the academy. As Mesquakie and Potawatomi's colleague, Tyeeme Clark (2004) states, "to Indigenize the academy means by necessity that Indigenous scholars and our non-Indigenous allies must identify and overpower anti-Indianism" (p. 219). When all faculty work toward ensuring that the workplace is a respectful and life-enforcing environment, it will become a nurturing community for all women and men, Indigenous and non-Indigenous people.

Despite the many challenges faced by Native studies departments, Kulchyski, McCaskill, and Newhouse (1999), from the Department of Native Studies at the University of Manitoba, claims that the discipline of Native studies has been responsible for some changes and gives Native elders a voice equivalent to non-Native authorities which are cited in scholarly practice. Kulchyski, McCaskill, and Newhouse (1999) feel that Native studies are about ethics and practice, about correcting history and knowing how to approach Native knowledge holders such as elders. He argues that "Native Studies involves the creation, recognition, or legitimization of new knowledge and new forms of knowledge" (Kulchyski, McCaskill, & Newhouse, 1999, p.14). I would argue that Indigenous knowledge is marginalized, not new to higher learning institutes. The conditions that exist within First Nations and Aboriginal communities require an urgent response by the academy where curriculum, research, and ultimately policy and development are created.

Native women face particular challenges when entering academia. Their wealth of knowledge systems, as well as developmental needs of their communities, require examination and action from the academy as well as other places. Women's stories are particularly poignant within both academic and community life:

> We continually look for ways to mesh our duties as scholars with our concerns about tribal interests and family. The lines between being female, Native, and scholar do indeed blur, and most of us are scholar-activists (Mihesuah, 2003, p. 22).

Bonita Lawrence (2003) describes the isolation she faced in being the only Aboriginal scholar in a mainstream university department. Lawrence (2003) longed to have writings by Aboriginal scholars and have those materials change the all-white workplace:

> I was troubled by the absence of Native people in my academic department, and at University of Toronto in general. When I began my research as a graduate student there were no Native faculty members at my university and, in general very few Aboriginal people in North America writing sociological theory from Native perspectives. Because of this, I was aware that my research on Native identity was treading on new ground, and yet there were no other Aboriginal academics to consult with about the implications of undertaking work that questions aspects of Native identity in a non-native environment. Indeed much of the existing academic work by Aboriginal people, primarily from the United States, has suggested that it is dangerous to explore native identity in an academic setting where there are no other Native people present to ensure that Aboriginal perspective will be well represented (p. 71).

Some have described the tension and feelings of inadequacy that are created by the academy. A tension exists between Indigenous academics feeling the need to write the stories and feeling that they won't be seen as worthy by the academy. Graveline (2004) in her chapter called "Encountering Academentia" describes the fear that gripped her before her PhD defense. "In a Eurocentric, patriarchal. Institution. Known to be continuously marginalizing Nehiyaw'ak. Women. Easy to feel less Than" (Graveline, 2004, p. 197). For many Aboriginal women scholars, our work is not separate from our identities and can be all encompassing. Many of us work from the belief that our workplaces must be more responsive to the material needs of community (Mihesuah, 2003). Within our department of Native studies we struggle to fit the requirements of academia to the needs of extended communities. Endless volunteer committees, increasing administrative requirements, expanded work loads requiring more of our time with fewer resources as well make for difficult balancing acts in the life of an Indigenous academic. The growing corporatization agenda of universities make for difficult situations for those of us who strive to ensure universities remain accountable to the public and society at large.

When I applied to do an interdisciplinary PhD program at my university, I faced what I thought was an unnecessary hurdle; an entire year passed from the date I applied to when I was approved to begin my program. This was an unprecedented event. I believe that it could be attributed to the fact the graduate studies department had few ideas of the nature of my proposed interdisciplinary research in Indigenous Knowledge Systems as it applies to agriculture and education. Maybe, it was because my research might raise some controversial or contentious issues about food security in a college that researches genetically modified foods? Oftentimes our Indigenous research needs and interests are not familiar to the research norms of the academy, which often narrows rather than extends the boundaries. Sometimes our research needs and interests challenge and run counter to the goals of higher learning and official knowledge.

Peter Kulchisky, from the Native Studies Department at the University of Manitoba states that by establishing the basis for Indigenous knowledge, we question and dismantle attitudes and practices that began with the Enlightenment era. These archaic attitudes and practices have no real application in education, nor are they reflective of diversity. Kulchisky (1999) questions the universality of non–Indigenous Knowledge Systems:

> A variety of challenges to the notion of a universal "man" who would continue to "progress" through the application of his rational powers have in the last few decades gained force within the humanities and social sciences. Feminists, anti-racists, and those involved in the struggle for decolonization have thrown the notion of a universal "man" into question, finding for the most part that where such a figure is presupposed it usually, on closer scrutiny, has been found to be a figure bound by values embedded in racial, class and gender privilege (p. 15).

Indigenous scholars bring new ideas and another worldview, which are often lacking in university disciplines. The academy can be enriched by the inclusion of Indigenous Knowledge Systems creating diverse, welcoming, inclusive workplaces where real democracies can be inspired and realized. But universities are well aware of the political ramifications of hiring Indigenous scholars who are politicized about equal rights. If they hire scholars who are activists, then they can expect disruption and pressure for change in the status quo.

In many ways, several of my colleagues and I have attempted to make a small difference in the institutionalization of Indigenous knowledge and to formulate some answers to these questions through our personal and academic journeys. The laborious task of producing *Expressions in Canadian Native Studies* (Laliberte et al., 2000) was the collective effort of a primarily University of Saskatchewan team of academics to define Indigenous knowledge. We, the editors, asked ourselves the questions who would be invited to write and what would the table of contents look like. The planning of this textbook with fellow colleagues was not a straightforward path. As a collective, we had to identify gaps that existed within the current collections. How could a local team decide what topics would be identified for a textbook that was intended to serve a national readership? The final product was a Native studies textbook called *Expressions in Canadian Native Studies* (Laliberte et al., 2000) that continues to be used for introductory Native studies courses. The textbook covers the range of North American Indigenous Knowledge Systems, including Indigenous people's intellectual property rights, biodiversity, women's knowledge, and international human rights. Other events in knowledge production that I coordinated were two international Aboriginal science conferences, two conferences on Indigenous knowledge and two on Indigenous food sovereignty. I have presented chapters at and listened to presenters at numerous conferences. Some of these have been scientific bodies and Indigenous knowledge conferences. My presentations included preserving Indigenous languages, research methodologies, sustainable development, water rights, curriculum development, and food sovereignty. The purpose of the majority of my academic work has been to bring Indigenous knowledge forward to the academy and to present it as legitimate knowledge.

The following is a quote from my paper "Indigenous Knowledge Systems, Global Food Systems and Community Sovereignty" presented at a symposium called The Globalization of Agricultural Biotechnology: Mutli-Disciplinary Views from the South at the Center for Globalization and Regionalization at the University of Warwick, England in May 2005:

> Indigenous peoples' knowledge systems have contributed greatly to global health in the area of foods and medicines. For the most part this knowledge is seldom acknowledged. Indigenous peoples have suffered devastating losses when they have had contact with colonizing forces. Today Indigenous peoples are going through a process that has been referred to as recolonization as a result of the forces of globalization. The loss of human rights among Indigenous peoples has resulted in a global struggle for sovereignty. However this time the issues involve more than just Indigenous peoples. Indigenous peoples, farmers and other concerned communities need to unite around issues of food sovereignty, food safety, and food security. The well-being of the earth and all who live on earth require concerted action (Settee, 2005, p. 16).

Similarly, my master's thesis in Education, entitled "Honoring Indigenous Science Knowledge as a Means of Ensuring Western Science Accountability," documented Indigenous knowledge in the sciences and described some of the tensions that exist between the two bodies of knowledge. "While it is indisputable that Indigenous knowledge in the sciences predates much of Western science, and forms the basis for many contemporary scientific wonders, recognition for these contributions is not evident" (Settee, 1999, p. 6). Through this process of learning to critique the conditions of dominant culture and the ensuing development of a critical mass of Indigenous scholars, curriculum is changed, and we educate our colleagues and students to appreciate Indigenous Knowledge Systems and to consider how we can become critical educators and learners.

In 2002, I served as an assessor for and later recommended a new degree program on Indigenous leadership and community development at Negahneewin College of Indigenous Studies at Confederation College in northern Ontario. That same year, the provincial government of Ontario approved the degree program. I have been advisor to many federal governmental processes which sought out the Indigenous voice on such matters as biodiversity, benefits sharing, and sustainable development. These consultations sought answers to how Indigenous Knowledge Systems and the Indigenous voice can be considered when discussing government interests. These conferences, consultations, and meetings attracted scholars and community representatives from various regions of the world and permitted us to exchange strategies and curriculum ideas for use within the academy. Unlike many academic conferences, our meetings, almost without exception, include the voices of the extended Indigenous communities. As educators, we must continue to listen to the voices from community—the source of Indigenous knowledge. This praxis helps to keep a critical perspective of the needs of community, to encourage civic participation, and to foster the development of democratic values. Or as Giroux (1992, p. 18) might query, are education and schooling "to uncritically serve and reproduce the existing society or challenge the social order to develop and advance its democratic imperatives?"

WHOSE KNOWLEDGE?

Critical theory makes it possible for Indigenous people to see the world in an enlarged perspective because we have removed the blinders that obscure knowledge. There are some troubling issues of knowledge creation that need to be addressed. As Indigenous peoples, we cannot understand or explain the world we live in or the real choices offered us as long as Western scientific and technological knowledge has deskilled us. We need to ask some hard questions. Who gives Indigenous knowledge-holders voice in the poorly laid-out path of globalization and the hallowed halls of academic research and development where that knowledge is subjugated? We are not the only ones who are questioning the relationship of globalization, knowledge creation, and democratic rights. How do communities who hold collective rights to knowledge cope with Western imposed concepts of intellectual property rights as private ownership? How do we handle the crises of the disappearance of Indigenous languages and their relationship to Indigenous knowledge? Western science generates technologies and applications that are not morally or politically neutral (Harding, 1991). Who has the rights to or stewardship of the earth and can call up the purveyors of unethical research practice, such as the atomic and nuclear bombs that now have capacities to wipe out virtually all life on earth? Some leaders now admit that they hold some regions of the world hostage through the proliferation of weapons of mass destruction. How do those knowledge keepers who have taken centuries to produce the well-adapted and life-giving hybrids comprehend the knowledge of suicide seeds, known by some as "terminator technology"? Research now has the capacity to clone human beings. One question should be, does this type of research need a formal policing and who will do this? Another question should be, how can we guarantee public accountability for questionable research? Lastly, how can we assure that community needs drive research? For these and other issues, Indigenous peoples are demanding a place in knowledge production. Indigenous peoples believe they have valuable contributions to make to ensure the survival of the planet. Some ways that Indigenous Knowledge Systems can be incorporated into higher learning would be first to have a critical mass of Indigenous scholars. In my experience, the majority of Indigenous scholars will work in transforming curriculum, methodologies, Indigenize research agendas as well as create innovative teaching and learning opportunities. Indigenous scholars are role models for Indigenous students and understand the importance of culture as well as the impact of poverty on the learning process. When you come from the eye of the storm you have a keener solution process. With appropriate role models Indigenous students will see themselves as future leaders within the academy. Ensuring a critical mass of Indigenous scholars will ensure that new relations will be made with extended learning communities. In order to create a critical mass of Indigenous scholars, universities need to identify money to make this a reality as most Indigenous learners have few financial resources. I know this from firsthand experience every day I see the impact of material poverty on my students. Non-Indigenous scholars need to work with their Indigenous colleagues where issues of class, race, and academic freedom arise. Indigenous scholars need the solidarity of justice-minded colleagues, to speak up, speak out, understand their issues, and help provide a climate of acceptance on thorny issues that challenge the academy. Tenure and promotion standards need to be examined for cultural relevancy, to ensure they reflect the needs of Indigenous communities. In regards to responsible development that responds to Indigenous community needs and preservation/respect for traditional Indigenous lands, researchers have a duty to consult with those impacted by development. This is the only way that Indigenous homelands will be developed respectfully with future generations in mind. In a world where neoliberalism has forced the natural world to the brink of disaster the academy needs to allow transformative leadership that work with the grinding poverty of Indigenous peoples. And lastly the academy needs to admit that hegemonic relations exist and be willing to critically examine the Western paradigm which locks out Indigenous perspectives and paradigms. Incorporating Indigenous Knowledge Systems, methodologies, and ways of knowing can create equity, challenge power relations, enhance learning, provide a sense of belonging for Indigenous scholars, and build bridges of understanding with our non-Indigenous colleagues. As Leonard Cohen (1992) states, "There is a crack in everything that's how the light gets in." Indigenous knowledge can be that crack of enlightenment which can help transform learning.

NOTE

1. Throughout this chapter, I use the terminology, Indigenous peoples, Aboriginal peoples, as well as First Nations, Inuit and Métis peoples, sometime interchangeably. The latter are legal terminologies that have been given by the government of Canada.

REFERENCES

Adams, H. (1975). *Prison of Grass: Canada from the Native Point of View.* Toronto: New Press.
Ahenakew, F. (1987). *Stories of the House People.* Winnipeg: The University of Manitoba Press.
Alfred, T. (1999). *Peace, Power, Righteousness, an Indigenous Manifesto.* Don Mills, Ontario: Oxford University Press.

Alfred, T. (2004). Warrior scholarship: seeing the university as a ground of contension. In D. Mihesuah & A. C. Wilson. (Eds.), *Indigenizing the Academy: Transforming Scholarship and Empowering Communities* (pp. 88–99). Nebraska: University of Nebraska.

Anderson, K. & Lawrence, B. (2003), Strong women stories: Native Vision and community survival. Toronto: Summach Press.

Anzaldua, G. (1999). *Borderlands/La Frontera: The New Mestiza.* San Francisco: Aunt Lute.

Cardinal, H., & Hildebrandt, W. (2000). *Treaty Elders of Saskatchewan: Our Dream Is That Our People Will One Day Be Clearly Recognized as Nations.* Calgary: University of Calgary Press.

Clark, D. A. T. (2004). Not the end of the stories, not the end of the songs. In D. Mihesuah, & A. C. Wilson (Eds.), *Indigenizing the Academy: Transforming Scholarship and Empowering Communities* (pp. 218–232). Nebraska: University of Nebraska Press.

Cleaver, E. (1968). *Soul on Ice.* New York: Dell.

Cohen, L. (1992).Anthem. *The Future* [record]. Canada: Columbia.

Couture, J. (1999). In P. Kulchyski, D. McCaskill, & D. Newhouse (Eds.). *In the Words of Elders: Aboriginal Cultures in Transition.* Toronto: University of Toronto Press.

Davis, A. Y. (1974). *Angela Davis: An Autobiography.* New York: Random House.

Dei, G. J. S. (1999). Knowledge and politics of social change: the implication of anti-racism. *British Journal of Sociology of Education 20*(3), 395–409.

Fanon, F. (1963). *The Wretched of the Earth.* New York: Grove.

Freire, P. (1970). *Pedagogy of the Oppressed.* New York: Herder and Herder.

Giroux, H. (1983). *Theory & Resistance in Education: A Pedagogy for the Opposition.* Westport, CT: Bergin & Garvey.

Giroux, H. (1992). *Border Crossings: Cultural Workers and the Politics of Education.* New York: Routledge.

Gramsci, A. (1971) *Selections from the Prison Notebooks.* New York: International.

Graveline, F. J. (2004). *Healing Wounded Hearts.* Halifax: Fernwood.

Harding, S. (1991). *Whose Science? Whose Knowledge? Thinking from Women's Lives.* Ithaca, NY: Cornell University Press.

hooks, b. (1984). *Feminist Theory: From Margin to Center.* Cambridge: South End.

Jensen, D. (2002). *Listening to the Land: Conversations about Nature, Culture, and Eros.* New York: Context.

King, T. (2003). *The Truth about Stories: A Native Narrative.* Toronto: House of Anansi.

Kovach, M. (2009). Being Indigenous in the academy: Creating space for Indigenous scholars. In A. M. Timpson (Ed.), *First Nations, First Thoughts,* (pp. 51–76). Vancouver: University of British Columbia Press.

Kulchyski, P., McCaskill, D., & Newhouse, D. (1999). *In the Words of Elders: Aboriginal Cultures in Transition.* Toronto: University of Toronto Press.

Kulchyski, P. McCaskill, D. & Newhouse, D. (1995) In the Words of elders: Aboriginal cultures in transition. Toronto: University of Toronto Press.

Laliberte, R. F., Settee, P., Waldram, J. B., Innes, R., MacDougall, B., McBain, L., & Barron, F. L. (Eds.). (2000). *Expressions in Canadian Native Studies.* Saskatoon: University of Saskatchewan Extension Press.

Mander, J., & Tauli-Corpuz, V. (2005). *Paradigm Wars, Indigenous Peoples' Resistance to Economic Globalization.* A special report of the International forum on Globalization Committee on Indigenous Peoples. San Francisco: International Forum on Globalization.

Memmi, A. (1974). *The Colonizer and the Colonised.* London: Condor/Souvenir.

Meyer, M., & Aluli, H. (2004). *Our Time of Becoming: Hawaiian Epistemology and Early Writings.* Honolulu: 'Ai Pohaku & Native.

Mihesuah, D. A. (1998). *Natives and Academics: Researching and Writing about American Indians.* Lincoln, NE: University of Nebraska Press.

Mihesuah, D. A. (2003). *Indigenous American Women: Decolonization, Empowerment, Activism.* Lincoln, NE: University of Nebraska Press.

Mihesuah, D. A., & Wilson A. C. (Eds.). (2004). *Indigenizing the Academy: Transforming Scholarship and Empowering Communities.* Lincoln, NE: University of Nebraska Press.

Odora Hoppers, C. A. (2002). *Indigenous Knowledge and the Integration of Knowledge Systems: Towards a Philosophy of Articulation.* South Africa: New Africa.

Settee, P. (1999). Honoring Indigenous science knowledge as a means of ensuring Western science accountability. (Master's thesis), University of Manitoba, Manitoba.

Settee, P. (2005, May). Indigenous knowledge systems, global food systems and community sovereignty. Paper presented at The Globalization of Agricultural Biotechnology: Multi-Disciplinary Views from the South, University of Warwick, Centre for Globalization and Regionalization, England.

Snyman, R. (2002). *From Africa to the World—The Globalisation of Indigenous Knowledge Systems*: Proceedings of the 15th standing conference of Eastern, Central Southern African Library and Information Associations. Pretoria (LIASA).

Contributors

Tope Adefarakan is a PhD candidate in the Collaborative Program in the Department of Sociology and Equity Studies and the Women and Gender Studies Institute at the Ontario Institute for Studies in Education of the University of Toronto. Her dissertation theorizes African Diasporic identities and particularly, how Yoruba migrants make meaning of and construct Yoruba Indigenous knowledges in the African diaspora, and more specifically, the geo-political space of Canada. Her interests also include Indigenous African spirituality in the multilayers of Diaspora and Eurocentric spaces, and the relationship between gendered social relations of Indigeneity and power.

Jeffrey D. Anderson (PhD, University of Chicago) is Associate Professor of Anthropology at Colby College. For the past twenty years his research has focused on the language, culture, and history of the Northern Arapaho tribe. He is an adopted member of the Spoonhunter family in the Northern Arapaho Nation of Wyoming. He is author of *The Four Hills of Life: Northern Arapaho Knowledge and Life Movement* (2001), *One Hundred Years of Old Man Sage: An Arapaho Life Story* (2003), and various articles. His topical interests include creativity, language shift, comparative ways of knowing, age grade systems, human rights, ethnohistory, and comparative human development.

Soenke Biermann, originally from northern Germany, is a PhD candidate with the Centre for Peace and Social Justice at Southern Cross University, Australia. His research focuses on social justice and decolonization in higher education, and he is particularly interested in the ways educators facilitate these ideals in their pedagogical practice.

Brennus BMJK is of Northern Irish and Canadian heritage. He is a freelance writer and researcher. His work in Indigenous education has been with the Oneida Nation Educators and Elders, predominantly in Oneida, Wisconsin, and partially the Oneida settlement just outside London, Ontario.

Martin Cannon is Onyota'a:ka (Oneida) from the Six Nations of Grand River Territory. He is Assistant Professor of sociology and equity studies in education at the Ontario Institute for Studies in Education in Toronto, Canada. His published work has focused on colonial dominance and racism, including sex discrimination in Canada's Indian Act. He has been an advocate for legislative changes to colonial policy and has worked with organizations like the Native Women's Association of Canada, Union of Ontario Indians, and the National Centre for First Nations Governance on this matter. His book, *Racism, Colonialism, and Indigeneity in Canada,* is co-edited with Dr Lina Sunseri (Western) and is expected to be published in January 2011.

Pauline W. U. Chinn and **Isabella Aiona Abbott** are Professor of Education and Professor Emerita, respectively, at the University of Hawai'i at Mānoa. Napua Barrows, Sabra Kauka, and Michelle Kapana-Baird include monitoring and restoration in their Hawaiian Studies programs. Doctoral student Huihui Kanahele-Mossman researches ancestral stories as sources for science inquiry. Archeologist Moana Lee works with several schools. Lila Lelepali and Mahina Hou Ross teach science and Ka'umealani Walk teaches geography in Hawaiian language immersion programs.

Peter Cole is a member of the Douglas First Nation (Xa'xtsa), has Welsh and Scottish ancestry and is an Assistant Professor in the Department of Curriculum and Pedagogy, Faculty of Education, University of British Columbia. His teaching and research interests include orality, narrativity, Aboriginal education, environmental thought, Indigenous self-determination, and Aboriginalizing methodology. He has published in national and international academic and literary journals and books and is the author of a book entitled, *Coyote and Raven Go Canoeing: Coming Home to the Village* (2006, McGill-Queen's University Press) and co-editor of *Speaking for Ourselves: Environmental Justice in Canada* (2009, UBC Press).

Michael Davis's academic background is in history and anthropology, with a BA Honors in Pacific and Aboriginal studies (La Trobe University). He submitted his PhD at the University of Technology Sydney (UTS) in March 2010. He has an established career in high level public policy formulation and critique, as well as in research and writing on Indigenous rights in cultural heritage, Indigenous knowledge, environment, and cultural and intellectual property. Michael has published in this area in a range of journals, and in 2007 produced a major work, *Writing Heritage: The Depiction of Indigenous Heritage in European-Australian Writings* (Australian Scholarly Publishing, and National Museum of Australia Press).

George J. Sefa Dei is Professor of sociology and equity studies, Ontario Institute for Studies in Education of the University of Toronto (OISE/UT). His teaching and research interests are in the areas of anti-racism, minority schooling, international development, Indigenous philosophies, and anti-colonial thought. He has researched and written extensively in these areas. In 2000, he co-edited *Indigenous Knowledges in Global Contexts: Multiple Readings of Our World* (2000, University of Toronto Press), with Budd Hall and Dorothy Goldin Rosenberg. His most recent books include*: Teaching Africa: Towards Transgressive Pedagogy* (2010, Springer Publishers), *Fanon and Education: Pedagogical Challenges,* co-edited with Marlon Simmons (2010, Peter Lang Publishing), *Fanon and the Counterinsurgency of Education* (2010, Sense Publishers), and *Learning to Succeed: Improving Educational Achievement for All* (2010, Teneo Press). In July 2007, he succeeded the occupant of the stool (Odikro) of Asokorekuma and was installed as a traditional chief in Ghana. His stool name is Nana Sefa Atweneboah I the Adomakwaahene of the town of Asokore, near Koforidua in the New Juaben Traditional Area of Ghana.

Cynthia B. Dillard is Professor of multicultural teacher education in the School of Teaching and Learning at the Ohio State University. Her major research interests include critical multicultural education, spirituality in teaching and learning, and African/African American feminist studies. She has published numerous book chapters and articles in journals including *International Review of Qualitative Research, Race, Ethnicity and Education, The Journal of Teacher Education, The International Journal of Qualitative Studies in Education* and *Urban Education.* Her first book, *On Spiritual Strivings: Transforming an African American Woman's Academic Life* was published in 2006 by SUNY Press and was selected for the 2008 Critics' Choice Book Award by the American Educational Studies Association (AESA). Most recently, her research and service is focused in Ghana, West Africa, where she has established a preschool, is building a new elementary school, and is enstooled Nana Mansa II, Queen Mother of Development in the village of Mpeasem, Ghana.

Kimberly A. Haverkos is a doctoral student at Miami University of Ohio in the Department of Educational Leadership. A former science educator, her research interests are science critique, girlhoods, and knowledge production.

Serena Heckler is a Research Fellow in the Department of Anthropology at Durham University. She has worked with the Piaroa of the Venezuelan Amazon and is currently researching Indigenous knowledge, endogenous development, and Indigenous higher education with the Shuar of Ecuador. She is editor of *Landscape, Process and Power: Re-evaluating Traditional Environmental Knowledge.* In 2009, she co-organized a symposium with Paul Sillitoe entitled "Indigenous Studies and Engaged Anthropology: Opening a Dialogue" at Durham University.

Judy Iseke is of Métis and Nehiyaw heritage along with European ancestry. She is a researcher, educator, and educational digital filmmaker from St. Albert, Alberta, Canada. Iseke is also the Canada Research Chair in Indigenous education and Associate Professor in the Faculty of Education, Lakehead University, where she teaches graduate courses in Indigenous education. She is also a member of the Métis Nation of Alberta.

Lloyd L. Lee is Diné of the Navajo Nation. He is of the Kinyaa'áanii (Towering House People) clan and born for the Tl'ááschí'í (Red Cheeks People) clan. His maternal grandfather's clan is Áshiihí (Salt) and his paternal grandfather's clan is Tábaahá (Water's Edge People). Originally from Albuquerque, New Mexico, he is an assistant professor in the Native American Studies Department at the University of New Mexico. His research focuses on Indigenous and Diné identity, Indigenous and Diné masculinities, Indigenous and Diné leadership, and Indigenous and Diné philosophy. He is the book review editor for the academic journal *American Indian Quarterly*.

Michael Marker is an Associate Professor in the Department of Educational Studies at the University of British Columbia, where he is director of Ts"kel First Nations Graduate Studies. His research has focused on the politics of Indigenous knowledge, ethnohistory of Aboriginal education, and cross-cultural concerns in ethnography.

Kimine Mayuzumi is a doctoral candidate at the Department of Sociology and Equity Studies in Education at OISE and the collaborative program with women and gender studies at University of Toronto. Her areas of interest include: Asian women faculty in higher education, Indigenous knowledge framework, and transnational feminist theory.

Dennis McPherson is an Ojibwa and a band member of the Couchiching First Nation at Fort Frances, Ontario. To better understand the issues concerning First Nations communities Mr.

McPherson has earned degrees in the arts (B.A.), in social work (H.B.S.W.), in philosophy (H.B.A.-Phil), and in law (LL.B. and LL.M.). Mr. McPherson was the coordinator and co-director of the Native Philosophy Project at Lakehead University and co-authored, with Dr. Douglas Rabb (retired), *Indian from the Inside: A Study in Ethno-Metaphysics* for use as a textbook in the delivery of Philosophy 2805, Native Canadian worldviews, the first course in Native philosophy to be offered in a Canadian university.

Ocean Ripeka Mercier (of the Ngāti Porou tribe) is the first Māori woman to complete a PhD in physics. She completed postdoctoral fellowships in superconducting tapes and in Antarctic sea ice, before swinging her academic interests in a different direction through a Bachelor of Arts in Māori language. She is a now a lecturer in Te Kawa a Māui (the School of Māori studies), Victoria University of Wellington, with teaching and research interests in confluences of Indigenous knowledge and science, te reo Māori, and film.

Zahra Murad is completing her MA in curriculum studies at the Ontario Institute for Studies in Education (UofT) where she will also be starting her Ph.D. in 2010. She is interested in integrative anti-racist curriculum and pedagogies, Indigenous knowledges in education, decolonization, and critical race theory. Some of her writing may be found in the online journal *Dark Matter* and the upcoming collection *Ruptures: Anti-colonial and Anti-racist Feminist Theorizing* (in press).

Pat O'Riley is Visiting Associate Professor, Department of Curriculum and Pedagogy, Faculty of Education, University of British Columbia. She is of Irish, French, and Mohawk heritage and married into Douglas First Nation. Her teaching and research interests include research methodology, equity studies, environmental education, and technology education. Pat is the author of *Technology, Culture and Socioeconomics: A Rhizoanalysis of Educational Discourses* (2003, Peter Lang Publishing), and co-editor of *Speaking for Ourselves: Environmental Justice in Canada* (2009, UBC Press).

Eric Ritskes is a Master's student in the Department of Sociology of Equity Studies in Education, Ontario Institute of Studies in Education at the University of Toronto. His background is in teaching internationally, and this informs his studies in Indigenous knowledges and anti-colonialism, especially in terms of seeking to bridge the gap between theory and practice.

Priscilla Settee is an Associate Professor in the Department of Native Studies at the University of Saskatchewan and a member of Cumberland House Cree First Nations from northern Saskatchewan. Priscilla believes that a better path needs to be made between the community and the academy and has initiated a number of projects locally and internationally, including a CIDA (Canadian International Development Agency) project with the University of San Marcos in Peru. This project supported Indigenous Amazonian and Andean students in making the transition from their home communities to the university. She is chair of Saskatoon's only Aboriginal high school, *Oskayak,* and is a member of the *Iskwewak* group, which focuses on disappeared and missing Indigenous women. She has developed youth leadership programs and internships which supports activities in the local (Saskatoon's annual Indigenous music festival) and international context (Fiji, the Philippines, Hawai'i internships). She is a member of the Indigenous Development Network for Heifer International and advises on Indigenous food sovereignty. Settee has published many journal articles, book chapters. Her current book in progress (Coteau Publishing) is called *Akemeyimow, Indigenous Women's Stories.* In 2008, Settee was awarded a Global Citizen's award by Saskatchewan Council for International Co-operation and was nominated for a teaching excellence award by her students. Dr. Settee is a board member for the Canadian Centre for Policy Alternatives, Canada's leading progressive think tank and publishing organization, and a Faculty Fellow at the Centre for Global Citizenship Education and Research at the University of Alberta.

Riyad A. Shahjahan is a Visiting Assistant Professor in the Department of Educational Leadership at the Miami University of Ohio. His research interests are in equity and social justice, spirituality and higher education, knowledge production, and anti-colonial thought.

Farah Mahrukh Coomi Shroff, PhD, is a thinker, educator, change maker who teaches yoga, meditation, and various mind/body practices. Working at the University of British Columbia in the Medical School in the area of public health, she believes passionately that ancient thought-forms of unity and oneness have important application in the world today. She lives in Vancouver with her husband and their two kids.

Paul Sillitoe is Professor of anthropology at Durham University and Shell Professor of sustainable development at Qatar University, Doha. He specializes in development and social change, subsistence and technology, land issues, environmental studies, human ecology, and ethno-science. He has conducted extensive fieldwork in Papua New Guinea, and has been involved in projects in South Asia, researching local agricultural knowledge and development programs, and is currently working in the Gulf region on sustainable development initiatives.

Gregory A. Smith is a professor in the Graduate School of Education and Counseling at Lewis and Clark College in Portland, Oregon, United States. He writes and speaks about the benefits of place- and community-based education and supports efforts to diminish the boundaries that stand between classrooms and the human and more-than-human world beyond. His most recent books include *Place- and Community-Based Education in Schools* (Routledge) written with David Sobel and *Place-Based Education in the Global Age: Local Diversity* (Routledge) co-edited with David Gruenewald.

Marcelle Townsend-Cross is a Biripi (Manning River, mid-coast, NSW), Worimi (Karuah River, Hunter region, NSW), and Irish woman and has been lecturing in Indigenous studies at Southern Cross University (SCU) in Bundjalung Country (North Coast, NSW) since 1999. She is a graduate of the Bachelor of Contemporary Music, SCU, and the Master of Education (Indigenous studies), University of Technology Sydney. Her research and professional activity focuses on defining and engaging Indigenous Australian philosophies in relation to teaching, learning, and practice in past, present, and future contexts. She is particularly dedicated to engaging Indigenous Australian values in mainstream Australian social and education policy and practice.

Njoki Nathani Wane, PhD, (University of Toronto), current Director of Office of Teacher Support at OISE & Associate Professor, sociology and equity studies in education, University of Toronto. Her teaching and research interests include: anti-racist pedagogy in teacher education; Indigenous knowledges; anti-colonial thought; spirituality and schooling; Black Canadian feminisms; and ethno-medicine. Her most recent selected works include a co-edited collection, *Theorizing Empowerment. Theorizing Empowerment: Canadian Perspectives on Feminist Thought* (2007, Massaquoi & Wane, refereed articles in *Journal Race Ethnicity and Education* (2009, 2008); *Atlantis Journal* (2009). *Contemporary Issues in Education Curriculum Inquiry* (2009); and book chapters in: *The Contested Academy* (2008, Wagner, A. E., Acker, S., & Mayuzumi, K); *Doing Democracy: Striving for Political Literacy and Social Justice* (2008, Darren E. Lund & Paul R. Carr); *Multicultural*

Education Policies in Canada and the United States (2007, Reva Joshee & Lauri Johnson); *Anti-Colonialism and Education: The Politics of Resistance* (2006, G. J. S. Dei & A. Kempf). She teaches both in graduate school and initial teachers education program.

Maria *Shaa Tláa* Williams is Tlingit, and is an Associate Professor at the University of New Mexico with a joint appointment in the Departments of Native American Studies and Music. She received her PhD from UCLA in Ethnomusicology. Her research interests include Alaska Native music, culture, and history. She recently edited *The Alaska Native Reader: History, Culture, Politics* (2009, Duke University Press).

Index

Aboriginal
    Claim to Alaskan land, 168, 192
    Communities, 115, 200, 443, 444
    Culture, 117, 118
    Discourse, 115
    Domination history of, 203
    Education, 72, 127, 131, 151, 164–65
    European discourses on, 114
    Heritage, 117, 118
    Knowledge, 113, 205, 207–8, 437
    Languages, 204, 405, 406
    Legislation, 118, 119–20
    People, 134, 158, 159, 163, 165, 201, 405
    Potlatching, 202
    Representation of, 122
    Scholars, 405, 442, 444, 445
    Stories, 204
    Students, 435
    Traditional Ecological Knowledge, 306
    Traditional Owners and Elders, 113
        Aboriginality, 16, 25, 26, 41, 73
Academia, 93, 107, 146, 147, 174, 308
Academic achievement, 226, 356
Activists
    Academic, 422–25, 429–30, 437, 446
    and Bering Strait theory, 183
    and Displacement, 37
    for Educational policy, 71, 142
    and Indigenous Knowledge, 116
    and Qatar University, 185
    and Research agenda, 9–10
    See also Bannerji, Himani
African
    Americans, 229
    Ascendants, 337, 338, 341, 344, 345–46
    Continent and European colonialism, 81, 82, 83–85
    Educational philosophy, 80–90, 281, 295–96
    Indigenous healing, 227–28, 280, 281, 284–86, 290–94
    Indigenous Knowledge, 81, 88–89, 283, 286–90, 333, 337
    Mental colonization, 80
    Political independence of, 86
    Post-colonial, 80, 86
    Renaissance, 441, 442
    Scholars, 442
    and the Slave trade, 339–42, 373
    Students, 81
    Systems of thought, 281, 282, 283
    Traditional society, 82, 83
    See also Kenya
Ahupua'a, 265, 266
Akula School, 234

Alaska legislature, 192–93, 194
Alaska National Wildlife Refuge (ANWR), 193
Alaska Native Claims Settlement Act (ANCSA), 168, 192, 193
Alaska Native Knowledge Network, 194, 229, 231–34, 300, 303, 439
Alaska Natives, 191
Alaska Rural Systemic Initiative, 229, 231–35, 238
Alexie, Sherman, 106
Alternative schools. *See* Schools, alternative
Anansi, 305
Ancestral insights, 198
Anchorage, Alaska, 192, 193, 194
Anderson, Benedict, 95
Animal stories, 256, 257
Anthropology
    Birth of, 390
    and the Collective consciousness, 103
    Cultural, 92
    Deloria on, 92
    and Ecological time, 99
    and Indigenous Knowledge, 116
    and Indigenous Studies, 72, 299, 443
    and Micro-cosmic systems, 102
    and Native American knowledge, 96
    and Post-colonialism, 315
    and Post-modernism, 93
    Theorists in, 355
Anti-colonial theory
    and African/Black feminist theory, 44
    and Anti-racism, 334, 422, 424
    Approaches to, 9
    as Critical Indigenous discursive framework, 29, 34, 42–43, 226
    Dei and Asgharzadeh on, 39, 43
    and Education, 226, 395, 396, 429
    and History, 368
    and Indigenous healing, 288
    and Indigenous Knowledge, 281–83
    Mignolo on, 316
    Pedagogy, 11–12, 137, 431
    Politics, 15
    Scholars/Sholarship, 9, 45, 368, 429, 430
    Social movements of, 35
    and Spirituality, 429, 430
    Strategy, 394
Anti-oppression, 412, 426
Anti-Racism
    in Academia, 424
    and Anti-colonialism, 334, 422–23, 424, 427

    in Communities, 423, 425
    Education, 150–51
    Post-foundational, 422, 423, 424, 427, 431, 432
    Post-modern, 430
Aotearoa/New Zealand
    Creation history of, 304
    and Indigenous Knowledge, 303, 307
    Non-Indigenous people in, 387
    and the Tuatara, 303
    Universities of, 311, 387
    West Wind Farm in, 307
Arapaho, 93, 94, 95, 105–6
ARCO, 192
Arnhem land, 306
Atua, 304
Australia
    and the Academy, 387
    and Alternative healing, 280
    Assimilation in, 68, 69–71, 72, 76
    and Colonialism, 37, 374, 388, 389
    and Decolonization, 393
    and Higher education in, 18, 69, 74, 75, 163
    and Indigenous education, 70–71, 416
    and Indigenous heritage, 117
    and Indigenous sites, 123
    and Indigenous Studies, 69, 72–76
    the Mirrar people in, 376
    Repression in, 73
    and Science education in, 313
    See also Dubbo; Schools, Australian; Tubba-Gah

Bacon, Francis, 105, 370, 417
Bannerji, Himani, 423, 424
Barbour, Ian, 95, 97, 102
Barnhardt, Ray, 231, 235, 300
Barriers
    in Deloria's work, 96
    to Education, 163, 171, 227, 276, 431
    to Goals, 171
    to Knowledge, 19
    Societal, 2, 270, 275
    to Transformation, 199
    Vapor, 233
Being in place, 115, 122
Bethel, Alaska, 194, 195n3, 195n6
Biophobia and biophilia, 206
Black Elk, 56, 105
Black feminism. *See* Feminism, Black
Bourdieu, Pierre, 89, 94, 96
British Petroleum, 192, 195n5

Burrawanga, Datjing, 306

Canoe, 203, 205, 209, 266, 304, 400
Canoe Plants Project, 275
Capitalism
    and Democracy, 401
    and Feminism, 44
    and Individualism, 372
    International/Global, 86, 360, 363, 374
    Rejection of, 172
    Rise of, 370, 374
    and Universal brotherhood, 101
    and Slavery, 339
    and Spirituality, 340
    and Western Modern Science, 319
Cassirer, Ernst, 95, 102, 104
Center for Research on Education, Diversity, and Excellence (CREDE), 235, 237, 239
Ceremonies banned, 161, 203, 373
Charter Schools. *See* Schools, Charter
Child Welfare Act, 7
Christianity
    on African Indigenous religion, 42
    and the Diné Marriage Act, 221
    and Indigenous belief systems, 206
    and Ireland, 246
    and Islam, 178
    and Philanthropy, 374
    and Secularism, 372, 374, 379
Chronos, 96, 98, 99, 100
Clare, John, 114, 116, 122
Coast Salish, 169, 199, 207, 209
Collaborative learning, 416, 417–19
Colonialism
    and Academia, 390–93
    African
        Diasporic Indigeneity, 43
        and Formal education in, 81, 82, 83–84, 88, 89, 90
        Indigenous experience, 37, 81, 82
        and "Sites of disempowerment," 43
        Theoretical base of, 441
    and Anti-racism, 424, 427, 429
    in Education, 135, 136, 395
    Effect of on constructions of gender, 45, 47–48
    Folklore as response to, 8
    and Healing practices, 290, 297
    History of, 129, 131, 157, 282, 370–71, 374–76
    and Imperialism, 41, 45
    and Indigeneity, 29
    and "Indigenous" (the term), 35
    and Indigenous Knowledge
        Discussions of, 5, 28
        Impact on, 45
        Positioned as non-intellectual, 16
        Predates, 24
    and Indigenous people
        Damage caused to, 16, 190, 194, 288, 396, 440
        Experiences under, 16, 38, 39, 134, 135, 138
        History shaped by, 132
    as Individualistic culture, 430
    and Land theft, 38
    and Legislation, 130
    Psychological impact of, 281
    Resistance to, 31, 32, 42, 133
    and Romanticism, 136
    Scholars/Scholarship on, 44, 45, 134, 136, 139, 387
    and "Settler" state, 388–90, 393–94
    Violence of, 47
    and Western discourse of, 412
    and Western Modern Science, 319
    See also Anti-colonialism, Post-colonialism
Colonially imposed border, 200
Community
    Academic, 356, 443, 444, 445, 447, 448
    and Anti-racism, 423, 426
    Capitalist class, 370
    and the Circle, 56
    and Colonialism, 17, 32
    and Critical pedagogy, 75
    and Decolonization, 394
    Development, 57
    and Education
        Anti-racist, 151, 152
        in Classrooms, 411–12, 415–16, 418, 419
        and Indigenous Knowledge, 177, 178, 380
        Informal, 82
        and Philosophy of, 83, 230
        Place-based, 230, 231, 232, 264, 269
        as Public good, 160
        Role of, 346
        Settings, 89
        and Social change, 334
        and Students, 307
        Teachers in, 277
    and Educators, 9–10
    and Elders, 135, 227, 291
    and Essentialisms, 42
    and Exchange of Knowledge, 105

Extended, 438
Global/glocal, 300, 303
Health and healing, 56, 283, 284, 285–86, 288, 290, 292
Imagined, 146
and Indigenous Knowledge, 167, 351, 380–1, 439, 441
and Indigenous scholars, 169, 197, 199, 201, 209
and Indigenous spirituality, 414–15
before Individual, 438
Integration, 9
and Intellectual property, 409
Involvement, 135, 138
as core of Knowledge, 332
of Learners, 331
Local knowledge in, 6, 29
Minorities in, 146–47
of Nations, 168
Partnerships, 111
Politics of, 150
Pre-contact, 169, 199, 205
Relationships, 249, 276
and Spirituality, 150, 414–15, 418
Storytelling, 245, 246, 251, 252, 254, 257, 258–59
Sustaining/sustainability, 5, 57, 334
Tensions of, 331
Traditional, 6–7
Unity of, 57
and Western thought, 346, 411
White, 70
See also Coast Salish; Hawai'ian Studies Program; Revitalization; Rough Rock Community School; Schools, alternative; STAR School
Conger, George P., 101, 102, 103
Connection to land, 254
Consciousness
  Collective, 97, 103, 150, 302
  Critical, 313, 344, 434, 435, 441
  Dynamic, 204
  Educated, 103
  and Eurocentrism, 391
  European, 118
  False, 229
  Human/universal, 43, 60, 103
  Indigenous, 8
  and Mythical space, 104
  of the Natural world, 269
  Participatory, 369, 370
  Popular, 41
  Public, 203
  Psycho-spiritual, 8
  and Reclamation,
  Socio-political, 3
  Spiritual, 150, 340, 344
  Wiradjuri, 119
Constructions of identity, 42, 119
Contemporary healing. See Kenya, Contemporary healing practices in
Cosmology
  Coast Salish, 201
  and Education, 178
  Indigenous, 198
  Islamic, 185
    Worldsense, 36
    Worldview, 35, 36
  Yoruba, 36
Creation science, 301
Cree
  Displacement of, 434
  Language, 134, 249, 437
  Relationship values of, 438
  in Residential school, 157
  in Saskatchewan, 134
  Scholar, 131
  and Smudging of sage, 438
  Stories, 139, 247
  Teachings, 438, 439
Critical pedagogy, 68, 73, 74–76, 146, 230, 395
Critical theory, 73, 447
Crocodile, 307
Cultural atlases, 233
Cultural diversity. See Diversity, Cultural
Cultural interface. See Interface, Cultural
Cultural restoration, 230
Cultural revitalization, 94, 95, 106, 137, 409
Cultural separation, 160
Cultural/symbolic meaning, 253
Culturally responsive schools. See Schools, culturally responsive
Culturally sensitive, 158, 316, 404
Culture
  African, 8, 22, 228, 338, 339
  American, 230, 263
  and Colonialism, 84, 374, 436
  Complexity, 136–8
  Consumer, 175
  Continuity of, 8
  Diné, 216, 218–19, 221
  and Dispowerment, 44
  Dominant, 18, 58, 68–69, 72, 89, 395

and Education, 10, 93, 146, 147, 227, 231, 263, 418
Folk, 8
and Glocalisation, 304
Hawai'ian, 238, 239, 241, 242, 262–78
and Indigeneity, 3, 110
Indigenous, 120, 393
and Indigenous Knowledge, 4, 5, 169
and Indigenous Science, 225
Individualistic, 430
Iranian, 53
Irish, 246
/Knowledge interface, 128
and Knowledge production, 4
Local, 4, 6–7, 232
Located spatially, 427
Loss, 94, 95, 132, 175
Material, 113, 114, 118
Native American, 96, 101
and Place, 22, 29
Political affirmation of, 24
and Postcolonialism, 361, 317, 318
and Postmodernism, 392
and Renewal efforts, 94
and Society-Nature nexus, 27, 29
Western, 29, 142, 269, 316, 380, 391
See also Australia, Indigenous Studies; Coast Salish; Eurocentric/Eurocentrism; Ghana; Haudenosaunee; Kenya; Oral cultures; Tubba-Gah Yoruba, Indigenous culture; UINPI

Curriculum
and Collaborative learning, 417
Colonial, 86
Design, 262, 276–77, 386, 392, 393
Diné courses in, 219, 223
and Eurocentric knowledge, 146–48
"Hidden," 206, 430
"Indigenization" of, 72
and Indigenous Knowledge, 7–9, 152, 177, 198, 419
and Indigenous languages, 204
K-12, 169, 195
Knowledge in, 149, 150
and Native control, 158, 163
and Non-Indigenous sources, 201
Place- and problem-based, 268, 274
and Pre-contact knowledge, 199, 201
Provincial, 407
Reforms of the 1960s, 312
Rejection of, 70
Relevance of, 274
and Science education, 313, 320
Simplified, 70
and Standards for teachers, 232
Studies, 430
Trends in, 263–64
University, 136, 139, 447, 448
Westernization of, 177
See also Schools, Alaska; STAR School; PRISM

Customary Care, 157, 158

Decolonization, 393–96
and the Academy, 128, 387, 393, 396
and Anti-racism, 427, 432
and Colonist independence, 388–89
and European knowledges, 432
Gruenewald on, 231
and Indigeneity, 40, 427
and Indigenous Knowledge, 2, 28, 30, 363, 423
and Indigenous spirituality, 411–19
Implications of, 15–19
Intellectual, 388
as Political, 352
Project of, 22, 24, 27
and Re-assertion, 26
and Revisiting history, 199
and Social transformation, 30
and Urgency of, 29
See also Hawai'ian Studies Program; PRISM

Deloria, Vine, Jr., 92–107
on American values, 230
and Indigenous communities, 212, 213
and Indigenous education, 230
on Indigenous humour, 256
on Indigenous students, 230
on Theologies, 206

Democracy, 73, 101, 401
Dialectics, 96, 107, 122
Dialogue
Critical, 226
Deloria's call for, 92, 93, 94
on Indigenous Knowledge, 333, 362, 395, 396
Intercultural, 320

Diaspora
African, 8, 25, 44, 341
of Black/African women, 344, 345
Conceptualization of, 39
and Indigenous Knowledge, 431
"Overlapping," 39
See also under Yoruba

Discourse
    of Aboriginality, 25, 115
    Academic, 362, 407, 417, 441
    Alternative, 115
    on Alternative development, 172
    Analysis, 426, 431
    Anthropological, 69
    Anti-colonial, 43, 44, 316, 316
    Anti-racist, 111, 143, 150, 151
    and Assimilationism, 68
    Authoritative, 114, 117, 118, 123, 124
    "Authorized heritage," 113, 117
    of a "Civilized human being," 379
    Classroom, 368
    Colonial, 17, 45, 207, 281, 333, 355, 361, 390
    Community-based, 264
    Counter-oppositional, 23
    Critical, 23, 430
    Destruction of, 426, 429, 432
    Development, 113, 174, 375, 378
    Dominant, 23, 74, 116, 371, 419
    Empancipatory, 3
    "Essentialist," 114
    Eurocentric, 22, 331, 333, 417, 424
    European, 114, 117–18, 119
    Feminist, 356
    Geographic, 119
    Hegemonic, 59
    Historical, 119
    of Identity, 26
    of Indigeneity, 15, 30, 31, 135, 415
    Indigenous, 107, 114
    on Indigenous Knowledge, 117
    Individualizing, 74
    International, 181
    on Japanese women, 356
    of Knowledge production, 27, 368
    Marginal, 312
    Metaphysical, 95
    and a Minority problematic, 144
    Modern, 203
    Moral, 373, 379
    Movement between, 115
    Oppositional, 23
    of "Otherness," 390
    Pedagogical, 81
    Philosophical, 81
    Political, 93
    Racialized, 150
    Religious, 59
    of Resistance, 9
    of Reductionism, 29
    Rights-based, 118
    Routines, 106
    Science education, 314
    Scientific, 69
    Secular, 369, 379
    Sites, 120
    State-authorized, 117, 124
    Trickster, 334
    Tubba-Gah, 114, 115, 121
    Western, 42, 46, 48, 110, 113, 282, 283, 333, 411–12
    Yoruba Indigenous, 36, 46
Disenfranchisement, 59, 389, 395, 436
Diversity
    and the Academy, 444, 445
    and Anti-colonialism, 412
    Bio-, 173
    and Collaborative learning, 418
    and Community, 414
    Cultural, 173, 313, 315, 387
        Literature, 317
        and the "Other," 317–18
        Scholarship on, 315, 316
        and Science education, 318, 321
    and Diné law, 218
    and Education, 151, 418
    Empowering, 412
    Epistemological, 319, 321, 322
    and Globalisation, 227, 300, 312
    of Indigenous Knowledge, 128, 304, 314–15
    and Indigenous people, 119
    of Knowledge systems, 127–28
    Linguistic, 312, 315
    and Resistance, 413
    and Students, 149, 182, 36
    and Teachers, 148, 264, 317
Doctrine of Discovery, 100, 101
Draft contract, 162
Dubbo, New South Wales, Australia, 110, 113, 114, 116, 120, 121
Dynamic consciousness. *See* Consciousness, Dynamic

Education
    Aboriginal, 406
    and Academia, 146–47, 199
    Anti-racist, 111, 150–51, 152, 431
    Anti-sexist, 130
    and Assimilationism, 69–71, 72–73, 76

and Collaborative learning, 418
and Colonialism, 136, 142, 152, 374
and Community, 199, 230–31, 259, 416
Controversial, 242
Decolonizing, 110–11, 199
Demographics of, 191–92 (Alaska)
and Dominant culture, 18, 68
Environmental, 9
Eurocentric, 190–91(Alaska)
Deloria, lessons on, 107
in Diné society, 218–19, 222–23
Disparity in, 68
Emancipatory, 69
and Endogenous development, 176–85
Environmental, 265
European, 82
Formal, 8, 81, 82, 399, 440
Funding, 193
Higher
African, 82
American, 354
Australian, 18, 69, 74, 75, 163, 416
and Colonialism, 379, 388, 389–90, 395–96
Culturally appropriate, 184
Decolonization of, 394, 395
and Endogenous development, 168, 176–80, 185
and the Indigenous, 395
and Indigenous Studies, 69, 72
Pedagogy, 386, 412
Profit-oriented, 307
Standardization in, 392, 394
Holistic, 218, 417
Ideologies of, 264
Inclusive, 418, 431
and Indian control of, 111, 158, 163–64
Indigenous
and the Academy, 131, 134, 135, 137–38
and Assimilationism, 69–72
and Critical theory, 76
Deloria and Wildcat on, 230
Differences in, 134–35, 139
History, 76, 160–63
and Identity, 144
Initiatives, 174
Materials, 139, 201
Place-based, 134, 138, 206, 230–31
Policy, 76
and Pre-contact knowledge, 205
Science, 225, 227, 263, 270–75, 277, 318–19
and Spirituality, 347, 419
and Storytelling, 259
and Indigenous Knowledge
as a "Marker," 123
Politics of, 7
and Science education, 11
and Indigenous Studies, 28, 68, 69, 71–73, 73–76
and Individualism, 438
Informal, 81, 82, 83
Japanese, 360, 361
K-12, 164, 169, 193, 277
Local, cultural, 94, 264
and Meritocracy, 151
Modernist, 198–99, 206–7
Multi-cultural, 148
Multiple intelligence-based, 9
Neo-colonial, 282
Non-formal, 81
Norms, Canadian, 158
and Parents, 237
and Power relations, 3
"Public," 116
and Race, 21, 146–47
as Resistance, 363
Resistance to change in, 10
and Revitalization, 93
as a Right, 218
and Ryerson, E., 159–60
Secular, 381, 382
Sociology of, 21
Transformative, 28, 419
Types of, 81–86
Universalism in, 198
US, 263–64
Waldorf model of, 360
Western, 168, 206, 207, 361
Whole child, 9
See also Africa, Educational philosophies; Alaska Native Claims Settlement Act; Alaska Native Knowledge Network; Coast Salish; Education, Science; Hawai'ian Studies Program; Holism; Indian Act; Kenya, Education in; STAR School; Students; Teachers
Elephant, 301, 302, 303
Empowerment
Collective, 30
of Communities, 184
and Decolonization, 394
in Education, 180–82, 185
in Ecuador, 179
against Eurocolonial oppression, 45

and Groups with little power, 149
and Identity, 168, 171, 185, 409
and Indigeneity, 40
and Indigenous Knowledge, 42, 116, 177
in Qatar, 174
Sites of, 22, 41
Enfranchisement, 160, 162. *See also* Disenfranchisement
Epistemological diversity, 227, 313, 319, 321
Epistemological pluralism, 93, 104, 105, 106, 107, 387
Epistemology
  African-centered, 344
  Diné, 215
  Diversity, 322
  Dominant, 72
  and Ethics, 32
  Euro-American, 143
  Eurocentric, 424
  Feminist, 343, 345
  Greek, 369
  Indigenous, 29, 76, 392
  and Indigenous Knowledge, 4, 28, 72, 226
  of Landscape, 204
  Nakata on, 128
  Objectivist, 370, 370
  Personal, for scholars, 144
  Philosophy as, 2
  Pointers on, 88
  Poles of, 370
  and Researchers, 201, 226, 247
  Secular, 367, 370, 371
  "of the South," 321
  Spiritual, 375
  Western, 282, 392, 442
  of Western Modern Science, 312
Equity
  and the Academy, 362, 382, 387, 396, 444
  and Anti-racism, 427, 432
  in Education, 150, 303, 314, 323
  Employment, 403
  Epistemological, 334, 388, 394, 395
  for Indigenous Australians, 71
Essentialism
  and Anti-essentialism, 42, 92
  and Colonialism, 32, 41
  and Indigenous Knowledge, 16, 426
  Primitive, 42
  Race, 21
  Strategic, 114, 352

Euclidean geometry, 100, 104
Eurocentric/Eurocentrism
  and the Academy, 415, 417, 426
  and Anti-colonialism, 388, 412
  and Anti-racism, 424, 427
  and Black Feminism, 44
  Challenges to, 23
  and Collective knowledge, 31
  Cultural control, 318
  and Curriculum, 146–48
  and Decolonization, 393, 396
  and Development, 168
  Essentialization, 25
  Hegemonic, 4, 22
  and Indigenous Knowledge, 319, 332, 429
  and Indigenous philosophy, 4
  and Indigenous prism, 23
  Institutions of, 137
  Knowledge, 425, 428, 430
  Knowledge production, 368
  Lattas on, 41
  "Metaphorical box," 11
  Need to eschew, 34
  as the Norm, 22
  and "Other" knowledges, 304
  and Postcolonialism, 317, 423
  and Postfoundationalism, 427
  Rejection of, 70
  and Residential schools, 132
  and Scholars, 35
  Science, 322
  and Secular vision, 333, 370, 371, 372
  and Spirit injury, 12
  and Spirituality, 331, 429
  Standards, 32
  and the term "Traditional," 27
  See also Yoruba, and Gender
Exxon/Conoco Phillips, 192, 195n5

Fabian, Johannes, 100
Facebook, 307, 408
Fairbanks, Alaska, 194, 195n6, 234
Falsifiability, principle of, 96
Feminism/feminist
  African, 337
  African/Black, 34, 44–46
  Black, 34, 49n6, 343
  and Dei and Asgharzadeh, 43
  and Japan, 356
  Men in, 130

Methodology, endarkened, 333, 337–47
and Postcolonialism, 315
Research, 404
and Science education, 314
Varieties of, 357
Yoruba, 36, 46–47
Feyerabend, Paul, 95
First Nations University of Canada, 159, 164
Fiscal debate, 163
Foucault, Michel
on Discredited Indigeneity, 42,
and Marxist thought, 424, 426
as Poststructuralist, 316
on Power, 144, 390, 392
and Subjugated knowledges, 148
Foundationalism, 428, 429. *See also* Post-foundationalism
Fowler, Loretta, 93
Freud, Sigmund, 102

Gender
Discrimination, 130, 162
and Diversity of experiences, 413
and Education, 147, 148, 149, 151
Eurocentric notions of, 47
and Feminisms, 45
and Identity, 31, 143
and Indigeneity, 5
and Indigenous Knowledge, 5, 11, 109, 381
and Intersectionality, 45, 151, 314
and Kenyan social structure, 295
and Knowledge construction, 144
and Power relations, 29, 45
Relations, Arab, 179, 80
and Researchers, 316
Struggles of, 110
Western construction of, 46, 47
See also Yoruba, and gender
Genocide, 123, 131, 133, 198, 374, 405, 436
Ghana
Creation story, 305
Education in, 295
Oral traditions in, 304
Proverbial ideal of, 346
Slavery in, 338, 345
Tour, 339–43
Philosopher Wiredu, 143
Giddens, Anthony, 101
Glocal framework, 301, 304, 306
Glocalisation, 228, 300, 301, 303, 304

Google Earth, 307
Gramsci, Antonio, 435, 437
Great Chain of Being, 102
Great Spirit, 305

Hallowell, A. Irving, 93
Hapū, 307
Haudenosaunee
and Colonialism, 128
Culture, 132, 442
and Great Law of Peace, 129
Identity, 133
and Indigenous Knowledge, 131
and Nation-to-nation agreements, 135
and Wampum, 130
Writers, 132
Hawai'ian Studies Program (Wai'anae High School), 238–39
Healing
Circles, men's, 249
and Coast Salish, 205
Collective, 95
from Colonization, 357, 381
Communities, 380
and Interconnectedness, 57
from Oppression, 41, 94, 95, 338, 429
Rituals, 56, 359
Sacred sites of, 376
Spirituality as, 10, 381
and Western practices, 285, 288, 295, 296–97
See under Kenya
Hegemony
and Australians, 73
Dilution of, 242
and Education, 180, 313
and Ethics, 373
Euro-American, 3, 31
Giroux on, 441
of Globalization, 322, 376
and Indigenous cultures, 440
and Knowledge production, 27, 361
and the Local, 145
of "Me," 413
and Post-colonial analysis, 316
Resistance to, 319, 352, 360, 415, 437
and Schools, 205, 207
as Starting point for discussion, 320
and Students, 74, 149, 151
Heisenberg, Werner, 95
Henry McKay Settee, 435–36, 440

Herbal medicine, 285, 290, 293, 294
Herbalists, 288. *See also* Kenya, Healing medicine
Higher education. *See* Education, Higher. *See also* Academia; Identity, and the Academy; Indigeneity, and the Academy; Knowledge, Indigenous, and the Academy
History (discipline)
    Birth of, 390
    Curriculum, 407
    and Indigenous Studies, 72, 442, 443
    and Alternative discourses, 115
    and Māori studies, 299
    and People of color, 147
    and Postcolonialism, 315
    Teaching of, 207, 218–19, 222, 225
Holism
    and Aboriginal storytelling, 204
    from Inside out, 54–55
    and Indigeneity, 65
    Indigenous concepts of, 55–57
    and *Punchamahabhutas,* 60–61
    and Systems Science, 63–65
    Transition from, 371
Homo academicus, 94
Hornet, 305
Hul'q'umin'um,' 204
Humor, 65, 245, 246, 257, 258, 439
Hunquminum, 208

Identity
    and the Academy, 2, 109, 134, 139
    Black, 45
    Categories of, 129, 130, 316, 316
    and Education, 21, 135, 138, 150, 225, 270, 318
    and Globalization, 26, 332
    and Indigeneity, 3
    Indigenous
    in Academia, 41, 174
    African, 296
    Claiming, 24, 27, 40
    and Colonialism, 132, 134
    Constructs of, 42, 118, 119
    Cultural, 271–72, 353
    Different, 39, 42
    Diné, 215, 222, 223
    Knowledge and, 168
    Lattas on, 41
    and Local culture, 8
    in Place, 4, 29, 121, 122, 123
    and Revitalization efforts, 94
    and Struggle, 168, 332
    Theorizing, 26
    and Knowledge production, 31, 110, 151
    and Location, 145–46
    as Parsi, 54–55
    Politics of, 39, 123, 176
    and Representation, 144–45
    Spiritual (and land-based), 22, 28
    Student, 147, 164, 208
    See also Haudenosaunee; Indigeneity; Storytelling; Tubba-Gah
Idols of the Mind, 105
Imagined community, 146
Imperialism
Indian Act, 129, 130–31, 160–63, 203, 435
Indian Control of Indian Education, 111, 157, 158, 163–64
Indian Residential School System, 157. *See also* Schools, Indian Residential
Indigeneity
    and Aboriginality, 25
    and the Academy, 3, 16, 197, 331
    African, 11, 38, 43, 48, 281
    and Ancestors, 10
    and Anti-colonial theory, 44
    and Anti-racist activists, 428
    and Black feminist principle, 43
    and Colonialism, 24, 25, 28, 30
    Critiques of, 16, 32, 42
    and Decolonization, 427
    Diasporic, 39, 43, 48
    Discourse on, 29, 31
    Diverse, 34, 35, 38, 39, 42
    and Education, 157–65, 226, 316, 317
    and Empowerment, 40, 41–42
    and Globalisation, 168
    and Holism, 53, 65
    and Identity (struggle for), 26
    and Indigenous Knowledge, 3, 4
    and Intellectual agency, 4
    and Knowledge, 27
    and the Land, 25, 37–38, 332
    Myth of, 137
    and Placeness, 28
    Politics of, 3, 27, 110
    and Resistance, 40, 41
    and Spirituality, 5
    Theorizing, 25
    See also Reclamation; Yoruba
Indigenous cosmology. *See* Cosmology, Indigenous

Indigenous cultural and intellectual property, 117
Indigenous education. *See* Education, Indigenous
Indigenous healing practices. *See* Healing, Indigenous;
   Herbal Medicine; Herbalists
Indigenous identity. *See* Identity, Indigenous
Indigenous inquiry. *See* Inquiry, Indigenous
Indigenous Knowledge. *See* Knowledge, Indigenous
Indigenous ontology. *See* Ontology, Indigenous
Indigenous pedagogy. *See* Pedagogy, Indigenous
Indigenous science. *See* Science, Indigenous
Indigenous spirituality. *See* Spirituality, Indigenous
Indigenous storytelling. *See* Storytelling
Individualism
    and Canadian government, 202
    in Japan, 360
    and Modernist education, 199, 201
    Philosophy of, 372, 374, 379
    Western ideology of, 277
Inquiry
    Barriers to, 96, 107
    Critical, 46, 95, 96
    Indigenous/Local, 227, 262–63, 266–77
    Intertribal, Intercultural, Interdisciplinary, 95
    Use of Metaphor as, 351
    Metaphysical, 95
    Philosophical, 18, 87
    Scientific, 58, 98, 265
    Socioecological, 266
    Student activities in, 233, 240
    and Western Modern Science, 313
Integration
    of Aboriginal arts, 118
    Community, 9, 236, 238, 411, 415, 416
    of Cultural interface, 26
    Global, 145, 168, 268
    in Hawai'ian schools, 238, 241, 269
    in Healing, 289
    of Knowledge, 26, 121, 200, 393, 441, 442
    for Learning (higher education), 178, 200
    of Local/place-based knowledge, 6, 138, 145, 268
    in Schools (of knowledge), 231, 235, 236, 380
    of Schools, 190, 201
    of Self-world, 97, 103
    Social, 56
    Spiritual, 55, 207, 417, 419
    and Systems Science, 63–64
    of Zones, 101
Interface
    Cultural, 26, 74, 75, 127, 128, 137, 303
    Defined, 302, 303
    Discomfit and Compromise at, 301–3
    and Indigenous Knowledge, 6, 180, 228, 301
    Research, 303, 308
Intersectionality, 45, 46, 111, 151
Investigating and Evaluating Environmental Issues
    and Actions (IEEIA), 240
Involvement
    Adult, 240
    Community, 135, 138, 414
    Elders, 248
    and Endogenous development, 171
    Equal, 411
    Governmental, 162
    Scholarly, 197

Jung, Carl, 94, 95, 98

Kairos, 96, 98, 99
Kamehameha Schools, 235
Kant, Immanuel, 84, 102, 103, 372
Kapu system, 265, 266–69
Kasigluk, Alaska, 233
Kawagley, Oscar, 229–30, 231, 241, 300
Kayak, 189, 307
k'e (kinship), 218, 235, 237
Kenya
    Colonial government, 281
    Contemporary healing practices in, 293–94, 295,
       296
    Education in
    Colonial, 280, 282, 295–96
    Western, 281, 295
    Healing knowledge in, 227, 283, 287–90, 293–94
    Indigenous Knowledge, 281, 286–87
    Malaria in, 291–93
    Research methods used in, 284–85
    Research setting in, 283–84
    Rural, 227, 280
    See also Africa, Philosophies of education
Knowledge
    Ancestral, 22, 173
    Animal, 106
    Arab, 185
    Buddhist and Hindu, 65
    Colonial, 2, 16, 24
    Current, 100, 105
    Dominant, 3, 42
    Eurocentric, 16
    Indian, 54
    Indigenous

and the Academy, 127–28, 134–38, 411–12
and Critical pedagogy, 74–76
Discourse in, 16
and the Dominant culture, 74–75, 415
as Emancipating, 69, 73
for a Multiplicity of, 3, 28
Spaces in, 72
Access to, 101
Acquisition of, 106
and Anti-racism, 423
and Colonialism, 27
and Communities, 7, 16, 26, 32, 332, 414, 415–16, 422
and Critical Methodologies, 9–10
Dei on, 16
Deloria and Treat on, 104
and Development, 116, 174–79
as Dynamic, 41, 128, 130, 167
and Education, 3, 7–9, 171, 180–82
Science, 225, 312–23
Framework of, 28–30, 350–53, 360–663
Generational transmission of, 37, 131, 133
and Humility, 44
and Indigenous peoples, 27
Key issues of, 23
Local, 11, 26
Multiple approaches to, 434–48
as Philosophy, 2, 3, 15, 22
Politics of, 24, 94, 167, 332
and Post-foundational anti-racism, 422–32
Reclaiming, 16, 24, 203
Reconceptualizing, 4–5
and Spirituality, 10
Studies, 30–32, 73–76
Threatened, 7, 11
in Transition, 212–23
as Tool of resistance, 41, 42, 351
in Western discourses, 113
and Metaphysics/metaphysical, 93, 353, 356, 357
Multiple, 2, 351
Oppositional, 332
and Power and Decolonization, 386–96
Production, 21, 26, 130, 142–52, 367
Secular fence of, 368–82
Systems of, 128
Traditional ecological/environmental, 116, 175, 189–90, 204, 232–33, 359, 406
Traditional local/cultural, 6, 11, 26, 95, 106, 173, 192, 197, 236
Unified, 93–98, 100, 101, 102–4, 105, 106, 107

Western, 101, 103, 105, 107
Scientific, 3, 5, 7
See also African Indigenous Knowledge; Alaska Native Knowledge Network; Australia; Clare, John; Glocalisation; Haudenosaunee; Kenya, Indigenous Knowledge; Native Hawai'ians; Place-based knowing (Indigenous); Pre-contact Local Knowledge; Storytelling; Tubba-Gah people; UINPI; Yoruba, Indigenous Knowledge
Kodiak, Alaska, 195n3
Kovach, M., 247–48
Kulchisky, Peter, 445
Kuleana, 227, 268, 271, 272, 276, 277

Lakota, 95, 96, 98, 99, 103, 134, 135
Land
Aboriginal claim to, 192
and the Academy, 199
Athabascan, 439
Coast Salish, 200, 201, 202, 204, 205
Cree, 438
Diné, 214
Displacement from, 31, 129
Expropriation of, 25, 282, 295, 374, 378
Hawai'ian, 240, 241, 268, 269
and Indigeneity, 25, 37, 38, 436, 440
and Indigenous identity, 24, 40
and Indigenous Knowledge, 23, 24, 37, 97, 134, 135, 428
and Indigenous peoples, 24, 27, 37, 39, 40, 137, 400, 437
Kenyan, 283
Locke on, 198
Native American metaphysics, 103
Navaho, 169
and non-Indians, 97
Privatization of, 378
Reclaiming, 381
Reconceptualization of, 39
Regaining a sense of belonging to, 28
Relationship with, 139, 240
Rights, 30, 118, 119–20, 332
Sea connection, 266
and Spirituality, 28, 29, 206
Storytelling about, 253, 254, 258, 259
of the Yoruba, 35
Language
African, 38
Coast Salish, 204, 208
Cree, 249, 437

Cultural interpretations of, 435
as Defining, 89
Deloria on, 94
Development of, 370
Diné, 215, 218–19, 222
Dominant, 30, 58, 68, 382
English, 355, 405
Hawai'ian, 238, 270, 277
and Identity, 114
Immersion, 262, 274
and Indigeneity, 23, 35
Japanese, 361
Literacy, 71
Loss of, 94, 95, 110, 132, 169, 406
and Residential schools, 133, 138
Lummi, 208
Michif, 249
Mohawk, 132
Müller on, 102
Oneida, 132
and Place, 121, 122, 123
Protection of, 194
Reduction of, 93
and Relationships, 53, 175
and Renewal efforts, 94, 131, 137, 194, 334, 376, 409
and Research, 405
Restrictions on, 168
Sami, 375
and Scholars, 183
and Secular humanistic vision, 369
Yup'ik, 233
and the Yoruba, 34, 46
Legislation
Child Welfare, 111, 158
and Colonial policy, 129, 130
and Diné Laws, 214, 221
Educational, 164
and Indigenous Knowledge, 117
Preservation, 117–19
Leopard, 305
Leupp, Arizona, 236–37
Lévy-Bruhl, Lucien, 102
Life histories, 251
Literacy and numeracy, 71, 158
Local, traditional knowledge. *See under* Knowledge
Lockean principles, 169, 198, 372, 373, 376
Lone Bear, Chief (Arapaho), 106
Loss
of Culture, 6, 94, 95, 138

of Epistemologies, 94
of Ethics, 94
through a Eurocentric framework, 393
of History, 6
Human, 95
of Identity, 6, 241
of Knowledge, 116, 295
of Land, 202
of Language, 94, 95, 110, 132, 406
and Residential schools, 133, 138
of Metaphysics, 94
of Native vegetation, 268
Resistance to, 26
of Respect, 175
of Territorial autonomy, 332
of Traditions, 6
Lukonen, Dara, 239
Lushootseed, 204

Malaria, 291–93
Manifest Destiny, 374
Manitu, 98
Māori
Academics, 299
Films, 307
Knowledge, 304
Monolingual, 194
Narratives, 306
People, 305
Protected Language/culture, 194
Science, 300
Steward-Harawira on, 198
Studies, 228, 299–301, 304, 307, 308–9
Traditions, 306
See also Wellington Māori Studies
Mapping, 254, 431
Marxism, 315, 316, 424, 425, 426, 427, 428
Mātauranga, 300, 304
Mathematics
Abstraction through, 103
Applied in classroom, 232
and Arab scholarship, 183
Fractal theory of, 102
Indian, 178
and Mythical thought, 104
Role models, 227
Mauri, 305
Mead, Hirini Moko, 299
Medicine Wheel, 56, 104
Metaphysics

Deloria on, 95, 97, 98
versus Experience, 96
Hopi, 96
James on, 98
Lakota, 95
Loss of, 94
Native American, 18, 93, 97, 101, 103
Western, 18, 96, 98, 101
Microcosmic thinking, 102
Migrant people, 423, 428
Mind-stuff, 98
Mitakuye oyasin, 99
Moʻolelo, 266, 267, 270, 272
Modernism, 300, 428
Mohawk, 130, 132, 134, 137, 305, 376, 438–39
Molokaʻi, 238, 239, 240, 274
Moon, 305, 320
Moss, Pius (Arapaho), 105
Müller, Max, 102
Multicultural science education, 225, 227, 263, 270–77, 317–23
Musqueam, 54, 208
Mysterium tremendum, 97
Myth(s)
in the Collective Consciousness, 302
and Fullness of time, 99
Hawaiʻian, 266
and Healing, 283
of Intrinsic Western knowledge, 295
in the MAOR371 classroom, 304
the "Native," 427
of the Noble savage, 165
Origin, 183
Pele, 267
of Physics, 301–2
as Source of knowledge, 5, 6, 31, 282
Undergraduate programs based on, 165
Mythical
Centered point, 97
Construction of Indigeneity, 137
Denigrated, 16
Elements in stories, 247
Space, 104
Thought, 102, 104

Nakata, Martin
on the "Cultural interface," 74, 128, 303
on Dynamic knowledge, 131, 135
on Indigenous Knowledge, 127, 128, 131, 136, 299, 301

Native Child Welfare Authority, 158
Native Hawaiʻian
and Ecological knowledge, 267–77
Students, 235, 238–41, 262–63
Studies, 207
Native Studies, 442–44, 445, 446
Navajos, 169, 213–23, 235–38
Neo-colonial
the Academy as, 387
Education, 280, 282
Government (Kenya), 281, 283
Health Systems (Africa), 281, 297
Melancholia, 168, 189–95
Situations and Indigenous Knowledge, 124
Netsilik, 306
Newberry, Vicki, 239–40
Newtonian principle, 65, 98, 282, 301–2, 371
Noa, 305
NOAA (National Oceanic and Atmospheric Administration), 263
No Child Left Behind (NCLB), 192, 194, 241–42, 262
Nome, Alaska, 195n3
Nome-Beltz Regional High School, 191
North Slope Borough, 192
Nunamiut, 305

Oʻahu, 238
Oil Industry, 168–69, 171, 175, 192–95, 220, 376
Olajubu, Oyeronke, 46, 47
ʻŌlelo noʻeau, 266, 267, 268, 270, 271
Ontology, 30, 175, 369, 372, 373
Indigenous, 175
Spiritual, 30
Oppression
African, 41, 283
and African/Black feminist theory, 44–45
and Anti-racism education, 150–51
Articulations of, 45
Colonial, 8, 45, 387
and Cultural knowledge, 427
in Ecuador, 178
in Education, 242, 318
Fear of, 158
Forms of, 43, 44, 62, 147
Healing from, 42
vs. Ideal society, 73
and Intersectionality, 45
and the Oppressors, 394
Patriarchal, 46
Pedagogy/Research on, 74, 77, 144, 199, 430

Resistance to, 29, 32, 114, 369, 412, 415, 425
and Scholars' role, 437, 440
Shared, 123
Sites of, 44
Speaking out against, 43
and Spirituality, 430
in Yoruba society, 47
Oral cultures, 123
Oral expressions, 332
Oral history, 95, 115, 265, 300–6
Oral knowledge, 88
Oral literature, 35
Oral narratives, 267, 282. *See also* Storytelling
Oral peoples, 123
Oral stories, 5, 123, 226, 245–60. *See also* Storytelling.
Oral tradition
   and Delgamuukw decision, 210n2
   Displaced, 370
   and Fundamental Laws, 215
   Generational sharing of, 247
   and Indigenous Knowledge, 8
   Legitimizing, 381
   and Literary tradition 6,
   and Merging of spiritual, 205
   and Native theatre, 250
   as Remembered landscape, 253
   as Training, 290
   Undermined/undermining, 377, 378, 380
Orenda, 98
Oyewumi, Oyeronke, 36, 46–48

Parents
   and Children's education, 197
   and Community Councils, 435
   Cultural knowledge of, 151, 182, 436
   and Culturally responsive educators, 232
   and Knowledge of remedies, 285
   and PRISM, 240
   and the STAR School, 237
   Surrogate, 438
Peat, David F., 302
Pedagogy
   Anti-colonial, 137
   Anti-racist, 137, 151, 430–31
   Critical, 73–74, 146, 395
   Critical Indigenous, 74–77
   Culturally responsive, 169, 199
   Decolonized, 199
   Ecuadorian, 183

   Euro-American, 179, 183
   Freire on, 158
   Holistic, 9, 431
   of Hope, 1, 331
   Indigenous, 195, 228, 259, 396, 416
   Nakata on, 128
   of Place, 199
   and Positioning oneself, 135, 425
   Practicing, 145
   Radical, 430, 435
   Research on, 248, 386–87, 392–93
   and Researchers, 148
   Spiritually centered, 419
   Standards for, 239,
   of Stories, 227, 257, 259
   Subversive, 2
   and Transformative Learning, 149–50
   Western conceptions of, 334
Philosophical incommensurability, 26, 320
Philosophy
   Buddhist, 358
   Classic liberal, 372
   Colonialism as, 282
   and Deloria, 93–94
   Eastern, 361
   of Education, 80, 83
   of the Great Law of Peace, 438–39
   Greek, 102, 178
   Healing, 288, 290, 293
   Hindu, 64
   Holistic, 65
   Indigenous, 9
   Indigenous Knowledge as, 2, 4, 15–19
   of Individualism, 372
   Liberation, 316
   Medicine wheel, 104
   Neo-liberal, 375
   Roman, 178
   Sage, 87
   samkhya, 62
   Western, 2, 101
   of Western science, 300
   Yogic, 55
   Yoruba, 35, 47
Physics (discipline), 58, 63, 64–65, 98, 103, 300–2
Pimatisiwin, 437
Place theory
   and the Academy, 134, 138
   Cannon on, 110–11
   and the Land, 206

and Storytelling, 204–5
Place-based ecological knowledge, 198, 268
Place-based education, 209, 265, 268, 274–75, 277
Place-based experiences, 264
Place-based genealogy, 270
Place-based identity, 121
Place-based knowing (Indigenous), 23, 29, 131, 137, 227
Place-based spirituality, 206, 208
Plato, 96, 97, 98, 102, 369
Polynesians, 238, 239, 262
Popper, Karl, 96,
Postcolonialism, 227, 313, 315–18, 321, 322
Post-foundationalism, 334, 422–32
Post-foundationalist anti-racism, 422–32
Postmodernism
    and Anthropology, 93
    Battiste on, 392
    Critique, 95
    and Indigenous Knowledge, 300
    and Politics of identity, 26
    and Postcolonialism, 315–16
    and Western scholars, 22, 299,
    Wong on, 314
Potlatch-feasts, 169, 191, 201–3
Pre-contact local knowledge, 169, 198, 199, 201, 205, 208, 209
Promoting Resolutions for a Sustainable Moloka'i (PRISM), 238–41
Providence, 100
Python, 305

Question of identity, 26, 164

Reclamation, 23, 24, 26, 27, 131–32, 283, 393
Recolonization, 446
Reinhabitation, 122, 231, 237, 239, 241
Relativism, 104, 105, 107, 320
Religion
    African, 42
    Celtic, 369
    Christianity, 42
    Deloria on, 92, 96, 104, 106
    Government, 215
    Greek (ancient), 369
    and Healers, 288
    Indigenous, 8
    Islam, 42
    and Mission schools, 190
    Native American, 98–102, 105
    and Secularism, 372
    and Spirituality and modernest education, 206–7
    Western, 97
    Zarathustrianism, 54–54
Religious bodies, 161
Religious denomination, 160
Remembered landscapes, 253
    Residential schools, Indian, 111, 133, 138, 157–58, 206, 440
Resource management, 169, 267, 269, 277, 440
Revitalization, 127–39
    African, 81
    of Community, 93
    of Indigenous culture, 94–95, 106
    of Indigenous languages, 30, 93, 219, 222, 277, 375
Role
    of Difference-making practices, 137
    of Educational system, 151, 168, 171–86
    of Hula, 270–71
    of Humor, 245
    of Indigenous identity, 270, 271–72
    of Indigenous Knowledge, 2, 116, 270
    Indian societal, 159, 161
    of Local culture, 4, 6
    Models, 227
    of Native Title Act 1993, 118
    of Place, 270, 272–75
    of Racism, 136
    of Sense of place, 123, 130
    of Storytelling, 248
    of Teachers, 148–49, 264
    of Tom McCallum, 258
    of Women and men, 5
Rough Rock Community School, 235

Saanich (elder), 205
Sacred spaces, 97–98, 339–42, 376
Salish Sea, 200, 209
Sapir, Edward, 93
Saskatchewan (Canada), 134–36, 249, 434. *See also* University of Saskatchewan
School climate, 238
School(s)
    African, 86, 89
    Afrocentric, 21
    Alaskan, 189–195
    Alternative, 435
    Australian, Indigenous, 71
    Bourdieu on, 96

Canadian
    Christian, 206
    and the Common School Act, 160
    and the Indian Act, 162–63
    Indigenous, 435
    Industrial, 161–62
    and Ryerson, 159
    Secondary, 15
Charter, 235
Coast Salish, 201, 205, 207–9
and Colonization, 226, 241, 242, 280, 435
and Community, 201, 331, 416
Competition in, 230
Contract grant, 219
Culturally responsive, 235
Curricula
    Hegemony in, 441
    and Indigenous Knowledge, 7–9, 321
    Indigenous science in, 318
    Knowledge in, 149, 150
    Revision, 147
    Trends in, 263–64
    Western science, 276
Critics of, 150
and Diné courses, 219, 222
and Dominant worldview, 242
Elementary, 169
English conversation, 354
and "Exclusion on Demand," 69
and Fundamental Laws, 223
Hawai'ian, 262–63
High school, 169, 189
Inclusive, 151, 418
Indigenous, 231
and Indigenous Knowledge, 10
Indigenous scholars in, 199
Multicultural, 145, 149
Navajo, 218–19
Place-based, 265, 275, 276
Public, 151
and Religion, 207
Residential, Indian, 111, 132, 133, 138, 206, 207, 440
Secular, 376, 379
Spirituality in, 347
Textbooks, 147
Western dominance of, 142
as "Working communities," 151
See also Alaska Native Knowledge Network; Alaska Rural Systemic Initiative; Education, Anti-racism; Effie Kokrine School; Hawai'ian Studies Program; Māori, Studies; PRISM; Rough Rock Community School; STAR School

Science
    "for All," 323
    Arab scholarship in, 178
    Claim to, 96
    in the Curriculum, 192, 194, 219, 227, 265
    Definition of, 322
    Education
        Contemporary agendas, 314
        and Indigenous Knowledge, 318–19, 321, 322
        Multiple approaches to, 317–18, 320, 321
        Overview, 312, 313–14
        and Postcolonialism, 316–17
        Reform, 322–23
        (*See also under* Education, Indigenous)
    and Holism, 60
    Indian, 178
    Indigenous, 4, 322
        and Artistic, 439
        Inquiry, 263
        and Revealed knowledge, 416
        and Western, 3, 228, 302, 303, 308, 446
    Language of, 370
    Linear, 267
    Local, 7
    Male-based, 5
    Modern, 7, 371
    Native, 189
    Natural, 299
    Political complexity of, 322
    Pursuit of, 31
    Reconstruction of, 322
    and *Red Earth, White Lies,* 92
    versus Religion, 96
    Researchers, 5, 8
    Role models in, 227
    Social, 9, 22, 23, 31, 95, 145, 149
    Standards, 32, 227, 268, 263
    Studies, 323
    and Sustainability, 227, 268
    Systems, 63–65
    Teachers, 195, 262, 269
    Terms for, 322
    Western
        and Entropy, 406
        Ethnocentric, 32
        Forced on students, 201
        Harding and Gough on, 322

and Indigenous, 3, 6, 228, 317
and Morality, 447
See also Education, Indigenous Science
Scientific racism, 198, 392
Self-identity, 250
Seniority, 46–47, 48
Sense of place, 114, 120, 123, 227, 253, 265
Sentient landscape, 199
Service learning, 238, 265, 416, 418
Settee, Henry McKay, 435–36, 440
Shell Oil, 171
Shooter (Lakota), 105
Snuneymuxw Nanaimo, 204
Social ecosystem, 265
Sorensen, Mark, 235–36
Soul wound, 95
South-West Coast, Wellington, 307
Sovereignty
    Continuing assertions of, 393, 394
    Diné, 213
    Epistemological, 98, 373–74, 392
    Flanagan, Tom, on, 165
    Food, 446
    Intellectual, 437
Space-time, 94, 98, 102, 103, 104, 107
Speaking position, 115
Spirit world, 36, 252, 254, 258
Spirituality
    African Indigenous, 42, 337–8, 340, 343–44, 347–48
    in the Classroom, 430–31
    as Evil, 16
    Indigenous and decolonization, 411–19
    Land-based, 29, 376
    and Religion and modernist education, 206–7
    as Resistance, 10–11, 428
    Shahjahan on, 429, 430, 431
    and Storytelling, 204
    Western, 374
    Yoruban, 34–36, 48
St. Denis, Verna, 131, 136
STAR (Service to All Relations) School, 235–38
Stevens, Ted, 194
Storm, Hyemeyohsts, 104
Storytelling
    African, 49
    Ecuadorian, 178, 181
    and McCallum, Tom, 226, 245–60
    as a Methodology, 436
Students
    of African civilization, 81
    Alaska native, 169, 190, 191–92, 194–95, 231–34
    Australian, 71, 72, 74, 75
    and Christian churches, 206
    Coast Salish, 201, 205, 207–9
    and Collaborative learning, 418–19
    and Colonialism, 139
    and Community, 237, 238, 239–40, 396, 416
    Deloria and Wildcat on, 230
    and Difference, learning about, 149
    Diné, 219
    Ghanaian, 295
    Graduation rates, 229
    Identity, 147, 241, 316, 317
    and Indian control of Indian, 111, 158
    Indigenous Hawai'ian, 227, 235, 238–41, 262, 276–77
    and Indigenous Knowledge systems, 226, 321, 381, 417
    of Indigenous-only schools, 69
    International, 363
    Japanese, 354
    and Knowledge construction, 149–50
    Māori, 228, 300, 303–4, 306, 307–8
    and Native Studies, 442, 443
    Navaho, 235–38
    and No Child Left Behind, 242
    Non-Indigenous, 135, 147
    and Place-based learning, 265
    of Residential schools, 133
    Resistant, 229
    Saskatchewan, 135
    and Science education, 314, 315, 321–22, 368
    and Segregated classes, 70
    and Storytelling, 246, 259
    and "Supporting Better Education Outcomes for First Nations," 164
    and Worldview theory, 316
    See also Education; Effie Kokrine School; PRISM: Qatar University; STAR School; Teachers
Sun, 235, 236, 305, 339
Sun Dance, 226, 245, 249, 251–55, 258, 438
Sustainability
    Community, 334
    and Development, 180
    Economic, 132
    Environmental, 184
    of Population groups, 241
    and Qatar, 180–82, 184–85

as a Science content standard, 227, 263, 267–69, 277
of a Way of life, 213
Suzuki, David, 302

Tahiti, 265, 304, 305
Tanana River, 189
Tāne Mahuta, 306
Tapu, 305
Teachers
    Aboriginal, 131
    as Cultural brokers, 317
    Dedicated, 194
    Education, 148–49, 233–34, 276–77
    Failure of, 152
    Native K-12, 194
    Non-Indigenous, 208, 396
    and Racism, 147
    Role (Righting the Wrong), 148–50
    Shortage of qualified, 158, 163, 192–93, 195
    Standards for (ADE), 231–32
    Science, 314
    Tools for, 8–9
    See also Effie Kokrine School; Hawai'ian Studies Program; STAR School
Teleology, 426
Telos, 98, 99
Theology, 92, 101
Thobani, Sunera, 131
Tikanga, 303
Tillich, Paul, 95, 102
Time (and Space and Unified Knowledge), 92–108
Time-space zones, 101
Tinker, George, 103
tl'aneq, 203
Tohunga, 304
Traditional ecological knowledge. *See under* Knowledge
Traditional Knowledge Conference (Ngā Pae o te Māramatanga), 307, 308
Traditional, local knowledge. *See under* Knowledge
Treat, James, 92, 97, 99–100, 103, 104–5
Trickster, 106, 189, 305, 334
Tuatara, 303
Tubba-Gah people, 110, 113–16, 119–22

UNESCO LINKS, 303
Unified knowledge, 18–19, 92–107
United States Geologic Survey (U.S.G.S.), 209
University, attainment of, 163

University of Alaska, Fairbanks, 193, 231, 300
University of British Columbia, 200, 208
University of California-Berkeley, 235
University of Hawai'i, 239
University of Manitoba, 444, 445
University of Qatar, 171, 179
University of Saskatchewan, 134, 138, 300, 307, 442
University of Southern Illinois, 240
University of Toronto, 21, 247
University of Warwick, 446

Values
    and Academia, 74, 75, 143, 147, 198, 207
    African, 227, 280
    American, 230, 235, 242, 267
    Arab, 175–85
    Core, universal, 28, 147, 212
    and Diné Bi Beenahaz'áanii, 217–18, 220–21
    Different, 94
    and the Ecosystem, 306
    Eskimo, 233
    and the Fundamental Laws, 215–16
    Hawai'an, 238, 265, 267, 269, 276–77
    Historically denied, 283, 295
    and Indigenous knowing, 3, 53,
    and Indigenous learning styles, 71, 111, 115
    Māori, 299
    Protestant, 159
    Salish, 201–2, 204, 209
    Transmission of, 159
    and UINPI, 177
    Western, 288, 375, 415
Victoria University of Wellington, 228, 303, 307, 309
Videoconference, 304, 307–8

wage economy, 202
Wakan, 98
Wakan Tanka, 105
wakohtowin, 438–41
Ways of being
    Alternative, 382
    Ecuadorian, 176
    Gandhi on, 375
    Indigenous, 133
    Multiple, 381, 382
    Secular vs. the rest, 369–71, 378, 379
Western, 263, 367, 368
Whānau, 307
Whitehead, Alfred N., 104
Whiteness, 24, 387, 395, 412, 424, 427

Whitestream, 199, 205
Whorf, Benjamin, 93
Wiradjuri Nation, 114, 119–21
Worldsense, 36, 41–42
Worldview, 35–36
    African, 228, 287–88
    Cobern on, 316
    Eurocentric/Western, 232, 242, 370, 375, 379, 415
    and Healing, 287
    and Indigenous Knowledge, 177, 185
    and Islam, 185
    Native, 193, 204, 439–40, 46
    and Personal experiences, 436

Xa:ls, 204
Xwelemi Chosen, 208

Yoruba
    Communities, 39
    Diaspora, 34, 35, 45
    and Gender, 34, 45–48
    Indigenous culture, 35
    and Indigenous identity, 35, 39, 43
    Indigenous Knowledge, 39, 44
    Oral literature, 35
    Philosophy, 35–36
    Spirituality, 36, 42
Yukon River/Territory, 189, 190, 205

Studies in the Postmodern Theory of Education

General Editor
Shirley R. Steinberg

Counterpoints publishes the most compelling and imaginative books being written in education today. Grounded on the theoretical advances in criticism, feminism, and postmodernism in the last two decades of the twentieth century, Counterpoints engages the meaning of these innovations in various forms of educational expression. Committed to the proposition that theoretical literature should be accessible to a variety of audiences, the series insists that its authors avoid esoteric and jargonistic languages that transform educational scholarship into an elite discourse for the initiated. Scholarly work matters only to the degree it affects consciousness and practice at multiple sites. Counterpoints' editorial policy is based on these principles and the ability of scholars to break new ground, to open new conversations, to go where educators have never gone before.

For additional information about this series or for the submission of manuscripts, please contact:

> Shirley R. Steinberg
> c/o Peter Lang Publishing, Inc.
> 29 Broadway, 18th floor
> New York, New York 10006

To order other books in this series, please contact our Customer Service Department:
> (800) 770-LANG (within the U.S.)
> (212) 647-7706 (outside the U.S.)
> (212) 647-7707 FAX

Or browse online by series:
> www.peterlang.com